Handbook of Re-Engineering Software Intensive Systems into Software Product Lines

Roberto E. Lopez-Herrejon • Jabier Martinez •
Wesley Klewerton Guez Assunção • Tewfik Ziadi •
Mathieu Acher • Silvia Vergilio
Editors

Handbook of Re-Engineering Software Intensive Systems into Software Product Lines

 Springer

Editors
Roberto E. Lopez-Herrejon
École de Technologie Supérieure
Universite du Québec
Montreal, QC, Canada

Jabier Martinez
Tecnalia, Basque Research and Technology
Alliance (BRTA)
Derio, Spain

Wesley Klewerton Guez Assunção
Pontifical Catholic University of Rio de
Janeiro
Rio de Janeiro, Brazil
Johannes Kepler University of Linz
Linz, Austria

Tewfik Ziadi
Sorbonne Universités & CNRS-LIP6
Paris, Paris, France

Mathieu Acher
IRISA-Inria
Institut Universitaire de France (IUF) &
University of Rennes 1
Rennes, France

Silvia Vergilio
Departamento de Informática
Federal University of Parana (UFPR)
Curitiba, Brazil

ISBN 978-3-031-11688-9   ISBN 978-3-031-11686-5   (eBook)
https://doi.org/10.1007/978-3-031-11686-5

This Springer imprint is published by the registered company Springer Nature Switzerland AG
The registered company address is: Gewerbestrasse 11, 6330 Cham, Switzerland

Foreword

For more than 30 years, I have been involved in Software Product Line Engineering. I started recording the good practices in a small department of Philips. These practices were adopted by larger departments, which led to the development of the platform presently in use everywhere in the company. We faced the same problems that companies still encounter when moving towards Software Product Line Engineering. For those who want to embark on the journey of re-engineering systems into Software Product Lines, this book provides several approaches for addressing some of these common issues. The focus of this book is on the technical/architecture side of the development. I recognise many of these practices and approaches within Philips as well as in other companies, which have been pioneered by many people.

In my experience, for successful introduction of a Software Product Line culture, the Business, Architecture, Process, and Organisation (BAPO) dimensions need to go in balance to ensure a good transition towards Software Product Line Engineering. The Business dimension needs to address not only how to market and sell the diverse products but also to select the right incentives for those that do Software Product Line Engineering. Also, additional incentives need to be selected for those that deliver internal value to the company but will not provide end products. In the Architecture dimension, variability need to be managed, from requirements up to testing and deployment. Good models are needed to show what is available and what can be added. The Process dimension deals with all activities, and their relationships, that need to be done during Software Product Line Engineering. The Organisation dimension deals with the mapping of the processes to the official and virtual departments in the organisation. It also deals with strategies for software outsourcing.

Over the years, I found it difficult to define what is a Product Line, although I can explain what Software Product Line Engineering is. For me, the simplest solution is to define a Software Product Line as the outcome of a specific instance of Software Product Line Engineering, which in practice is a continuously evolving set of more or less similar products. In the Philips case, it has been evolving over the last 25 years. I have seen, several times, that Product Lines from different origins are merged into one. Because of this, I prefer to use the term "Software Product Line Engineering" over "Software Product Line". During the evolution of the Philips' Software Product Line Engineering, the way to handle it also has evolved. In practice, it has been able to incorporate any new trend that was introduced in software engineering. During this evolution, in the Business dimension, the development moved from only a single platform team to the whole of Philips. In the Architecture dimension, the platform was initially defined with components and then moved to services. This service architecture allowed cloud and edge processing, and introduced dependability solutions for the whole family. Parallel to this architectural evolution, programming languages used in the platform also changed from Objective-C towards Java, C#, and Python among others. Regarding the Process dimension, agility and lean development was introduced. This meant adopting extensive automated testing, and supporting maintenance with a logging system and error prediction. In the Organisation dimension, we introduced inner source development that became the main way of adapting the code base.

In the following, I describe shortly my experience with Software Product Line Engineering, illustrating it along the way with examples of the issues addressed in this book. In 1991, I became involved in the Philips telecom-switch department in Nürnberg, Germany, where they wanted to modernise their way to create software. At that time, they wanted to know whether object-oriented design might be a good idea for them or even if they were close to doing object-oriented development. My impression was that they were not doing something related to object-oriented design, but they included all best software engineering ideas of the 1970s and 1980s in their development process. They applied all these technologies to be able to deliver high dependable real-time systems in a niche market that had a large amount of variety in number of subscribers, hardware configurations, legal rules, and commercial requirements. In fact, they were doing Software Product Line Engineering, even before that term was coined.

The development at Phillips had the following characteristics: component-oriented, aspect-oriented design with code generation for several dependability aspects, plug-in architecture, call-back interfaces, a digital twin of the hardware and software configuration to support error management, maintenance, reconfiguration, and load balancing. Note that many of these terms were not yet coined in 1991. The development was largely supported by the use of CHILL, at that time, a common programming language in the telecommunications domain. The modular structure of the programs makes it easy to develop components as separate entities for development, testing, and deployment, a critical aspect of their development. Although the development was not object-oriented, we evaluated it higher, because of the aspects mentioned above, which were not easily available in the object-oriented languages at that time. Of course, if they wished they could have used object-orientation in parts of the development, because it was possible to have a CHILL module border around foreign language code. However, we recommended not to do so because that would not give a lot of profit.

A variability model was crucial for the development of Phillips' system. In this system, the variability model was captured in the digital twin, which in turn was configured from a generated script for its initialisation, and that was active at runtime for describing the actual variant. Error messages could alter the status of the twin, leading to repair functions. There was a global model that described all possible configurations, and each running system had its own running models. The running models describe, in their own terminology, the abstract resources in the system. The global model described mainly the plug-in points to be used (variation points). Each one was called a generic resource, and there was a list of actual resource components that could be plugged-in, constructing in this way the possible system variants. The global model was the origin of the development of new systems. First, the components already available were selected, and then, the decision was taken on what new components to develop. Once completed, the specific make-file of variant was automatically generated based on these decisions.

Two years later, Philips decided to sell to telecommunication department to AT&T (later AVAYA). This means that we lost contact with the developers after that. However, we have captured enough knowledge to introduce product family engineering, as we called it at that time, in another department. We started with the TV-set development, which was a very important product for Philips, and that involved a large variety in the systems. The development at that time was based of formal methods (COLD) and code generation. The most important improvement was the creation of components, and the definition of ways for combining them differently. The variability model was part of the formal description. There was massive code generation, not only to ensure that the system was build according to the chosen variant but also to ensure enough performance. Notably, the variability model described the coupling of the components, and the code generation removed the majority of indirections in calls. Until Philips sold the TV-set development department in 2010, this Software Product Line Engineering was in use.

In 1997, we started to introduce Software Product Line Engineering in the medical department of Philips. This group provided supporting software for medical image processing and transfer. They transformed their software into a platform to be used by departments that applied medical image processing. Initially, a set of core components were defined and a road map was set to incorporate more software into components. The architecture was set up in a way that facilitated plug-in components, and also required for separate interfaces for different development aspects, some related to dependability. In about 8 years, all software was either transformed or rewritten into the new format. Of course, also new software was added, mainly related to dependability aspects, Internet access, and interchange standards and requests from new departments using the platform. Because of requests made by several departments, the architecture needed to be able to work in a service-oriented environment. At the same time, experiments were done to introduce open source in development and products, and also open source practices in the Process dimension. This led to "inner source" development within Philips. All platform sources were open in the company, thus anybody who needed a change could do it on their own.

Of course management was involved to set the right priorities. This decision enabled people from separate departments to form short-term virtual teams to address specific software needs. By that time, agility and lean development were introduced. Their introduction was eased by the existing inner source development as this can easily be done in an agile way. In the meantime, Philips was moving many product divisions out of the company, but the medical department remained. Since then, the platform became the standard way of developing and using software in Philips. The architect that started the first architecture in 1997 is still in Philips as "Chief architect". During this whole evolution, Philips acquired many companies in the medical domain. All had their own software architecture. So one of the first steps in integrating them was to ensure that they were merged efficiently into the product line business, architecture, processes, and organisation. This always led to an important step in the evolution of the architecture and platform.

For the readers of the book. My conviction is that Software Product Line Engineering is presently the best way of developing software for a set of products. My experience is that it can incorporate almost all new trends in software engineering but still stay strong because of its focus on variability and the ways to manage and implement it. If you plan to transform your development into a product line engineering, the benefits will allow profits in the future, by reducing the engineering effort. There are no specific road blocks, as Software Product Line Engineering can deal with many different development styles, architectures, languages, etc. Only, if you are not dealing with enough variability, a move towards Software Product Line Engineering may not pay off. However, in all the cases, plan well and make future-proof decisions on the architectures. Ensure the availability of future-proof interfaces, and involve the Business dimension at an early point. Finally, I encourage you to apply the technologies presented in this book at the moment you encounter the related problems.

Eindhoven, the Netherlands   Frank van der Linden
February 2022

Preface

Software Product Lines (SPLs) are families of systems that share common assets allowing a disciplined software reuse. The adoption of SPLs practices has been shown to enable significant technical and economic benefits for the companies that employ them. However, successful SPLs rarely start from scratch. Instead, they usually start from a set of existing legacy systems that must undergo a well-defined re-engineering process.

Many approaches to conduct such re-engineering processes have been proposed and documented in the literature. This handbook is the result of the collective community expertise and knowledge acquired in conducting theoretical and empirical research also in partnership with industry. The topic discussed in this handbook is a recurrent and challenging problem faced by many companies. Conducting a re-engineering process could unlock new levels of productivity and competitiveness. The chapter authors are all experts in different topics of the re-engineering process, which brings valuable contributions to the content of this handbook. Additionally, organizing the international workshop on REverse Variability Engineering (REVE) has contributed to this topic during the last decade. REVE has fostered research collaborations between Software Re-engineering and SPL Engineering (SPLE) communities. Thus, this handbook is also a result of our expertise and knowledge acquired from the fruitful discussions with the attendants of REVE.

Our handbook aims to bring together into a single, comprehensive, and cohesive reference the wealth of experience and expertise in the area of re-engineering software intensive systems into SPLs. We cover the entire re-engineering life-cycle, from requirements gathering to maintenance and evolution tasks. Also, we provide future directions and perspectives. The handbook is the result of our collective effort over the last 3 years. It underwent a rigorous and careful selection and edition process. The selected contributors are worldwide experts in their field, and all chapters were peer reviewed.

What Is This Handbook About?

The scope of the book includes different aspects of re-engineering software systems into SPLs: processes and activities involved, techniques, support tools, and empirical studies related to extraction or refinement of SPLs.

The handbook comprises four parts with a total of 20 chapters divided as illustrated in the next figure. The first part, Feature Location and Variability Model Extraction (Chaps. 1–7), focuses on a core aspect of SPLE and the re-engineering process, related to the variability management and mining existing assets. This part gathers an assemble of approaches based on different techniques. Chapter 1 describes an Information Retrieval (IR) approach for feature location from variants. The approaches described in Chaps. 2 and 3 are based, respectively, on natural language requirements and software version history slicing. Chapter 4 introduces approaches for feature location in models, by using a Genetic Algorithm at design time, and architectural models and IR at runtime. Synthesis of variability models is addressed in Chaps. 5 and 6, which describe, respectively, a multi-objective optimization approach for reverse engineering of feature models and a Formal Concept Analysis approach for extracting complex variability relationships from non-boolean descriptions. The approach of Chap. 7 uses Machine Learning to prevent the derivation of invalid products through the synthesis of feature constraints.

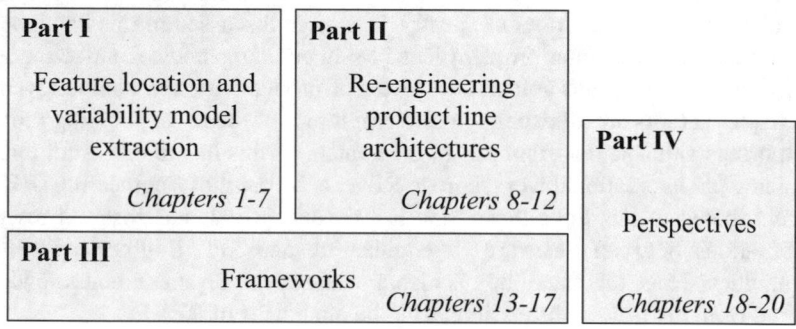

The second part, Re-engineering Product Line Architectures (Chaps. 8–12), focuses on the extraction of SPL architectures (SPLAs) from existing software variants. Chapter 8 discusses challenges and good practices proposed in the state of the art of the SPLA extraction. The approach of Chap. 9 allows the generation of UML models to represent the SPLA, such as class diagrams. Chapter 10 presents a study for extraction and evolution of a software product line from existing Web-based systems. Chapter 11 describes an approach to extract a microservices-based product line that combines the feature diagram with the UML class diagram from existing systems to design the architecture. The approach of Chap. 12 explores ideas of traditional software architectural recovery for the SPL context.

The third part, Frameworks (Chaps. 13–17), describes tools for supporting different aspects of the re-engineering process. The framework of Chap. 13 allows planning of the re-engineering process considering the characteristics of distinct scenarios. The framework of Chap. 14 allows integration of more than 20 algorithms and techniques for the re-engineering activities such as feature identification and location, feature constraints discovery, feature model synthesis, and the construction of reusable assets. Chapter 15 presents data structures and operations for creation of variants using clone-and-own practice with automated reuse and centralized maintenance. The framework of Chap. 16 supports the extraction of SPLs from clones, by analysing variants of control software implemented using the IEC 61131-3 family of programming languages. The tool of Chap. 17 supports SPL evolution by means of a filtered editing model, which is inspired by the checkout-modify-commit workflow established in version control systems. The tool allows successive modifications in single-variant workspaces for integrating the changes according to the affected variants.

The fourth part, Perspectives (Chaps. 18–20), overviews related themes that can encourage future research and provide insights in the field. Chapter 18 presents results of an empirical study to investigate the potential to adopt SPLE in start-ups, including motivations, benefits, challenges, barriers, best practices, and experiences revealed in the migration process. Chapter 19 shows that variability is a key criterion for structuring microservices and presents results from a survey and interviews conducted to identify how professionals perform microservice extraction to conduct the re-engineering process. Chapter 20 overviews the main processes and activities involved in SPL evolution, focusing on processes for synchronizing core assets and products. This book also includes an index of terms that makes it easy to trace back the particular sections or chapters in which specific topics have been addressed.

Who Should Read This Handbook?

This handbook is intended for all those interested in software engineering, and more particularly, software reuse variability management, SPLs, as well as reverse engineering and modernization. The book can be a resource for a wide variety of people including software and system engineers, designers, architects, developers, researchers, educators, and undergraduate and graduate students. Researchers will find in the chapters an overview of the most recent research results covering different research aspects of re-engineering for SPL. The book can benefit practitioners who will find possible solutions and support for solving problems they face. We also believe this book has a great potential to be used in teaching advanced (graduate or undergraduate) software engineering courses on, e.g., software architecture, software re-engineering, software reuse, variability management, and SPLE.

For all the readers, the main features of this handbook can be summarized as:

- Comprehensive overview of re-engineering legacy systems across the entire Software Product Line lifecycle
- Description of multiple and competing state-of-the art approaches to provide a broader perspective for the researchers and practitioners to select existing approaches according to their needs
- Evaluation results of the approaches and case studies, as well as perspectives for future research

We would like to thank the authors and reviewers for their contributions. Without their expertise and effort, this book would never come to fruition. Springer editors and staff also deserve our sincere recognition for their support throughout the project.

We hope you find the contributed chapters useful for your endeavours and that you enjoy reading this handbook!

Montreal, QC, Canada   Roberto E. Lopez-Herrejon
Bilbao, Spain   Jabier Martinez
Linz, Austria   Wesley Klewerton Guez Assunção
Paris, France   Tewfik Ziadi
Rennes, France   Mathieu Acher
Curitiba, Brazil   Silvia Vergilio
March 2022

Acknowledgements

We thank all supporters, the authors, the grant funding schemes, and the Software Product Line community in general. Special thanks to the attendants of the REVE series of workshops (Reverse Variability Engineering) as your contributions and discussions helped to advance the field.

Apart from the editors themselves, the following persons have helped with the peer reviews of the chapters: Iris Reinhartz-Berger, Leonardo Tizzei, Xhevahire Tërnava, Leopoldo Teixeira, Anas Shatnawi, Javier Troya, Rick Rabiser, Rafael Capilla, Ivan Machado, José Galindo, Leticia Montalvillo, Uirá Kulesza, Ruben Heradio, and Jaime Font. Thanks for helping with your suggestions for improvement.

Roberto Erick Lopez-Herrejon's work is partially supported by the Natural Sciences and Engineering Research Council of Canada (NSERC) grant RGPIN-2017-05421. Wesley Klewerton Guez Assunção's work is partially supported by the Carlos Chagas Filho Foundation for Supporting Research in the State of Rio de Janeiro (FAPERJ), under the PDR-10 program, grant 202073/2020.

Contents

11   Re-Engineering Microservice Applications into Delta-Oriented Software Product Lines 275
Maya R. A. Setyautami, Hafiyyan S. Fadhlillah, Daya Adianto, Ichlasul Affan, and Ade Azurat

12   Understanding the Variability on the Recovery of Product Line Architectures 293
Crescencio Lima, Mateus Cardoso, Ivan do Carmo Machado, Eduardo Santana de Almeida, and Christina von Flach Garcia Chavez

Part III   Frameworks

13   **PAxSPL: A Framework for Aiding SPL Reengineering Planning** 319
Luciano Marchezan, Elder Rodrigues, João Carbonell,
Maicon Bernardino, Fábio Paulo Basso, and Wesley K. G. Assunção

14   **Bottom-Up Technologies for Reuse: A Framework to
Support Extractive Software Product Line Adoption Activities** 355
Jabier Martinez, Tewfik Ziadi, Tegawendé F. Bissyandé,
Jaques Klein, and Yves le Traon

Editors and Contributors

Editors

Roberto E. Lopez-Herrejon École de Technologie Supérieure, Université du Québec, Montreal, QC, Canada

Jabier Martinez Tecnalia, Basque Research and Technology Alliance (BRTA), Derio, Spain

Wesley Klewerton Guez Assunção Pontifical Catholic University of Rio de Janeiro, Rio de Janeiro, Brazil
Johannes Kepler University of Linz, Linz, Austria

Tewfik Ziadi Sorbonne University, UPMC Paris VI, Paris, France

Mathieu Acher Institut Universitaire de France (IUF) & University of Rennes 1, IRISA-Inria, DiverSE project, Rennes, France

Silvia Vergilio Federal University of Paraná (UFPR), Departamento de Informática Centro Politécnico, Jardim das Américas, Curitiba, Brazil

Contributors

Mathieu Acher Univ Rennes, IRISA, CNRS, Rennes, France

Eiji Adachi Federal University of Rio Grande do Norte, Natal, Brazil

Daya Adianto Faculty of Computer Science, Universitas Indonesia, Depok City, Indonesia

Ichlasul Affan Faculty of Computer Science, Universitas Indonesia, Depok City, Indonesia

Juliana Alves Pereira Pontifical Catholic University of Rio de Janeiro, PUC-Rio, Rio de Janeiro, Brazil

Lorena Arcega Universidad San Jorge, SVIT Research Group, Zaragoza, Spain

Wesley K. G. Assunção Pontifical Catholic University of Rio de Janeiro, Rio de Janeiro, Brazil
Johannes Kepler University of Linz, Linz, Austria

Ade Azurat Faculty of Computer Science, Universitas Indonesia, Depok City, Indonesia

Fábio Paulo Basso Laboratory of Empirical Studies in Software Engineering - Federal University of Pampa, Alegrete, Brazil

Maicon Bernardino Laboratory of Empirical Studies in Software Engineering - Federal University of Pampa, Alegrete, Brazil

Tegawendé F. Bissyandé University of Luxembourg, Esch-sur-Alzette, Luxembourg

Rodrigo Bonifácio University of Brasília, Brasília, Brazil

João Carbonell Laboratory of Empirical Studies in Software Engineering - Federal University of Pampa, Alegrete, Brazil

Mateus Cardoso Federal University of South of Bahia, Salvador, Brazil

Luiz Carvalho Pontifical Catholic University of Rio de Janeiro, Rio de Janeiro, Brazil

Renato Cerqueira IBM Research, Rio de Janeiro, Brazil

Carlos Cetina Universidad San Jorge, SVIT Research Group, Zaragoza, Spain

Marsha Chechik Department of Computer Science, University of Toronto, Toronto, ON, Canada

Elder Cirilo Federal University of São João del-Rei, São João del-Rei, Brazil

Carlos Eduardo da Silva Department of Computing, Sheffield Hallam University, Sheffield, UK

Rafael de Mello Federal Center for Technological Education of Rio de Janeiro, Rio de Janeiro, Brazil

Thelma Elita Colanzi State University of Maringá, Maringá, Brazil

Oscar Díaz University of the Basque Country, Leioa, Spain

Christophe Dony Lirmm Laboratory, Montpellier, France

Ivan do Carmo Machado Federal University of Bahia, Salvador, Brazil

Serge Demeyer University of Antwerp – Flanders Make vzw, Antwerp, Belgium

Alexander Egyed Johannes Kepler University Linz, Linz, Austria

Hafiyyan S. Fadhlillah Faculty of Computer Science, Universitas Indonesia, Depok City, Indonesia

Stefan Fischer Software Competence Center Hagenberg, Hagenberg, Austria

Jaime Font Universidad San Jorge, SVIT Research Group, Zaragoza, Spain

Jessie Galasso Université de Montréal, Montréal, ON, Canada

Alessandro Garcia Pontifical Catholic University of Rio de Janeiro, Rio de Janeiro, Brazil

Paul Grünbacher Johannes Kepler University Linz, Linz, Austria

Øystein Haugen Østfold University College, Faculty of Computer Science, Halden, Norway

Marianne Huchard LIRMM, University of Montpellier, CNRS, Montpellier, France

Jean-Marc Jézéquel Univ Rennes, IRISA, CNRS, Rennes, France

Jaques Klein University of Luxembourg, Esch-sur-Alzette, Luxembourg

Uirá Kulesza Federal University of Rio Grande do Norte, Natal, Brazil

Yves le Traon University of Luxembourg, Esch-sur-Alzette, Luxembourg

Yang Li pure-systems GmbH, Magdeburg, Germany

Yi Li School of Computer Science and Engineering, Nanyang Technological University, Singapore, Singapore

Crescencio Lima Federal Institute of Bahia, Salvador, Brazil

Lukas Linsbauer Institute of Software Engineering and Automotive Informatics, Technische Universität Braunschweig, Braunschweig, Germany

Roberto E. Lopez-Herrejon École de Technologie Supérieure, Universite du Québec, Montreal, QC, Canada

Carlos Lucena Pontifical Catholic University of Rio de Janeiro, Rio de Janeiro, Brazil

Luciano Marchezan Institute for Software Systems Engineering - Johannes Kepler University Linz, Computer Science SP3, Linz, Austria

Hugo Martin Univ Rennes, IRISA, CNRS, Rennes, France

Jabier Martinez Tecnalia, Basque Research and Technology Alliance (BRTA), Mendaro, Spain

Gabriela Karoline Michelon Johannes Kepler University Linz, Linz, Austria

Leticia Montalvillo Ikerlan Technology Research Centre, Basque Research and Technology Alliance (BRTA), Mendaro, Spain

Mercy Njima University of Antwerp, Antwerp, Belgium

Erick Sharlls Ramos de Pontes Federal University of Rio Grande do Norte, Natal, Brazil

Márcio Ribeiro Federal University of Alagoas, Maceió, Brazil

Elder Rodrigues Laboratory of Empirical Studies in Software Engineering - Federal University of Pampa, Alegrete, Brazil

Kamil Rosiak Institute of Software Engineering and Automotive Informatics, Technische Universität Braunschweig, Braunschweig, Germany

Julia Rubin Department of Electrical and Computer Engineering, University of British Columbia, Vancouver, BC, Canada

Houari Sahraoui DIRO, Université de Montréal, Montreal, QC, Canada

Hamzeh Eyal Salman Mutah University, Al-Karak, Jordan

Eduardo Santana de Almeida Federal University of Bahia, Salvador, Brazil

Ina Schaefer Testing, Validation and Analysis of Software-Intensive Systems (TVA), Karlsruhe Institute of Technology (KIT), Karlsruhe

Sandro Schulze Otto-von-Guericke Universität Magdeburg, Faculty of Computer Science, Magdeburg, Germany

Felix Schwägerl University of Bayreuth, Applied Computer Science I, Bayreuth, Germany

Abdelhak-Djamel Seriai University of Montpellier, CNRS, LIRMM, Montpellier, France

Maya R. A. Setyautami Faculty of Computer Science, Universitas Indonesia, Depok City, Indonesia

Anas Shatnawi University of Montpellier, CNRS, LIRMM, Montpellier, France

Paul Temple University of Namur, Namur, Belgium

Leonardo P. Tizzei IBM Research, Rio de Janeiro, Brazil

Silvia R. Vergilio Dinf, Federal University of Paraná, Curitiba, Brazil

Birgit Vogel-Heuser Institute of Automation and Information Systems, Technische Universität München, Munich, Germany

Christina von Flach Garcia Chavez Federal University of Bahia, Salvador, Brazil

Bernhard Westfechtel University of Bayreuth, Applied Computer Science I, Bayreuth, Germany

Tewfik Ziadi Sorbonne University, Paris, France

Acronyms

ABS	Abstract Behavioral Specification
AE	Application Engineering
AHC	Agglomerative Hierarchal clustering
ANOVA	Analysis of Variance
AOC-poset	Attribute-Object Concept partially ordered set
AOP	Aspect-Oriented Programming
aPs	Automated Production System
AST	Abstract Syntax Tree
BFS	Breadth First Search
BIG	Binary Implication Graphs
BPMN	Business Process Model and Notation
BRCG	Branch-Reserving Call Graph
BS	Banking System
BUT4Reuse	Bottom-up Technologies for Reuse
CART	Classification and Regression Trees
CBOW	Continuous Bag-of-Words
CDT	Eclipse C/C++ Development Tooling
CIA	Change Impact Analysis
CIT	Combinatorial Interaction Testing
CLI	Command Line Interface
CM	Class Mandatory
CNF	Conjunctive Normal Form
CO	Class Optional
COQ	Question Options Criteria
COTS	Commercial Off-The-Shelf
CPS	Cyber-Physical System
CRR	Component Reuse Rate
CSV	Comma-Separated Values
CTC	Cross-Tree Constraint
CVL	Common Variability Language
DE	Domain Engineering

DM	Decision Model
DNF	Disjunctive Normal Form
DOP	Delta-Oriented Programming
DPL	Draw Product Line
DSL	Domain-Specific Language
DSM	Design Structure Matrix
DSM	Distributional Semantic Models
ECCO	Extraction and Composition for Clone-and-Own
ECFD	Equivalence Class Feature Diagrams
ECU	Elementary Construction Unit
ED	Euclidean Distance
EMF	Eclipse Modelling Framework
ERP	Enterprise Resource Planning
ESPLA	Software Product Line Adoption case studies
FBD	Function Block Diagram
FCA	Formal Concept Analysis
FD	Feature Diagram
FLiM	Feature Location in Models
FLiMEA	FLiM at Design time
FLiMRT	FLiM at Runtime
FM	Feature Model
FN	False Negative
FOP	Feature-Oriented Programming
FP	False Positive
GA	Genetic Algorithm
GOL	Game Of Life
GP	Genetic Programming
GQM `	Goal/Question/Metric
GRAFCET	Graphe Fonctionnel de Commande Etape Transition
GUI	Graphical User Interface
IHDSL	DSL to specify the Induction Hobs
IHs	Induction Hobs
IL	Instruction List
IR	Information Retrieval
J48	Decision Tree C4.5
JDT	Eclipse Java Development Tools
JSF	Java Server Face
JVM	Java Virtual Machine
LCS	Longest Common Subsequence
LD	Ladder Diagram
LDA	Latent Dirichlet Allocation
LoC	Lines of Code
LSA	Latent Semantic Analysis
LSI	Latent Semantic Indexing
MCS	Mihalcea, Corley, and Strapparava's measure

MDG	Module Dependency Graph
MDSE	Model-Driven Software Engineering
MDSPLE	Model-Driven SPL Engineering
MLP	Multilayer Perceptron
MM	MobileMedia
MOF	Meta Object Facility
MPL	Multi-Product Line
MS	Model Similarity
NER	Named Entity Recognition
NLP	Natural Language Processing
NSGA-II	Non-Dominated Sorting Genetic Algorithm
OO	Object-Oriented
OSGi	Java Open Services Gateway Initiative
OVM	Orthogonal Variability Model
PART	Pruning Rule-Based Classification
PAxSPL	Prepare, Assemble, and Execute Framework for SPL Reengineering
PCM	Product Comparison Matrices
PDA	Prune Dependency Analysis
PFKnown	Pareto Front Known
PFTrue	Pareto Front True
PLA	Product Line Architecture
PLAR	Product Line Architecture Recovery
PLC	Programmable Logic Controller
PLTV	Product Line Total Variability
POS	Parts-of-Speech
POU	Program Organization Unit
PPU	Pick and Place Unit
QM	Quality Metrics
RCP	Rich Client Platform
ReqIF	Requirements Interchange Format
SAR	Software Architecture Recovery
SBSE	SBSE
SCM	Software Configuration Management
SFC	Sequential Function Chart
SFS	Strict Feature-Specific location
SPEA2	Strength Pareto Evolutionary Algorithm
SPL	Software Product Line
SPLA	Software Product Line Architecture
SPLE	Software Product Line Engineering
SPR	Scenario-based Probabilistic Ranking
SRL	Semantic Role Labelling
SRS	Software Requirements Specification
SSC	Structure Similarity Coefficient
ST	Structured Text
SVC	Structure Variability Coefficient

SVD	Singular Value Decomposition
TF-IDF	Term Frequency-Inverse Document Frequency
TFM	Technical Feature Model
TN	True Negative
TP	True Positive
TVL	Textual Variability Language
UML	Unified Modeling Language
UVM	Uniform Version Model
VAT	Variability Analysis Toolkit
VCS	Version Control System
VM	Virtual Machine
VM	Variability Model
VOD	Video On Demand
VS	Variability Safety
VSM	Vector Space Model
WISE	Weather InSights Environment
xPPU	Extended Pick and Place Unit

Part I
Feature Location and Variability Model Extraction

Chapter 1
Feature Location in Software Variants Toward Software Product Line Engineering

Hamzeh Eyal Salman, Abdelhak-Djamel Seriai, and Christophe Dony

Abstract Feature location is the process of finding or locating a segment of code that implements a specific software function (i.e., feature). Feature location in a collection of software variants is an important step for transition from ad-hoc development to systematic development (software product line engineering). In this chapter, we present in a pedagogical order the concept of feature location, types of feature location and feature location in the software variants. Then, we present an illustrative approach for feature location based on information retrieval (IR).

1.1 Introduction

Feature location is the process of finding or locating a segment of code that implements a specific software function (i.e., feature). A feature is "a prominent or distinctive user-visible aspect, quality or characteristic of a software system or systems" [18]. Feature location is one of the most important and common activities performed by programmers during software maintenance, evolution and re-engineering, as any maintenance activity can not be performed with first understanding and locating the code relevant to the task at hand [6]. Feature location plays a pivot role in re-engineering legacy product variants into a Software Product Line (SPL). There is a large body of research on feature location approaches [6, 8]. There are different distinguishing factors between these approaches. These factors are: (1) type of analysis used, (2) type of input artifacts, (3) automation, and (4) objective. Figure 1.3 shows our taxonomy of the feature location approaches. In the following two sections, we detail this taxonomy. Also, there is also literature in feature location

H. Eyal Salman (✉)
Mutah University, Al-Karak, Jordan
e-mail: hamzehmu@mutah.edu.jo

A.-D. Seriai · C. Dony
Lirmm Laboratory, Montpellier, France
e-mail: seriai@lirmm.fr; dony@lirmm.fr

© Springer Nature Switzerland AG 2023
R. E. Lopez-Herrejon et al. (eds.), *Handbook of Re-Engineering Software Intensive Systems into Software Product Lines*, https://doi.org/10.1007/978-3-031-11686-5_1

3

for other assets such as requirements, models, etc. [36]. In this chapter, we focus on locating features in the source code implementation.

1.2 Product Variants

It is common for companies developing variants of a software product to accommodate different customer needs. These variants provide common features (mandatory) but they also differ from one another by providing unique features or feature combinations. These products are known as *product variants* [46]. Often, product variants evolve from an initial product developed for, and successfully used by, the first customer. Unfortunately, product variants are not developed and maintained in a systematic way. They are often developed by using ad-hoc reuse approaches such as "clone-and-own" [45]. Companies develop separate product variants where a new product is built by ad-hoc copying and modifying various existing variants to fit new purposes. Figure 1.1 shows five variants of the Wingsoft Financial Management System (WFMS) [45], developed for Fudan (WFMS^{Fudan}) University. The initial product of this system attracted new customers, such as Zhejiang University and Shanghai University. Then, WFMS were used in over 100 universities in China. When there was a need to create a new variant, the WFMS's developers clone-and-modify existing variants. For example, WFMS^{Chongqing} was developed by using WFMS^{Fudan} and WFMS^{Zhejiang}.

Separately maintaining product variants causes challenges. Changes in the code of common features must be repeated across product variants. Moreover, software engineers must know how the feature (i.e., its implementation) is supposed to interact (or not interact) with other features at source code level in every product variant independently [7]. As the number of features and the number of product variants grow, developing product variants in such a way becomes more challenging and costly. Therefore, companies should change their software development strategy by a transition to systematic reuse approach such as, Software Product Line Engineering (SPLE) [33].

Fig. 1.1 An example of five software variants [46]

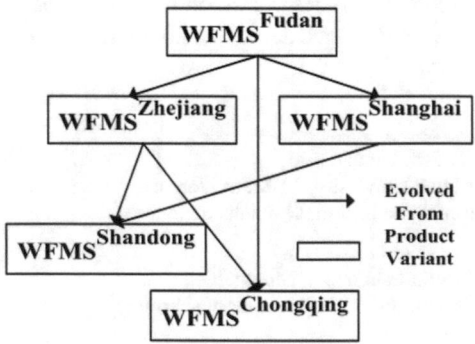

Fig. 1.2 Accumulated costs for SPL and independently systems [33]

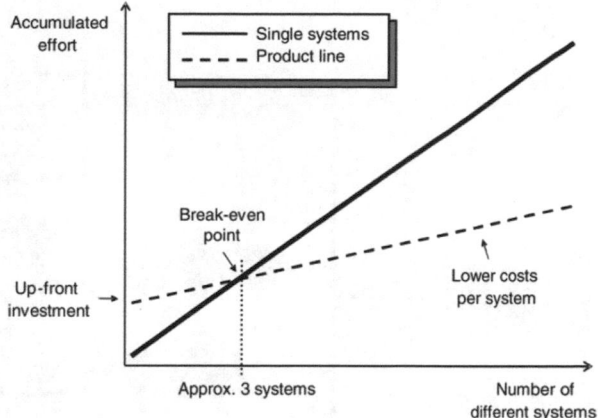

SPL's core assets play a pivotal role in SPLE. However, building SPL's core assets from scratch is a costly task and requires a long time, which leads to increase time-to-market [33]. Figure 1.2 shows the accumulated costs required to develop n software products in both SPLE and the traditional way of software development (one software system at a time). The solid line represents the costs of developing software products independently, while the dashed line represents the development costs using SPLE. In the case of the development of a few products, the costs of SPLE are high. This is because the SPL's core assets are built from scratch to generate not only small number of products but also to support generation of the full scope of products required for the foreseeable horizon. Thus, this increases up-front investment. However, these costs are significantly reduced for the development of many products. The location at which both curves intersect represents the break-even point. At this point, the costs are the same for developing the systems independently as for developing them using SPLE (Fig. 1.3).

Generally, companies cannot afford to start developing a SPL's assets from scratch, and hence they have to reuse as much existing software assets of product variants as possible. The existing assets represent a starting point for building SPL's assets. In product variants, features and source code are available assets. Features are available due to the need for product customization, as product variants are a series of customized products to meet specific needs of different customers. These needs can be features provided by these variants. Source code is always available. These assets (features and source code) should be linked together to be a part of SPL's core assets, as core assets in SPLE are linked.

Locating feature implementations are necessary to understand source code of product variants, and then reuse right features (with their implementations) for building SPL's assets and developing new products taking advantages of SPLE [23]. Also, feature location is essential for facilitating and automating new product derivation from SPL's core assets, when the re-engineering process is completed.

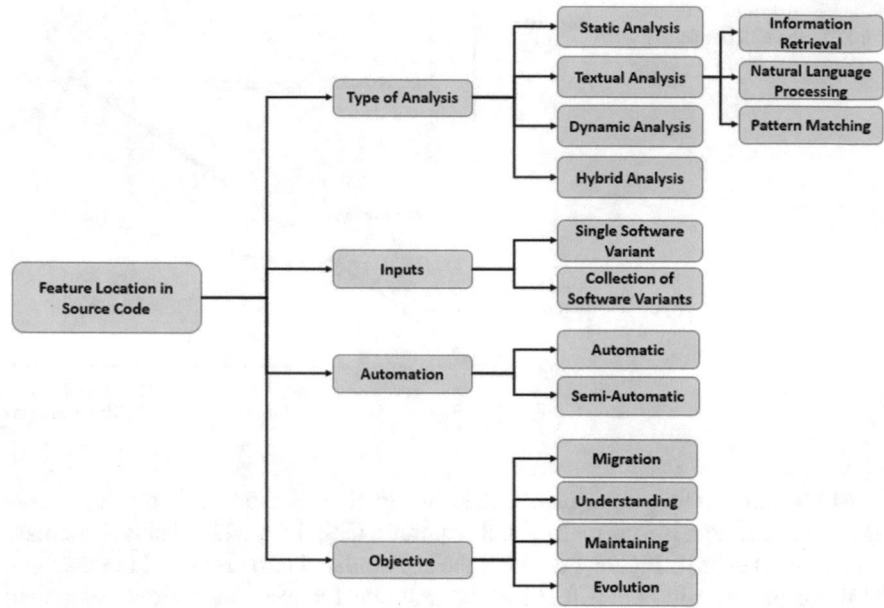

Fig. 1.3 Taxonomy scheme of feature location approaches

The application of Information Retrieval (IR) techniques in software engineering has been considered by several studies [27, 34, 35, 44]. One of the most important applications of IR in software engineering is the feature location [23]. For the importance of the IR for re-engineering product variants into SPL, we present a new classification of IR-based feature location techniques. This classification divides feature location techniques into two categories based on how they deal with product variants. The first category includes all techniques that consider product variants as singular independent products. We call this category *feature location in single software product*. The second category includes all techniques considering product variants as a collection of similar and related products. We call this category *feature location in a collection of product variants*.

1.3 Types of Feature Location

Feature location techniques are classified into four types based on the type of analysis used by these techniques: dynamic-based feature location, static-based feature location, textual-based feature location and hybrid among them [6].

1.3.1   Static-Based Feature Location

Feature location using static analysis refers to the analysis of the source code to explore structural information such as control or data flow dependencies [13], formal concept analysis [49]. Static feature location approaches require not only dependence graphs, but also a set of source code elements which serve as a starting point for the analysis. This initial set is relevant to features of interest and usually specified by maintainers. The role of static analysis is to determine other source code elements relevant to the initial set using dependency graphs [21].

Static approaches allow maintainers to be very close to what they are searching for in the source code, as they start from source code elements (initial set) specific to a feature of interest. However, these approaches often exceed what is pertinent to a feature and are prone to returning irrelevant code [6]. This is because following all dependencies of a section of code that is relevant to a feature may catch source code elements that are irrelevant. In addition, static approaches need maintainers who are familiar with the code in order to determine the initial set.

1.3.2   Textual-Based Feature Location

Textual information embedded in source code comments and identifiers provides important guidance about where features are implemented. Feature location using textual analysis aims to analyze this information to locate a feature's implementation [39]. This analysis is performed by three different ways: *pattern matching*, *Natural Language Processing (NLP)* and *Information Retrieval (IR)* [6].

1.3.2.1   Pattern Matching

Pattern matching usually needs a textual search inside a given source code using a utility tool, such as *grep* [32]. Maintainers formulate a query that describes a feature to be located and then they use a pattern matching tool to investigate lines of code that match the query. Pattern matching is not very precise due to the vocabulary problem; the probability of choosing a query's terms, using unfamiliar source code maintainers, that match the source code vocabulary is relatively low [14].

1.3.2.2   Natural Language Processing (NLP)

NLP-based feature location approaches analyze the parts of the words (such as noun phrases, verb phrases and prepositional phrases) used in the source code [41]. They rely on the assumption that verbs in object-oriented programs correspond to methods, whereas nouns correspond to objects. As an input for these approaches, the maintainer formulates a query describing the feature of interest and then the content of the query is decomposed into a set of pairs *(verb, object)*. These approaches work by finding methods and objects inside the source code, which are similar to the input verbs and objects, respectively. NLP is more precise than pattern matching but relatively expensive [6].

1.3.2.3 Information Retrieval (IR)

IR-based techniques, such as **L**atent **S**emantic **I**ndexing (LSI) and vector space model (VSM), are textual matching techniques to find textual similarity between a query and given corpus of textual documents. For the purpose of locating a feature's implementation, a feature's description represents the subject of a query while source code documents represent corpus documents. A feature description is a natural language description consisting of short paragraph(s). A source code document contains textual information of certain granularity of source code, such as a method, a class or a package. IR-based feature location approaches find a code portion that is relevant to the feature of interest by conducting a textual matching between identifiers and comments of a given source code portion and the description of the feature to be located [23].

IR lies between NLP and pattern matching in terms of accuracy and complexity [6]. Regardless of the type of textual analysis used (pattern matching, NLP and IR), generally the quality of these approaches mainly depends on the quality of the source code naming conventions and the query.

1.3.3   Dynamic-Based Feature Location

Dynamic analysis refers to collecting information from a system during runtime. For the purpose of feature location, it is used to locate feature implementations that can be called during runtime by test scenarios [4, 19]. It can be test scenarios strictly speaking about testing, but it can also be just executions trying to exercise the feature (without being a test) [30]. Feature location using dynamic analysis depends on the analysis of execution traces. An execution trace is a sequence of source code entities (classes, methods, etc.). Usually, one or more feature-specific scenarios are developed that invoke only the implementation of feature of interest. Then, the scenarios are run and execution traces are collected, recording information about the code that was invoked. These traces are obtained by instrumenting the system code. Using dynamic analysis, the source code elements pertaining to a feature can be determined in several ways. Comparing the traces of the feature of interest to other feature traces in order to find source code elements that only are invoked in the feature-specific traces [11, 43]. Alternatively, the frequency of execution parts of source code can be analyzed to determine the implementation of a feature [12, 38]. For example, a method exercised multiple times and in different situations by test scenarios relevant to a feature is more likely to be relevant to the feature being located than a method used less often.

Feature location by using dynamic analysis has some limitations. The test scenarios used to collect traces may invoke some but not all the code portions that are relevant to a given feature; this means that some of the implementation of that feature may not be located. Moreover, it may be difficult to formulate a scenario that invokes only the required feature, which leads to obtain irrelevant source code elements. Additionally, developing test scenarios involves well-documented systems to understand the system functionalities [6]. Such maintainers may be not always available, especially in legacy product variants.

1.4   Feature Location in Software Variants

In this section, we present how the feature location is used as a first step to re-engineer from software product variants to software product line development. Therefore, we present the feature location process in a collection of product variants for the re-engineering purpose.

1.4.1   Feature Location with IR in Product Variants: Conventional Application

All approaches that belong to this category represent the conventional application of IR for the purpose of locating feature implementations. In [6], Bogdan et al. survey the techniques of this category. Figure 1.4 shows an example of the conventional application of IR in a collection of three product variants. We notice that this application involves conducting a textual matching between all features (i.e., their descriptions) and entire source code of each product in product variants independently. These features and the source code represent the *IR search spaces*. In case of having a large-scale system, such an application of IR may lead to retrieve irrelevant source code elements for features, especially in case of having similar features and trivial descriptions. In the literature, different strategies have been proposed to improve the performance of this conventional application of IR concerned with locating feature implementations. In the beginning, vector space model (VSM) was used for this purpose. Then, latent semantic indexing (LSI) was proposed to overcome polysemy and synonymy problems that occur in VSM. Then, the performance of both LSI and VSM is improved using other source code information such as static information, dynamic information or their combinations. Below, we list the approaches of this category based on the strategy used in chronological order.

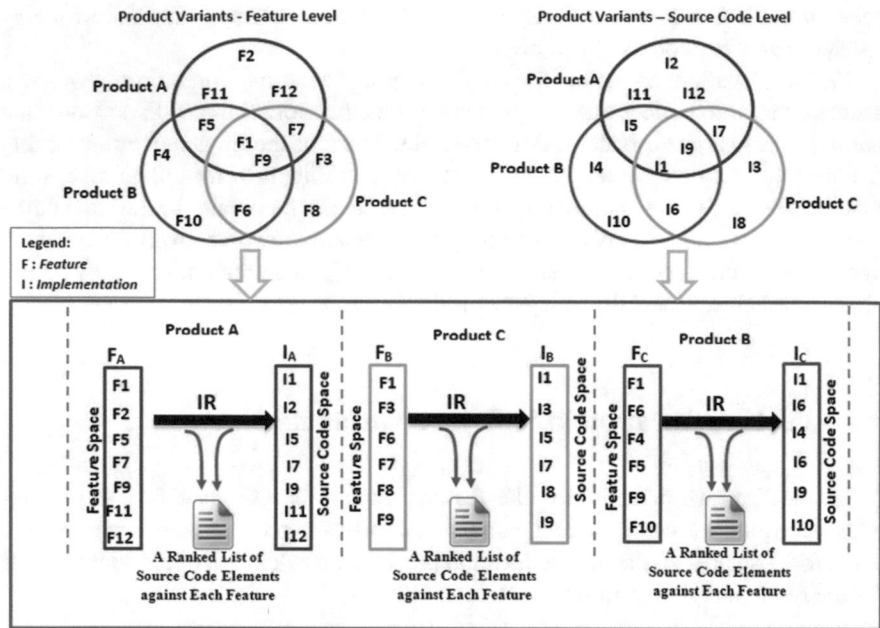

Fig. 1.4 An example of the conventional application of IR for locating feature implementations in a collection of three product variants

1.4.1.1 VSM-Based Feature Location

In [3], Antoniol et al. was the first used VSM to recover traceability links between source code and free text documentation (e.g., requirement specifications, design documents, error logs, etc.). In their approach, VSM is applied to trace C++ and Java source classes to manual pages and functional requirements, respectively. In their approach, documentation pages were used to create IR's corpus documents while source code files are used as queries. They compare the identifiers in source code and the words in corpus documents to recover traceability links.

In [15], Gay et al. introduce the notion of relevance feedback from maintainers into feature location process to improve VSM results. Relevance feedback represent a maintainer feedback about the list of source code elements retrieved by VSM. After VSM returns a ranked list of source code elements relevant to a query (e.g., feature description), the maintainer ranks the top n source code elements as relevant or irrelevant. Then, a new query is automatically formulated by modifying the previous one and new ranked list is returned, and the process repeats until achieving satisfactory results.

In [2], Ali et al. propose an approach, called COPARVO, to improve the performance of VSM for recovering traceability links between source code and requirements by partitioning the source code into different sources of information (class names, comments, methods names and class variables). Each information source acts as an expert recommending traceability links established between requirements and code classes using VSM. The top rated experts score each existing link and decide via majority voting if the link is still valid or should be rejected due to evolution in source code, requirements or both.

1.4.1.2 LSI-Based Feature Location

In [26], Marcus and Maletic use for the first time LSI for recovering traceability links between documentation and source code. In their approach, source code files without any parsing are used to create LSI's corpus while sections of documentation pages are used as queries. These sections may describe functional requirements, error logs, etc. The experiments prove that the performance of LSI is at least as well as VSM in spite of LSI do not use source code comments. In addition, it requires less preprocessing of the source code and documentation. In [27], Marcus et al. use LSI to link features with their respective source code functions. Maintainers formulate a query describing a feature. Then, LSI is applied to return a list of functions ranked by the relevance to the query. Maintainers inspect this list to decide which ones are actually parts of the feature implementation.

In [35], Poshyvanyk and Marcus propose combining LSI and FCA to link features of a given system to their respective source code methods. LSI is used to return a ranked list of source code methods against each feature. This list may contain a set of irrelevant methods to the feature being located. Therefore, FCA is employed to reduce this list by analyzing the relation between methods and terms that appear in these methods. The top k terms of the first n methods ranked by LSI are used to construct FCA's formal context and create a lattice. The objects of the formal context are methods while the attributes are terms. Concepts in the generated lattice associate terms and methods. Therefore, programmers can focus on the nodes with terms similar to their queries (feature descriptions) to find feature-relevant methods.

In [20], Kuhn et al. propose an approach to identify *linguistic topics* that reveal the intention of the source code. A *linguistic topic* is a cluster of similar object-oriented source code elements that are grouped together based on their contents. These *linguistic topics* can be composed of different source code granularity (package, class and method). The authors interpret these *linguistic topics* as features implemented by source code. They rely on LSI to compute similarity among a given set of methods, classes or packages. Then, hierarchical clustering is used to cluster similar elements together as *linguistic topics*.

In [25], De Lucia et al. present an incremental LSI-based approach to link requirements with their respective source code classes. Requirements represent queries while class documents represent LSI's corpus. They use a threshold on the similarity value to cut the ranked list of class documents returned by LSI against requirements. In their approach, the similarity threshold value is incrementally decreased to give maintainers control of the number of validated correct classes and the number of discarded false positives classes. This is why their approach is called incremental LSI-based approach. Furthermore, they conduct a comparative study between *one-shot* and *incremental* approaches. In *one-shot* approach, a full ranked list of classes that are textually similar to a requirement is submitted to maintainers for checking. The results prove that the incremental process reduces the effort required to complete a traceability recovery task compared with one-shot approaches.

Lucia et al. [24] develop a tool called *ADAMS Re-Trace* to recover traceability links between software artifacts of different levels of abstraction by using LSI. Based on this tool, traceability links are recovered by following three steps. In the first step, the software engineer selects artifacts that represent the source (e.g., requirements, sequence diagrams, test cases, code classes). In the second step, he/she selects the artifacts that represent the target. Finally, the software engineer selects the mechanism that is used to show the list of candidate links: threshold based or full ranked list. As a final output, the tool links the source artifacts to their target artifacts.

1.4.1.3 Feature Location by Combining IR with Static Analysis

In [47], Zhao et al. use VSM and static analysis to link each feature with their relevant source code functions. Their proposal consists of a two-phase process. In the first phase, VSM is applied to return a ranked list of functions that are similar to a given feature. Then, this list is reduced to a set of feature-specific functions using some algorithm. In the second phase, the authors use a static representation of the source code called Branch-Reserving Call Graph (BRCG). This representation is explored using theses feature-specific functions to identify other relevant functions for these feature-specific functions. In [40], *Shao and Smith* combine LSI and static analysis for supporting feature location. First, LSI is applied to rank all methods of a given software system against a given query (feature description). Next, a call graph for each method in the ranked list is created. Next, a method's call graph is investigated to assign it a score. The score represents the number of a method's direct neighbors that are listed in LSI's ranked list. Finally, the cosine similarity from LSI and the scores of call graphs are combined using predefined transformation to produce a new ranked list.

In [31], Peng et al. propose an iterative context-aware approach to link features with their source code elements (classes and methods). Their approach employs an iterative process with several rounds of feature-to-code mapping. The initial round is based on textual similarity only, and in following rounds textual and structural similarities are combined. Textual similarity between feature descriptions and source code is computed using LSI. The structural similarity between a feature (f) and a program element (P) was computed by evaluating how much of f's neighboring features and their relations can be mapped to P's neighboring program elements and their relations according to predefined mapping schema.

1.4.1.4   Feature Location by Combining IR with Dynamic Analysis

In [34], *Poshyvanyk et al.* propose an approach to combine LSI and a dynamic technique called *scenario-based probabilistic ranking (SPR)* to link features with their respective source code methods. Both LSI and SPR return a ranked list of code methods relevant to a feature. Each method in both lists takes a weight expressing the maintainer's confidence about LSI and SPR. Their approach combines both LSI and SPR results to overcome the uncertainty in decision making of feature-to-method linking because methods that are classified as relevant by using LSI can be irrelevant by using SPR.

In [22], Liu et al. propose a feature location approach called SITIR (SIngle Trace + Information Retrieval). Their approach combines dynamic analysis (i.e., execution traces) and LSI so that for each feature there is only a single execution trace. Then, LSI is used to rank only executed methods in the obtained trace against a given feature instead of ranking all methods in the software system.

In [4], Asadi et al. propose to combine LSI, dynamic-analysis and a search-based optimization technique (genetic algorithms) to locate cohesive portions of execution traces that correspond to a feature. Their approach is based on the assumptions that methods implementing a feature are likely to have shared terms and called close to each other in an execution trace. Their approach takes as input a set of scenarios (test cases) that exercise the features. The approach starts by executing the system using these scenarios to collect execution traces so that each trace is a sequence of methods and each feature has one execution trace. Finally, genetic algorithms (GAs) are used to separate methods of an execution trace into segments in order to find the segment that maximizes the cosine similarity between its methods. Similarity between methods is computed using LSI. This is performed by creating a document for each method containing method information (identifiers and comments). Method documents represent at the same time queries and corpus. The similarity between two method document vectors in LSI sub-space is quantified using the cosine similarity. The methods of the obtained segment implement the feature of interest.

In [10], Eaddy et al. propose a feature location approach called *Cerberus*. Their approach uses three types of analysis: dynamic, static and textual. Their approach is the only approach that leverages together all three types of analysis. The core of *Cerberus* is a technique called prune dependency analysis (PDA). By using PDA, a relationship between a program element and a feature exists if the program element should be removed or altered, when that feature is pruned (removed) from the software system. They use the approach proposed by [34] to combine rankings of program elements from execution traces, with rankings from IR to produce seeds for PDA. Then, PDA finds additional relevant elements by analyzing different kinds of relationships (such as a method call, inheritance, composition dependency among classes, etc.).

1.4.2 Feature Location with IR in Product Variants: Variability Awareness

Considering product variants together as a set of similar and related products allows the reduction of IR search spaces. This reduction refers to the division of all features and source code elements of given product variants into minimal portions so that this reduction allows to conduct a textual matching between a few features and source code elements that only implement those features. This helps to reduce the number of irrelevant source code elements returned by IR-based feature location approaches due to similar feature descriptions and implementations. Such a reduction is performed by exploring commonality and variability across product variants at feature and source code levels. Commonality refers to features (resp. their source code elements) that are part of each product while variability refers to features (resp. their source code elements) that are part of one or more (but not all) products.

In the literature, there are only two works that exploit commonality and variability across product variants to support feature location [37, 44]. One of them uses IR, namely LSI while the other is applicable to any feature location approach.

In [44], Xue et al. use LSI to link features and their source code units (functions and procedures) in a collection of product variants. They explore commonality and variability of product variants using software differencing tools and formal concept analysis (FCA) to improve the effectiveness of LSI. In their approach, LSI spaces (i.e., feature and source code spaces) are reduced into minimal disjoint partitions of feature and source code units. These partitions represent groups of features (resp. their source code elements) that can not be divided further and also without shared members between these groups. Figure 1.5 shows an example of feature and source

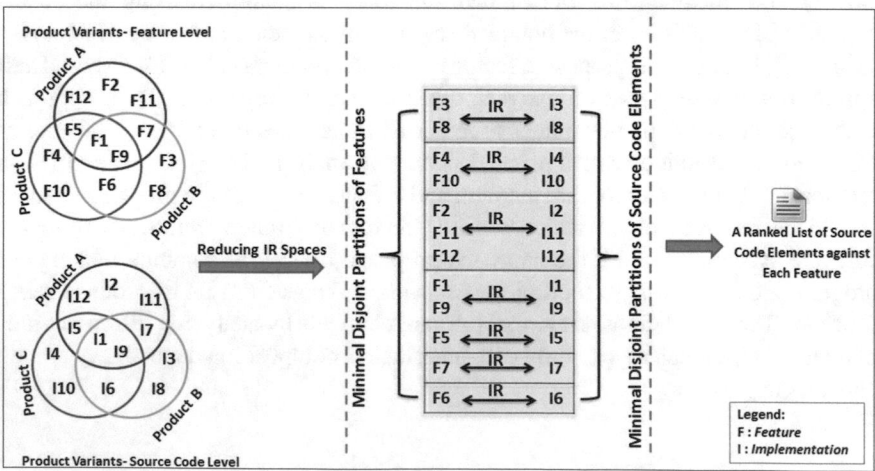

Fig. 1.5 An example of feature and implementation partitions for IR according to [44]

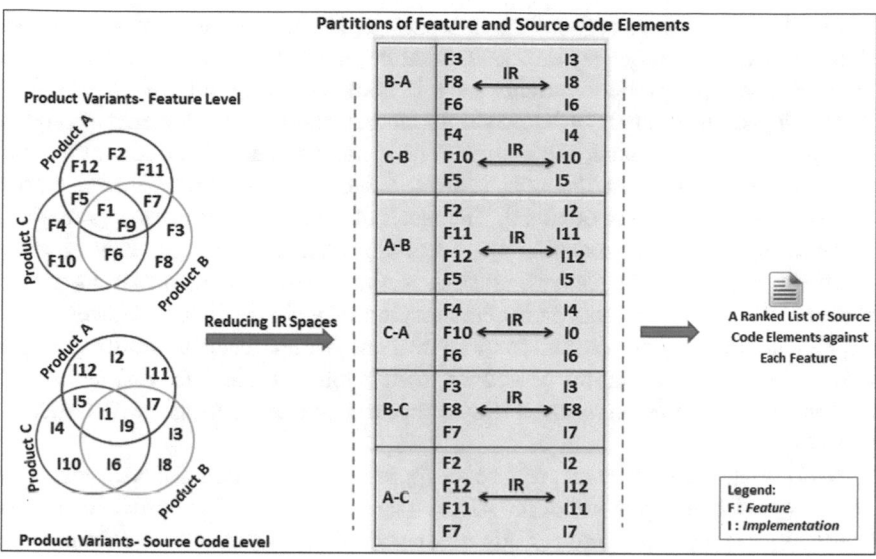

Fig. 1.6 An example of feature and implementation partitions for IR according to [37]

code partitions of a collection of three product variants according to their approach. Each slot in this figure represents a minimal disjoint partition of features and source code elements.

In [37], *Rubin and Chechik* suggest two heuristics to improve the accuracy of feature location approaches when these approaches are used to locate implementations of distinguishing features–those that are present in one product variant while absent in another. Their heuristics are based on identifying a code region that has a high potential to implement distinguishing features. This region is called *set diff* and identified by comparing pair-wisely the code of a variant that provides distinguishing features to one that does not. Figure 1.6 shows an example of all possible partitions (*set diffs*) of features and source code elements obtained by pair-wise comparison of a collection of three product variants according to their approach. In this figure, for example, (B-A) means a set of features (resp. their source code elements) that are present in *B* and absent in *A* ({F3, F8, F6}, {I3, I8, I6}). Although their approach helps to reduce IR's search spaces, the achieved reduction is not minimal comparing with Xue et al.'s work. For example, F7 (resp. its code elements) is grouped with other features (resp. their code elements) while F7 (resp. its code elements) in Xue et al.'s work is grouped alone (see Fig. 1.5). Additionally, their work does not pay attention to how code portion that implements shared features among all product variants can be obtained.

In the literature, there are two works [1, 49] similar to some extent to approaches mentioned in this category, in spite of the fact that they do not use feature descriptions and IR for determining feature implementations. We consider these works because they exploit what product variants have in common at the source code level to identify feature implementations. These works are as follows:

In [49], Ziadi et al. propose an approach to identify portions of source code elements that potentially may implement features in a collection of product variants. They exploit what product variants have in common at the source code level by performing several rounds of intersections among source code elements of product variants. In the first round, the source code elements shared between all product variants are obtained. In the next rounds, source code elements shared among some product variants are obtained. The result of each intersection may potentially represent feature implementation(s). According to their approach, they consider source code elements (packages, classes, methods and attributes) that are shared between all product variants as implementation of a single feature. However, this implementation may correspond to more than one feature when all product variants share two features or more. Moreover, their approach does not distinguish the implementation of features that always appear together, such as AND-Group of features.

In [1], Al-Msie'Deen et al. propose an approach similar to Ziadi et al.'s approach. Their approach exploits common source code elements across product variants to identify segments of source code elements, which potentially may implement features. They rely on FCA for conducting several intersections between source code elements of product variants to identify these segments. The formal context is defined as follows: objects represent names of product variants, attributes represent all unique source code elements of product variants and the relation between objects and attributes refers to which products possess which source code elements. Based on their approach, the intent of each concept in the generated lattice may correspond to the implementation of one or more features. Therefore, they rely on LSI and again on FCA to divide intent of each concept into sub-segments of textual similar source code elements. The idea behind this division is that code elements that collaborate to implement a feature share similar terms, and hence they can be grouped together as a feature implementation. However, it is not necessary that the intent of each concept represent implementation of feature(s) because source code elements that are shared between two or more features appear as a separated concept. This leads to identify features more than the features actually provided by a given collection of product variants, and hence missing source code elements that are relevant to features that actually are provided by this collection.

Martinez et al. create a tool called BUT4Reuse [28, 29]. The BUT4Reuse tool is for extractive SPL adoption by providing a framework and techniques for feature location, feature mining, mining feature constraints, extraction of reusable artifacts, feature model mining and visualization, etc. This tool is built to be generic and extensible to allow researcher to include their proposals.

Also in [48], Zhou et al. have proposed an approach and developed a tool (called INFOX) to identify cohesive code changes as a feature implementation in forks of a given C/C++ project. Their proposed approach incorporates three techniques to support such an overview: ClusterChanges technique, community-detection technique and IR technique. Such feature identification process provides new developers with overview about what development activities happened in active forks. Moreover, their approach labels the implementation of each identified feature by representative keywords extracted from source code of that feature.

In [9], Cruz et al. present a literature review to compare between three information retrieval techniques and evaluate them against the ground-truth of the ArgoUML-SPL benchmark for feature location. These techniques were compared based on their ability to correctly identify the source code of several features from the ArgoUML-SPL ground truth. The results suggest that latent semantic indexing outperforms the other two techniques. However, latent semantic indexing is should be used in combination with other methods such as, static or dynamic as using it alone leads to poor precision, recall and f-measure values.

Table 1.1 compares and summarizes techniques of both categories (feature location in a single and a collection of product variants with IR) based on predefined criteria related to the type of information that they used during the feature location process.

1.5   An Illustrative Approach for Feature Location with IR: Variability Awareness

In this chapter, we present an approach to improve the conventional application of IR for locating feature implementations in a collection of object-oriented product variants. These improvements involves following two strategies.

Firstly, we exploit commonality and variability across product variants for reducing IR spaces (i.e., feature and source code spaces) into portions of features and their corresponding portions of source code elements. These portions represent minimal disjoint sets of features and their corresponding source code elements. Each set at the feature level represent the smallest number of features that can be isolated together with their implementations. Moreover, these sets are disjoint (i.e., no shared features among them).

Secondly, we reduce the abstraction gap between the feature and source code levels in each new obtained IR spaces by introducing the concept of *code-topic*. A *code-topic* is a cluster of similar classes that have common terms and they also are called near to each other. A *code-topic* can be a functionality implemented by the source code and provided by a feature. A *code-topic* allows the grouping of terms describing a feature implemented by code-topic's classes together rather than scattering these terms over many source code elements.

1.5.1   An Overview of the Feature Location Process

To implement the strategies mentioned in the previous section, we propose the process shown in Fig. 1.7. This figure shows that our feature location process

Table 1.1 Summary of IR-feature location approaches

	Studied work	Awareness of commonality and variability	Using static source code information	Using textual information describing features	Using well-known metrics for evaluation	Source code granularity	Technique used
Single software product	[2]	No	No	Yes	Yes	Class	VSM
	[35]	No	No	Yes	No	Method	LSI, FCA
	[47]	No	Yes	Yes	Yes	Function	LSI, static analysis
	[27]	No	No	Yes	Yes	Function	LSI
	[25]	No	No	Yes	Yes	Class	LSI
	[31]	No	Yes	Yes	Yes	Class, method	LSI, static analysis
	[22]	No	No	Yes	No	Method	LSI, dynamic analysis
	[40]	No	Yes	Yes	Yes	Method	LSI, static analysis
	[15]	No	No	Yes	No	Method	VSM
	[34]	No	No	Yes	No	Method	LSI, dynamic analysis
	[10]	No	Yes	Yes	Yes	Method, attribute	LSI, dynamic analysis, static analysis
	[4]	No	No	No	Yes	Method	LSI, dynamic analysis, genetic algorithm
	[20]	No	No	No	No	Package, class, method	LSI, hierarchal clustering
	[3]	No	No	Yes	Yes	Class	VSM, probabilistic model
	[26]	No	No	Yes	Yes	Class	LSI
	[24]	No	No	Yes	Yes	Class	LSI
Product variants	[44]	Yes	No	Yes	Yes	Function	LSI
	[37]	Yes-partially	No	No	Yes	Code region (class, method, attributes, function, procedure)	Own algorithm
	[1]	Yes-partially	No	No	Yes	Package, class, method, attributes	LSI, FCA
	[49]	Yes-partially	No	No	No	Package, class, method, attributes	Own algorithm

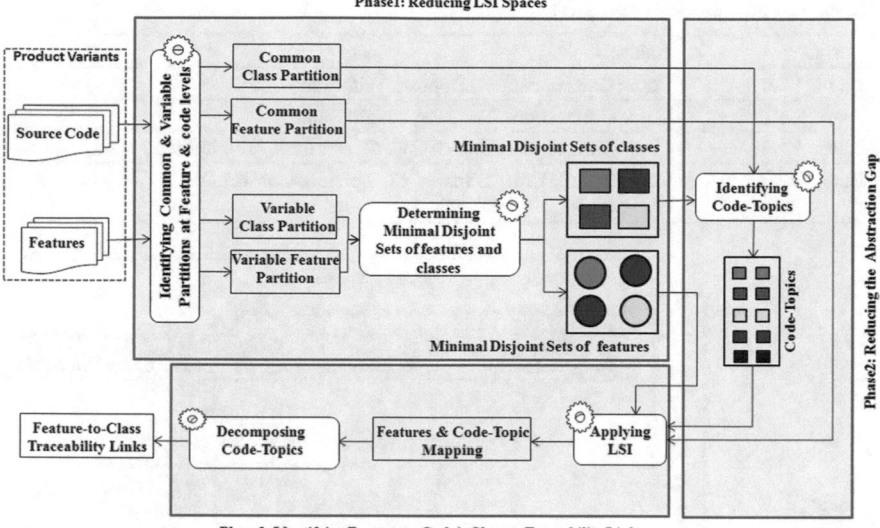

Fig. 1.7 An overview of our feature location process

consists of three phases: *reducing IR (namely, LSI) spaces*, *reducing the abstraction gap between feature and source code levels* and *linking feature-to-code's classes*.

In the first phase, we group all features (with their classes) of a given set of product variants into common and variable partitions at feature and source code levels. At the feature level, common and variable partitions respectively consist of all mandatory and optional features across product variants. At the source code level, common and variable partitions respectively consist of source code classes that implement mandatory and optional features. Also in this phase, the variable partitions at both levels are further fragmented into minimal disjoint sets. Each minimal disjoint set at feature level corresponds to its minimal disjoint set at source code level. In the second phase, we identify *code-topics* from the partition of common classes and each minimal disjoint set of classes. In the third phase, we link features and their possible corresponding *code-topics* using LSI. Such linking is used as a means to connect features with their source code classes by decomposing each code-topic to its classes. In the coming sections, we detail these phases.

As an illustrative example, we consider four variants of a bank system, as it is shown in Table 1.2, *Bank_V1.0* supports just core features for any bank system: *CreateAccount, Deposit, Withdraw* and *Loan. Bank_V1.1* has, in addition to the core features, *OnlineBank, Transfer* and *MobileBank* features. *Bank_V1.2* supports not only core features but also new features: *OnlineBank, Conversion, Consortium* and *BillPayment. Bank_V2.0* is an advanced application. It supports all previous features together.

Table 1.2 Feature set of four text bank systems

Variant	Features
Bank_V1.0	Core (CreateAccount, Deposit, Withdraw, Loan).
Bank_V1.1	Core, OnlineBank, Transfer, MobileBank.
Bank_V1.2	Core, OnlineBank, Conversion, Consortium, BillPayment.
Bank_V2.0	Core, OnlineBank, Transfer, Conversion, Consortium, BillPayment, MobileBank.

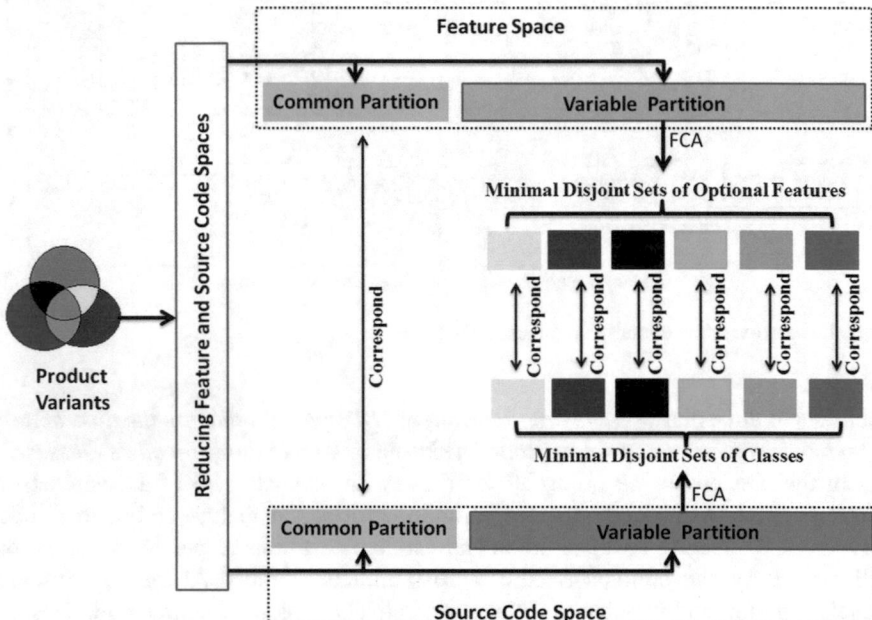

Fig. 1.8 Commonality and variability analysis across product variants

1.5.2   Reducing IR Search Spaces

In this section, we address how to improve the conventional application of IR techniques (namely, LSI) for locating features in a collection of product variants by reducing feature and source code spaces. For this, we need to analyze and understand the commonality and variability distribution across product variants. Such analysis allows the reduction of IR spaces into fragments.

We follow two steps at feature and source code levels for performing the reduction. The first step at both levels aims to determine common and variable partitions of features and source code's classes by analyzing commonality across product variants. The second step at both levels aims to fragment variable partitions of features and classes into minimal disjoint sets by analyzing variability using FCA. Figure 1.8 highlights how commonality and variability analysis can be used to reduce feature and source code spaces. In this figure, green portions refer to commonality while other colored portions refer to variability distribution across product variants. Each colored portion at the feature level is composed of one or more features while the colored portion at the source code level is composed of source code classes that implement the corresponding portion of features. Below, we detail these steps.

1.5.2.1   Determining Common and Variable Partitions at the Feature Level

As the common partition at the feature level is composed of mandatory features of product variants, we do textual matching among all feature names of product variants to find these mandatory features. The features that are part of each product in product variants form the common partition while the remaining features (i.e., optional features) in each variant form together the variable partition. In our illustrative example, all core features form the common partition while *OnlineBank, Transfer, Conversion, Consortium, BillPayment and MobileBank* features form the variable partition.

1.5.2.2   Determining Common and Variable Partitions at the Source Code Level

To group the source code classes of a given collection of product variants into common and variable partitions, we need to compare classes of product variants. Such comparison helps to determine classes that are part of each product (common partition of classes), and hence the remaining classes form the variable partition. For this, we first represent the source code classes for each variant as a set of Elementary Construction Units (ECUs). Each ECU has the following format:

$ECU = PackageName@ClassName$

This representation is necessary to be able to compare source code classes of product variants. Each product variant P_i is abstracted as a set of *ECUs* as follows: $P_i = \{ECU_1, ECU_2, \ldots, ECU_n\}$. In this way, an *ECU* reveals differences in source code's packages and classes from one variant to another variant (e.g., adding or removing packages or classes). These differences at the source code level occur due to adding or removing features to create a new variant. Common *ECUs* shared by all product variants represent common classes that form the common partition at source code level. The remaining *ECUs* in each variant represent classes that form together the variable partition at source code level. The common *ECUs* are computed by conducting a textual matching among *ECUs* of all product variants, as we assume that developers use the same vocabulary to name source code identifiers. The representation of source code as ECUs is inspired from [5].

1.5.2.3 Fragmentation of the Variable Partitions into Minimal Disjoint Sets

In this step, we reduce further the variable partitions at the feature and source code levels computed in the previous step. Our approach aims to fragment these partitions into minimal disjoint sets of optional features and their respective minimal disjoint sets of classes by using FCA (see Fig. 1.8). These sets represent the final output of the process of reducing IR spaces. These sets are minimal because each set can not be reduced more. They also are disjointed because there are no shared members among them.

Minimal disjoint sets of optional features can be obtained by analyzing optional features distribution across product variants. This analysis involves comparing all optional features of product variants. Referring again to Fig. 1.8, we can see an example of optional features distribution across product variants. *Blue*, *red* and *orange* portions in this figure refer to features (resp. their classes) that are specific to *Product1*, *Product2* and *Product3* respectively. Black, yellow and grey portions refer to features that are shared between products pair-wisely. Such analysis allows determining minimal disjoint of features. We rely on FCA to perform such analysis in order to group optional features via concept lattice into minimal disjoint sets.

We apply FCA to all variant-differences extracted from a collection of product variants. For two product variants P_1 and P_2, we create three variant-differences. $P_1 - P_2$ (a set that contains features existing only in P_1 but not in P_2), $P_2 - P_1$ (a set that contains features existing only in P_2 but not in P_1) and $P_1 \cap P_2$ (a set that contains all the optional features that P_1 and P_2 have in common). If we consider, for example, variants Bank_V1.2 (V1.2) and Bank_V2.0 (V2.0) of our illustrative example, three variant-differences can be created as follows: V1.2-V2.0 = $\{\phi\}$, V2.0-V1.2 = {*Transfer, MobileBank*} and V1.1 $\cap$ V1.2 = {*OnlineBank, Conversion, Consortium, BillPayment*}. The variant-differences aim at identifying all possible common and differences between each pair of variants in terms of provided features taking into account all combinations between product variants pair-wisely.

After extracting all variant-differences of a given collection of product variants, we define the formal context of FCA as follows:

- Variant-differences represent objects (extent)
- Optional features represent attributes (intent)
- The relation between an object and attribute refers to which optional feature is possessed by which variant-difference.

Table 1.3 shows the formal context of optional features and variant-differences corresponding to our illustrative example. Figure 1.9 shows the resulting concept lattice corresponding to the formal context defined in Table 1.3. Such a lattice shows the distribution of optional features across product variants. Each concept in this lattice consists of three fields. The upper field refers to a concept name (generated automatically). The middle field represents a set of optional features (intent). The bottom field shows variant-differences (extent). We are interested in the concepts

Table 1.3 Formal context for describing variant-differences of bank systems

	OnlineBank	Transfer	Consortium	BillPayment	Conversion	MobileBank
$V1.2 - V1.0$	X		X	X	X	
$V1.0 - V2.0$						
$V2.0 - V1.0$	X	X	X	X	X	X
$V1.1 - V1.2$		X				X
$V1.2 \cap V2.0$	X		X	X	X	
...						

Fig. 1.9 GSH-lattice for the formal context of Table 1.3

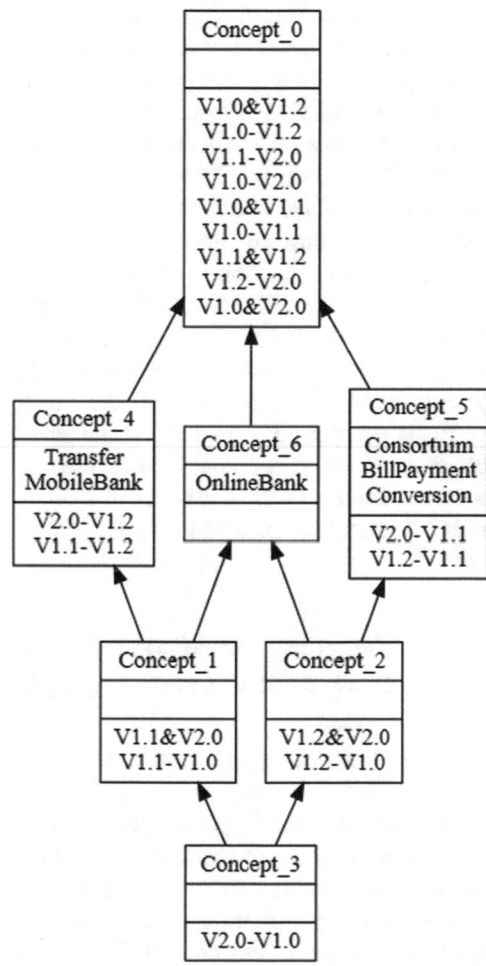

associated with a set of optional features (such as the *Concept_5* in Fig. 1.9) because these features represent the minimal disjoint set of features. The variant-differences of these concepts determine which product variants should be compared to obtain the implementation of these features.

For a given concept having a minimal disjoint set of features as intent, the extent (i.e. variant-differences) of such a concept determine which product variants should be compared to determine classes that implement only those features in that concept. The obtained classes represent the minimal disjoint set of classes corresponding to the minimal disjoint set of features in that concept. In this way, we encounter two cases. Firstly, if the concept's extent is not empty, we randomly select only one variant-difference from the variant-differences listed in its extent. For instance, to compute the minimal disjoint set of classes corresponding to the minimal disjoint set of features for $Concept\_5$ in Fig. 1.9, we can select the first variant-difference ($V2.0 - V1.1$) to identify a set of classes that are present in $Bank\_V2.0$ but absent in $Bank\_V1.1$. The resulting set of classes implements only the features located in the $Concept\_5$ ($Consortium$, $BillPayment$ and $Conversion$). Secondly, if the concept's extent is empty. i.e., it does not have own variant-differences but it inherits in a down-up manner variant differences from other concepts. In this case, we randomly select only one variant-difference from each concept located immediately below and directly related to this concept. For example, to compute the minimal disjoint set of classes corresponding to the minimal disjoint set of features for $Concept\_6$ in Fig. 1.9, we select randomly a variant-difference from $Concept\_1$ and another one from $Concept\_2$. Considering that the selected variant-differences are (V1.1 $\bigcap$ V2.0 and V1.2 $\bigcap$ V2.0). According to these variant-differences, classes that implement the $OnlineBank$ feature located in $Concept\_6$ are present at the same time in $Bank\_V1.1$, $Bank\_V2.0$ and $Bank\_V1.2$.

In both cases, commonalities and differences among source code classes of product variants are computed by lexically comparing their ECUs. For example, the corresponding classes of features of $Concept\_5$ are a set of $ECUs$ that are present in $V1.2$ but are not present in $V1.1$.

1.5.3 Reducing the Abstraction Gap Between Feature and Source Code Levels Using Code-Topic

In this section, we present how to reduce the abstraction gap between feature and source code levels using code-topic in a collection of product variants. For this, we propose to identify code-topics from the common partition's classes and any minimal disjoint set of classes in order to benefit from the reduction of IR spaces. As the code-topic is a cluster of classes, we first formulate the identification of the code-topic as a partitioning problem. Next, we compute similarity among a given set of classes, as the code-topic is a cluster of similar classes. Then, we cluster similar classes together as code-topics by using a clustering technique.

Figure 1.10 shows an example to simplify the code-topics identification process. In this figure, we assume that a given collection of product variants provides a set of features {$F1$, $F2$, ..., $F13$} and contains a set of classes {$C1$, $C2$, ..., $C47$}. This figure shows that similarity among the common partition's classes and each

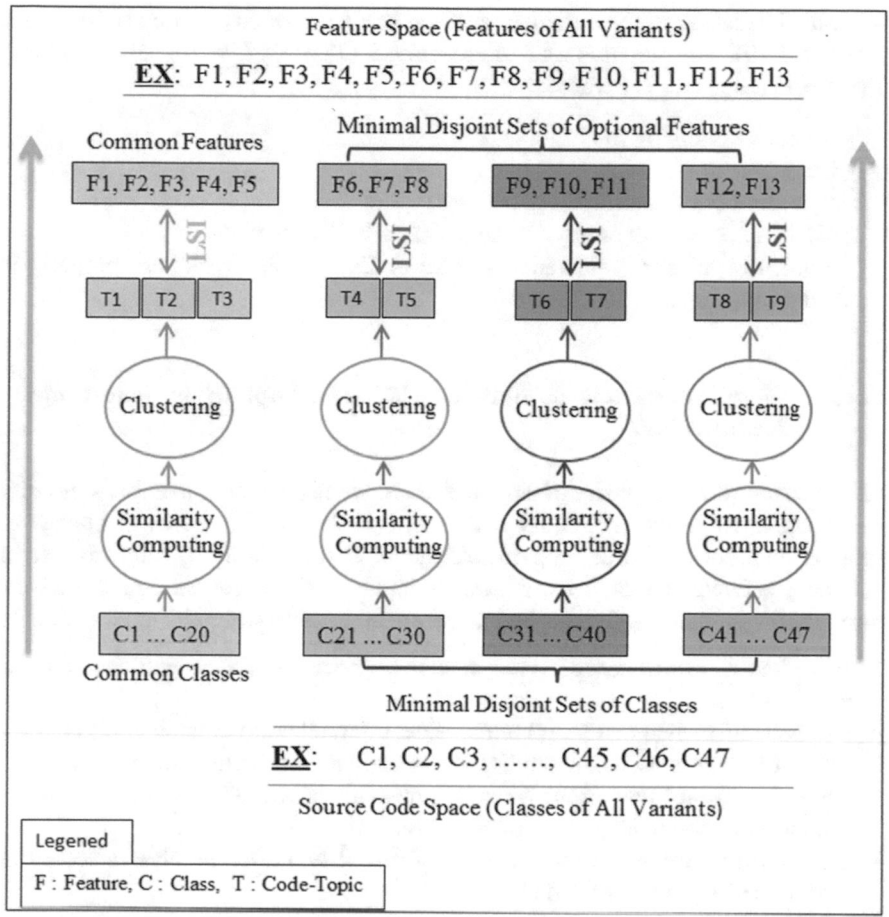

Fig. 1.10 An overview of the code-topic identification process

minimal disjoint set of classes is separately computed. Next, similar classes are clustered together to identify code-topics. Then, LSI is used to link the identified code-topics to their features.

1.5.3.1 Code-Topic Identification as a Partitioning Problem

According to our definition of the *code-topic*, the content of the *code-topic* matches a set of classes. Therefore, in order to determine a set of classes that can represent a *code-topic*, it is important to formulate the code-topic identification as a partitioning problem. This is because we need to group the classes of the common partition and any minimal disjoint set into groups. Each resulting group (partition) can be a candidate code-topic. The input of the partition process is a set of classes (C). This set could be classes of the common partition or classes of any minimal disjoint set (see Fig. 1.10). The output is a set of *code-topics* (T) of C. $C = \{c_1, c_2, \ldots, c_n\}$ and $T(C) = \{T_1, T_2, \ldots, T_k\}$ where:

- c_i is a class belonging to C.
- T_i is a subset of C.
- k is the number of identified *code-topics*.
- $T(C)$ does not contain empty elements: $\forall T_i \in T(C), T_i \neq \Phi$.
- The union of all $T(C)$ elements is equal to C: $\bigcup_{i=1}^{k} T_i = C$. This property is called completeness.

1.5.3.2 Computing Similarity Between Classes for Supporting Code-Topic Identification

As the code-topic is a cluster of similar classes, we need to compute this similarity which refers to textual similarity and structural dependency between classes to support the process of code-topic identification. Textual similarity refers to textual matching between terms derived from identifiers of the source code's classes. Structural dependency refers dependencies among classes which include:

1. **Inheritance relationship:** when a class inherits attributes and methods of another class.
2. **Method call:** when method(s) of one class use method(s) of another class.
3. **Attribute access:** when method(s) of one class use attribute(s) of another class.
4. **Shared method invocation:** when two methods of two different classes invoke the same method belonging to a third class.
5. **Shared attribute access:** when two methods of two different classes access an attribute belonging to a third class.

1.5.3.3 Clustering Classes as Code-Topics

After computing the similarity between classes of a given set, we cluster similar classes together as a candidate code-topic. Clustering techniques group similar classes together and aggregate them into clusters [17]. Each cluster is considered as a code-topic. Different clustering technique can employed in this step such as, Formal Concept Analysis (FCA) [42] and Agglomerative Hierarchal clustering (AHC) [16].

1.5.4 Locating Features by LSI

In this section, we present how to link features with their implementing classes taking advantage of reducing IR search spaces and abstraction gap between feature and source code levels. This is achieved by following two steps: establishing a mapping between features and their corresponding code-topics and then decomposing the code-topics to their classes.

1.5.4.1   Establishing a Mapping Between Features and Code-Topics

LSI is used to link features to their code-topics, as shown in Fig. 1.10. Features of the common partition are linked to the code-topics extracted from this partition. Also, Features of each minimal disjoint set are linked to code-topics extracted from its corresponding minimal disjoint set of classes.

LSI takes *code-topic* and feature documents as input. Then, LSI measures the similarity between the *code-topics* and features using the cosine similarity. LSI returns a list of *code-topics* ordered by their cosine similarity values against each feature. The *code-topics* retrieved should have a cosine similarity value greater than or equal to *0.70*, as this value represents the most widely used threshold for the cosine similarity [26].

1.5.4.2   Decomposing Code-Topics to their Classes

After linking each feature to all its corresponding *code-topics*, we can easily determine relevant classes for each feature by decomposing each *code-topic* to its classes. For instance, imagine that we have a feature (F1) that is linked to two *code-topics*: *code-topic1= {c1, c4}* and *code-topic2= {c7, c6}*. By decomposing these code-topics into their classes; we find that *F1* is implemented by five classes *{c1, c4, c7, c6}*.

1.6   Conclusions

The general goal of this chapter is to re-engineer software product variants into software product line engineering based on feature location. Locating features implantation is essential for understanding source code of product variants, and then reusing features (with their implementations) for developing new products taking advantage of SPLE. It is also necessary for facilitating and automating new product derivation from SPL's core assets when the re-engineering process is completed. We analyzed the state of the art to identify good practices to locate feature implementation in a collection of product variants.

As examples of good practices for locating features implementation, we can find the ones use information retrieval techniques. They are used widely for feature location. We have presented an approach to improve the effectiveness of IR namely LSI, as a feature location technique in a collection of product variants. Our approach followed two strategies to achieve this improvement: reducing IR search spaces (feature and source code spaces) and reducing the abstraction gap between feature and source code levels. Firstly, we analyzed commonality and variability distribution across product variants to reduce features and source code of a collection of product variants into a minimal disjoint set of features and their corresponding minimal disjoint set of classes. Secondly, we introduced the concept code-topic to reduce the abstraction gap between feature and source code levels.

References

1. Al-Msie'Deen, R., Seriai, A., Huchard, M., Urtado, C., Vauttier, S., Eyal Salman, H.: Mining features from the object-oriented source code of a collection of software variants using formal concept analysis and latent semantic indexing. In: The 25th International Conference on Software Engineering and Knowledge Engineering, p. 8. Knowledge Systems Institute Graduate School (2013)
2. Ali, N., Gueheneuc, Y.G.a., Antoniol, G.: Requirements traceability for object oriented systems by partitioning source code. In: 18th Working Conf. on Reverse Engineering, pp. 45–54. IEEE Computer Society (2011)
3. Antoniol, G., Canfora, G., Casazza, G., De Lucia, A., Merlo, E.: Recovering traceability links between code and documentation. IEEE Trans. Softw. Eng. 28(10), 970–983 (2002)
4. Asadi, F., Penta, M., Antoniol, G., Gueheneuc, Y.G.: A heuristic-based approach to identify concepts in execution traces. In: Proceedings of the 2010 14th European Conference on Software Maintenance and Reengineering, CSMR '10, pp. 31–40. Washington, DC, USA (2010)
5. Blanc, X., Mounier, I., Mougenot, A., Mens, T.: Detecting model inconsistency through operation-based model construction. In: Proceedings of the 30th international conference on Software engineering, ICSE '08, pp. 511–520. New York, NY, USA (2008)
6. Bogdan, D., Meghan, R., Malcom, G., Denys, P.: Feature location in source code: a taxonomy and survey. Journal of Evolution and Process 25(1), 53–95 (2013)
7. Calder, M., Kolberg, M., Magill, E.H., Reiff-Marganiec, S.: Feature interaction: A critical review and considered forecast. Comput. Netw. 41(1), 115–141 (2003)
8. Cornelissen, B., Zaidman, A., van Deursen, A., Moonen, L., Koschke, R.: A systematic survey of program comprehension through dynamic analysis. IEEE Trans. Software Eng. 35(5), 684–702 (2009)
9. Cruz, D., Figueiredo, E., Martinez, J.: A literature review and comparison of three feature location techniques using ArgoUML-SPL. In: Proceedings of the 13th International Workshop on Variability Modelling of Software-Intensive Systems, VAMOS 19. Association for Computing Machinery, New York, NY, USA (2019).
10. Eaddy, M., Aho, A.V., Antoniol, G., Guéhéneuc, Y.G.: Cerberus: Tracing requirements to source code using information retrieval, dynamic analysis, and program analysis. In: Proceedings of the 16th IEEE International Conference on Program Comprehension, ICPC '08, pp. 53–62. Washington, DC, USA (2008)
11. Eisenbarth, T., Koschke, R., Simon, D.: Locating features in source code. IEEE Trans. Softw. Eng. 29(3), 210–224 (2003)
12. Eisenberg, A.D., De Volder, K.: Dynamic feature traces: Finding features in unfamiliar code. In: Proceedings of the 21st IEEE International Conference on Software Maintenance, ICSM '05, pp. 337–346. Washington, DC, USA (2005)
13. Eyal-Salman, H., Seriai, A., Hammad, M.: Quality-driven feature identification and documentation from source code. Journal of Theoretical and Applied Information Technology 84 (2016)
14. Furnas, G.W., Landauer, T.K., Gomez, L.M., Dumais, S.T.: The vocabulary problem in human-system communication. Commun. ACM 30(11), 964–971 (1987)

15. Gay, G., Haiduc, S., Marcus, A., Menzies, T.: On the use of relevance feedback in ir-based concept location. In: ICSM, pp. 351–360. IEEE (2009)
16. Haifeng, Z., Zijie, Q.: Hierarchical agglomerative clustering with ordering constraints. In: WKDD, pp. 195–199 (2010)
17. Jain, A.K., Murty, M.N., Flynn, P.J.: Data clustering: A review. ACM Comput. Surv. **31**(3), 264–323 (1999)
18. Kang, K.C., Cohen, S.G., Hess, J.A., Novak, W.E., Peterson, A.S.: Feature-oriented domain analysis (FODA) feasibility study (1990)
19. Koschke, R., Quante, J.: On dynamic feature location. In: Proceedings of the 20th IEEE/ACM international Conference on Automated software engineering, ASE '05, pp. 86–95. New York, NY, USA (2005)
20. Kuhn, A., Ducasse, S., Gírba, T.: Semantic clustering: Identifying topics in source code. Inf. Softw. Technol. **49**(3), 230–243 (2007)
21. Kunrong, C., Vaclav, R.: Case study of feature location using dependence graph. In: Proceedings of the 8th International Workshop on Program Comprehension, pp. 241–249. IEEE Computer Society (2000)
22. Liu, D., Marcus, A., Poshyvanyk, D., Rajlich, V.: Feature location via information retrieval based filtering of a single scenario execution trace. In: Proceedings of the Twenty-second IEEE/ACM International Conference on Automated Software Engineering, ASE '07, pp. 234–243. New York, NY, USA (2007)
23. Lucia, A.D., Fasano, F., Oliveto, R., Tortora, G.: Recovering traceability links in software artifact management systems using information retrieval methods. ACM Trans. Softw. Eng. Methodol. **16**(4) (2007)
24. Lucia, A.D., Oliveto, R., Tortora, G.: Adams re-trace: traceability link recovery via latent semantic indexing. In: ICSE, pp. 839–842. ACM (2008)
25. Lucia, A.D., Oliveto, R., Tortora, G.: IR-based traceability recovery processes: An empirical comparison of "one-shot" and incremental processes. In: Proceedings of the 2008 23rd IEEE/ACM International Conference on Automated Software Engineering, ASE '08, pp. 39–48. Washington, DC, USA (2008)
26. Marcus, A., Maletic, J.I.: Recovering documentation-to-source-code traceability links using latent semantic indexing. In: ICSE, pp. 125–137. IEEE Computer Society (2003)
27. Marcus, A., Sergeyev, A., Rajlich, V., Maletic, J.I.: An information retrieval approach to concept location in source code. Working Conference on Reverse Engineering **0**, 214–223 (2004)
28. Martinez, J., Ziadi, T., Bissyande, T.F., Klein, J., Le Traon, Y.: Bottom-up adoption of software product lines: A generic and extensible approach. In: Proceedings of the 19th International Conference on Software Product Line, SPLC 15, p. 101–110. Association for Computing Machinery, New York, NY, USA (2015)
29. Martinez, J., Ziadi, T., Bissyande, T.F., Klein, J., Traon, Y.L.: Bottom-up technologies for reuse: Automated extractive adoption of software product lines. In: Proceedings of the 39th International Conference on Software Engineering Companion, ICSE-C 17, p. 67–70. IEEE Press (2017)
30. Michelon, G.K., Linsbauer, L., Assunção, W.K., Fischer, S., Egyed, A.: A hybrid feature location technique for re-engineeringsingle systems into software product lines. In: 15th International Working Conference on Variability Modelling of Software-Intensive Systems, VaMoS'21. Association for Computing Machinery, New York, NY, USA (2021)
31. Peng, X., Xing, Z., Tan, X., Yu, Y., Zhao, W.: Improving feature location using structural similarity and iterative graph mapping. J. Syst. Softw. **86**(3), 664–676 (2013)
32. Petrenko, M., Rajlich, V., Vanciu, R.: Partial domain comprehension in software evolution and maintenance. In: The 16th IEEE Int'l Conf. on Program Comprehension, pp. 13–22. IEEE (2008)
33. Pohl, K., Bckle, G., van der Linden, F.J.: Software product line engineering: Foundations, principles and techniques. Springer Publishing Company, Incorporated (2010)

34. Poshyvanyk, D., Gueheneuc, Y.G., Marcus, A., Antoniol, G., Rajlich, V.: Feature location using probabilistic ranking of methods based on execution scenarios and information retrieval. IEEE Trans. Softw. Eng. **33**(6), 420–432 (2007)
35. Poshyvanyk, D., Marcus, A.: Combining formal concept analysis with information retrieval for concept location in source code. ICPC '07, pp. 37–48. Washington, DC, USA (2007)
36. Reinhartz-Berger, I., Itzik, N., Wand, Y.: Analyzing variability of software product lines using semantic and ontological considerations. In: M. Jarke, J. Mylopoulos, C. Quix, C. Rolland, Y. Manolopoulos, H. Mouratidis, J. Horkoff (eds.) Advanced Information Systems Engineering, pp. 150–164. Springer International Publishing, Cham (2014)
37. Rubin, J., Chechik, M.: Locating distinguishing features using diff sets. In: Proceedings of the 27th IEEE/ACM International Conference on Automated Software Engineering, ASE 2012, pp. 242–245. New York, NY, USA (2012)
38. Safyallah, H., Sartipi, K.: Dynamic analysis of software systems using execution pattern mining. In: ICPC, pp. 84–88. IEEE Computer Society (2006)
39. Savage, T., Revelle, M., Poshyvanyk, D.: Flat3: feature location and textual tracing tool. In: ICSE'2, pp. 255–258. ACM (2010)
40. Shao, P., Smith, R.K.: Feature location by ir modules and call graph. In: Proceedings of the 47th Annual Southeast Regional Conference, ACM-SE 47, pp. 70:1–70:4. New York, NY, USA (2009)
41. Shepherd, D., Pollock, L., Vijay-Shanker, K.: Towards supporting on-demand virtual remodularization using program graphs. In: Proceedings of the 5th International Conference on Aspect-oriented Software Development, AOSD '06, pp. 3–14. New York, NY, USA (2006)
42. Valtchev, P., Missaoui, R., Godin, R.: Formal concept analysis for knowledge discovery and data mining: The new challenges. pp. 352–371. Springer (2004)
43. Wilde, N., Scully, M.C.: Software reconnaissance: mapping program features to code. Journal of Software Maintenance: Research and Practice **7**(1), 49–62 (1995)
44. Xue, Y., Xing, Z., Jarzabek, S.: Feature location in a collection of product variants. In: WCRE, pp. 145–154. IEEE Computer Society (2012)
45. Ye, P., Peng, X., Xue, Y., Jarzabek, S.: A case study of variation mechanism in an industrial product line. In: Proceedings of the 11th International Conference on Software Reuse: Formal Foundations of Reuse and Domain Engineering, ICSR '09, pp. 126–136. Springer-Verlag, Berlin, Heidelberg (2009)
46. Yinxing, X., Zhenchang, X., Stan, J.: Understanding feature evolution in a family of product variants. Reverse Engineering, Working Conference on **0**, 109–118 (2010)
47. Zhao, W., Zhang, L., Liu, Y., Sun, J., Yang, F.: Sniafl: Towards a static noninteractive approach to feature location. ACM Trans. Softw. Eng. Methodol. **15**(2), 195–226 (2006)
48. Zhou, S., Stanciulescu, S., Lebenich, O., Xiong, Y., Wasowski, A., Kästner, C.: Identifying features in forks. In: Proceedings of the 40th International Conference on Software Engineering, ICSE '18, pp. 105–116. ACM, New York, NY, USA (2018)
49. Ziadi, T., Frias, L., da Silva, M.A.A., Ziane, M.: Feature identification from the source code of product variants. In: Proceedings of the 15th European Conference on Software Maintenance and Reengineering, pp. 417–422 (2012)

Chapter 2
Feature and Variability Extraction from Natural Language Requirements

Sandro Schulze and Yang Li

Abstract Requirements or requirement specifications are usually the very first artifact that is created when starting a software project. It results from intensive discussions with customers about all facets of the software system to be developed, mostly in form of plain text. Hence, if properly done, requirement specifications reflect on all features of a software system as well as how these features depend on each other. Consequently, requirements are a valuable source for extracting variability to support systematic reuse in variant-rich software systems. We research on techniques that employ syntactical as well as semantical information from such textual requirements in order to (1) *extract features* and map requirements to them, and (2) *extract variability* to understand how features are related to each other, and thus, which variants can be possibly created.

2.1 Introduction

Software reuse has been proposed a long time ago as a pivotal aspect of software maintenance and evolution. While lots of concepts have been proposed for reuse in-the-small (e.g., classes, inheritance, higher-order functions), developing systems for reuse over time and in order to support diverse customer requirements is the grand challenge of today. Most notably, it is hard to reason about reusable parts (i.e., features) from the beginning (i.e., during requirements analysis) as it is impossible to foresee, which parts should be reused and how should they be modularized for future requirements. Moreover, there is usually no time to perform an in-depth domain analysis that would be necessary for such reasoning.

S. Schulze (✉)
Faculty of Computer Science, Otto-von-Guericke Universität Magdeburg, Magdeburg, Germany
e-mail: sanschul@iti.cs.uni-magdeburg.de

Y. Li
Pure-systems GmbH, Magdeburg, Germany
e-mail: yang.li@ovgu.de

© Springer Nature Switzerland AG 2023
R. E. Lopez-Herrejon et al. (eds.), *Handbook of Re-Engineering Software Intensive Systems into Software Product Lines*, https://doi.org/10.1007/978-3-031-11686-5_2

Think about the following (even though hypothetical) scenario: You are running a software company that is working in an increasingly important domain with competitors all over the world. You are lucky enough to get an offer for developing a software system that would be amazingly important for your business, but you need to be fast enough as your competitors picked up your trail. Hence, it all breaks down to the following decision:

Alt1   Just get started with the project, achieving the goal with incremental refinement and extensions and continuous prototyping, or

Alt2   Start with high efforts in discussing and eliciting the requirements with the customer, and thereupon, coming up with a proper *software requirements specification (SRS)* as a basis for any further project activity (no matter which type of project management is applied)?

Which alternative would you choose? Obviously, it is tempting to go with *Alt1*, as it promises to deliver a first product relatively fast that can be shown to the customer, and thus, convince her to stay with your company. However, what if your first prototype is far away from what the customer wants? What if crucial features are not even close to be planned and realized? What if future customer's requirements are diverging or even conflicting with your initial system?

The take away message from this short story is that requirements engineering (and its results) are one of the most crucial yet underestimated parts of the software engineering process since they capture all of the features that should be developed for a particular system. Of course, this information is not for free: the process of collecting and eliciting requirements is usually a tedious and long-lasting activity, involving many stakeholders, such as customers, managers, developers, and encompassing a series of workshops and interviews. At the end, the resulting document is a *software requirements specification (SRS)* that constitutes a comprehensive description of any characteristic of the software system that should be developed [12]. As such, it is a valuable source of information to reason about the system, its features and how they are related.

However, an SRS document also comes with some specialities that pose challenges on the analysis of such a document. First of all, requirements are *textual* documents mostly written in *natural language* with only some basic structure among them. Second, compared to other artifacts such as code or models, requirements are rather informal with at most following a certain template or boilerplate [12]. However, they barely follow any strict rules regarding their syntax or composition; in worst case, it is just plain text. Consequently, analyzing such requirements with the aim of information retrieval is a non-trivial task, as it requires both, syntactic as well as semantic analysis techniques.

Nevertheless, the advantages of requirements for feature and variability extraction outweigh their shortcomings; if properly maintained, an SRS encompasses all functional and non-functional properties of a system. Moreover, traceability links to other artifacts in later development stages are usually maintained, and thus, allow for a mapping of such artifacts to their corresponding requirements. Hence, any information about features that we extract from requirements can be propagated throughout all later development phases. In particular, we are interested in two different application scenarios for extracting features & variability from requirements:

(A) Software systems that initially start as single program, but over time, features are added that also allow for creating different instances of this system. However, the information about what can be/should be combined and what better not to put into a common program has never been explicated, and thus, needs to be recreated.

(B) A software system evolves over time to fulfill the requirements for a particular customer or market. At some point, a different customer or market should be satisfied. To this end, the original system is copied and from there on, has its own life (i.e., evolves independently). This process is called *clone-and-own*, can be repeated several times, and is a common reuse mechanism in practice [7], resulting in multiple similar, yet related systems that evolve independently. However, with this kind of reuse, all information about differences and commonalities among the resulting variants is usually not documented, and thus, this information is lost or at least hidden from any prospective stakeholder.

In this chapter, we will have a closer look on techniques that allow to derive valuable information for both of the aforementioned scenarios from SRS documents. In particular, we focus on two main challenges that are of superior interest in this context:

How can Features be Identified in Natural Language Requirements?

Answering this question is imperative, as features constitute the (logical) building blocks of any product line or variant-rich software system. Without this knowledge, any task that requires reasoning about features—testing, specifying feature dependencies, exploring feature interactions—is impossible.

Unfortunately, there is no universal technique that enables this feature extraction task. However, since requirements are textual and rather informal, the rise of *natural language processing (NLP)* [13] techniques bear a huge potential to support this task. We will introduce NLP in general in Sect. 2.2 and provide details about techniques for feature extraction (using NLP) in Sect. 2.3.

How can Variation Points Between Features be Identified?

Even if we know about the features (and their mapping to the artifacts), we still miss information about their *relationships* and *dependencies* among each other. This is inevitable, for instance, to reason about valid configurations, apply sampling algorithms [29], or to analyze inconsistencies among such relations.

However, since requirements do rarely follow a certain scheme, it is a non-trivial and challenging task to identify those parts that indicate a variation point such as an alternative group or, even harder, a cross-tree constraint. Only few work exists for this task, which we introduce in more detail in Sect. 2.4.

2.2 Natural Language Processing in a Nutshell

Natural language processing (NLP) is indispensable for feature and variability information extraction from NL documents. It supports computers to analyze, interpret and manipulate human language, paving the way for computer's understanding the human communication. In this section, we will briefly introduce how NLP techniques can be generally utilized to enable feature identification and variation point extraction in SPLs. The general process is shown in Fig. 2.1.

First of all, NL documents are pre-processed by implementing tokenization, assigning parts of speech to each word, removing stop words and so on, which is named *Text Pre-processing*. Given a character sequence, tokenization is the task of breaking it up into pieces, such as words, symbols and other elements called tokens, which makes it easy for computers to identify and analyze NL documents. Moreover, these tokens can be tagged with their type of word (e.g., noun, verb, object, etc.) using *Part-Of-Speech* tagging (POS tagging). Lemmatization can be used to transform different forms of a word into the common base form of this word. For example, the semantically related words, "activates", "activated", "activating", all with similar meaning, are converted into the word "activate". Additionally, stop words which usually refer to the most common words in a vocabulary (e.g., "the", "at", "a") are removed in this phase, as they lack any linguistic information. Note that there doesn't exist a single universal list of stop words that can be selected by means of the specific given purpose. An example for tokenization is as follows:

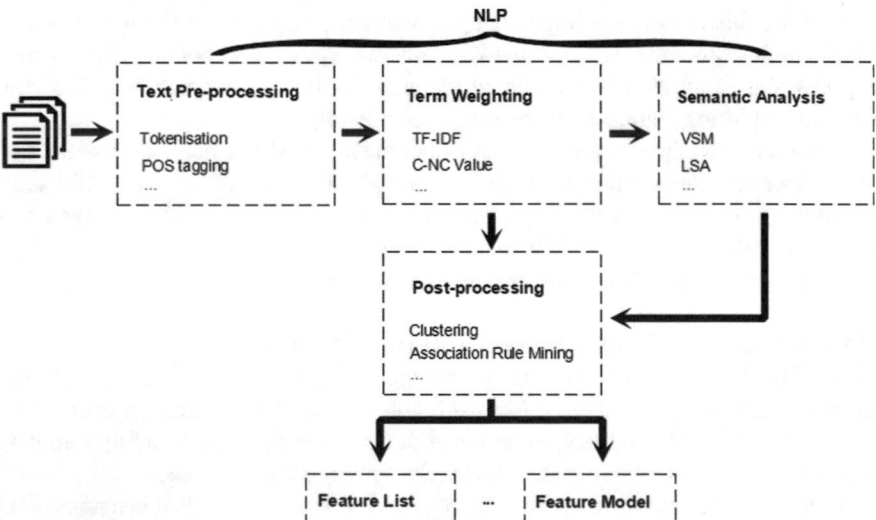

Fig. 2.1 Example graphic, showing a general NLP process for variability extraction

> Requirement:
> "When the alarm system is activated, this is indicated by the light of the LED."
> The corresponding tokens obtained after tokenization:
> "When", "the", "alarm", "system", "is", "activated", ",", "this", "is", "indi-cated", "by", "the", "light", "of", "the", "LED", "."

Second, some *Term weighting* techniques are typically used to assess the importance of terms in NL documents usually based on numerical statistics, such as, computing the frequency of their occurrence in different NL documents. Term Frequency-Inverse Document Frequency (TF-IDF) and C/NC value are two commonly used techniques. Generally speaking, TF-IDF relies on the term frequency in a given document and inverse document frequency relies on a collection of documents as a whole, in which the term is considered significant if it appears frequently in a document, but infrequently in other documents. In contrast, C/NC value is a more sophisticated statistical measure which combines linguistic and statistical information [10].

Third, *Semantic Analysis* is optionally applied to achieve the semantic information of the NL documents. Several techniques, such as, Vector Space Model (VSM) and Latent Semantic Analysis (LSA) are widely used to conduct a semantic analysis. More precisely, semantic analysis in this context mostly refers to the distributional semantics research field that analyzes the semantic similarities between linguistic items in terms of the corresponding word vector similarity, while the vector representation is calculated and modelled by words distributional properties in NL documents. Moreover, the cosine value between the vectors are typically used to measure the similarity called cosine similarity.

Finally, after the general NLP process, a *post-processing* step is indispensable to further analyze the processed NL documents with specific focus on identifying features and extracting variation points. Certainly, various techniques regarding information retrieval and machine learning can be used in this step, such as, Clustering Approaches and Association Rule Mining. Cluster approaches are adopted to group similar features with a feature being a cluster of tight-related requirements. Association rule mining is used to discover affinities among features across products and to augment and enrich the initial product profile. In addition, there are also some rule-based methods in terms of the transformed data by NLP.

After post-processing, various outputs can be obtained depending on the goal of the analysis and further usage, such as, a feature list, some variation points or an entire feature model. Note that the NLP techniques that are appicable in this research area are not limited to aforementioned methods. Moreover, advances in NLP, information retrieval, or deep learning promote the development of feature and variability extraction from NL documents in SPLs.

2.3   Feature Extraction

A feature is the initial and smallest artifact in a feature model. While diverse approaches have been utilized for extracting features from NL documents, we introduce the three most commonly used methods, that is, similarity-based, graph-based, and term-based feature extraction.

2.3.1   Similarity-Based Feature Extraction

Similarity-based feature extraction is the most popular method. Here, the similarity information among words and sentences is an indispensable property that can be analyzed and utilized for feature extraction from NL documents. In order to achieve the similarity value for each pair of words, sentences or requirements, various similarity measures can be employed, such as, string-based, corpus-based and knowledge-based similarity [11]. In the context of feature extraction from requirements, the most commonly used similarity measures are *corpus-based* and *knowledge-based* similarity [17]. The reason is that the similarity value for each pair of requirements highly depends on the semantic information of the requirements, while string-based similarity measures lack the capability of achieving accurate semantic information.

In Fig. 2.2, we show the general work flow regarding similarity-based feature extraction. Besides tokenization, lemmatization, and removing stop words, a POS filter is commonly used during pre-processing in order to select the most meaningful words, such as nouns, adjectives, and verbs. After the pre-processing step, different similarity measures can be applied to achieve the similarity information encompassing the similarity values and a similarity matrix regarding the words, sentences, or requirements. Then, the obtained similarity information is further analyzed using different approaches, such as clustering algorithms or even manual analysis. Certainly, *clustering algorithms* are the most commonly used methods to automate the analysis, where similar information (e.g., words, sentences, requirements) are grouped in terms of the *similarity matrix* of the requirements. Finally, features can

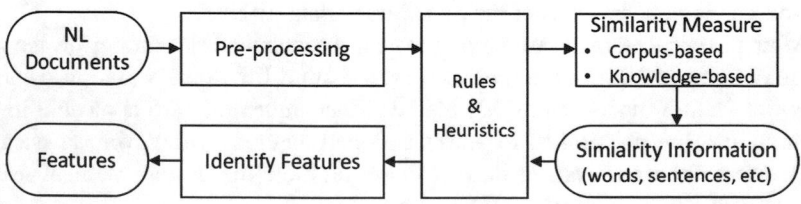

Fig. 2.2 A general process for similarity-based feature extraction

be identified based on the resulting clusters (i.e., groups of similar information), taking different rules or heuristics into account.

2.3.1.1   Similarity Measures

Corpus-Based Similarity The semantic similarity of words, sentences or texts is obtained in terms of a numeric representation learned from the semantic information of a large text collection, called corpus-based similarity. In our case, the corpora can be any text collection regarding the products or systems in a specific domain, such as SRS. There are two kinds of corpus-based similarity measures commonly used to achieve the similarity: traditional distributional semantic models (DSMs) and neural word embedding.

Traditional DSMs Traditional DSMs can be considered as count models, since they operate on co-occurrence matrices to initialize the vector representation of words, such as counting co-occurrences of words appearing in a specific corpus. VSM and LSA are traditional DSMs that are commonly applied in the research area for feature extraction from requirements [1, 16, 32].

The basic idea behind VSM is to transform the text content to vector operations in vector space. To this end, spatial similarity (i.e., the similarity of vectors) is used to express semantic similarity of texts, which is intuitive and easy to understand [27]. When a document is represented as a vector, the similarity between documents can be measured by calculating the similarity between the vectors. The most commonly used measure of similarity in text processing is the cosine distance. Next, we briefly introduce how to obtain the vector representation of requirements. Given a set of requirements R and a dictionary D, a requirement is represented as the bag of its words (i.e., the bag-of-words model), and then a value is calculated for each word according to the TF-IDF. Given the size of dictionary D being m, the requirement is converted into an m-dimensional vector. If a word in the dictionary does not appear in a particular requirement, the corresponding element of the word in the vector is 0. If a word appears in the requirement, the corresponding element value of the word in the vector is the TF-IDF value of the word. This way, the requirement is represented as a vector, which forms the foundation the vector space model.To put it differently, the vector space model does not catch the relationship between terms, but rather assumes that terms are independent of each other.

LSA also treats the text as a document-term matrix and calculates the similarity between documents by vectors (e.g., based on the angle), which is the same as VSM. The difference is that LSA assumes that some latent structures exist in word usage to express a topic, but these latent structures may be partially obscured by the variety of word selections. Hence, LSA utilizes singular value decomposition (SVD) to the document-term matrix and takes the first k largest singular values and corresponding singular vectors to form a new matrix [8]. The new matrix reduces the ambiguity of the semantic relationship between terms and text, which is beneficial to figure out the meaning of text.

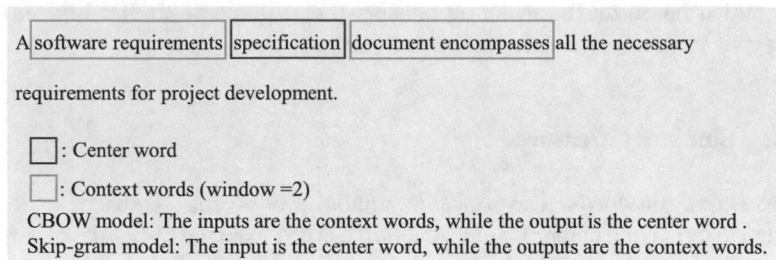

Fig. 2.3 An example for sketching the CBOW and Skip-gram models

Neural Word Embedding Neural word embedding is a neural-network-based natural language processing architecture which can be seen as prediction models, since the vector representations of words or texts can be gained from a pre-trained language model, trained on a large text collections by using neural network technique. To this end, various techniques exist to achieve accurate neural word embedding models, such as word2vec [21], GloVe [25] and FastText [4].

Word2vec applies a two-layer neural network to train a large-scale corpus, which results in a vector space where the words in the corpus are transformed into vector representation in the vector space. Its basic idea is that two words with similar context (i.e., surrounding words) should have similar word vectors. According to the difference of using the context, word2vec provides two methods to achieve the representations of languages: the Continuous Bag-of-Words (CBOW) and Skip-gram models. As shown in Fig. 2.3, the CBOW predicts the target word based on the context, while based on the word, Skip-gram predicts the target context.

Word2vec is trained on a local corpus, and its text characteristic extraction is based on sliding windows, while GloVe's sliding windows are used to build a co-occurance matrix, which is based on a global corpus. As a consequence, GloVe needs to count the co-occurrence probability in advance. FastText treats each word as a bag of n-grams rather than the word itself. For example, the n-gram representation of word "apple" for $n = 3$ is "<ap", "app", "ppl", "ple", "le>" with boundary symbols "<" and ">". As a result, we can use these tri-grams to represent the word "apple". Moreover, the sum of these five tri-grams vectors can be used to represent the word vector of "apple". Additionally, Fasttext can learn the vector of the character n-grams in a word and sum these vectors to generate the final vector of the word itself, and thus, generate a vector for a word that does not appear in the training corpus.

Knowledge-Based Similarity The similarity among words depends on the degree of the words' semantic relatedness drawn from semantic networks or knowledge bases, called knowledge-based similarity [20]. WordNet as a large knowledge base has been extensively used to achieve the semantic relatedness of words in various research areas. It is a large lexical database of English in which nouns, verbs, adjectives and adverbs are grouped into sets of cognitive synonyms, each expressing a distinct concept [22]. In WordNet, synsets denote the sets of cognitive synonyms, interlinked by means of conceptual-semantic and lexical relations. There exist some approaches that uses WordNet in the process of feature extraction. For example, WordNet can be applied to identify synonyms to group verbs with similar senses [30, 31], while in research [14, 15], WordNet is utilized to compute the similarity of two words based on the depth of the two senses in the taxonomy in WordNet ontology. Besides achieving the similarity, WordNet is employed to extract the hierarchy of features by taking advantage of the hypernyms and hyponyms of the feature names [19].

2.3.1.2 Rules & Heuristics

Rule-based methods and heuristics are typically used to analyze and process the requirements in order to extract features, taking the different kinds of similarity information into account.

Semantic Roles In some research [14, 26], the requirements are further analyzed and processed to extract some predicated semantic roles (e.g., agent, action, object, ect) from each individual requirement based on Semantic Role Labelling (SRL) technique. The similarity of each pair of requirements relies on the weighted average similarity of the predicated semantic roles in the requirements.

The SRL task refers to the predicate of the sentence as the center. However, it does not analyze the semantic information contained in the sentence in depth, but only analyzes the relationship between each component (i.e., semantic argument) in the sentence and the predicate (i.e., verb), namely the Predicate-Argument structure. Moreover, SRL describes these structural relationships with semantic roles, such as Agent, Patient, Theme, Experiencer, Beneficiary, Instrument, Location, Goal, Source, and so on [24].

Clustering Algorithms Commonly used methods to analyze the similarity information automatically are clustering algorithms, such as, K-means, hierarchical clustering and DBSCAN. The indispensable assumption is that, for example, if we assume that several requirements related to similar functionality belong to a particular feature, we can observe that a cluster denotes a feature.

Moreover, hierarchical clustering algorithms are not only used to extract features from requirements, but can also be applied to achieve the hierarchy of features by inheriting the cluster tree (i.e., a dendrogram), such as in several proposed approaches [1, 14, 18, 32]. More precisely, we can cut the tree at a predefined distance to gain features (i.e., clusters) and keep the hierarchy information. For example, in Fig. 2.4, given the distance threshold as 20, we can achieve three concrete features marked as green, red and peacock blue, respectively. According to the cluster tree, we can also infer that there might exist an abstract feature that is the parent feature of the two concrete features marked as red and peacock blue.

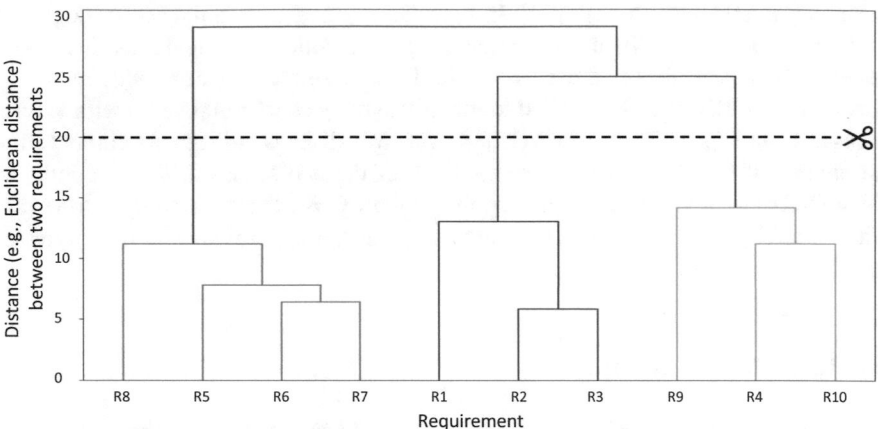

Fig. 2.4 The dendrogram in the HAC

2.3.2 Graph-Based Feature Extraction

Graph-based approaches constitute another method for feature extraction. In graph theory, a graph is a network of a set of objects, where some pairs of objects are related with each other in a certain, well-defined way. Generally, we use vertices (i.e., points or nodes) to represent the objects and edges (i.e., lines) to represent the relation between (pairs of) vertices. In other words, a graph is a set of vertices connected with edges, denoted as $G = (V, E)$. Moreover, a graph can have further properties such as being *directed/undirected* or a *weighted graph*.

As an example for graph-based extraction approaches, we briefly introduce a technique by Chen et al. that uses a weighted, undirected graph for feature extraction [5]. In particular, they use this graph to illustrate several dedicated relationships between individual requirements. To this end, vertices denote individual requirements, while edges represent the dedicated relationships between pairs of requirements. Moreover, the weight of each edge is used to measure the strength of the relationships between requirements. In particular, they predefined five relationships between requirements in terms of whether the two requirements access or modify the same data, while the weight of each relationship is determined by domain engineers. Since there may exist more than one relationship between two requirements, the weight value of each edge is the sum of the weights of all relationships of the corresponding two requirements.

After the graph construction, requirements are clustered by a comparison between the weight values of each edge and a preset threshold value that must be exceeded. As a result, the finally created cluster constitutes the features with the threshold determining the granularity of features. The rationale behind this technique is that strongly related requirements (by means of data flow) belong to the same feature. Furthermore, the hierarchy of features is obtained by means of comparing whether a feature is another feature's subset. For example, let us assume that there is a feature *A* containing three requirements *R*1, *R*2 and *R*3, while feature *B* comprises *R*2 and *R*3. Then, the described technique identifies feature *A* as the parent feature of feature *B*, because feature *B* comprises a subset of the requirements of feature *A*. The method mentioned above can be used to initially achieve application feature trees by analyzing the functional requirements of different but similar applications. Afterwards, the application feature trees are merged into a single domain feature tree by the occurrence of features in both application feature trees and domain feature tree. Eventually, manual intervention is necessary to refine the results of the application feature trees and domain feature tree.

Moreover, the graph-based method is not only able to identify features, but also capable of extracting variability information (cf. Sect. 2.4), especially by the application of *directed graphs*.

2.3.3   Feature Term Extraction

In NL documents, there usually exist some domain specific terms representing the concrete functionality in a system. Hence, it is possible to use the specific term to denote a feature, called *feature term*. For example, consider the requirement below:

> "The interior monitoring is deactivated as soon as the alarm system is deactivated."

Since the terms, "interior monitoring" and "alarm system", denote the specific functionality of the system, both terms can be considered as feature terms. These feature terms not only constitute possible feature names, but also can be used to detect variability information, taking the syntax of the requirements into consideration.

Generally, different NLP techniques are capable of extracting feature terms, such as keyword extraction or Named Entity Recognition (NER). In the context of SPLs, *POS pattern* is a common keyword extraction method to identify meaningful terms. For example, "alarm system" can be identified by a *<noun, noun>* pattern, whereas "interior monitoring" can be identified by a *<adj, noun>* pattern. The NER technique is utilized for identifying the named entities of things in NL documents, such as people and organization names, or gene and protein names. In the context of SPLs, a feature term is regarded as a named entity. Since we lack open source pre-trained NER models for feature term extraction, we first of all have to train a NER model by using a labelled dataset. In related work [2], there is an example of how the requirements are labeled in the context of NER for feature extraction:

"A graph is an abstract mathematical representation that is used for exemplifying inter-entity relationships. Graphs can have different types. They can be <u>directed</u> or <u>indirected</u>; <u>weighted</u> or <u>unweighted</u>. A graph cannot be both directed and undirected. A graph can either be weighted or unweighted. One of the most desirable operations on a graph is the <u>search</u> operation. Graphs can be searched using <u>depth-first</u> or <u>breadth-first</u> strategies..."

The underlined terms are labeled as potential features. Moreover, we also need to identify the characteristics[1] of these labeled requirements for the learning step, such as, the word level characteristics (e.g., n-gram, lowercase, uppercase, token length, POS) [23].

2.3.4 Evaluation Metric

In order to properly conduct a quantitative analysis of the results, the measures *precision*, *recall* and *F1 score* are usually used to evaluate the results of the extracted features. The equations for each measure are shown below:

$$Precision = \frac{The\ number\ of\ extracted\ true\ features}{The\ number\ of\ all\ extracted\ features} \tag{2.1}$$

$$Recall = \frac{The\ number\ of\ extracted\ true\ features}{The\ number\ of\ features\ in\ ground\ truth} \tag{2.2}$$

$$F1 = 2 \times \frac{Precision \times Recall}{Precision + Recall} \tag{2.3}$$

From the equations above, we can see that if we intend to achieve the quantitative analysis of the results by using precision, recall and F1 score, the ground truth of the features in a particular SPL is indispensable.

---

[1] In machine learning, features are observable or derived properties of a phenomenon in a specific domain. In order to distinguish from the features in the context of SPLs, we utilize *characteristics* to denote features in machine learning.

2.4   Variability Extraction

While features are the building blocks of the envisioned domain-feature model, we also need to know about their corresponding variability, that is, how and when a feature must (not) be selected for a certain configuration. Extracting such variability information requires multiple NLP tasks to reveal different relations among features. While *heuristics* or *rule-based* methods are predominantly utilized to further analyze the information from the *occurrence* of requirements and terms, *lexical analysis, syntactic analysis, association rule mining* and *NER* are used to infer the potential variability information from requirements.

2.4.1   Optionality

Several approaches exist to detect the optionality (i.e., mandatory and optional). We introduce the three most common methods below.

Occurrence The most popular method is to apply heuristics or pre-defined rules to detect the optionality based on the occurrence of requirements or domain-specific terms in different variants. For example, we can simply define the following rule: if a feature has been extracted from some requirements and these requirements are present in all the variants, the feature is mandatory; otherwise, the feature is optional. Although the rules vary depending on the concrete research topic, the foundation of the rules is the distribution of features across different variants, which can be considered as *traceability link* between features and variants.

The general process for establishing such traceability links is as follows:

1. If the set of requirements contains the corresponding variants information (i.e., in which variants certain requirements are present), we can directly obtain a mapping between requirements and variants.
2. After feature extraction, the approach we used is capable of achieve a mapping between features and requirements.
3. Based on the aforementioned two mappings, we can achieve a traceability link between feature and variants.
4. Regarding the distribution of features across different variants, we know whether a variant includes a certain feature or not. Hence, different methods such as heuristics can now be applied to extract the optionality.

It is worth to mention that the two-step mapping approach is kind of a bridge used to connect the features and variants. Generally, such a bridge can be constructed by other mappings as well, such as a mapping between domain-specific terms and variants [9]. The underlying idea is that the distribution of different features across different variants can be regarded as a kind of domain knowledge, while we use statistics to quantify this kind of domain knowledge in order to further detect the optionality.

Lexical Analysis Another regularly applied method is to analyze some specific words appearing in the requirements, such as adjectives (e.g., "possible"), model verbs (e.g., "must"), adverbs (e.g., "optionally") and etc.. For example, in the requirement below [28]:

> "The publishing module **can** be configured using a custom reports module."

The model verb "can" represent a possibility, from which the relationship between the two feature terms, "publishing module" and "custom reports module", are able to be deduced as optional.

Association Rule Mining The optionality can also be detected by identifying associations between features based on association rule mining, one of the popular data mining techniques. For example, Davril et al. proposed to use an implication graph, a *directed graph*, where vertex denotes a feature and edge denotes the confidence between the two connected features to determine whether a feature is mandatory or not [6].

2.4.2   Group Constraints

The methods for group constraints (e.g., Or-Group and XOR-Group) extraction are predominantly related to the techniques used for optionality extraction.

Occurrence In previous work of Itzik et al. [14], feature models are generated by grouping similar requirements based on a hierarchical clustering algorithm, including some abstract and concrete features. Moreover, in their model, each concrete feature denotes an individual functional requirement. Moreover, two rules are pre-defined for group constraints extraction:

> 1. If at least two requirements that are grouped under the same parent node appear in the same input document, then the corresponding requirements are *OR-grouped*.
> 2. If requirements originating from different input files are grouped under the same parent node, we consider the corresponding requirements as *XOR-grouped*.

In the two rules above, the input documents/files can be regarded as variants. Moreover, the parent node of the feature model constitutes an abstract feature, while each requirement constitutes a concrete feature. Hence, similarly to extracting optionality, the distribution of features across variants can also be applied to extract the group constraints. Note that further rules are defined in abovementioned paper [18].

Lexical Analysis For extracting group constraints based on lexical analysis, we also illustrate an example from Sree-Kumar et al. [28]:

> "We believe that proof of individuality (POI) *can* be better solved with biometrics than what is currently being proposed in the Ethereum community—a series of video calls."

We can deduce that there two potential sub-features, "biometrics" and "a series of video calls", belonging to "proof of individuality". In terms of the specific model verb "can", we can deduce that the two sub-features may or may not coexist when the parent feature is configured. Hence, the two sub-features are possibly or-grouped.

Association Rule Mining As the aforementioned optionality extraction based on implication graphs drawn by association rule mining [6], the or-group relation can also be detected by the vertex (i.e., concrete feature) of an implication graph. If an abstract feature can be comprised of concrete features from the vertices in the implication graph, these concrete features are regarded as or-grouped features.

2.4.3   Cross-Tree Constraints

Lexical and Syntactic Analysis Based on the feature term extraction (cf. Sect. 2.3.3), we can further analyze the lexical and syntactic information of requirements containing feature terms in order to detect the cross-tree constraints between features.

For lexical analysis, here is an example from Sree-Kumar et al. [28].

> "Headphones are generally provided for *all* devices with FM radio capability."

They assume that the predeterminers assists the inference of cross-tree constraints between feature terms. Hence, in the requirement above, the predeterminer "all" is regarded as presenting a require relation between "headphones" and "FM radio".

For usage of syntactic information, we can simply define a rule that there exist potential cross-tree constraints between feature terms in main clause and modifier clause (e.g., temporal or adverbial clause).

"When the alarm system is activated, this is indicated by the light of the LED."

In the above example, there is requirement including a temporal clause. Based on the pre-defined rules we can observe that the light of "LED" require the activated "alarm system".

NER While we introduced NER as a technique to extract features, it is also possible to apply NER for detecting cross-tree constraints. First of all, if there is no pre-trained NER model, we need to train a NER model by a labelled dataset. In this labelled dataset, the requirements containing specific cross-tree constraints are assigned a dedicated label. An example of labelled requirements [2] is shown below:

"A graph cannot be both directed and undirected" and "A graph can either be weighted or unweighted" are labelled as *ic*.

The label *ic* denotes integrity constraints (i.e., cross-tree constraints). The label is just a symbol used to indicate that there are potential cross-tree constraints in the requirements.

2.4.4 Evaluation Metric

We can also use the *precision*, *recall* and *F1 score* to conduct the quantitative analysis of the extracted variability information. The equations are shown below:

$$Precision = \frac{The\ number\ of\ extracted\ true\ variation\ points}{The\ number\ of\ all\ extracted\ variation\ points} \quad (2.4)$$

$$Recall = \frac{The\ number\ of\ extracted\ true\ variation\ points}{The\ number\ of\ variation\ points\ in\ ground\ truth} \quad (2.5)$$

$$F1 = 2 \times \frac{Precision \times Recall}{Precision + Recall} \tag{2.6}$$

Likewise, the ground truth of the variability information is required in the process of achieving the quantitative analysis.

2.5 Related Work

All the techniques introduced above are used to process natural language requirements documents for extracting features and variability information, which allows for a more efficient way to conduct domain analysis than only depending on manual analysis for processing textual requirements. In order to understand the general applicability of these techniques for feature and variation points extraction, we categorize related work in terms of the type of *input* documents, the type of *output* and the specific *supposition*. We list the different kinds of inputs, outputs and suppositions in Table 2.1.

Con1, In2 and In4, Out2, Sup1 Dubinsky et al. [1] apply VSM and LSA to achieve similarity matrices of requirements documents with different structures and formats. Subsequently, the similarity matrices are fed into HAC to achieve different initial feature trees. Finally, the different initial feature trees are merged into the final feature model by manual analysis. In the evaluation, they apply two different requirements specification documents from a Smart Home case study

Table 2.1 The types of inputs, outputs, and suppositions

Interests/goals	Types	Descriptions
Condition	Con1	The formal SRS documents are reachable.
	Con2	The formal SRS documents are not reachable.
Input	In1	Functional requirements with simple and uniform format.
	In2	Requirements specification documents written by different formats.
	In3	Other informal textual documents.
	In4	The requirements specification documents (or other informal textual documents) come from different products or applications in a particular domain.
Output	Out1	(list of) Features.
	Out2	Feature model.
Supposition	Sup1	A feature as a high-level abstraction of a group of requirements semantically similar to each other.
	Sup2	A feature as a high-level abstraction of a group of requirements that are similar not only semantically but also from a specific perspective.
	Sup3	A feature as a term comprised of words or phrases.

as input.Moreover, they compare the clustering results between VSM+HAC and LSA+HAC, reporting the observation that for the small size of the individual requirements, VSM might outperform LSA. However, there is no evaluation regarding the features, variability information, and feature model. As an alternative approach, Li et al. combine BM25+ and word2vec instead of VSM and LSA to obtain the similarity of each pair of requirements [18].

Con1, In1 or In2, Out2, Sup1 In [32], LSA and HAC are also applied to cluster similar requirements into features. Afterwards, the features grouped using HAC are directly regarded as mandatory features, resulting in an initial feature tree. The variant features are identified manually with the assistance of the results of variability lexicon and grammatical pattern identifier, thereby obtaining the final feature model.

Con1, In1 and In4, Out2, Sup2 Itzik and Reinhartz-Berger et al. conducted a series of research [14, 15, 26] on extracting features and analyzing the variability information in terms of behaviors of the software products extracted from functional requirements. They identify behavioral vectors from the requirements, while each behavioral vector contains six semantic roles extracted by semantic role labeling. In the next step, the extracted behavioral vectors are classified into different behavioral elements (i.e., initial state, external event, and final state) that are used to denote the initial/final state of a system before/after a behavior occurs, and the corresponding external event triggering the behavior. Afterwards, the similarity of the requirements is computed by using Mihalcea, Corley, and Strapparava's (MCS) measure that is based on WordNet. Moreover, MCS also takes the behaviors into account when calculating the similarity, for example, assigning different weights for the semantic roles and behavioral elements. This approach also relies on HAC to obtain the initial feature tree. Additionally, the variability information, such as optionality and group constraints, is detected by predefined rules which are created by taking into account the occurrence of the individual requirements in the requirements documents from different applications. We can observe that (a) in order to achieve accurate behaviors, the requirements should be well written in a uniform format, especially for the automated extraction; and (b) The input requirements should come from different applications in the same domain. Otherwise, the rules for detecting variation points can not be used.

Con1, In1 and In4, Out2, Sup3 In [19], Mefteh et al. use a dedicated semantic model to process the requirements to achieve the corresponding mapping rules that are able to present each sentence in the requirements in a formal and unique way. By using such mapping rules, information such as the type of sentences, syntax, and semantic roles can be extracted. Moreover, they perceive the *terms* identified from the mapping rules and denoting the specific functionalities as *features*. After extracting the initial feature terms, they also use a similarity method (i.e., a combination of TF-IDF and cosine similarity) to group the initial feature terms into several clusters in order to achieve the unified features that can be shown in different variants. The variability information is extracted by using different methods: 1. formal concept analysis, 2. heuristics based on hyponymy relationship from WordNet, 3. heuristics based on the characteristics of the semantic model (i.e., using the lexical and syntactical analysis).

Sree-Kumar et al. [28] also treat the terms extracted from functional requirements as features, while the terms are identified by the part-of-speech and syntax information (i.e., the terms are noun phrases as the subject/object in a sentence). The variability information is detected by heuristics defined by using lexical and syntactical analysis. Moreover, it is worth to note that the input requirements are of rather simple format, and there might be very few sentences in each individual requirement. The reason is that the rules and heuristics used to extract features and variation points are strictly based on the predefined patterns (lexicon pattern, POS patter, and syntax pattern), while the fixed patterns are not capable of processing all kind of requirements due to the diverse writing style of natural language.

Con2, In3 and In4, Out2, Sup1 In [6], Davril et al. describe a scenario in which a company or organization does not possess existing requirements specification documents for certain products. They use the online product descriptions (e.g., the publicly available data from Softpedia[2]) to extract potential features to initiate and support the domain analysis for building an SPL. In this process, Spherical k-Means is used to cluster similar descriptions into a group to form a feature, and the feature name is mined by finding frequent itemsets in each cluster. Afterwards, they build a product-by-feature matrix that is taken advantage of to obtain the final feature model. In particular, the implication graph formed by using association rule mining plays an important role to detect the variant points.

Con2, In3 and In4, Out1, Sup3 Bakar et al. [3] also propose an approach to automatically analyze the online reviews of products (e.g., the compilation of software reviews by experts from website[3]) to identify features. In their research, the terms extracted by using POS patterns are considered to represent features.

2.6   Challenges and Risks

Although research on feature and variability information extraction has been developed for around twenty years, we are still confronted with many challenges. In particular, we consider the following challenges to be essential for making a step forward in the automation of feature and variability extraction from requirements.

1. The accuracy of feature and variation points detection still needs to be improved. While all current approaches perform rather low on this aspect, we

---

[2] https://www.softpedia.com/.
[3] https://www.toptenreviews.com/.

consider this crucial to establish a comprehensive domain model and to reason about validity and derivation of variants.

2. The majority of the existing approaches lacks the capability of processing different types of requirements, which is probably caused by the widely used pre-defined rules that are not able to cover all the situations due to the variety of natural language writing. However, in real world, there is no standard vocabulary or structure for requirements, and thus, reliable extraction techniques should be robust against different types of requirements.

3. The lack of accessible requirements, especially of a large and publicly available requirements dataset, considerable hinders the forthcoming of this research topic for researchers. Hence, only with industrial partners there may be a chance to get access to a larger amount of SRS documents. However, for a real step forward, we need join forces of researchers, and thus, it is inevitable to release such a dataset, most likely with support by industry.

4. Feature and variability information extraction heavily relies on NLP techniques. While these techniques that have considerably improved thanks to the development of deep learning techniques, the latter requires a rather large set of unlabelled or labelled data to train a model. However, we not only lack enough unlabelled data, but also lots of work regarding creating dedicated labelled dataset for multiple feature and variability information extraction tasks needs special attentions and strenuous endeavors to make progress in this field of research.

All the aforementioned challenges result in the risks of making feature and variability information extraction techniques inapplicable in practice. Hence, only by addressing these challenges together, we can push the idea of feature and variablity extraction from SRS documents forward to a level where it can be applied in a real-world setting, and thus, contribute to a more automated domain analysis.

References

1. Alves, V., Schwanninger, C., Barbosa, L., Rashid, A., Sawyer, P., Rayson, P., Pohl, C., Rummler, A.: An exploratory study of information retrieval techniques in domain analysis. In: Proceedings of the International Software Product Line Conference (SPLC), pp. 67–76. IEEE (2008)
2. Bagheri, E., Ensan, F., Gasevic, D.: Decision support for the software product line domain engineering lifecycle. Automated Software Engineering **19**, 335–377 (2012)
3. Bakar, N.H., Kasirun, Z.M., Salleh, N., Jalab, H.A.: Extracting features from online software reviews to aid requirements reuse. Applied Soft Computing **49**, 1297–1315 (2016)
4. Bojanowski, P., Grave, E., Joulin, A., Mikolov, T.: Enriching word vectors with subword information. arXiv preprint arXiv:1607.04606 (2016)
5. Chen, K., Zhang, W., Zhao, H., Mei, H.: An approach to constructing feature models based on requirements clustering. In: Proceedings of the International Conference on Requirements Engineering (RE), pp. 31–40. IEEE (2005)
6. Davril, J., Delfosse, E., Hariri, N., Acher, M., Cleland-Huang, J., Heymans, P.: Feature model extraction from large collections of informal product descriptions. In: Proceedings

of the European Software Engineering Conference/Foundations of Software Engineering (ESEC/FSE), pp. 290–300. ACM (2013)

7. Dubinsky, Y., Rubin, J., Berger, T., Duszynski, S., Becker, M., Czarnecki, K.: An exploratory study of cloning in industrial software product lines. In: Proceedings of the European Conference on Software Maintenance and Reengineering (CSMR), pp. 25–34. IEEE (2013)

8. Dumais, S.T.: Latent semantic analysis. Annual Review of Information Science and Technology **38**(1), 188–230 (2004)

9. Ferrari, A., Spagnolo, G.O., Dell'Orletta, F.: Mining commonalities and variabilities from natural language documents. In: Proceedings of the International Software Product Line Conference (SPLC), p. 116. ACM (2013)

10. Frantzi, K., Ananiadou, S., Mima, H.: Automatic recognition of multi-word terms: The c-value/nc-value method. pp. 115–130 (2000)

11. Gomaa, W.H., Fahmy, A.A.: A survey of text similarity approaches **68**, 13–18 (2013)

12. IEEE: Ieee recommended practice for software requirements specifications (1998)

13. Indurkhya, N., Damerau, F.J.: Handbook of Natural Language Processing. Chapman & Hall/CRC (2010)

14. Itzik, N., Reinhartz-Berger, I.: Generating feature models from requirements: Structural vs. functional perspectives. In: Proceedings of the International Software Product Line Conference (SPLC), pp. 44–51. ACM (2014)

15. Itzik, N., Reinhartz-Berger, I., Wand, Y.: Variability analysis of requirements: Considering behavioral differences and reflecting stakeholders' perspectives. IEEE Transactions on Software Engineering (TSE) **42**, 687–706 (2016)

16. Kumaki, K., Tsuchiya, R., Washizaki, H., Fukazawa, Y.: Supporting commonality and variability analysis of requirements and structural models. In: Proceedings of the International Software Product Line Conference (SPLC), pp. 115–118. ACM (2012)

17. Li, Y., Schulze, S., Saake, G.: Reverse engineering variability from natural language documents: A systematic literature review. In: Proceedings of the International Systems and Software Product Line Conference, pp. 133–142. ACM (2017)

18. Li, Y., Schulze, S., Saake, G.: Reverse engineering variability from requirement documents based on probabilistic relevance and word embedding. In: SPLC, pp. 121–131 (2018)

19. Mefteh, M., Bouassida, N., Ben-Abdallah, H.: Mining feature models from functional requirements **59**, 1784–1804 (2016)

20. Mihalcea, R., Corley, C., Strapparava, C.: Corpus-based and knowledge-based measures of text semantic similarity. In: Proceedings of the National Conference on Artificial Intelligence, pp. 775–780. AAAI Press (2006)

21. Mikolov, T., Sutskever, I., Chen, K., Corrado, G.S., Dean, J.: Distributed representations of words and phrases and their compositionality. pp. 3111–3119. Curran Associates, Inc. (2013)

22. Miller, G.A.: Wordnet: A lexical database for english. Communications of the ACM **38**, 39–41 (1995)

23. Nadeau, D., Sekine, S.: A survey of named entity recognition and classification. Linguisticae Investigationes **30**(1), 3–26 (2007)

24. Palmer, M., Gildea, D., Kingsbury, P.: The proposition bank: An annotated corpus of semantic roles. Computational Linguistics **31**(1), 71–106 (2005)

25. Pennington, J., Socher, R., Manning, C.: Glove: Global vectors for word representation. In: Proceedings of the Conference on Empirical Methods in Natural Language Processing (EMNLP), pp. 1532–1543 (2014)

26. Reinhartz-Berger, I., Itzik, N., Wand, Y.: Analyzing variability of software product lines using semantic and ontological considerations. In: Proceedings of the International Conference on Advanced Information Systems Engineering (CAiSE), pp. 150–164. Springer (2014)

27. Salton, G., Wong, A., Yang, C.S.: A vector space model for automatic indexing. Commun. ACM **18**(11), 613–620 (1975)

28. Sree-Kumar, A., Planas, E., Clarisó, R.: Extracting software product line feature models from natural language specifications. In: Proceedings of the International Systems and Software Product Line Conference, pp. 43–53 (2018)

29. Varshosaz, M., Al-Hajjaji, M., Thüm, T., Runge, T., Mousavi, M.R., Schaefer, I.: A classification of product sampling for software product lines. In: Proceedings of the International Systems and Software Product Line Conference, pp. 1–13. ACM (2018)
30. Wang, Y.: Semantic information extraction for software requirements using semantic role labeling. In: Proceedings of the International Conference on Progress in Informatics and Computing (PIC), pp. 332–337. IEEE (2015)
31. Wang, Y.: Automatic semantic analysis of software requirements through machine learning and ontology approach. Journal of Shanghai Jiaotong University (Science) **21**, 692–701 (2016)
32. Weston, N., Chitchyan, R., Rashid, A.: A framework for constructing semantically composable feature models from natural language requirements. Proceedings of the International Software Product Line Conference (SPLC) pp. 211–220 (2009)

Chapter 3
Semantic History Slicing

Yi Li, Julia Rubin, and Marsha Chechik

Abstract Feature location techniques aim to locate software artifacts that implement a specific program functionality, a.k.a. a feature. In this chapter, we introduce a technique called *semantic history slicing*, to locate features in software version histories. The key insight is that the information embedded in version histories can be used to establish a connection between features and changes implementing the features. We present the formal definitions as well as the general principles of semantic history slicing and provide details on a specific history slicing algorithm based on change dependency analysis. The identified feature implementing changes are fully functional and guaranteed to preserve the desired behaviors.

3.1 Introduction

Feature location techniques aim to locate pieces of code that implement a specific program functionality, a.k.a. a *feature*. These techniques support developers during various maintenance tasks, e.g., locating code of a faulty feature that requires fixing, and are extensively studied in the literature [8, 28]. The techniques are based on static or dynamic program analysis, information retrieval (IR), change set analysis, or some combination of the above.

Y. Li (✉)
School of Computer Science and Engineering, Nanyang Technological University, Singapore,
Singapore
e-mail: yi_li@ntu.edu.sg

J. Rubin
Department of Electrical and Computer Engineering, University of British Columbia, Vancouver,
BC, Canada
e-mail: mjulia@ece.ubc.ca

M. Chechik
Department of Computer Science, University of Toronto, Toronto, ON, Canada
e-mail: chechik@cs.toronto.edu

© Springer Nature Switzerland AG 2023
R. E. Lopez-Herrejon et al. (eds.), *Handbook of Re-Engineering Software Intensive
Systems into Software Product Lines*, https://doi.org/10.1007/978-3-031-11686-5_3

Recently, a number of techniques for identifying features in the Software Product Line context have been proposed [1, 2, 20–22, 33, 34, 36]. Such techniques are primarily based on intersecting code of multiple product variants in order to identify code fragments shared by variants with a particular feature. The identified code fragments can then be attributed to that feature. These intersection-based techniques operate in a static manner and are effective when a large number of product variants are available.

Often, we cannot rely on the availability of a large number of variants. For example, consider a family of related software products realized via *cloning* (a.k.a. the "clone-and-own" approach)—a routinely used practice where developers create a new product by copying/branching an existing variant and later modifying it independently from the original [9]. Such variants are commonly maintained in a version control system, e.g., Git [11]. Their number can be relatively small, e.g., 3 to 10 products, while intersection-based techniques [22], are typically evaluated for tens or even hundreds of variants.

Identifying features in cloned software product variants is important for a variety of software development tasks. For example, developers often need to share features between variants. That becomes a challenging task as it is often unclear which commits correspond to the particular feature of interest [3, 14, 31]. Refactoring cloned variants into *single-copy* SPL representations also relies on the ability to identify and extract code that implements each feature [3, 27, 29–31].

3.1.1 Locating Features in Software Histories

As a step towards addressing these problems, this chapter contributes a dynamic technique for locating features in software version histories. Our technique differs from other work in that it (a) traces features to historical information about their evolution, (b) leverages version histories to improve the accuracy of feature location, and (c) is efficient even if the number of available product variants is small.

Software version histories are often organized not in terms of features, but as a sequence of incremental development activities, ordered by timestamps. This usually results in a history mixed with changes to multiple features which may or may not be related to each other. To categorize changes according to the features they contribute to, we rely on the availability of a test suite T_f exercising a feature of interest f; such test suites are commonly provided by developers for validating features. We also assume that the execution trace of a test is deterministic. Given a piece of history H known to implement a set of features F, and each feature $f \in F$ exercised by a test suite T_f, we would like to identify the set of relevant changes for each feature f.

Example 3.1 We take a history fragment from the release version 1.3 of an open source software project commons-csv [6]. The simplified commit history is shown in Fig. 3.1 as a sequence of commits $\langle \Delta_1, \Delta_2, \Delta_3, \Delta_4 \rangle$. There are three

Fig. 3.1 Features identified
as a set of commits from a
history fragment

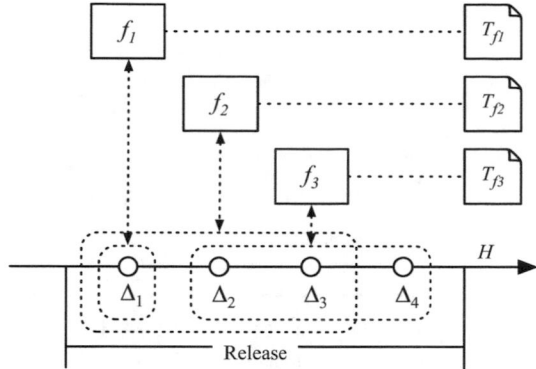

features implemented in this fragment: "CSV-159" (f_1: add IgnoreCase option for accessing header names), "CSV-179" (f_2: add shortcut method for using first record as header to CSVFormat), and "CSV-180" (f_3: add withHeader(Class? extends Enum>) to CSVFormat). The corresponding test cases for the three features are T_{f_1}, T_{f_2}, and T_{f_3}, respectively. The goal is to identify a set of commits for each feature which allows the corresponding test cases to pass.

We assume that the features introduced within the history fragment are given and each feature is implemented by one or more commits from the history. As shown in Fig. 3.1, the commits implementing f_1, f_2 and f_3 are $\{\Delta_1\}$, $\{\Delta_1, \Delta_2, \Delta_3\}$, and $\{\Delta_2, \Delta_3, \Delta_4\}$, respectively. Notice that a single commit can be related to multiple features. For example, Δ_1 (adding the "IgnoreCase" option for accessing head names) implements the feature f_1 and at the same time is also a prerequisite for f_2.

This also means that the identified commits, when applied at the beginning of the given history segment, pass the corresponding test cases. Once such correspondence between features and feature-implementing changes (or *feature changes* for short) is established, it can be used in the reverse engineering of SPLs from cloned products maintained in a version control system.

3.1.2 Semantic History Slicing

The problem of identifying a set of changes from a history fragment in order to preserve a given *semantic property* (such as passing certain test cases) is known as *semantic history slicing*. To address this problem, Li et al. introduced a technique CSLICER [14] based on change dependency analysis and many other techniques [15, 17, 18, 35] have been proposed in the literature since then. We illustrate the concept of semantic history slicing on a simple example.

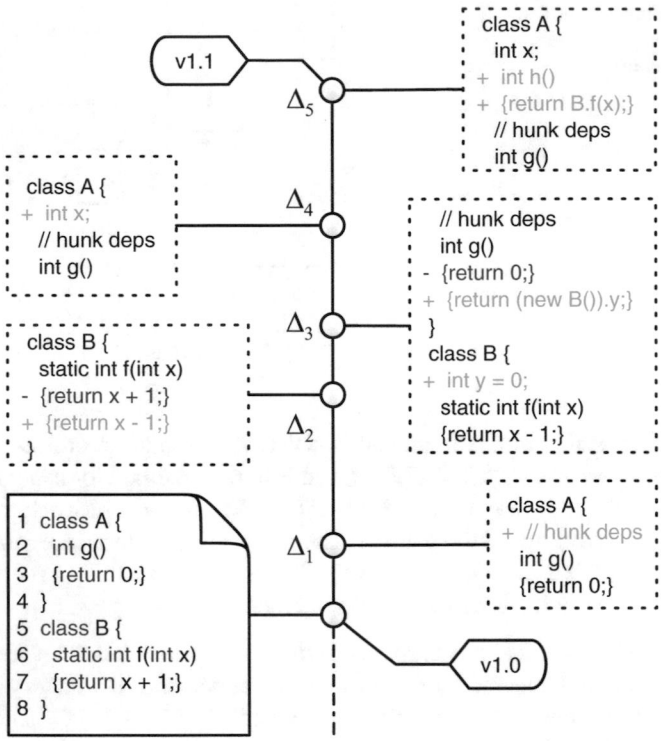

Fig. 3.2 History fragment between v1.0 and v1.1 of Foo.java

Example 3.2 Figure 3.2 shows a fragment of the change history between versions v1.0 and v1.1 for the file Foo.java. Initially, as shown in version v1.0, the file contains two classes, A and B, each having a member method g and f, respectively. Later, in change set Δ_1, a line with a textual comment was inserted right before the declaration of method A.g. Then, in change set Δ_2, the body of B.f was modified from {return x+1;} to {return x-1;}. In change set Δ_3, the body of A.g was updated to return the value of a newly added field y in class B. In change set Δ_4, a field declaration was inserted in class A and, finally, in change set Δ_5, a new method h was added to class A. The resulting program in v1.1 is shown in Fig. 3.3a on the left.

Each dashed box in Fig. 3.2 encloses a commit written in the *unified format* (the output of command diff -u). The lines starting with "+" are inserted while those starting with "-" are deleted. Each bundle of changed lines is called a *hunk* and comes with a *context*—a certain number of lines of surrounding text that stay unchanged. In Fig. 3.2, these are the lines which do not start with "+" or "-". The context that comes with a hunk is useful for ensuring that the change is applied at the correct location even when the line numbers change. A *conflict* is reported if the

```
1    class A {                          1    class A {
2        int x;                         2        int x;
3        int h()                        3        int h()
4        {return B.f(x);}               4        {return B.f(x);}
5        // hunk deps                   5        // hunk deps
6        int g()                        6        int g()
7        {return (new B()).y;}          7        {return 0;}
8    }                                  8    }
9    class B {                          9    class B {
10       int y = 0;                     10       static int f(int x)
11       static int f(int x)            11       {return x - 1;}
12       {return x - 1;}                12   }
13   }
```

(a)   (b)

Fig. 3.3 Foo.java before and after semantic slicing in Example 3.2. (a) Foo.java at v1.1. (b) Foo.java at v1.0 with the sliced sub-history $\langle \Delta_1, \Delta_2, \Delta_4, \Delta_5 \rangle$

context cannot be matched. In Example 2, the maximum length of the contexts is four lines: up to two lines before and after each change.

Slicing Criteria In order to perform semantic history slicing on the given history fragment, a *slicing criteria* need to be defined. Suppose the feature of interest is that the method A.h() returns "-1". Although this feature was introduced in Δ_5, cherry-picking Δ_5 alone back to v1.0 would result in test failure for the following reasons:

- the body of method B.f was changed in Δ_2, and the change is required to produce the correct result;
- the declaration of field A.x was introduced in Δ_4 but was missing in v1.0, which would cause compilation errors; and
- a merge conflict would arise due to the missing context of Δ_5—the text that appears immediately after the change. This text was introduced in Δ_1.

Slicing Result Therefore, in order to identify the set of feature-implementing commits and compute a history slice satisfying the slicing criteria, we need to identify all the dependencies among changes. We provide more details on the change dependency analysis of CSLICER in Sect. 3.4.

In this example, applying $\{\Delta_1, \Delta_2, \Delta_4, \Delta_5\}$ in sequence on top of v1.0 produces a new program shown in Fig. 3.3b on the right. It is easy to verify that the call to A.h in both programs returns the same value. Changes introduced in commit Δ_3—an addition of the field B.y and a modification of the method A.g—do not affect the test results and are not part of any other commit context. Thus, this commit can be omitted. The final semantic slicing result is a sub-history of four commits $\langle \Delta_1, \Delta_2, \Delta_4, \Delta_5 \rangle$.

3.1.3   Chapter Organization

The rest of this chapter is structured as follows. Section 3.2 provides the necessary background and definitions. Section 3.3 defines semantics-preserving history slices and introduces general approaches of semantic history slicing. In Sect. 3.4, we describe the change dependency-based history slicing technique in more details. Finally, in Sect. 3.5, we present a web-based semantic history slicing framework.

3.2   Representing Programs and Program Changes

The techniques presented in this chapter are not limited to any particular programming languages or tools. Without loss of generality, we choose Java as an example in our demonstrations. And to keep the presentation of algorithms concise, we step back from the complexities of the full Java language and concentrate on its core object-oriented features.

3.2.1   Program Representation

We adopt a simple functional subset of Java from *Featherweight Java* [12], denoting it by P. The syntax rules of the language P are given in Fig. 3.4. Many advanced Java features, e.g., interfaces, abstract classes and reflection, are stripped from P, while the typing rules which are crucial for the compilation correctness are retained [13].

We say that p is a *syntactically valid program* written in language P, denoted by $p \in P$, if p follows the syntax rules. A program $p \in P$ consists of a list of class declarations $(\overline{L})$, where the overhead bar $\overline{L}$ stands for a (possibly empty) sequence $L_1, \ldots, L_n$. We use $\langle \rangle$ to denote an empty sequence and comma for sequence concatenation. We use $|L|$ to denote the length of the sequence. Every class declaration has *members* including *fields* $(\overline{C\ f})$, *methods* $(\overline{M})$ and a single *constructor* (K). A method *body* consists of a single *return* statement; the returned expression can be a variable, a field access, a method lookup, an instance creation or a type cast.

Fig. 3.4 Syntax rules of the
P language [12]

$$P ::= \overline{L}$$

$$L ::= \texttt{class}\ C\ \texttt{extends}\ C\{\overline{C\ f};\ K\ \overline{M}\}$$

$$K ::= C\,(\overline{C\ f})\,\{\texttt{super}\,(\overline{f})\,;\ \overline{\texttt{this}.f = f;}\,\}$$

$$M ::= C\ m\,(\overline{C\ x})\,\{\texttt{return}\ e;\}$$

$$e ::= x\ \mid\ e.f\ \mid\ e.m\,(\overline{e})\ \mid\ \texttt{new}\ C\,(\overline{e})\ \mid\ (C)\,e$$

$$C <: C \qquad \frac{C <: D \quad D <: E}{C <: E} \qquad \frac{\text{class } C \text{ extends } D\{\ldots\}}{C <: D}$$

Fig. 3.5 Subtyping rules of the P language [12]

$$\text{FIELDS}(\text{Object}) = \langle\rangle$$

$$\frac{\text{class } C \text{ extends } D\{\overline{C}\ \overline{f};\ K\ \overline{M}\} \quad \text{FIELDS}(D) = \overline{D}\ \overline{g}}{\text{FIELDS}(C) = \overline{D}\ \overline{g}, \overline{C}\ \overline{f}}$$

$$\frac{\text{class } C \text{ extends } D\{\overline{C}\ \overline{f};\ K\ \overline{M}\} \quad B\ m(\overline{B}\ \overline{x})\{\text{return } e;\} \in \overline{M}}{\text{METHODS}(m, C) = (\overline{B} \to B, \overline{x}.e)}$$

$$\frac{\text{class } C \text{ extends } D\{\overline{C}\ \overline{f};\ K\ \overline{M}\} \quad m \notin \overline{M}}{\text{METHODS}(m, C) = \text{METHODS}(m, D)}$$

Fig. 3.6 Fields and methods lookup rules of the P language [12]

The subtyping rules of P, shown in Fig. 3.5, are straightforward. We write $C <: D$ when class C is a subtype of D. As in full Java, subtyping is the reflexive and transitive closure of the immediate subclass relation implied by the `extends` keyword. In Featherweight Java [12], the field and method lookup rules are slightly different from the standard ones (see Fig. 3.6)—field *overshadowing* and method *overloading* are not allowed while method *overriding* is allowed. For example, when resolving a method call $C.m$, the method list $\overline{M}$ of class C is first consulted. If m is defined in C then its type and body are returned as a pair $(\overline{B} \to B, \overline{x}.e)$. Otherwise, the lookup continues recursively on the super class of C. Note that $\text{METHODS}(m, C)$ is a partial function. Since in P, the special class `Object` is assumed to have no method, $\text{METHODS}(m, \text{Object})$ is undefined.

3.2.2   Changes and Change Histories

Based on the program representations used, either structured ASTs or unstructured plain texts, we define the AST- and line-based views of changes and change histories.

3.2.2.1   AST-Based View

Let Γ be the set of all ASTs. Below we define changes, change sets and change histories as AST transformation operations.

Fig. 3.7 Types of atomic changes [10]. Refer to Sect. 3.2.1 for AST-related symbols

$$\frac{y \in V(r)}{V(r') \leftarrow V(r) \cup \{x\} \quad \text{PARENT}(x) \leftarrow y} \quad \text{INS}((x,n,v),y)$$
$$id(x) \leftarrow n \quad v(x) \leftarrow v$$

$$\frac{x \in V(r)}{V(r') \leftarrow V(r) \setminus \{x\}} \quad \text{DEL}(x) \qquad \frac{x \in V(r)}{v(x) \leftarrow v} \quad \text{UPD}(x,v)$$

Fig. 3.8 Visualizing a change set C as a sequence of atomic changes applied on ASTs

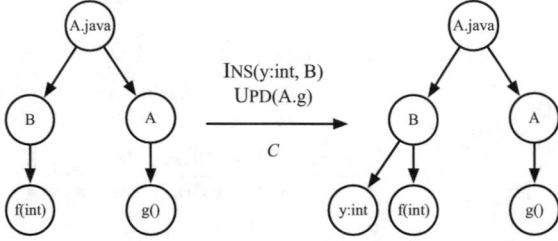

Atomic Change An *atomic change* operation $\delta : \Gamma \mapsto \Gamma$ is a partial function which transforms $r \in \Gamma$ producing a new AST r' such that $r' = \delta(r)$. An atomic change operation can be either an *insert*, *delete* or *update* (see Fig. 3.7).

An insertion $\text{INS}((x, n, v), y)$ inserts a node x with an identifier n and a value v as a child of a node y. A deletion $\text{DEL}(x)$ removes a node x from the AST. An update $\text{UPD}(x, v)$ replaces the value of a node x with v. A change operation is *applicable* on an AST if its preconditions are met. For example, an insertion $\text{INS}((x, n, v), y)$ is applicable on r if and only if $y \in V(r)$. Insertion of an existing node is treated the same as an update.

Change Set Let r and r' be two ASTs. A *change set* $\Delta : \Gamma \mapsto \Gamma$ is a sequence of atomic changes $\langle \delta_1, \ldots, \delta_n \rangle$ such that $\Delta(r) = (\delta_n \circ \cdots \circ \delta_1)(r) = r'$, where $\circ$ is a standard function composition. A change set $\Delta = \Delta_{-1} \circ \delta_1$ is applicable to r if δ_1 is applicable to r and Δ_{-1} is applicable to $\delta_1(r)$. Change sets between two ASTs can be computed by tree differencing algorithms [5]. For instance, in Fig. 3.8, the change set C consists of an insertion of a new node y under B, followed by an update of the node g.

Change History and Sub-history A *history of changes* is a sequence of change sets, i.e., $H = \langle \Delta_1, \ldots, \Delta_k \rangle$. A *sub-history* is a sub-sequence of a history, i.e., a sequence derived by removing change sets from H without altering the ordering. We write $H' \subseteq H$ indicating H' is a sub-history of H and refer to $\langle \Delta_i, \ldots, \Delta_j \rangle$ as $H_{i..j}$. The applicability of a history is defined similarly to that of change sets. We use $SH(H)$ to denote the set of all sub-histories of H.

Fig. 3.9 Line-based view of
changes represented as a
hunk

```
// hunk deps
int g()
-   {return 0;}
+   {return (new B()).y;}
}
class B {
+   int y = 0;
    static int f(int x)
    {return x - 1;}
```

3.2.2.2   Line-Based View

Software Configuration Management (SCM) tools represent changes using the *line-based view*. The smallest unit for line-based changes is a *hunk*.

Hunk   Let P be the set of all program texts. A *hunk* $\hat{\delta} : P \rightarrowtail P$ is a partial function which transforms $p \subset P$ producing a new program text p' such that $p' = \hat{\delta}(p)$. For example, Fig. 3.9 shows a hunk of one line deletion and two line insertions, marked by "-" and "+", respectively. The *context* (the lines not marked by "-" or "+" in Fig. 3.9) that comes with a hunk is useful for ensuring that the hunk can be applied at the correct location even when the line numbers change for the target program texts. A *conflict* happens if the context cannot be matched when applying a hunk. In the current example, the maximum length of the contexts is four lines: up to two lines before and after each change.

Commit and Commit History   A *commit* is a collection of hunks, in no particular order, which takes a program text p and transforms it to produce a new program text $\hat{\Delta}(p)$. Applying a commit is equivalent to composing its corresponding hunks, each representing a set of line changes with an approximate locality. More formally, let p and p' be two program texts. A *commit* $\hat{\Delta} : P \rightarrowtail P$ is a set of hunks $\{\hat{\delta}_1, \ldots, \hat{\delta}_n\}$ such that $\hat{\Delta}(p) = (\hat{\delta}_1 \circ \cdots \circ \hat{\delta}_n)(p) = p'$, where $\circ$ is standard function composition. A *commit history* is a sequence of commits, i.e., $H = \langle \hat{\Delta}_1, \ldots, \hat{\Delta}_k \rangle$.

For simplicity, in the rest of this chapter, we use the same notations for both AST-based and line-based changes where the context is clear.

3.2.3   Tests and Test Suites

We assume that semantic functionalities can be captured by tests and the execution trace of a test is deterministic [26]. For simplicity, a test can be abstracted into two parts—the setup code which initializes the testing environment and executes the target functionalities using specific inputs, as well as the oracle checks which verify that the produced results match with the expected ones. A test execution *succeeds* if all checks pass.

More formally, a *test t* is a predicate $t : P \mapsto \mathbb{B}$ such that for a given program p, $t(p)$ is true if the test succeeds, and false otherwise. A *test suite* is a collection of tests that can exercise and demonstrate the functionality of interest. Let test suite T be a set of test cases $\{t_i\}$. We write $p \models T$ if and only if program p passes all tests in T, i.e., $\forall t \in T \cdot t(p)$.

3.3 Semantics-Preserving History Slices

As shown in Fig. 3.1 of Example 3.1, the problem of identifying feature-implementing changes can be effectively solved by semantic history slicing using feature tests as the slicing criteria. In this section, we define *Semantics-Preserving History Slices* and discuss general properties about them.

We refer to a sub-history which preserves certain semantic properties of the original history as a *semantics-preserving slice*. The preserved semantic properties are referred to as *slicing criteria*. In this chapter, we focus on using feature tests as one concrete instantiation of the slicing criteria. Thus, the computed semantics-preserving slices guarantee that the runtime behaviors of the corresponding feature tests are preserved.

Consider a program p_0 and its k subsequent versions $p_1, \ldots, p_k$ such that $p_i \in P$ and p_i is well-typed for all integers $0 \leq i \leq k$. Let H be the change history from p_0 to p_k, i.e., $H_{1..i}(p_0) = p_i$ for all integers $0 \leq i \leq k$. Let T be a set of tests passed by p_k, i.e., $p_k \models T$; T is fixed once chosen.

Definition 3.1 (Semantics-Preserving Slice) A semantics-preserving slice of history H with respect to T is a sub-history $H' \subseteq H$ such that the following properties hold:

1. $H'(p_0) \in P$,
2. $H'(p_0)$ is well-typed,
3. $H'(p_0) \models T$.

The problem of semantic history slicing is to identify such a *semantics-preserving slice* given change history H and target tests T. We sometimes refer to semantics-preserving slice as *semantic slice* for short. A trivial and uninteresting solution to this problem is the original history H itself. Shorter slicing results are preferred over longer ones, and the optimal slice is the shortest sub-history that satisfies the above properties.

However, the optimality of the sliced history cannot always be guaranteed by polynomial-time algorithms. Since the test case can be arbitrary, it is not hard to see that for any program and history, there always exists a worst case input test that requires enumerating all 2^k sub-histories to find the shortest one. The naïve approach of enumerating sub-histories is not feasible as the compilation and running time of each version can be substantial. Even if a compile and test run takes just one minute, enumerating and building all sub-histories of only twenty commits would

Fig. 3.10 Relationships
between various history slices

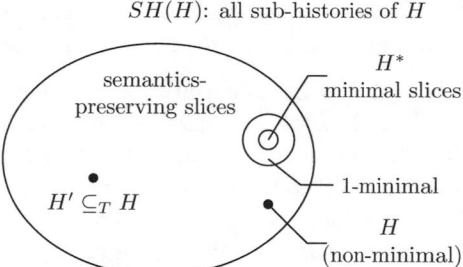

take approximately two years. In fact, it can be shown that the optimal semantic slicing problem is NP-complete by reduction from the set cover problem. We omit the details of this argument [18] here.

An optimal algorithm which runs the test only once cannot exist in any case: in order to determine whether to keep a change set or not, it needs to at least be able to answer the decision problem, "given a fixed program p and test t, for any arbitrary program p', will the outputs of t be different on both?" which is known to be undecidable [25].

Therefore, we are often more interested in an approximation of the optimal solution, which can be efficiently computed in practice. We say that a sub-history H^* of H is a *minimal semantic slice* if H^* is semantics-preserving and it cannot be further shortened without losing the semantics-preserving properties (see Definition 3.1).

As shown in Fig. 3.10, there are several special kinds of semantics-preserving slices. First, H is a semantics-preserving slice of itself, but it may not be *minimal*. Second, minimal semantic slices (H^*) are slices which are semantics-preserving and cannot be reduced further. Finally, computing minimal semantics-preserving slices is expensive, so we often compute an approximation known as the *1-minimal* semantic slice—a slice which cannot be further reduced by removing *any single commit*. In practice, 1-minimal slices are often minimal.

Definition 3.2 (Minimal Semantics-Preserving Slice) Let H^* be semantics-preserving, i.e., $H^* \subseteq_T H$. H^* is a minimal semantic slice of H if, $\forall H_{sub} \subset H^* \cdot H_{sub} \not\models T$.

Definition 3.3 (1-Minimal Semantic Slice) Let H^* be semantics-preserving, i.e., $H^* \subseteq_T H$. H^* is a *1-minimal semantic slice* of H if, $\forall \delta \in H^* \cdot (H^* \setminus \{\delta\}) \not\models T$.

3.4   Semantic History Slicing

Since solutions are often intractable for the problem of finding optimal semantics-preserving slices, there are mainly two types of semantic history slicing techniques which trade off optimality for efficiency, namely, the change dependency analysis and the dynamic delta refinement approaches.

Change Dependency Analysis The change dependency approach mostly relies on static analysis of dependencies between change sets and is therefore much cheaper in terms of running time. CSLICER [18] is an efficient semantic history slicing algorithm which requires only a one-time effort for compilation and test execution.

The actual slicing process consists of two phases, a generic history slicing algorithm which is independent of any specific SCM system in use, and an SCM adaptation component that adapts the output produced by the slicing algorithm to specifics of SCM systems. The slicing algorithm conservatively identifies all atomic changes in the given input history that contribute to the *functional* and *compilation* correctness of the functionality of interest. The SCM adaptation component then maps the collected set of atomic changes back to the commits in the original change history. It also takes care of merge conflicts that can occur when cherry-picking commits in text-based SCM systems such as SVN and Git. CSLICER is designed to be conservative in the first phase and thus can be imprecise, producing non-minimal slices.

Dynamic Delta Refinement In contrast, the dynamic delta refinement approach [15, 16] executes tests multiple times and directly observes the test results while attempting to shorten the history slices iteratively. The semantic history slices found by this kind of approaches are guaranteed to be 1-minimal, but the running time is usually much longer. The high-level idea is to partition the input history by dropping some subset of the commits and opportunistically reduce the search space when the target tests pass on one of the partitions, until a minimal partition is reached. The observed test pass/fail results can also be used to predict the significance of changes with respect to the target tests to speed up the history slicing process.

3.4.1 CSLICER *by Example*

In the remaining part of this section, we describe CSLICER, a history slicing algorithm based on change dependency analysis.

3.4.1.1 Dependency Hierarchy

The core of the algorithm is to identify the three types of change dependencies given a slicing criteria, namely the *functional*, *compilation* and *hunk* dependencies. These dependencies together guarantee the semantic correctness and well-formedness of the sliced feature changes, and the applicability of the feature slices in text-

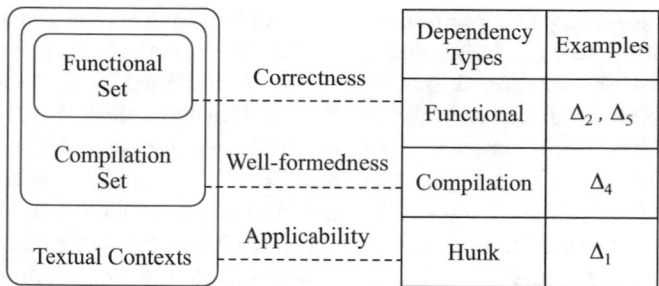

Fig. 3.11 Change dependency hierarchy in Example 3.2

based SCM systems. In fact, changes within a semantics-preserving slice form a dependency hierarchy with respect to the target feature (see Fig. 3.11).

At its core, the *functional set* contains program components which directly participate in the test execution to deliver the functionalities of the target feature, e.g., methods "A.h" and "B.f" in Example 3.2. The changes made to the functional set are called the *functional dependencies*, e.g., Δ_2 and Δ_5. They are essential for the semantic correctness of the target feature. In addition, the *compilation set* connects the functional core with its structural supporting components, i.e., classes "A", "B" and the field declaration "int x" in the class "A". Similarly, the corresponding contributing changes are called the *compilation dependencies*, e.g., Δ_4. They are necessary to guarantee program well-formedness including syntactic correctness and type safety. Finally, to ensure the selected changes can be applied using a text-based SCM system, some additional changes which provide textual contexts should be included as well. We call these changes the *hunk dependencies*, e.g., Δ_1.

3.4.1.2 CSLICER Workflow

There are mainly three steps involved in computing a semantic history slice, essentially to find the three types of dependencies. We illustrate the workflow of CSLICER on Example 3.2.

Step 1: Computing Functional Set CSLICER executes the test on the latest version of the program (left-hand side of Fig. 3.3a), which triggers method A.h. It dynamically collects the program statements traversed by this execution. These include the method bodies of A.h and B.f. The set of source code entities (e.g., methods or classes) containing the traversed statements is called the *functional set*, denoted by Λ. The functional set in the current example is {A.h, B.f}. Intuitively, if (a) the code entities in the functional set and (b) the execution traces in the program after slicing remain unchanged, then the test results will be preserved. Special attention has to be paid to any class hierarchy and method lookup changes that might alter the execution traces, as discussed in more detail in Sect. 3.4.2.

Step 2: Computing Compilation Set To avoid causing any compilation errors in the slicing process, we also need to ensure that all code entities referenced by the functional set are defined even if they are not traversed by the tests. Towards this end, CSLICER statically analyzes all the reference relations based on p_k and transitively includes all referenced entities in the *compilation set*, denoted by Π. The compilation set in our case is {A, A.x, B}. Notice that the classes A and B are included as well since the fields and methods require their enclosing classes to be present. During the slicing process, CSLICER ensures that all entities in the compilation set are present in the sliced program, albeit their definitions may not be the most updated version. Because the entities in the compilation set are not traversed by the tests, differences in their definitions do not affect the test results.

Step 3: Computing Hunk Dependencies In the last stage, CSLICER iterates backwards from the newest change set Δ_5 to the oldest one Δ_1, collecting changes that are required to preserve the "behavior" of the functional and compilation set elements. Each change is divided into a set of *atomic changes* (see Sect. 3.2.2.1). Having computed the functional and compilation set (highlighted in Fig. 3.2), CSLICER then goes through each atomic change and decides whether it should be kept in the sliced history (H') based on the entities changed and their change types. In our example, Δ_2 and Δ_5 are kept in H' since all atomic changes introduced by these commits—B.f and A.h—are in the functional set. Δ_4 contains an insertion of A.b which is in the compilation set. Hence, this change is also kept in H'. Δ_3 can be ignored since the changed entities are not in either set. Even if Δ_1 does not belong to functional or compilation dependencies, it is still included as a hunk dependencies because Δ_4 cannot be applied correctly without it.

After the three steps, the computed history slice $\langle \Delta_1, \Delta_2, \Delta_4, \Delta_5 \rangle$ is guaranteed to be applicable on Foo.java at v1.0 and results in an executable program as shown in Fig. 3.3b. The behaviors of the target feature test are also preserved by the resulting program. Therefore, the computed semantic history slice is effectively an executable feature implementation which is fully compatible with text-based SCM systems.

3.4.2 The Semantic History Slicing Algorithm

Now we present in detail the semantic slicing algorithm which is independent of the underlying SCM systems and it follows essentially the workflow depicted in Fig. 3.12. First, the functional set (Λ) and compilation set (Π) are computed based on the latest version p_k and the input tests T. The original version history H is then distilled as a sequence of change sets $\langle \Delta_1, \ldots, \Delta_k \rangle$ through AST differencing. This step removes cosmetic changes (e.g., formatting, annotations, and comments) and only keeps in Δ_i atomic changes over code entities. Each such set Δ_i then goes through the core slicer component which decides whether to keep a particular

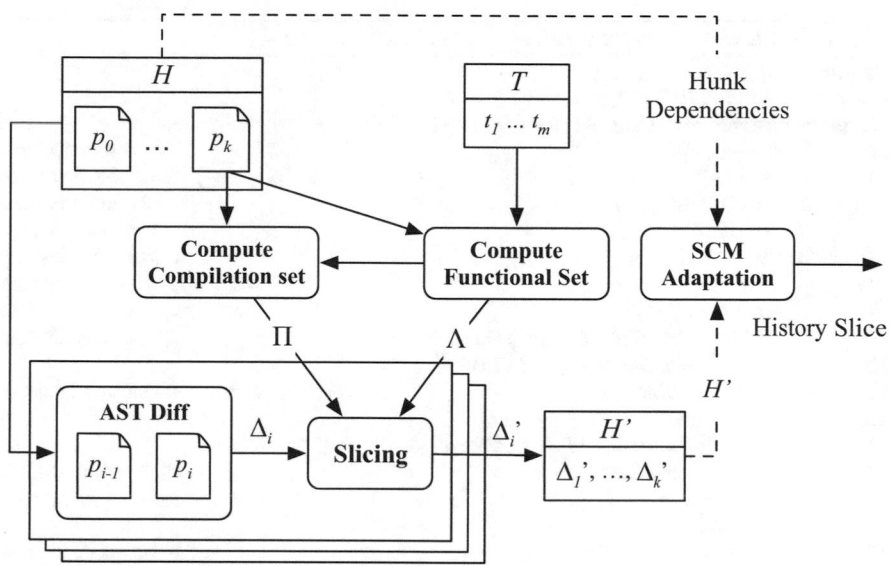

Fig. 3.12 High-level overview of the semantic slicing algorithms

atomic change or not. This component outputs a sliced change set Δ_i', which is a subsequence of Δ_i. Finally, the sliced change sets are concatenated and returned as a sub-history H'. Optionally, a post-processing step (SCM Adaptation) of H' is needed if the sliced history is to be applied using text-based SCM systems (Sect. 3.4.3).

3.4.2.1   Algorithm Description

The main SEMANTICSLICE procedure is shown in Algorithm 1. It obtains as the input the base version p_0, the original history $H = \langle \Delta_1, \ldots, \Delta_k \rangle$, and a set of test cases T. It then computes the functional and compilation set Λ and Π, respectively (Lines 4 and 5).

FUNCDEP(p_k, T) Based on the execution traces of running T on p_k, the procedure FUNCDEP returns the set of code entities (AST nodes) traversed by the test execution. This set (Λ) includes all fields assigned and all methods (and constructors) called during runtime. Although not allowed in Featherweight Java, field declarations with explicit inline initializations are also included when analyzing real Java code because these also involve assignments to fields.

COMPDEP(p_k, Λ) The procedure COMPDEP analyzes *reference* relations in p_k and includes all code entities referenced by the elements of Λ into the compilation set Π. We borrow the set of rules for computing Π from Kästner and Apel [13],

---

Algorithm 1 The semantic history slicing algorithm

Require: $|H| > 0 \wedge H(p_0) \in P \wedge H(p_0) \models T$
Ensure: $H' \subseteq H \wedge H'(p_0) \in P \wedge H'(p_0) \models T$

```
1:  procedure SEMANTICSLICE (p_0, H, T)
2:      H', k ← ⟨⟩, |H|                                              ▷ initialization
3:      p_k ← H(p_0)                                        ▷ p_k is the latest version
4:      Λ ← FUNCDEP(p_k, T)                                        ▷ functional set
5:      Π ← COMPDEP(p_k, Λ)                                       ▷ compilation set
6:      for i ∈ [k, 1] do                                         ▷ iterate backwards
7:          Δ'_i ← ⟨⟩                                    ▷ initialize sliced change set
8:          for δ ∈ Δ_i do
9:              if ¬LOOKUP(δ, H_{1..i}(p_0)) then                     ▷ keep lookup
10:                 if δ is DEL ∨ id(δ) ∉ Π then
11:                     continue                       ▷ skip non-comp and deletes
12:                 end if
13:                 if δ is UPD ∧ id(δ) ∉ Λ then
14:                     continue                            ▷ skip non-test updates
15:                 end if
16:             end if
17:             Δ'_i ← Δ'_i, δ                              ▷ concatenate the rest
18:         end for
19:         H' ← H', Δ'_i                                              ▷ grow H'
20:     end for
21:     return H'
22: end procedure
```

$$\frac{C <: D \quad C \in \Pi}{D \in \Pi} \text{ [L.1]} \qquad \frac{f : C \in \Pi}{C \in \Pi} \text{ [L.2]}$$

$$\frac{C(\overline{D\,f})\{\texttt{super}(\overline{f}); \texttt{this}.f = f;\} \in \Pi}{C \in \Pi \quad \overline{D} \in \Pi \quad \overline{f} \in \Pi} \text{ [K1]} \qquad \frac{C\ m(\overline{D\ x})\{\texttt{return } e;\} \in \Pi}{C \in \Pi \quad \overline{D} \in \Pi} \text{ [M1]}$$

$$\frac{\ldots\{\texttt{return } e.f;\} \in \Pi}{f \in \Pi} \text{ [E1]} \qquad \frac{\ldots\{\texttt{return } e.m(\overline{e});\} \in \Pi}{m \in \Pi} \text{ [E2]}$$

$$\frac{\ldots\{\texttt{return new } C(\overline{e});\} \in \Pi}{C \in \Pi} \text{ [E3]} \qquad \frac{\ldots\{\texttt{return } (C)e;\} \in \Pi}{C \in \Pi} \text{ [E4]}$$

$$\frac{x \in \Pi}{\text{PARENT}(x) \in \Pi} \text{ [P1]} \qquad \frac{x \in \Lambda}{x \in \Pi} \text{ [T1]}$$

Fig. 3.13 COMPDEP reference relation rules

where the authors formally prove that their rules are complete and ensure that no reference without a target is ever present in a program. Applying these rules, which are given in Fig. 3.13 and described below, allows us to guarantee type safety of the sliced program.

L1   a class can only extend a class that is present;

L2   a field can only have type of a class that is present;

K1   a constructor can only have parameter types of classes that are present and access to fields that are present;

M1   a method declaration can only have return type and parameter types of classes that are present;

E1   a field access can only access fields that are present;

E2   a method invocation can only invoke methods that are present;

E3   an instance creation can only create objects from classes that are present;

E4   a cast operation can only cast an expression to a class that is present;

P1   an entity is only present when the enclosing entities are present;

T1   an entity is in the compilation set if it is in the functional set.

We iterate backwards through all the change sets in the history (Lines 6 to 20) and examine each atomic change in the change set. An atomic change δ is included into the sliced history if it is an insertion or an update to the functional set entities, or an insertion of the compilation set entities. Updates to the compilation set entities (that are not in the functional set) are ignored since they generally do not affect the test results.

Our language P does not allow method overloading or field overshadowing, which limits the effects of class hierarchy changes. Exceptions are changes to subtyping relations or casts which might alter method lookup (Line 9). Therefore, we define function LOOKUP to capture such changes,

$$\text{LOOKUP}(\delta, p) \triangleq \exists m, C \cdot \text{METHODS}(m, C) \neq \text{METHODS}'(m, C),$$

where METHODS and METHODS$'$ are the method lookup function for p and $\delta(p)$, respectively. Finally, the sliced history H' is returned at Line 21.

3.4.2.2   Correctness of Algorithm 1

Assume that every intermediate version of the program p is syntactically valid and well-typed. We show that the sliced program p' produced by the SEMANTICSLICE procedure maintains such properties. The proofs of Lemmas 3.1 and 3.2 can be found in Ref. [18].

Lemma 3.1 (Syntactic Correctness) $H'(p_0) \in P$.

Lemma 3.2 (Type Safety) $H'(p_0)$ *is well-typed.*

Theorem 3.1 (Correctness of Algorithm 1) *Let* $\langle p_1, \ldots, p_k \rangle$ *be* k *consecutive subsequent versions of a program* p_0 *such that* $p_i \in P$ *and* p_i *is well-typed for all indices* $0 \leq i \leq k$. *Let* $H = \langle \Delta_1, \ldots, \Delta_k \rangle$ *such that* $\Delta_i(p_{i-1}) = p_i$ *for all indices* $1 \leq i \leq k$. *Let* T *be a test suite such that* $p_k \models T$. *Then the sliced history* $H' = \text{SEMANTICSLICE}(p_0, H, T)$ *is semantics-preserving with respect to* T.

Proof According to Definition 3.1, we need to show that H' satisfies the following properties,

1. $H'(p_0) \in P$,
2. $H'(p_0)$ is well-typed,
3. $H'(p_0) \models T$.

From Lemmas 3.1 and 3.2 we know that $(H' \circ H_{1..i})(p_0)$ satisfies (1) and (2) is an invariant for the outer loop (Lines 6 to 20) of Algorithm 1. The original history H has a finite length k, so upon termination, we have $H'(p_0)$ satisfies (1) and (2). Since all functional set insertions and updates are kept in H', any functional set entity that exists in $H(p_0)$ can be found identical in $H'(p_0)$. Because all changes that alter method lookups are also kept (Line 9), the execution traces do not change either. Due to that reason, and by the definition of functional set, (3) also holds. Thus, $H'(p_0)$ satisfies (1), (2) and (3).

3.4.3   SCM Adaptation

The presented semantic history slicing algorithm operates on the atomic change level using AST-based view, which can be directly used with semantic-based tools such as SemanticMerge [32]. As an optional step, SCM adaptation integrates the generic Algorithm 1 with text-based SCM systems such as Git.

The line-based view used by text-based SCM tools represents changes between versions as a set of *hunks* (Sect. 3.2.2.2). For example, Fig. 3.14 shows an abstract view of the changes made between p_{i-1} and p_i, where blocks with "-" represent lines removed and blocks with "+" represent lines inserted. Grey blocks surrounding the changed lines represent the contexts. From the line-based view, the difference between p_{i-1} and p_i consists of three hunks, i.e., δ_1, δ_2 and δ_3. We define two auxiliary functions, $left(\delta)$ and $right(\delta)$, which return the lines involved before and after the hunk δ, respectively. Special cases are $right(\delta)$ when δ is a deletion and $left(\delta)$ when δ is an insertion: in both cases, the functions return a zero-length placeholder at the appropriate positions.

In order to apply the sliced results with text-based SCM tools where changes are represented as hunks, it is needed to ensure that no conflict arises due to unmatched contexts. Informally, a commit Δ_i *directly hunk-depends* on another commit Δ_j, denoted by $\Delta_i \rightsquigarrow \Delta_j$, if and only if Δ_j *contributes* to the hunks or their contexts in Δ_i. In contrast, if Δ_i does not directly hunk-depend on Δ_j, we say they *commute* [7], i.e., reordering them in history does not conflict. The procedure HUNKDEP(H') returns the transitive hunk dependencies for all commits in H', i.e.,

$$\text{HUNKDEP}(H') \triangleq \bigcup_{\Delta_i \in H'} \{\Delta_j \in H/H' | \Delta_i \rightsquigarrow^* \Delta_j\}.$$

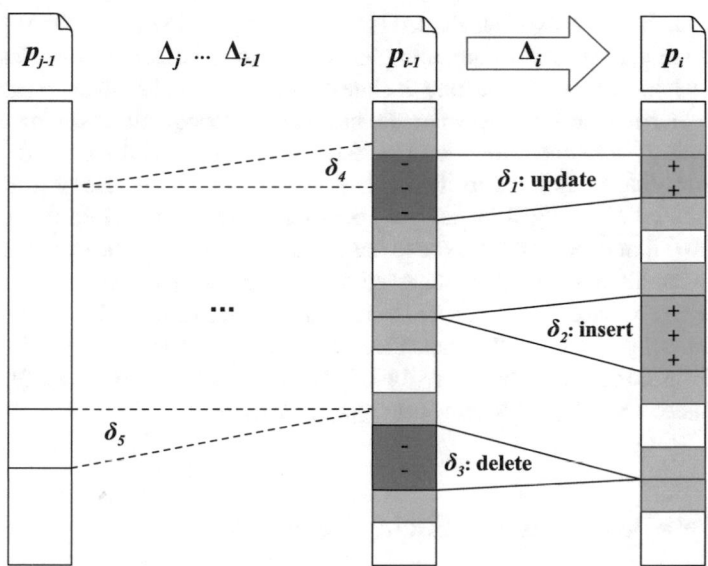

Fig. 3.14 Illustration of direct hunk dependencies. Commit Δ_i directly hunk-depends on a previous commit Δ_j. Hunk δ_4 provides contexts for hunk δ_1. Hunk δ_5 provides contexts for hunk δ_3

Once a sub-history H' is computed and returned by Algorithm 1, we augment H' with HUNKDEP(H') and the result is guaranteed to apply to p_0 without edit conflicts.

Given a commit Δ_i, we collect a set of text lines B_i which are required as the *basis* for applying Δ_i. For example, B_i for Δ_i includes $left(\delta)$ for all $\delta \in \Delta_i$ and

---

Algorithm 2 The DIRECTHUNK procedure

Require: B_i is the basis set for Δ_i
Ensure: $D = \{\Delta \in H_{1..(i-1)} | \Delta \leadsto \Delta_i\}$
 1: **procedure** DIRECTHUNK$(B_i, H_{1..i})$
 2:     $D \leftarrow \emptyset$ ▷ initialize the direct hunk set
 3:     $B_{i-1} \leftarrow B_i$ ▷ initialize B_{i-1}
 4:     **for** $\delta \in \Delta_{i-1}$ **do**
 5:         **if** δ is DEL $\wedge$ $right(\delta) \subseteq B_i$ **then**   ▷ deletion falls within the range of B_i
 6:             $D \leftarrow D \cup \{\Delta_{i-1}\}$
 7:         **else if** δ is INS $\wedge$ $right(\delta) \cap B_i \neq \emptyset$ **then**   ▷ insertion contributes to B_i
 8:             $D \leftarrow D \cup \{\Delta_{i-1}\}$
 9:             $B_{i-1} \leftarrow B_{i-1} \setminus right(\delta)$
10:         **end if**
11:     **end for**
12:     $D \leftarrow D \cup$ DIRECTHUNK$(B_{i-1}, H_{1..(i-1)})$ ▷ calls DIRECTHUNK recursively on $H_{1..(i-1)}$
13:     **return** D
14: **end procedure**

---

their surrounding contexts (all shaded blocks under p_{i-1} in Fig. 3.14). Algorithm 2 describes the algorithm for computing the set of direct hunk dependencies ($\leadsto$) by tracing back in history and locating the latest commits that contribute to each line of the basis. Starting from Δ_{i-1}, we iterate backwards through all preceding commits. If a commit Δ contains a deletion that falls in the range of the basis (Line 5) or an insertion that adds lines to the basis (Line 7), then Δ is added to the direct dependency set D. In Fig. 3.14, $\Delta_i \leadsto \Delta_j$ because Δ_j has both an insertion (δ_4) and a deletion (δ_5) that directly contribute to the basis at p_{i-1}. When the origin of a line is located in the history, the line is removed from the basis set (Line 9). The algorithm then recursively traces the origin of the remaining lines in B_{i-1}. Upon termination, D contains all direct hunk dependencies of Δ_i. In the worst case, HUNKDEP calls DIRECTHUNK for every change set in H'. Thus, the running time of HUNKDEP is bounded above by $O(|H'| \times |H| \times \max_{\Delta \in H}(|\Delta|))$.

3.5 Web-Based History Slicing Framework

A number of semantic history slicing techniques, including CSLICER presented in Sect. 3.4, are implemented and encapsulated within a web-based framework—CSLICERCLOUD [19]. The main features of CSLICERCLOUD are:

- CSLICERCLOUD is a Web-based application built upon the Node.js JavaScript runtime [24]. It requires no downloading, installation, or configuration. All parameters for performing history slicing can be configured through a graphical user interface.
- It supports Java projects hosted on GitHub. For projects using Maven [23] as their build system, the history slicing process is completely automated. It may require further configurations for other types of projects.
- The framework unifies a number of underlying history slicing algorithms and can be applied in many different feature-oriented development and maintenance activities.

The tool and more detailed information are available at: https://github.com/ntu-SRSLab/CSlicer-Cloud.

3.5.1 User Interface

The user interface of CSLICERCLOUD consists of three main components—the *slicing parameter panel*, the *history view*, and the *test view*.

Imagine that a developer wants to migrate a feature—"Adding a placeholder in the Lexer and CSV parser to store the end-of-line string" which was introduced in version 1.5 of the Apache Common CSV project [6]—to another branch, but he/she is unsure which commits are required for the target feature to work correctly on the target branch.

Slicing Parameter Panel In order to use CSLICERCLOUD for identifying the commits required, a user must specify a number of slicing parameters. Figure 3.15 shows the slicing parameter panel of CSLICERCLOUD. A user defines a history range by specifying the "start commit" and the "end commit", in this case, the commits "#99be47e" and "#259812e", respectively. This can also be done by directly clicking on the commits in the history view.

Test View Then, a set of feature test cases needs to be provided as the slicing criteria. The test view visualizes the unit tests of a Java project, and a user can select the tests he/she wants to use for history slicing tasks. Figure 3.16 gives a screenshot of the test view showing the test cases organized in an expandable tree structure. Each top-level node represents a Java test file, e.g., "CSVParserTest.java". The leaf nodes become visible when a test file

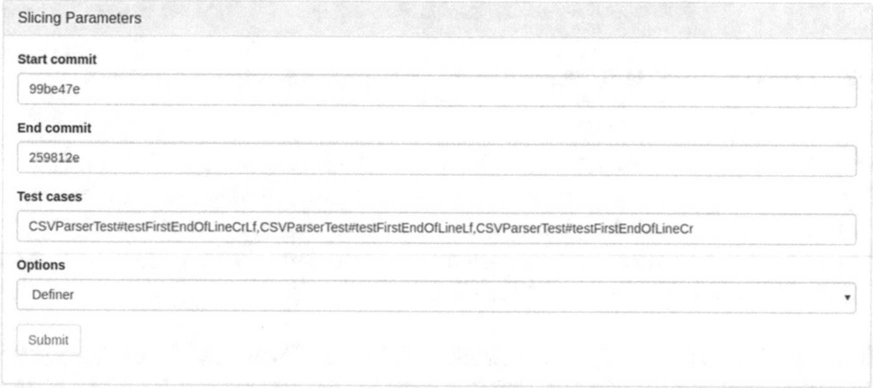

Fig. 3.15 Setting slicing parameters: start commit, end commit, test cases, and slicing algorithm

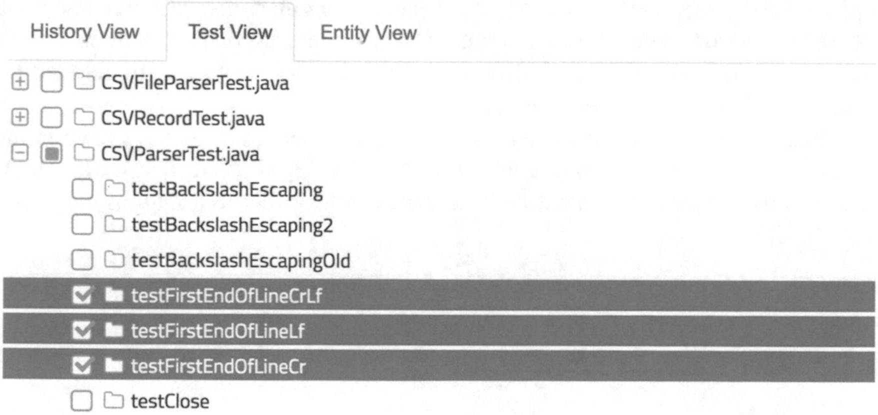

Fig. 3.16 The test view of CSLICERCLOUD

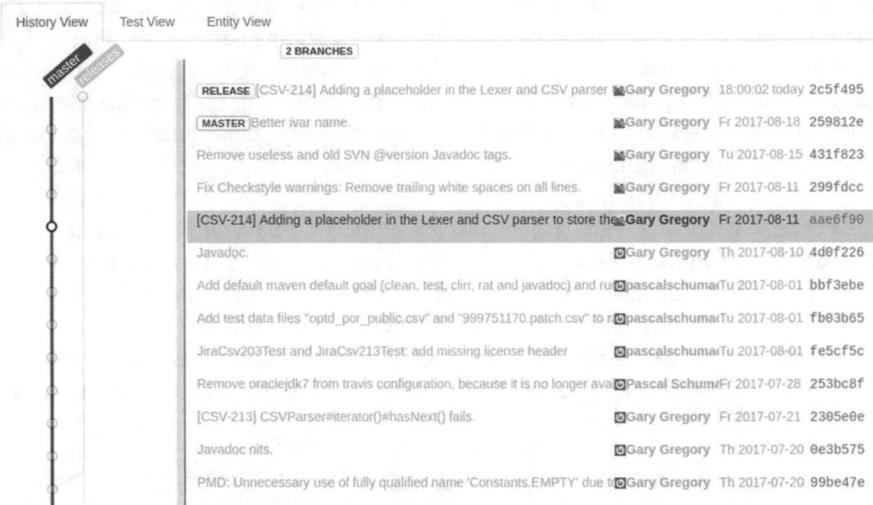

Fig. 3.17 The history view of CSLICERCLOUD. Slicing results are highlighted

node is expanded. They represent the test methods contained in the corresponding test file. For instance, there are three test cases associated with the target
feature, "testFirstEndOfLineCrLf", "testFirstEndOfLineLf", and
"testFirstEndOfLineCr". Each method also comes with a check box which
allows it to be included as one of the slicing criteria.

History View The history view visualizes the version histories of a given software
repository and allows users to define a history range for the subsequent history
slicing tasks. Figure 3.17 shows a screenshot of the history view displaying the
version histories of the Common CSV project. The left pane depicts the branches
and commits graphically while the right pane lists other metadata including log
messages, authors, and SHA-1 commit IDs of the corresponding commits. Each
item in the commit list is clickable such that a history range can be defined by
selecting a starting and an ending commit.

When the history slicing process is finished, the slicing results are shown in the
history view; in our case, the commit #aae6f90 is highlighted. CSLICERCLOUD
can also create a new branch with the computed history slice as a migration dry-run
(see Fig. 3.17).

3.5.2   Use Cases in SPL

We see applications of CSLICERCLOUD in many software development and maintenance scenarios under the SPL settings.

A1. Porting Features Across Versions Often, a developer works on multiple features at the same time which could result in mixed commit histories concerning different features. However, when submitting pull requests for review, contributors should refrain from including unrelated changes as suggested by many project contribution guidelines. Despite the efforts of keeping the development of each feature on separate branches, isolating each functional unit as a self-contained pull request is still a challenging task. For a particular pull request, the test cases created for validation can be used as slicing criteria to identify relevant commits from the developers' local histories in their forked repositories, i.e., it can facilitate creation of logically clean and easy-to-merge pull requests

A2. Creating Pull Requests CSLICERCLOUD can identify the set of commits required for back-porting a feature to earlier versions of a software project. Even in very disciplined projects, when such commits can be identified by browsing their associated log messages, the feature of interest might depend on earlier commits in the same branch. To ensure correct execution of the desired feature, all dependencies have to be identified and migrated as well, which is a tedious and error-prone manual task. Given test cases for the features to be ported, CSLICERCLOUD can automatically compute the required changes and, at the same time, effectively avoid including unnecessary changes.

A3. Cutting New Releases Many software projects periodically cut releases by cherry-picking commits corresponding to desired features from the develop branch to the release branches, e.g., Bazel [4]. CSLICERCLOUD analyses the change history since the last release and uses feature test cases to locate the desired set of commits which guarantee not to cause merge conflicts and pass the tests when moved to the release branch.

3.6 Conclusion

In this chapter, we presented semantic history slicing, a feature location technique designed to work on software version histories. We also described a particular history slicing algorithm, called CSLICER, and illustrated it with examples. Finally, we introduced a Web-based history slicing framework CSLICERCLOUD and discussed its use cases in software development and maintenance under SPL settings.

References

1. Al-Msie'deen, R., Seriai, A., Huchard, M., Urtado, C., Vauttier, S.: Mining features from the object-oriented source code of software variants by combining lexical and structural similarity. In: Proceedings of the 2013 IEEE 14th International Conference on Information Reuse & Integration, pp. 586–593 (2013)

2. Al-Msie'deen, R., Seriai, A., Huchard, M., Urtado, C., Vauttier, S., Salman, H.E.: Feature location in a collection of software product variants using formal concept analysis. In: Proceedings of the 13th International Conference on Software Reuse, vol. 7925, pp. 302–307 (2013)
3. Antkiewicz, M., Ji, W., Berger, T., Czarnecki, K., Schmorleiz, T., Lämmel, R., Stănciulescu, S., Wąsowski, A., Schaefer, I.: Flexible product line engineering with a virtual platform. In: Companion Proceedings of the 36th International Conference on Software Engineering, pp. 532–535. ACM, New York, NY, USA (2014)
4. Bazel support policy. https://bazel.build/support.html#releases (2020)
5. Chawathe, S.S., Rajaraman, A., Garcia-Molina, H., Widom, J.: Change detection in hierarchically structured information. In: Proceedings of the 1996 ACM SIGMOD International Conference on Management of Data, pp. 493–504 (1996)
6. Using Apache Commons CSV. https://commons.apache.org/proper/commons-csv (2020)
7. Understanding Darcs/patch theory. http://en.wikibooks.org/wiki/Understanding_Darcs/Patch_theory (2020)
8. Dit, B., Revelle, M., Gethers, M., Poshyvanyk, D.: Feature location in source code: A taxonomy and survey. Journal of Software: Evolution and Process **25**(1), 53–95 (2013)
9. Dubinsky, Y., Rubin, J., Berger, T., Duszynski, S., Becker, M., Czarnecki, K.: An exploratory study of cloning in industrial software product lines. In: Proceedings of the 2013 17th European Conference on Software Maintenance and Reengineering, pp. 25–34 (2013)
10. Fluri, B., Gall, H.C.: Classifying change types for qualifying change couplings. In: Proceedings of the 14th IEEE International Conference on Program Comprehension, pp. 35–45. IEEE (2006)
11. Git version control system. https://git-scm.com (2016)
12. Igarashi, A., Pierce, B.C., Wadler, P.: Featherweight Java: A minimal core calculus for Java and GJ. ACM Transactions on Programming Languages and Systems **23**(3), 396–450 (2001)
13. Kästner, C., Apel, S.: Type-checking software product lines – a formal approach. In: Proceedings of the 23rd IEEE/ACM International Conference on Automated Software Engineering, pp. 258–267. IEEE Computer Society, Washington, DC, USA (2008)
14. Li, Y., Rubin, J., Chechik, M.: Semantic slicing of software version histories. In: Proceedings of the 30th IEEE/ACM International Conference on Automated Software Engineering, pp. 686–696. Lincoln, NE, USA (2015)
15. Li, Y., Zhu, C., Gligoric, M., Rubin, J., Chechik, M.: Precise semantic history slicing through dynamic delta refinement. Automated Software Engineering **26**(4), 757–793 (2019)
16. Li, Y., Zhu, C., Rubin, J., Chechik, M.: Precise semantic history slicing through dynamic delta refinement. In: Proceedings of the 31st IEEE/ACM International Conference on Automated Software Engineering, pp. 495–506. Singapore, Singapore (2016)
17. Li, Y., Zhu, C., Rubin, J., Chechik, M.: FHistorian: Locating features in version histories. In: Proceedings of the 21st International Systems and Software Product Line Conference - Volume A, pp. 49–58. ACM, New York, NY, USA (2017)
18. Li, Y., Zhu, C., Rubin, J., Chechik, M.: Semantic slicing of software version histories. IEEE Transactions on Software Engineering **44**(2), 182–201 (2017)
19. Li, Y., Zhu, C., Rubin, J., Chechik, M.: CSlicerCloud: A web-based semantic history slicing framework. In: Proceedings of the 40th International Conference on Software Engineering (2018)
20. Linsbauer, L., Angerer, F., Grünbacher, P., Lettner, D., Prähofer, H., Lopez-Herrejon, R.E., Egyed, A.: Recovering feature-to-code mappings in mixed-variability software systems. In: Proceedings of the 2014 IEEE International Conference on Software Maintenance and Evolution, pp. 426–430 (2014)
21. Linsbauer, L., Lopez-Herrejon, R.E., Egyed, A.: Recovering traceability between features and code in product variants. In: Proceedings of the 17th International Software Product Line Conference, pp. 131–140 (2013)
22. Linsbauer, L., Lopez-Herrejon, R.E., Egyed, A.: Variability extraction and modeling for product variants. Software & Systems Modeling pp. 1–21 (2016)

23. Apache Maven project. https://maven.apache.org (2020)
24. Node.js. https://nodejs.org (2020)
25. Rothermel, G., Harrold, M.J.: A framework for evaluating regression test selection techniques. In: Proceedings of the 16th International Conference on Software Engineering, pp. 201–210. IEEE Computer Society Press, Los Alamitos, CA, USA (1994)
26. Rothermel, G., Harrold, M.J.: Analyzing regression test selection techniques. IEEE Transactions on Software Engineering **22**(8), 529–551 (1996)
27. Rubin, J., Chechik, M.: A framework for managing cloned product variants. In: Proceedings of the 35th International Conference on Software Engineering, pp. 1233–1236 (2013)
28. Rubin, J., Chechik, M.: A survey of feature location techniques. In: I. Reinhartz-Berger et al. (ed.) Domain Engineering: Product Lines, Conceptual Models, and Languages, pp. 29–58. Springer (2013)
29. Rubin, J., Czarnecki, K., Chechik, M.: Managing cloned variants: A framework and experience. In: Proceedings of the 17th International Software Product Line Conference, pp. 101–110 (2013)
30. Rubin, J., Czarnecki, K., Chechik, M.: Cloned product variants: From ad-hoc to managed software product lines. Journal on Software Tools for Technology Transfer **17**(5), 627–646 (2015)
31. Rubin, J., Kirshin, A., Botterweck, G., Chechik, M.: Managing forked product variants. In: Proceedings of the 16th International Software Product Line Conference, vol. 1, pp. 156–160. ACM, New York, NY, USA (2012)
32. The diff and merge tool that understands your code – SemanticMerge. https://www.semanticmerge.com (2020)
33. Tsuchiya, R., Kato, T., Washizaki, H., Kawakami, M., Fukazawa, Y., Yoshimura, K.: Recovering traceability links between requirements and source code in the same series of software products. In: Proceedings of the 17th International Software Product Line Conference, pp. 121–130. New York, NY, USA (2013)
34. Xue, Y., Xing, Z., Jarzabek, S.: Feature location in a collection of product variants. In: Proceedings of the 2012 19th Working Conference on Reverse Engineering, pp. 145–154. IEEE Computer Society, Washington, DC, USA (2012)
35. Zhu, C., Li, Y., Rubin, J., Chechik, M.: GenSlice: Generalized semantic history slicing. In: Proceedings of the 36th IEEE International Conference on Software Maintenance and Evolution (2020)
36. Ziadi, T., Frias, L., da Silva, M.A.A., Ziane, M.: Feature identification from the source code of product variants. In: 2012 16th European Conference on Software Maintenance and Reengineering, pp. 417–422 (2012)

Chapter 4
Feature Location in Models (FLiM): Design Time and Runtime

Lorena Arcega, Jaime Font, Øystein Haugen, and Carlos Cetina

Abstract In this chapter, we apply feature location to automate the identification and extraction of the features existing among a family of product models and re-engineering them into a model-based SPL. To address the feature location in software models (FLiM) challenge, we present two approaches: at design time (FLiMEA) and at runtime (FLiMRT). Both FLiMEA and FLiMRT approaches are different but complementary. FLiMEA takes information from design time models while FLiMRT takes information from runtime models. The FLiMEA approach combines Genetic Operations and Information Retrieval. Given a model and a description of a possible feature, model fragments extracted from the model are generated using genetic operation and are assessed using an information retrieval technique to rank the candidates based on the similarity with the feature description. The FLiMRT approach leverages the use of software architecture models at runtime. The information is collected in the software architecture model at runtime and each model element is assessed based on its similarity to the feature description. We evaluated our approaches in two real-world industrial case studies: BSH and CAF. The application of FLiMEA shows that the mean values of recall and precision are 72.99 per cent for BSH and 68.34 per cent for CAF while FLiMRT ranks the relevant elements in the top ten positions of the ranking in 84 per cent of the cases.

4.1 Introduction

Software Product Lines (SPLs) aim at reducing development cost and time to market while improving quality of software systems by exploiting commonalities and managing variabilities across a set of software applications [52]. The SPL engineering

L. Arcega (✉) · J. Font · C. Cetina
Universidad San Jorge, SVIT Research Group, Zaragoza, Spain
e-mail: larcega@usj.es; jfont@usj.es; ccetina@usj.es

Ø. Haugen
Faculty of Computer Science, Østfold University College, Halden, Norway
e-mail: oystein.haugen@hiof.no

© Springer Nature Switzerland AG 2023
R. E. Lopez-Herrejon et al. (eds.), *Handbook of Re-Engineering Software Intensive Systems into Software Product Lines*, https://doi.org/10.1007/978-3-031-11686-5_4

paradigm separates two processes; domain engineering (where the commonalities are identified and realized as reusable assets) and application engineering (where specific software products are derived by reusing the variability of the SPL) [12]. Traditionally, a domain analysis is performed to build a feature model that captures the variability of the system in terms of features [13, 29]. The domain knowledge from the experts is captured and used to build the library of reusable assets.

A recent survey [6] reveals that most of the SPLs are built when there are already products; therefore, the set of existing products is re-engineered into an SPL [34]. This is known as the extractive approach to SPLs [34]; it capitalizes on existing systems to initiate a product line, formalizing variability among a set of similar products into a variability model. The resulting SPL is capable of generating the products used as input (among others) with the benefit of having the variability among the products formalized, enabling a systematic reuse.

Feature Location is known as the process of finding the set of software artifacts that realize a particular feature. This topic has gained momentum during recent years [16, 56]. However, most of the research efforts in feature location have been directed towards the location of features into source code artifacts, neglecting other software artifacts such as models [43, 44, 66]. In addition, Search-Based Software Engineering (SBSE) has had notable successes and there is an increasingly widespread application of SBSE across the full spectrum of Software Engineering activities and problems [25].

The task of feature location in models may appear easy, however it becomes very complex in the models of our industrial partners [51]. For example, suppose we ask the domain experts of one of our industrial partners, CAF in this case, to manually locate the model elements that correspond to the 121 features of the data set provided. Taking into account that the data set comprises 23 trains and the model of each train has more than 1200 model elements, at least 27,600 model elements should be evaluated. To assess a model element, it is reasonable to consider its properties. In the data set, each element has about 15 properties. Therefore, about 414,000 properties of model elements should be considered. Assuming that a domain expert only needs 1 second to consider a property of a model element, the domain expert needs 4.79 days to manually locate each feature. Considering the 121 features and 19 domain experts, the result is 30.17 years.

Domain experts could make use of simple text search tools in the models, but these tools would not prevent domain experts from first knowing the models of the trains. There is no domain expert who knows all models completely in CAF. Although we ignore that domain experts can forget models that belong to trains manufactured over two decades as is the case in CAF, the models have always been created by different domain experts. Moreover, the models may have been maintained by other domain experts who have not participated in the creation. Time improvements because of the learning effect, or locating several features simultaneously are not accounted here, but these improvements could also be source of errors which take time to fix.

In addition, the 30.17 years do not include the time that is necessary to reach a consensus on 19 solutions for each of the 121 features. In an industrial environment like in CAF, the domain experts are distributed in three different parts of Spain (Zaragoza, Beasain and Bizkaia). This geographical distribution implies that the domain experts are not used to carrying out consensus tasks, which can negatively influence the time they need to agree on the solutions.

Therefore, feature location in real-world models is not a trivial task. From the 121 features of the data set, only the model elements of 43 features are documented in CAF. The documentation of these 43 features is the result of months of manual work with external consultants to address certification needs or bugs. Moreover, this data set is made up of tramway models, but the need to locate features is also present in more CAF models of similar complexity as subway models, or in more complex models such as suburban and high speed.

We can apply feature location to automate the identification and extraction of the features existing among a family of product models and re-engineering them into a model-based SPL (an SPL whose final products are models) by establishing precisely the variability between the features. To address this challenge we present an approach that turns a set of similar but different product models with no variability specification into a set of product models with a formal variability definition that specifies the commonalities and variability among them [23].

In addition, we can apply feature location in systems that work with models at runtime. We use the information extracted from software architecture models at runtime to perform feature location. In our dynamic feature location approach [3], the software engineer executes a scenario, which uses the desired feature to be located. The information is collected in the software architecture model at runtime. Then, our approach filters the trace in order to extract the relevant elements of the software models.

In the evaluation, we have applied our approaches to two industrial domains: BSH and CAF. BSH is one of the largest manufacturers of home appliances in Europe. Its induction division has been producing induction hobs under the brands of Bosch and Siemens for the last 15 years. CAF produces a family of PLC software to control the trains they manufacture, which has been under development for more than 25 years. The firmware for their products is generated from models using a model-based approach. The results of the evaluations show a good performance of our approaches. The application of FLiMEA shows that the mean values of recall and precision are around 72.99% for BSH and 68.34% for CAF. Our FLiMRT approach ranks the relevant elements in the top ten positions of the ranking in 84% of the cases.

4.2   Background

This section provides some basic background for understanding this chapter. Specifically, we present Software Product Lines (SPLs), feature location, information retrieval, and evolutionary algorithms. In addition, the Domain-Specific Language (DSL) used by our industrial partner to formalize their products, the IHDSL. It will be used through the rest of the chapter to present a running example. Then, the Common Variability Language (CVL) is presented, CVL is the language used by our approach to formalize the model fragments.

4.2.1 Software Product Lines

Mass production was popularized by Henry Ford in the early twentieth century. McIlroy coined the term software mass production in 1968 [45]. It was the beginning of SPLs. In 1976, Parnas introduced the notion of software program families as a result of mass production [50]. The use of features (to drive mass production) was proposed by Kang in the early 1990s [29]. Shortly, the first conferences appeared turning SPL into a new body of research [37].

SPLs are defined as "a set of software-intensive systems, sharing a common, managed set of features that satisfy the specific needs of a particular market segment or mission and that are developed from a common set of core assets in a prescribed way" [12, 17]. This definition can be redefined into five major issues:

1. **Products**. SPL shift the focus from single software system development to SPL development. The development processes are not intended to build one application, but a number of them (e.g., 10, 100, 10,000, or more). This forces a change in the engineering processes where a distinction between domain engineering and application engineering is introduced. Doing so, the construction of the reusable assets (platform) and their variability is separated from production of the product-line applications.
2. **Features**. Features are units (i.e., increments in application functionality) by which different products can be distinguished and defined within an SPL [5].
3. **Domain**. An SPL is created within the scope of a domain. A domain is a specialized body of knowledge, an area of expertise, or a collection of related functionality [48].
4. **Core Assets**. A core asset is an artifact or resource that is used in the production of more than one product in an SPL [12].
5. **Production Plan**. It states how each product is produced. The production plan is a description of how core assets are to be used to develop a product in a product line and specifies how to use the production plan to build the end product [9]. The production plan ties together all the reusable assets to assemble (and build) end products. Synthesis is a part of the production plan.

SPLs (or system families) provide a highly successful approach to strategic reuse of assets within an organization. A standard SPL consists of a product line architecture, a set of software components and a set of products. A product consists of a product architecture, derived from the product line architecture, a set of selected and configured product line components and product specific code.

Therefore, SPL engineering is about producing families of similar systems rather than the production of individual systems. SPL engineering consists of three main processes: domain engineering (also called core asset development), application engineering (also called product development) and management. These three processes are complementary and provide feedback to each other.

Domain engineering is, among others, concerned with identifying the commonality and variability for the products in the product line and implementing the shared artifacts such that the commonality can be exploited while preserving the required variability. Using a "design-for-reuse" approach, domain engineering (core asset development [12]) is on charge of determining the commonality and the variability among product family members. In general, domain engineering is divided into domain analysis, domain design and domain implementation.

During application engineering, individual products are developed by selecting and configuring shared artifacts and, where necessary, adding product specific extensions. To achieve this, it reuses the reusable assets developed previously. This process is subdivided into application analysis, application design and application implementation.

Management is responsible for giving resources, coordinating, and supervising domain and application engineering activities. See [12, 52] for more details about the processes.

In SPL processes, variability is made explicit through variation points. A variation point represents a delayed design decision. When the architect or designer decides to delay the design decision, he or she has to design a variation point. The design of the variation point requires several steps: (1) the separation of the stable and variant behaviour, (2) the definition of an interface between these types of behaviour, (3) the design of a variant management mechanism and (4) the implementation of one or more variants. Given a variation point, it can be bound to a particular variant. For each variation point, the set of variants may be open, i.e. more variants can be added, or closed, i.e. no more variants can be added. Overall, during domain engineering new variation points are introduced, whereas during application engineering these variation points are bound to selected variants

4.2.2   Feature Location

In software systems a feature represents a functionality that is defined by requirements and accessible to developers and users [16]. Identifying an initial location in the software artifacts that corresponds to a specific functionality is known as feature location [7].

The majority of existing approaches for feature location in program code can be divided in three categories: static, dynamic, and hybrid. Static feature location approaches examine structural information such as control or data flow dependencies. These approaches require a set of software artifacts which serve as a starting point for the analysis in order to generate program elements relevant to the initial set. This initial set is usually specified by the software engineer. Dynamic feature location approaches examine a software system's execution. They are often used for feature location when features can be invoked and observed during runtime. Typically, these approaches rely on a post-mortem analysis of an execution trace. The combination of more than one type of analysis results in a hybrid approach for feature location.

Existing approaches for feature location in models rely on mechanical comparisons to find model differences. First, several comparisons among the product models are performed. Then, a set of model fragments is extracted based on the differences and common parts spotted among the models. Identical elements are extracted as common parts of the product line, similar elements are extracted as variable alternative parts, and unmatched elements are extracted as variable optional parts. As a result, the variability existing among the set of similar product models is formalized.

4.2.3 Information Retrieval

Information Retrieval (IR) is the task, given a set of documents and a user query, of finding the relevant documents. There are many information retrieval techniques: program analysis dependencies [11, 19, 20, 33], textual similarity [38, 42, 55, 59], trace analysis [21, 53, 64, 65], type systems [18, 30–32] or propositional logic [2, 14, 46, 47]. In these approaches, we focus on information retrieval techniques based on textual similarity.

The IR techniques based on textual similarity, are based on mathematical and statistical methods to determine the similarity between different collections of texts. Three of the most popular IR techniques are: Vector Space Model (VSM) [58], Latent Semantic Analysis (LSA) [36] or Latent Dirichlet Allocation (LDA) [8].

The current results are ambiguous and contradictory about which technique provides the best performance [63]. However, some works state that LSI performs better working with bug reports [10] or with text [54], while VSM works better with source code. This is due to the reason that VSM works very well in case of exact match while LSI retrieves relevant documents based on the semantic similarity.

We decided to apply Latent Semantic Analysis (LSA) to analyze the relationships between the description of the features and the bugs provided by the user and the model. This decision is because of product models are representations at a higher abstraction level than the source code, and the language used to build them is closer to the bug description language; similar to text.

4.2.4 Evolutionary Algorithms

The approach for feature location in models at design time explained in this chapter comes in the form of an Evolutionary Algorithm. In Evolutionary Algorithms, a population of individuals (candidate solutions for the problem) is evolved and assessed through several iterations in the search for the best possible individual. When applied to model artifacts, the population of individuals will be in the form of model fragments. These individuals need to be properly encoded, enabling the evolutionary algorithm to work efficiently with them. Next, each candidate solution from the population is evaluated using a fitness function (a formalization of the overall quality goal) to determine how well it performs as a solution to the problem. As a result, the population of solutions is ranked depending on their fitness value and, based on the ranked population, some genetic manipulations are performed over the individuals. This cycle of genetic manipulations and assessment will be repeated until some stop criteria is met.

As we said, each possible solution to the problem (called individual) needs to be encoded so the genetic operations can be applied to them. Traditionally, individuals are encoded as a fixed-size string of binary values, but other encodings can be used such as tree encodings. In fact, it is suggested [15] to use an encoding natural for the problem and then devise genetic operations capable of working for that specific encoding. The individuals of our problem are model fragments (extracted from some product model); therefore, the encoding must be able to represent a model fragment extracted from a product model.

Next, the fitness function is used as an heuristic to guide the search performed by the evolutionary algorithm. To do so, the function assigns a fitness value to each of the model fragments based on their quality as feature realization. This information can be used in two ways: to determine that the algorithm should terminate as a desirable level of fitness has been reached and to determine the best candidates to be used as parents for the next generation.

Finally, different operations are performed to manipulate the individuals, with the hope that manipulated individuals (so-called offspring) will perform better after manipulation. Then, to perform the genetic manipulations some parents are selected based on previous fitness assessment, giving priority to the solutions with higher fitness values. Then two types of genetic operations can be performed: crossover, that combines two parents into a new individual; mutation, the individual is evolved and some of its characteristics are modified (added or removed).

4.2.5   The Induction Hob Domain

Traditionally, stoves have a rectangular shape and feature four rounded areas that become hot when turned on. Therefore, the first Induction Hobs (IHs) created provided similar capabilities. However, the induction hobs domain is constantly evolving and, due to the possibilities provided by the induction phenomena and the electronic components present in the induction hobs, a new generation of IHs has emerged.

For instance, the newest IHs feature full cooking surfaces, where dynamic heating areas are automatically calculated and activated or deactivated depending on the shape, size, and position of the cookware placed on top. There has been an

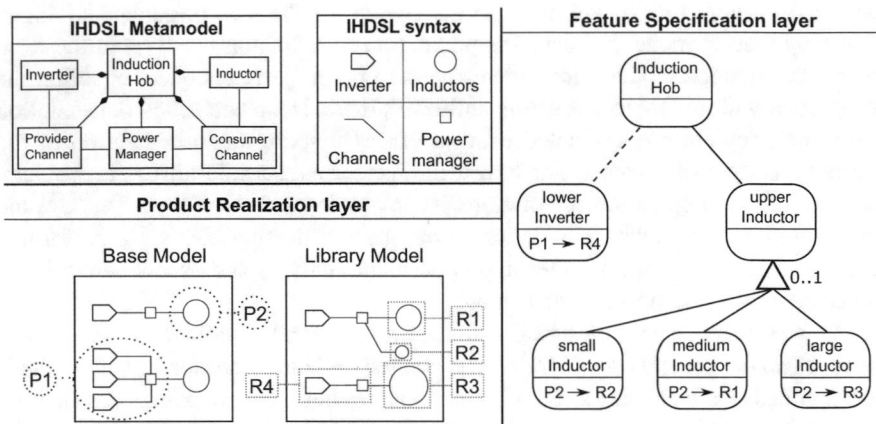

Fig. 4.1 IHDSL and CVL applied to it

increase in the type of feedback provided to the user while cooking, such as the exact temperature of the cookware, the temperature of the food being cooked, or even real-time measurements of the actual consumption of the IH. All of these changes are being possible at the cost of increasing the software complexity. The Domain-Specific Language (DSL) used by our industrial partner to specify the Induction Hobs (IHDSL) is composed of 46 meta-classes, 74 references among them and more than 180 properties. However, in order to gain legibility and due to intellectual property rights concerns, in this section we use a simplified subset of the IHDSL (see the top of Fig. 4.1).

Inverters are in charge of converting the input electric supply to match the specific requirements of the induction hob. Specifically, the amplitude and frequency of the electric supply needs to be precisely modulated in order to improve the efficiency of the IH and to avoid resonance. Then, the energy is transferred to the hotplates through the channels. There can be several alternative channels, which enable different heating strategies depending on the cookware placed on top of the IH at runtime. The path followed by the energy through the channels is controlled by the power manager.

Inductors are the elements where energy is transformed into an electromagnetic field. Inductors are composed of a conductor that is usually wound into a coil. However, inductors vary in their shape and size, resulting in different power supply needs in order to achieve performance peaks. Inductors can be organized into groups in order to heat larger cookware while sharing the user interface controllers. Each group of inductors can have different particularities; for instance, some of them can be divided into independent zones or others can grow in size adapting to the size of the cookware being placed on top of them. Some of the groups of inductors are made at design time, while others can occur at runtime (depending on the cookware placed on top).

Bottom left part of Fig. 4.1 depicts an example of a product model specified with the IHDSL. The product model contains four inverters used to power two different inductors. The upper inductor is powered by a single inverter while the lower inductor is powered by the combination of three different inverters. Power managers act as hubs to perform the connection between the inverters and the inductors.

4.2.6   The Common Variability Language Applied to Induction Hobs

Our approach formalizes the features located as model fragments, the subset of model elements from a whole model that realizes a particular feature. We use the Common Variability Language (CVL) to formalize the model fragments used as features.

The Common Variability Language (CVL) [26, 49, 62] was recommended for adoption as a standard by the Architectural Board of the Object Management Group and is our industrial partner's choice for specifying and resolving variability. CVL defines variants of a base model (conforming to MOF) by replacing variable parts of the base model by alternative model replacements found in a library model.

The variability specification through CVL is divided across two different layers: the feature specification layer (where variability can be specified following a feature model syntax) and the product realization layer (where variability specified in terms of features is linked to the actual models in terms of placements, replacements and substitutions).

The base model is a model described by a given Domain-Specific Language (DSL) which serves as a base for different variants defined over it. In CVL the elements of the base model that are subject to variations are the placement fragments (hereinafter placements). A placement can be any element or set of elements that is subject to variation. To define alternatives for a placement we use a replacement library, which is a model described in the same DSL as the base model that will serve as basis to define alternatives for a placement. Each one of the alternatives for a placement is a replacement fragment (hereinafter replacement). Similarly to placements, a replacement can be any element or set of elements that can be used as variation for a replacement.

CVL defines variants of the base model by means of fragment substitutions. Each substitution references to a placement and a replacement and includes the information necessary to substitute the placement by the replacement. In other words, each placement and replacement is defined along with its boundaries, which indicate what is inside or outside each fragment (placement or replacement) in terms of references among other elements of the model. Then, the substitution is defined with the information of how to link the boundaries of the placement with the boundaries of the replacement. When a substitution is materialized, the base model (with placements substituted by replacements) continues to conform to the same metamodel.

Figure 4.1 shows an example of variability specification of IH through CVL. In the product realization layer, two placements are defined over an IH base model (P1 and P2). Then, four replacements are defined over an IH library model (R1, R2, R3, and R4). In the feature specification layer, a Feature Model is defined that formalizes the variability among the IH based on the placements and replacements previously defined. For instance, P1 can only be substituted by R4 (which is optional), but P2 can be replaced by R1, R2, or R3. Note that each fragment has a signature, which is a set of references going from and towards that replacement. A placement can only be replaced by replacements that match the signature. For instance, the P2 signature has a reference from a power manager (outside the placement) to an inductor (inside the placement), while the R4 signature is a reference from a power manager (inside the replacement) to an inductor (outside the replacement). P2 cannot be substituted by R4 since their signatures do not match.

4.3   Relation Between FLiMEA and FLiMRT

The approaches presented in this chapter need some model elements in order to work. To perform feature location with FLiMRT, we need a system with at least, design time models and runtime models. And to perform feature location with FLiMEA, we need a system with at least design time models. In addition, taking into account the results obtained in our evaluations, we realized that our approaches are complementary. In the real word, before locating a feature, in most cases, we do not know the source of the feature for sure.

We recommend to apply specific approaches taking into account the problem to be solved and the system where the feature is located. If the results are not satisfactory, then we can manually refine the solutions or apply other approaches. For example, if we want to locate a feature and we have a system with models at runtime. Our recommendation is to use the FLiMRT approach as the starting point. If the results obtained by FLiMRT are not useful, other approaches can be launched since they explore a larger solution space than FLiMRT.

4.4   FLiM at Design Time (FLiMEA)

In this section we explain our approach for feature location in product models. As we said before, the objective of the approach is to provide a subset of elements from a given product model that realizes a particular feature being requested by the user. Then, we are going to use Genetic Operations to iterate over a population of model fragments and evolve them using genetic operations. The output is a list of model fragments that might realize the feature. This list is assessed and ranked taking into

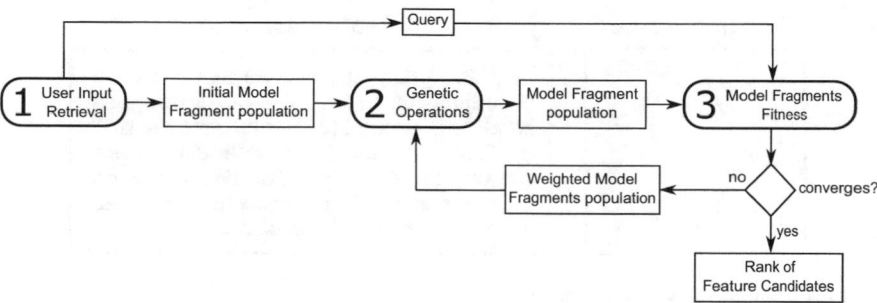

Fig. 4.2 Overview of the FLiM approach at design time

account the information provided by the user as input. The entire explanation of the approach can be found in [23].

Figure 4.2 shows an overview of the approach. Rounded boxes represent the different steps of the approach while rectangular boxes represent the inputs and outputs of each of the steps. Lines indicate that an element is an input or output of one of the steps.

The input of the approach is the product model where the feature is going to be located. Then, the user provides a description of the target feature in terms of an initial seed fragment and a textual description of the feature. The initial seed and the product model are used to generate some candidate fragments. Then, those candidates are assessed taking into account the textual description of the feature being located. These two steps (generation and assessment) are repeated until some stop condition is met. When the stop condition is fulfilled the process returns the list of fragment candidates ranked according to the assessments.

4.4.1   User Input

The first step is to gather input for the feature location. The input will consist of the product model and information about the target feature provided by the user. In particular, the user will provide:

- A **seed fragment** of the target feature is an element or set of elements that the engineer believes that could be part of the feature being located. To do so, the engineer applies her/his knowledge of the domain and the product models to point to some elements that will be used as the starting point of the process.
- A **feature description** of the target feature, using natural language. Typically these descriptions can come from textual documentation of the products, comments in the code, bug reports or oral descriptions from the engineers. Therefore, the query will include some domain-specific terms similar to those used when specifying the product models. The knowledge of the engineers about the domain

Fragment Seed	Feature Description
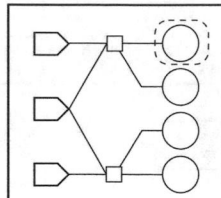	Hotplate: group of inductors that can work in conjunction to heat the cookware. Each hotplate is controlled by a power level that is then translated to different power outputs for each inductor depending on their size and position. Inductors activated depend on the detection of cookware.

Fig. 4.3 Input provided to the approach

and the product models will be useful to select the textual description from the sources available. Figure 4.3 presents an example of input for the approach. Left part presents the seed fragment proposed by the user (a model fragment of the product model where the feature is going to be located). The user believes that the selected inductor is going to be part of the feature realization. Then, the right part of the figure shows a textual description for the feature being located, the hotplate. It is a simplified version of a text description that has been extracted from the internal documentation used by our industrial partner to describe their products.

The textual description provided by the user is turned into a query by using some well-established Information Retrieval (IR) techniques:

1. The textual description is tokenized (divided into words). Usually a white space tokenizer can be applied (that splits the strings whenever it finds a white space), but for some sources more complex tokenizers need to be applied. For instance, when the description comes from documents that are close to the implementation of the product some words can be following CamelCase naming.
2. We apply the Parts-of-Speech (POS) tagging technique. POS tagging analyses the words grammatically and infers the role of each word into the text provided. As a result, each word is tagged enabling the removal of some categories that do not provide relevant information. For instance, conjunctions (e.g. 'or'), articles (e.g. 'a') or prepositions (e.g. 'at') are words commonly used and do not contribute with relevant information that describe the feature, so they are removed.
3. Stemming techniques are applied to unify the language used in the text. This technique consists in reducing each word to its roots enabling that different words referring to similar concepts can be grouped together. For instance, plurals are turned into singulars ("inductors" to "inductor") or verbs tenses are unified ("using" and "used" are turned into "use").

The User Input Retrieval step generates as a result an initial population of fragments (that contain the model fragment provided as seed) and the query that will be used for the comparisons (obtained from the textual description). Then, the model fragment from the initial population will be evolved into several model fragments through the use of the genetic operations.

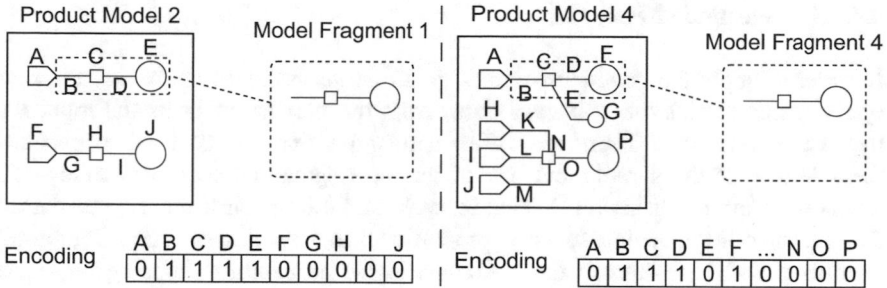

Fig. 4.4 Representation of model fragments

4.4.2 Encoding

We use a binary string encoding where each position of the string has two possible values: 0 or 1. However, encoding each model fragment as a string of binary values is not straightforward. Each individual of our proposed approach will be a model fragment that is defined in one of the product models. In other words, each individual is a set of model elements that are present in one of the product models.

Figure 4.4 shows two examples of our representation of model fragments. We denote each model element of the product model with a letter. In the example of the left part of Fig. 4.4, the letters A and F correspond to inverters, the letters B, D, G, and I correspond to channels, and the letters E and J correspond to inductors. Therefore, the string of binary values that represents the model fragment from this product model has the positions that correspond to each letter with a value of 0 or 1. If the model element appears in the model fragment, the value will be 1; if the model element does not appear in the model fragment the value will be 0.

Each model fragment representation depends on the product model that it came from. Both of the examples in Fig. 4.4 represent the same model fragment, but they come from different product models. Throughout the rest of the paper, we will refer to each individual as a model fragment that is part of a product model.

4.4.3 Genetic Operations

The second step is to generate a set of model fragments that could be realizing the feature. The generation of model fragments is done by applying genetic operators adapted to work over model fragments. That is, new fragments based on the existing ones (the seed fragment during the first execution) are generated through the use of three genetic operators: the selection of parents, the mutation and the crossover.

4.4.3.1   Selection of Parents

In order to apply the genetic operators, it is first necessary to apply the selection operator that selects the best candidates from the population to be the input for the rest of operators. There are different methods that can be used to perform the selection of the parents, but one of the most spread choices is to follow the wheel selection mechanism [1]. That is, each model fragment from the population has a probability of being selected proportional to their fitness score. Therefore, candidates with high fitness values will have higher probabilities of being chosen as parents for the next generation. Top part of Fig. 4.5 shows an example of application of the selection operator.

4.4.3.2   Crossover

The crossover operator is used to imitate the sexual reproduction followed by some living beings in nature to breed new individuals. That is, two individuals mix their genomic information to give birth a new individual that holds some genetic information from one parent and some from the other one. This could make it adapt better (or worse) to her/his living environment depending on the genetic information inherited from her/his parents.

Following this idea, our crossover operator applied to model fragments takes as input two model fragments and a randomly generated mask to combine them into two new individuals. The mask determines how the combination is done, indicating for each element of the model fragments if the offspring should inherit from one parent or the other (including the element or not if the element is present on the parent or not). A model fragment is a subset of the elements present in a product model. As both model fragments have been extracted from the same product model the combination (applying the mask) of them will always return a model fragment that is part of the product model. As a result, two individuals will be generated, one by applying directly the mask and another one by applying the inverse of the mask as it is usually done in genetic algorithms [15].

Figure 4.5 shows an example of application of the crossover operator. The input of the operator is the first parent (MF1), a mask indicating two sets of elements (one regular and one marked in black) and the second parent (MF3). To create the first of the new individuals we interpret the mask selecting the blacked out elements from the first parent (MF1) and the regular elements from the second parent (MF3). That is, the elements on the top part of the product model that are in black in this mask are selected depending on whether they are part of MF1 or not, while the rest of the elements that are not blacked out in the mask are selected depending on whether they are part of MF3 or not. As a result, the new MF5 contains some elements from the first parent (power group connected to the inductor) and some others from the second parent (the inverter that connects with the power group).

In addition, the mask is also interpreted in the opposite way, selecting the blacked out elements form the second parent and the regular elements from the first parent.

Fig. 4.5 Genetic operations: selection, crossover, and mutation over model fragments

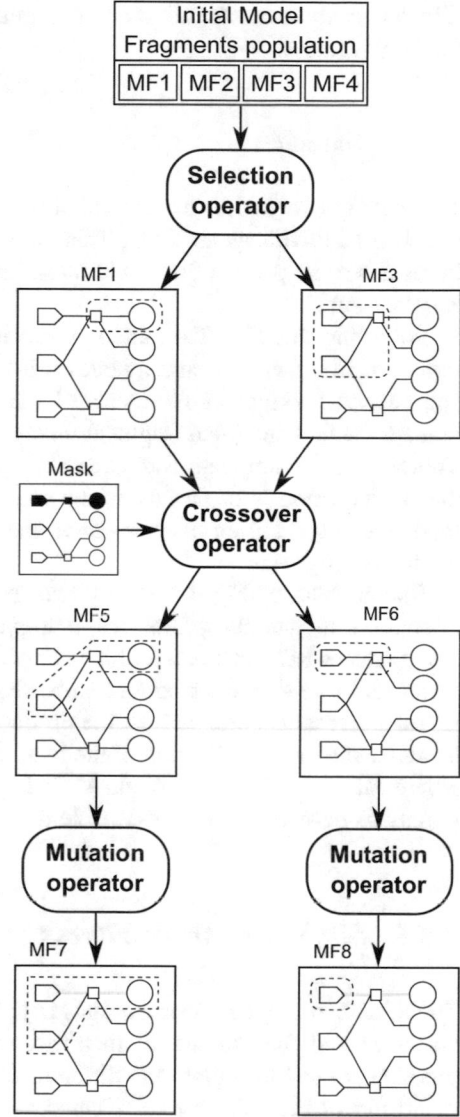

This produces MF6 (see middle-right part of Fig. 4.5), where an inverter connected to a power manager has been inherited from the second parent (MF3) and nothing has been inherited from parent 1 (MF1) as all the elements not blacked out in the mask are not part of MF1.

For the crossover operation to work, it is not necessary to have elements shared by both parents. It is possible to perform crossovers that return fragments where not all the elements are connected. Indeed, the feature being located could be realized by several model elements that are not directly connected in the model. Therefore, it is necessary to create this kind of fragments as they could be the ones realizing the target feature.

4.4.3.3 Mutation

The mutation operator is used to imitate the mutations that randomly occur in nature when new individuals are born. That is, a new individual holds a small difference in regards to its parents that could make him adapt better (or worse) to their living environment.

Following this idea, the mutation operator applied to model fragments takes as input a model fragment and mutates it into a new one produced as output. As the approach is looking for fragments of the product model that realize a particular feature, the new modified fragment must remain being a part of the product model. Therefore, the modifications that can be done to the model fragment are driven by the product model. In particular, the mutation operator can perform two kind of modifications, addition of elements to the fragment, or removal of elements from the model fragment.

Bottom part of Fig. 4.5 shows two examples of application of the mutation operator. Left part shows the first example, MF5 is used as input of the operator that produces M7 as output. In this example, the mutation operation has added some elements (a new inverter connected to the power manager). The resulting model fragment remains being part of the product model that is driving the mutation, so it is a candidate as realization of the feature. Right part shows the second example, where MF6 is used as input and MF8 is produced as output. In this example the mutation operator has removed an element (the power manager).

4.4.4 Model Fragment Fitness

The third step of the process consists in the assessment of each candidate fragment produced and the ranking of them according to a fitness function. The fitness function is used to imitate the different degrees of adaptation to the environment that different individuals have. Therefore, individuals that result of mutations and crossovers that contribute to their adaptation to the environment will have higher chances of survival than others.

Following this idea, the fitness function is used to determine the suitability of each candidate as solution to the problem, enabling to rank them from the best candidate to the worst. The fitness function is based on the comparison between the feature description query and the identifier names and other natural language items present in the model fragments. The input of this step is a population of candidate fragments, and the feature description query; the output produced is a ranking where each candidate has been assigned with a fitness value.

To assess the relevance of each model fragment in relation to the feature description provided by the user, we apply methods that are based on Information Retrieval (IR) techniques. Specifically, we apply Latent Semantic Analysis (LSA) [36] to analyze the relationships between the description of the feature provided by the user and the model fragments previously obtained. Recent studies have shown that there is not a statistically significant difference among different IR techniques [24, 40] when applied to software artifacts [28]. Hence, we chose LSA because it provides results that are similar to other IR techniques for software documents.

LSA constructs vector representations of a query and a corpus of text documents by encoding them as a *term-by-document co-occurrence matrix* (i.e., a matrix where each row corresponds to terms, each column corresponds to documents, and the last column corresponds to the query). We use the *term-frequency (tf)* as the term weighting schema to construct the matrix. In other words, each cell holds the number of occurrences of a term (row) inside either a document or the query (column).

In our approach, all documents are model fragments (i.e., a document of text is generated from each of the model fragments). The text of the document corresponds to the names and values of the properties and the methods of each model fragment. The query is constructed from the terms that appear in the feature description. The text from the documents (model fragments) and the text from the query (feature description) are homogenized by applying the Natural Language Processing techniques previously described in Sect. 4.4.1.

The union of all of the keywords extracted from the documents (model fragments) and from the query (feature description) are the terms (rows) used by our LSA fitness operation.

Once the matrix is built, we normalize and decompose it into a set of vectors using a matrix factorization technique called Singular Value Decomposition (SVD) [36]. SVD projects the original term-by-document co-occurrence matrix in a lower dimensional space k. We use the value of k suggested by Kuhn et al. [35], which provides good results [60]. One vector that represents the latent semantics of the document is obtained for each model fragment and the query. Finally, the similarities between the query and each model fragment are calculated as the cosine between the two vectors. The fitness value that is given to each model fragment is obtained as the cosine similarity between the two vectors, obtaining values between -1 and 1.

Let p_1 be an individual of the population; let A be the vector representing the latent semantic of p_1; let B be the vector representing the latent semantics of the query where the angle formed by the vectors A and B is θ. The fitness function can be defined as:

$$fitness(p_1) = \cos(\theta) = \frac{AB}{\|A\|\|B\|} \tag{4.1}$$

Finally, after the cosines are calculated, we obtain a value for each of the model fragments, indicating its similarity with the query.

4.4.4.1 Loop

At this point, if the stop condition is met, the process will stop returning the rank of model fragment. If the stop condition is not met yet, the genetic algorithm will keep its execution one generation more. The next time that the genetic operators are applied, it will be necessary to select the best candidates as parents for the new generation. This will be done based on the score obtained by each model fragment. As a result, model fragments with higher similarities will have more chances to be selected as parents of the new generation.

The process of generation of fragments is repeated until the stop condition is met. Usually, the stop condition can be a time slot, a fixed number of generations or a trigger value of the fitness that makes the process finish when reached. In addition, it is also possible to monitor the fitness values and determine when they are converging and no further improvements are being made by new generations. The stop condition highly depends on the domain and the problem being solved; therefore, it is adjusted depending on the results being outputted by the process.

As a result, FLiMEA provides a ranking of model fragments. The ranking is ordered following the similarity of the model fragment to the feature description, i.e. the fitness value obtained by each model fragment. Then, the domain experts will select the model fragment from the ranking, using their knowledge of the domain. At the end, the experts will be the ones working and manipulating these features as part of their daily work. Hence, they are the ones that understand and recognize them well. In a previous work [22], we conducted a usability test to know why the domain experts can discard a model fragment suggested as feature.

4.5   FLiM at Runtime (FLiMRT)

Figure 4.6 shows an overview of our feature location approach at runtime (FLiMRT). In the Dynamic Analysis phase, the software engineer executes a scenario, which uses the target feature to be located. The information from the executed scenario is stored by means of models at runtime.

Models at runtime provide a kind of formal basis for reasoning about the current system state, for reasoning about necessary adaptations, and for analyzing the consequences of possible system adaptation. This is possible because there is a causal connection between the system and the runtime model. Then, we can use the runtime architecture model obtained from the running scenario. This model contains the elements of the model that are related to the target feature.

In the Information Retrieval phase, the approach filters the runtime architecture model to extract the relevant elements of the target feature to be located. To achieve the filtering, we adapt the same Information retrieval (IR) technique used in the design time approach, LSA [36], which allows the software engineers to write queries that describe the feature to be located. The result is a ranked list of model elements that are related to the feature based on the similarity to the provided query.

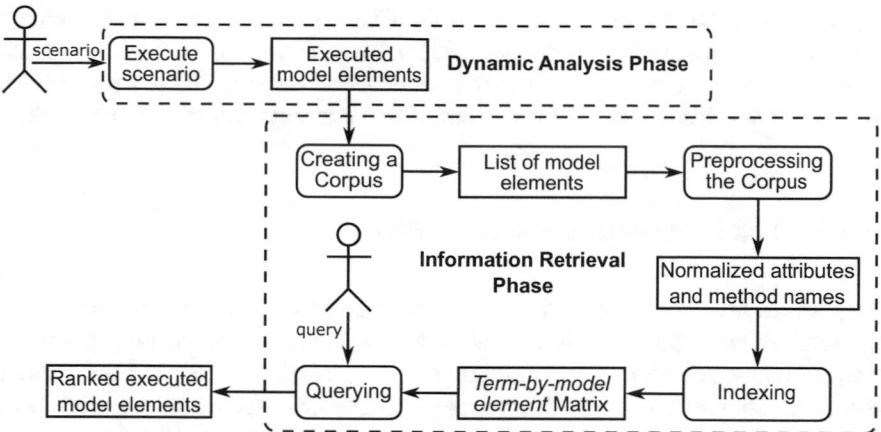

Fig. 4.6 Overview of the FLiM approach at runtime

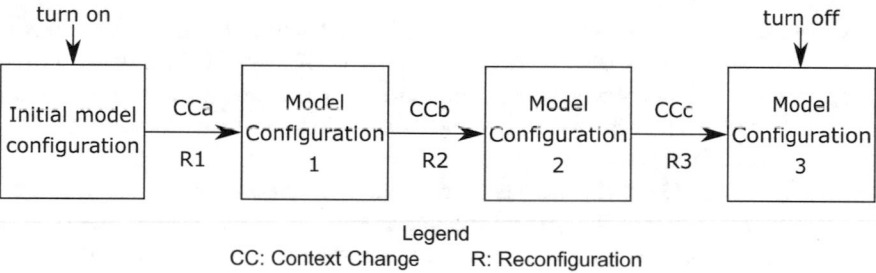

Legend
CC: Context Change   R: Reconfiguration

Fig. 4.7 Induction Hob at runtime

4.5.1 The Dynamic Analysis Phase

Dynamic Analysis is used to delimit the search space. Execution information is gathered via dynamic analysis (see Fig. 4.6), which is commonly used in program comprehension and involves executing a software system under specific conditions. In our case, we design scenarios that run the target features in order to obtain model traces in which the target features are involved. In other words, executing the target feature during runtime generates a feature-specific execution trace.

Our approach implies that the software engineer input is needed and of course, results are sensitive to that input. The software engineer has to decide on a scenario that will run the desired feature.

Figure 4.7 shows the behavior of an induction hob at runtime. The induction hob is turned on in an initial configuration with a known model. In the face of changes in the context (CCs in Fig. 4.7), reconfigurations (Rs in Fig. 4.7) are triggered in order to change the configuration of the induction hob. Then, the induction hob is in a different configuration and therefore in a different model (Model Configurations in Fig. 4.7). Some examples of scenarios for different features can include putting a pot on top, the pot reaches the set temperature, the pot is moved to other place on the induction hob, or liquid spills from the pot onto the surface. The reconfigurations activate or deactivate inductors and inverters and connect them through channels.

4.5.2 The Information Retrieval Phase

To perform Information Retrieval, we use the same technique used in the previous approach. Our approach follows the same five main steps: creating a corpus, preprocessing, indexing, querying, and generating results (see Fig. 4.6 Information Retrieval phase). We adapted each step of the LSA technique to work with architecture models. We used the architecture model that contains the executed model elements from the dynamic analysis. The adaptation is performed as follows:

- Creating a corpus. In the first step of LSA, a document granularity needs to be chosen to form a corpus. A corpus consists of a set of documents. In this approach, each document corresponds to a model element of the architecture model. Each document (model element) includes text from the names of the attributes and methods.
- Preprocessing. Once the corpus is created, it is preprocessed. Preprocessing involves normalizing the text of the documents. In this approach, the type of the attributes and the type of the parameters in the methods are removed.
- Indexing. The corpus is used to create a *term-by-document matrix*. Each row of the matrix corresponds to each term in the corpus, and each column represents each document. Each cell of the matrix holds a measure of the weight or relevance of the term in the document. The weight is expressed as a simple count of the number of times that the term appears in the document. In other words, each term-document pair has a number that indicates the number of times this term appears as part of the names of attributes or methods of this model element. In this work, in the term-by-document co-occurrence matrix, the terms (rows) correspond to the names of the attributes or operations (i.e., intensity) of the runtime model and the documents (columns) correspond to the model elements that have appeared in the runtime model.

  Figure 4.8 shows a term-by-document co-occurrence matrix. Each row in the matrix stands for each one of the unique words (terms) extracted from the runtime model. Figure 4.8 shows a set of representative keywords in the domain such as 'provider', 'coil', or 'intensity' as the terms of each row. Each column in the matrix stands for the model elements of the runtime model. Figure 4.8 also shows the model elements in the columns, which represent the model elements of the runtime model. Each cell in the matrix contains the frequency with which the

Model Elements

Terms	ME1	ME2	ME3	ME4	...	MEn	Query
size	6	12	9	6	...	12	6
provider	12	6	4	0	...	24	10
coil	36	30	0	0	...	0	0
small	24	12	2	0	...	6	4
intensity	0	8	10	2	...	0	6
high	6	0	2	0	...	6	8
...	...	...	...	...	...	...	0
name	8	2	1	12	...	3	0

LSI Results

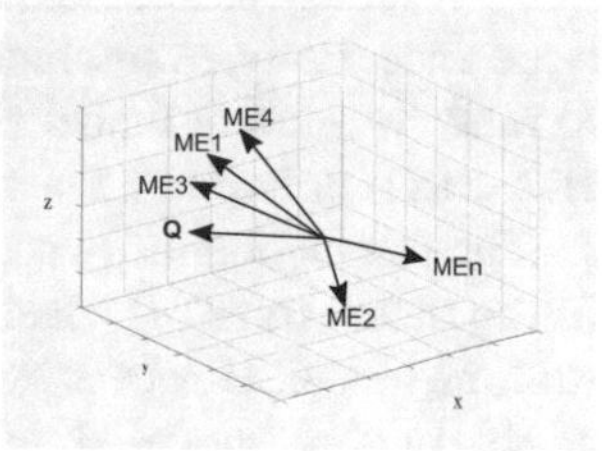

Fig. 4.8 Information retrieval via latent semantic indexing (LSI)

keyword of its row appears in the document denoted by its column. For instance, in Fig. 4.8, the term 'size' appears 9 times in the 'ME3' model element.

- Querying. A user formulates a query in natural language consisting of words or phrases that describe the feature to be located. Since LSI does not use a predefined grammar or vocabulary, users can originate queries in natural language. In this work, we use the requirements to formulate the queries. Only the relevant terms are taken into account, and words such as determinants and connectors from the language are avoided.

In Fig. 4.8, the query column represents the words that appear in the requirement. Each cell contains the frequency with which the keyword of its row appears in the query. For instance, the term 'provider' appears 10 times in the query.

- Generating results. In LSA, the query and each document correspond to a vector. We use the same matrix factorization technique as in the design time approach. The cosine of the angle between the query vector and a document vector is used as the measure of the similarity of the document to the query. The closer the cosine is to 1, the more similar the document is to the query. A cosine similarity value is calculated between the query and each document, and then the documents are sorted by their similarity values. The user inspects the ranked list to determine which of the documents are relevant to the feature.

A three-dimensional graph of the LSI results is provided in Fig. 4.8. The graph shows the representation of each one of the vectors, labeled with letters that represent the names of the model elements, which are referenced in the box below the graph. The graph reflects the 'ME3' model element vector as being the closest to the query vector, followed by the 'ME1' model element vector.

After applying the two phases of our approach, the output produced is a ranking where each model element has been assigned with a value. Only those model elements that have a similarity measure greater than x must be taken into account to measure the quality of the results. A good heuristic that is widely used is x = 0.7. This value corresponds to a 45% angle between the corresponding vectors. This threshold has yielded good results in other similar works [42, 57]. Determining a more generally usable heuristic for the selection of the appropriate threshold is an issue under study, over which further research is needed. The goal of our approach is to rank the relevant model elements within the top positions. The ranking of model elements is ordered by the values of the cosines.

The results obtained can be influenced by the amount of information contained in the model trace [4]. Each execution trace is related to a set of snapshots of the runtime model. However, we can have different criteria to decide when a snapshot of the runtime model should be added to the trace. For example, we could add a snapshot to the trace only when the model at run time corresponds to a valid configuration of the system, or we could add a snapshot each time a change in the architecture model at runtime is performed.

4.6 Evaluation

In this section, we present the evaluations performed to test the Feature Location in Models (FLiM) approaches. We have followed a process for evaluating each of the approaches on each of the case studies.

Figure 4.9 shows an overview of the generic setup of the evaluation. The process is composed of: (1) an oracle obtained from our industrial partner; (2) a set of test cases extracted from the oracle; (3) an approach that is being evaluated; (4) the set of results obtained when applying the approach to the test cases; (5) the measure (or measures) that we want to evaluate; and (6) the measurements obtained based on the results yielded by the approach and the information available from the oracle.

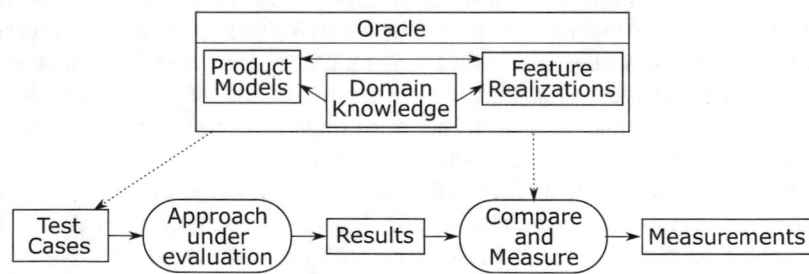

Fig. 4.9 Overview of the process followed in each evaluation

4.6.1   The Induction Hobs Domain

The first case study where we applied our approach is BSH.[1] Their induction division has been producing Induction Hobs under the brands of Bosch and Siemens for the last 15 years.

They have 46 induction hob models where, on average, each product model is composed of more than 500 elements. Their induction hobs include 96 different features that can be part of a specific product model. Those features correspond to products that are currently being sold or will be released to the market in the near future.

4.6.2   Train Control and Management Domain

The second case study where we applied our approach was CAF, a worldwide provider of railway solutions.[2] Their trains can be seen all over the world and in different forms (regular trains, subway, light rail, monorail, etc.). A train unit is furnished with multiple pieces of equipment through its vehicles and cabins. These pieces of equipment are often designed and manufactured by different providers, and their aim is to carry out specific tasks for the train. Some examples of these devices are: the traction equipment, the compressors that feed the brakes, the pantograph that receives power from the overhead wires, or the circuit breaker that isolates or connects the electrical circuits of the train. The control software of the train unit is in charge of making all the equipment cooperate in providing the train with functionality while guaranteeing compliance with the specific regulations of each country.

The DSL of our industrial partner has the required expressiveness to describe the interaction between the main pieces of equipment installed in a train unit. Moreover, this DSL also has the required expressiveness to specify non-functional aspects related to regulation, such as the quality of signals from the equipment or the different levels of installed redundancy. This results in a DSL that is composed of around 1000 different elements.

As an example, the high voltage connection sequence can be described using the DSL. This high voltage connection sequence is initiated when the train driver requests its start by using interface devices fitted inside the cabin. The control software is in charge of raising the pantograph to receive power from the overhead wire and of closing the circuit breaker so the energy can get to converters that adapt the voltage to charge batteries which, in turn, power the traction equipment.

---

[1] https://youtu.be/nS2sybEv6j0.

[2] https://youtu.be/Ypcl2evEQB8.

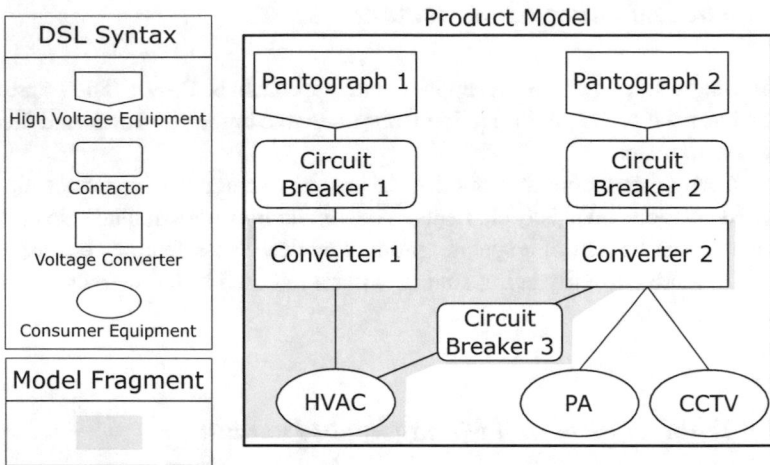

Fig. 4.10 Example of product model and model fragment (colored part) of CAF

Figure 4.10 shows an example of a product model from a real-world train. It shows two separate pantographs (High Voltage Equipment) that collect energy from the overhead wires and send it to their respective circuit breakers (Contactors), which, in turn, send it to their independent Voltage Converters. The converters then power their assigned Consumer Equipment: the HVAC on the left (the train's air conditioning system), and the PA (public address system) and CCTV (television system) on the right.

An example of model fragment is also shown in Fig. 4.10. The elements of the model fragment are highlighted in green, which are the realization of the feature: HVAC Assistance. This feature allows the passing of current from one converter to the HVAC that is assigned to its peer for coverage in case of overload or failure of the first converter.

They have 23 train models where, on average, each product model is composed of around 1200 elements. The product models are built using 121 different features that can be part of a specific product model. They provide us with documentation of their features and the model fragments that implement each feature.

4.6.3 Oracle Preparation

The oracle is the mechanism that we will use to evaluate the results provided by our approach. The oracle will be considered the ground truth and the results provided by the approach will be compared (when needed) with the oracle in terms of the measures that we want to obtain. In addition the oracle will be used to obtain the test cases used for the evaluation.

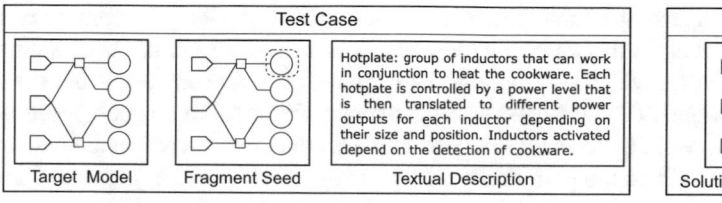
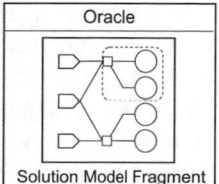

Fig. 4.11 Test case example

The oracle will be mainly composed by a set of product models and a set of features located over those product models. That is, a set of features whose realizations are model fragments and a set of product models built using those model fragments. Therefore, we have the traceability information between the features, the model fragments realizing those features, and the features being used by each product model. In addition, the oracle includes domain knowledge in different forms, such as descriptions and technical documentations for each product model, descriptions about the features, etc.

The oracle is extracted directly from the family of models of our industrial partner, that is being used to manage the products that are under production. Therefore, we consider it to be the best version available. The domain experts of each of the companies provide us with documentation and the model fragments that implements each of the features.

4.6.4   Test Cases

A set of test cases is extracted from the oracle, so the approach under evaluation can be applied to them. Figure 4.11 shows an example of a test case. It includes a feature description in the format required by the approach (in this case, a seed fragment and a textual description of the feature) and the target product model (where the feature will be located). In addition, the test case has been extracted from the oracle and there is a corresponding model fragment for that feature description (that will be used to compare with the output provided by the approach).

4.6.5   Comparison and Measure

Once the results from applying the approach to the test cases are obtained, we proceed to compare them with the oracle and measure them in terms of some software quality properties [41]. To compare the model fragments obtained and the solution from the oracle we are going to use an error matrix [61], also known as confusion matrix.

A confusion matrix is a table that is often used to describe the performance of a classification model (in this case, our algorithms) on a set of test data (the resulting model fragments) for which the true values are known (from the oracle). In our case, each solution outputted by the algorithms is a model fragment that is composed of a subset of the model elements that are part of the product model (where the feature is being located). Since the granularity will be at the level of model elements, the presence or absence of each model element will be considered as a classification. The confusion matrix distinguishes between the predicted values and the real values by classifying them into four categories:

- True Positive (TP): values that are predicted as true (in the solution) and are true in the real scenario (the oracle).
- False Positive (FP): values that are predicted as true (in the solution) but are false in the real scenario (the oracle).
- True Negative (TN): values that are predicted as false (in the solution) and are false in the real scenario (the oracle).
- False Negative (FN): values that are predicted as false (in the solution) but are true in the real scenario (the oracle).

Then, some performance metrics are derived from the values in the confusion matrix. Specifically, we will create a report that includes four performance metrics (precision, recall, the F-measure, and the MCC) for each of the test cases for each search algorithm.

Precision measures the number of elements from the solution that are correct according to the ground truth (the oracle) and is defined as follows:

$$Precision = \frac{TP}{TP + FP} \tag{4.2}$$

Recall measures the number of elements of the oracle that are correctly retrieved by the proposed solution and is defined as follows:

$$Recall = \frac{TP}{TP + FN} \tag{4.3}$$

The F-measure corresponds to the harmonic mean of precision and recall and is defined as follows:

$$F\text{-}measure = 2 * \frac{Precision * Recall}{Precision + Recall} \tag{4.4}$$

Finally, the MCC is a correlation coefficient between the observed and predicted binary classifications that takes into account all of the observed values (TP, TN, FP, FN) and is defined as follows:

$$MCC = \frac{TP * TN - FP * FN}{\sqrt{(TP + FP)(TP + FN)(TN + FP)(TN + FN)}} \tag{4.5}$$

4.6.6   Evaluation of FLiM at Design Time (FLiMEA)

In Table 4.1, we outline the results of our algorithm in BSH and CAF. We also show the F-measure and the MCC performance indicators. The algorithm provides a precision value of 76.47% in the BSH case study and a precision value of 71.75% in the CAF case study. The Recall achieved is 72.41% for BSH and 67.96% for CAF. The combined F-measure is 72.99% for BSH and 68.34% for CAF. Finally, the MCC achieved is 0.67 for BSH and 0.62 for CAF.

4.6.6.1   Analysis of the Results

The recall and precision values suggest that the fitness function is performing well and guiding the algorithm to find feature realization candidates close to the target feature. Following the classification of the results in precision and recall presented in [27], we can state that our approach presents excellent results (range 50–100%) in precision in both BSH and CAF, good results in recall (range 70–79%) in BSH, and acceptable results in recall (range 60–69%) in CAF.

Input data   The presented approach relies on two pieces of information given by the engineer performing the feature location, the seed fragment and the query. These two elements will have an impact on the ranking of model fragments produced and must be chosen carefully by the engineer performing the feature location.

To test out the impact of the seed fragment in the results, we have executed the approach with different kind of seed fragments containing one element (single element belonging to the feature being located or single element not belonging to the feature being located). But those executions did not produce noticeable differences in the resulting ranking of model fragments or in the number of generations needed to converge.

However, when selecting seed fragments of sizes closer to the size of the feature being located, the effect is noticeable. The number of generations needed by the GA to converge was reduced when a seed fragment close to the feature being located was chosen. In particular, when the fragment seed contained about 50% of the elements belonging to the feature being located, the number of generations needed for the GA to converge was reduced up to 15%.

To test out the impact of the query in the results, we have also executed the approach varying the text description used as input (using longer and smaller

Table 4.1 Mean values and standard deviations for precision, recall, F-measure, and MCC for the search algorithm in BSH and CAF

	Precision $\pm\sigma$	Recall $\pm\sigma$	F-measure $\pm\sigma$	MCC $\pm\sigma$
BSH	76.47 ± 13.39	72.41 ± 13.79	72.99 ± 9.35	0.67 ± 0.13
CAF	71.75 ± 12.54	67.96 ± 15.07	68.34 ± 10.24	0.62 ± 0.13

queries by subsetting the original description, including more or less domain terms and including more or less meta-element terms).

The search query used to locate the feature is in charge of driving the search and greatly impacts on the precision and recall results. In fact, depending on the level of detail of the query, the recall and precision values obtained will change. When the query provided is too broad, the precision decreases as there are several model elements matching the query not belonging to the target feature. Anyhow, the elements belonging to the feature will be also matched positively so the recall value will be high. However, when the query provided is too specific, some of the elements relevant for the feature being located can be missed out. Thus, the recall value is decreased although the precision values remain high.

Two examples of queries can be: (1) "A double hot plate is a group of two inductors that are heated together" and (2) "A double hotplate is formed by an inductor of small size and an inductor of big size that are connected to the same power group". The second query is completer and more concise than the first query. Hence, the second query will obtain better results than the first one.

To achieve good precision and recall values, it is important to avoid the usage of words included into the meta-elements of the model elements. That is, if we refer to the metaclass name of one of the model elements, all instances of this class will match to that word (e.g. any inductor class model element will match the query "inductor"). By contrast, by using words specific for the model element (as the value of the name property or values of some of the parameters contained in those model elements), those model elements (and not others with the same class) will be included into the model fragments, affecting positively to the precision values (e.g. only some inductors will match the query "doubleTwistedCoil" as it is the value of a property of the inductor class). In fact, when removing the usage of metaelement names in the queries, the approach obtained similar values of recall but the precision raised up to a 20% for best cases.

Generalization   The presented approach has been designed to be applied, not only to our industrial partners domain, but to any domain. The only requisite to apply the approach is that the set of models where features have to be located conform to MOF (the OMG metalanguage for defining modeling languages). The query must be provided as a textual description.

The generation and management of fragments is performed using the Common Variability Language (CVL), which can be applied to any MOF-based languages. With the use of CVL, the approach is able to work with the model fragments provided as seed and evolve them applying the genetic algorithms. As output, the approach produces a ranking in the form of CVL model fragments.

Furthermore, the fitness function can also be applied to any MOF-based model. The text elements associated to the models are extracted automatically by the approach using the reflective methods provided by the Eclipse Modeling Framework. That is, there is no need of knowledge about the domain of application in order to extract the relevant terms.

However, the approach can be tailored to fit the needs of different domains if necessary. For instance, the naming conventions used by companies for model elements, properties and functions can follow different formats, but the approach can be tailored to handle them. In our case studies some model elements follow the CamelCase convention while others follow the Underscore convention. To address that, we applied different tokenizers in order to obtain the terms properly. Similarly, the Part-of-Speech tagger that is used to eliminate non-relevant words based on their grammatical category is language dependant, but can be configured to other languages when necessary.

In summary, the approach can be applied to locate features on any MOF-based model from any domain. If necessary, some tweaks and modifications can be applied to tailor the approach to particular needs of the domains, but the core of the approach will remain unchanged.

4.6.7   Evaluation of FLiM at Runtime (FLiMRT)

In this case, instead of using precision, recall, F-measure and MCC, we evaluate the position of the first model element in the ranking. It is accepted by the feature location community [39, 55] that a feature location approach is considered better than another feature location when it produces a ranking where the elements that belongs to the feature are in higher positions than in the ranking of the other approach.

We performed this evaluation with thirty-nine features of BSH. We defined the scenarios based on bug reports of each one of the features. Figure 4.12 shows the position of the first model element that belong to the target feature in the ranking for each one of the thirty-nine features. The x-axis represents the features, and the y-axis represents the position in the ranking. The blue dots represent the first model element for each feature. The position of the first model element that belongs to each one of the features has values between 1 and 28, where the 84% of the results are in the top ten positions.

4.6.7.1   Analysis of the Results

Figure 4.13 shows the graphical representation of the ranking for one feature (feature number five in Fig. 4.12). Due to space constraints, we only show the graphical representation for one feature, however, all the rankings follow a similar distribution in the results.

The query is the vector that is on the x-axis. The remainder of the vectors are model elements. Those that have been tagged by the oracle have a r_i label at the end of the arrow, while those that have not been tagged have nothing at the end of the arrow. The angle corresponds to the cosine with which we calculated the position in the ranking (see Sect. 4.5.2); the closer the model element is to the query, the higher the position in the ranking. The length of each vector indicates the number of times that the terms appear in each model element. The longer the vector is, the more

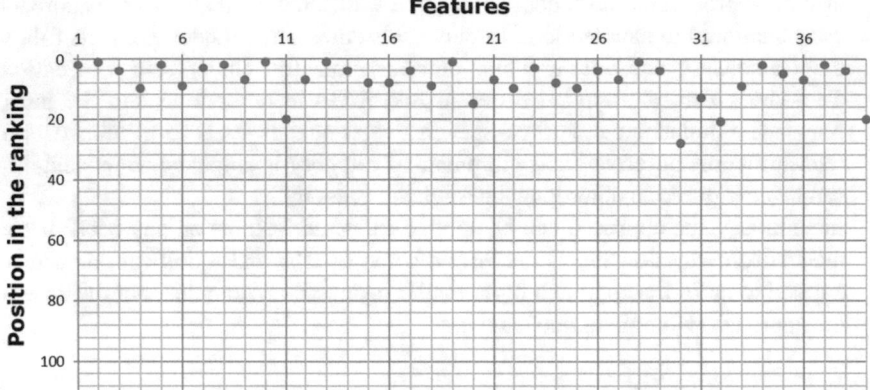

Fig. 4.12 Position of the first model element that belong to the target feature in the ranking for each one of the features

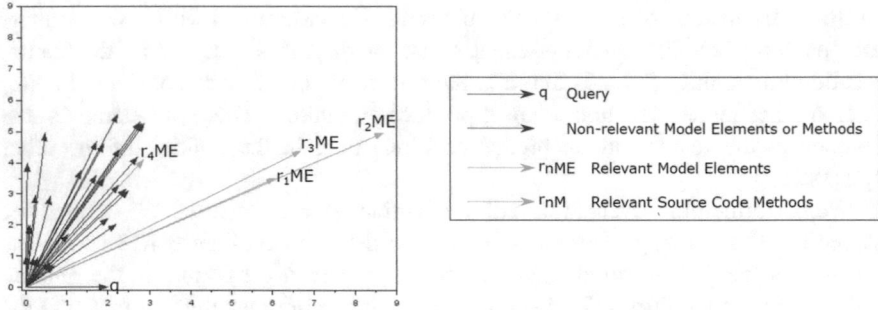

Fig. 4.13 Vectorial representation of the model elements in the Ranking of one feature

terms appear in the model element. The graph only shows the thirty-three which have positive cosines, the rest, thirteen, are in the left of the y-axis and have few relevance for the query.

The goal of a feature location technique is to reduce the effort required by software engineers to find the desired feature. Our approach on average requires searching in less than fifty model elements while a source-code-based approach on average requires searching in more than three thousand eight hundred methods.

The graphical representation of Fig. 4.13 allows us to see that the approach performs a good discrimination between relevant and non-relevant model elements. The majority of the model elements that belong to the feature achieve better results than the ones that do not belong.

Since architecture models at runtime allow working on a high level of abstraction, the words used at the model level are closer to the query. By raising the level of abstraction with the architecture model, we can prevent auxiliary methods and variables from interfering with the feature location.

Finally, we realized that the model elements that contained few attributes and methods got worse positions in the ranking than the ones that contained more attributes and methods. For example, one of the elements related to the feature in Fig. 4.13 obtained position 27 in the ranking. This is because this element corresponds to a channel element. This particular channel only has three attributes that describe the information that goes through the channel. The information required by this element was not as detailed as the other model elements when specifying the model. For this reason, the model element corresponding to this channel got a lower position in the ranking. In contrast, other kinds of channels got better positions since, on average, they have about twenty attributes and methods.

4.7 Conclusion

In this chapter, we presented approaches for Feature Location in Models (FLiM) at design time (FLiMEA) and at runtime (FLiMRT). Specifically, we have presented a Genetic Algorithm for FLiM at design time, and an approach that combines architecture models and information retrieval for FLiM at runtime.

Software systems are becoming more increasingly complex, and systems with models are not an exception. Hence, software maintenance is becoming more and more important. In particular, the feature location area has gained significant attention and cannot be neglected in the models area.

The results show that our design time (FLiMEA) and runtime approaches (FLiMRT) can be applied to address the challenge of feature location in models (FLiM). Specifically, the use of genetic operations for models provided good results in our studies. In addition, this demonstrates that FLiMEA and FLiMRT for feature location at the model level can be applied in real world environments.

References

1. Affenzeller, M., Winkler, S., Wagner, S., Beham, A.: Genetic Algorithms and Genetic Programming: Modern Concepts and Practical Applications, 1th edn. Chapman & Hall/CRC (2009)
2. Alves, V., Schwanninger, C., Barbosa, L., Rashid, A., Sawyer, P., Rayson, P., Pohl, C., Rummler, A.: An exploratory study of information retrieval techniques in domain analysis. In: 2008 12th International Software Product Line Conference, pp. 67–76 (2008)
3. Arcega, L., Font, J., Haugen, Ø., Cetina, C.: Feature location through the combination of run-time architecture models and information retrieval. In: J. Grabowski, S. Herbold (eds.) System Analysis and Modeling. Technology-Specific Aspects of Models : 9th International Conference, SAM 2016, Saint-Malo, France, October 3-4, 2016. Proceedings, pp. 180–195. Springer International Publishing (2016)
4. Arcega, L., Font, J., Haugen, Ø., Cetina, C.: On the influence of models at run-time traces in dynamic feature location. In: Modelling Foundations and Applications - 13th European Conference, ECMFA 2017, Held as Part of STAF 2017, Marburg, Germany, July 19-20, 2017, Proceedings (2017)

5. Batory, D., Sarvela, J.N., Rauschmayer, A.: Scaling step-wise refinement. In: Proceedings of the 25th International Conference on Software Engineering, ICSE '03, pp. 187–197. IEEE Computer Society, Washington, DC, USA (2003)
6. Berger, T., Rublack, R., Nair, D., Atlee, J.M., Becker, M., Czarnecki, K., Wasowski, A.: A survey of variability modeling in industrial practice. In: Proceedings of the Seventh International Workshop on Variability Modelling of Software-intensive Systems, VaMoS '13, pp. 7:1–7:8. ACM, New York, NY, USA (2013)
7. Biggerstaff, T.J., Mitbander, B.G., Webster, D.: The concept assignment problem in program understanding. In: Proceedings of the 15th International Conference on Software Engineering, ICSE '93, pp. 482–498. IEEE Computer Society Press, Los Alamitos, CA, USA (1993)
8. Blei, D.M., Ng, A.Y., Jordan, M.I., Lafferty, J.: Latent dirichlet allocation. Journal of Machine Learning Research 3(4/5), 993 – 1022 (2003)
9. Chastek, G., McGregor, J.: Guidelines for developing a product line production plan. Tech. Rep. CMU/SEI-2002-TR-006, Software Engineering Institute, Carnegie Mellon University, Pittsburgh, PA (2002)
10. Chawla, I., Singh, S.K.: Performance evaluation of vsm and lsi models to determine bug reports similarity. In: 2013 Sixth International Conference on Contemporary Computing (IC3), pp. 375–380 (2013)
11. Chen, K., Rajlich, V.: Case study of feature location using dependence graph. In: Proceedings IWPC 2000. 8th International Workshop on Program Comprehension, pp. 241–247 (2000)
12. Clements, P., Northrop, L.: Software Product Lines: Practices and Patterns, 3rd edn. SEI Series in Software Engineering. Addison-Wesley Longman Publishing Co., Inc., Boston, MA, USA (2001)
13. Czarnecki, K., Eisenecker, U.W.: Generative Programming: Methods, Tools, and Applications. ACM Press/Addison-Wesley Publishing Co., New York, NY, USA (2000)
14. Czarnecki, K., Wasowski, A.: Feature diagrams and logics: There and back again. In: 11th International Software Product Line Conference (SPLC 2007), pp. 23–34 (2007)
15. Davis, L.: Handbook of Genetic Algorithms. Van Nostrand Reinhold, New York (1991)
16. Dit, B., Revelle, M., Gethers, M., Poshyvanyk, D.: Feature location in source code: a taxonomy and survey. Journal of Software: Evolution and Process 25(1), 53–95 (2013)
17. Donohoe, P.: Proceedings of the 1st International Software Product Lines Conference (SPLC 2000). ISBN 0-7923-7940-3. Denver, Colorado, USA (2000)
18. Duszynski, S., Knodel, J., Becker, M.: Analyzing the source code of multiple software variants for reuse potential. In: 2011 18th Working Conference on Reverse Engineering, pp. 303–307 (2011)
19. Eaddy, M., Aho, A., Antoniol, G., Gueheneuc, Y.G.: Cerberus: Tracing requirements to source code using information retrieval, dynamic analysis, and program analysis. In: Program Comprehension, 2008. ICPC 2008. The 16th IEEE International Conference on, pp. 53–62 (2008)
20. Eisenbarth, T., Koschke, R., Simon, D.: Locating features in source code. IEEE Transactions on Software Engineering 29(3), 210–224 (2003)
21. Eisenberg, A., De Volder, K.: Dynamic feature traces: finding features in unfamiliar code. In: Software Maintenance, 2005. ICSM'05. Proceedings of the 21st IEEE International Conference on, pp. 337–346 (2005)
22. Font, J., Arcega, L., Haugen, Ø., Cetina, C.: Building software product lines from conceptualized model patterns. In: Proceedings of the 19th International Conference on Software Product Line, SPLC 2015, Nashville, TN, USA, July 20-24, 2015, pp. 46–55 (2015)
23. Font, J., Arcega, L., Haugen, Ø., Cetina, C.: Feature location in models through a genetic algorithm driven by information retrieval techniques. In: Proceedings of the ACM/IEEE 19th International Conference on Model Driven Engineering Languages and Systems, MODELS '16, pp. 272–282. ACM, New York, NY, USA (2016)
24. Gethers, M., Oliveto, R., Poshyvanyk, D., Lucia, A.D.: On integrating orthogonal information retrieval methods to improve traceability recovery. In: IEEE 27th International Conference on Software Maintenance, ICSM 2011, Williamsburg, VA, USA, September 25-30, 2011, pp. 133–142 (2011)

25. Harman, M.: Why the virtual nature of software makes it ideal for search based optimization. In: Proceedings of the 13th International Conference on Fundamental Approaches to Software Engineering, FASE'10, pp. 1–12. Springer-Verlag, Berlin, Heidelberg (2010)
26. Haugen, Ø., Møller-Pedersen, B., Oldevik, J., Olsen, G.K., Svendsen, A.: Adding standardized variability to domain specific languages pp. 139–148 (2008)
27. Hayes, J.H., Dekhtyar, A., Sundaram, S.K.: Advancing candidate link generation for requirements tracing: the study of methods. IEEE Transactions on Software Engineering 32(1), 4–19 (2006)
28. Hindle, A., Barr, E.T., Su, Z., Gabel, M., Devanbu, P.: On the naturalness of software. In: Proceedings of the 34th International Conference on Software Engineering, ICSE '12, pp. 837–847. IEEE Press, Piscataway, NJ, USA (2012)
29. Kang, K., Cohen, S., Hess, J., Novak, W., Peterson, A.: Feature-oriented domain analysis (FODA) feasibility study. Tech. Rep. CMU/SEI-90-TR-021, Software Engineering Institute, Carnegie Mellon University, Pittsburgh, PA (1990). URL http://resources.sei.cmu.edu/library/asset-view.cfm?AssetID=11231
30. Kästner, C., Dreiling, A., Ostermann, K.: Variability mining: Consistent semi-automatic detection of product-line features. IEEE Transactions on Software Engineering 40(1), 67–82 (2014)
31. Kästner, C., Giarrusso, P.G., Rendel, T., Erdweg, S., Ostermann, K., Berger, T.: Variability-aware parsing in the presence of lexical macros and conditional compilation. In: Proceedings of the 2011 ACM International Conference on Object Oriented Programming Systems Languages and Applications, OOPSLA '11, pp. 805–824. ACM, New York, NY, USA (2011)
32. Kästner, C., Ostermann, K., Erdweg, S.: A variability-aware module system. In: Proceedings of the ACM International Conference on Object Oriented Programming Systems Languages and Applications, OOPSLA '12, pp. 773–792. ACM, New York, NY, USA (2012)
33. Koschke, R., Quante, J.: On dynamic feature location. In: Proceedings of the 20th IEEE/ACM International Conference on Automated Software Engineering, ASE '05, pp. 86–95. ACM, New York, NY, USA (2005)
34. Krueger, C.W.: Easing the transition to software mass customization. In: Revised Papers from the 4th International Workshop on Software Product-Family Engineering, PFE '01, pp. 282–293. Springer-Verlag, London, UK, UK (2002)
35. Kuhn, A., Ducasse, S., Gírba, T.: Semantic clustering: Identifying topics in source code. Inf. Softw. Technol. 49(3), 230–243 (2007)
36. Landauer, T.K., Foltz, P.W., Laham, D.: An introduction to latent semantic analysis. Discourse Processes 25(2-3), 259–284 (1998)
37. van der Linden, F. (ed.): Software Product-Family Engineering, 4th International Workshop, PFE 2001, Bilbao, Spain, October 3-5, 2001, Revised Papers, *Lecture Notes in Computer Science*, vol. 2290. Springer (2002)
38. Liu, D., Marcus, A., Poshyvanyk, D., Rajlich, V.: Feature location via information retrieval based filtering of a single scenario execution trace. In: Proceedings of the Twenty-second IEEE/ACM International Conference on Automated Software Engineering, ASE '07, pp. 234–243. ACM, New York, NY, USA (2007)
39. Liu, D., Marcus, A., Poshyvanyk, D., Rajlich, V.: Feature location via information retrieval based filtering of a single scenario execution trace. In: Proceedings of the Twenty-second IEEE/ACM International Conference on Automated Software Engineering, ASE '07, pp. 234–243. ACM, New York, NY, USA (2007)
40. Lucia, A., Penta, M., Oliveto, R., Panichella, A., Panichella, S.: Labeling source code with information retrieval methods: An empirical study. Empirical Softw. Engg. 19(5), 1383–1420 (2014)
41. Manning, C.D., Raghavan, P., Schütze, H.: Introduction to Information Retrieval. Cambridge University Press, New York, NY, USA (2008)
42. Marcus, A., Sergeyev, A., Rajlich, V., Maletic, J.: An information retrieval approach to concept location in source code. In: Proceedings of the 11th Working Conference on Reverse Engineering, pp. 214–223 (2004)

43. Martinez, J., Ziadi, T., Bissyandé, T.F., Klein, J., l. Traon, Y.: Automating the extraction of model-based software product lines from model variants (t). In: Automated Software Engineering (ASE), 2015 30th IEEE/ACM International Conference on, pp. 396–406 (2015)
44. Martinez, J., Ziadi, T., Bissyandé, T.F., Le Traon, Y.: Bottom-up adoption of software product lines: A generic and extensible approach. In: Proceedings of the 19th International Software Product Line Conference, SPLC '15. Nashville, TN, USA. (2015)
45. McIlroy, M.D.: Mass-produced software components. In: J.M. Buxton, P. Naur, B. Randell (eds.) Software Engineering Concepts and Techniques (1968 NATO Conference of Software Engineering), pp. 88–98. NATO Science Committee (1968)
46. Nadi, S., Berger, T., Kästner, C., Czarnecki, K.: Mining configuration constraints: Static analyses and empirical results. In: Proceedings of the 36th International Conference on Software Engineering, ICSE 2014, pp. 140–151. ACM, New York, NY, USA (2014)
47. Niu, N., Easterbrook, S.: On-demand cluster analysis for product line functional requirements. In: 2008 12th International Software Product Line Conference, pp. 87–96 (2008)
48. Northrop, L.M.: SEI's software product line tenets. IEEE Softw. **19**(4), 32–40 (2002)
49. OMG: Common variability language (CVL), OMG revised submission 2012. OMG document: ad/2012-08-05 (2012)
50. Parnas, D.L.: On the design and development of program families. IEEE Trans. Softw. Eng. **2**(1), 1–9 (1976)
51. Pérez, F., Font, J., Arcega, L., Cetina, C.: Collaborative feature location in models through automatic query expansion. Autom. Softw. Eng. **26**(1), 161–202 (2019)
52. Pohl, K., Böckle, G., Linden, F.J.v.d.: Software Product Line Engineering: Foundations, Principles and Techniques. Springer-Verlag New York, Inc., Secaucus, NJ, USA (2005)
53. Poshyvanyk, D., Gueheneuc, Y.G., Marcus, A., Antoniol, G., Rajlich, V.: Feature location using probabilistic ranking of methods based on execution scenarios and information retrieval. IEEE Transactions on Software Engineering **33**(6), 420–432 (2007)
54. Rahman, M.M., Chakraborty, S., Ray, B.: Which similarity metric to use for software documents?: A study on information retrieval based software engineering tasks. In: Proceedings of the 40th International Conference on Software Engineering: Companion Proceedings, ICSE '18, pp. 335–336. ACM, New York, NY, USA (2018)
55. Revelle, M., Dit, B., Poshyvanyk, D.: Using data fusion and web mining to support feature location in software. In: IEEE 18th International Conference on Program Comprehension (ICPC), pp. 14–23 (2010)
56. Rubin, J., Chechik, M.: A survey of feature location techniques. In: I. Reinhartz-Berger, A. Sturm, T. Clark, S. Cohen, J. Bettin (eds.) Domain Engineering, pp. 29–58. Springer Berlin Heidelberg (2013)
57. Salman, H.E., Seriai, A., Dony, C.: Feature location in a collection of product variants: Combining information retrieval and hierarchical clustering. In: The 26th International Conference on Software Engineering and Knowledge Engineering, Hyatt Regency, Vancouver, BC, Canada, July 1-3, 2013., pp. 426–430 (2014)
58. Salton, G., McGill, M.J.: Introduction to Modern Information Retrieval. McGraw-Hill, Inc., New York, NY, USA (1986)
59. She, S., Lotufo, R., Berger, T., Wasowski, A., Czarnecki, K.: Reverse engineering feature models. In: Proceedings of the 33rd International Conference on Software Engineering, ICSE '11, pp. 461–470. ACM, New York, NY, USA (2011)
60. van der Spek, P., Klusener, S., van de Laar, P.: Complementing Software Documentation. Views on Evolvability of Embedded Systems pp. 37–51. Springer Netherlands, Dordrecht (2011)
61. Stehman, S.V.: Selecting and interpreting measures of thematic classification accuracy. Remote Sensing of Environment **62**(1), 77–89 (1997)
62. Svendsen, A., Zhang, X., Lind-Tviberg, R., Fleurey, F., Haugen, Ø., Møller-Pedersen, B., Olsen, G.K.: Developing a software product line for train control: A case study of cvl. In: Proceedings of the 14th International Conference on Software Product Lines: Going Beyond, SPLC'10, pp. 106–120. Springer-Verlag, Berlin, Heidelberg (2010)

63. Thomas, S.W., Hassan, A.E., Blostein, D.: Mining Unstructured Software Repositories, pp. 139–162. Springer Berlin Heidelberg, Berlin, Heidelberg (2014)
64. Wilde, N., Scully, M.C.: Software reconnaissance: Mapping program features to code. Journal of Software Maintenance **7**(1), 49–62 (1995)
65. Wong, W.E., Gokhale, S.S., Horgan, J.R., Trivedi, K.S.: Locating program features using execution slices. In: Proceedings 1999 IEEE Symposium on Application-Specific Systems and Software Engineering and Technology. ASSET'99 (Cat. No.PR00122), pp. 194–203 (1999)
66. Zhang, X., Haugen, Ø., Møller-Pedersen, B.: Model comparison to synthesize a model-driven software product line. In: 15th International Software Product Line Conference (SPLC), pp. 90–99 (2011)

Chapter 5
Search-Based Variability Model Synthesis from Variant Configurations

Wesley K. G. Assunção, Silvia R. Vergilio, Roberto E. Lopez-Herrejon, and Lukas Linsbauer

Abstract The parallel maintenance of independent system variants, developed to supply a wide range of customer-specific demands, is a complex activity. To alleviate this problem and ease the creation of new products, the consolidation of such variants into a Software Product Line (SPL) is an effective solution. For this, a fundamental step is to construct a variability model that represents the combinations of features of all the existing variants. However, the process of extracting an SPL from independent variants, and consequently constructing a variability model, is acknowledged as costly and error-prone. Instead of starting from scratch, many approaches have been proposed for reverse engineering variability models, but they have two limitations. These approaches usually optimize a single objective that does not allow software engineers to consider design trade-offs and do not exploit knowledge from implementation artifacts. This chapter presents our approach to address these limitations. Our approach applies a multi-objective optimization strategy and uses source code dependencies to reverse engineer variability models. The resulting model not only represents the desired feature combinations but are also well-formed regarding source code dependencies, i.e., variability safe. The approach, using two multi-objective evolutionary algorithms, namely NSGA-II and SPEA2, and a single-objective algorithm was evaluated with twelve subject systems.

W. K. G. Assunção (✉)
Pontifical Catholic University of Rio de Janeiro, Rio de Janeiro, Brazil

Johannes Kepler University of Linz, Linz, Austria
e-mail: wesley.assuncao@jku.at

S. R. Vergilio
Dinf, Federal University of Paraná, Curitiba, Brazil
e-mail: silvia@inf.ufpr.br

R. E. Lopez-Herrejon
École de Technologie Supérieure, Universite du Québec, Montreal, QC, Canada
e-mail: roberto.lopez@etsmtl.ca

L. Linsbauer
ISF, Technische Universität Braunschweig, Braunschweig, Germany
e-mail: l.linsbauer@tu-bs.de

© Springer Nature Switzerland AG 2023
R. E. Lopez-Herrejon et al. (eds.), *Handbook of Re-Engineering Software Intensive Systems into Software Product Lines*, https://doi.org/10.1007/978-3-031-11686-5_5

For comparisons, we rely on widely adopted performance indicators. The results indicate that the performance of the multi-objective algorithms is similar in most cases, and that both clearly outperform the single-objective algorithm. Also, the trade-off among different solutions is important to support engineers during decision making.

5.1   Introduction

Software Product Lines (SPLs) have been receiving wide attention from software companies due to their advantages such as higher software quality and shorter time-to-market for new products [27]. In summary, an SPL is an approach to create families of software products with focus on reuse of artifacts and systematic variability management [9]. In the literature we can observe different strategies to adopt SPLs [25, 26]. The most common one, used in industrial settings, is the extractive strategy, in which system variants existing in a company are consolidated into an SPL. The extraction of SPLs from systems variants is conducted by employing a re-engineering process that consists of different phases using and generating different artifacts [4, 7].

One of the main artifacts to support the development of SPLs is the Feature Model (FM) [24]. An FM is the most common representation for modeling variability and commonality in SPLs [10]. An FM is composed of SPL features and their relationships in a tree-like structure that denotes the set of valid configurations of features that constitute the products of an SPL. FMs are essential for analysis, design, and evolution of SPLs, supporting stakeholders in making technical and managerial decisions about the portfolio of products [8]. Due to this importance, FMs are usually one of the first assets to be created during the re-engineering of system variants into an SPL [4, 7]. Since the system variants have different configurations, reverse engineering of FMs from such configurations can provide useful information to stakeholders in the re-engineering process.

In the literature, we can find many pieces of work proposing or evaluating strategies for reverse engineering of FMs based on system variants. These strategies cover different artifacts and rely on different techniques. For instance, they are based on configuration scripts [38], propositional logic expressions [16, 39], natural language [44], ad hoc algorithms [1, 22, 23], and search-based techniques [29, 31, 33, 40, 41]. Search-based techniques have presented promising results. However, in previous work we identified two main limitations [5]:

- **Conflict optimization:** most studies based on search-based techniques do not consider multiple objectives to capture the trade-offs that software engineers must consider for the reverse engineering task. A multi-objective perspective has advantages in situations where there are conflicts among the goals of the software engineer. For instance, obtaining an FM that represents a set of desired product configurations can lead to a model that also generates a surplus of configurations, which are not desired. Nevertheless, if we tweak the FM to avoid such additional configurations, we might lose some desired configurations. A multi-objective algorithm aims to optimizing both goals and enables the engineer to make a decision based on an analysis of the different trade-offs of importance in the problem domain.

- **Use of source code as source of information:** existing approaches do not exploit any knowledge on how the system variants are actually implemented. The use of knowledge available in implementation artifacts helps to generate FMs in accordance with the already existing software variants.

In this chapter we present our approach to cope with these limitations [3]. Our approach to reverse engineer FMs is based on multi-objective algorithms and uses a graph to represent dependencies in the source code artifacts of the existing system variants. The approach provides sets of FMs with different trade-offs to the software engineers. We also describe an empirical evaluation that relies on two well-known multi-objective evolutionary algorithms, namely NSGA-II and SPEA2, which are compared to a single-objective evolutionary algorithm used as baseline. The evaluation was performed using 12 subject systems. The results highlight the benefits and advantages of using a multi-objective approach over a single-objective one. Furthermore, NSGA-II outperforms SPEA2, but in most of the cases they present similar performance. To motivate the practical use of our approach, we present an illustrative example on how obtained solutions can be used to support software engineers in the decision-making process during the extractive adoption of SPLs.

5.2   Running Example

To illustrate our approach, we present a running example based on a simple family of software products for a drawing application. Let us assume the goal is to use these variants as a starting point to obtain a product line called *Draw Product Line (DPL)*. This application has the features to allow users to handle a drawing area (feature BASE), draw lines (feature LINE), draw rectangles (feature RECT), draw filled rectangles (feature FILL), select a color for the line or rectangle (feature COLOR), and clean the drawing area (feature WIPE). From the combination of these six features, 16 product variants were developed, as presented in Table 5.1. The symbol ✓ indicates the selected features per variant. In the context of this work, we refer to each feature combination as a *feature set* (often also referred to as a configuration), formally defined as [29]:

Definition 5.1 (Feature Set) A *feature set* is a 2-tuple [sel,$\overline{\text{sel}}$] where sel and $\overline{\text{sel}}$ are respectively the set of selected and not-selected features of a system variant. Let FL be the list of features of a feature model, such that sel, $\overline{\text{sel}} \subset$ FL, sel $\cap$ $\overline{\text{sel}} = \emptyset$, and sel $\cup \overline{\text{sel}} =$ FL.

Table 5.1 Feature sets for DPL

Products	BASE	LINE	RECT	COLOR	FILL	WIPE
Product$_1$	✓	✓				✓
Product$_2$	✓	✓		✓		
Product$_3$	✓	✓	✓	✓		
Product$_4$	✓	✓	✓	✓	✓	
Product$_5$	✓	✓	✓			✓
Product$_6$	✓	✓				
Product$_7$	✓	✓		✓		✓
Product$_8$	✓	✓	✓			
Product$_9$	✓		✓			
Product$_{10}$	✓		✓			✓
Product$_{11}$	✓		✓	✓		
Product$_{12}$	✓		✓	✓	✓	
Product$_{13}$	✓		✓	✓		✓
Product$_{14}$	✓		✓	✓	✓	✓
Product$_{15}$	✓	✓	✓	✓		✓
Product$_{16}$	✓	✓	✓	✓	✓	✓

5.3   Source Code Dependency Graphs

This section describes the concept of source code dependencies and how they are represented in a dependency graph. This dependency graph, which is a weighted directed graph, is the basis for considering implementation artifacts to reverse engineer FMs. To create this graph we use the terminology and the tool from previous work [19, 28]. Since we deal with system variants, common and variable implementation artifacts are grouped in two kinds of *modules*, as follows:

Definition 5.2 (Base Module) A *base* module implements a feature regardless of the presence or absence of any other features and is denoted with the feature name written in lowercase.

Definition 5.3 (Derivative Module) A *derivative* module $m = \delta^n(c_0, c_1, ..., c_n)$ implements feature interactions, where c_i is F (if feature F is selected) or ¬F (if not selected), and n is the order of the derivative.

In our approach, Base and Derivative modules are extracted from the implementation of each variant based on a deterministic algorithm [28, 30]. This algorithm computes traces from the modules to their implementing source code fragments and identifies dependencies between the modules. Figure 5.1 illustrates some traces computed by the algorithm. The traces are indicated using comments at the end of the lines. For example, recalling our running example, the field defined in Line 5 traces to the base module *Color* of the corresponding feature Color, which is present in all variants with feature Color, regardless the existence of other features.

```
 1  public class Canvas ... {
 2    List<Shape> shapes = new LinkedList<Shape>();
 3    Point start;
 4    Line newLine = null; // Line
 5    Color color = Color.BLACK; // Color
 6    ...
 7    void mousePressedLine(MouseEvent e) { // Line
 8    if (newLine == null) {
 9        start = new Point(e.getX(), e.getY());
10        newLine=new Line(color,start);//δ¹(Color,Line)
11        shapes.add(newLine);
12    }
13    }
14  }
```

Fig. 5.1 Source code snippet for DPL example

On the other hand, in Line 10 we can observe a derivative module $\delta^1(Color, Line)$, which means that the corresponding line of code will be part of its containing method only when the variant has both features `Color` and `Line`.

In addition to Base and Derivative modules, there are potential dependencies between modules. To define such dependencies and their representation in a graph, we first introduce the concept of a module expression:

Definition 5.4 (Module Expression) A module expression is the propositional logic representation of modules. For a base module b, the module expression is its own literal b. For a derivative module $m = \delta^n(c_0, c_1, ..., c_n)$ its module expression is $c_0 \wedge c_1 \wedge ... \wedge c_n$.

For illustration, the module expression of base module `Color` is *Color*. For the derivative module δ^1(`Color`, `Line`) the module expression representation is *Color* $\wedge$ *Line* which indicates the interaction between features `Color` and `Line`.

Based on the definitions of modules and expressions presented above, we can describe how the deterministic algorithm identifies the dependencies between fragments of source code. In this way, let us consider the following definitions.

Definition 5.5 (Dependency) A dependency establishes a requires relationship between two sets of modules and it is denoted with a three-tuple (`from`, `to`, `weight`), where `from` and `to` each are a set of modules (or module expressions) of the related modules, and `weight` expresses the strength of the dependency, i.e. the number of dependencies of structural elements in modules `from` on structural elements in modules `to`. We use the dot (`.`) operator to refer to elements of a tuple, e.g., the weight of a dependency `dep` is denoted by `dep.weight`. A dependency's propositional logic representation is defined as:

$$\bigvee_{\text{mfrom}\in\text{dep.from}} \text{mfrom} \Rightarrow \bigwedge_{\text{mto}\in\text{dep.to}} \text{mto}$$

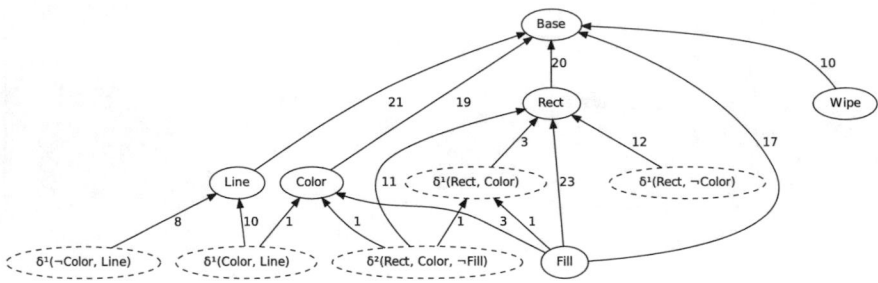

Fig. 5.2 Dependency graph for DPL

Definition 5.6 (Dependency Graph) A dependency graph is a set of dependencies, where each node in the graph corresponds to a set of modules (or module expressions), and every edge in the graph corresponds to a dependency as defined above. Edges are annotated with natural numbers that represent the dependencies' weights.

Figure 5.2 presents the dependency graph of our running example considering all its feature sets. The base modules have solid borders and the derivative modules have dashed borders. Only the lowest order modules are presented, since they are the most relevant to our approach, and self-dependencies are removed for better readability. We can observe that the strongest dependencies, i.e., those with the highest weights, are those that go to base modules. As mentioned before, weights in the graph represent the number of structural dependencies between source code elements belonging to different features. For example, in Fig. 5.2 there are 10 dependencies from the source code elements of WIPE to the source code elements of BASE. In this example, dependencies are field accesses (4) and containment relationships (6), i.e a field belongs to a class.

To ease the computation of metrics based on the dependencies, the dependency graph can also be represented as a dependency matrix, as presented in Table 5.2. Each row represents a dependency. In addition to the weight of the dependency (fourth column), the fifth column presents a normalized weight in order to keep the sum of all weights of the graph equal to 1.0. This normalization enables a better interpretation of the values in the optimization process.

To illustrate the representation of dependencies using propositional logic, we refer to the source code presented in Fig. 5.1. Let us consider the dependency that exists between the module $\delta^1(Color, Line)$ and the module $Color$. This dependency exists because the field color defined in Line 5 belongs to the module $Color$ and it is used by newLine = new Line(color,start); in Line 10 which belongs to the module $\delta^1(Color, Line)$. The propositional logic expression for this dependency is $(Color \wedge Line) \Rightarrow Color$. Another example is the module $\delta^1(Color, Line)$ that depends on module $Line$, because the statement in Line 10 is contained in the method void mousePressedLine(MouseEvent e) which belongs to module $Line$. In this case, the propositional logic expression is

Table 5.2 Dependency matrix for DPL

ID	From	To	Weight	Normalized
1	Line	Base	21	0.1304
2	Wipe	Base	10	0.0621
3	Color	Base	19	0.1180
4	Rect	Base	20	0.1242
5	Fill	Base	17	0.1056
6	Fill	Rect	23	0.1429
7	Fill	Color	3	0.0186
8	Fill	δ^1(Rect, Color)	1	0.0062
9	δ^1(Rect, ¬Color)	Rect	12	0.0745
10	δ^1(Rect, Color)	Rect	3	0.0186
11	δ^1(¬Color, Line)	Line	8	0.0497
12	δ^1(Color, Line)	Color	1	0.0062
13	δ^1(Color, Line)	Line	10	0.0621
14	δ^2(Rect, Color, ¬Fill)	δ^1(Rect, Color)	1	0.0062
15	δ^2(Rect, Color, ¬Fill)	Rect	11	0.0683
16	δ^2(Rect, Color, ¬Fill)	Color	1	0.0062
Total:			161	1.0000

$(Color \wedge Line) \Rightarrow Line$. The propositional logic constraints of some dependencies are tautologies, hence they always hold. The two examples illustrate this situation, since $(Color \wedge Line \Rightarrow Line) \Leftrightarrow TRUE$.

5.4   Multi-Objective Search-Based Variability Model Synthesis

Next, we present our multi-objective approach for synthesis of variability models. This approach relies on our previous work [3, 29]. Since the approach is based on search-based techniques, we describe the representation of solutions, the fitness functions used to evaluate the quality of the solutions, and the operators to improve the solutions and explore the search space.

5.4.1   Variability Model Representation

The representation of solutions in our approach is based on a simplified version of the SPLX metamodel[1] [35]. Figure 5.3 presents an overview of the structure and

---

[1] http://www.splot-research.org/.

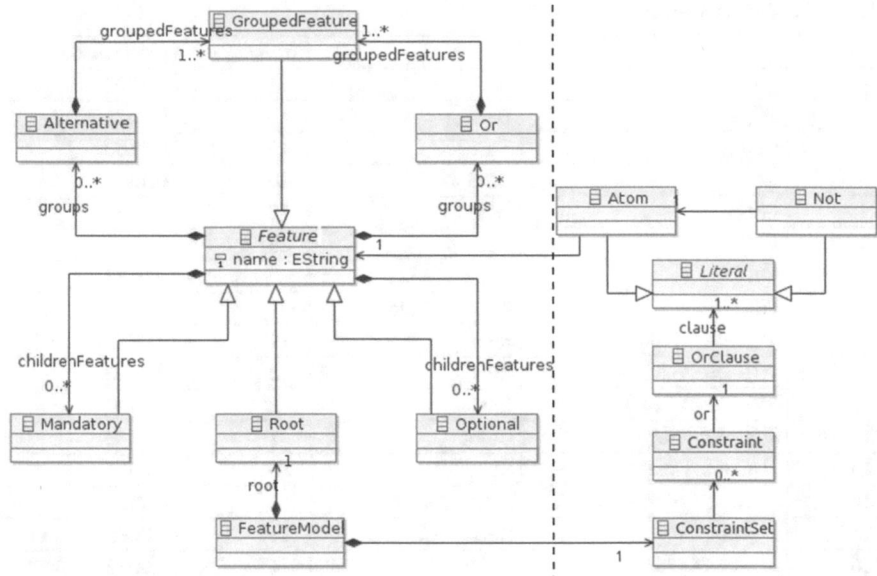

Fig. 5.3 Representation used to describe the structure and semantics of solutions, based on the SPLX metamodel. Extracted from [29]

semantics used to represent the FMs. In summary, the elements on the left side of the figure correspond to the tree-like structure of an FM. The elements on the right side correspond to the cross-tree constraints (CTCs) between the features. A detailed explanation of this metamodel can be found in [29]. Using this representation, the initial population is generated by creating random feature trees and random CTCs. Additionally, some domain constraints are also taken into account (see Sect. 5.4.3). To create the random solutions, we use the tools FaMa [11] and BeTTy [37].

5.4.2   Fitness Functions

In a previous work we could observe the multi-objective nature of the reverse engineering of FMs [3, 5]. Based on that, we have proposed a multi-objective search-based approach to deal with this problem. Our approach deals with three objectives, i.e., fitness functions, that use auxiliary function, which are described next.

Let us consider $\mathscr{FM}$ as the universe of feature models, $\mathscr{SFS}$ the universe of set of feature sets, and sfs the set of feature sets available for the variability model synthesis (sfs is illustrated in Table 5.1). Using these definitions, we introduce the first auxiliary function:

Definition 5.7 $featureSets$ returns the set of feature sets denoted by a feature model.

$$featureSets : \mathcal{FM} \rightarrow \mathcal{SFS}$$

Among all feature sets denoted by an FM, we have to check which ones are in conformance with the dependencies of the dependency graph. This is required to measure the variability safety of an FM. For that, we define the second auxiliary function:

Definition 5.8 $holds(dep, fs)$ returns 1 if dependency dep holds on the feature set (of a system variant) fs and 0 otherwise. A dependency dep holds for a feature set fs if:

$$(\bigwedge_{f \in fs.sel} f \wedge \bigwedge_{g \in fs.\overline{sel}} \neg g) \Rightarrow (dep.from \Rightarrow dep.to)$$

As illustration of $holds$ using our running example, let us consider the dependency $Fill \Rightarrow Rect$ and the feature set, i.e., system variant, with the features Base and Line. For this case, the function $holds$ returns 1, since the propositional logic formula $(Base \wedge Line \wedge \neg Fill \wedge \neg Rect \wedge \neg Wipe \wedge \neg Color) \Rightarrow (Fill \Rightarrow Rect)$ is true.

The functions $featureSets$ and $holds$ are used to compute the three fitness functions of our multi-objective approach, namely Precision (P), Recall (R), and Variability Safety (VS). These fitness functions are described in the following.

Definition 5.9 $precision(sfs, fm)$ expresses how many feature sets denoted by a reverse engineered feature model fm are among the desired feature sets sfs.

$$precision(sfs, fm) = \frac{|sfs \cap featureSets(fm)|}{|featureSets(fm)|}$$

Definition 5.10 $recall(sfs, fm)$ expresses how many of the desired feature sets sfs are denoted by the reverse engineered feature model fm.

$$recall(sfs, fm) = \frac{|sfs \cap featureSets(fm)|}{|sfs|}$$

Definition 5.11 $variabilitySafety(fm, dg)$ expresses the degree of *variability-safety* of a reverse engineered feature model fm with respect to a dependency graph dg.

$$variabilitySafety(fm, dg) =$$

$$\sum_{dep \in dg} dep.weight \times \left(\frac{\sum\limits_{fs \in featureSets(fm)} holds(dep, fs)}{|featureSets(fm)|} \right)$$

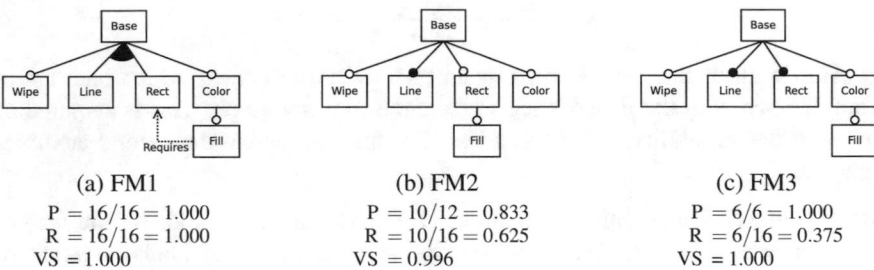

(a) FM1

$P = 16/16 = 1.000$
$R = 16/16 = 1.000$
VS = 1.000

(b) FM2

$P = 10/12 = 0.833$
$R = 10/16 = 0.625$
VS = 0.996

(c) FM3

$P = 6/6 = 1.000$
$R = 6/16 = 0.375$
VS = 1.000

Fig. 5.4 Examples of extracted feature models for DPL

The first two fitness functions are based on measures from the information retrieval field [34] and the third measure is based on our definition of variability safety.

Next, we present examples of solutions to show the multi-objective nature of variability model synthesis and illustrate the use of the three fitness functions. Figure 5.4 presents three FMs that are solutions for the drawing application variants. Below each FM, we present the values computed for P, R, and VS. These values were obtained based on the set of feature sets in Table 5.1 and the dependencies in Table 5.2.

FM1 in Fig. 5.4a is an ideal solution, as $|featureSets(FM1) \cap sfs| = 16$, leading to P and R being equal to 1.000. This means that its valid configurations are exactly the same as the desired feature sets. VS is also 1.000, indicating that there is no broken dependency in any configuration denoted by FM1. On the other hand, FM2 in Fig. 5.4b denotes $|featureSets(FM2)| = 12$ feature sets of which $|sfs \cap featureSets(FM2)| = 10$ are in the desired feature sets, leading to P = 0.833 and R = 0.625. Still, some feature sets denoted by this feature model do not satisfy all dependencies, leading to VS = 0.996. An example of broken dependencies is with the feature set $[\{Base, Line, Rect, Fill\}, \{Wipe, Color\}]$, for which the dependency with ID 7 (Fill $\Rightarrow$ Color) (see Table 5.2) is not satisfied. This dependency indicates that when the feature Fill is selected in the feature set, the feature Color must also be selected. Finally, FM3 presented in Fig. 5.4c denotes six feature sets in which all of them are desired feature sets. Thus, $|featureSets(FM3)| = 6$ and $|sfs \cap featureSets(FM3)| = 6$, leading to P = 1.000 and R = 0.375. No dependency is broken by its feature sets, leading to VS = 1.000.

This illustrative example presents the potential trade-off among the fitness functions. FM1 has the best values for the three objectives and is the best solution. However, for most practical cases, there is no ideal solution (see the results of our empirical study in Sect. 5.6), requiring practitioners to reason about the trade-offs among different solutions.

5.4.3   Evolutionary Operators

The evolutionary operators are responsible for modifying the individuals, i.e., solutions, in order to explore the search space. To apply such changes, the first operator is responsible for selecting individuals from the populations. Our approach adopts the standard tournament selection as selection operator. After selecting the individuals from the population, the mutation and crossover operators perform the changes on the individuals. Before presenting these operators in detail, we present some domain constraints that are taken into account in the evolutionary process to guarantee the semantics of FMs:

- Each feature is identified by its name, so every feature appears exactly once in the FM tree;
- All FMs have a fixed set of feature names, so in different FMs only the relations between features are different;
- CTCs can only be either *requires* or *excludes*, i.e., exactly two literals per clause with at least one being negated;
- CTCs must not contradict each other, i.e., the corresponding CNF of the entire constraint set must be satisfiable;
- There is a maximum number of CTCs (given as a percentage of the number of features) that must not be exceeded.

Note that there might exist rare cases of contradictions between CTCs and the FM tree. Our approach does not consider this domain constraint, as their detection and repair is computationally expensive. However, when individuals with these characteristics are created, the evolutionary process itself weeds them out because of their bad fitness value.

Once the individuals have been selected from the population, the changes to the solutions take place. The *mutation* operator in our approach is designed to apply small changes in the FM. This operator changes randomly selected parts of the tree or in the CTCs of the feature model. The mutation uses a probability to decide if the change is applied in the tree part, in the CTCs, or in both. The possible changes applied by this operator are randomly selected from the list presented below.

- Mutations performed on the tree:

  - Randomly swaps two features in the feature tree;
  - Randomly changes an *Alternative* relation to an *Or* relation or vice-versa;
  - Randomly changes an *Optional* or *Mandatory* relation to any other kind of relation (*Mandatory, Optional, Alternative, Or*);
  - Randomly selects a subtree in the feature tree and puts it somewhere else in the tree without violating the metamodel or any of the domain constraints.

- Mutations performed on the CTCs:

  - Adds a new, randomly created CTC that does not contradict the other CTCs and does not already exist;
  - Randomly removes a CTC.

Similarly to the mutation operator, the *crossover* operator also generates off-spring in conformance to the metamodel (see Fig. 5.3) and to the domain constraints. Differently from mutation, that operates in a single parent, the crossover requires the selection of two parents. The steps performed by the crossover are the following:

1. The offspring is initialized with the root feature of $Parent_1$. If the root feature of $Parent_2$ is a different one, then it is added to the offspring as a mandatory child feature of its root feature.
2. Traverse the first parent depth first starting at the *root* node and add to the offspring a random number r of features that are not already contained by appending them to their respective parent feature already contained in the offspring using the same relation type between them (the parent feature of every visited feature during the traversal is guaranteed to be contained in the offspring due to the depth first traversal order).
3. Traverse the second parent exactly the same way as the first one.
4. Go to Step 2 until every feature is contained in the offspring.

The steps above generate the first child from the two parents. The second child is generated by performing the same process but with reversed parents, i.e., the position of the parents is swapped.

To obtain the CTCs of the offspring, all constraints of both parents are merged in a set, and then a subset of these CTCs is randomly selected and assigned to the first child. The remaining subset of CTCs is assigned to the second child.

5.5   Evaluation

This section describes the algorithms with their experimental configuration, the subject systems, and the information collected to evaluate our multi-objective approach for the synthesis of variability models. A replication package is made available for further studies.[2]

For evaluating our approach, we considered three different algorithms. *Non-Dominated Sorting Genetic Algorithm (NSGA-II)* [17] and *Strength Pareto Evolutionary Algorithm (SPEA2)* [46] are multi-objective algorithms that apply the Pareto concepts to find a set of non-dominated solutions for the given problem. The NSGA-II and SPEA2 algorithms are widely used in multi-objective optimization of software engineering problems [21]. Additionally, we also applied a single-objective *Genetic Programming (GP)* algorithm from related work [29], to serve as baseline comparison. This GP algorithm uses a weighted measure of precision and recall with same weight for both values. The three algorithms were implemented on top of the ECJ Framework.[3] The parameters used for configuring the algorithms are presented

---

[2] http://www.inf.ufpr.br/gres/IS/MORevEngFMs.zip.

[3] http://cs.gmu.edu/~eclab/projects/ecj/.

Table 5.3 Algorithm's parameters

Parameter	GP	NSGA-II	SPEA2
Number of generations	1000	1000	1000
Population size	200	200	200
Archive size	–	–	10
Crossover	0.7	0.7	0.7
Feature tree mutation	0.5	0.5	0.5
CTCs mutation	0.5	0.5	0.5
Number of elites	25%	25%	25%
Selection method	Tournament	Tournament	Tournament
Tournament size	6	6	6
Maximum CTC percentage for builder[a]	0.1	0.1	0.1
Maximum CTC percentage for mutator[a]	0.5	0.5	0.5
Independent runs	30	30	30

[a]Relative to number of features

Table 5.4 Subject systems overview

System	#F	#P	LoC	#Nodes	#Edges
ArgoUML	11	256	264K–344K	49	114
DPL	6	16	282–473	12	27
GOL	15	65	874–1.9K	12	24
VOD	11	32	4.7K–5.2K	7	11
ZipMe	7	32	5K–6.2K	29	60
MM-V1	5	3	2.1K	5	4
MM-V2	6	6	2.3K–2.4K	6	6
MM-V3	7	12	2.3K–2.5K	9	12
MM-V4	8	24	2.6K–2.9K	10	14
MM-V5	9	48	2.7K–3.8K	14	25
MM-V6	10	96	2.8K–4.1K	22	43
MM-V7	13	240	2.9K–4.3K	31	70

#F: number of features, #P: number of products, LoC: lines of code,
#Nodes: number of nodes in the dependency graph,
#Edges: number of Edges, i.e. dependencies, in the dependency graph

in Table 5.3. The execution of the algorithms are performed on a laptop with an Intel® Core^{TM} i7-4900MQ CPU with 2.80 GHz, 16 GB of memory, running on a Linux platform.

The evaluation uses as input 12 subject systems with different sizes and from diverse domains. Table 5.4 presents the systems. ArgoUML is an open source tool for UML modelling [15]. Draw Product Line (DPL), introduced in the running example, is a simple drawing application. Game Of Life (GOL) is a family of games. Video On Demand (VOD) implements algorithms for streaming on demand.

ZipMe is a compression application. Finally, MobileMedia (MM) is an application to manipulate media files on mobile devices [18], of which seven different revisions exist.

For an easy interpretation and analysis of the results of this evaluation, the values of *Precision (P)*, *Recall (R)*, and *Variability Safety (VS)* are normalized values in the interval between 0 and 1. The goal is to maximize all objective functions so that an ideal solution has the values $P = 1.0$, $R = 1.0$, and $VS = 1.0$. Additionally, to the objective functions, we also collected the runtime of each independent run for all algorithms. The goal is to observe the impact of adopting a multi-objective optimization such as NSGA-II and SPEA2 in comparison to a single-objective optimization, namely GP.

Since our experiment is based on different algorithms and types of optimizations, to support the analysis of the results obtained by the algorithms, we computed two different sets of solutions [6], These sets of solutions are commonly used in studies with multi-objective optimization [13].

- *Pareto Front True (PF_{True})*: this set represents ideal solutions for a given problem. However, as we do not know the real Pareto Front True for our subject systems, we use an approximation of PF_{True}. In this study, this set consists of the best solutions reached by all algorithms for each case study. These best solutions are found by the union of all the solutions of all independent runs of the three algorithms together, then removing all dominated solutions.
- *Pareto Front Known (PF_{Known})*: this set contains the best solutions reached by each algorithm for each subject system. To compute PF_{Known} we merged all the solutions of all runs for each algorithm and then we keep only the non-dominated solutions.

To investigate the two multi-objective algorithms, i.e., NSGA-II and SPEA2, we used the well known quality indicator called Hypervolume [47]. Hypervolume is a performance indicator to measure the n-dimensional volume between a Pareto front, namely a set of solutions found by each multi-objective algorithm, and a specific reference point. To compute the Hypervolume, the reference point for all case studies was P = 1.1, R = 1.1, and VS = 1.1. Since our problem is a maximization problem, lower values of Hypervolume are better. To check statistical difference we applied the Wilcoxon test [12]. To corroborate our analysis we also compute the effect size with the Vargha-Delaney's $\hat{A}_{12}$ statistic [42], used for assessing randomized algorithms in Software Engineering [2].

5.6 Results and Analysis

The results of runtime are presented in Table 5.5. GP is the fastest algorithm in all case studies, followed by NSGA-II and then SPEA2. This is an expected result, since the multi-objective algorithms compute the Pareto fronts in each generation. However, this cost in computation brings other advantages, as discussed below.

Table 5.5 Average runtime per run

System	GP			NSGA-II			SPEA2		
	min	sec	msec	min	sec	msec	min	sec	msec
ArgoUML		25	275	13	59	911	17	35	300
DPL		23	512		35	802	1	30	583
GOL		56	934	2	15	991	3	3	531
VOD			906		1	882		2	247
ZipME		1	131	1	50	576	2	57	495
MM-V1		4	816		10	468		20	258
MM-V2		8	502		15	321		38	451
MM-V3		17	212		22	325		45	628
MM-V4		29	327		30	624		58	208
MM-V5		52	962		59	342	1	44	310
MM-V6	1	27	442	3	28	598	4	18	747
MM-V7	2	35	35	10	53	762	11	2	444

min = minutes, sec = seconds, msec = milliseconds

To discuss the advantages of using a multi-objective perspective for reverse engineering FMs, we compare the solutions obtained from multi-objective algorithms against solutions from a single-objective algorithm. Table 5.6 presents in the second column the cardinality of PF_{True} and in the fourth column the cardinality of PF_{Known}. We can observe that for seven subject systems, there is only one single solution in PF_{True}. This means that the three objectives could be optimized independently. For the other five subject systems, we can confirm that there are conflicts among the objectives. For Mobile Media, we can see that the objectives became conflicting after MM-V6. Additionally, the results of PF_{True} show that MM-V6 and MM-V7 have many solutions in comparison with the other subject systems. After MM-V6 big changes were introduced in the source-code of MobileMedia [18]. MM-V6 and MM-V7 introduced the two alternative features Music and Video, and the mandatory feature Photo was made optional, impacting the whole system. These modifications lead to a large and complex dependency graph (see Table 5.4) directly impacting the number of solutions found.

The results in Table 5.6 also allow us to analyze how good the algorithms are in finding diverse solutions, namely non-dominated solutions. For that, we consider: (i) the number of solutions in PF_{known} that are also in PF_{True}, shown in the fifth column; and (ii) the average number of solutions found per run that are/were in PF_{True}, show in the sixth column. To illustrate this analysis, we rely on ArgoUML. This subject system has a PF_{True} composed of four solutions, from which GP found two solutions, NSGA-II found three, and SPEA2 two. On average, GP can find almost one solution in PF_{True} per run, which is expected because it is a single-objective approach. NSGA-II and SPEA2 found 1.9 and 2.0 solutions per run on average, respectively.

Table 5.6 Pareto fronts

System	PF$_{True}$ cardinality	Search algorithm	PF$_{known}$ cardinality	# of solutions in PF$_{True}$	Average in PF$_{True}$ per run
ArgoUML	4	GP	2	2 (50%)	0.966
		NSGA-II	3	3 (75%)	1.9
		SPEA2	2	2 (50%)	2.0
DPL	1	GP	1	1 (100%)	0.033
		NSGA-II	1	1 (100%)	0.166
		SPEA2	1	1 (100%)	0.066
GOL	8	GP	6	0 (0%)	0.0
		NSGA-II	8	8 (100%)	0.966
		SPEA2	6	5 (62%)	0.933
VOD	1	GP	1	0 (0%)	0.0
		NSGA-II	1	1 (100%)	1.0
		SPEA2	1	1 (100%)	1.0
ZipME	4	GP	1	1 (25%)	1.0
		NSGA-II	4	4 (100%)	3.033
		SPEA2	3	3 (75%)	3.0
MM-V1	1	GP	1	1 (100%)	0.5
		NSGA-II	1	1 (100%)	0.5
		SPEA2	1	1 (100%)	0.566
MM-V2	1	GP	1	1 (100%)	0.3
		NSGA-II	1	1 (100%)	0.366
		SPEA2	1	1 (100%)	0.433
MM-V3	1	GP	2	0 (0%)	0
		NSGA-II	1	1 (100%)	0.333
		SPEA2	1	1 (100%)	0.333
MM-V4	1	GP	1	1 (100%)	0.066
		NSGA-II	1	1 (100%)	0.333
		SPEA2	1	1 (100%)	0.3
MM-V5	1	GP	1	1 (100%)	0.1
		NSGA-II	1	1 (100%)	0.233
		SPEA2	1	1 (100%)	0.166
MM-V6	42	GP	5	1 (2%)	0.033
		NSGA-II	42	42 (100%)	4.66
		SPEA2	20	13 (30%)	1.033
MM-V7	801	GP	5	3 (0.37%)	0.333
		NSGA-II	796	760 (92%)	36.0
		SPEA2	155	61 (7%)	3.833

Considering both the final cardinality of PF$_{True}$ and the average number of solutions in PF$_{True}$ per run presented in Table 5.6, we can observe that GP only has similar results as NSGA-II and SPEA2 in two subject systems, namely MM-

Table 5.7 Hypervolume and effect size

| System | Hypervolume | | Wilcoxon | $\hat{A}_{12}$ Effect size | |
	NSGA-II	SPEA2	p-value	NSGA-II	SPEA2
ArgoUML	0.0036 (0.0005)	0.0035 (0.0000)	1.61E−01	46.67	53.33
DPL	0.0064 (0.0025)	0.0071 (0.0017)	1.42E−01	56.56	43.44
GOL	0.0365 (0.0080)	**0.0340 (0.0041)**	**3.62E-02**	34.22	**65.78**
VOD	0.0010 (0.0000)	0.0010 (0.0000)	NA[a]	50.00	50.00
ZipME	0.0038 (0.0000)	0.0038 (0.0000)	NA[a]	50.00	50.00
MM-V1	0.0050 (0.0042)	0.0037 (0.0032)	1.69E−01	40.56	59.44
MM-V2	0.0097 (0.0075)	0.0083 (0.0073)	4.33E−01	44.50	55.50
MM-V3	0.0121 (0.0086)	0.0109 (0.0083)	4.33E−01	44.33	55.67
MM-V4	0.0124 (0.0089)	0.0104 (0.0083)	3.49E−01	43.22	56.78
MM-V5	0.0126 (0.0089)	0.0129 (0.0088)	5.06E−01	45.06	54.94
MM-V6	0.0399 (0.0128)	0.0435 (0.0123)	1.78E−01	60.17	39.83
MM-V7	0.1125 (0.0015)	**0.1038 (0.0059)**	**1.86E-09**	4.78	**95.22**

[a]NA = Not Available, because the two sets of values are identical

V1, MM-V2, and never reached the best results. NSGA-II and SPEA2 reached the same results and outperform GP in four systems, namely VOD, MM-V3, MM-V4, and MM-V5. Finally, in six systems NSGA-II is better than GP and SPEA2, namely ArgoUML, DPL, GOL, ZipMe, MM-v6, and MM-V7.

In our experiment, we observed that five subject systems have conflicting objectives, which means that for getting better values for one objective, another objective is penalized. These conflicts lead to a set of possible solutions with different trade-offs. For these cases, the multi-objective algorithms are better than the single-objective algorithm. On average, NSGA-II and SPEA2 algorithms found a set of good solutions per run, while GP could find only one. Yet, considering the solutions obtained in each independent run, GP still was not competitive against NSGA-II and SPEA2. GP commonly finds the same solution in each run, not exploring the search space, in contrast to the multi-objective algorithms. For the seven subject systems without conflicting objectives, NSGA-II and SPEA2 performed similar to GP, finding the best solution. We can conclude with our experiment that a multi-objective approach is the best choice to reverse engineer FMs.

Now we focus on comparing the results of NSGA-II and SPEA2 for the three selected objective functions. Based on the 30 independent runs, Table 5.7 presents the average values of Hypervolume in the second and third columns with the standard deviation in parentheses. The p-value obtained with the statistical test is presented in the fourth column of the table. The effect size is presented in the last two columns. The results in Table 5.7 show a difference between the two algorithms only for GOL and MM-V7. In two cases (highlighted in bold), the best algorithm was SPEA2, with lower values of Hypervolume on average. The results for the case studies VOD and ZipME are exactly the same. Despite some differences in the average Hypervolume for the other case studies, they are statistically similar.

In summary, taking into account the number of good solutions found on average and after the 30 runs, NSGA-II outperformed SPEA2. However, both can properly explore the search space. Relying on the Hypervolume indicator, we observed that for ten subject systems, there are no significant differences. For the two cases with significant difference, SPEA2 was the best. In conclusion, both multi-objective algorithms can satisfactorily solve the problem of reverse engineering of FMs using our three objectives.

5.7   Example of Use

This section is devoted to illustrate how solutions obtained by our approach can be used in practice. The goal is to qualitatively analyse the solutions obtained by NSGA-II and SPEA2. Table 5.8 presents solutions in the set PF_{known}. Due to the large number of solutions for MM-V6 and MM-V7, only some of them are presented. For these two subject systems, we selected the solutions with the value 1.0 for at least one of the objectives.

As previously discussed, the solutions of NSGA-II and SPEA2 are the same for seven subject systems, namely DPL, VOD, MM-V1, MM-V2, MM-V3, MM-V4, and MM-V5. These single solutions must be selected for use in practice, as they represent the best trade-off for these systems. However, for the remaining case studies, we can observe how conflicting the three objective functions can be. For instance, in ArgoUML the conflict occurs only between recall and variability safety and all solutions have the value 1.0 for precision. Also, this is a similar situation for GOL, but in this system the value variability safety is 1.0 in all solutions. On the other hand, ZipMe, MM-V6 and MM-V7 have solutions with different trade-offs among the three objectives. Independently of the number of objectives, the software engineer has to decide which measure is more important and then select the corresponding solution.

Figure 5.5 presents four FMs from MM-V7 obtained by SPEA2 to exemplify the decision-making process involving multiple solutions. These FMs were selected based on two criteria: *(i)* solutions with value equal to 1.0 for at least one objective, and *(ii)* solutions with the best value for a second objective. For example, the solution in Fig. 5.5a has P=1.0, satisfying the first criterion, and R=0.8000000119 is the best value of recall among solutions with P=1.0, satisfying the second criterion. The FM in Fig. 5.5a has 192 valid configurations and all of them are desired products, leading to a precision equal to 1.0. However, the total number of desired products for this case study is 240, so the recall of this FM is not 1.0. The value of variability safety equal to 0.999162264 means that there are 324 broken dependencies among the valid configurations for this FM. The FMs in Fig. 5.5b and c have the best values for variability safety, but with very low value of recall. Taking into account Fig. 5.5b, only four valid configurations are

Table 5.8 Non-dominated solutions

System	NSGA-II			SPEA2		
	P	R	VS	P	R	VS
ArgoUML	1.0	1.0	0.9999629741.0	1.0	1.0	0.9999629741.0
	1.0	0.765625	0.9999682636	1.0	0.75	1.0
	1.0	0.75	1.0			
DPL	1.0	1.0	1.0	1.0	1.0	1.0
GOL	1.0	0.5538461804	1.0	1.0	0.5538461804	1.0
	0.8333333135	0.6153846383	1.0	0.8333333135	0.6153846383	1.0
	0.8000000119	0.7384615541.0	1.0	0.8000000119	0.7384615541.0	1.0
	0.4851485193	0.7538461685	1.0	0.4851485193	0.7538461685	1.0
	0.4193548262	0.8000000119	1.0	0.3081081212	0.8769230843	1.0
	0.4117647111.0	0.8615384698	1.0	0.2941176593	1.0	1.0
	0.380952388	0.9846153855	1.0			
	0.2941176593	1.0	1.0			
VOD	1.0	1.0	1.0	1.0	1.0	1.0
ZipMe	1.0	1.0	0.9999533669	1.0	1.0	0.999953669
	1.0	0.875	0.9999600288	1.0	0.75	1.0
	1.0	0.75	1.0	0.9696969986	1.0	0.99995478
	0.9696969986	1.0	0.99995478			
MM-V1	1.0	1.0	1.0	1.0	1.0	1.0
MM-V2	1.0	1.0	1.0	1.0	1.0	1.0
MM-V3	1.0	1.0	1.0	1.0	1.0	1.0
MM-V4	1.0	1.0	1.0	1.0	1.0	1.0
MM-V5	1.0	1.0	1.0	1.0	1.0	1.0

(continued)

Table 5.8 (continued)

System	NSGA-II			SPEA2		
	P	R	VS	P	R	VS
MM-V6	1.0	1.0	0.9988592489	1.0	1.0	0.9988592489
	1.0	0.8333333135	0.9990873991.0	1.0	0.75	0.9996489996
	1.0	0.75	0.9996489996	1.0	0.6666666865	0.9997367497
	1.0	0.6666666865	0.9997367497	1.0	0.625	1.0
	1.0	0.625	1.0	0.75	1.0	0.9988592489
	0.8571428657	1.0	0.9988592489	0.6666666865	1.0	0.9992394992
	0.8000000119	1.0	0.9989469989	0.5	1.0	0.9992541243
	0.6666666865	1.0	0.9992394992	...		
	0.5	1.0	0.9992541243			
MM-V7	1.0	0.6000000238	0.9989360141.0	1.0	0.8000000119	0.999162264
	1.0	0.400000006	0.9989360141.0	1.0	0.6000000238	0.9993559012
	1.0	0.3625000119	0.99966602	1.0	0.4666666687	0.9994112262
	1.0	0.2333333343	0.9997554055	1.0	0.400000006	0.9997431758
	1.0	0.1000000015	0.9998858559	1.0	0.200000003	0.9999021622
	1.0	0.0666666701.0	0.999266217	1.0	0.0833333358	0.9999217298
	1.0	0.0500000007	0.999347748	1.0	0.0500000007	0.9999347748
	1.0	0.0333333351.0	0.999510811.0	1.0	0.0333333351.0	0.9999510811.0
	1.0	0.0250000004	1.0	1.0	0.0250000004	0.9999673874
	0.625	1.0	0.9991153834	1.0	0.020833334	0.9999804324
	0.46875	1.0	0.9992723315	1.0	0.0166666675	1.0
	0.375	1.0	0.9993762841.0	0.625	1.0	0.9991153834
	0.25	1.0	0.9994374327	0.46875	1.0	0.9992723315
	0.1666666716	1.0	0.9994700453	0.375	1.0	0.9993347031.0
	0.8000000119	0.0333333351.0	1.0	0.2727272809	1.0	0.9993751723
	0.75	0.0500000007	1.0	0.25	1.0	0.9994374327
	...			0.2307692319	1.0	0.9994393142
				0.2083333284	1.0	0.9994700453
				0.75	0.0500000007	1.0
				...		

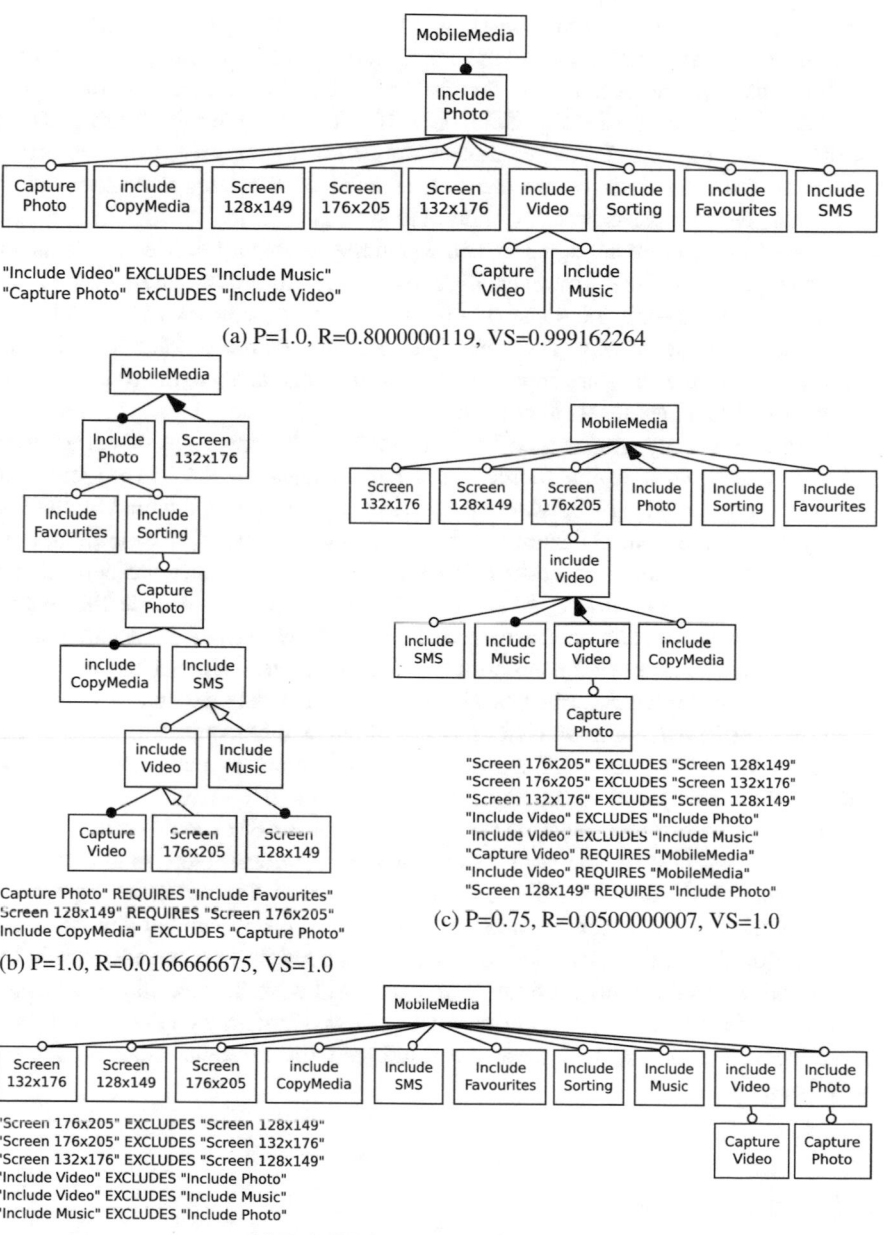

(a) P=1.0, R=0.8000000119, VS=0.999162264

"Include Video" EXCLUDES "Include Music"
"Capture Photo" ExCLUDES "Include Video"

"Capture Photo" REQUIRES "Include Favourites"
"Screen 128x149" REQUIRES "Screen 176x205"
"Include CopyMedia" EXCLUDES "Capture Photo"

(b) P=1.0, R=0.0166666675, VS=1.0

"Screen 176x205" EXCLUDES "Screen 128x149"
"Screen 176x205" EXCLUDES "Screen 132x176"
"Screen 132x176" EXCLUDES "Screen 128x149"
"Include Video" EXCLUDES "Include Photo"
"Include Video" EXCLUDES "Include Music"
"Capture Video" REQUIRES "MobileMedia"
"Include Video" REQUIRES "MobileMedia"
"Screen 128x149" REQUIRES "Include Photo"

(c) P=0.75, R=0.0500000007, VS=1.0

"Screen 176x205" EXCLUDES "Screen 128x149"
"Screen 176x205" EXCLUDES "Screen 132x176"
"Screen 132x176" EXCLUDES "Screen 128x149"
"Include Video" EXCLUDES "Include Photo"
"Include Video" EXCLUDES "Include Music"
"Include Music" EXCLUDES "Include Photo"

(d) P=0.625, R=1.0, VS=0.9991153834

Fig. 5.5 MM-V7 feature models. (**a**) P = 1.0, R = 0.8000000119, VS = 0.999162264. (**b**) P = 1.0, R = 0.0166666675, VS = 1.0. (**c**) P = 0.75, R = 0.0500000007, VS = 1.0. (**d**) P = 0.625, R = 1.0, VS − 0.9991153834

possible, mainly because of the constraint "Include_CopyMedia EXCLUDES Capture_Photo" that makes all the configurations after the third level of the tree invalid. This happens because the feature Include_CopyMedia is mandatory for Capture_Photo. In Fig. 5.5c only 16 valid configurations are possible as the constraint "Include_Video EXCLUDES Include_Music" makes invalid all configurations below the second level of the tree, since the feature Include_Music is a mandatory child of feature Include_Video. In Fig. 5.5d we have an FM with recall equal to 1.0, which means that all desired products are valid configurations here. However, it denotes more valid configurations than the input, hence decreasing the value of precision. In this same FM, the number of broken dependencies is 624. These are four examples of multi-objective solutions that are given to the software engineers, so that they can analyze the trade-offs and select the one that best meets their needs.

Using dependency graphs also helps to identify the existence of compilation errors or incoherence in the source code. For instance, in the FM presented in Fig. 5.5a the precision is 1.0, which means that all feature sets denoted by the FM belong to the set of desired feature sets. However, there are configurations that, even though they are valid, have broken dependencies. For example, the dependency $Include\_SMS \Rightarrow Capture\_Photo$ means that in the source code the feature Include_SMS depends on Capture_Photo. However, in the set of desired configurations, there are 72 configurations that have the feature Include_SMS but do not have Capture_Photo. This represents a broken dependency.

From a practical point of view, the benefit of a multi-objective approach is to provide to the software engineer a set of good solutions with different trade-offs among the objectives. Based on these solutions, the software engineer can reason about the different measures used to evaluate the FMs, and is able to select the solution that best fits the needs. Additionally, the multi-objective optimization process can obtain solutions that call the attention of the software engineer to characteristics that are not considered in advance. We illustrated this situation about the identification of possible inconsistencies between the dependencies in the source code and valid configurations of products. Although the identification of such inconsistencies was not a goal, our approach allowed software engineers to reason about inconsistencies by looking at the solutions with different values among the objectives.

5.8 Related Work

SPLs have been the focus of many studies using optimization techniques such as feature selection, architectural improvement, products testing, and feature model construction [20, 32]. More specifically, Lopez-Herrejon et al. [31, 33] also use optimization algorithms to reverse engineer FMs [31, 33]. These authors applied a single-objective evolutionary algorithm that uses as input a set of desired feature sets and maximizes the number of the configuration denoted by a feature model, disregarding any surplus feature sets [31, 33]. Based on this work, Thianniwet and Cohen [40] proposed a new fitness function to balance both additional and missing products. Additionally, Thianniwet and Cohen also create a new representation and evolution operators to deal with complex cross-tree constraints. Another work applied single-objective genetic programming for reverse engineering feature models [29]. This study was replicated with a larger set of feature models to investigate the effects of various genetic programming parameters and operators on the results [43]. We notice here that none of these pieces of work includes the information from the implementation artifacts or a multi-objective perspective.

Haslinger et al. [22, 23] also used feature sets as input, but for the purpose of identifying patterns in the selected and not selected features mapped in parent-child relations of feature models [22]. These same authors extended this approach to consider basic CTCs, i.e., requires and excludes [23]. Still, the authors do not consider the implementation artifacts. On the other hand, Czarnecki and Wasowski used as input for their approach a set of propositional logic formulas for the reverse engineering task [16, 39]. In their work, an ad hoc algorithm was proposed to extract multiple feature models from a single propositional logic formula preserving the original formula and reducing redundancy [16]. This same algorithm was improved to deal with CNF and DNF constraints [39]. In contrast to our work their starting point is configuration files, documentation files, and constraints expressed in propositional logic instead of feature sets and source code.

Acher et al. [1] presented an interactive process to map features of a single variant into a feature model. Then, all the feature models of all variants are merged into a global feature model. Sannier et al. [36] consider as input product matrices from Wikipedia. Differently from the works described above, these matrices can have other values besides selected or not selected. These matrices are the basis for analysis to identify variability patterns. However, these authors only mention the benefits of exploiting that information to extract models such as feature models. None of these works used genetic programming or a multi-objective optimization in their approaches.

There are many pieces of work that use multi-objective optimization algorithms in the field of search-based software engineering [14]. For instance, software modularization, testing integration, resource allocation, software project scheduling, project effort estimation, program repair, or software defect prediction [21, 45]. However, they do not address reverse engineering of FMs.

5.9   Concluding Remarks

This chapter presents a multi-objective approach to reverse engineer feature models from a set of feature sets and a dependency graph, extracted from the source code. The set of feature sets is used to compute the precision and recall of the feature models. The dependency graph is used to compute the variability safety. The goal of this multi-objective approach is to deal with the three different measures independently. Based on this, the approach can find a set of solutions with trade-offs among considered objectives, supporting the software engineers in the decision-making process.

We conducted an experiment to evaluate our approach regarding the benefits and advantages of using a multi-objective approach, the performance of two multi-objective evolutionary algorithms for reverse engineering of FMs, and on the practical use of a multi-objective perspective by the software engineers. This evaluation was based on twelve subject systems and used two multi-objective algorithms, namely NSGA-II and SPEA2, and a single-objective algorithm, namely GP.

The results showed that the multi-objective algorithms and the single-objective algorithm have the same performance for only two subject systems. NSGA-II and SPEA2 had the same performance for four subject systems, both also being better than GP. Finally, NSGA-II was better than GP and SPEA-2 for six systems. However, the statistical test using the Hypervolume values revealed that they do not have a difference in ten case studies, and in the other two the algorithm SPEA2 has better Hypervolume values, because it better explores the search space.

When conducting this study, we identified some possible directions for future work. For instance, the use of different types of constraints in addition to the source code dependencies, exploring new sources of information like non-functional properties, using new metrics as objective functions, dealing with ambiguity in input artifacts, and developing more robust and interactive tools and techniques.

Acknowledgments This work was supported by the Brazilian Agencies CAPES: 7126/2014-00; CNPq: 453678/2014-9, 305358/2012-0, 408356/2018-9 and 305968/2018-1; and the Carlos Chagas Filho Foundation for Supporting Research in the State of Rio de Janeiro (FAPERJ), under the PDR-10 program, grant 202073/2020. This work is partially funded Natural Sciences and Engineering Research Council of Canada (NSERC) grant RGPIN-2017-05421.

References

1. Acher, M., Cleve, A., Perrouin, G., Heymans, P., Vanbeneden, C., Collet, P., Lahire, P.: On extracting feature models from product descriptions. In: International Workshop on Variability Modelling of Software-Intensive Systems (VaMoS), pp. 45–54 (2012)
2. Arcuri, A., Briand, L.: A hitchhiker's guide to statistical tests for assessing randomized algorithms in software engineering. Software Testing, Verification and Reliability 24(3), 219–250 (2014)
3. Assunção, W.K.G., Lopez-Herrejon, R.E., Linsbauer, L., Vergilio, S.R., Egyed, A.: Multi-objective reverse engineering of variability-safe feature models based on code dependencies of system variants. Empirical Software Engineering 22(4), 1763–1794 (2016)
4. Assunção, W.K.G., Lopez-Herrejon, R.E., Linsbauer, L., Vergilio, S.R., Egyed, A.: Reengineering legacy applications into software product lines: a systematic mapping. Empirical Software Engineering 22(6), 2972–3016 (2017)
5. Assunção, W.K., Lopez-Herrejon, R.E., Linsbauer, L., Vergilio, S.R., Egyed, A.: Extracting variability-safe feature models from source code dependencies in system variants. In: Genetic and Evolutionary Computation Conference (GECCO), pp. 1303–1310. ACM, New York, NY, USA (2015)

6. Assunção, W.K.G., Colanzi, T.E., Vergilio, S.R., Pozo, A.: A multi-objective optimization approach for the integration and test order problem. Information Sciences **267**, 119 – 139 (2014)
7. Assunção, W.K.G., Vergilio, S.R.: Feature location for software product line migration: A mapping study. In: 18th Software Product Line Conference - 2nd International Workshop on REverse Variability Engineering (REVE), pp. 1–8 (2014)
8. Batory, D.: Feature models, grammars, and propositional formulas. In: H. Obbink, K. Pohl (eds.) Software Product Lines, pp. 7–20. Springer Berlin Heidelberg, Berlin, Heidelberg (2005)
9. Batory, D.S., Sarvela, J.N., Rauschmayer, A.: Scaling step-wise refinement. IEEE Transactions on Software Engineering **30**(6), 355–371 (2004)
10. Benavides, D., Segura, S., Cortés, A.R.: Automated analysis of feature models 20 years later: A literature review. Information Systems **35**(6), 615–636 (2010)
11. Benavides, D., Segura, S., Trinidad, P., Cortés, A.R.: FAMA: Tooling a framework for the automated analysis of feature models. In: K. Pohl, P. Heymans, K.C. Kang, A. Metzger (eds.) International Workshop on Variability Modelling of Software-Intensive Systems (VaMoS), *Lero Technical Report*, vol. 2007-01, pp. 129–134 (2007)
12. Bergmann, R., Ludbrook, J., Spooren, W.P.J.M.: Different Outcomes of the Wilcoxon-Mann-Whitney Test from Different Statistics Packages. The American Statistician **54**(1), 72–77 (2000)
13. Coello, C.A.C., Lamont, G., van Veldhuizen, D.: Evolutionary Algorithms for Solving Multi-Objective Problems, 2nd edn. Genetic and Evolutionary Computation. Springer, Berlin, Heidelberg (2007)
14. Colanzi, T.E., Assunção, W.K., Vergilio, S.R., Farah, P.R., Guizzo, G.: The symposium on search-based software engineering: Past, present and future. Information and Software Technology **127**, 106,372 (2020)
15. Couto, M.V., Valente, M.T., Figueiredo, E.: Extracting software product lines: A case study using conditional compilation. In: Conference on Software Maintenance and Reengineering (CSMR), pp. 191–200 (2011)
16. Czarnecki, K., Wasowski, A.: Feature diagrams and logics: There and back again. In: International Software Product Line Conference (SPLC), pp. 23–34. IEEE Computer Society (2007)
17. Deb, K., Pratap, A., Agarwal, S., Meyarivan, T.: A fast and elitist multiobjective genetic algorithm: NSGA-II. IEEE Transactions on Evolutionary Computation **6**(2), 182–197 (2002)
18. Figueiredo, E., Cacho, N., Sant'Anna, C., Monteiro, M., Kulesza, U., Garcia, A., Soares, S., Ferrari, F., Khan, S., Castor Filho, F., Dantas, F.: Evolving software product lines with aspects: An empirical study on design stability. In: International Conference on Software Engineering (ICSE), pp. 261–270. ACM, New York, NY, USA (2008)
19. Fischer, S., Linsbauer, L., Lopez-Herrejon, R.E., Egyed, A.: Enhancing clone-and-own with systematic reuse for developing software variants. In: International Conference on Software Maintenance and Evolution (ICSME) (2014)
20. Harman, M., Jia, Y., Krinke, J., Langdon, W.B., Petke, J., Zhang, Y.: Search based software engineering for software product line engineering: A survey and directions for future work. In: 18th International Software Product Line Conference - Volume 1, SPLC '14, pp. 5–18. ACM, New York, NY, USA (2014)
21. Harman, M., Mansouri, S.A., Zhang, Y.: Search-based software engineering: Trends, techniques and applications. ACM Computing Surveys **45**(1), 11:1–11:61 (2012)
22. Haslinger, E.N., Lopez-Herrejon, R.E., Egyed, A.: Reverse engineering feature models from programs' feature sets. In: Working Conference on Reverse Engineering (WCRE), pp. 308–312 (2011)
23. Haslinger, E.N., Lopez-Herrejon, R.E., Egyed, A.: On extracting feature models from sets of valid feature combinations. In: International Conference Fundamental Approaches to Software Engineering (FASE), pp. 53–67 (2013)
24. Kang, K., Cohen, S., Hess, J., Novak, W., Peterson, A.: Feature-Oriented Domain Analysis (FODA) Feasibility Study. Tech. Rep. CMU/SEI-90-TR-21, SEI, CMU (1990)

25. Krueger, C.W.: Software reuse. ACM Computing Surveys (CSUR) **24**(2), 131–183 (1992)
26. Krueger, C.W.: Easing the transition to software mass customization. In: Software Product-Family Engineering, pp. 282–293. Springer (2002)
27. van d. Linden, F.J., Schmid, K., Rommes, E.: Software Product Lines in Action: The Best Industrial Practice in Product Line Engineering. Springer (2007)
28. Linsbauer, L., Lopez-Herrejon, R.E., Egyed, A.: Recovering traceability between features and code in product variants. In: International Software Product Line Conference (SPLC), pp. 131–140 (2013)
29. Linsbauer, L., Lopez-Herrejon, R.E., Egyed, A.: Feature model synthesis with genetic programming. In: International Symposium on Search Based Software Engineering (SSBSE), pp. 153–167 (2014)
30. Linsbauer, L., Lopez-Herrejon, R.E., Egyed, A.: Variability extraction and modeling for product variants. Software & Systems Modeling **16**(4), 1179–1199 (2017)
31. Lopez-Herrejon, R.E., Galindo, J.A., Benavides, D., Segura, S., Egyed, A.: Reverse engineering feature models with evolutionary algorithms: An exploratory study. In: International Symposium on Search Based Software Engineering (SSBSE), pp. 168–182 (2012)
32. Lopez-Herrejon, R.E., Linsbauer, L., Egyed, A.: A systematic mapping study of search-based software engineering for software product lines. Journal of Information and Software Technology (2015)
33. Lopez-Herrejon, R.E., Linsbauer, L., Galindo, J.A., Parejo, J.A., Benavides, D., Segura, S., Egyed, A.: An assessment of search-based techniques for reverse engineering feature models. Journal of Systems and Software **103**(0), 353 – 369 (2015)
34. Manning, C.D., Raghavan, P., Schütze, H.: Introduction to information retrieval. Cambridge University Press (2008)
35. Mendonca, M., Branco, M., Cowan, D.: S.p.l.o.t.: Software product lines online tools. In: 24th ACM SIGPLAN Conference Companion on Object Oriented Programming Systems Languages and Applications, OOPSLA '09, p. 761–762. Association for Computing Machinery, New York, NY, USA (2009)
36. Sannier, N., Acher, M., Baudry, B.: From comparison matrix to variability model: The wikipedia case study. In: International Conference on Automated Software Engineering (ASE), pp. 580–585. IEEE (2013)
37. Segura, S., Galindo, J., Benavides, D., Parejo, J.A., Cortés, A.R.: BeTTy: benchmarking and testing on the automated analysis of feature models. In: U.W. Eisenecker, S. Apel, S. Gnesi (eds.) International Workshop on Variability Modelling of Software-Intensive Systems (VaMoS), pp. 63–71. ACM (2012)
38. She, S., Lotufo, R., Berger, T., Wasowski, A., Czarnecki, K.: Reverse engineering feature models. In: International Conference on Software Engineering (ICSE), pp. 461–470. ACM (2011)
39. She, S., Ryssel, U., Andersen, N., Wasowski, A., Czarnecki, K.: Efficient synthesis of feature models. Information and Software Technology **56**(9), 1122–1143 (2014)
40. Thianniwet, T., Cohen, M.: SPLRevO: Optimizing complex feature models in search based reverse engineering of software product lines. In: North American Search Based Software Engineering Symposium (NasBASE) (2015)
41. Thianniwet, T., Cohen, M.B.: Scaling up the fitness function for reverse engineering feature models. In: F. Sarro, K. Deb (eds.) Search Based Software Engineering, pp. 128–142. Springer International Publishing, Cham (2016)
42. Vargha, A., Delaney, H.: A critique and improvement of the CL common language effect size statistics of McGraw and Wong. Journal of Educational and Behavioral Statistics **25**(2), 101–132 (2000)
43. Vescan, A., Pintea, A., Linsbauer, L., Egyed, A.: Genetic programming for feature model synthesis: a replication study. Empirical Software Engineering **26**(4) (2021)
44. Weston, N., Chitchyan, R., Rashid, A.: A framework for constructing semantically composable feature models from natural language requirements. In: International Software Product Line Conference (SPLC), pp. 211–220 (2009)

45. Yao, X.: Some Recent Work on Multi-objective Approaches to Search-Based Software Engineering, pp. 4–15. Springer Berlin Heidelberg, Berlin, Heidelberg (2013)
46. Zitzler, E., Laumanns, M., Thiele, L.: SPEA2: Improving the Strength Pareto Evolutionary Algorithm. Tech. Rep. 103, Swiss Federal Institute of Technology (ETH) Zurich, Gloriastrasse 35, CH-8092 Zurich, Switzerland (2001)
47. Zitzler, E., Thiele, L., Laumanns, M., Fonseca, C.M., da Fonseca, V.G.: Performance assessment of multiobjective optimizers: An analysis and review. IEEE Transactions on Evolutionary Computation 7, 117–132 (2003)

Chapter 6
Extending Boolean Variability Relationship Extraction to Multi-valued Software Descriptions

Jessie Galasso and Marianne Huchard

Abstract Extracting variability information from software product descriptions is crucial when reverse engineering a software product line, e.g., for variability model synthesis. Existing methods are predominantly designed for feature-oriented product lines, where products are described by the set of distinguishable features they implement, and variability information may be expressed by logical relationships over these features. However, limits of such boolean feature-based variability modeling approaches have been highlighted, notably regarding their expressive power. In this chapter, we take a step towards more complex variability extraction and focus on extracting non-boolean variability relationships from multi-valued software descriptions. We first analyze software descriptions, variability relationships and extraction methods used in the boolean case. We attract attention to a knowledge engineering framework supporting a sound and complete feature-based variability relationship extraction method. The benefits of this framework include several extensions enabling to take into account more complex datasets than boolean ones. We explore one of these extensions to extend the traditional boolean extraction method and handle variability relationships including both boolean features and attribute values that can be used to synthesize extended variability models.

6.1 Introduction

Reducing the development time and cost of a software portfolio while increasing its overall quality and scope may be achieved through systematic reuse and mass-customization; it is the core of the Software Product Line Engineering (SPLE) approach [48]. SPLE is a development paradigm based on a set of reusable

J. Galasso (✉)
Université de Montréal, Montreal, QC, Canada
e-mail: jessie.galasso-carbonnel@umontreal.ca

M. Huchard
LIRMM, University of Montpellier, CNRS, Montpellier, France
e-mail: marianne.huchard@lirmm.fr

© Springer Nature Switzerland AG 2023
R. E. Lopez-Herrejon et al. (eds.), *Handbook of Re-Engineering Software Intensive Systems into Software Product Lines*, https://doi.org/10.1007/978-3-031-11686-5_6

software artifacts and a common architecture with which the artifacts may be combined: different combinations lead to different software products that share similarities. Altogether, the common architecture, the reusable artifacts and the derivable products form a software product line (SPL). A central task of SPLE is to document the SPL *variability*, i.e., documenting the accepted artifact combinations and thus the derivable software products. This task produces *variability models* which are crucial for the understanding, implementation, management, maintenance and evolution of the SPL. Variability models can operate at several levels of abstraction but most commonly group artifacts under distinguishable software characteristics or behaviours called *features*. Feature-oriented product line engineering [4, 34] is a widely adopted approach for SPL implementation, where feature diagrams (FDs) [33] are the most commonly studied variability models. FDs are a family of description languages that enable to express constraints (also called *variability relationships*) over a set of features and thus delimit the scope of an SPL. In other words, FDs describe derivable software intensive systems through boolean descriptions being accepted combinations of features. However, limitations regarding the expressiveness of these "boolean" FDs have been encountered, and FD extensions were proposed to overstep them, e.g., to represent feature cardinalities [16], group cardinalities [16, 50], or multi-valued attributes [7, 16]. Aside from these extended FDs, other types of variability models try to tackle the problem of representing more detailed variability information, such as orthogonal variability models [48] or the common variability language [31].

Proactive adoption of an SPL [37] instructs to first determine its scope (i.e., establishing which artifacts will be needed and which combinations should be allowed through variability models), then implement the architecture and the artifacts, and finally begin to derive software products. However, this adoption process takes time before being able to propose working products to customers, that is why a large part of companies working with SPLE prefer to adopt an extractive approach [11]. Extractive SPL adoption [37] is about capitalizing on similar software products already developed to fasten the definition of the common software architecture, the set of reusable artifacts and the variability models through reverse engineering methods. A detailed overview of current research in SPL reverse engineering can be found in [6] in the form of a mapping study. An abundant literature addresses automated or semi-automated extraction of variability relationships between features from (boolean) software intensive-system descriptions, mostly to synthesize boolean FDs [2, 3, 20, 21, 29, 30, 38, 41, 45, 51]. Variability extraction that goes beyond boolean feature relationships is addressed by few authors: Becan et al. consider boolean features and multi-valued attributes [9], and Carbonnel et al. consider boolean features, UML-like cardinalities and multi-valued attributes [15].

In this chapter, we present a method to extract variability relationships involving more than boolean features from product descriptions. More specifically, we focus on the types of relationships to be extracted to synthesize the three prevalent FD extensions that were proposed to enhance their expressiveness. We study product descriptions that take the form of multi-valued matrices containing both boolean and non-boolean characteristics. The proposed method leverages existing boolean variability relationships extraction methods based on Formal Concept Analysis (FCA) [25], a framework for knowledge engineering and knowledge representation. Even though the value of FCA may be difficult to apprehend at first, it is one-of-a-kind in the variability reverse engineering landscape; FCA offers a structural, reusable and extensible framework which formalizes variability extraction and representation, and thus includes most of the existing variability extraction approaches found in the literature. In the following, we first present a boolean variability extraction method based on FCA (Sect. 6.2), and then a way to extend this framework to handle multi-valued variability extraction (Sect. 6.3). In each section, we present the input product descriptions, the variability relationships to be extracted, the reverse engineering approaches found in the literature, and a sound and complete FCA-based extraction method (i.e., all variability relationships that are true for the considered set of input product descriptions are extracted, and all extracted relationships are true). We do not address the problem of synthesizing variability models such as FDs extended with attributes or cardinalities; we focus on extracting variability information independently from any representation, but that can be used to build different kinds of variability models. The soundness and completeness of the extraction method provide strong foundations for the synthesis of variability models which are consistent with the input descriptions, but do not guarantee the legibility and/or maintainability of the produced models as these quality attributes depend on the synthesis method. We conclude in Sect. 6.4 by summarizing the approach and drawing a few perspectives.

6.2 Variability in Boolean Descriptions

Descriptions composed of boolean feature sets have been extensively studied from the very first research works on product line engineering [33]. In this section, we focus on the variability relationships which can be extracted from this type of descriptions, and how. Feature-based boolean descriptions are discussed in Sect. 6.2.1, where we introduce an illustrative example derived from the robot battle programming game Robocode[1] [43]. Section 6.2.2 reviews the main variability relationships between features that have been studied in the literature, and Sect. 6.2.3 reports the main approaches for feature relationship extraction. The key principles and benefits of an extraction process involving Formal Concept Analysis are exposed in Sect. 6.2.4.

---

[1] https://robocode.sourceforge.io/.

6.2.1 Boolean Feature-Based Descriptions

In SPLE, a *feature* corresponds to a high level product's part or behavior which is relevant to any stakeholder [4]. Features are intended to be easily understandable contrary to artifacts of lower level that only experts may comprehend. They represent noticeable characteristics which help distinguish similar products from one another; a feature is associated to a unique name and may be implemented by various (concrete) artifacts. Let us consider an example about Robocode, a programming game where developers have to implement the behaviour of their own bots (i.e., the products to be described) in order to fight bots implemented by other developers. Examples of features characterizing a bot may be its strategies of movement on the battlefield (e.g. random movement, minimum risk movement, stop&go, wave surfing), the kinds of fights it is designed for (one-on-one fighting or melee fighting), if it takes part to some community events (such as the roborumble competition), or the software license of the code source (open source or closed license). Let us note that all features may not be at the same level of abstraction: for instance, the feature license is more abstract (or generalised) than the feature open source.

In a feature-oriented approach [34], a product is designated by the set of features it possesses. Such a set of features is called a product *configuration* and may be considered an abstract, high level description of the product. For example, {one-on-one fighting, melee fighting, roborumble} is a configuration. However, some configurations may not be admitted, for instance, if the artifacts implementing the features are not compatible regarding some domain or business constraints. For instance, a product cannot have both an open source and a closed license. Accepted combinations of features may be delineated through constraints defining a set of valid configurations, also called the product line scope. Constraints over a finite set of features restricting the way they can be combined are called variability relationships and express what is called the *variability* of the product line, which is traditionally documented through variability models.

6.2.2 Boolean Variability Relationships

Feature Relationships If one maps features to propositional variables in propositional logic [42], then any propositional formula may be used to express variability relationships in the form of constraints between features (also called feature dependencies or feature relationships). However, for a product designer, a simplified dependency language is more suitable to highlight the principal feature relationships. Hence, four kinds of feature relationships gathered most of the attention of practitioners. These relationships express situations where: ① a feature requires another feature, ② two features are mutually exclusive, ③ a feature should be

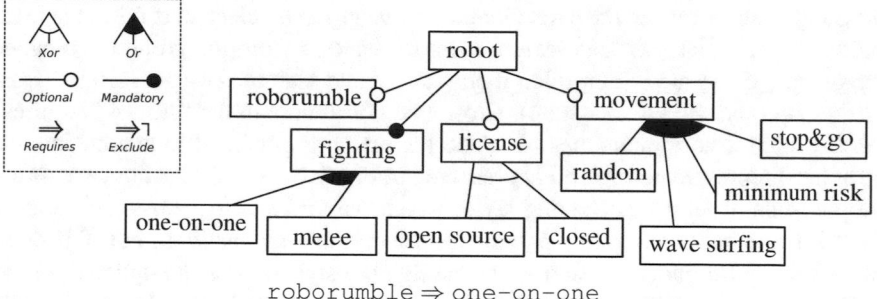

$$roborumble \Rightarrow one\text{-}on\text{-}one$$

Fig. 6.1 Excerpt of a possible FD depicting the variability of Robocode bots

refined by selecting at least one feature in a group and ④ a feature should be refined by selecting exactly one feature in a group. For example, to document Robocode variability, one may want to define feature relationships stating that: a bot participating in the `roborumble` competition requires to be designed for `one-on-one fighting`; a `random movement` strategy is not appropriate for `melee fighting`; the implemented movement strategies should be specified amongst the feature group {`random, wave surfing, stop&go, minimum risk`} (at least one but possibly more); the source code `license` should be specified amongst the group {`open-source, closed`} (exactly one). These four kinds of relationships may be expressed by propositional formulas using respectively: binary implications for "requires" relationships (`roborumble` ⇒ `one-on-one fighting`), binary implications with negations for "exclude" relationships (`random movement` ⇒ ¬ `melee fighting`), equivalences with or-connectives for "at least one" feature refinement (`movement` ⟺ (`random` ∨ `wave surfing` ∨ `stop&go` ∨ `minimum risk`)) and equivalences with xor-connectives for "exactly one" feature refinement (`license` ⟺ (`open-source` ⊕ `closed`)). Those are thus the basic feature relationships usually expressed in boolean variability models.

Feature Diagram The *de facto* standard for representing a product line variability in a diagram-like representation is a type of variability model called *feature diagram* (FD) [33, 57]. Figure 6.1 presents an example of FD representing a possible view of the variability of Robocode bots.

The box-shaped nodes represent the features. They are structured in a tree representing child-parent (or refinement) relationships. The edges of the tree must be decorated to express some constraints (amongst the four depicted in the top part of the box in the left-hand side of Fig. 6.1) restricting the way the features may be selected when choosing a valid configuration. A white disc states that the child-feature may be optionally selected when the parent-feature is present in the configuration, and a black disc forces the child-feature to be selected. Arcs are used to group features; when the parent feature of the group is selected: if the arc is filled with black then at least one feature must be selected from the group (also called or-group); if the arc is non-filled then exactly one feature must be selected from the group (also called xor-group). Cross-tree constraints in the form of "requires" and "exclude" constraints may be added (textually or graphically) to complete the graphical representation. The FD presented in Fig. 6.1 states that: a bot necessarily implements at least one fighting style, which may be `melee`, `one-on-one` or both. It can optionally participate to the roborumble competition, but if it does, then it should implement the one-on-one fighting style. A bot can optionally have a license which is either open source or closed, but not both. Finally, it optionally implements at least one movement strategy amongst four possible strategies.

Link with Propositional Logic The relationships expressed in feature diagrams may be mapped to the four basic feature relationships discussed at the beginning of the section, and therefore to their representations in propositional logic [10, 20, 42]. Straightforwardly, mutually exclusive features (situation ②) are expressed through "exclude" cross-tree constraints, and feature group refinement (situations ③ and ④) are expressed through or- and xor-groups, respectively. Child-parent relationships implicitly express "require" relationships (situation ①); for instance, if one wants to select `open source` (which is a *kind-of* license) in a configuration, he or she needs to select the feature `license` beforehand, thus `open source` $\Rightarrow$ `license`. Note that such "require" relationships may also be expressed through cross-tree constraints (such as `roborumble` $\Rightarrow$ `one-on-one`) and mandatory relationships (all bots have a fighting style, thus `robot` $\Rightarrow$ `fighting`). The first two columns of Table 6.2 depict this mapping: the first column shows the feature relationships in their propositional form with a particular case of situation ① when there are symmetric binary implications (i.e., logical equivalences) denoted by ①', and the second column shows the FD syntax of the corresponding variability relationships. Third and fourth columns will be addressed later in the section. We can see that: a binary implication (①) may correspond to a child-parent relationship, an optional relationship or a "require" cross-tree constraint; an equivalence (①') may correspond to a mandatory relationship (because it is the combination of two binary implications: one comes from the child-parent relationship and the other comes the mandatory constraint) or may correspond to two symmetric "require" cross-tree constraints; mutual exclusions (②) and groups (③ and ④) have only one representation in the feature diagram syntax.

Semantics The conjunction of the "propositional logic forms" of feature relation-ships depicted in an FD outlines a propositional formula (called the FD's *logical semantics*). The formula's models correspond to the FDs' set of valid configurations (called its *configuration semantics*). Another semantics, called the *ontological semantics*, is given by the tree structure of the diagram that conveys meanings to the modeled domain. For instance, a situation where a feature f_1 requires another feature f_2 (logically represented by $f_1 \Rightarrow f_2$) may be represented in an FD by different relationships having different meanings, e.g., through the feature hierarchy

(f_2 refines f_1), a mandatory relationship (f_2 is a necessary refinement of f_1), or through a cross-tree constraint (f_1 necessitates f_2 but does not generalize nor specialize it).

Other Boolean Variability Models In some cases, when one needs to express more complex feature relationships, the expressiveness of FD graphical syntax is not sufficient. A *feature model* is a *feature diagram* supplemented by a complex propositional logic formula capturing the constraints which cannot be expressed by an FD [57]. In this context, a "complex" propositional formula is a formula which cannot be written as a conjunction of "require" and "exclude" cross-tree constraints; if it is the case, then it is considered an FD (as the one of Fig. 6.1). Other formalisms have been introduced. Binary Implication Graphs (BIG), as their name suggests, graphically represent binary implications [1, 2, 20, 21, 56, 57]. Directed hypergraphs have been presented in [20]. In this representation, each binary implication is represented by a directed binary edge, while other constraints (feature groups and mutex) are represented by hyperedges. Mutex graphs [56, 57] only show pairwise incompatibilities between features. Feature Diagram Generalized Notation and Feature Graphs [20] represent binary implications and groups, while relaxing the tree-structure constraint of traditional FDs. She et al. [57] add mutex to these representations. Equivalence Class Feature Diagrams (ECFD) have been proposed in [14] as a canonical structure for variability representation. They represent binary implications, groups, mutex as the other structures, but may also highlight generalized exclusions (i.e., groups of features that never appear together).

6.2.3 Feature Relationship Extraction in the Literature

Becan et al. empirically show that variability model extraction approaches based on (1) logical heuristics extracting the logical semantics combined with (2) ontological heuristics relying on user or expert decisions for associating meaningful knowledge to the extracted logical relationships outperform other approaches [8]. In fact, the first one guarantees correct configuration and logical semantics, while the second one guarantees a correct ontological semantics. In this chapter, we mainly focus on the first step of this type of variability model synthesis, i.e., the extraction of variability information (feature relationships) in the form of logical relationships. A sound and complete feature relationship extraction method is crucial to ensure correct foundations for meaningful variability model synthesis.

In the literature, feature relationships extraction has been studied from various perspectives. As feature diagrams may not represent all configuration sets, most authors synthesize feature models. Several dedicated algorithms to build a feature model from a set of valid configurations can be found. She et. al [57] propose a sound and complete feature relationship extraction by enhancing the method defined by Czarnecki and Wasowski [20] which originally did not extract mutually exclusive features; these methods rely on binary decision diagrams to extract interim variability representations in the form of binary implication graph and mutex graph. Acher et al. [2] also present a dedicated algorithm for a sound and complete extraction using binary implication graphs. Haslinger et al. [29, 30] propose a recursive algorithm to build feature models without extracting feature relationships beforehand; the soundness and completeness of the extraction method is not assessed. Davril et al. [21] extract relevant features from informal documents to produce a configuration-by-feature matrix, and all valid implications. They use text-mining techniques and feature co-occurrences to identify meaningful implications. The feature group extraction is sound but not complete, and these properties are not assessed for the other feature relationships. Ferrari et al. [23] analyze product descriptions in the form of commercial texts to propose candidate optional and mandatory features to an expert. Search-based techniques are applied in several works. The authors in [38] and [41] explore these techniques and build FMs whose configuration semantics approximate a given configuration set. Assunção et al. [5] propose to use 2 multi-objective evolutionary algorithms for reverse engineering feature models. The multi-objective perspective allows the expert to tune the reverse engineering process depending on the objectives (e.g., correct configuration semantics, legibility) they identified as important in a given context. They take into account knowledge from existing variants' source code (in the form of a weighted directed graph representing source code dependencies) to ensure that the output models' configurations correspond to well formed software variants with regard to their source code. Czarnecki et al. propose an algorithm based on data-mining techniques to build Probabilistic Feature Models in [19]. These extraction methods are not deterministic. In [58], Temple et al. elaborate a technique to build a variability model that can be configured for different contexts, using classification trees [40] and constraint solving. Other approaches use the conceptual structures built by Formal Concept Analysis (FCA), a mathematical knowledge engineering framework, to benefit from their ability to encode variability in a systematic and canonical way [3, 14, 39, 51]. FCA framework supports a sound and complete extraction of the four prevalent feature relationships, and stands out among the other proposed methods in the literature. In fact, it is not a method specifically designed for variability extraction, but rather an identification of variability information naturally embedded in a unique and canonical structure whose construction relies on mathematical properties applied on the input software descriptions. FCA encompasses most of the aforementioned extraction methods, as well as their interim variability representations (e.g., binary implication graphs, mutex graphs, FDs) used for variability analysis, as the constructed structures contain the essence of variability [14]. The elements composing these structures express, as pointed out by Uta Priss, *"a natural feature of information representation which is as fundamental to hierarchies and object/attribute structures as set theory or relational algebra are for relational databases"* [49]. This explains the spreading of Formal Concept Analysis in knowledge engineering [47] or even software reverse engineering [59]. In what follows, we detail a sound and complete variability relationship extraction in the form of logical relationships based on the FCA framework and its associated conceptual structures.

6.2.4   A Sound and Complete FCA-Based Feature Relationships Extraction

Formal Concept Analysis (FCA) [25] is a knowledge engineering framework for data structuring and knowledge representation. FCA enables the elaboration of concept hierarchies, where concepts group a maximal set of objects (or entities, documents) sharing a maximal set of attributes (or properties, descriptors). Applying this framework on a set of objects described by a set of attributes enables to build data structures organizing objects depending on the attributes they share.

Input FCA input is a *formal context* $K = (O, A, J)$ with O a set of objects, A a set of attributes and $J \subseteq O \times A$ a binary relationship, where $(o, a) \in J$ when "o owns a". A formal context may be represented by a binary table where a cross in a cell represents attribute (feature) ownership for an object (product). Table 6.3 shows a formal context with 7 existing Robocode bots (objects as rows) described by 11 features (attributes as columns) taken from the RoboWiki.[2] It states for instance that the bot named `Aristocles` owns the `one-on-one fighting` feature, but not the `melee fighting` one. Formal contexts may conveniently represent configuration sets in an extensional way (e.g., the bot `Centaur` corresponds to the configuration {`melee fighting, one-on-one fighting, roborumble`}).

Step 1—Building Concepts A concept $C = (E, I)$ associates a maximal group of objects E, with a maximal group of attributes I they share. $E = \{o \in O \mid \forall a \in I, (o, a) \in J\}$ is the concept's extent and $I = \{a \in A \mid \forall o \in E, (o, a) \in J\}$ is the concept's intent. For example, the concept gathering "all bots having open source license" is $C_{os} = (E_{os}, I_{os})$ with $I_{os} = \{$`one-on-one fighting, license, open-source, movement`$\}$ and $E_{os} = \{$`Aristocles, Coriantumr, Decado, DrussGT`$\}$. There is no other bot than the ones in E_{os} that share all attributes of I_{os}, and there is no other attribute than the ones in I_{os} shared by all bots of E_{os}.

Step 2—Ordering Concepts The specialization order $\leq_{CL}$ between concepts is based on extent inclusion (and intent containment): for two concepts $C_1 = (E_1, I_1)$ and $C_2 = (E_2, I_2)$, $C_1 \leq_{CL} C_2$ if and only if $E_1 \subseteq E_2$ (and equivalently $I_1 \supseteq I_2$). For example, C_{os} is a super-concept of concept $C_{rand} = (E_{rand}, I_{rand})$, with $I_{rand} = \{$`one-on-one fighting, license, open-source, movement, random movement`$\}$ and $E_{rand} = \{$`Aristocles, Decado`$\}$, which is the concept gathering all bots implementing the random movement strategy. Indeed, $E_{rand} \subseteq E_{os}$ and $I_{os} \subseteq I_{rand}$. This order enables to organize concepts in a specialization/generalization fashion.

---

[2] http://robowiki.net/, last access July 2019.

Output Conceptual Structures The *concept lattice* is the set of all the concepts C_K of the formal context K, provided with the order $\leq_{CL}$. In some applications, it is not necessary to study all the concepts that can be extracted: some of them may be more valuable than others regarding the analysis to be applied. This is the case when investigating the variability information naturally embedded in concept lattices. To analyze variability information highlighted by means of FCA, it is enough to work with an output conceptual structure restricted to two types of concepts, namely *attribute-concepts* and *object-concepts*. An attribute-concept is the concept gathering all objects having a given attribute: we say that this attribute is introduced in this concept. For instance, the concept C_{os} is the attribute-concept introducing the attribute open source. An *object-concept* is the concept gathering the exact attribute set of a given object (i.e., its associated configuration): we say that this object is introduced in this concept. The concept $C_{cent} = (E_{cent}, I_{cent})$ with $E_{cent} = $ {Centaur, Coriantumur, Durandal} and $I_{cent} = $ {melee fighting, one-on-one fighting, roborumble} (corresponding to the configuration of Centaur) is the object-concept introducing Centaur. The AOC-poset (for *Attribute-Object Concept partially ordered set*) is the concept lattice restricted to these specific concepts. Using AOC-posets instead of concept lattices brings a considerable improvement in terms of scalability. In fact, given $|O|$ and $|A|$ the numbers of objects and attributes, respectively, a concept lattice may have at most $2^{(min(|O|,|A|))}$ concepts, whereas the AOC-poset is bounded by $|O| + |A|$, thus avoiding an eventual exponential growth of the output conceptual structures. A graphical representation of the AOC-poset associated with the formal context of Table 6.1 is shown in Fig. 6.2; it is built with the tool RCAExplore [22]. Note that for a given formal context, there exists only one concept lattice and only one AOC-poset (i.e., they are canonical structures).

Note that, if the products and/or features are numerous, the associated AOC-poset will likely be very wide, the extracted relationships too numerous, and the resulting model difficult to read. Experiments assessing the size of conceptual structures and the number of extracted relationships [14, 15] show that the method scales even with large inputs and outputs. However, the aforementioned issue is not inherent to FCA-based relationship extraction, but is related to the necessity to use separation of concerns to avoid synthesizing huge monolithic variability models. Relational Concept Analysis [27], another FCA extension that is not discussed here, provides solutions to extract variability relationships between several configuration sets, that can be obtained, for instance, by splitting a large configuration set depending on concerns. In this way, it may support the synthesis of several smaller interconnected variability models that enhance the legibility of represented variability information.

Reading the AOC-poset In this graph-like representation, a concept is a 3-part box showing: the concept identifier (top-part), the concept intent (middle-part displaying attributes), and the concept extent (bottom-part displaying objects). The specialization order is represented by arrows between concepts: an arrow from a concept A (sub-concept) to a concept B (super-concept) states that "concept A specializes concept B". Organizing concepts by specialization/generalization

Table 6.1 Formal context about 7 Robocode bots gathered from RoboWiki (2019)

Robocode	Melee fighting	One-on-one fighting	License	Closed	Open-source	Movement	Min-risk-movement	Random-movement	Stop-and-go	Wave-surfing	Roborumble
Aristocles	×	×	×		×	×		×			×
B26354	×	×	×	×		×	×			×	
Centaur	×	×									×
Coriantumr	×	×	×		×	×	×				×
Decado		×	×		×	×		×	×		
DrussGT	×	×	×		×	×				×	×
Durandal	×	×	×	×		×				×	×

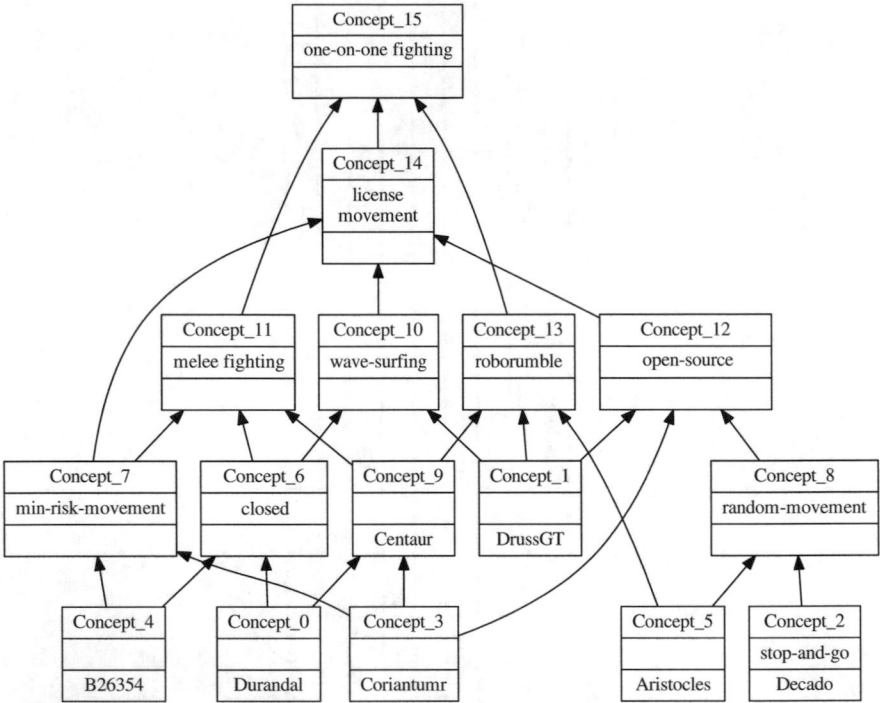

Fig. 6.2 AOC-poset associated with the formal context of Table 6.1

allows to represent factorized concepts' intents and extents by displaying only the introduced elements: full intents and extents may be reconstituted by inheritance, from top to bottom for attributes (a concept possesses all attributes of its super-concepts) and from bottom to top for objects (a concept possesses all objects of its sub-concepts). In Fig. 6.2, the attribute-concept C_{os} introducing open source corresponds to $Concept\_12$: attributes one-on-one fighting, license and movement are introduced in its super-concepts, and all objects of its extent are introduced in its sub-concepts. C_{rand} corresponds to $Concept\_8$ and C_{cent} to $Concept\_9$.

Extracting Feature Relationships By organizing objects depending on their attributes, conceptual structures naturally highlight the common and variable features amongst a set of configurations. By analyzing the structure, one can detect patterns corresponding to the feature relationships that hold in the input configuration set. Table 6.2 (columns 3 and 4) shows how the four prevalent feature relationships appear in the AOC-posets. We detail them in what follows, and we consider that f_i, $i \in \{0, 1, \ldots, n\}$ denotes a feature and C_{f_i} the attribute-concept introducing f_i.

Table 6.2 Mapping between the representations of the four prevalent feature relationships: propositional formulas (Prop. form.), feature diagrams (FD syntax) and AOC-posets adapted from [14]. The extent of a context C is denoted by $Ext(C)$

Prop. form.	FD syntax	AOC-posets
① $f_2 \Rightarrow f_1$	f_1 f_2 f_1 f_2 $f_2 \Rightarrow f_1$	$C_{f_2} \leq_{CL} C_{f_1}$
①' $f_1 \Leftrightarrow f_2$	f_1 f_2 f_2 or f_1 $f_1 \Rightarrow f_2;$ $f_2 \Rightarrow f_1$	$C_{f_1} =_{CL} C_{f_2}$
② $f_1 \Rightarrow \neg f_2$ or $f_2 \Rightarrow \neg f_1$	$f_1 \Rightarrow \neg f_2$	$Ext(C_{f_1}) \cap Ext(C_{f_2}) = \varnothing$
③ $f_0 \Leftrightarrow$ $(f_1 \vee ... \vee f_k)$	f_0 f_1 $..$ f_k	$\forall f_i \in \{f_1,..f_k\}, C_{f_i} \leq_{CL} C_{f_0}.$ $Ext(C_{f_1}) \cup ... \cup Ext(C_{f_k}) = Ext(C_{f_0}).$ $C_{f_0} \notin O^{C}$
④ $f_0 \Leftrightarrow$ $(f_1 \oplus ... \oplus f_k)$	f_0 f_1 $..$ f_k	$\forall f_i \in \{f_1,..f_k\}, C_{f_i} \leq_{CL} C_{f_0}.$ $Ext(C_{f_1}) \cup ... \cup Ext(C_{f_k}) = Ext(C_{f_0}).$ $C_{f_0} \notin O^{C}$ $Ext(C_{f_1}) \cap ... \cap Ext(C_{f_k}) = \varnothing.$

Situation ① (binary implications representing features that "require" other features) can be extracted from the AOC-poset by analyzing the specialization order between attribute-concepts. In fact, if an attribute-concept C_{f_2} is a subconcept of another attribute-concept C_{f_1} (denoted by $C_{f_2} \leq_{CL} C_{f_1}$), then the set of configurations having f_2 is included in the set of configurations having f_1 (because $E_{f_2} \subseteq E_{f_1}$). Thus, all configurations having f_2 also have f_1 and ($f_2 \Rightarrow f_1$) holds. In Fig. 6.2, we can see for instance that min-risk-movement $\Rightarrow$ melee fighting (because $Concept\_7 \leq_{CL} Concept\_11$) and closed $\Rightarrow$ license (because $Concept\_6 \leq_{CL} Concept\_14$). When such a pattern is detected in an AOC-poset built upon a configuration set, then we have candidates for refinement, optional or "require" cross-tree constraints during the synthesis of an FD. Deciding whether the minimum risk movement feature *requires* the fighting melee feature or *refines* it is left to the expert or to further processes relying on domain ontology. Situation ①' is a special case of situation ① where two features require each other. Because there is a double binary implication, then $C_{f_2} \leq_{CL} C_{f_1}$ and $C_{f_1} \leq_{CL} C_{f_2}$, meaning that C_{f_1} and C_{f_2} are the same concept ($C_{f_2} =_{CL} C_{f_1}$). Therefore, if two features are introduced in the same concept, then they are always present together in any configuration (co-occurring features) and ($f_1 \Leftrightarrow f_2$) holds. In Fig. 6.2, we observe that license $\Leftrightarrow$ movement because they are both introduced in *Concept*_14, meaning that if a bot defines movement strategies, it also specifies a license, and conversely.

Situation ② (mutually exclusive features) is revealed in the AOC-poset by analyzing the intersection of the extents of two attribute-concepts. If the intersection of C_{f_1} extent and C_{f_2} extent is empty (denoted by $Ext(C_{f_1}) \cap Ext(C_{f_2}) = \varnothing$), then it means that the configurations having f_1 and the configurations having f_2 are disjoint. In other words, f_1 and f_2 never appear together in any configuration and ($f_1 \Rightarrow \neg f_2$) holds. In Fig. 6.2, we can see that wave-surfing $\Rightarrow \neg$ random-movement (because $Ext(Concept\_10) \cap Ext(Concept\_8) = \varnothing$).

Situation ③ ("at least one" feature group refinement, also called or-groups) is more complex to identify. Let $\{f_1, \dots, f_k\}$ be the features involved in an or-group, and f_0 the parent-feature of this group. A first property characterizing or-groups is that each configuration having one feature in $\{f_1, \dots, f_k\}$ should also have f_0. Thus, in the AOC-poset, the concepts $\{C_{f_1}, \dots, C_{f_k}\}$ must be sub-concepts of C_{f_0}. A second or-group property is that each configuration possessing the parent-feature f_0 must also have at least one feature of the or-group. This can be seen in the AOC-poset when the union of the extents of concepts $\{C_{f_1}, \dots, C_{f_k}\}$ is equal to the extent of C_{f_0}. A "true" or-group would respect a third property, stating that all $\{f_1, \dots, f_k\}$ combinations appear amongst the objects (configurations) in the AOC-poset. However, as we consider possibly incomplete configuration sets as input, having product descriptions documenting all possible combinations is very unlikely. Thus, we relax this third constraint and look for patterns corresponding to the two first or-group properties in the AOC-poset. In other words, we look for an attribute-concept and a set of its sub-concepts such that a) the latter are also attribute-concepts and b) the union of their extents is equal to the extent of the first attribute-concept. For example, let us consider in Fig. 6.2 *Concept*_7 (min-risk-movement), *Concept*_8 (random-movement) and *Concept*_10 (wave-surfing): the union of their extents is the configuration set corresponding to the set of bots having identified movement strategies (all bots except Centaur). They form a candidate or-group with parent movement introduced in their super-concept *Concept*_14. Thus, (movement $\Leftrightarrow$ (min-risk-movement $\vee$ wave-surfing $\vee$ random-movement)) holds. Notice that the candidate does not contain the feature stop-and-go (*Concept*_2) but that it could be integrated in the group; the feature could also refine random-movement due to a complementary constraint establishing that stop-and-go implies random-movement. Notice also that *Concept*_12 (open source) may replace *Concept*_7 and satisfy the or-group properties: (movement $\Leftrightarrow$ (min-riskmovement $\vee$ wave-surfing $\vee$ open source)) holds too. The candidates or-groups may be numerous and need an ontological evaluation in order to detect the meaningful ones. Other constraints may be added

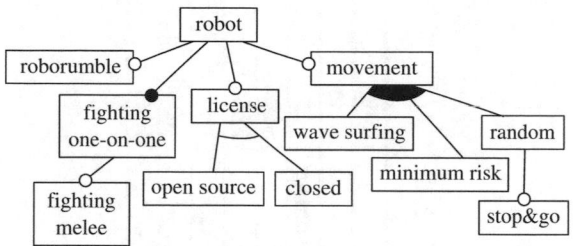

random ⇒ open source ; minimum risk ⇒ fighting melee
closed ⇒ wave surfing ; closed ⇒ melee ; license ⇔ movement
random ⇒ ¬ fighting melee ; random ⇒ ¬ wave surfing ; minimum risk ⇒ ¬ random

Fig. 6.3 Example of FD synthesized from the AOC-poset built upon Robocode configurations of Table 6.3

to help select the best candidates, e.g., set of candidates that do not overlap, minimal groups.

Situation ④ ("exactly one" feature group refinement, also called xor-group) is a particular sub-case of the situation ③ where all pairs of features of $\{f_1, \ldots, f_k\}$ are mutually exclusive. In addition to the two aforementioned or-group properties, concepts $\{C_{f_1}, \ldots, C_{f_k}\}$ must have disjoint extents. In Fig. 6.2, *Concept_14* (license) with its sub-concepts *Concept_6* (closed) and *Concept_12* (open source) form a xor-group candidate: (license ⇔ (closed ⊕ open source)) holds.

By analyzing concepts and how they are situated to each other, we can identify variability information that can be represented by propositional formulas over the set of features. Lattice theory guarantees that all detected relationships are true in the considered input, and that all true relationships can be read in FCA conceptual structures [25]. This enables the sound and complete extraction of all prevalent feature relationships from a configuration set; variability model synthesis methods using these relationships can thus guarantee a logical semantics and a configuration semantics consistent with the input descriptions.

Feature Diagram Synthesis Thanks to the mapping established in Table 6.2, it is possible to guide an expert during a feature diagram synthesis, a task that can be seen as choosing an FD syntax for each feature relationship identified in the AOC-poset. Figure 6.3 presents an example of FD that can be extracted from the configurations gathered in Table 6.3 by building and analyzing the associated AOC-poset. It differs from the one exposed in Fig. 6.1 because it is based on existing configurations and ontological choices corresponding to feature relationship patterns identified in the AOC-poset. For instance, Table 6.3 does not contain any fighting feature stating if the bot has at least one identified fighting styles, but it does contain two more specific fighting styles: thus, fighting one-on-one and fighting melee are not grouped in Fig. 6.3. Moreover, in the studied set of Robocode configurations, all bots are defined for one-on-one fighting style: the corresponding feature may be

Table 6.3 PCM about the 7 previous robots of Robocode Wiki (2018) with their roborumble PWIN. Some boolean attributes (features) about movement strategy were transformed into one multi-valued attribute having symbolic values

Robocode	One-on-one fighting	Melee fighting	Roborumble	License	Open-source	Closed	Movement	PWIN
Aristocles	×		×	×	×		Random	86.47
B26354	×	×		×		×	Minimum risk, wave surfing	*
Centaur	×	×	×				*	80.00
Coriantumr	×	×	×	×	×		Minimum risk	77.24
Decado	×			×	×		Random, stop & go	*
DrussGT	×		×	×	×		Wave surfing	100.00
Durandal	×	×	×	×		×	Wave surfing	79.48

identified as mandatory in this case. Also, as feature stop&go implies random, we decided to put it as an optional feature of random, but we could have chosen to add stop&go in the or-group and to add a "require" cross-tree constraint. Some extracted constraints may be seen as "accidental", i.e., true for the considered set of configurations but not for the domain. For instance, the constraint closed $\Rightarrow$ wave surfing, stating that if the bot's source code is proprietary, then it must implement the wave surfing movement strategy, is likely to be coincidental. Note that, because FD syntax cannot represent all configuration sets, the configuration semantics of this FD is not exactly the same as the one presented in the input Table 6.1. However, as the extraction of the FD logical relationships is sound and complete, the configuration semantics of the resulting model is as close as possible as the input configuration set. If the domain expert building the FD from the extracted logical relationships considers that some of them should not appear in the graphical part of the model (e.g., for pertinence or legibility concerns), they can be kept as complex cross-tree constraints to preserve a consistent configuration semantics.

Other Variability Information Contained in AOC-posets AOC-posets and more generally conceptual structures highlight different types of information which are useful regarding variability management in general. If we look at the intent of each concept (i.e., the middle part), these sub-sets of features actually represent either a valid configuration (if the concept is an object-concept) or a partial configuration, i.e., a sub-set of features shared by several valid configurations. This information may be useful for feeding decision processes, e.g., to guide a user when choosing a product configuration, or to imagine new possible configurations which can be easy to build from existing artifacts. Also, if we analyze the place of the concepts in the structure, it may give information on the usage and distribution of features in the configuration set. For instance, if a feature is introduced in a concept in the top of the structure, then it is more likely to be inherited by numerous concepts, and therefore to be commonly found in configurations. Conversely, if a feature is introduced in the bottom of the structure, then it will be present in possibly less configurations and could be identified as a specific or unpopular feature. Conceptual structures result from the application of a data analysis framework: their construction is *structural*; they are not built for variability analysis, but by following some mathematical properties that naturally highlight the intrinsic variability of a configuration set. They offer a unique dual view of variability, by organizing both features and configurations in one structure, that makes them a suitable representation to study the variability of existing products developed without any reuse strategy. Besides, FCA conceptual structures are not only interim representations of variability: they come with a framework relying on strong mathematical foundations, a set of management operations and numerous extensions enabling to take into account more complex input than boolean datasets.

6.3 Variability in Non-Boolean Descriptions

In the previous section, we focused on variability relationships in the form of constraints over a set of features, and how to extract them from boolean descriptions. However, representing product line variability through boolean features and feature diagrams has shown some limits regarding expressiveness. This is even more the case with the increasing complexity of software intensive systems, which give birth to new issues about complex product lines and complex variability modeling [32]. In this section, we study more expressive variability relationships (used in FD extensions) which may be extracted from multi-valued descriptions. We first introduce product descriptions containing multi-valued characteristics (Sect. 6.3.1). These non-boolean descriptions necessitate a more complex modeling framework that the one previously presented for boolean feature sets in order to fully apprehend their intrinsic variability. Then, we present three prevalent FD extensions that seek to enhance the expressiveness of traditional boolean models, and we identify the new variability relationships introduced by these extensions (Sect. 6.3.2). We also discuss other types of variability models that may take into account more than boolean features. Then, we survey main directions in non-boolean variability extraction (Sect. 6.3.3) before discussing how to extend FCA-based variability extraction to take into account the expressive variability relationships (Sect. 6.3.4).

6.3.1 Multi-Valued Descriptions

Software descriptions may include boolean features but also more complex information: characterizing products using multi-valued attributes such as numerical ones, or with symbolic values enhanced with metadata is a common practice. Product comparison matrices (PCMs) are representative of such complex product configurations [46, 53]. PCMs describe product properties in a tabular form where rows show the product configurations, columns show the product characteristics and cells contain values. A PCM characteristic can be associated with a type (that may be boolean, numerical or symbolic) and a scope for its corresponding set of possible values. Examples of such PCMs used in the product line community include Wikipedia PCMs[3] [53], gathered descriptions of variants generated with JHipster v3.6.1[4] [28], and the Robocode descriptions[5] [43] used here. Table 6.3 is a multi-valued matrix (PCM) that extends and adapts the previous boolean example about Robocode. Features (boolean characteristics) are shown in the first six columns. Movement strategies now are described in one column representing a multi-valued

---

[3] https://en.wikipedia.org/wiki/Category:Software_comparisons, last accessed July 2019

[4] https://github.com/xdevroey/jhipster-dataset/tree/master/v3.6.1

[5] https://github.com/but4reuse/RobocodeSPL_teaching

attribute with symbolic values. The last column indicates numerical values for the roborumble PWIN (probability of win). When a product possesses several values for one characteristic, they are split by a coma; the symbol '*' states that there is no known value.

Modeling complex variability necessitates to express more than only *feature relationships*: we now consider *multi-valued relationships* that should involve boolean attributes (features) as well as multi-valued attributes.

6.3.2   Multi-valued variability relationships

In the same way as the literature identified feature relationships corresponding to the prevalent variability information, we identify the multi-valued relationships necessary to model more complex variability. This is done through the analysis of the three FD extensions that seek to enhance the boolean case expressiveness, as we consider that these extensions represent the designers' needs in terms of non-boolean variability.

FD with Attributes A first extension associates *multi-valued attributes* to features [16]. The attribute has a type, such as string, enumeration or integer. Attributes enable to define more detailed information without making the model more complex. In fact, modeling the same variability information with only boolean features would end up with a large model more difficult to read, as illustrated in Fig. 6.4.

With this extension, we can write (in addition to feature relationships) binary implications, co-occurrences and mutex either between a feature and an attribute value, or between two attribute values (denoted by `attribute:value`). As or- and xor-groups represent feature refinements, attribute values cannot be involved in such groups.

FD with Feature Cardinalities A second extension introduces UML-like cardinalities on features [18], stating that a feature may occur several times in a configuration and defining the minimum and maximum number of these occurrences. A number of

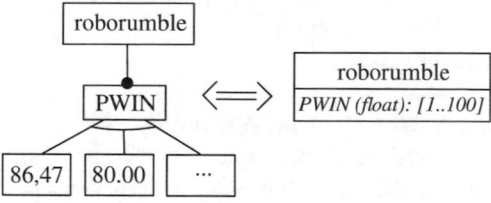

Fig. 6.4 Representing detailed information without making the model more complex by using attributes: (left) representation of PWIN values with features only, (right) representation of PWIN values with a multi-valued attribute

variability relationships	:= *relationship**
relationship	:= *binary implication* | *co-occurrence* | *mutex* | *group*
binary implication	:= *element '⇒' element*
co-occurrence	:= *element '⇔' element*
mutex	:= *element '⇒' '¬' element*
group	:= *'(' feature ',' '{' feature_set '}' ',' cardinality ')'*
feature_set	:= *feature | feature_set ',' feature*
element	:= *feature | attribute*
feature	:= **feature_name**
attribute	:= **attribute_name: value**
cardinality	:= **'⟨' nb_min '-' nb_max '⟩'**

Fig. 6.5 Grammar of variability relationships for representing FD extensions

occurrences associated with a feature may be seen as an attribute with integer values: the variability relationships necessary to represent this extension are the same as for FDs with attributes.

FD with Group Cardinality The third extension proposes to refine feature groups with *feature-group cardinality* in the form $\langle min - max \rangle$ indicating that a product can contain between *min* and *max* child features in the group. The boolean FD notations for xor-groups and or-groups are respectively replaced by $\langle 1 - 1 \rangle$ groups and $\langle 1 - n \rangle$ groups. Thanks to this extension, feature relationships ③ and ④ exposed at the beginning of Sect. 6.2.2 may be merged in one kind of more abstract feature relationship, stating that a feature should be refined by "between *min* and *max*" features in a group. Instead of representing the logical semantics of or- and xor-groups with ∨-connectives and ⊕-connectives respectively, one may now specify which combinations of features from a group are allowed by the cardinality. For instance, a group with parent p, a cardinality $\langle 2 - 3 \rangle$ and children $\{f_1, f_2, f_3\}$ is represented through the following formula:

$$p \Leftrightarrow ((f_1 \wedge f_2 \wedge \neg f_3) \vee (f_1 \wedge f_3 \wedge \neg f_2) \vee (f_2 \wedge f_3 \wedge \neg f_1) \vee (f_1 \wedge f_2 \wedge f_3))$$

To consider these three extensions, it is necessary to extend the previous four feature relationships so that binary implications, co-occurrences and mutual exclusions can involve attribute values as well as features. Figure 6.5 presents the grammar of these variability relationships. We simplify the logical relationships representing feature-groups by introducing the notation $(p, \{f_1, ..., f_n\}, \langle min - max \rangle)$ to be used instead of the one introduced before.

Other Formalisms for Non-Boolean Variability We survey a few alternative formalisms for complex variability description without pretending to be exhaustive. A survey on variability modeling in Cyber-Physical Systems (CPSs) and pointers to other surveys can be found in [52]. Decision Models (DMs) are textual descriptions focusing only on variability decisions [17, 55]. They are organized in tabular form, where each row includes a question (such as *"has PWIN?"*), the type of the expected answer (such as *Integer*) and its range (such as *[0,100]*). It may also present constraints about the required form of the answer (e.g., cardinality or implication) and conditions on when to consider the question. Variability relationships expressed by such models are the same as the three aforementioned FD extensions. An Orthogonal Variability Model (OVM) also focuses on variability only [48]. It introduces variation points (e.g. `movement`) and their variants (e.g. `random`, `wave surfing`). Variation points can be optional or mandatory. Optional variants may be part of a group with a cardinality. Therefore, the variability relationships of Fig. 6.5 are sufficient to represent OVM variability. Common Variability Modeling (CVL) [31] proposes three interrelated models: base model (UML model or any MOF based Domain Specific Language model), variability model, and resolution model (for selection). It allows the description of cardinalities on features and groups and the introduction of attributes (under the name of *variable*). CVL models rely on separation of concerns to split one variability model in several smaller models referencing each other: this notion of references is not taken into account in Fig. 6.5. Constraint Satisfaction Problem [54] and Constraint Logic Programming [35] also have been used to consider non-boolean descriptions. Variability relationships of Fig. 6.5 may be used to build such models, but the models may represent more complex constraints as the one studied here.

6.3.3 Multi-Valued Variability Extraction in the Literature

Becan et al. [9] and Carbonnel et al. [15] both extract variability relationships involving features and attributes. Becan et al. [9] propose dedicated algorithms to extract attributed feature models. They start from configuration matrices: they compute feature groups, implications between features and mutually exclusive features; then they extract all implications involving an attribute value. They use different structures: a binary implication graph and a mutex-graph. Carbonnel et al. [15], in addition, compute mutex between features and/or attribute values, and co-occurrences between features and/or attributes. They use a single structure, which is a conceptual structure and do not synthesize an attributed feature model. This approach is detailed in the next section. The MoVa2PL approach [44] extracts dependencies as well as *requires* and *exclude* constraints from feature spanning over several model variants graph decomposition (including cardinalities), and may define CVL compliant models. To the best of our knowledge, there is no approach for extracting OVM models from product descriptions. Constraint satisfaction problem acquisition [12] is a promising field which should be investigated and connected to complex variability extraction in the future.

6.3.4 A Sound and Complete FCA-Based Multi-Valued Variability Extraction

As real datasets are often more complex than boolean descriptions, many extensions have been proposed over the years for the FCA data analysis framework. To process multi-valued attributes, we can mention the scaling of numerical data [25], the use of value taxonomies [26], and the more general and complete framework extension called Pattern Structures [24]. These approaches may overlap and have common theoretical foundations that may lead to some mappings between them. Dealing with a PCM information as the one presented in Table 6.3 (called a *multi-valued context* in FCA) can be done with several of these frameworks. In this chapter, we choose to explore the approach based on value taxonomies, for pedagogical purposes and to avoid introducing a full complex data analysis framework such as Pattern Structures.

Value Taxonomies The key principle of the value taxonomy approach is the elaboration of taxonomies (partial orders, or scales) on the attribute values. This task may be summarized by "establishing, naming and organizing groups of values in a hierarchy". The goal of this approach is to group the different values of a given attribute under more abstract values; in this way, relationships may be established not only on the attribute values present on the multi-valued descriptions, but also between groups of these values. Value taxonomies may come from different sources depending what the variability analysis aims to highlight. They may be based on *is-a* relationships for symbolic values, or extracted from external resources such as ontologies or other documents. For example, if we consider Robocode movement strategies, one may introduce the new value several opponents, that is more abstract than the ones introduced in Table 6.3 and encompasses all strategies suited for dealing with several bots during a fight. When studying the RoboWiki, one may determine that minimum risk movement belongs to this group, while random movement, wave surfing and stop&go rather belong to a group that could be identified by the value one opponent. Alternatively they could be organized depending on the complexity of their implementation algorithms, or by other movement strategies they were inspired from. Movement strategies grouped by the number of opponents against which they are more efficient are presented in Fig. 6.6 ❶. It states that a bot which implements the wave surfing strategy (third level) thus implements a strategy suited for fighting one opponent (second level) and thus implement a movement strategy (first level).

Taxonomies for numerical values correspond to strict or partial ordering of the values. Several schemes have been studied in FCA for building these orders [25]. In nominal scaling, each value v of a multi-valued attribute m is converted to an attribute m : v. It is used in our example for movement values, generating 5 columns labeled with the prefix "movement : ". Nominal scaling may be seen as an approach to apply by default when no groups of values may be defined or retrieved. In ordinal scaling, the ordinary number order is used. Values of a multi-valued attribute m are described by expressions of the form m > n. It is shown in Fig. 6.6 ❸ for PWIN

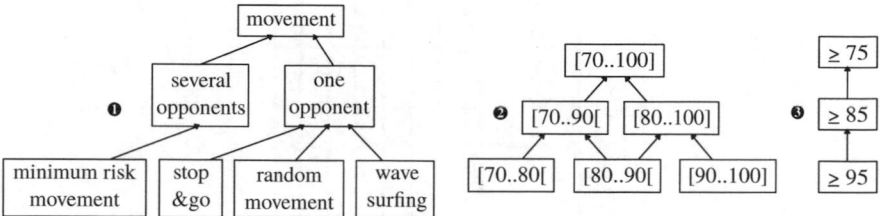

Fig. 6.6 Examples of a taxonomy for the symbolic values of the attribute movement, and two taxonomies for the numerical values of the attribute PWIN

values. The figure indicates that a value described by attribute PWIN ≥ 95q is also described by attribute PWIN ≥ 85 and by attribute PWIN ≥ 75. Notice that, to elaborate this scale, design choices are required to define the bounds that serve in the description. Here, 75, 85 and 95 have been chosen. Figure 6.6 ❷ describes another type of scale on PWIN values. It is based on a description of values by their membership to intervals that split the value set. Here again, the interval bounds have to be determined by domain experts or using techniques like box-plot [36]. Moreover, the intervals are grouped and organized through a hierarchical structure in order to enrich the description and allow more similarities to be discovered between values. For example 75 and 85 cannot be grouped with using the bottom intervals, but they can be grouped using the level 2 interval [70..90[. Other kinds of scales can be found in [25, 36]. In general, any similarity/distance relationships between values both symbolic or numerical, can be used to form a scale.

Binary Conversion These value taxonomies may be used to convert the multi-valued context in a binary context. In this way, theoretical properties and algorithms of the standard FCA scheme (as presented in Sect. 6.2.4) apply on the transformed dataset. To achieve the binary conversion, each element from the scale (i.e., each value in the taxonomy) becomes a boolean attribute of the final binary context. Compared to a naive solution which does not use value taxonomies and where each attribute value is transformed in a boolean feature, this allows to extract additional relationships taking into account groups of attributes values. Let us choose the scale ❶ for values of movement and the scale ❸ for values of PWIN. Then, the boolean attributes of Table 6.3 along with the values of attributes movement and PWIN enhanced with the taxonomy values form the boolean attributes of the equivalent binary context of Table 6.4; its associated AOC-poset is presented in Fig. 6.7.

Rows of the final context still correspond to the product configurations from the multi-valued context shown Table 6.3. A relation between a product configuration c and an attribute a is then established (and shown with a cross in the table) depending on the attribute kind. For a boolean attribute a, c owns a in the final context when c owns a in the multi-valued context. This is illustrated by the 6 first columns (Table 6.4). For a nominal scale, c owns $m : v$ in the final context when c owns m with value v in the multi-valued context. This is illustrated by columns 7-11 for movement. For an ordinal scale, c owns the attribute $m > n$ in the final context when

Table 6.4 Formal context obtained after applying binary conversion to the multi-valued context of Table 6.3

Robocode	One-on-one fighting	Melee fighting	Roborumble	License	Open-source	Closed	Movement: random	Movement: min-risk	Movement: wave-surfing	Movement: stop-and-go	PWIN:≥95	PWIN:≥85	PWIN:≥75	Movement	Movement: one-opponent	Movement: several-opponents
Aristocles	×		×	×	×		×					×			×	×
B26354	×	×		×		×		×	×					×	×	×
Centaur	×	×	×										×			
Coriantumr	×	×	×	×	×			×					×	×		×
Decado	×			×	×		×			×				×	×	
DrussGT	×		×	×	×				×		×	×	×	×	×	
Durandal	×	×	×	×		×			×				×	×	×	

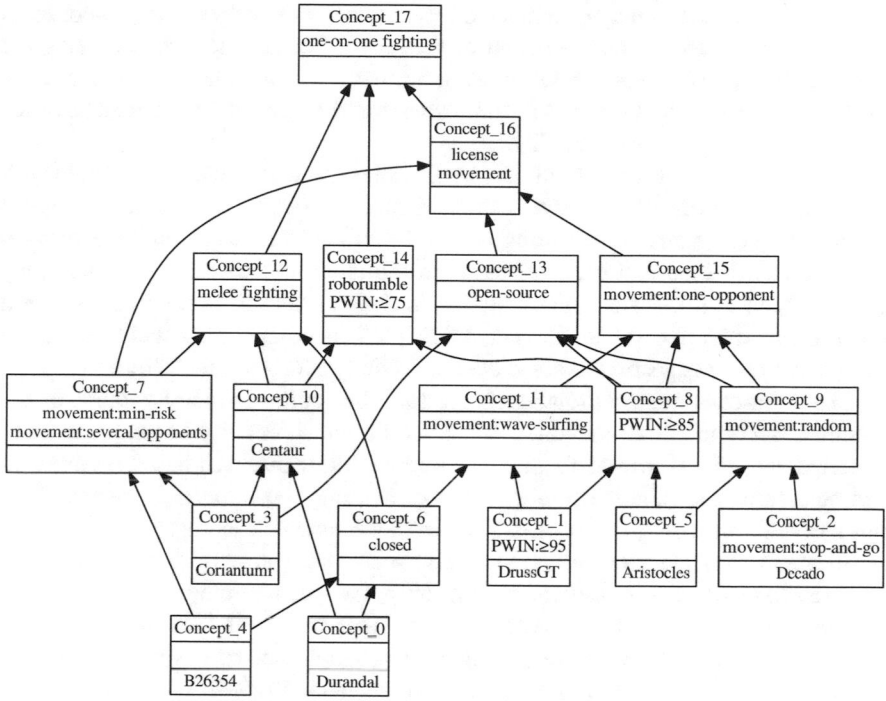

Fig. 6.7 AOC-poset associated with the context of Table 6.4

c owns for m a value $v \succ n$ in the multi-valued context. The last 4 columns illustrate the ordinal scale for PWIN. A (c, a) relation in this scheme verifies the following general property: if we have (c, a_l) and a_g more general than a_l in the taxonomy, (c, a_g) is also true. This applies to all value taxonomies, beyond the examples we have shown in this section.

Reading Multi-valued Relationships in the AOC-poset The AOC-poset can be interpreted as in the boolean case. As a consequence of the value taxonomies, a concept introducing an attribute a_g, with a_g more general than another attribute a_l in the taxonomy, is a super-concept of the concept introducing a_l (if one exists). For example, in Fig. 6.7, *Concept_15*, introducing PWIN: ≥ 75, is a super-concept of *Concept_10* which introduces PWIN: ≥ 85. Therefore, the taxonomies are included in the AOC-poset.

The mapping between propositional formulas and the AOC-poset still applies in this context. For example, applying the rule from Table 6.2, row ①, we can deduce PWIN: $\geq 85 \Rightarrow$ open-source because *Concept_10* introduces PWIN: ≥ 85 and its super-concept *Concept_14* introduces open-source. From Table 6.2, row ②, as *Concept_11* (introducing movement:random) and *Concept_11* (introducing PWIN≥ 95) have disjoint extents, we can deduce movement:random $\Rightarrow \neg$ PWIN≥ 95.

Group cardinalities may be extracted by analyzing the intent of the sub-concepts of the concept introducing the parent of the group. For instance, by analyzing the sub-concepts of *Concept_*16 introducing movement, one may notice that a bot never possesses more than two initial values for the attribute movement, hence suggesting a $< 1 - 2 >$ cardinality.

In the FD extended with multi-valued attributes, each attribute is associated with a feature of the FD. In the AOC-poset, when the most general value of a value taxonomy (i.e., group representing all values of an attribute) implies a feature, then we can deduce that the attribute corresponding to the value taxonomy may be associated to this feature. For instance, in *Concept_*14 of Fig. 6.7, the element representing all values of PWIN (i.e., PWIN$\geq$75) is co-occurrent with the feature roborumble, suggesting to associate the attribute PWIN to this feature.

The extracted logical relationships may be quite numerous due to the sound and complete extraction method based on potentially incomplete input descriptions [15]. However, redundancy elimination techniques based on grouped attribute values introduced through taxonomies may be applied to reduce their number without losing information. For instance, one can extract the two binary implications PWIN:$\geq$95 $\Rightarrow$ movement:one opponent and PWIN:$\geq$85 $\Rightarrow$ movement:one opponent, but only the second may be kept as the first one is included in it. Depending on whether the input descriptions possess numerous features or attributes having values which can be easily organized in taxonomies, redundancy elimination may reduce up to 50% of some types of variability relationships. Redundancy elimination combined with filtering methods allowing the expert to ignore or focus on relationships between given features and/or attributes may help their analysis. A previous study shows that a filtering method as simple as removing relationships between features and/or attributes considered unrelated by the expert reduces their number from 30% to 65%.

FCA is a structural framework which naturally highlights variability and that can be extended to take into account more complex input descriptions. We have seen how value taxonomies may help handle multi-valued descriptions more efficiently and extract multi-valued variability relationships represented by extended FDs. The more complete FCA extension called Pattern Structure generalizes the taxonomy approach to take into account any description on which similarities may be defined. In this way, one can imagine handling more complex artifacts such as slices of FDs, or versioning data. Other extensions such as Relational Concept Analysis [27] can be investigated to extend the extracted variability relationships and build interconnected variability models such as FDs with references or CVL models [13].

6.4   Conclusion

In this chapter, we focused on the process of extracting variability information in the form of logical relationships from product descriptions. More specifically, we tackled the concern of extracting complex variability relationships from non-boolean descriptions. To do so, we extend existing extraction methods focusing on the traditional boolean case to complex variability representations. Thus, this chapter was divided in two main symmetric parts: the first part discussed the traditional boolean case, and the second part examined the extraction in a more complex case.

In the first part, we presented the boolean product descriptions as defined in feature-oriented product line approaches. Then, we summarized the four main studied feature relationships (i.e., variability relationships based on boolean descriptions) to express variability in terms of features. After that, we reviewed methods found in the literature that seek to extract these feature relationships. As revealed by a study on feature model synthesis, methods that first focus on extracting the logical foundation of descriptions' intrinsic variability before relying on experts to breath ontological meaning to them outperform the other methods. Thus, we directed attention to Formal Concept Analysis, a knowledge engineering framework for knowledge representation and extraction, as it includes and formalizes existing methods extracting variability information in the form of logical relationships. We then presented a sound and complete extraction method based on Formal Concept Analysis and its associated conceptual structures. An advantage of using this framework in the boolean case is that it is extensible, and thus may be applied to more complex datasets (i.e., not necessarily boolean).

In the second part, we focused on multi-valued input descriptions, i.e., representing software products by both boolean features and multi-valued characteristics. As traditional feature relationships are not sufficient to capture the intrinsic variability of this type of multi-valued descriptions, we identified new variability relationships which take into account multi-valued characteristics. For that, we analyzed the three FD extensions that were proposed to enhance the expressiveness of the feature-based variability representations. Then, we discussed the few existing methods that tackle this type of extraction, and we show how Formal Concept Analysis may be extended to be applied in the multi-valued case. We relied on the definition of value taxonomies (i.e., grouping values under more abstract values) for non-boolean attributes, which enable the extraction of more precise variability relationships and the definition of redundancy elimination techniques. We mentioned other Formal Concept Analysis extensions that may be useful to go further in the problem of complex variability extraction, e.g., by relying on more complex descriptions or even interconnected ones.

References

1. Acher, M., Baudry, B., Heymans, P., Cleve, A., Hainaut, J.: Support for reverse engineering and maintaining feature models. In: The Seventh International Workshop on Variability Modelling of Software-intensive Systems, VaMoS '13, Pisa , Italy, January 23–25, 2013, pp. 20:1–20:8 (2013)

2. Acher, M., Cleve, A., Perrouin, G., Heymans, P., Vanbeneden, C., Collet, P., Lahire, P.: On extracting feature models from product descriptions. In: Sixth International Workshop on Variability Modelling of Software-Intensive Systems, Leipzig, Germany, January 25–27, 2012. Proceedings, pp. 45–54 (2012)
3. Al-Msie'deen, R., Huchard, M., Seriai, A., Urtado, C., Vauttier, S.: Reverse engineering feature models from software configurations using formal concept analysis. In: Proceedings of the Eleventh International Conference on Concept Lattices and Their Applications, Košice, Slovakia, October 7-10, 2014., pp. 95–106 (2014)
4. Apel, S., Batory, D.S., Kästner, C., Saake, G.: Feature-Oriented Software Product Lines - Concepts and Implementation. Springer (2013)
5. Assunção, W.K.G., Lopez-Herrejon, R.E., Linsbauer, L., Vergilio, S.R., Egyed, A.: Multi-objective reverse engineering of variability-safe feature models based on code dependencies of system variants. Empirical Software Engineering 22(4), 1763–1794 (2017)
6. Assunção, W.K.G., Lopez-Herrejon, R.E., Linsbauer, L., Vergilio, S.R., Egyed, A.: Reengineering legacy applications into software product lines: a systematic mapping. Empirical Software Engineering 22(6), 2972–3016 (2017)
7. Batory, D.S.: Feature models, grammars, and propositional formulas. In: Software Product Lines, 9th International Conference, SPLC 2005, Rennes, France, September 26-29, 2005, Proceedings, pp. 7–20 (2005)
8. Bécan, G., Acher, M., Baudry, B., Nasr, S.B.: Breathing ontological knowledge into feature model synthesis: an empirical study. Empirical Software Engineering 21(4), 1794–1841 (2016)
9. Bécan, G., Behjati, R., Gotlieb, A., Acher, M.: Synthesis of attributed feature models from product descriptions. In: Proceedings of the 19th International Conference on Software Product Line, SPLC 2015, Nashville, TN, USA, July 20-24, 2015, pp. 1–10 (2015)
10. Benavides, D., Segura, S., Cortés, A.R.: Automated analysis of feature models 20 years later: A literature review. Inf. Syst. 35(6), 615–636 (2010)
11. Berger, T., Rublack, R., Nair, D., Atlee, J.M., Becker, M., Czarnecki, K., Wasowski, A.: A survey of variability modeling in industrial practice. In: The Seventh International Workshop on Variability Modelling of Software-intensive Systems, VaMoS '13, Pisa , Italy, January 23 - 25, 2013, pp. 7:1–7:8 (2013)
12. Bessiere, C., Daoudi, A., Hebrard, E., Katsirelos, G., Lazaar, N., Mechqrane, Y., Narodytska, N., Quimper, C., Walsh, T.: New approaches to constraint acquisition. In: Data Mining and Constraint Programming - Foundations of a Cross-Disciplinary Approach, pp. 51–76 (2016)
13. Carbonnel, J., Huchard, M., Nebut, C.: Exploring the Variability of Interconnected Product Families with Relational Concept Analysis. In: Proceedings of 7th International Workshop on Reverse Variability Engineering (REVE 2019) @ SPLC (2019)
14. Carbonnel, J., Huchard, M., Nebut, C.: Modelling equivalence classes of feature models with concept lattices to assist their extraction from product descriptions. Journal of Systems and Software 152, 1–23 (2019)
15. Carbonnel, J., Huchard, M., Nebut, C.: Towards Complex Product Line Variability Modelling: Mining Relationships from Non-Boolean Descriptions. Journal of Systems and Software (2019)
16. Czarnecki, K., Eisenecker, U.W.: Generative programming - methods, tools and applications. Addison-Wesley (2000)
17. Czarnecki, K., Grünbacher, P., Rabiser, R., Schmid, K., Wasowski, A.: Cool features and tough decisions: a comparison of variability modeling approaches. In: Sixth International Workshop on Variability Modelling of Software-Intensive Systems, Leipzig, Germany, January 25-27, 2012. Proceedings, pp. 173–182 (2012)
18. Czarnecki, K., Helsen, S., Eisenecker, U.W.: Staged configuration using feature models. In: Software Product Lines, Third International Conference, SPLC 2004, Boston, MA, USA, August 30-September 2, 2004, Proceedings, pp. 266–283 (2004)
19. Czarnecki, K., She, S., Wasowski, A.: Sample spaces and feature models: There and back again. In: Proceedings of the 12th International Conference on oftware Product Lines (SPLC'08), pp. 22–31 (2008)

20. Czarnecki, K., Wasowski, A.: Feature diagrams and logics: There and back again. In: Software Product Lines, 11th International Conference, SPLC 2007, Kyoto, Japan, September 10-14, 2007, Proceedings, pp. 23–34 (2007)
21. Davril, J., Delfosse, E., Hariri, N., Acher, M., Cleland-Huang, J., Heymans, P.: Feature model extraction from large collections of informal product descriptions. In: Joint Meeting of the European Software Engineering Conference and the ACM SIGSOFT Symposium on the Foundations of Software Engineering, ESEC/FSE'13, Saint Petersburg, Russian Federation, August 18-26, 2013, pp. 290–300 (2013)
22. Dolques, X., Braud, A., Huchard, M., Ber, F.L.: Rcaexplore, a FCA based tool to explore relational data. In: Supplementary Proceedings of ICFCA 2019 Conference and Workshops, Frankfurt, Germany, June 25-28, 2019., pp. 55–59 (2019)
23. Ferrari, A., Spagnolo, G.O., Gnesi, S., Dell'Orletta, F.: CMT and FDE: tools to bridge the gap between natural language documents and feature diagrams. In: Proceedings of the 19th International Conference on Software Product Line, SPLC 2015, Nashville, TN, USA, July 20-24, 2015, pp. 402–410 (2015)
24. Ganter, B., Kuznetsov, S.O.: Pattern structures and their projections. In: Conceptual Structures: Broadening the Base, 9th International Conference on Conceptual Structures, ICCS 2001, Stanford, CA, USA, July 30-August 3, 2001, Proceedings, pp. 129–142 (2001)
25. Ganter, B., Wille, R.: Formal Concept Analysis - Mathematical Foundations. Springer (1999)
26. Godin, R., Mili, H.: Building and maintaining analysis-level class hierarchies using Galois lattices. In: Conference on Object-Oriented Programming Systems, Languages, and Applications (OOPSLA), Eighth Annual Conference, Washington, DC, USA, September 26 - October 1, 1993, Proceedings., pp. 394–410 (1993)
27. Hacene, M.R., Huchard, M., Napoli, A., Valtchev, P.: Relational concept analysis: mining concept lattices from multi-relational data. Ann. Math. Artif. Intell. 67(1), 81–108 (2013)
28. Halin, A., Nuttinck, A., Acher, M., Devroey, X., Perrouin, G., Heymans, P.: Yo variability! jhipster: a playground for web-apps analyses. In: Proceedings of the Eleventh International Workshop on Variability Modelling of Software-intensive Systems, VaMoS 2017, Eindhoven, Netherlands, February 1-3, 2017, pp. 44–51 (2017)
29. Haslinger, E.N., Lopez-Herrejon, R.E., Egyed, A.: Reverse engineering feature models from programs' feature sets. In: 18th Working Conference on Reverse Engineering, WCRE 2011, Limerick, Ireland, October 17-20, 2011, pp. 308–312 (2011)
30. Haslinger, E.N., Lopez-Herrejon, R.E., Egyed, A.: On extracting feature models from sets of valid feature combinations. In: Fundamental Approaches to Software Engineering - 16th International Conference, FASE 2013, Held as Part of the European Joint Conferences on Theory and Practice of Software, ETAPS 2013, Rome, Italy, March 16-24, 2013. Proceedings, pp. 53–67 (2013)
31. Haugen, Ø., Wasowski, A., Czarnecki, K.: CVL: common variability language. In: 17th International Software Product Line Conference, SPLC 2013, Tokyo, Japan - August 26 - 30, 2013, p. 277 (2013)
32. Holl, G., Grünbacher, P., Rabiser, R.: A systematic review and an expert survey on capabilities supporting multi product lines. Information & Software Technology 54(8), 828–852 (2012)
33. Kang, K., Cohen, S., Hess, J., Novak, W., Peterson, A.: Feature-Oriented Domain Analysis (FODA) Feasibility Study. Tech. Rep. CMU/SEI-90-TR-021 (1990)
34. Kang, K.C., Lee, J., Donohoe, P.: Feature-oriented project line engineering. IEEE Software 19(4), 58–65 (2002)
35. Karatas, A.S., Oguztüzün, H., Dogru, A.H.: From extended feature models to constraint logic programming. Sci. Comput. Program. 78(12), 2295–2312 (2013)
36. Kaytoue, M., Kuznetsov, S.O., Napoli, A.: Revisiting numerical pattern mining with formal concept analysis. In: Proceedings of the 22nd International Joint Conference on Artificial Intelligence (IJCAI'11), pp. 1342–1347 (2011)
37. Krueger, C.W.: Easing the transition to software mass customization. In: Software Product-Family Engineering, 4th International Workshop, (PFE'01) Revised Papers, pp. 282–293 (2001)

38. Linsbauer, L., Lopez-Herrejon, R.E., Egyed, A.: Feature model synthesis with genetic programming. In: Search-Based Software Engineering - 6th International Symposium, SSBSE 2014, Fortaleza, Brazil, August 26-29, 2014. Proceedings, pp. 153–167 (2014)
39. Loesch, F., Ploedereder, E.: Restructuring variability in software product lines using concept analysis of product configurations. In: 11th European Conference on Software Maintenance and Reengineering, Software Evolution in Complex Software Intensive Systems, CSMR 2007, 21-23 March 2007, Amsterdam, The Netherlands, pp. 159–170 (2007)
40. Loh, W.: Classification and regression trees. Wiley Interdiscip. Rev. Data Min. Knowl. Discov. 1(1), 14–23 (2011)
41. Lopez-Herrejon, R.E., Linsbauer, L., Galindo, J.A., Parejo, J.A., Benavides, D., Segura, S., Egyed, A.: An assessment of search-based techniques for reverse engineering feature models. Journal of Systems and Software 103, 353–369 (2015)
42. Mannion, M.: Using first-order logic for product line model validation. In: Software Product Lines, Second International Conference, SPLC 2, San Diego, CA, USA, August 19-22, 2002, Proceedings, pp. 176–187 (2002)
43. Martinez, J., Tërnava, X., Ziadi, T.: Software product line extraction from variability-rich systems: the Robocode case study. In: Proceeedings of the 22nd International Systems and Software Product Line Conference - Volume 1, SPLC 2018, Gothenburg, Sweden, September 10-14, 2018, pp. 132–142 (2018)
44. Martinez, J., Ziadi, T., Bissyandé, T.F., Klein, J., Traon, Y.L.: Automating the extraction of model-based software product lines from model variants (T). In: Proceedings of the 30th IEEE/ACM International Conference on Automated Software Engineering (ASE'15), pp. 396–406. IEEE Computer Society (2015)
45. Martinez, J., Ziadi, T., Bissyandé, T.F., Klein, J., Traon, Y.L.: Bottom-up technologies for reuse: automated extractive adoption of software product lines. In: Proceedings of the 39th International Conference on Software Engineering, (ICSE'17), Companion Volume, pp. 67–70. IEEE Computer Society (2017)
46. Nasr, S.B., Bécan, G., Acher, M., Filho, J.B.F., Sannier, N., Baudry, B., Davril, J.: Automated extraction of product comparison matrices from informal product descriptions. Journal of Systems and Software 124, 82–103 (2017)
47. Poelmans, J., Ignatov, D.I., Kuznetsov, S.O., Dedene, G.: Formal concept analysis in knowledge processing: A survey on applications. Expert Syst. Appl. 40(16), 6538–6560 (2013)
48. Pohl, K., Böckle, G., van der Linden, F.: Software Product Line Engineering - Foundations, Principles, and Techniques. Springer (2005)
49. Priss, U.: Formal concept analysis in information science. ARIST 40(1), 521–543 (2006)
50. Riebisch, M., Böllert, K., Streitferdt, D., Philippow, I.: Extending feature diagrams with uml multiplicities. In: Proceedings of the 6th World Conference on Integrated Design & Process Technology (IDPT'02) (2002)
51. Ryssel, U., Ploennigs, J., Kabitzsch, K.: Extraction of feature models from formal contexts. In: Software Product Lines - 15th International Conference, SPLC 2011, Munich, Germany, August 22-26, 2011. Workshop Proceedings (Volume 2), p. 4 (2011)
52. Safdar, S.A., Yue, T., Ali, S., Lu, H.: Evaluating variability modeling techniques for supporting cyber-physical system product line engineering. In: Proceedings of the 9th International Conference on System Analysis and Modeling. Technology-Specific Aspects of Models (SAM'16), pp. 1–19 (2016)
53. Sannier, N., Acher, M., Baudry, B.: From comparison matrix to variability model: The wikipedia case study. In: 2013 28th IEEE/ACM International Conference on Automated Software Engineering, ASE 2013, Silicon Valley, CA, USA, November 11-15, 2013, pp. 580–585 (2013)
54. Sawyer, P., Mazo, R., Diaz, D., Salinesi, C., Hughes, D.: Using constraint programming to manage configurations in self-adaptive systems. IEEE Computer 45(10), 56–63 (2012)
55. Schmid, K., John, I.: A customizable approach to full lifecycle variability management. Sci. Comput. Program. 53(3), 259–284 (2004)

56. She, S., Lotufo, R., Berger, T., Wasowski, A., Czarnecki, K.: Reverse engineering feature models. In: Proceedings of the 33rd International Conference on Software Engineering, ICSE 2011, Waikiki, Honolulu , HI, USA, May 21-28, 2011, pp. 461–470 (2011)
57. She, S., Ryssel, U., Andersen, N., Wasowski, A., Czarnecki, K.: Efficient synthesis of feature models. Information & Software Technology **56**(9), 1122–1143 (2014)
58. Temple, P., Acher, M., Jézéquel, J., Barais, O.: Learning contextual-variability models. IEEE Software **34**(6), 64–70 (2017)
59. Tilley, T., Cole, R., Becker, P., Eklund, P.W.: A survey of formal concept analysis support for software engineering activities. In: Formal Concept Analysis, Foundations and Applications, pp. 250–271 (2005)

Chapter 7
Machine Learning for Feature Constraints Discovery

Hugo Martin, Paul Temple, Mathieu Acher, Juliana Alves Pereira, and Jean-Marc Jézéquel

Abstract Constraints among features are central to the success and quality of software product lines (SPLs). Unfortunately, the number of potential interactions and dependencies, materialized as logical constraints, grows as the number of features increases in an SPL. In particular, it is easy to forget a constraint and thus mistakenly authorizes invalid products. Developers thus struggle to identify and track constraints throughout the engineering of more and more complex SPLs.

In this chapter, we show how to leverage statistical machine learning (and more specifically decision trees) to automatically prevent the derivation of invalid products through the synthesis of constraints. The key principle is to try and test some product of an SPL and then identify what individual features or combinations of features (if any) are causing their non-validity (e.g., a product does not compile). A sample of derived products is used to train a classifier (here a decision tree but other classifiers might also be used as long as constraints can be easily extracted) that can classify any remaining products of the SPL. We illustrate the chapter through different application domains and software systems (a video generator, parametric programs for 3D printing, or the Linux kernel). We also discuss the cost, benefits, and applicability of the method.

H. Martin · M. Acher (✉) · J.-M. Jézéquel
University of Rennes, IRISA, CNRS, Rennes, France
e-mail: hugo.martin@irisa.fr; mathieu.acher@irisa.fr; jean-marc.jezequel@irisa.fr

P. Temple
University of Namur, Namur, Belgium
e-mail: paul.temple@unamur.be

J. A. Pereira
Pontifical Catholic University of Rio de Janeiro, PUC-Rio, Rio de Janeiro, Brazil
e-mail: juliana@exacta.inf.puc-rio.br

© Springer Nature Switzerland AG 2023
R. E. Lopez-Herrejon et al. (eds.), *Handbook of Re-Engineering Software Intensive Systems into Software Product Lines*, https://doi.org/10.1007/978-3-031-11686-5_7

7.1 Introduction

Not all combinations of features (a.k.a. configurations) are possible in a software product line (SPL). An unauthorized composition of features may indeed lead to an invalid product that: does not compile, does not build, is not executable, does not pass the test suite, or fails to meet a performance objective. For technical or marketing reasons, constraints among features are central to the success and quality of SPLs. Without proper constraints and a too permissive configuration space, users may derive invalid products and developers would deliver products full of bugs or of bad quality.

Unfortunately, the specification of constraints is known to be a time-consuming and error-prone task. The number of potential interactions and dependencies grows as the number of features increases in an SPL. In particular, it is easy to forget a constraint and thus mistakenly authorize some invalid products. Developers thus struggle to identify and track constraints throughout the (re-)engineering of more and more complex SPLs. Mining constraints is needed in several engineering scenarios [20, 37]: (1) *reverse engineering:* dependencies among features are either implicit, scattered, or not correctly formalized, and consequently the logic behind these dependencies are often lost; (2) *evolution and re-engineering:* the SPL has evolved with the addition of new features and the removal of deprecated features, and then begs the question of specifying new constraints to keep the SPL consistent; (3) *domain knowledge:* possible combinations of features are technically possible but do not make sense from a marketing or domain point of view.

In essence, capturing constraints of an existing SPL boils down to anticipate all possible combinations of features and to make explicit the configuration *knowledge* that is somewhat implicit in various kinds of artefacts (documentation, code, test cases, etc.). The domain knowledge of experts and developers may not be sufficient or up-to-date to capture all constraints. Furthermore, the static analysis of artefacts, though extremely useful and effective in many situations, may be hard to develop or exhibit limitations [3, 9, 18, 21, 22, 28, 31]. A possible consequence is that the synthesis of feature models [6, 8, 12] can be incomplete or unsound since constraints are not fully discovered.

Another approach, that gains more and more interests, is to dynamically execute the software system (or the SPL under development) over different configurations and statistically *learn* what combinations of features are not appropriate and thus should be used to further constrain the system. In practice, a first key step is to gather a sample of configurations together with their observations (e.g., acceptable or not). Such observations will serve as *labels* for the machine learning algorithm (see Sect. 7.2.2). Gathering labels requires compiling (or executing) some configurations. The resulting qualities of the derived product (e.g., whether it builds or fails) are automatically observed and labels are attached to configurations. Then, statistical machine learning algorithms can identify what individual features or combinations of features (if any) are causing their non-validity (e.g., a product does not build). The generated sample from the first step is exploited to train a classifier (e.g., a decision tree) that can classify any remaining products of the SPL, especially those that have never been tested. Some constraints can eventually be extracted out of a classifier to avoid the derivation of products classified as invalid.

In this chapter, you will learn:

- some basics of supervised machine learning needed to understand and implement the approach (Sect. 7.2);
- the process of "sampling, labelling, learning" for eventually mining constraints (Sect. 7.3);
- concrete applications for different use-cases and software systems: a generator capable of synthesizing videos used to benchmark video processing pipelines, VaryLaTeX for generating documents that meet page restriction constraints, parametric programs for 3D printing that indeed produce valid 3D models, and the Linux kernel for preventing build failures (Sect. 7.4);
- the benefits, but also the costs and underlying challenges for making the process applicable (Sect. 7.5).

7.2 Machine Learning in a Nutshell

Machine learning refers to a set of techniques and algorithms that allow computers to perform tasks without being explicitly programmed for. These techniques are statistical as they analyse data and provide a mathematical model (that can be arbitrarily complex), which can be used to give the most likely outcome to previously unseen data regarding a given problem. This outcome can be categorical (and the tackled problem is called classification) or numerical (tackling a regression problem). In this section, we will present some basics of machine learning and quickly focus on the ones we use for the purpose of discovering constraints inside configurable software: supervised learning using decision trees.

7.2.1 Data Representation and Model Generation

Data that are used to learn patterns, knowledge, correlation, etc. have to be transformed to provide the same kind of information. For instance, in the case of object recognition in images, images that are fed to the machine learning algorithm must be represented in the same color space, have the same dimension or must be transformed to provide a vector of information of the same size for all the images. Therefore, the intermediate representation between raw data and data used by the machine learning algorithm is very important: it must provide an homogeneous representation (e.g., a vector of a unique size) which will provide as much information as possible to the algorithm.

Based on this intermediate representation, the typical process of learning a mathematical model begins with the gathering of a collection of relevant data for the task at hand. Only a part of this collection is given to the algorithm such that it can build its model. It is called the training set. The remaining part is then used for validation and performance assessment (respectively called the validation set and the test set).

7.2.2   Supervised and Unsupervised Learning

Numerous algorithms exist in machine learning and are usually classified in two categories: supervised techniques and unsupervised techniques. Both aim to predict a label (i.e., a category or a numerical value) out of predictive variables (also known as *features* following the machine learning terminology), that are represented by the vector of information mentioned earlier. Note that the term "feature" is also used in the software product line. While the communities are different, we can see some similarities in the use of this term: features in machine learning are used to represent data as a summary of characteristics while features in software are an abstraction that represents some functionalities and capabilities of the system. Features are used as a way to discriminate/differentiate data or system instances. Because of that, we do not make any distinction in the following between the two terms. Yet, to use reading, whenever felt necessary we specify which term is used.

Once all needed data are gathered, a part of them is used to train a predictive model. In the case of unsupervised techniques, labels are not available a priori in the dataset. In the case of supervised learning, labels are given to the algorithm as additional information to build its mathematical model. In the rest of this chapter, we are interested only in supervised techniques.

While gathering relevant data can be difficult in itself (because sometimes they are rare, need to be preprocessed, etc.), being able to annotate them is another difficulty to cope with. It calls back to the oracle problem [5]. While asking a domain expert or humans to manually review and annotate data is still feasible (e.g., using Amazon Mechanical Turk [15, 42], a service proposed by Amazon where people can submit small jobs, like annotating data, that will be taken care of by anybody (sometimes several person can work on the same job) willing to contribute in exchange of some money), the amount of data to review makes it very time-consuming, hence, difficult for humans to stay focused. Moreover, depending on the task and the reviewer/annotator, results may be inconsistent (e.g., defining bounding boxes around objects in an image) thus introducing "noise". That is why manual reviewing ask for multiple checks. When possible, it is preferable to use an automatic procedure to annotate data directly since it will be consistent over time, fast and completely automatic. Fortunately, there are numerous software engineering contexts in which it is indeed possible to automatically measure an information about the software system and thus assign a label to a software configuration.

7.2.3   Decision Trees

Many different algorithms lie in the family of supervised learning techniques. Decision tree learning is a set of algorithms, such as CART [7], able to create (Binary) search trees. Creating a decision tree is about creating a hierarchy of splits that goes from the root to leaves. Splits are decided based on data and a feature representation in the training set. The most discriminate splits come first (i.e., at higher levels of the tree) and they can be composed of one or several features of the data representation. The selection of a split at a given level of the tree is defined by a split criterion. The two most popular criteria are: Gini impurity and Shannon entropy [13]. The former finds the best cut to better isolate one class at each level while the latter uses the information gain to split the dataset. Depending on the selected splitting strategy, the order of the splits (or the order of importance of features for splits) can be different even if the training set remains the same. Without any further restrictions, the algorithm will create a tree that perfectly clusters the training set depending on these classes, without any mistake, but will likely have a high error rate when evaluated on the test set. This phenomenon is called *overfitting* and is not really suitable as the decision tree may be very efficient over the training set but will not be capable of generalizing predictions to unknown data (e.g., used in the test set). To be able to cluster perfectly, the tree can be arbitrary large and complex. To limit the expansion of a tree, other parameters need to be defined such as: maximum depth, maximum nodes, maximum number of leaves, splitting only if there is a certain number of examples in the node, etc.

Interpretability   Decision trees are probably the most humanly interpretable models among usual models generated by popular machine learning algorithms. They come in the form of a tree and thus one simply needs to follow the path leading to a leaf to understand how the classification decision has been taken for a specific data. This path can be read as a propositional formula (right part of Fig. 7.1). However, as said before, a tree can grow large and be complex which can make its interpertability difficult. It is near impossible for humans to grasp completely a decision tree composed of hundreds or thousands of nodes. Such tree can be suitable when a program breaks down the complexity, such as measuring the feature importance among others, or when used for debugging purposes where a human

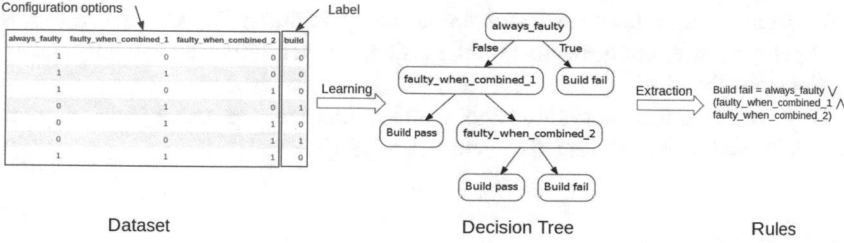

Fig. 7.1   From data to rules with machine learning

reviewer can follow a precise example through the tree. However, if the purpose is to have a tree that is fully understandable by humans, it should not exceed three or four nodes in depth. Such restriction brings a drop in the performance of the decision tree in most cases.

7.2.4 Metrics

After a model has been trained completely, its prediction performance needs to be assessed on a test set (composed of data that the model has never seen before). The model is asked to predict the outcome (that we will call a *class*) of all the data in the test set and these results are compared to the known expected outcome (i.e., the groundtruth). In the case of a binary classification task, the classifier will determine statistically to which class[1] a data is most likely to belong to out of the two labels. In the case of binary classification, the comparison between the label of a data and the class given by the classifier can lead to four different situations. Let the two possible labels (and associated classes) be 'Pos' and 'Neg'. If the class and the label agree on 'Pos', the model succeeded to perform a True Positive (TP); on the other hand if they agree on 'Neg', the model performed a True Negative (TN). When the class and the label disagree, if the class states 'Pos' instead of 'Neg', we call it a False Positive (FP) and if it states 'Neg' instead of 'Pos' a False Negative (FN).

With these values, several metrics can be calculated. The most popular is called accuracy:

$$accuracy = \frac{TP + TN}{TP + TN + FP + FN} \tag{7.1}$$

and computes the ratio of good prediction (when classes and labels agree, i.e., TP and TN) over the total number of predictions. While this metric shows the general prediction performance of the model, it may not be sufficient to properly assess the model. Consider a dataset composed of 95% of data from label 'Pos'. The data set is split randomly into the training set and the test set. Statistically, a model trained on this training set has high probabilities to state that every thing should be assigned with class 'Pos' (since 'Neg' data will be considered as rare events). When assessing the model's performances, the test set is used (suppose that it is also composed of 95% of data from label 'Pos') and the accuracy is thus 95%. Overall, it seems a good performance, but it means that the trained model will systematically failed to predict label 'Neg'.

To have a better overview, among other metrics, we use precision, recall, specificity and negative predictive value (aka NPV):

---

[1] The difference between a class and a label lies in the fact that labels are determined by the annotator or an "oracle" while classes are predicted by a classifier.

$$precision = \frac{TP}{TP + FP} \qquad recall = \frac{TP}{TP + FN} \tag{7.2}$$

$$specificity = \frac{TN}{TN + FP} \qquad NPV = \frac{TN}{TN + FN} \tag{7.3}$$

In the case of a model classifying every example in the 'Pos' class, specificity and NPV would be 0%, a classification fault that accuracy, precision and recall would not be able to reveal. This illustrative example shows the need for multiple metrics to assess the performances of a machine learning model.

7.3 Sampling, Labeling, Learning

The use of machine learning techniques for feature constraints discovery follows a 3-stage process: (1) sampling; (2) labeling; and (3) learning. The stages are sketched in Fig. 7.2. The dashed-line boxes denote the inputs and outputs of each stage. The process starts by building and labeling an initial sample of configurations. Then, these labels are used to learn a prediction model, in our case a decision tree, on which logical constraints can be extracted. These constraints are used to precisely define the space of valid configurations of an SPL, typically through variability models [27]. The ultimate goal of using decision trees (or any other machine learning algorithm) is to design an accurate and complete variability model that would exclude unacceptable configurations (e.g., configurations that do not build or run under an excessive amount of time).

Overall, estimating the system behavior based on a small sample of configurations is a critical step since, in practice, the sample may not contain important feature interactions nor reflect the system real behavior accurately. To overcome this issue, numerous sampling and learning approaches have been proposed in the last years. Next, we describe in detail each stage and point out a few existing state-of-the-art sampling and learning techniques.

7.3.1 Sampling

Sampling is realized either out of an enumerated set of configurations or a variability model. In Fig. 7.2, let $C = \{C_1, C_2, ..., C_n\}$ be the set of n enumerated configurations, and $C_i = \{f_1, f_2, ..., f_m\}$ with $f_j \in \{0, 1\}$ a combination of m selected and deselected features.[2] A straightforward way to determine whether we have an invalid combination of features is to label all possible combinations of features of a system, and then define a set of logical constraints that leads to invalid

---

[2] We call a feature selected if its value is set to 1; if it is set to 0, the feature is deselected.

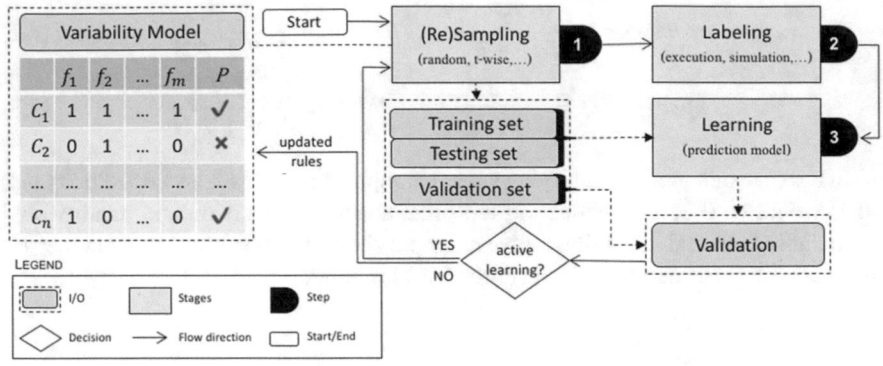

Fig. 7.2 Employed machine learning stages for feature constraints discovery in SPLs

combinations. However, it is usually unfeasible to benchmark all possible variants, due to the extremely large configuration space. Machine learning techniques address this issue making use of a small labeled *sample* of configurations $S_C = \{s_1, ..., s_k\}$, where $S_C \subseteq C$ and trying to find correlations between selected features and the labels assigned to configurations. With the promise to balance labeling effort and prediction accuracy, several sampling strategies have been reported in the literature.

Random sampling is the most used sampling strategy. The current studies consider different notions of randomness. Uniform random sampling aims to select a distribution of configurations reasonably closed to uniform [26]. Guo et al. [11] consider four sizes of random samples for training: N, $2N$, $3N$, and M, where N is the number of features of a system, and M is the number of minimal valid configurations covering each pair of features. They choose size N, $2N$, and $3N$, because measuring a sample whose size is linear in the number of features is likely feasible and reasonable in practice, given the high cost of measurements by execution. Instead of randomly choosing configurations as part of the sample, several heuristics have been developed, such as knowledge-wise, feature-coverage, feature-frequency, and distance-based.

In the knowledge-wise heuristic, the configuration samples are selected based on their influence on the target property, e.g. known feature interactions defined by a domain expert. Experts may detect feature interactions by analyzing the specification of features, implementation assets, and source code. The tool SPLConqueror [35] provides engineers with an environment that they can document and in which they can incorporate known feature interactions. For each defined feature interaction, a single configuration is automatically added to the set of sample for measurement.

Feature-coverage heuristic is used to detect automatically all first order feature interactions. For instance, Siegmund et al. [33, 34] use a pair-wise measurement heuristic which assumes the potential existence of a feature interaction between each pair of features in an SPL. It includes a minimal valid configuration for each pair of features being selected. Pair-wise requires a number of measurements that is quadratic in the number of optional features. Some authors [14, 17, 30] also use a 3-wise feature coverage heuristic to discover interactions among 3 features. Yilmaz et al. [44] use a 5 and 6-wise heuristic. As there are n-th order feature coverage heuristics, the sample set might be unnecessarily large which increases labeling effort substantially. However, not every generated sample contains features that interact with each other. Thus, the main problem of this strategy is that it requires prior knowledge to select a proper coverage criterion. To overcome this issue, approaches might combine this heuristic with the knowledge-wise heuristic.

Distance-based heuristic [14] consists in covering the configuration space by selecting configurations according to a given probability distribution (typically a uniform distribution) and a distance metric. The underlying benefit is that distance-based sampling can better scale compared to an enumerative-based random sampling, while the generated samples are closed to those obtained with a uniform random. Diversified distance-based sampling is a variant of distance-based sampling [14, 23]. The principle is to increase diversity of the sample set by iteratively adding configurations that contain the least frequently selected options. The intended benefit is to avoid missing the inclusion of some (important) options in the process.

There are several others sampling heuristics, such as *Plackett-Burman design* [32] for reasoning with numerical options; *Breakdown* [43] (random breakdown, adaptive random breakdown, adaptive equidistant breakdown) for breaking down (in different sectors) the parameter space; *Constrained-driven sampling* [10] (constrained combinatorial interaction testing, combinatorial interaction testing of constraint validity, constraints violating combinatorial interaction testing, combinatorial union, unconstrained combinatorial interaction testing) to verify the validity of combinatorial interaction testing (CIT) models; sampling based on adversarial learning [40]; and many others [24]. Overall, the objective of these heuristics is to cover the configuration space with the lowest sampling size. Another expected property is to isolate and pinpoint the root cause of configuration issues out of sample (see, e.g., [40]). Ideally, a sample is representative of the whole configuration space: learning techniques can be used to train an accurate model out of it.

7.3.2 Labeling

In this stage, the goal is to label the sample set of configurations of a configurable system $S_C = \{s_1, ..., s_k\}$ with quantitative or qualitative properties $\{p_1, ..., p_k\}$. Such properties are typically the fact that the configuration does build or to assess the execution time. Systems are labeled either by *execution, static analysis, user feedback* or *synthetic labeling. Execution* consists of executing the configurations' sample and monitoring their behaviour at compile-time or runtime. Execution is the most used strategy (see [24]). In addition to execution, *static analysis* infers labels only by examining the code, model, or documentation. For example, practitioners can label a configuration failure of Linux by checking a missing dependency between two options specified in its documentation. Finally, instead of labeling configurations statically or dynamically, some approaches also make use of user feedback. *User feedback* relies only on domain experts knowledge to label configurations (e.g., whether the configuration is acceptable or not).

Next, the labelled sample is partitioned into training, testing, and (optionally) validation sets which are used to train and validate the machine learning prediction model.

7.3.3 Learning

In this stage, a prediction model is learnt based on a given sample of labeled configurations $C(S_C)$ to infer the behavior of non-labeled configurations $C(C - S_C)$. Table 7.1 summarizes a few state-of-the-art learning techniques reported in the literature for feature constraint discovery [24]. These techniques tackle a classification problem (see Sect. 7.2.2). They aim at constructing machine learning models to predict a categorical value of non-labeled configurations. As an example, Temple et al. [38, 39], Acher et al. [2], and Martin et al. [19] use *classification and regression trees* (CART). CART are a specific decision tree algorithm as presented in Sect. 7.2. Many different implementations exist but they all provide a tree which can be interpreted as a set of decisions to go from the root to a leaf. The approach creates new constraints in the variability model by building the negation of the conjunction of a path to reach a faulty leaf (i.e., a leaf gathering configurations that do not show expected performances/properties).

For learning, the sampling set S_C is divided into a *training set* S_{Tr} and a *test set* S_{Ts}, where $S_C = S_{Tr} + S_{Ts}$ (see Fig. 7.2). The training set is used as input to learn a prediction model, i.e. describe how configuration options and their interactions

Table 7.1 Learning techniques reported in the literature of constraints discovery

Reference	Learning technique
[2, 16, 19, 38, 39, 44]	Classification and regression trees (CART)
[36]	Kernel density estimation and NSGA-II
[4]	Random forest
[4, 40]	Support vector machine
[4]	Decision tree C4.5 (J48)
[4]	Multilayer perceptrons (MLPs)
[10]	CitLab model
[40]	Evasion attack
[4]	Hoeffding tree, K*, kNN, logistic model tree, logistic regression, naive bayes, PART decision list, random committee, REP tree, RIPPER
[29]	Pruning rule-based classification (PART)

influence the behavior of a system. The test set is used to quantitatively analyse the quality of the tree for prediction using an evaluation metric on the outcomes of each configuration of S_{Ts} (see Sect. 7.2.4). To be practically useful, an ideal model is obtained at low cost with a reasonable labeling effort from a computational or human point of view; and the model exhibits low prediction errors and high interpretability (e.g. small number of rules in a decision tree).

7.4   Applications

The framework presented in Sect. 7.3, Fig. 7.2 can be applied on various case studies and adapted in different ways. This section is about giving a glimpse on these different possible adaptations and applications. In the following, we first instantiate the framework to other case studies than the Linux kernel before trying to generalize how the framework could be adapted.

7.4.1   Learning Constraints of an Industrial Video Generator

Let us take the example of an industrial video sequence generator called MOTIV [39]. MOTIV is a system allowing users to select values from features which will configure the content of an output video sequence. MOTIV is supposed to generate video sequences to benchmark computer-vision-based systems that would recognize entities in images. Among these features, there are the number of people that will walk around in the video, another feature will state which path they will follow, and others will define the amount of camera movement in the video, whether there is fog or whether the scene is filmed during the day or during the night, etc. All these features are gathered into an intermediate representation (*i.e., a feature vector*) that can be processed by machine learning algorithms. Let's suppose that some users are interested in generating video sequences that do not exceed a specific size (for instance 120 Mb) because they want these videos to be used on distributed systems such that videos will be streamed on a network. Multiple configurations of video sequence are created by setting values for all the features; and the output sizes of the resulting videos are measured.

From the configurations, MOTIV is able to assemble and generate all the frames of the video sequences and save them into video files, measurements only consists in reporting the size of the video files. The sampling step is done. From the measurements, we can tell automatically whether a video sequence associated with its configuration exceeds the predefined size threshold of 120Mb. The answer to this question will serve as a label to learn a model. Once all the videos are labeled, the training of the model starts. After training, the decision tree can be exploited to retrieve new constraints which were not discovered before. For instance, we are able to retrieve small video files when features controlling the amount of noise is set

```
1  !(signal_quality.dynamic_noise_level > 0.171472 &&
2    signal_quality.compression_artefact_level <= 0.180349)
3
4  !(signal_quality.dynamic_noise_level > 0.171472)
```

Fig. 7.3 A set of constraints helping to know which features are involved in the size of a MOTIV video file. Each constraint begins by a logical negation (!) indicating what follows should not be allowed

to a low value. The size can be even more decreased if the features controlling the compression level is set too high which will make details disappear at the cost of the visual quality of the video (because of visual artifacts appearing). This may seem rather obvious but these constraints are domain specific and they make sense for practitioners that try to minimize the size of a video. Figure 7.3 shows an example of retrieved constraints.

While, in Fig. 7.3, the exact float values do not really matter, the important elements are the options involved in the constraints and the order of magnitude of the float value. For instance, here, all options are bounded between 0 and 1 which means that having a float value set to 0.17 is rather low. In the end, the constraints can be read as follows: "To generate low size video files, the noise level needs to be set to a low value or the compression level needs to be high".

7.4.2 VaryLaTeX: Generating Text Documents That Does Not Exceed a Fixed Number of Pages

In another context, let suppose that some documentation need to be written. In order to avoid the document to be too long, authors have a page limit (for instance 50 pages). While writing they are wondering whether some paragraphs or sections are necessary, they are trying to find an optimal size for images, etc. They specify that these paragraphs and sections are optional and they state five different image sizes. In the end, with all the content they produced a 56 pages long document which is too much with regards to the initial constraint. They need to reduce the number of pages and start by reducing the size of images, the document is now 54 page-long. By removing all the paragraphs and sections marked as optional and setting the size of images to the minimum value they choose, they get a document which is 30 page-long. This new document meets the constraint but a lot of details are missing and the images are barely readable. After a couple of try-and-errors, the result remains not satisfying and finding a combination of content to add or remove and a large enough size of images remains difficult. Instead, authors can use the framework we present in Sect. 7.3. Configurations of the document are represented by a set of Boolean representing whether a section or paragraph is included and another set representing the size of images. A sample of all these possible configurations is drawn and the number of pages is measured for each of them. Then, as in the previous example, the number of pages is compared to the threshold limit and a Boolean answer is reported serving as the label. A machine learning model can now learn which options can produce documents with a page number that does not exceed the 50 pages limit. Of course, the threshold can be refined and instead of having a strict upper bound, the limit can be expressed as: "the number of pages must be between 45 and 50".

In the end, using our framework, the process of finding a satisfying document (meeting the page limit constraints) can be done automatically and only the selection of the best one according to authors needs to be done. This application has been already explored with the writing of scientific papers that need to meet strict constraints regarding page limit [2].

7.4.3   Other Applications

We briefly mention two additional applications in which the learning-based discovery of feature constraints has been applied.

Linux Kernel   The Linux kernel offers more than ten thousand features that can be combined to build a large number of kernel variants. In the community, it is considered as a benchmark for sampling techniques given its complexity [25, 41]. In practice, developers and contributors spend significant effort and computational resources to continuously track configurations that lead to build failures. Another error-prone and time-consuming task is to maintain the numerous constraints among features of the kernel. Numerous commits and patches are added to fix such constraints in the variability model of the kernel, through Kconfig files. While validating the correctness of the kernel across its entire configuration space is desirable, exhaustive testing of all configurations is simply impossible at the scale of Linux. Furthermore, the build process of Linux involves different layers and languages (CPP, Make and Kconfig) that are hard to statically analyze. Hence, an approach is to adopt the method presented in the chapter. A sample of configurations is first build: some fail, some pass. Then, thanks to the labels attached to Linux configurations, it is possible to learn combinations of features that lead to a failure. Such combinations can be lifted as constraints to reinforce the variability model of the kernel. More details can be found in [1].

Parametric Programs for 3D Printing   In the 3D printing industry, *parametric* programs are developed to derive custom 3D object models that can be printed. Such programs contain the list of parameters and their value domains, but no explicit constraints. This calls for a complementary approach that learns what configurations are valid based on previous experiences. In this context, validity refers to the fact that the object can actually be printed. This definition can be refined to include also the fact that it must not be fragile and thus avoid very tiny and small piece of plastic that make the whole object sticks together. An example is a junction that is so thin that the object is printable but the weight of the structure on top of the junction would make it collapse within a few seconds. Again, we can apply the method presented in the chapter: (1) a sample of a subset of all possible parameterizations is first computed; (2) an oracle to determine the validity of any parameterization of a given sample is executed; and (3) classifiers are trained on the sample to predict the validity of parameterizations that were not part of the sample. As reported in [4] experiments reveal that in most of the cases, the classifiers manage to achieve high scores. It can be used to enforce parametric programs with constraints and avoid the case of 3D object models that are simply not valid.

7.4.4 Applicability

The applicability of the proposal is broad and multiple domains are concerned. In essence, it can be any configurable systems for which multiple configurations can be sampled and observed. As presented before, it can well be the configurations of an operating system at compile time; a video sequence generator that produces videos that can be used to benchmark autonomous vehicles behaviors; a trans-coding system (such as x264) that turns an input video into a different format that can be lighter or played on modern screens; or a LaTeX paper variant generator that will try to tweak some parameters (for instance the size of images or whether to remove some paragraphs or parts of the text) to meet page limits. The only thing that matters is that multiple configurations can be created and that they can be represented as a vector of features such that it can be processed by a machine learning algorithm. Of course, the more the configuration that can be generated and the more complex the system is, the bigger the reward of using this framework since it was thought as a way to automate the task of retrieving constraints for a specific goal.

This specific labelling phase can also be different from simply "it builds or not". The example of the LaTeX paper variant generator tells that we can label variants based on the number of pages. However, we cannot use directly the number of pages since we are answering a binary classification problem: "Does the configuration meet a constraint or not?"; but, it is easy to go from the number of pages to a binary classification problem. Instead of considering directly the number of pages, we can set a threshold which must not be exceeded and answer the following question: "Does the number of pages of this specific configuration exceed the predefined threshold?"

Based on this transformation, an analysis of any quantity can be turned into a binary question. Instead of considering the number of pages, the amount of energy or memory can be measured and used as a quantity to check. The execution time, the size of the output artefact (code, video sequences, etc.), the visual quality of a video, whether a 3D model of an object to print is printable are just a few examples of quantities that could be considered as a criteria to claim that a configuration should be forbidden or not.

7.5   Benefits, Risks, and Challenges

Using such kind of automation and framework is tempting and shows high benefits when it can be applied properly. However, because of the statistical nature of machine learning algorithms and automation, there are also risks and problems that exist. The last part of this chapter is dedicated to show what benefits and risks can be expected from using machine learning techniques to discover feature constraints in SPLs and we also briefly describe open challenges that remain and open the road for further research directions.

7.5.1   Benefits

Automation Process vs Manual Effort Probably the biggest and most direct benefits of trying to use machine learning techniques to discover new constraints is its automation capability. While asking domain experts to state explicitly all the knowledge that they may have over a system is probably the most accurate way to start constraining system configurability. Yet it remains time-consuming for experts that may have difficulties to verbalise or write all these knowledge. A practical consequence is that the resulting set of constraints might be unsound and complete.

Taking the example of video generation, trying to define properly what is an acceptable video quality is hard. How much amount of noise exactly is too noisy? When is the night too dark? On the contrary, asking experts to state whether an already produced video is of sufficient quality is easy; they only have to look at a few frames of the sequence and they are able to decide. However, even if perfectly identifying what features values (and their combinations) produce a video of bad quality, excluding combinations that do not make sense is already helping to reduce the number of possible configurations. The more accurate the first constraints will be, the more the configuration space will be restricted. Nonetheless, we cannot expect experts to state a lot of constraints but we can expect them to provide a "warm start" such as the fact that the distribution of colors in the video is wide enough to provide contrasts (in turn becoming constraints over the mean and standard deviation of the colors). Experts may also state that a parameter that controls the noise level in the video cannot exceed 25% for instance otherwise, the noise is too much disturbing and nothing can be distinguished anymore. This threshold of 25% is important: being too cautious and only precise 90% would be already a useful piece of information but if 25% is too much, probably that 50% is already way too much and thus more savings could be done; on the other hand, being too restrictive and stating that "to be sure" 5% is already enough would prevent to generate video sequences in which noise would not be challenging enough and thus would prevent to apply video transcoders, for instance, on an "unusual" video sequence. In the end, maybe 25% is not the exact threshold—it can be 20 or 23%. We expect the constraints extractor to refine this threshold with the help of experts.

While experts may miss lots of constraints at first, our framework makes the promise to explore broadly and in an objective way the configuration space. It should help in covering more combinations of features, including the ones that are usually not considered. In addition, it can help discovering new constraints that will be eventually added to a variability model. The discovery process is iterative and requires the continuous involvement of experts throughout the evolution of a domain or a software project (see hereafter).

Scoping the Configuration Space On-Demand Besides the fact that using an automatic framework might give more systematic results and thus provide a more complete set of constraints, the ultimate goal of this framework is to reduce the number of configurations to consider when tackling a specific task (with specific expectations about systems' properties). Being able to reduce automatically and drastically the number of possible configurations is important and the expected outcome is that only configurations that meet expectations remain. While the original SPL was more general and was offering a more diverse set of configurations, after applying the framework, remaining configurations may be similar but have higher chances to meet expected properties. In the end, choosing one configuration randomly in the remaining set of configurations may help reduce waste of time and resources spent in deriving configurations that would be not used because of a mismatch with these user requirements. In other words, the solution space is scoped by the addition of extracted constraints.

Saving Resources in the Long Run From a global view, the sampling and measuring steps of our framework may seems costly as they require the selection and generation of actual products in order to measure them. However, once this first effort is made (hopefully on a tiny portion of the configuration space), there are no measures that have to be done anymore. Once the classifier is trained, a prediction is perform only by comparing the input configuration with the others that have been already seen and measured. Thus, the decision is done quickly and without having to generate the actual product, resulting in tremendous savings in time and resources as the number of queries on the classification model increases.

7.5.2 Risks

Completeness of Constraints Despite experts' knowledge, we cannot expect them to review all the features of the variability model. Some of the constraints may be missed. Intuitively, missing constraints can be: the most trivial ones, that experts will not think about as, for them, such constraints are common knowledge, and thus should be written by default. Taking the example of videos, colors should never be uniform (i.e., all the pixels have the same color) which results in images that do not change and thus on which we cannot see anything of the actual scene; regarding the generation of text documents, produced documents should not be 0 pages long.

Of course, such documents meet the page limit constraint but they are not really useful. Other constraints that can be missed by experts are the ones preventing from extremely rare combinations of features or those that never happened before. Because of their low chances of occurrences, experts may have trouble thinking about them. These combinations can involve a high number of features, which explain their rarity as the probability to select these specific combinations may decrease as more and more features are involved in the combinations. The fact that some combinations are implied in unpopular configurations can explain why some combinations were never seen before. For instance, when generating a video sequence, maybe the use of a night setup is not very popular because it is really difficult to properly parameterize. However, while night setup with enhanced contrasts can be acceptable, adding more than 10% of noise may end-up with videos that are too complex to analyze. Because of the addition of all these conditions in the features, and because the use of night is rarely used, experts may have missed such kind of constraints on the generator. Nonetheless, the use of our framework may explore broadly different combinations of features, including the ones rarely used, in order to better cover the configuration space and capture automatically such kind of constraints.

Efforts Need to be Put in the Oracle Definition The framework is based on checking that a specific configuration shows quantitative properties that are conform to the wish of end users (i.e., the number of pages in a document or the size of a kernel). Based on observations of such quantities, the machine learning algorithm is able to build a statistical model that will grasp features that need to be taken into account to retrieve new constraints. However, the threshold on the quantitative properties need to be carefully chosen. An example, which is not really dramatic but show that it must be done properly, is the Vary LATEX example. In this case, we defined a maximum number of pages, but usually, users do not want to get the minimal configuration which would reduce too much information. They want the machinery (i.e., the generator) to help them find a "good enough" configuration that will generate a product close to what they have in mind but they are not able to describe properly. Such a definition is hard to precisely express since aesthetics aspects should be considered.

Similarly, we gave examples of constraints that are rather easily implementable. But in the case of the video sequence generator, instead of considering the size of the output video file, one might want to generate video sequences that are *realistic*, similar to videos that could be captured by physical cameras. In this case, a lot of options need to be constrained: compression artifacts must not be perceivable, noise must not be too high, colors must be realistic, so must be objects' trajectories, etc. This poses the problem of providing an automatic routine that can check all these constraints. It implies that expectations can be stated precisely and that can be turned into a program while sometimes it is easier to present the result to a manual reviewing.

Finding Configurations Representing Both Labels Before learning the statistical model, a training set needs to be created. A proper training set is composed of a "sufficient" number of configurations but also configurations that represent both labels (ideally balanced between the two labels). While the problem of the number of configurations (i.e., how much is "sufficient"?) is task-specific, the problem of providing configurations from both labels is more general and remains difficult. Because we do not know the distribution of the labels a priori, we cannot know whether the constraints allow for both labels to be represented. Even if configurations can represent both labels, it can be difficult to find configurations of one label or the other because some configurations' labels occur rarely and are more rare. Or the way to sample configurations is biased and does not allow to explore all the space forbidding to find configurations of the missing label. For instance, based on the defined options such as the size of images and numerous optional paragraphs, maybe finding configurations of LaTeXdocuments that fit in 11 pages is easy. Yet synthesizing documents with 10 pages is much more challenging. Because of such threshold (here: equal or below 10 pages), it is challenging to automatically produce a balanced training set that would contain the right amount of configurations' labels.

7.5.3 Challenges

Limit Computations While Keeping a High Accuracy To retrieve constraints, the machine learning model needs a training set that contains a "large enough" number of configurations representing both classes. To be statistically representative, the training set may have to include configurations that will make the task of finding a separation between the two classes difficult. With such a dataset, the amount of computations, time, and resources will increase and, perhaps, will provide a high level of accuracy. On the other hand, wanting to avoid this increase of computations at all cost will provide a minimalist training set which is unlikely to grasp the subtleties defining both classes, affecting the machine learning model and leading to poor accuracy performances when it will be used in the wild. Thus, there is a trade-off to find in the size and configurations gathered in the training set. The definition of such trade-off has to be performed for each task at hand.

Finding Machine Learning Models That Are Powerful Yet Exploitable So far, we have only used decision trees as machine learning models since they can be exploited directly (i.e., they are humanly readable and the tree is parsed to retrieve constraints). However, such models can produce limited models (separations are parallel to the dimensional of the feature space) which may not be enough to find the best possible separation between classes. Other machine learning models can probably be used that would be more powerful but at the cost of putting more efforts in their exploitation (i.e., retrieve constraints as easily as with decision trees). Finding such models as well as simple ways to extract constraints remain to be defined.

Coping with Multiple Constraints We have presented our framework with examples that are fairly simple yet that show the different problems that can be encountered. However, all our examples were using only one kind of constraints (that were more or less easy to define) while other applications may be more complex and require to cope with several constraints at the time. This will make the learning task even more challenging and we foresee that the sampling method will be a key component. In addition to make the configuration space more complex, some of these constraints may be contradictory resulting in an unsolvable problem when trying to strictly satisfy all of them. In such applications, the need to define constraints that have to be satisfied and other that can be satisfied is very important and is likely to impact the overall quality of the machine learning model.

7.6   Conclusion

In this chapter, we have presented the "Sampling, Measuring, Learning" framework that leverages machine learning models on a set of configurations for adding new constraints to a software product line. The practical outcome is to restrict the configuration space to a better scope in which remaining configurations are valid. Constraining the configuration space is a challenging task as the space is usually too large to derive and assess all configurations and find the valid ones or the most suited ones. One advantage of using machine learning in this context is that the learned model can be applied on new configurations that were never derived before and decide whether it meets functional or performance expectations while only reasoning on the configuration's definition (i.e., without derivation but only considering feature values). Machine learning models require a set of configurations to be trained on. In our framework, we have used decision trees that come from the supervised family. In addition to the training set, supervised algorithms require configurations to be annotated by the use of an oracle. This oracle is task-dependent and can be easy to define (e.g., the page limit of a document) but in more complex setting can be hard to assess (e.g., defining an acceptable quality for synthetic video generation) which may make the use of this framework difficult in some domains at the moment. As described in this chapter, there are numerous domains and software product line engineering contexts in which this framework has already been applied. We believe the applicability of the method is broad and can be used to discover the subtle constraints of configurable systems.

References

1. Acher, M., Martin, H., Alves Pereira, J., Blouin, A., Eddine Khelladi, D., Jézéquel, J.M.: Learning From Thousands of Build Failures of Linux Kernel Configurations. Technical report, Inria ; IRISA (2019). URL https://hal.inria.fr/hal-02147012

2. Acher, M., Temple, P., Jezequel, J.M., Galindo, J.A., Martinez, J., Ziadi, T.: Varylatex: Learning paper variants that meet constraints. In: Proceedings of the 12th International Workshop on Variability Modelling of Software-Intensive Systems, pp. 83–88. ACM (2018)
3. Al-Msie'Deen, R.A., Huchard, M., Seriai, A.D., Urtado, C., Vauttier, S.: Concept lattices: a representation space to structure software variability. In: ICICS: International Conference on Information and Communication Systems. Irbid, Jordan (2014)
4. Amand, B., Cordy, M., Heymans, P., Acher, M., Temple, P., Jézéquel, J.M.: Towards learning-aided configuration in 3d printing: Feasibility study and application to defect prediction. In: Proceedings of the 13th International Workshop on Variability Modelling of Software-Intensive Systems, p. 7. ACM (2019)
5. Barr, E.T., Harman, M., McMinn, P., Shahbaz, M., Yoo, S.: The oracle problem in software testing: A survey. IEEE transactions on software engineering 41(5), 507–525 (2014)
6. Bécan, G., Acher, M., Baudry, B., Nasr, S.B.: Breathing ontological knowledge into feature model synthesis: an empirical study. Empir. Softw. Eng. 21(4), 1794–1841 (2016)
7. Breiman, L., Friedman, J.H., Olshen, R.A., Stone, C.J.: Classification and Regression Trees. Wadsworth and Brooks, Monterey, CA (1984)
8. Czarnecki, K., Wasowski, A.: Feature diagrams and logics: There and back again. In: SPLC'07 (2007)
9. Dietrich, C., Tartler, R., Schröder-Preikschat, W., Lohmann, D.: A robust approach for variability extraction from the linux build system. In: Proceedings of the 16th International Software Product Line Conference-Volume 1, pp. 21–30 (2012)
10. Gargantini, A., Petke, J., Radavelli, M.: Combinatorial interaction testing for automated constraint repair. In: 2017 IEEE International Conference on Software Testing, Verification and Validation Workshops (ICSTW), pp. 239–248. IEEE (2017)
11. Guo, J., Czarnecki, K., Apel, S., Siegmund, N., Wasowski, A.: Variability-aware performance prediction: A statistical learning approach. In: ASE (2013)
12. Haslinger, E.N., Lopez-Herrejon, R.E., Egyed, A.: On extracting feature models from sets of valid feature combinations. In: FASE (2013)
13. James, G., Witten, D., Hastie, T., Tibshirani, R.: An Introduction to Statistical Learning: with Applications in R. Springer (2013). URL https://faculty.marshall.usc.edu/gareth-james/ISL/
14. Kaltenecker, C., Grebhahn, A., Siegmund, N., Guo, J., Apel, S.: Distance-based sampling of software configuration spaces. In: Proceedings of the IEEE/ACM International Conference on Software Engineering (ICSE). ACM (2019)
15. Kittur, A., Chi, E.H., Suh, B.: Crowdsourcing user studies with mechanical turk. In: Proceedings of the SIGCHI conference on human factors in computing systems, pp. 453–456 (2008)
16. Krismayer, T., Rabiser, R., Grünbacher, P.: Mining constraints for event-based monitoring in systems of systems. In: ASE, pp. 826–831. IEEE Press (2017)
17. Lillack, M., Müller, J., Eisenecker, U.W.: Improved prediction of non-functional properties in software product lines with domain context. Software Engineering 2013 (2013)
18. Lora-Michiels, A., Salinesi, C., Mazo, R.: A Method based on Association Rules to Construct Product Line Model. In: 4th International Workshop on Variability Modelling of Software-intensive Systems (VaMos), p. 50. Linz, Austria (2010). URL https://hal.archives-ouvertes.fr/hal-00707527
19. Martin, H., Pereira, J.A., Acher, M., Jézéquel, J.: A comparison of performance specialization learning for configurable systems. In: SPLC '21: 25th ACM International Systems and Software Product Line Conference. ACM (2021)
20. Martinez, J., Ziadi, T., Bissyandé, T.F., Klein, J., Le Traon, Y.: Bottom-up adoption of software product lines: a generic and extensible approach. In: Proceedings of the 19th International Conference on Software Product Line, pp. 101–110 (2015)
21. Martinez, J., Ziadi, T., Mazo, R., Bissyandé, T.F., Klein, J., Le Traon, Y.: Feature Relations Graphs: A Visualisation Paradigm for Feature Constraints in Software Product Lines. In: IEEE Working Conference on Software Visualization (VISSOFT 2014), pp. 50–59. Victoria, Canada (2014)

22. Nadi, S., Berger, T., Kästner, C., Czarnecki, K.: Mining configuration constraints: Static analyses and empirical results. In: ICSE (2014)
23. Pereira, J.A., Acher, M., Martin, H., Jézéquel, J.: Sampling effect on performance prediction of configurable systems: A case study. In: J.N. Amaral, A. Koziolek, C. Trubiani, A. Iosup (eds.) ICPE '20: ACM/SPEC International Conference on Performance Engineering, Edmonton, AB, Canada, April 20-24, 2020, pp. 277–288. ACM (2020)
24. Pereira, J.A., Martin, H., Acher, M., Jézéquel, J.M., Botterweck, G., Ventresque, A.: Learning software configuration spaces: A systematic literature review (2019)
25. Pett, T., Thüm, T., Runge, T., Krieter, S., Lochau, M., Schaefer, I.: Product sampling for product lines: The scalability challenge. In: Proceedings of the 23rd International Systems and Software Product Line Conference-Volume A, pp. 78–83 (2019)
26. Plazar, Q., Acher, M., Perrouin, G., Devroey, X., Cordy, M.: Uniform sampling of SAT solutions for configurable systems: Are we there yet? In: ICST 2019 - 12th International Conference on Software Testing, Verification, and Validation, pp. 1–12. Xian, China (2019). URL https://hal.inria.fr/hal-01991857
27. Pohl, K., Böckle, G., van der Linden, F.J.: Software product line engineering: foundations, principles and techniques. Springer, Berlin Heidelberg (2005)
28. Ryssel, U., Ploennigs, J., Kabitzsch, K.: Extraction of feature models from formal contexts. In: I. Schaefer, I. John, K. Schmid (eds.) Software Product Lines - 15th International Conference, SPLC 2011, Munich, Germany, August 22-26, 2011. Workshop Proceedings (Volume 2), p. 4. ACM (2011)
29. Safdar, S.A., Lu, H., Yue, T., Ali, S.: Mining cross product line rules with multi-objective search and machine learning. In: Proceedings of the Genetic and Evolutionary Computation Conference, pp. 1319–1326. ACM (2017)
30. Sarkar, A., Guo, J., Siegmund, N., Apel, S., Czarnecki, K.: Cost-efficient sampling for performance prediction of configurable systems (t). In: ASE, pp. 342–352. IEEE (2015)
31. Shatnawi, A., Seriai, A., Sahraoui, H.: Recovering architectural variability of a family of product variants. In: International Conference on Software Reuse, pp. 17–33. Springer (2015)
32. Siegmund, N., Grebhahn, A., Apel, S., Kästner, C.: Performance-influence models for highly configurable systems. In: Proceedings of the 2015 10th Joint Meeting on Foundations of Software Engineering, ESEC/FSE 2015, pp. 284–294 (2015)
33. Siegmund, N., Kolesnikov, S.S., Kästner, C., Apel, S., Batory, D.S., Rosenmüller, M., Saake, G.: Predicting performance via automated feature-interaction detection. In: ICSE, pp. 167–177 (2012)
34. Siegmund, N., Rosenmüller, M., Kästner, C., Giarrusso, P.G., Apel, S., Kolesnikov, S.S.: Scalable prediction of non-functional properties in software product lines. In: 15th International Software Product Line Conference (SPLC), pp. 160–169 (2011)
35. Siegmund, N., Rosenmüller, M., Kuhlemann, M., Kästner, C., Apel, S., Saake, G.: SPL Conqueror: Toward optimization of non-functional properties in software product lines. Software Quality Journal 20(3), 487–517 (2012)
36. Siegmund, N., Sobernig, S., Apel, S.: Attributed variability models: outside the comfort zone. In: Proceedings of the 2017 11th Joint Meeting on Foundations of Software Engineering, pp. 268–278. ACM (2017)
37. Strüber, D., Mukelabai, M., Krüger, J., Fischer, S., Linsbauer, L., Martinez, J., Berger, T.: Facing the truth: Benchmarking the techniques for the evolution of variant-rich systems. In: Proceedings of the 23rd International Systems and Software Product Line Conference-Volume A, pp. 177–188 (2019)
38. Temple, P., Acher, M., Jézéquel, J., Barais, O.: Learning contextual-variability models. IEEE Software 34(6), 64–70 (2017)
39. Temple, P., Galindo Duarte, J.A., Acher, M., Jézéquel, J.M.: Using Machine Learning to Infer Constraints for Product Lines. In: Software Product Line Conference (SPLC). Beijing, China (2016)
40. Temple, P., Perrouin, G., Acher, M., Biggio, B., Jézéquel, J.M., Roli, F.: Empirical assessment of generating adversarial configurations for software product lines. Empirical Software Engineering 26(1), 1–49 (2021)

41. Thüm, T.: A bdd for linux? the knowledge compilation challenge for variability. In: Proceedings of the 24th ACM Conference on Systems and Software Product Line: Volume A-Volume A, pp. 1–6 (2020)
42. Turk, A.M.: Amazon mechanical turk. Retrieved August **17**, 2012 (2012)
43. Westermann, D., Happe, J., Krebs, R., Farahbod, R.: Automated inference of goal-oriented performance prediction functions. In: ASE, pp. 190–199. ACM (2012)
44. Yilmaz, C., Cohen, M.B., Porter, A.A.: Covering arrays for efficient fault characterization in complex configuration spaces. IEEE Transactions on Software Engineering **32**(1), 20–34 (2006)

Part II
Reengineering Product Line Architectures

Chapter 8
Extraction of Software Product Line Architectures from Many System Variants

Anas Shatnawi, Abdelhak-Djamel Seriai, and Houari Sahraoui

Abstract Software Product Line Architecture (SPLA) describes the architecture of a set of software variants by describing (1) what components can be included in the product configuration based on the selected features of this product (2) how these components can be configured to form a concrete architecture of the product, (3) shared components, and (4) individual architecture characteristics of each product. However, developing SPLA from scratch is known a highly, costly and risky task. The alternative is to exploit the already developed *legacy* software variants to reverse engineer SPLA. This reduces the cost of Software Product Line (SPL) development and allows to manage software variants as a SPL. In this chapter, we discuss the extraction of SPLA based on the analysis of several software variants. Precisely, we discuss the variability in SPLA. Then, we discuss challenges in extracting variability of SPLA and highlight a number of good practices proposed in the-state-of-the-art of the SPLA extraction. Next, we discuss one example approach that completely extracts SPLA of software variants.

8.1 Introduction

Software Product Line Architecture (SPLA) represents one of the most important software elements of a Software Product Line (SPL). In the literature, many definitions have been proposed for SPLA. These definitions consider SPLA as a core architecture that captures the variability of a set of software products at the architecture level. However, they differ in terms of the variability definition. For instance, DeBaud et al. [11] defined SPLA as an architecture shared by their member products and has such a variability degree. This is a very general definition since it

A. Shatnawi (✉) · A.-D. Seriai
University of Montpellier, CNRS, LIRMM, Montpellier, Montpellier, France
e-mail: shatnawi@lirmm.fr; seriai@lirmm.fr

H. Sahraoui
DIRO, Université de Montréal, Montreal, QC, Canada
e-mail: sahraouh@iro.umontreal.ca

© Springer Nature Switzerland AG 2023
R. E. Lopez-Herrejon et al. (eds.), *Handbook of Re-Engineering Software Intensive Systems into Software Product Lines*, https://doi.org/10.1007/978-3-031-11686-5_8

does not specify the nature of the architecture variability. In contrast, Pohl et al. [37] provide a more precise definition by specifying the nature of architecture variability. In this definition, SPLA includes variation points and variants that are presented in such a variability model. Gomaa [19] links the architecture variability with the architectural-elements. Thus, in his definition, SPLA describes the variability in terms of mandatory, optional, and variable components, and their connections. As a synthesis of these definitions, we propose the following one:

Definition 1 Software Product Line Architecture (SPLA) describes the high level structures, and the commonality and the variability related to components and architectural configuration of a set of software variants of a SPL.

Companies rely on three approaches to develop SPLA of a SPL: *proactive*, *reactive* and *extractive* [18, 41].

- **Proactive approach:** companies develop SPLA from scratch. They need to understand the commonality and the variability of the SPL in advance. However, developing SPLA from scratch is known to be a highly costly and risky task.
- **Reactive approach:** companies incrementally develop SPLA during the development of a SPL. This can reduce the cost and the risk compared to the proactive strategy.
- **Extractive approach:** companies exploit the already developed *legacy* software variants to reverse engineer SPLA. This is based on the analysis of the commonality and the variability between the software artifacts of software variants to extract the SPLA. This allows companies to significantly reduce the cost of SPLA development compared to the proactive and reactive approaches. The Extractive approach was used by 50% of companies according to the industrial survey of SPL adaptation [3].

In many cases, companies usually develop several software variants with functional and technical variations without using SPLs [12, 16]. In their recent studies, Fischer et al. [16] reported that it becomes an industrial practice to rely on the *clone-and-own* approach to develop similar software variants based on copying functionalities from existing software variants and by customizing these functionalities to meet the varied requirements of new customers [16]. Nevertheless, managing the software reuse and maintenance of these software variants and their cloned functionalities is a very hard task when the number of software variants is increased [12]. Therefore, it is important to systematically manage the commonality and variability between software variants using SPLs. One of the main challenges is to manage the commonality and variability between software variants at the architecture level by extracting SPLA.

In this chapter, we discuss the extraction of SPLA based on the analysis of several software variants. We present an illustrative example in Sect. 8.2. We discuss the variability in SPLA in Sect. 8.3, including the different types of SPLA variability. Next, we discuss challenges concerning the extraction of SPLA from many software variants in Sect. 8.4. Then, in Sect. 8.5, we discuss the process of SPLA extraction and highlight a number of good practices of this extraction. Next, to illustrate the whole extraction process, we present an approach that completely identifies SPLA of software variants in Sect. 8.6. Finally, we conclude the chapter in Sect. 8.7.

8.2 An Illustrative Example

We provide an illustrative example presented in Fig. 8.1 to better understand the architecture variability of software variants. This example includes the architecture of three software variants from the audio player software family. The first software

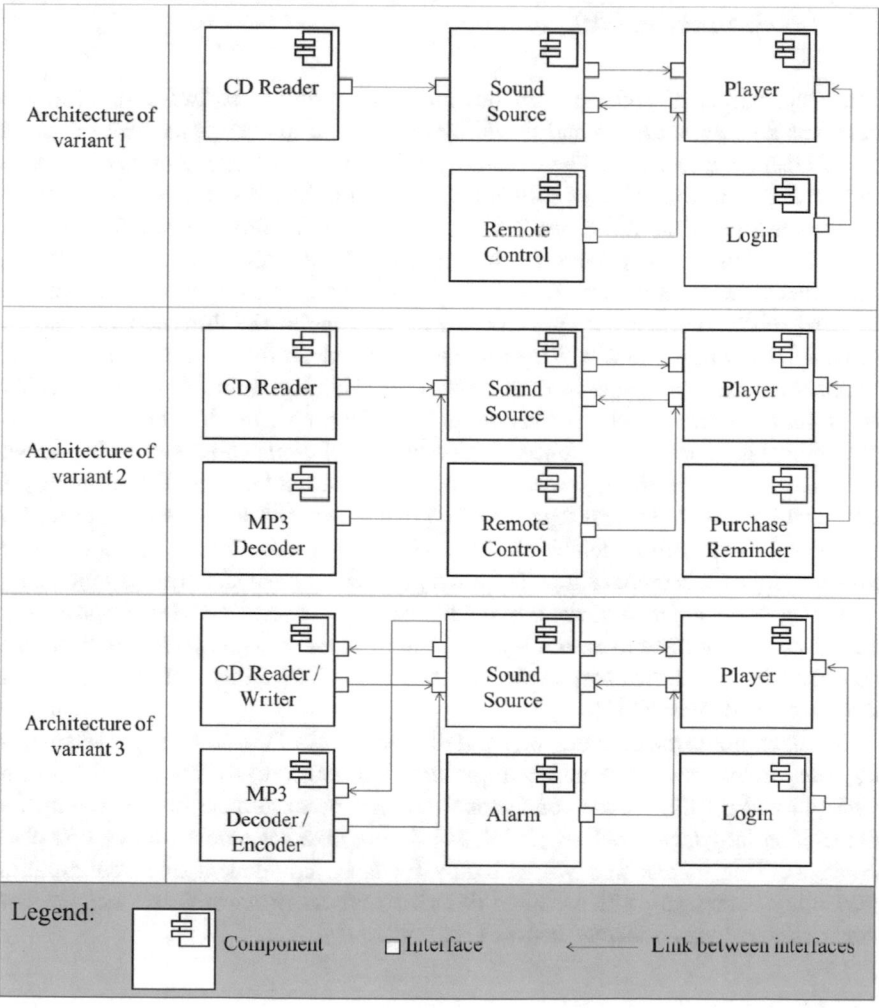

Fig. 8.1 An illustrative example of architecture variability

architecture consists of five components: *CD Reader, Sound Source, Player, Login* and *Remote Control* components. The second software architecture contains six components: *CD Reader, Sound Source, Player, Remote Control, MP3 Decoder* and *Purchase Reminder*. The third software architecture has six components: *CD Reader, Sound Source, Player, MP3 Decoder, Login* and *Alarm*.

To show different types of variability in SPLA, we include diversity related to the components composing each architecture, the functionalities implemented by the same component in different software variants (*MP3 Decoder* and *MP3 Decoder/Encoder*), the interfaces (provided and required) of components and the links between these components.

8.3   Variability in SPLA

The main theme of software product line engineering is software variability. It concerns the *susceptibility* and *flexibility* of software to change to meet the needs of different customers [9]. The variability exists at *different levels of abstraction* of the development life cycle of software variants of a SPL (e.g. requirement, design, implementation) [9]. At the *requirement level*, the variability is instituted from the *diversity in customers' wishes*. Each customer selects a different set of features to be included in the software variant. In the illustrative example, the customer of the first software variant selects *CD Reader* and one of the third software variant selects *CD Reader*, and *CD Writer* features. This variability is documented by the feature modeling language in most cases [20]. This variability at the requirement level *does not carry technical concerns* [37]. Starting from the *design level*, the variability has more details concerning *technical solutions about how to implement the features to form the software architectures*. It describes how the variability is built and implemented with regard to the point of view of software architects [37]. The technical variability details concerns *what software components are included in the software architecture* (e.g., *CD Reader, Sound Source* and *Player* components), *how these components interact through their interfaces* (e.g., *CD Reader* provides a sound stream interface to *Sound Source*), and *what topology forms the architectural configuration* (i.e. how components are composed) [35]. SPLA should describe all these technical details [41].

SPLA explores the commonality and the variability of the architectural elements, i.e. *component, connector* and *configuration* variability to realize the architecture variability. We will exclude connector variability because most of the architecture description languages such as [5, 29, 30] do not take the connectors as first class concepts. This means that we will only focus on component and configuration variability. Therefore, SPLA should describe *component variability, configuration variability* and *dependencies between the components*.

8.3.1 Component Variability

Components represent the main building elements of the software architecture that define the functionalities of the corresponding software. The component variability starts from the existence of many software components that have the same architectural meaning in terms of their implemented functionalities compared to the big picture of the software architectures of several software variants. *MP3 Decoder* and *MP3 Decoder/Encoder* are examples of these components in Fig. 8.1. We call these similar software components as *component variants* and we define them as follows:

Definition 2 Component variants are a collection of components that have the same architectural meaning across software variants by offering the same features with technical or functional variations.

We also need to enable capturing the commonality and the variability between component variants to understand the similarities and differences in their implemented functionalities. This requires to provide a mechanism to identify the *structure variability* and the *interface variability*.

Component structure variability concerns the differences compared to the implementation details of component variants. This is related to the variability in the set of functionalities (e.g., *Decoder* or *Decoder/Encoder*) implemented by these component variants. This component structure variability can be presented at the class, method, attribute or even statement levels. The choice of the level is left to software architects. We should identify the *common elements* that belong to all component variants, and the *variable elements* that do not belong to all component variants. We define component structure variability as follows:

Definition 3 Component structure variability concerns the differences in the structure of the component variants identified at the implementation level.

Component interface variability is related to the interaction between component variants with other components in different architectures. This is based on the variability in the component interfaces: provided and required ones. Each component provided interface provides an abstract description to access the functionalities of the component based on a set of method invocations. Component variants could be variable in their provided interfaces in the different software variants. In Fig. 8.2, *CD Reader* and *CD Reader/Writer* are component variants that are variable in their interfaces. *CD Reader* provides a single interface to read the *CD* content, while *CD Reader/Writer* has an additional required interface related to the additional functionalities of writing on a CD that requires a source of information. We need to distinguish between mandatory and optional interfaces. Mandatory interfaces exist in all component variants. Optional interfaces exist in some component variants. We define component interface variability as follows:

Definition 4 Component interface variability is the interaction variability between components through their provided and required interfaces.

Fig. 8.2 An example of
variability of two component
variants

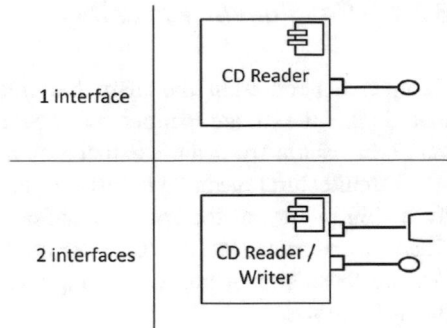

8.3.2 Architecture Configuration Variability

The architectural configuration defines the collection of software components to be included in the software architecture, and the topology of how components are linked through their interfaces. Therefore, the configuration variability is represented in terms of the *component existence variability*, as well as the *component-to-component link variability*. We define configuration variability as follows:

Definition 5 Configuration variability determines the mandatory and optional components as well as the mandatory and optional component-to-component links to be included in different architectures of software variants.

Component existence variability concerns the presence and absence of components in the software architectures of different software variants. We define this variability in terms of the collection of *mandatory* and *optional* components. Mandatory components should be included in any software architecture of software variants. Optional components are not mandatory to be included in the software architecture of a software variant. In the illustrative example in Fig. 8.1, *Sound Source* is a mandatory component because it is a part of all software architectures, and *Purchase Reminder* is an optional component because it is only a part of the second software architecture. We define component existence variability as follows:

Definition 6 Component existence variability refers to the mandatory or optional existence of a given component in the architecture of a specific software variant.

The component-to-component link is the connection of two components based on their interfaces. With variability, a component can be linked with various components in different software variants. A component could be linked with a group of components in one software variant, and it could be linked with a different group of components in other software variants. In Fig. 8.1, we show an example of component-to-component link variability where *CD Reader* has only one link with

Sound Source in the first and the second software architectures, while *CD Reader* has two links with *Sound Source* and *MP3 Decoder/Encoder* in the third software architecture.

The component-to-component link variability is related to the *component existence variability*. For instance, the existence of a link between *CD Reader* and *MP3 Decoder/Encoder* is related to the selection of *CD Reader* and *MP3 Decoder/Encoder* in the architecture of software variant. Therefore, we consider a component-to-component link as a mandatory link if and only if it occurs in the architecture as well as the connected components are included in the architecture. Otherwise, it is considered as optional component-to-component link. We define component-to-component link variability as follows:

Definition 7 Component-to-component link variability refers to the mandatory or optional existence of a particular link between two components, i.e., interface connection, in the architecture of a specific software variant as well as the corresponding components are included in the architecture of this software variant.

8.3.3   Component Dependencies

The component and configuration variabilities, discussed earlier, are not enough to define a valid architecture of a software variant. We also need the dependencies, i.e. constraints, between components. Such dependencies are related to the feature variability. They can be of five types: *Require, And, Exclude, Alternative,* and *Or* dependencies between the components [41]. We define these dependencies as follows:

Definition 8 Required dependency refers to the necessary selection of a component to select another one; i.e. *Component B* is required to select *Component A*.

Definition 9 And dependency is the bidirectional form of the required one; i.e. *Component A* requires *Component B* and vice versa. More generally, the selection of one component among a set of components requires the selection of all the other components.

Definition 10 Exclude dependency refers to the antagonistic relationship; i.e. *Component A* and *Component B* cannot occur in the same architecture.

Definition 11 Alternative dependency generalizes the exclude one by exclusively selecting only one component from a set of components.

Definition 12 Or dependency refers to the obligation to select at least one component between a set of components to be included in a software variant.

To better understand a large number of *Require*, *And*, *Exclude*, *Alternative*, and *Or* dependencies between different components, we analyze these dependencies to identify their relationships in terms of *groups of variability*. Such relationships are the overlapping between dependencies. Several dependencies are the constraints of a common set of components. For example, a component has an *Or* dependency with components having *And* dependencies among themselves. We represent these dependencies using a hierarchical tree (e.g. feature model of components) to help support software architects to perform their tasks. We define groups of variability as follows:

Definition 13 Groups of variability organizes the overlapping of dependencies between components based on a feature model of components.

8.4 Challenges in Extracting SPLA from Software Variants

In the previous section, we defined the SPLA and explained the different types of variability of architectural elements of the SPLA. In this section, we discuss challenges related to the extraction of SPLA based on the analysis of many software variants.

Unlike the extraction of the software architecture of single software, the extraction of SPLA from multiple software variants requires the analysis of all these software variants. In most cases, these software variants are developed using the clone-and-own approach in an ad-hoc manner. Meaning, the cloning of software variants from existing ones is done without preserving contorting the commonalty and the variability across software variants. That makes the comparison of software artifacts of different software variants hard due to the loss of the architectures of some software variants because there is no a rigorous coordination process to enforce the development teams to provide architectures of their software variants with respect to the previously developed software variants. Furthermore, the tractability links between software artifacts of software variants are not well-documented at different levels of abstraction including source code, architectures and features. For example, this complicates the identification of software components implementing each feature.

For some extreme cases, software variants could be developed by different international teams [4] where developers could use their native-languages to document the software artifacts of software variants [6]. For example, an Arabic developer writes documents in Arabic, while a French one writes documents in French. In such cases, we will have difficulties analyzing the software artifacts of different software variants to identify a mapping between the different human-languages. Moreover, developers could use different programming languages to extend the software variants that could lead to the case of multilanguage software variants. In [40], we identify five challenges that make the analysis of source code difficult for multilanguage software variants. Such challenges are: (1) the diversity of meta-models of their source code, (2) the mixing of multilanguage source code in one single file, (3) different languages rely on various patterns to codify dependencies, (4) different frameworks provide different container services, and (5) the usage of string literals to describe dependencies.

8.5 Toward SPLA Extraction from Many Software Variants: Good Practices

The SPLA extraction[1] refers to the process of recovering the commonality and the variability at the architecture level based on the analysis of other software artifacts of software variants (e.g., source code) [8]. It includes the recovery of an abstract model that describes the architecture variability and concrete software components that can be directly reused in the future development. We identify good practices related to the extraction of SPLA based on our experience in the extraction of variability in software variants and on the study of the-state-of-the-art of architecture extraction [1, 13, 27]. We follow a process-oriented analysis to define these practices similar to [1, 13]. Following the life cycle of a SPLA extraction approach shown in Fig. 8.3, the approach starts from the input software variant artifacts to be analyzed for extracting SPLA. Then, we should define a suitable process to be performed on the input artifacts. Next, we should specify the output desired from the SPLA extraction approach.

8.5.1 The Input Artifacts to Be Analyzed for Extracting SPLA

The input software artifacts of the SPLA extraction approach are used to extract the information related to the variability of software variants and to allow us to

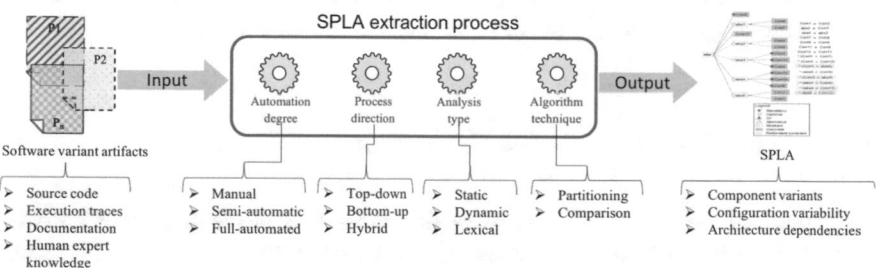

Fig. 8.3 The good practices of SPLA extraction approach

---

[1] In the literature, researchers have used many synonyms of extraction like reverse engineering [41], identification [32], mining [45], recovery [36] and reconstruction [34].

recover the SPLA. The input software artifacts can be *source code*, *execution traces*, *documentations* and/or *human expert knowledge*.

- **Source code** is used to determine the functionalities to be implemented by computers. For object-oriented software, the source code consists of classes including methods (e.g., operations) and attributes (e.g, data). The dependencies between classes are method invocations, attribute accesses, inheritance, and so on. All these information allow identifying the variability at the implementation level that reflects the architecture variability. Due to its availability, source code is the most commonly used input artifact to be analyzed by the existing software architecture extraction approaches. These extraction approaches relied on the dependencies between classes to cluster them into disjoint groups representing the component-based architecture (i.e., to identify high cohesive and low coupling partitions) [31, 32, 34].
- **Execution traces** represent the system behavior at runtime such that dependencies between software elements are collected during the program execution. They allow one to identify the dynamic variability between the software variants following different usage scenarios. We can identify these usage scenarios based on use cases, sequence diagram and test cases [14, 33, 42].
- **Software documentations** include descriptions of the software variants at different level of abstractions [26]. It can be text-based (e.g., configuration files) or model-based documents (e.g., use cases). We can derive functional components from use cases [42]. Configuration files help to extract information about the previous architecture [43]. Design documents are used to provide information about how components have been designed [23].
- **Human expert knowledge** is related to persons who have relevant information about the design and the implementation of software variants. Their knowledge can be used to select the main architecture view to be the core of SPLA in [36], and to guide the extraction process by classifying the architectural elements and identifying their dependencies [21].

The selection of which input artifacts to be analyzed in the process of SPLA extraction approach is based on: (1) the availability of artifacts, (2) the ease to execute the program, and (3) the decision of software architects.

8.5.2 The Process of SPLA Extraction

The approach process of SPLA extraction aims to analyze the input software artifacts in order to recover the variability of software variants at the architecture level and to identify reusable components composing the recovered SPLA. We see that the process is based on four aspects. These aspects are the *automation degree* of the extraction process, the *direction* of the analysis process, the *type of analysis* to be performed, and the *algorithm* determining the procedure of the process.

- **The automation degree of the extraction process** refers to the degree in which human expert interactions are required to perform this process. It can be *manual, semi-automatic* and *fully-automatic* processes.

  - **Manual process** totally depends on human experts. In this context, we provide guides for the experts, such as a visual analysis of the source code that allows identifying architectural elements [25, 44].
  - **Semi-automatic process** needs human experts for recommendations to perform the SPLA extraction process [21]. Such recommendations are to select the main architecture view to be the core of SPLA [21], to manually analyze design documents [36], and to interact with the approach steps to refine the results [15].
  - **Fully-automated process** does not require human expert interactions to identify SPLA, excluding the need to determine some threshold values [31, 41].

- **The direction of the analysis process** can be *top-down, bottom-up* and *hybrid*. In top-down, the process analyzes software requirements to extract SPLA. In bottom-up, the process analyzes the source code of software variants to extract SPLA [17, 21, 24, 41]. Hybrid process refers to the analysis of software requirements (top-down) and source codes (bottom-up) to identify the corresponding software architecture [2].

- **The type of analysis** to be performed can be *static, dynamic* or *lexical* to identify the relationships between artifacts, in order to extract SPLA.

  - **Static analysis** does not require executing software variants to perform the analysis [36, 41, 43]. We can statically extract graph structures representing the elements (classes, methods, attributes) of the software variants and their related dependencies (calls and references) from the source code [40]. These graph structures are used to identify the architecture of each software variants and the variability between these identified architectures [36, 41]. Note that static analysis does not address polymorphism and dynamic binding, and it does not allow to distinguish between the used and unused source code.
  - **Dynamic analysis** refers to the use of program execution traces to identify the relationships between elements of software variants at the run-time. This allows us to collect actual dependencies between elements. For example, by executing a feature, we can identify software components related to this feature by collecting the executed elements. However, the limitations against the use of dynamic analysis are: (1) it requires to cope with complex setup of software variants for execution, and (2) the difficulty to identify all execution scenarios that cover all dependencies in the software variants. To help deal with the second limitations, we can rely on use cases, usage logs and sequence diagrams to identify execution scenarios [14, 33, 42].

- **Lexical analysis** relies on the textual information in the software variant artifacts to identify their related dependencies. This analysis supports the identification of cloned functionalities between the software variants [17, 22–24, 31, 32].

• **The algorithms that support the extraction process** depend on the formulation of the computational problems of SPLA extraction. The SPLA extraction can be viewed as *partitioning problem* and *comparison problem*.

   - **The partitioning problem** aims to recover the software architectures corresponding to all software variants. For this purpose, one can use clustering algorithms [41], or search-based algorithms [38] to partition classes.
   - **The comparison problem** aims to identify the variability between these recovered software architectures. Several algorithms can be used like formal concept analysis [7, 41] and clone detection algorithms [17, 23, 24] to identify pieces of source code existing in many software variants.

8.6 Illustrative Approach to Extract SPLA

In this section, we provide example techniques to extract each type of architecture variability of SPLA. We rely on our previous work [41] because it provides techniques that cover all types of architecture variability related to SPLA.

8.6.1 Input and Goal

For simplicity, let us consider that we have as input the component-based architecture of each single software variant. Each component-based architecture is a set of disjoint groups of classes such that each group of classes represents the implementation of a component in this architecture. This component-based architecture can be extracted based on any architecture recovery approach by analyzing the object-oriented source code of each single software variant. A comprehensive survey of these approaches could be found at [1, 13, 27].

The goal is to find the commonality and variability between the component-based architectures respectively recovered from individual software variants. This is based on: (1) the extraction of component variability including the component variants and their related structure and interface variability, and (2) the extraction of configuration variability including the component existence variability, component-to-component link variability, and component dependencies.

8.6.2   *Extraction of Component Variability*

8.6.2.1   Extraction of Component Variants

Component variants are extracted based on the identification of components providing the same, or at least similar, core functionalities. Since that these functionalities are implemented based on the object-oriented source code, a group of components sharing the majority of their source code is considered as components providing similar functionalities. Software architects should define the similarity degree to consider this group of components to be components variants.

Textual analysis allows identifying the semantic relationships between the classes of different components. Each component is seen as a text document that contains the implementation of classes composing this component. Then, a text-based clustering algorithm is used to identify similar components that are considered as component variants of the same architectural element. Note that two components from the same software variant should not be grouped together in the same cluster. The clustering algorithm should adhere to this condition to forbid this situation.

8.6.2.2   Extraction of Component Structure Variability

At this stage, the source code of component variants is used to extract their structure variability in terms of common and variable classes. Formal Concept Analysis (FCA) allows one to identify common and variable classes as well as the distribution of variable classes in the component variants. The formal context of FCA considers component variants and classes as objects and attributes respectively. The objects of this formal context have attributes based on the classes distribution in the implementation of the corresponding component variants. We give an example of a formal context of three component variants in Table 8.1 where X refers to that the *variant* includes the corresponding *class* in its implementation. Then, FCA generates a *lattice* based on this formal context that is presented in Fig. 8.4. Following this lattice, the common classes are grouped in the root node of the lattice, while the variable ones are distributed in other nodes. A component variant has all classes included in all nodes placed in the path to the root node.

Table 8.1 An example of formal context of three component variants

	CD	Reader	Transformer	StreamManager	Helper	Writer	Encoder	Decoder
Variant 1	X	X	X	X	X			X
Variant 2	X	X	X	X	X	X		
Variant 3	X	X	X	X			X	X

Fig. 8.4 A lattice example of
three component variants

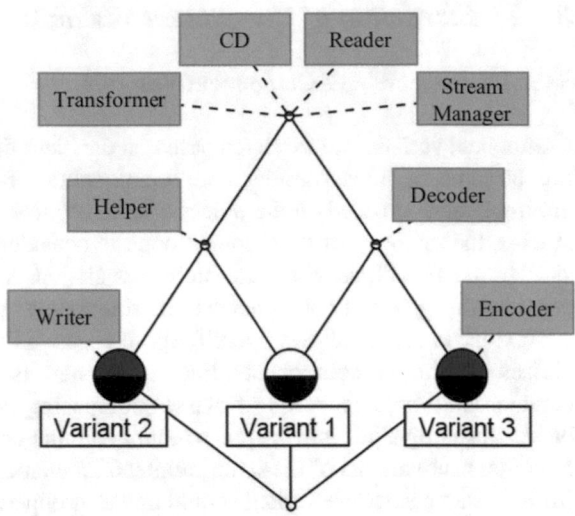

8.6.2.3 Extraction of Component Interface Variability

Now that the structure variability is extracted, the next step is to extract the
mandatory and optional interfaces of component variants. The interfaces of each
component variant are identified as they are structured in the corresponding software
variant where the component variant has been extracted. One can use any approach
of Seriai et al. [39] or Lui et al. [28] to extract groups of methods representing
the component interfaces. The textual analysis allows one to identify the semantic
similarity between interfaces of component variants to determine similar interfaces.
This textual analysis compares the methods of each interface with ones of other
interfaces based on the header and body of methods. Software architects can use
a pre-defined threshold similarity value to decide whether interfaces are similar or
not. Once similar interfaces are detected in the different variants of a component, the
intersection determines the mandatory interfaces. The remaining ones are optional
interfaces.

8.6.3 Extraction of Configuration Variability

8.6.3.1 Extraction of Component Existence Variability

Formal Concept Analysis (FCA) is also used to analyze the component existence
variability. In the formal context, each software architecture of a software variant
is represented in terms of an object that has a set of components as attributes. FCA
generates a lattice of concepts representing the distribution of the components in the
different architectures. Based on this lattice, the mandatory components are grouped
in the root node of the lattice, while the variable components are in the other nodes.

Fig. 8.5 A lattice example of three architectural configurations

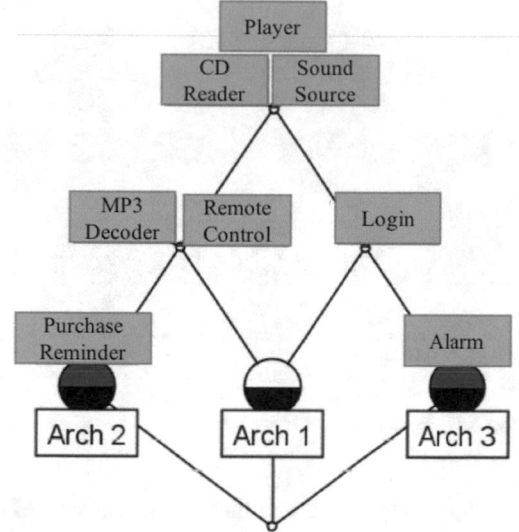

In Fig. 8.5, we provide an example of a lattice for architectures of three software variants related to our illustrative example of the audio player family presented in Fig. 8.1. The mandatory components are *CD Reader*, *Sound Source* and *Player*, and the optional components are *Remote Control*, *MP3 Decoder*, *Purchase Reminder*, *MP3 Decoder*, *Login* and *Alarm*.

8.6.3.2 Extraction of Component-to-Component Link Variability

For each component, the set of components that have links with this component in each software variant are identified. The mandatory component-to-component links are identified based on the intersection between the links of this component in different software variants. The other component-to-component links are optional ones.

8.6.3.3 Extraction of Component Dependencies

The identification of dependencies between optional components is done using the same lattice generated by FCA in Fig. 8.5. The intent of each node in this lattice contains a group of components (e.g. *MP3 Decoder* and *Remote Control*) and the extent of each node is a group of architectural configurations (e.g. *Arch 2*). The architecture configurations can be reverse-engineered from this lattice based on paths identified starting from their nodes to the root of the lattice. Each path consists of an ordered series of nodes. This order is based on the hierarchical distribution of the nodes called sub-concept to super-concept relationships.

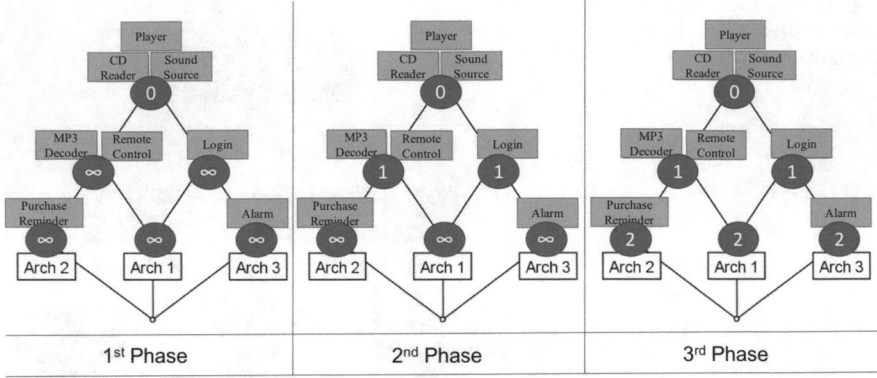

Fig. 8.6 An example of BFS process

The process to extract these paths consists of two steps as follows.

1. **Node numbering** is based on the *Breadth First Search (BFS)* algorithm [10]. BFS helps extracting a tree-based representation from the lattice starting from its root node. BFS will visit the nodes at distance *1*, then it will visit the nodes at distance 2 and so on. Figure 8.6 shows the steps of BFS for numbering nodes. The number of a node denotes to the distance of visiting a given node and ∞ refers to unvisited nodes.

2. **Path extraction** starts from each node holding an extent (e.g. *Arch 1*). It goes in a bottom-up direction based on the numbers identified in the previous step to nodes having a lower numbering. It performs this process recursively until reaching the root node that has *0* numbering. We provide in Fig. 8.7 the three paths identified based on our example in Fig. 8.5. These three paths are respectively presented by solid, dashed and double dashed arrows. For example, the path corresponding to *Arch 1* includes the node of *Login*, the node of *MP3 Decoder* and *Remote Control* and the node of *CD Reader Sound Source*, and *Player*.

The next process is to extract the dependencies between components based on these identified paths.

- **Required dependency extraction.** It is based on *parent-to-child relationships* between the nodes. A node requires another node if this node appears after the other node in all of the identified paths. Due to the sub-concept and the super-concept between these nodes, the first node cannot be reached without passing the required node in the lattice. Considering our example in Fig. 8.5, *Purchase Reminder* requires *Remote Control* and *MP3 Decoder*.

- **Exclude dependency extraction.** It is based on the identification of nodes that do not have any sub-concept to super-concept relationship in all paths. Two nodes are considered having exclude dependency if they never appear together

Fig. 8.7 An example of paths extracted from FCA lattice

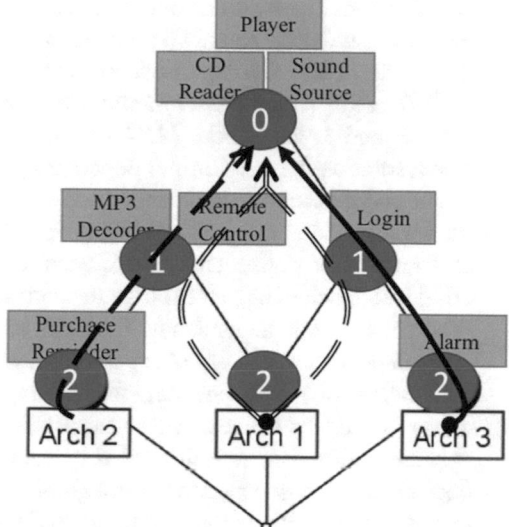

in all paths. Considering our example in Fig. 8.5, *Purchase Reminder* and *Alarm* exclude each other as they never appear together in paths identified in Fig. 8.7.

- **Alternative dependency extraction.** It is the generalized form of the exclude one by exclusively choosing one component from a group of components having the alternative dependencies between each other. Therefore, the identification of alternative dependency is based on a group of nodes that hold exclude dependency with each node in this group. This is based on the set cover extraction algorithm from the graph theory [10]. For example, if node *A* is excluded with nodes *B* and *C* on the one hand, and node *B* is excluded with node *C* on the other hand, then the group of *A, B* and *C* forms an alternative dependency.

- **And dependency extraction.** It is based on a group of components grouped in the same node in the lattice. *Remote Control* and *MP3 Decoder* have an And dependency in our example in Fig. 8.5.

- **Or dependency extraction.** When some components are concerned by an OR dependency, this means that at least one of them should be selected; i.e., the architectural configuration may contain any combination of these components. Therefore, in the case of absence of other dependencies any pair of components is concerned by an OR dependency. Thus, pairs concerned by required, exclude, alternative, or AND dependencies are ignored as well as those concerned by transitive require dependencies; e.g., *Purchase Reminder* and *Alarm* are ignored since they are exclusive.

The process of identifying the OR groups is as follows. Firstly, we check the dependencies between each pair of nodes. Pairs that have required, exclude, alternative, and AND dependencies are ignored. All pairs having transitive require dependencies are also ignored. The reason of the exclusion is that these dependencies break the OR one. Then, the remaining pairs of nodes are assigned an OR dependency. Next, we analyze these pairs by testing the dependency of their nodes. Pairs sharing a node need to be resolved (e.g., in Fig. 8.5, a pair of *MP3 Decoder-Remote Control* and *Alarm*, and a pair of *MP3 Decoder-Remote Control* and *Login*, where *MP3 Decoder-Remote Control* is a shared node). The resolution is based on the dependency between the other two nodes (e.g., *Login* and *Alarm*). If these nodes have a require dependency, then we select the highest node in the lattice (i.e., the parent causes the OR dependency to its children). If the dependency is excluded or alternative one, then we remove all OR dependencies (i.e., an exclude dependency violates an OR one). In the case of sharing an OR dependency, the pairs are grouped to one OR dependency. AND dependency will not occur in this case according to the AND definition.

- **Extraction of groups of variability** aims to identify dependencies among groups of dependencies. Since an AND group can be considered as one coherent entity, it is not allowed for its components to partially have internal dependencies, e.g. dependent through an OR with other groups. This implies that all components belonging to an AND group should have the dependency. For alternative and OR dependencies, it is allowed to take AND ones as a member. In addition, the internal dependencies between alternative and OR dependencies are allowed. In other words, an alternative dependency can be a member of an OR dependency and vice versa. According to that, the AND dependency has a high priority to be added before the others while OR and alternative have the same priority. The identification of the hierarchical tree starts from the root of the tree by directly connecting all mandatory components to it (e.g., *CD Reader*, *Sound Source* and *Player*). At this stage, the tree does not have a hierarchy. Then, optional components are added based on their relationships. Groups of components having AND dependencies are added by creating an abstract node that carries out these components (e.g., *Remote Control* and *MP3 Decoder* are added using a group of an AND dependency). The relation between the parent and the children is an AND dependency. Next, alternative dependencies are represented by an abstract node that carries out these components (*Purchase Reminder* and *Alarm*). Next, OR dependencies are applied by adding an abstract node as a parent to components having an OR. In the case where the relation is between a set of components having AND dependency as well as alternative dependency, the connection is made with their abstract nodes (i.e. the abstract nodes corresponding to the AND dependency and the alternative one become children of the OR parent). Next, the remaining components are directly added to the root with optional notation. Finally, the cross-tree dependencies are added (i.e. required and exclude ones).
  In Fig. 8.8, we present the architecture variability related to the dependencies between components of the audio player software family presented in Fig. 8.1

For more details regarding the approach and the evaluation results, please refer to [41].

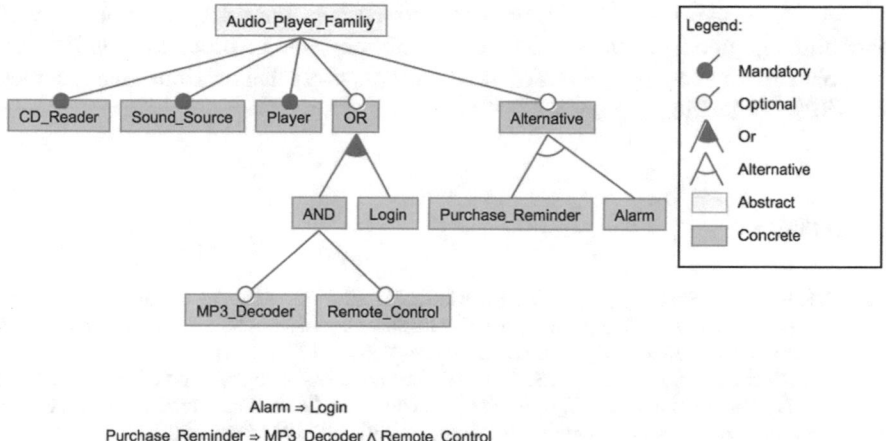

Alarm ⇒ Login

Purchase_Reminder ⇒ MP3_Decoder ∧ Remote_Control

Fig. 8.8 The resulting component dependencies in terms of feature modeling representation of the illustrative example presented in Fig. 8.1

8.7   Conclusion

To support the reengineering of existing software variants into SPLs, we discussed in this chapter the extraction of the Software Product Line Architecture (SPLA) based on the analysis of several software variants. We defined the different types of architecture variability of SPLA elements including component variability, configuration variability and dependencies between components.

We analyzed the-state-of-the-art of architecture extraction to identify good practices related to the extraction of SPLA. We found that the input artifacts of a SPLA extraction approach could be source code, execution traces, documentations and human expert knowledge. The processes used to analyze these input artifacts are based on several automation degrees, directions, analysis types to be performed, and the algorithms determining the procedure of the process.

As examples of the implementation of some good practices, we presented an illustrative approach for extracting SPLA based on the analysis of many software variants using Formal Concept Analysis. This approach identifies mandatory and optional components as well as the dependencies among components and draw them in terms of Feature Modeling language. However, this illustrative approach is sensitive to the input software variants as dependencies between components are identified based on component occurrences in the software architectures of these software variants. To cope with this sensitivity, we suggest to carefully select software variants covering a large number of dependencies. Also, to improve the resulting SPLA, we recommend to rely on other software artifacts such as documentations and feature models.

As future directions, we recommend researchers consider the evaluation of the different good practices presented in this chapter, in order to identify best combinations and configurations of these good practices that maximize the accuracy of a SPLA extraction approach.

References

1. Abdellatif, M., Shatnawi, A., Mili, H., Moha, N., El Boussaidi, G., Hecht, G., Privat, J., Guéhéneuc, Y.G.: A taxonomy of service identification approaches for legacy software systems modernization. Journal of Systems and Software. Volume 173. (2021)
2. Allier, S., Sahraoui, H.A., Sadou, S.: Identifying components in object-oriented programs using dynamic analysis and clustering. In: Proceedings of the 2009 Conference of the Center for Advanced Studies on Collaborative Research, pp. 136–148. IBM Corp. (2009)
3. Berger, T., Rublack, R., Nair, D., Atlee, J.M., Becker, M., Czarnecki, K., Wasowski, A.: A survey of variability modeling in industrial practice. In: Proceedings of the Seventh International Workshop on Variability Modelling of Software-intensive Systems, p. 7. ACM (2013)
4. Businge, J., Openja, M., Nadi, S., Bainomugisha, E., Berger, T.: Clone-based variability management in the android ecosystem. In: 2018 IEEE International Conference on Software Maintenance and Evolution (ICSME), pp. 625–634. IEEE (2018)
5. Canal, C., Pimentel, E., Troya, J.M.: Specification and refinement of dynamic software architectures. In: Software Architecture, pp. 107–125. Springer (1999)
6. Capiluppi, A., Ajienka, N.: National boundaries and semantics of artefacts in open source development. In: 2018 IEEE/ACM 1st International Workshop on Software Health (SoHeal), pp. 33–39. IEEE (2018)
7. Carbonnel, J., Huchard, M., Miralles, A., Nebut, C.: Feature model composition assisted by formal concept analysis. In: ENASE: Evaluation of Novel Approaches to Software Engineering, pp. 27–37. SciTePress (2017)
8. Chikofsky, E.J., Cross, J.H., et al.: Reverse engineering and design recovery: A taxonomy. Software, IEEE 7(1), 13–17 (1990)
9. Clements, P., Northrop, L.: Software product lines: practices and patterns, vol. 3. Addison-Wesley Reading (2002)
10. Cormen, T.H., Leiserson, C.E., Rivest, R.L., Stein, C.: Introduction to algorithms. MIT press (2009)
11. DeBaud, J.M., Flege, O., Knauber, P.: Pulse-dssa-a method for the development of software reference architectures. In: Proceedings of the third international workshop on Software architecture, pp. 25–28. ACM (1998)
12. Dubinsky, Y., Rubin, J., Berger, T., Duszynski, S., Becker, M., Czarnecki, K.: An exploratory study of cloning in industrial software product lines. In: Software Maintenance and Reengineering (CSMR), 2013 17th European Conference on, pp. 25–34. IEEE (2013)
13. Ducasse, S., Pollet, D.: Software architecture reconstruction: A process-oriented taxonomy. IEEE Transactions on Software Engineering 35(4), 573–591 (2009)
14. Dugerdil, P., Sennhauser, D.: Dynamic decision tree for legacy use-case recovery. In: Proceedings of the 28th Annual ACM Symposium on Applied Computing, SAC '13, pp. 1284–1291. ACM, New York, NY, USA (2013)
15. Erdemir, U., Tekin, U., Buzluca, F.: Object oriented software clustering based on community structure. In: 2011 18th Asia Pacific Software Engineering Conference (APSEC), pp. 315–321. IEEE (2011)
16. Fischer, S., Linsbauer, L., Lopez-Herrejon, R.E., Egyed, A.: Enhancing clone-and-own with systematic reuse for developing software variants. In: Software Maintenance and Evolution (ICSME), 2014 IEEE International Conference on, pp. 391–400. IEEE (2014)

17. Frenzel, P., Koschke, R., Breu, A.P., Angstmann, K.: Extending the reflexion method for consolidating software variants into product lines. In: 14th Working Conference on Reverse Engineering (WCRE), pp. 160–169. IEEE (2007)
18. Gasparic, M., Janes, A., Sillitti, A., Succi, G.: An analysis of a project reuse approach in an industrial setting. In: Software Reuse for Dynamic Systems in the Cloud and Beyond, pp. 164–171. Springer (2014)
19. Gomaa, H.: Designing software product lines with UML. In: Software Engineering Workshop - Tutorial Notes, 2005. 29th Annual IEEE/NASA, pp. 160–216 (2005)
20. Kang, K.C., Cohen, S.G., Hess, J.A., Novak, W.E., Peterson, A.S.: Feature-oriented domain analysis (FODA) feasibility study. Tech. rep., Carnegie-Mellon Univ Pittsburgh Pa Software Engineering Inst (1990)
21. Kang, K.C., Kim, M., Lee, J., Kim, B.: Feature-oriented re-engineering of legacy systems into product line assets–a case study. In: Software Product Lines, pp. 45–56. Springer (2005)
22. Kolb, R., Muthig, D., Patzke, T., Yamauchi, K.: A case study in refactoring a legacy component for reuse in a product line. In: Proceedings of the 21st IEEE International Conference on Software Maintenance (ICSM 2005), pp. 369–378. IEEE (2005)
23. Kolb, R., Muthig, D., Patzke, T., Yamauchi, K.: Refactoring a legacy component for reuse in a software product line: a case study. Journal of Software Maintenance and Evolution: Research and Practice 18(2), 109–132 (2006)
24. Koschke, R., Frenzel, P., Breu, A.P., Angstmann, K.: Extending the reflexion method for consolidating software variants into product lines. Software Quality Journal 17(4), 331–366 (2009)
25. Langelier, G., Sahraoui, H., Poulin, P.: Visualization-based analysis of quality for large-scale software systems. In: Proceedings of the 20th IEEE/ACM international Conference on Automated software engineering, pp. 214–223. ACM (2005)
26. Lethbridge, T.C., Singer, J., Forward, A.: How software engineers use documentation: The state of the practice. IEEE Software 20(6), 35–39 (2003)
27. Lima, C., Chavez, C., de Almeida, E.S.: Investigating the recovery of product line architectures: an approach proposal. In: International Conference on Software Reuse, pp. 201–207. Springer (2017)
28. Liu, C., van Dongen, B., Assy, N., van der Aalst, W.M · Component interface identification and behavioral model discovery from software execution data. In: Proceedings of the 26th Conference on Program Comprehension, pp. 97–107. ACM (2018)
29. Luckham, D.: Rapide: A language and toolset for simulation of distributed systems by partial orderings of events. Tech. rep. (1996)
30. Magee, J., Kramer, J.: Dynamic structure in software architectures. In: ACM SIGSOFT Software Engineering Notes, vol. 21, pp. 3–14. ACM (1996)
31. Mende, T., Beckwermert, F., Koschke, R., Meier, G.: Supporting the grow-and-prune model in software product lines evolution using clone detection. In: 12th European Conference on Software Maintenance and Reengineering (CSMR), pp. 163–172. IEEE (2008)
32. Mende, T., Koschke, R., Beckwermert, F.: An evaluation of code similarity identification for the grow-and-prune model. Journal of Software Maintenance and Evolution: Research and Practice 21(2), 143–169 (2009)
33. Mishra, S., Kushwaha, D.S., Misra, A.K.: Creating reusable software component from object-oriented legacy system through reverse engineering. Journal of object technology 8(5), 133–152 (2009)
34. Moshkenani, Z.S., Sharafi, S.M., Zamani, B.: Improving naïve bayes classifier for software architecture reconstruction. In: Instrumentation & Measurement, Sensor Network and Automation (IMSNA), 2012 International Symposium on, vol. 2, pp. 383–388. IEEE (2012)
35. Nakagawa, E.Y., Antonino, P.O., Becker, M.: Reference architecture and product line architecture: A subtle but critical difference. In: European Conference on Software Architecture, pp. 207–211. Springer (2011)
36. Pinzger, M., Gall, H., Girard, J.F., Knodel, J., Riva, C., Pasman, W., Broerse, C., Wijnstra, J.G.: Architecture recovery for product families. In: Software Product-Family Engineering, pp. 332–351. Springer (2004)

37. Pohl, K., Böckle, G., Van Der Linden, F.: Software product line engineering, vol. 10. Springer (2005)
38. Rathee, A., Chhabra, J.K.: A multi-objective search based approach to identify reusable software components. Journal of Computer Languages **52**, 26–43 (2019)
39. Seriai, A., Sadou, S., Sahraoui, H., Hamza, S.: Deriving component interfaces after a restructuring of a legacy system. In: 2014 IEEE/IFIP Conference on Software Architecture (WICSA), pp. 31–40. IEEE (2014)
40. Shatnawi, A., Mili, H., El Boussaidi, G., Boubaker, A., Guéhéneuc, Y.G., Moha, N., Privat, J., Abdellatif, M.: Analyzing program dependencies in java ee applications. In: Mining Software Repositories (MSR), 2017 IEEE/ACM 14th International Conference on, pp. 64–74. IEEE (2017)
41. Shatnawi, A., Seriai, A.D., Sahraoui, H.: Recovering software product line architecture of a family of object-oriented product variants. Journal of Systems and Software **131**, 325–346 (2017)
42. Shatnawi, A., Shatnawi, H., Saied, M.A., Shara, Z.A., Sahraoui, H., Seriai, A.: Identifying software components from object-oriented apis based on dynamic analysis. In: Proceedings of the 26th Conference on Program Comprehension, pp. 189–199. ACM (2018)
43. Weinreich, R., Miesbauer, C., Buchgeher, G., Kriechbaum, T.: Extracting and facilitating architecture in service-oriented software systems. In: 2012 Joint Working IEEE/IFIP Conference on Software Architecture (WICSA) and European Conference on Software Architecture (ECSA), pp. 81–90 (2012)
44. Wu, Y., Yang, Y., Peng, X., Qiu, C., Zhao, W.: Recovering object-oriented framework for software product line reengineering. In: Top Productivity through Software Reuse, pp. 119–134. Springer (2011)
45. Yuan, E., Esfahani, N., Malek, S.: Automated mining of software component interactions for self-adaptation. In: Proceedings of the 9th International Symposium on Software Engineering for Adaptive and Self-Managing Systems, SEAMS 2014, pp. 27–36. ACM, New York, NY, USA (2014)

Chapter 9
ModelVars2SPL: From UML Class Diagram Variants to Software Product Line Core Assets

Wesley K. G. Assunção, Silvia R. Vergilio, and Roberto E. Lopez-Herrejon

Abstract Software Product Line (SPL) is a reuse-oriented approach to create families of related system variants. SPLs are commonly adopted as a way to overcome problems emerged with the use of opportunistic reuse. In the existing literature of extractive adoption of SPLs, most of the studies only focus on source code, limiting engineers to reason about high-level architectural design decisions. Also, the vast majority of approaches are partially automated, or do not reflect domain constraints, such as feature interactions, and include or exclude relationships, which requires extensive human intervention and is error-prone. These limitations hamper a widely adoption of SPLs in industry. To tackle these limitations, in this chapter we present ModelVars2SPL (*Model Variants to SPL Core Assets*), an automated approach to aid the re-engineering of SPLs from existing system variants. ModelVars2SPL uses as input a set of *Unified Modeling Language* (UML) class diagrams and the list of features they implement. The approach generates as output two SPL core assets: (1) Feature Model (FM), which represents the combinations of features, and (2) Product Line Architecture (PLA), which represents a global structure of the variants. ModelVars2SPL is composed of four automated steps. The approach was evaluated regarding the artifacts it generates and its performance. The results show that the FMs well-represent the features organization, providing useful information to define and manage commonalities and variabilities. The PLAs represent a global structure of current variants, facilitating the understanding of existing implementations of all variants. An advantage of ModelVars2SPL is to exploit the use of UML design

W. K. G. Assunção (✉)
Pontifical Catholic University of Rio de Janeiro, Rio de Janeiro, Brazil

Johannes Kepler University of Linz, Linz, Austria
e-mail: wesley.assuncao@jku.at

S. R. Vergilio
Dinf, Federal University of Paraná, Curitiba, Brazil
e-mail: silvia@inf.ufpr.br

R. E. Lopez-Herrejon
École de Technologie Supérieure, Montreal, QC, Canada
e-mail: roberto.lopez@etsmtl.ca

© Springer Nature Switzerland AG 2023   221
R. E. Lopez-Herrejon et al. (eds.), *Handbook of Re-Engineering Software Intensive Systems into Software Product Lines*, https://doi.org/10.1007/978-3-031-11686-5_9

models, being programming language agnostic. In addition, our approach supports the re-engineering process in the design level, allowing practitioners to have a broader view of the SPL.

9.1 Introduction

Software reuse is a strategy widely used to increase productivity and quality while reducing cost of software development [5, 11, 23, 36]. By reusing existing artifacts rather than building them from scratch, companies can keep their investment put in pieces of software. Any artifact built during the software development can be reused, including source code, design models, test cases, to cite some [22]. Software reuse in practice is done mostly opportunistically [36]. Opportunistic reuse—also known as clone-and-own reuse, copy-and-paste reuse, or ad hoc reuse—refers to the use of artifacts among different software systems which were not designed for being reused [12, 21, 36, 37]. Usually, when companies need a new variant of a system, existing software artifacts are cloned/copied and adapted/modified to fulfill the new requirements. Opportunistic reuse is an easy way to reuse software artifacts, does not require an upfront investment, and helps to quickly obtain the desired results and products.

Despite some benefits, opportunistic reuse leads to the need of extensive refactoring, usually adds technical debt, creates unanticipated behavior, violated constraints, conflicts in assumptions, fragile structure, and software bloat [24]. Furthermore, the resulting duplication of software artifacts makes systems maintenance and evolution a complex activity [16]. Furthermore, usually developers do not have architectural nor domain information related to the reused artifacts to allow them to understand how the different implementations are spread along the product variants. These are well-know and widely studied problems related to opportunistic reuse [1, 27]. A recommended solution for such a scenario is the adoption of a systematic reuse approach. A proven and well-established approach to tackle this problem is the extractive adoption of a Software Product Line [1, 38]. A *Software Product Line (SPL)* is a set of system variants developed by integrating common and variable parts for deriving software products designed for a specific domain [13, 28].

The extractive adoption of SPLs fits the scenario in which an organization has a large base of artifacts already developed using opportunistic reuse. These artifacts are the source of information to construct an SPL, in order to achieve a systematic reuse and easier maintenance and evolution, because the systems will no longer be maintained or evolved individually but as a group considering both commonalities and variabilities. The extraction of an SPL encompasses a re-engineering process that is a complex activity and involves many steps to deal with a great diversity of artifacts in different levels of abstraction [1]. This process requires extensive human effort and is an error-prone task [10]. The extraction of SPLs from system variants has attracted interest from industry and academia [1, 20, 23, 27]. Based on the findings reported on these secondary studies, we identified some limitations of the existing works. Firstly, we found that most pieces of work have focus exclusively on source code [31]. Source code enables detailed analysis of system variants, however, it limits engineers to reason about high-level architectural design decisions. Hence, there is a lack of approaches considering other types of artifacts, such as design models. Design models are essential artifacts to understand, develop, evolve and maintain SPLs [15]. Secondly, we also observed that existing studies address specific phases of the re-engineering process, most of them have focus only on the traceability between features and implementation artifacts [34, 35, 42, 47, 49]. There is a lack of approaches and tools to widely support the re-engineering process. Most approaches require extensive human expertise and participation [7, 9, 25, 33] and generally do not consider domain constraints among features [39, 45]. A proper feature management is fundamental to deal with domain constraints. However, this is a challenging activity, because of the potential large number of possible feature combinations and the lack of explicit information about features interactions/dependencies that may exist even in small SPLs.

To overcome these limitations, in a recent work we have introduced Model-Vars2SPL (*Model Variants to SPL core assets*) [3]. It is an automated approach to address the problem of automatically extracting SPL core design assets from model variants, covering the re-engineering phases (detection, analysis, and transformation) and taking into account domain constraints existing in the variants under consideration. ModelVars2SPL uses as input UML class diagrams and feature sets of the variants, and generates two SPL core design assets: (1) the *Product Line Architecture (PLA)*, that allows reasoning about the generation of the products and enables practitioners to better understand, maintain, and evolve a system family; and (2) the *Feature Model (FM)*, a standard artifact for variability modeling and management, expressing common and variable characteristics of a product family to support stakeholders in making technical and managerial decisions about the portfolio of products [6].

In this chapter we present details of ModelVars2SPL, an overview of its application in an illustrative example, and a summary of its evaluation for ten applications. The results show that ModelVars2SPL can automatically produce FMs and PLAs that well-represent the model variants provided as input. In addition, we present the existing literature for those who want to go deeper in this topic. To motivate the extractive adoption of SPLs in industry, we describe practical ways to use solutions generated by ModelVars2SPL.

9.2 Background and Related Work

SPL engineering approaches allow reuse of a common infrastructure composed of *core assets*, which are shared to create different system variants. Two kinds of assets are identified in Software Product Line Engineering, the *common assets* (also known as commonalities) that are reused in all products, and the *variable assets* (also known as variabilities) that are related to those features provided only by some variants. Examples of core assets are components, domain models, design models, requirements statements, documents, plans, test cases or any other useful reusable artifact of the software production process. One of the main core assets of an SPL is its architecture. The *Product Line Architecture (PLA)* helps the generation of the products and allows practitioners to better understand, maintain, and evolve a system family. Another fundamental core asset is the variability model, such as the *Feature Model (FM)*, which has become the *de facto* standard artifact used for *variability modeling* and *variability management* [38]. An FM expresses common and variable characteristics of a product family and are used to support stakeholders in making technical and managerial decisions about the portfolio of products. To generate and maintain these artifacts, namely PLA and FM, is essential for re-engineer product variants into an SPL, and for its future evolution.

Obtaining both PLAs and FMs from existing system variants by an extractive adoption of SPLs is a problem neither simple nor trivial. An automated approach for the re-engineering process requires some fundamental phases such as detection of features, organization of variabilities, and transformation of artifacts; that have different goals and deal with specific information and artifacts. In some cases, the input artifacts have implicit information or are partially incomplete, for example, the existing domain constraints in terms of feature combinations are not clearly described, or only a small set of variants is available. These situations require a well-designed re-engineering strategy. Furthermore, design models are commonly complex artifacts used to describe system structures. Consequently, dealing with many of these artifacts, each one representing a different variant, can be challenging. Complex problems like this have been effectively and efficiently solved in the Search-Based Software Engineering (SBSE) field [19], where software engineering problems are modeled as optimization problems and then solved with search-based techniques [14]. Search-based techniques are beneficial for the automation of several tasks of the re-engineering process. For such tasks, developers most times can recognize a good solution, but to obtain it can be very difficult.

In the literature we can find several pieces of work dealing with extraction of PLAs and FMs from system variants [1, 20, 31]. However, few studies deal with re-engineering UML models, mostly focusing on feature identification, which is only the first step of the re-engineering process towards an SPL. The approach called MoVaC was proposed by Martinez et al. to identify commonalities and variabilities among model variants [34]. MoVaC allows visualization of features among the variants and their model elements and also presents feature interactions, allowing practitioners to reason about how complex are the feature implementations. A study focusing on identifying variability among models was proposed by Wille et al. [47]. However, they only deal with state-charts, since this was a requirement in the domain they are interested in. Another work performed by Rubin and Chechik also has focus on comparing UML state-charts with the goal of refactoring them into an SPL [42]. This work performs identification of similar model elements to generate a single model representation, without describing feature implementations or interactions. In the work of Ziadi et al., the authors use class diagrams as additional artifact for feature location [49]. However, the main input artifact for their approach is the source code. The class diagrams are used only as a simplified representation of the implementation artifacts. Mefteh et al. proposed a method that uses UML models as source of information to extract FMs [35]. Here, the authors extract an initial version of an FM from UML use case diagrams and natural language description of existing scenarios.

With respect to the re-engineering process presented above, only two studies deal with the entire re-engineering process of UML models variants to an SPL [40, 41]. However, these studies deal with illustrative small size subject systems, namely Microwave Oven and Washing Machine. Yet, these studies do not consider organization of existing features in an FM. Furthermore, in the catalog of Extractive Software Product Line Adoption case studies (ESPLA)[1] only 13 case studies deal with models of which eight are UML models. Thus, in this regard, we identified two important gaps: *(1) few studies deal with artifacts other than source code and a small fraction among them uses UML models*, and *(2) UML models research is focused mostly on the detection step of the re-engineering process.*

Identifying domain requirements and representing them in software systems is also the goal of some studies. For example, Reinhartz-Berger and Kemelman propose an automated extractive method, named CoreReq, to identify core reusable requirements [39]. From system requirements written in natural language, CoreReq clusters similar descriptions, analyses variability among them, and generates core requirements by using natural language processing techniques. However, they do not take into account the domain constraints. In an SPL, these requirements will be implemented as features, which are mostly represented in FMs. The reverse engineering of FMs is subject of the work of She et al. [45]. Using as input a set of feature names, feature descriptions, and features dependencies, some heuristics are applied, and an FM is built. However, their work does not focus on dealing with system variants. In addition, despite using features dependencies, they do not infer other possible constraints that domain requirements could impose. These limitations of existing studies constitutes a third gap: *(3) discovery of domain constraints existing among features and representing them into an FM.*

In the literature, we can also find studies focusing on high-level artifacts such as FM and PLA. For example, Bayer et al. introduce an approach, called PuLSETM-DSSA, to integrate software artifacts in different abstraction levels to obtain a reference architecture [7]. The reference architecture gives guidance for migrating the system variants into an SPL. However, PuLSETM-DSSA is not fully automated, requiring human expertise. The work of Kumaki et al. has a goal of generating variability models and architectures [25]. The input of their approach is also a set of UML class diagram variants, but instead of using feature sets, they use a set of requirements. Their approach uses overlap analysis to identify common and variable sentences in the requirements. The same overlap analysis is done in the class diagram variants. An algorithm based on vector space model is applied to recommend traceability between requirement sentences and class diagram elements. Using this traceability, an SPL expert develops the variability model and a reference

---

[1] https://but4reuse.github.io/espla_catalog/ visited on July 7th, 2021.

architecture that best represents the variants. Despite being very related to our goals, this approach still requires human intervention.

Martinez et al. propose an approach called MoVa2PL to support model-based adoption of SPLs [33]. MoVa2PL first identifies common and variable parts of model elements, called blocks, from a set of model variants. Then, these blocks of model elements are mapped manually to their corresponding features. The model-based SPL is obtained by describing variabilities using the Common Variability Language [9]. Taking into account the re-engineering process steps, MoVa2PL deals only with the feature identification activity. Hence, the analysis and transformation steps are not the focus of this approach. Taking into account this limitation, and the ones mentioned in previous paragraph, the fourth limitation identified is: *(4) extensive manual effort for conduction of the entire re-engineering process.*

The four gaps found in the literature and described above lead us to propose ModelVars2SPL [3]. This approach deals with UML models and feature sets, discovers domain constraints among features, and automates the entire re-engineering process, reducing the need for manual effort to generate the FM and PLAs. Next we present the details of our approach.

9.3   ModelVars2SPL

ModelVars2SPL is an approach designed to automate the extraction of PLAs and FMs from existing UML class diagram variants. ModelVars2SPL is model-based, which makes it independent of programming languages, allowing practitioners to focus on the SPL design. Our aim is to aid architects, engineers, and developers to communicate, plan, reason, and estimate on how to extract an SPL from existing system variants.

The main goal is to aid the re-engineering process. ModelVars2SPL has the following characteristics:

1. It uses UML models as both input and output. The input for the approach is a set of UML class diagram variants, artifacts that are commonly available in the software development organizations. UML is the most used language in industry to represent software architectures [26, 30]. The output is the FM and a UML-based PLA, composed of a class diagram with feature annotations. Such output has in purpose to ease the communication, comprehension, planning, maintenance, and future evolution of the extracted SPL;
2. It covers three common phases of the re-engineering process, namely detection, analysis, and transformation, by generating outputs for each phase, allowing practitioners to follow and understand the process;
3. Each step of the approach is automated, and the outputs are produced with minimal human intervention. The most complex tasks are solved with search-based techniques. The use of such techniques is justified because such tasks are associated to a large search space, that is, there exists a great number

of solutions representing different combinations of features and relationships between them. In many situations, information of constraints and feature interactions are missing or are poorly described;
4. It is implemented with widely used tools, e.g. Eclipse Modeling Framework (EMF), to fit better in industrial scenarios.

Our approach contributes to reduce manual low-level effort, such as analysis of pieces of source code, and allows practitioners to focus on high-level activities, such as managerial decisions, time-to-market, and customer satisfaction.

9.3.1   Approach Overview

Figure 9.1 presents an overview of ModelVars2SPL. The input for the approach is composed of UML class diagrams and the features sets. The output of the steps are used by the other steps or intended to support practitioners in all the re-engineering activities. The phases of the re-engineering process, namely detection, analysis, and transformation, associated to each step are represented in Fig. 9.1 by swim lanes. The phases of detection and analysis encompass one step each, whereas the transformation phase two. To present our approach, an illustrative example with the required input and output artifacts, and details of each step are presented below.

Figure 9.2 presents an illustrative example with four variants of a Banking System (BS) [49]. In the context of this example, we assume these variants were created by opportunistic reuse, and now it is desired to move to an SPL. For ModelVars2SPL, the input consists of *UML class diagrams* that provides a static

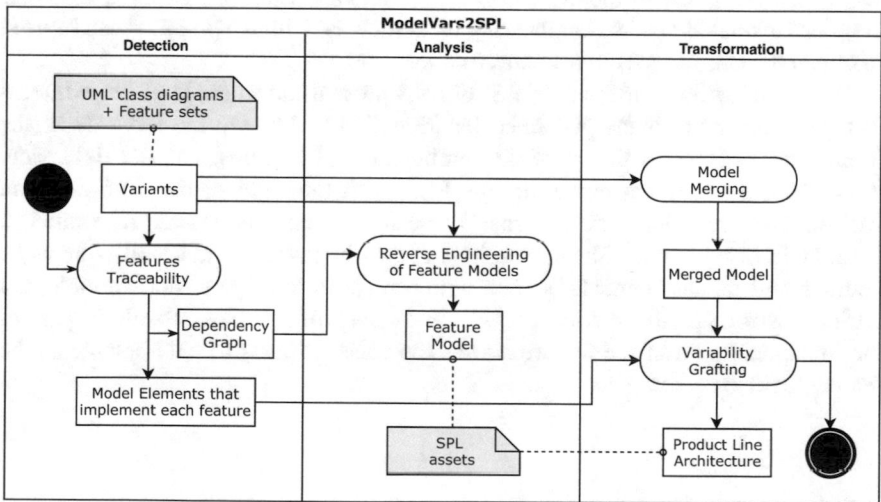

Fig. 9.1 Input, steps, and output overview of ModelVars2SPL

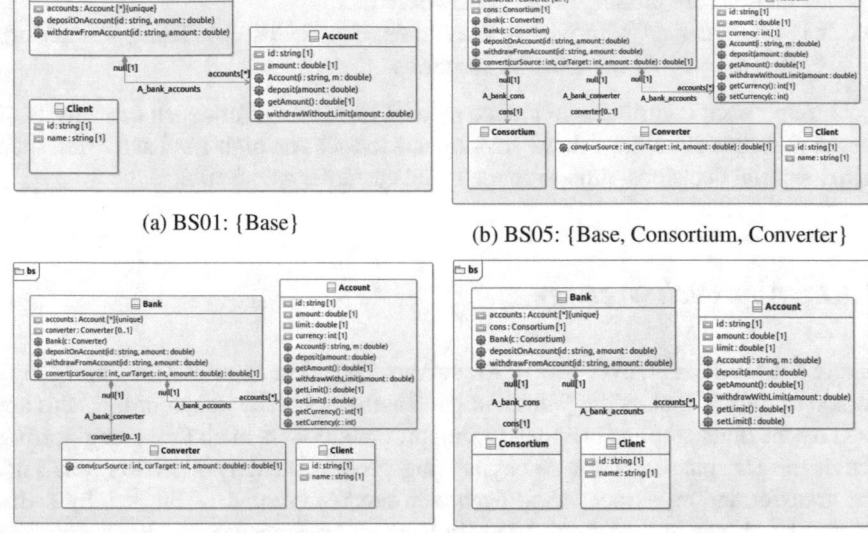

(a) BS01: {Base}

(b) BS05: {Base, Consortium, Converter}

(c) BS06: {Base, WithdrawLimit, Converter}

(d) BS07: {Base, WithdrawLimit, Consortium}

Fig. 9.2 Four variants of Banking System used as input to illustrate the steps of ModelVars2SPL

view of the structure of the system variant, and *feature sets* that denotes the configuration of features provided by the variant. In this example, BS has four variants in which each one has a UML class diagram and the corresponding feature set, which are given in the captions of Fig. 9.2. In a context without UML class diagrams available, reverse engineering tools such as Eclipse MoDisco[2] can be used to obtain the diagrams from the source code.

Based on the input artifacts of BS, Fig. 9.3 presents an example of the extracted SPL with design artifacts generated by ModelVars2SPL. On the left side of the figure, the FM shows the possible combination of features. On the right side, the UML class diagram represents the PLA with model elements from all input variants and the feature annotations. These feature annotations are illustrated in the middle of the figure. The annotations allow observing the traceability between features and model elements, shown with arrows in the figure. For example, the attribute `accounts: Account[*]{unique}` of the class `Bank` is part of the implementation of the feature `Base`, the class `Consortium` implements the feature `Consortium`.

---

[2] https://eclipse.org/MoDisco.

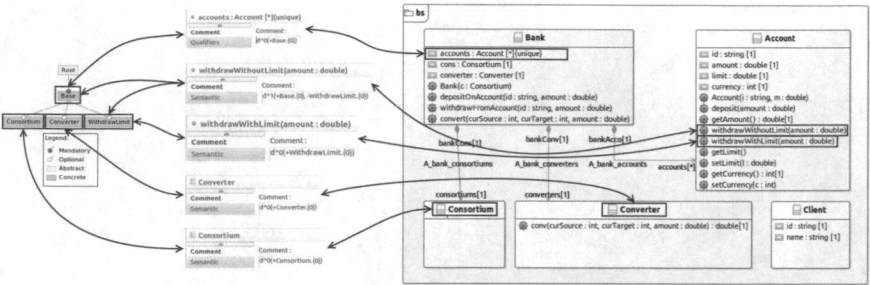

Fig. 9.3 Example of FM and PLA Banking System obtained by ModelVars2SPL

9.3.2   Features Traceability

The first step of ModelVars2SPL (see Fig. 9.1) aims at identifying the model elements that implement each feature and consists of two activities: the decomposition of the model variants in atomic elements and traceability discovery. Atomic elements are parts of the models with low granularity that are relevant to the reengineering process, similar to the principles adopted by BUT4Reuse [32]. For our approach, we consider as atomic elements the following class diagram elements: classes, interfaces, attributes, methods/operations, and all relationships such as inheritance and composition. After the decomposition, the traceability discovery is conducted to map such atomic elements to the features they implement. An ideal result of the traceability is to identify each set of elements that implement each distinct feature. However, in practice, some implementation elements are only present or absent when two or more features interact. These elements are responsible for providing a proper feature interaction.

To deal with features interactions, ModelVars2SPL relies on the strategy presented by Linsbauer et al. [29]. These authors introduced a strategy to perform feature location and traceability based on the identification of two kinds of *modules* in the system variants, namely Base and Derivative modules, defined as follows:

Definition 9.1 (Base Module) A *base* module $m = d^0(+c.\{v\})$ implements a feature regardless of the presence or absence of any other features. This module is represented by a derivative of order 0 (d^0), where $+c$ is a feature, and $\{v\}$ is an optional number related to the version of the variant when the feature was included.

Definition 9.2 (Derivative Module) A *derivative* module $m = d^n(c_0.\{v\}, c_1.\{v\}, \ldots, c_n.\{v\})$ implements feature interactions, where c_i is $+F$ (if feature F is selected) or $-F$ (if not selected), and n is the order of the derivative.

Based on the above definitions, the goal of the traceability discovery activity is to automatically produce a set of traces between both types of modules and artifacts that implement them (i.e., atomic elements). The traces are produced by matching

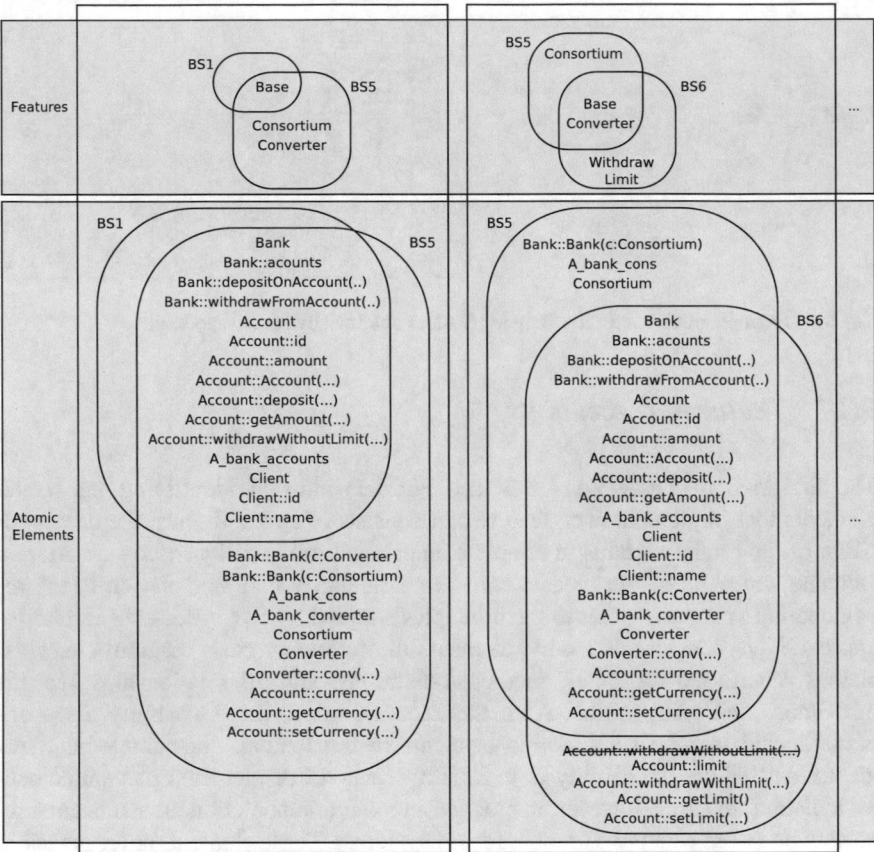

Fig. 9.4 Example of overlap analysis for BS1 vs BS5 and BS5 vs BS6

atomic elements overlaps and feature overlaps. Each variant is incrementally analyzed, comparing overlaps already analyzed with new variant artifacts provided.

To illustrate the traceability discovery employed by our approach, Fig. 9.4 presents the overlap analysis between feature sets and the atomic model elements of BS1, BS5, and BS6. Recalling this is an incremental analysis, firstly BS1 and BS5 are analyzed, as presented on the left side of the figure. These variants have in common the feature Base and 15 model elements, leading to the mapping of these model elements to the implementation of Base. Furthermore, only BS5 has Consortium and Converter, and 10 model elements. At this point, we cannot separate the model elements of each of these features. On the analysis of BS5 and BS6, on the right side of the figure, the variants have in common the features Base and Converter, and 21 model elements. Considering this, and the previous analysis, we can refine the traceability and assume which are the models elements

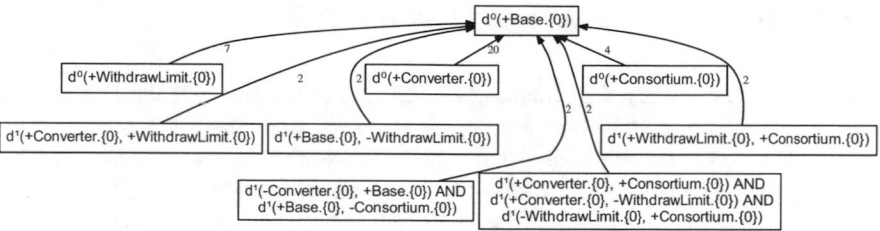

Fig. 9.5 Example of modules and relationships represented as a dependency graph

that implement `Converter`, since we had the model elements that compose `Base`. We can corroborate this analysis with the analysis of `Consortium`, which is in BS5, but not in BS6. Another important analysis is regarding the feature `WithdrawLimit`. We can observe that `WithdrawLimit` in BS6 implies the exclusion of the method `Account::widthdrawWithoutLimit(...)` in the variant. Then, we can assume that the inclusion of the feature `WithdrawLimit` leads to the exclusion of one method, and inclusion of three methods and one attribute. In systems with many variants, this incremental analysis is performed among all pairs of variants to compute the traceability of all features and their interactions.

In addition to identify base and derivative modules, in this step our approach also identifies relationship between modules. The relationships between modules are represented in a dependency graph, which allows us to use this information in the next step of ModelVars2SPL. The definitions of relationship and dependency graph are based on our previous work and defined below [4]. An example of a dependency graph for our illustrative example is presented in Fig. 9.5. In this figure, we can see that the traceability discovery activity has identified four base modules and five derivative modules. Eight relationships were identified, where all of them are relationships to the module $d^0(+Base.\{0\})$.

Definition 9.3 (Dependency) A dependency establishes a relationship between two sets of modules and it is denoted with a triple (`from`, `to`, `weight`), where `from` and `to` are a set of modules (or module expressions) of the related modules, and `weight` expresses the strength of the dependency, i.e., the number of dependencies of structural elements in modules `from` on structural elements in modules `to`.

Definition 9.4 (Dependency Graph) A dependency graph is defined as a set of dependencies, where each node in the graph corresponds to a set of modules (or module expressions), and each edge corresponds to a dependency as defined above. Edges are annotated with natural numbers that represent the dependencies weights.

9.3.3 Reverse Engineering of Feature Models

This step is responsible for obtaining an FM that best represents the feature sets. Reverse engineering of FMs is a complex problem, since there is a huge number of possible feature combinations, and existing constraints between features are not explicitly described, facts that justify the use of search-based techniques. This step of reverse engineering of FMs of our approach is based on our previous work that relies on a search-based technique [4]. This step of reverse engineering of FMs involves a complex problem for two reasons: (1) there is a huge number of possible feature combinations, and (2) existing constraints between features are not explicitly described. These problem characteristics are the motivation to use a search-based technique [14]. This task requires two inputs: (1) a set of feature sets from the input variants, and (2) the dependency graph obtained in the previous step. Next, we describe the concepts and details of the search-based technique employed in this step.

9.3.3.1 Representation of Individuals

Our search-based technique to automatize this step relies on an evolutionary algorithm [48]. Individuals are represented by a meta-model with the nodes *Root*, *Mandatory*, *Optional*, and *GroupedFeature* that are children of *Feature*. The FM tree of an individual can have only one *Root*, and the features *Mandatory* and *Optional* have the cardinality of zero or more. The number of *Alternative* and *Or* groups is arbitrary; however, each group must have at least one *GroupedFeature*. An FM has exactly one *ConstraintSet* that describes the propositional formula in Conjunctive Normal Form (CNF). A *Constraint* has one *OrClause* that has at least one *Literal*. A literal can be an *Atom* or a *Not*.

9.3.3.2 Objective Functions

Our search-based technique to reverse engineer FMs is based on a multi-objective perspective. A multi-objective evolutionary algorithm evaluates candidate solutions, computing more than one objective function simultaneously. For this step of ModelVars2SPL we use three objective functions to evaluate solutions. To introduce these functions, let us consider $\mathcal{FM}$ as the universe of candidate feature models, $\mathcal{SFS}$ the universe of feature sets, and sfs the feature sets from the system variants, dep a dependency in the dependency graph created in the previous step. Based on that, we define two auxiliary function, as follows:

Definition 9.5 (featureSets) Function *featureSets* returns the set of feature sets denoted by a feature model.

$$featureSets : \mathcal{FM} \rightarrow \mathcal{SFS}$$

Definition 9.6 (holds) Function $holds(dep, fs)$ returns 1 if dependency dep holds on the feature set fs and 0 otherwise. A dependency dep holds for a feature set fs if:

$$\left(\bigwedge_{f \in fs.selected} f \wedge \bigwedge_{g \in \overline{fs.selected}} \neg g \right) \Rightarrow (dep.from \Rightarrow dep.to)$$

These two auxiliary functions presented above are used for computing three metrics used as objective functions, which are described below. The first two functions are based on feature sets, and the third function is based on dependencies between features. The three fitness functions are designed to keep the computed values between 0 and 1, where value 1 is the best value for each objective.

Definition 9.7 (Precision (P)) Precision expresses how many of the feature sets denoted by a reverse engineered feature model fm are among the desired feature sets sfs.

$$precision(sfs, fm) = \frac{|sfs \cap featureSets(fm)|}{|featureSets(fm)|}$$

Definition 9.8 (Recall (R)) Recall expresses how many of the desired feature sets sfs are denoted by the reverse engineered feature model fm.

$$recall(sfs, fm) = \frac{|sfs \cap featureSets(fm)|}{|sfs|}$$

Definition 9.9 (Variability Safety (VS)) Variability Safety expresses the degree of *variability-safety* of a reverse engineered feature model fm with respect to a dependency graph dg.

$$variabilitySafety(fm, dg) =$$

$$\sum_{dep \in dg} dep.weight \times \left(\frac{\sum_{fs \in featureSets(fm)} holds(dep, fs)}{|featureSets(fm)|} \right)$$

9.3.3.3   Evolutionary Operators

In order to modify individuals to obtain better solutions, the operators are designed to be applied along the evolutionary process. In our search-base technique of this step of ModelVars2SPL, the evolutionary operators must adhere to the following constraints to guarantee the semantics of FMs:

- Each feature is identified by its name, so every feature appears exactly once in the FM tree;
- All FMs have a fixed set of feature names, so in different FMs only the relations between features are different;
- *Cross-Tree Constraints (CTCs)* can only be either *requires* or *excludes*, i.e., exactly two literals per clause with at least one being negated;
- CTCs must not contradict each other, i.e., the corresponding CNF of the entire constraint set must be satisfiable;
- There is a maximum number of CTCs (given as a percentage of the number of features) that must not be exceeded.

Below, we introduce the process performed to apply the operators of crossover and mutation. The individuals chosen to participate in the crossover/mutation are selected by standard tournament selection. The initial population is a set of initial FMs created by generating random feature trees and random CTCs. Domain constraints are also taken into account to generate random FMs.

The *crossover* operator generates offspring following the meta-model representation and in conformance to the domain constraints. The crossover process is:

1. Initialize the offspring with the root feature of $Parent_1$. If the root feature of $Parent_2$ is a different one, then it is added to the offspring as a mandatory child feature of its root feature.
2. Traverse the first parent depth first starting at the *root* node and add to the offspring a random number r of features that are not already contained by appending them to their respective parent feature already contained in the offspring using the same relation type between them (the parent feature of every visited feature during the traversal is guaranteed to be contained in the offspring due to the depth first traversal order).
3. Traverse the second parent exactly the same way as the first one.
4. Go to Step 2 until every feature is contained in the offspring.

The second child is obtained by swapping the order of the parents. The CTCs offspring are assigned randomly from a set of constraints obtained by merging all the constraints of both parents. First, a subset of CTCs are selected and assigned to the first offspring and then the remaining to the second offspring.

The *mutation* operator applies minor modifications in the tree or in the CTCs of the FM. A probability value is used to choose if the change is applied in the tree part, in the CTCs, or in both. The modifications applied in an FM are:

- Mutations performed on the tree:

    - Randomly swaps two features in the feature tree;
    - Randomly changes an *Alternative* relation to an *Or* relation or vice-versa;
    - Randomly changes an *Optional* or *Mandatory* relation to any other kind of relation (*Mandatory, Optional, Alternative, Or*);
    - Randomly selects a sub-tree in the feature tree and puts it somewhere else in the tree without violating the metamodel or any of the domain constraints.

Table 9.1 Feature sets of the illustrative example

Variants	Feature Sets			
	Base	Consortium	Converter	WithdrawLimit
BS01	✓			
BS05	✓	✓	✓	
BS06	✓		✓	✓
BS07	✓	✓		✓

Table 9.2 Dependency matrix of the illustrative example

From	To	Weight	Normalized
d^0(+WithdrawLimit.{0})	d^0(+Base.{0})	7	0.170731707
d^0(+Converter.{0})	d^0(+Base.{0})	20	0.487804878
d^0(+Consortium.{0})	d^0(+Base.{0})	4	0.097560976
d^1(+Converter.{0}, +WithdrawLimit.{0})	d^0(+Base.{0})	2	0.048780488
d^1(+Base.{0}, −WithdrawLimit.{0})	d^0(+Base.{0})	2	0.048780488
d^1(+WithdrawLimit.{0}, +Consortium.{0})	d^0(+Base.{0})	2	0.048780488
d^1(−Converter.{0}, +Base.{0}) AND d^1(+Base.{0}, −Consortium.{0})	d^0(+Base.{0})	2	0.048780488
d^1(+Converter.{0}, +Consortium.{0}) AND d^1(+Converter.{0}, −WithdrawLimit.{0}) AND d^1(−WithdrawLimit.{0}, +Consortium.{0})	d^0(+Base.{0})	2	0.048780488
	Total:	41	1.0000

- Mutations performed on the CTCs:
  - Adds a new randomly created CTC that does not contradict the other CTCs and does not already exist;
  - Randomly removes a CTC.

To illustrate the reverse engineering of FMs we recall the BS variants (Fig. 9.2), where the set of feature sets for our illustrative example is presented in Table 9.1. The dependencies of this illustrative example are presented in Fig. 9.5, however we represented the dependency graph with normalized values in Table 9.2. This normalization keeps the sum of all weights of the graph equal to 1.0, enabling a better interpretation of the values in the optimization process. The information of Tables 9.1 and 9.2 are provided as input for the search-based technique.

Figure 9.6 presents two FMs reached by the algorithm. Briefly, we can observe that both FMs have VS equal to 1.0, which means they do not violate any dependency of the dependency graph. Regarding the objectives of precision and recall, there is a trade-off between the solutions. FM1 (Fig. 9.6a) has R=1.0, which means the four configurations of Table 9.1 are possible with this FM, however, the same FM denotes more products than desired, decreasing the values of precision (P) to 0.5. On the other hand, the value of precision for FM2 (Fig. 9.6b) is 1.0, therefore all products of this FM are in the desired feature sets, however it represents only

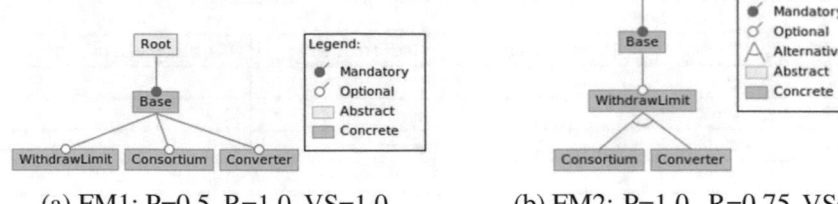

(a) FM1: P=0.5, R=1.0, VS=1.0   (b) FM2: P=1.0, R=0.75, VS=1.0

Fig. 9.6 Example of reverse engineered FMs

three products, missing one desired configuration, leading to a recall value equal to 0.75. The software engineer can choose the FM that best fits his/her needs. With this example, we observe the benefits of having a multi-objective solution.

9.3.4 Model Merging

This step is responsible for combining multiple class diagram variants into a global class diagram. The goal is to synthesize a UML class diagram that contains all possible model elements present in different variants. The merging of multiple models is a NP-hard problem, and the comparison among all model elements for a big set of variants can lead to a huge search space [43]. Based on that, this task is performed by a search-based technique that evaluates the merged class diagrams, considering the number of differences from the candidate individual to all input model variants. We used as basis our previous work [2]. This is the first step towards the PLA.

9.3.4.1 Representation of the Individuals

In this step, the individuals are represented using the same structure of the step Features Traceability, namely a UML class diagram following UML2 meta-model. This representation allows programmatically comparison, modification, and storage of UML models.

9.3.4.2 Objective Function

Differently from the previous step, here we adopted a single-objective evolutionary algorithm. The individuals are evaluated according to their differences to the UML class diagram variants. We can find some tools to compare UML models, but they are able to deal with only two models at once (or three models if we include an ancestor model). Differently, in our approach an individual is evaluated in comparison to a set of several UML class diagram variants. Considering this, the proposed objective function is composed of the sum of differences from one model to all input model variants. The definition below presents the metric called *Model Similarity*. The function *diff* represents the number of differences found by using common UML model comparing tools. We sum only the set of differences indicating that the elements exist in the variant *v* but are missing on the *candidate_model*.

Definition 9.10 (Model Similarity (MS)) Model Similarity expresses the degree of similarity of the candidate architecture model to a set of model variants.

$$M = \sum_{v \in Variants} diff(candidate\_model, v)$$

9.3.4.3 Evolutionary Operators

The initial population of individuals is created by copying the input UML models variants. The only constraint is that all the input models must be included in the initial population at least once. The selection of solutions to apply crossover and mutation is done by the tournament strategy. To introduce the modifications in the individuals, the set of differences found between the models is also used to perform crossover and mutation.

For the *crossover*, the starting point are two candidate models. From these two models, we generate two children: one with the differences merged and one without the differences. For instance, let us consider two parent models X and Y. The children will be created as described below. The strategy adopted to *Child Model 1* aims at creating a model that has more elements, going to the direction of the system architecture. On the other hand, the strategy used for *Child Model 2* has the goal of eliminating possible conflicting elements from a candidate architecture.

- *Crossover Child Model 1*: this model has the differences between its parents merged. For example, the elements of X that are missing on Y are merged in this latter, or vice versa. This operator is commutative.
- *Crossover Child Model 2*: this child is generated by removing the differences between the parents. For example, the differences of X that are missing on Y are removed, or vice versa. This operator is commutative.

Mutation applies only one modification in each model parent. The starting point of the mutation operator is two candidate architectures, and the result is also two children. The process to create children for any parent models X and Y is described below. The mutation process can select a difference that is owned, i.e., is part of another difference. In such cases, the entire owning difference is moved to the child.

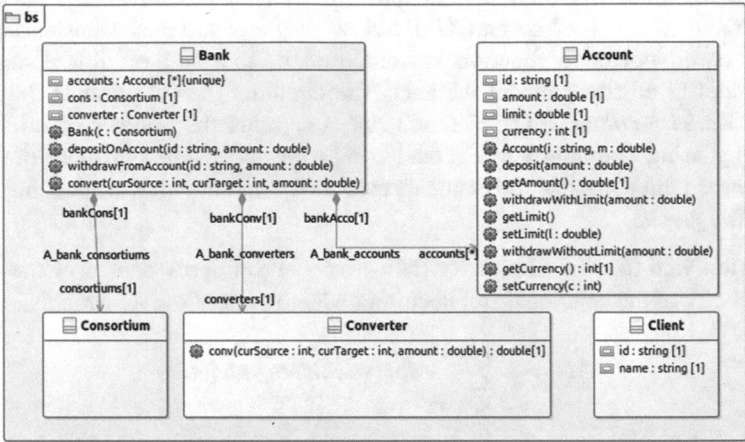

Fig. 9.7 Example of merged UML class diagram

For example, when a mutation selects a parameter owned by an operation, the entire operation is moved to the child.

- *Mutation Child Model 1*: the first child is created by merging one difference of the model Y in the model X. After randomly selecting one element of the model Y, but missing on the model X, this element is added in the model X.
- *Mutation Child Model 2*: here, the same process described above is performed, however, including one element of the model X in the model Y.

An example of output generated by our model merging approach is presented in Fig. 9.7, considering the four variants of the illustrative example (Fig. 9.2). We can observe that all model elements of the input variants are merged in one global UML class diagram.

9.3.5 Variability Grafting

This step aims at enriching the merged class diagram obtained in the previous step with information about features and variability to produce a PLA. In the context of this work, a PLA is a structural representation of model variants with annotations regarding the features of the variants. Each model element of the merged UML class diagram is annotated with the feature, or set of features, it corresponds. This task is done by adding a UML comment to each model element. To generate such representation, the traceability discovered in the step Features Traceability is used to graft information regarding the features in the merged model obtained in the previous step. The task of variability grafting is done by labeling each model element to the module (i.e., features) it belongs to. The strategy to graft variability

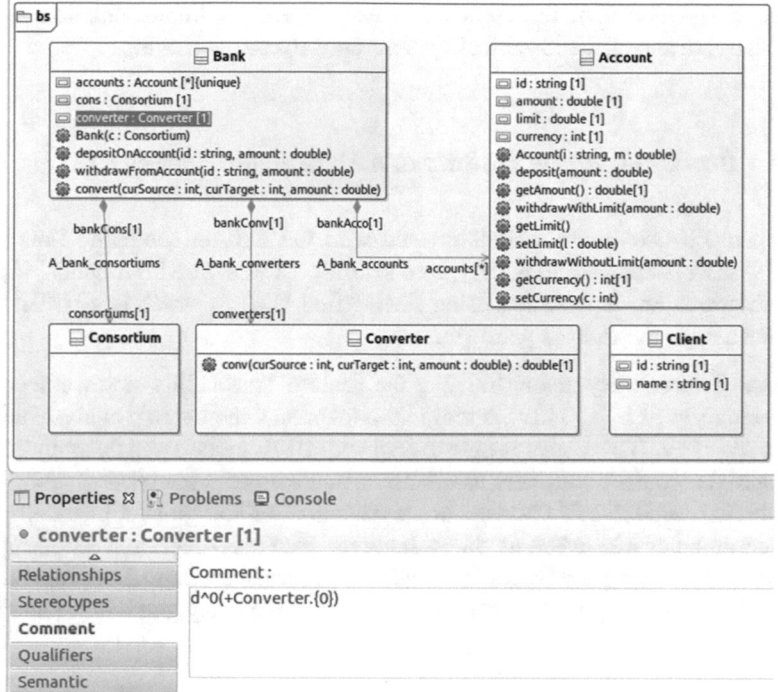

Fig. 9.8 Example of variabilities in the PLA

information consists of adding UML owned comments to every element of a UML class diagram. By adopting this strategy, the obtained PLA can be viewed in any UML editor.

Figure 9.8 presents a PLA for our BS illustrative example. Basically, the merged model presented in Fig. 9.7 and the traceability obtained in the first step of ModelVars2SPL were used for obtaining this artifact. The figure presents the variability information of an attribute of Bank with the comment that indicates it belongs to $d^0(+Converter.\{0\})$.

9.4 Evaluation

We evaluated ModelVars2SPL[3] with the goal of investigating two aspects: (1) capacity to represent all input variants in the PLA and in the FM that are generated,

---

[3] The applications, tools, and an illustrative example are publicly available at: https://wesleyklewerton.github.io/reengineering.html.

and (2) performance of the approach. Next we present implementation aspects, algorithms parameters, and subject systems used for the evaluation.

9.4.1 Implementation Details and Parameter Settings

Our approach deals with models created with the Eclipse Modeling Framework (EMF),[4] a well-known and widely used set of tools to deal with models [46]. The class diagrams are represented using EMF-based UML2, which is a UML^{TM} 2.x meta-model for the Eclipse platform.

Features Traceability algorithm For the Feature Traceability step we developed a parser on top of ECCO [29], a tool that implements the overlap analysis used by ModelVars2SPL. This parser is able to deal with UML models and decompose class diagrams. The parser considers as atomic model elements the class diagram types available in the UML2 EMF-based implementation. ECCO tool automatically identifies dependencies between modules, however, for class diagram relationships we adapted ECCO using our parser for UML2 EMF-based models. After representing the relationships using ECCO internal types, the dependency graph is automatically generated.

Reverse Engineering of FMs—Algorithm and Parameters Here the individuals are represented using a simplified version of the SPLX meta-model.[5] This meta-model defines the structure and semantics of FMs [4]. The random FMs for the initial population are created using the tools FaMa [8] and BeTTy [44]. The adopted multi-objective evolutionary algorithm adopted was the Non-Dominated Sorting Genetic Algorithm (NSGA-II) available on the ECJ Framework.[6] The parameters used to configure the algorithm are: number of fitness evaluations = 200,000, population size = 200, crossover probability = 0.7, feature tree mutation probability = 0.5, CTCs mutation probability = 0.5, number of elites = 25%, tournament size = 6, maximum CTC percentage for builder[7] = 0.1, maximum CTC percentage for mutator[7] = 0.5, and independent runs = 30. The maximum number of fitness evaluations is the stop criterion.

Model Merging—Algorithm and Parameters The implementation of this step is based on EMF Diff/Merge. The search-based technique was implemented on top of jMetal.[8] We selected the mono-objective generational Genetic Algorithm (gGA).

---

[4] https://eclipse.org/modeling/emf/.

[5] http://www.splot-research.org/.

[6] http://cs.gmu.edu/~eclab/projects/ecj/.

[7] Relative to number of features.

[8] http://jmetal.sourceforge.net/.

The parameters used to configure gGA are: number of fitness evaluations = 4000, population size = 200, crossover probability = 0.95, mutation probability = 0.2, number of elites = 2%, tournament size = 4, and independent runs = 30. The maximum number of fitness evaluations is the stop criterion.

Variability Grafting Algorithm For this step, we implemented our own algorithm on top of the ECCO Tool. In summary, the algorithm uses the trace links information discovered by the tool and enriches UML class diagrams with owned comments in the model elements.

Hardware Settings The experiments were executed on a machine with an Intel® Core™ i5-3570 CPU with 3.40 GHz × 4, 16 GB of memory, and running a 64-bit Linux platform.

9.4.2 Target Applications

For the evaluation, we selected applications composed of a set of different UML class diagram variants which implement different features. The applications are: Banking System (BS) [33], Draw Product Line (DPL) [18], Mobile Media (MM) [17, 29], Video On Demand (VOD) [29], ZipMe (ZM) [18], and Game Of Life (GOL) [18]. Table 9.3 presents the total number of features, number of mandatory features, number of variants, and mean and standard deviation values of features implemented in each variant. We reverse engineered the models from Java code using Eclipse MoDisco, except the BS application, which was originally a set of UML model variants.

Table 9.3 Information of the applications

| Application | Features | | Variants | Mean (Std deviation) features per variant |
	Total	Mandatory		
BS	4	1	8	2.50 (0.93)
DPL	6	1	16	3.75 (1.13)
MMv1	5	2	3	3.00 (0.00)
VOD	11	6	32	8.50 (1.14)
ZM	7	2	32	4.50 (1.14)
GOL	15	3	28	6.93 (1.46)
MMv2	6	2	4	3.25 (0.50)
MMv3	7	2	9	3.67 (0.50)
MMv4	8	2	12	3.75 (0.45)
MMv5	9	2	33	4.45 (0.67)

9.4.3 Evaluation Metrics

To evaluate how the generated FMs and PLAs represent the input variants, intending to keep the behavior of existing products, we use the following metrics:

- *FM Metrics*: Precision (P), Recall (R), and Variability Safety (VS) as presented in Sect. 9.3.3.
- *PLA Metric*: Model Similarity (MS) as presented in Sect. 9.3.4;

Taking into account that a relevant factor to adopt an approach in practice is how long it takes to obtain solutions and the number of alternative solutions the architects and engineers have to deal with, we use the following metrics:

- *Time to obtain solutions:* during the execution of each step of our approach, we measured the time performance. For the steps using exact techniques (deterministic algorithms), namely Features Traceability and Variability Grafting, the runtime of each single run for each application was collected. For the steps using search-based techniques (stochastic algorithms), namely Reverse Engineering of FMs and Model Merging, we computed the mean runtime for 30 independent runs;
- *Number of candidate solutions:* our approach is designed to reach a set of candidate solutions, since we have a step of multi-objective reverse engineering of FMs. Hence, diverse good solutions might be possible. One of the solutions could be better considering one or more objectives, and other solutions considering the remaining objectives. These solutions are called non-dominated and form the Pareto front. In the evaluation, we constructed the Pareto Front based on non-dominated solutions reached considering the 30 independent runs;
- *Euclidean Distance from Ideal Solution (ED):* ED is a quality indicator that measures how close a solution is from an optimal point (i.e., the ideal solution). An ideal solution has optimal values for each criteria under consideration.

9.5 Results and Analysis

This section presents a summary of the results obtained during the evaluation of ModelVars2SPL. For a more detailed description of the results, we refer the reader to our original paper [3].

9.5.1 Capacity to Rederive Input Variant

Table 9.4 presents an overview of the results regarding the FMs and PLAs obtained by ModelVars2SPL. The basis for the comparison is the number of feature sets used as input (second column) and the number of model elements of the baseline

Table 9.4   Results for the obtained FMs and PLAs

| Application | Input feature sets | Baseline model elements[a] | Obtained FM | | | Obtained PLA | | |
			Present feature sets	Absent feature sets	Violated deps	Model elements[a]	Differences baseline to PLA	Differences PLA to baseline
BS	8	32	8	0	0	34	16	3
DPL	16	72	16	0	0	72	303	2
MMv1	3	180	3	0	0	180	827	0
VOD	32	675	32	0	0	759	2122	36
ZM	32	656	32	0	0	715	2588	99
GOL	28	178	18	10	0	186	1954	521
MMv2	4	210	4	0	0	210	953	0
MMv3	9	214	9	0	0	215	1989	712
MMv4	12	245	12	0	12	244	2195	819
MMv5	33	313	27	6	27	313	2788	1038

[a] (Classes + Interfaces + Attributes + Operations + Relationships)

class diagram (third column). The baseline of each application is the most complete UML class diagram variant used as input (i.e., that implements the greatest number of features).

To analyze the instantiation of the same input variants as products of the SPL, we consider the obtained FM for each application. Comparing the feature sets used as input (second column) and the feature sets present in the obtained FMs (fourth column) of Table 9.4, we can see that ModelVars2SPL is able to represent exactly the same input configurations of products for eight out of ten applications. Despite not finding optimal solutions for two applications, the obtained FMs have more present feature sets than absent ones (fifth column). For example, in the GOL application the obtained FM denotes 18 input feature sets, and only ten feature sets are absent. This happens for the applications GOL and MMv5, which have the largest number of features and variants respectively. Regarding the violated dependencies, only two FMs denote feature sets that do not satisfy some dependencies of the dependency graph, namely MMv4 and MMv5. For these two applications, there are only two optional features and the configurations of products have less than 50% of features on average (see Table 9.3). This means that there is not much available information on the evolutionary process of NSGA-II. In spite of that, we can say our approach is able to generate variability-safe FMs, or in other words, our approach is consistent to the design artifacts.

With respect to the PLAs, we analyze the baseline in comparison to the PLAs obtained by ModelVars2SPL. In Table 9.4 the number of model elements in the PLA (seventh column) is greater than the model elements in the baseline (third column) except for MMv4. A greater number of model elements means that the PLA is more complete than the baseline. To corroborate our findings, Fig. 9.9 presents the graphs with the number of model elements. We can observe that the number of model elements in the PLA is very similar to the number in the baseline in the applications

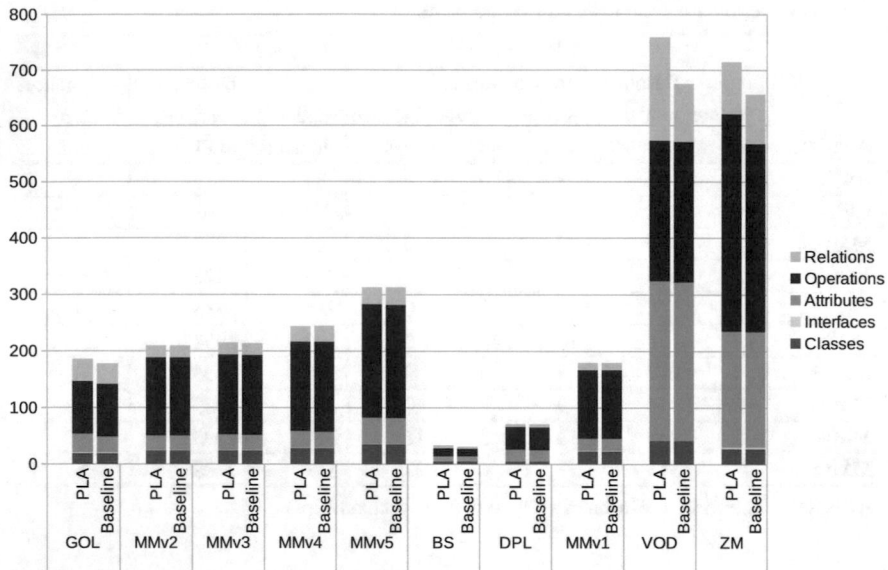

Fig. 9.9 Baselines and PLAs

BS, DPL and MMV1, the smallest applications. For the applications GOL, VOD and ZM, the PLAs have more model elements than the baseline, which is expected.

In the last two columns of Table 9.4 we can see the number of differences between the baseline and PLA taking into account the two directions of comparison. For example, considering the BS application, the baseline has 16 different model elements in comparison to the PLA. On the other hand, the PLA has only 3 differences in comparison to the baseline. Analyzing these differences, we can see in all applications that the PLA is more similar to the baseline than the other way around.

Based on the results presented above, we can attest that the FMs generated with ModelVars2SPL in most of the cases represent the exact input variants, since most of the time (8 out of 10) the FMs represent exactly the desired input feature sets. Also, only in two applications (2 out of 10) the FMs have violated dependencies. In general, ModelVars2SPL can reach solutions in accordance to the design artifacts. In all applications, the PLA is similar or more complete than the baselines, indicating our approach is able to merge the input UML class diagram variants properly. In summary, we can say that the PLAs and FMs represent well the input variants.

9.5.2 Performance for Obtaining Solutions

To evaluate the overall performance of our approach, we consider the solutions for every step. In summary, the step Features Traceability obtains solutions as expected,

Table 9.5 Approach runtime for each step of ModelVars2SPL and their total

	Feature traceability		Reverse engineer of FMs			Model merging				Variability grafting		Total runtime			
Application	s	ms	min	s	ms	h	min	s	ms	s	ms	h	min	s	ms
BS	1	987			234		1	24	724	1	481		1	28	426
DPL	2	206	1	0	252		9	6	269	1	811		10	10	538
MMv1	2	58		5	180		7	11	326	2	806		7	21	370
VOD	13	570			746	2	11	2	673	8	972	2	11	25	962
ZM	17	394		1	395	2	18	19	501	9	31	2	18	47	322
GOL	12	373	5	37	642		34	31	417	4	524		40	25	956
MMv2	2	230		3	740		10	5	797	2	899		10	14	667
MMv3	2	930		4	820		20	0	752	2	927		20	11	429
MMv4	3	723	5	9	975		28	50	764	3	204		34	7	667
MMv5	6	875	39	49	388	1	23	49	51	3	958	2	3	49	272

discovering properly the base and derivative modules, and dependencies. The FMs reverse engineered in the second step describe well the input feature sets, as shown by the values of P, R, and VS. The majority of the solutions found with the search-based technique are optimal solutions in the Pareto front with the best ED values. The evolutionary process in the step of Model Merging is able to reach good global UML class diagrams by exploring the search space. As previously discussed, the solutions are very similar to the baseline variants. Finally, we observed that our algorithm in the Variability Grafting step can successfully include annotations in model elements to generate good PLAs.

Regarding the time needed to obtain a solution, Table 9.5 presents the runtime of the four steps of the approach and the total runtime. The runtime of the reverse engineering of FMs is related to the input information as shown in Table 9.3, i.e., a lower runtime is observed when an application has few optional features (low variability). This low variability implies simpler FMs which are easier to reach. The bottleneck regarding the runtime is the step of model merging. As we can see in Table 9.5, for the applications VOD, ZM, and MMv5 ModelVars2SPL took more than 2 h in this step. On closer inspection, these applications have larger number of variants and model elements (see Table 9.3), fact that causes the computation of the fitness functions (based on model diffing) to take longer.

With respect to the artifacts obtained in each step, we can attest that Model-Vars2SPL can successfully aid the extraction of SPL core design artifacts. The good representativeness of the FMs and PLAs obtained is a consequence of the good results obtained throughout all the steps in ModelVars2SPL. Furthermore, the runtime spent in the steps allows the approach to be applied in practice, thus providing developers a sound FM and a PLA that serves as launchpad for the re-engineering process.

9.6 Practical Usage of ModelVars2SPL Solutions

In order to motivate practical use of ModelVars2SPL, below we present some ways to use the generated FMs and PLAs, showing the approach's benefits for practitioners.

Being Source of Information for Technical and Managerial Decision FMs generated can support the communication among stakeholders, allowing better managerial decision regarding the migration of existing variants to an SPL. PLAs allow a better understanding of the implementation, presenting commonalities and variabilities, in this way, this artifact can provide information for technical decisions.

Plan Re-engineering Activities The FMs and PLAs can be used as a source of information to support practitioners on deciding a sequence of products to be migrated to an SPL. For instance, practitioners can identify outlier variants, i.e., those variants that became too different, and remove these variants from the re-engineering process. Furthermore, FMs and PLAs allow the estimation of financial and human resources to perform the re-engineering process.

Ease Maintenance of the Variants The core design assets generated by ModelVars2SPL can be used as a source of information for bug fixing, providing a global view of the whole system family, easing the identification of the parts to be maintained/fixed. For example, the ModelVars2SPL solutions can help in the identification of bad smells, and consequently their removal.

Support System Evolution Practitioners can reason on FMs and plan the release of new a product with new configuration of features, or decide the development of a new functionality to fulfill domain gaps to be more competitive. The PLA can support the platform migration of existing products, e.g. from desktop to mobile, cloud, or microservices.

Aid the Design of Test Cases By using FMs and PLAs, software engineers and testers can observe the interaction among different parts that implement a feature. In this way, the practitioners can design better test cases to exercise such different parts.

9.7 Concluding Remarks

This chapter presented ModelVars2SPL, an approach to extract SPL core design assets. ModelVars2SPL is composed of four steps covering all three phases of the re-engineering process of system variants into SPLs. ModelVars2SPL takes as input a set of UML class diagrams, with a description of the features implemented in each variant, and generates FMs that describe the configuration of the variants and PLAs that represent the model elements related to each feature.

A distinguishing characteristic of ModelVars2SPL is the use of design models. This makes our approach independent of programming language and supports the re-engineering process at the design level. Another benefit is that the SPL core design artifacts are obtained automatically. ModelVars2SPL uses search-based techniques to better solve the complex activities as the identification of domain constraints. In this way, ModelVars2SPL can reduce effort to extract SPLs from system variants and make the adoption of SPL using an extractive approach more attractive.

We evaluated ModelVars2SPL with ten applications from different domains and complexities. The results indicate that ModelVars2SPL is effective to obtain FMs and PLAs that represent the input variants, and it does so within an acceptable runtime. Concerning the benefits of ModelVars2SPL, in terms of practical use of its generated FMs and PLAs, we argued that they can be used to aid the communication between practitioners and stakeholders, the re-engineering planning, maintenance of existing products, to support system evolution for development of new products and platform migration, and to improve quality by easing derivation of better test cases.

Acknowledgments This work was supported by the Brazilian Agencies CAPES: 7126/2014-00; CNPq: 453678/2014-9, 305358/2012-0, 408356/2018-9 and 305968/2018-1; and the Carlos Chagas Filho Foundation for Supporting Research in the State of Rio de Janeiro (FAPERJ), under the PDR-10 program, grant 202073/2020. This work is partially funded Natural Sciences and Engineering Research Council of Canada (NSERC) grant RGPIN-2017-05421.

References

1. Assunção, W.K.G., Lopez-Herrejon, R.E., Linsbauer, L., Vergilio, S.R., Egyed, A.: Reengineering legacy applications into software product lines: A systematic mapping. Empirical Software Engineering **22**(6), 2972–3016 (2017)
2. Assunção, W.K.G., Vergilio, S.R., Lopez-Herrejon, R.E.: Discovering Software Architectures with Search-Based Merge of UML Model Variants. In: G. Botterweck, C. Werner (eds.) Mastering Scale and Complexity in Software Reuse: 16th International Conference on Software Reuse (ICSR), pp. 95–111. Springer (2017)
3. Assunção, W.K., Vergilio, S.R., Lopez-Herrejon, R.E.: Automatic extraction of product line architecture and feature models from uml class diagram variants. Information and Software Technology **117**, 106,198 (2020)
4. Assunção, W.K.G., Lopez-Herrejon, R.E., Linsbauer, L., Vergilio, S.R., Egyed, A.: Multi-objective reverse engineering of variability-safe feature models based on code dependencies of system variants. Empirical Software Engineering pp. 1–32 (2016)
5. Barros-Justo, J.L., Pinciroli, F., Matalonga, S., Martínez-Araujo, N.: What software reuse benefits have been transferred to the industry? A systematic mapping study. Information and Software Technology **103**, 1–21 (2018)
6. Batory, D.: Feature models, grammars, and propositional formulas. In: H. Obbink, K. Pohl (eds.) Software Product Lines, pp. 7–20. Springer Berlin Heidelberg, Berlin, Heidelberg (2005)
7. Bayer, J., Forster, T., Ganesan, D., Girard, J.F., John, I., Knodel, J., Kolb, R., Muthig, D.: Definition of reference architectures based on existing systems. Tech. Rep. Report No. 034.04/E, Fraunhofer IESE-Report No. 034.04/E (2004)

8. Benavides, D., Segura, S., Trinidad, P., Cortés, A.R.: FaMa: Tooling a framework for the automated analysis of feature models. In: International Workshop on Variability Modelling of Software-Intensive Systems (VaMoS), pp. 129–134 (2007)
9. Berger, T., She, S., Lotufo, R., Wasowski, A., Czarnecki, K.: A study of variability models and languages in the systems software domain. IEEE Transactions on Software Engineering **39**(12), 1611–1640 (2013)
10. Canfora, G., Di Penta, M., Cerulo, L.: Achievements and challenges in software reverse engineering. Commun. ACM **54**(4), 142–151 (2011)
11. Capilla, R., Gallina, B., Cetina, C., Favaro, J.: Opportunities for software reuse in an uncertain world: From past to emerging trends. Journal of Software: Evolution and Process **31**(8), e2217 (2019)
12. Ciborowska, A., Kraft, N.A., Damevski, K.: Detecting and characterizing developer behavior following opportunistic reuse of code snippets from the web. In: 15th International Conference on Mining Software Repositories, MSR '18, pp. 94–97. Association for Computing Machinery, New York, NY, USA (2018)
13. Clements, P., Northrop, L.: Software Product Lines: Practices and Patterns. Addison-Wesley Longman Publishing Co., Inc., Boston, MA, USA (2001)
14. Colanzi, T.E., Assunção, W.K., Vergilio, S.R., Farah, P.R., Guizzo, G.: The symposium on search-based software engineering: Past, present and future. Information and Software Technology **127**, 106,372 (2020)
15. Colanzi, T.E., Vergilio, S.R.: A feature-driven crossover operator for multi-objective and evolutionary optimization of product line architectures. Journal of Systems and Software **121**, 126–143 (2016)
16. Faust, D., Verhoef, C.: Software product line migration and deployment. Software: Practice and Experience **33**(10), 933–955 (2003)
17. Figueiredo, E., Cacho, N., Sant'Anna, C., Monteiro, M., Kulesza, U., Garcia, A., Soares, S., Ferrari, F., Khan, S., Castor Filho, F., Dantas, F.: Evolving software product lines with aspects: An empirical study on design stability. In: International Conference on Software Engineering (ICSE), pp. 261–270. ACM (2008)
18. Fischer, S., Linsbauer, L., Lopez-Herrejon, R.E., Egyed, A.: Enhancing clone-and-own with systematic reuse for developing software variants. In: IEEE 30th International Conference on Software Maintenance and Evolution, ICSME, pp. 391–400. IEEE Computer Society, Washington, DC, USA (2014)
19. Harman, M., Mansouri, S.A., Zhang, Y.: Search-based software engineering: Trends, techniques and applications. ACM Computing Surveys (CSUR) **45**(1), 11:1–11:61 (2012)
20. Hasbi, M., Budiardjo, E.K., Wibowo, W.C.: Reverse engineering in software product line - a systematic literature review. In: 2Nd International Conference on Computer Science and Artificial Intelligence, CSAI '18, pp. 174–179. ACM, New York, NY, USA (2018)
21. Holmes, R., Walker, R.J.: Systematizing pragmatic software reuse. ACM Transactions on Software Engineering and Methodology **21**(4), 20:1–20:44 (2013)
22. Krueger, C.W.: Software reuse. ACM Computing Surveys **24**(2), 131–183 (1992)
23. Krüger, J., Berger, T.: An empirical analysis of the costs of clone- and platform-oriented software reuse. In: 28th ACM Joint Meeting on European Software Engineering Conference and Symposium on the Foundations of Software Engineering, ESEC/FSE 2020, pp. 432–444. Association for Computing Machinery, New York, NY, USA (2020)
24. Kulkarni, N., Varma, V.: Perils of opportunistically reusing software module. Software: Practice and Experience **47**(7), 971–984 (2017)
25. Kumaki, K., Tsuchiya, R., Washizaki, H., Fukazawa, Y.: Supporting commonality and variability analysis of requirements and structural models. In: 16th International Software Product Line Conference, SPLC, pp. 115–118. ACM (2012)
26. Lago, P., Malavolta, I., Muccini, H., Pelliccione, P., Tang, A.: The road ahead for architectural languages. IEEE Software **32**(1), 98–105 (2015)
27. Laguna, M.A., Crespo, Y.: A systematic mapping study on software product line evolution: From legacy system reengineering to product line refactoring. Science of Computer Programming **78**(8), 1010–1034 (2013)

28. Linden, F.J.v.d., Schmid, K., Rommes, E.: Software Product Lines in Action: The Best Industrial Practice in Product Line Engineering. Springer-Verlag New York, Inc., Secaucus, NJ, USA (2007)
29. Linsbauer, L., Lopez-Herrejon, E.R., Egyed, A.: Recovering traceability between features and code in product variants. In: 17th International Software Product Line Conference, SPLC 2013, pp. 131–140. ACM, New York, NY, USA (2013)
30. Malavolta, I., Lago, P., Muccini, H., Pelliccione, P., Tang, A.: What industry needs from architectural languages: A survey. IEEE Transactions on Software Engineering **39**(6), 869–891 (2013)
31. Martinez, J., Assunção, W.K.G., Ziadi, T.: ESPLA: A catalog of extractive SPL adoption case studies. In: Proceedings of the 21st International Systems and Software Product Line Conference - Volume B, SPLC '17, pp. 38–41. ACM, New York, NY, USA (2017)
32. Martinez, J., Ziadi, T., Bissyandé, T.F., Klein, J., Le Traon, Y.: Bottom-up adoption of software product lines: A generic and extensible approach. In: 19th International Conference on Software Product Line, SPLC '15, p. 101–110. Association for Computing Machinery, New York, NY, USA (2015)
33. Martinez, J., Ziadi, T., Bissyandé, T.F., Klein, J., le Traon, Y.: Automating the extraction of model-based software product lines from model variants. In: 30th IEEE/ACM International Conference on Automated Software Engineering (ASE), pp. 396–406 (2015)
34. Martinez, J., Ziadi, T., Klein, J., le Traon, Y.: Identifying and visualising commonality and variability in model variants. In: J. Cabot, J. Rubin (eds.) Modelling Foundations and Applications, pp. 117–131. Springer International Publishing, Cham (2014)
35. Mefteh, M., Bouassida, N., Ben-Abdallah, H.: Implementation and evaluation of an approach for extracting feature models from documented uml use case diagrams. In: 30th Annual ACM Symposium on Applied Computing, SAC'15, pp. 1602–1609. ACM, New York, NY, USA (2015)
36. Mikkonen, T., Taivalsaari, A.: Software reuse in the era of opportunistic design. IEEE Software **36**(3), 105–111 (2019)
37. Mäkitalo, N., Taivalsaari, A., Kiviluoto, A., Mikkonen, T., Capilla, R.: On opportunistic software reuse. Computing **102**(11), 2385–2408 (2020)
38. Pohl, K., Böckle, G., Linden, F.J.v.d.: Software Product Line Engineering: Foundations, Principles and Techniques. Springer-Verlag New York, Inc., Secaucus, NJ, USA (2005)
39. Reinhartz-Berger, I., Kemelman, M.: Extracting core requirements for software product lines. Requirements Engineering (2019)
40. Rubin, J.: Cloned product variants: From ad-hoc to well-managed software reuse. Ph.D. thesis, University of Toronto, Graduate Department of Computer Science (2014)
41. Rubin, J., Chechik, M.: From products to product lines using model matching and refactoring. In: 2nd International Workshop on Model-driven Approaches in Software Product Line Engineering (MAPLE '10), collocated with the 14th International Software Product Line Conference (SPLC '10) (2010)
42. Rubin, J., Chechik, M.: Combining related products into product lines. In: J. de Lara, A. Zisman (eds.) Fundamental Approaches to Software Engineering, pp. 285–300. Springer Berlin Heidelberg, Berlin, Heidelberg (2012)
43. Rubin, J., Chechik, M.: N-way model merging. In: 9th Joint Meeting on Foundations of Software Engineering (ESEC/FSE), pp. 301–311. ACM (2013)
44. Segura, S., Galindo, J., Benavides, D., Parejo, J.A., Cortés, A.R.: BeTTy: benchmarking and testing on the automated analysis of feature models. In: International Workshop on Variability Modelling of Software-Intensive Systems (VaMoS), pp. 63–71 (2012)
45. She, S., Lotufo, R., Berger, T., Wąsowski, A., Czarnecki, K.: Reverse engineering feature models. In: 33rd International Conference on Software Engineering, ICSE'11, pp. 461–470. ACM, New York, NY, USA (2011)
46. Steinberg, D., Budinsky, F., Merks, E., Paternostro, M.: EMF: eclipse modeling framework. Pearson Education (2008)

47. Wille, D., Schulze, S., Schaefer, I.: Variability mining of state charts. In: 7th International Workshop on Feature-Oriented Software Development, FOSD'16, pp. 63–73. ACM, New York, NY, USA (2016)
48. Yu, X., Gen, M.: Introduction to evolutionary algorithms. Springer Science & Business Media (2010)
49. Ziadi, T., Frias, L., da Silva, M.A.A., Ziane, M.: Feature identification from the source code of product variants. In: 16th European Conference on Software Maintenance and Reengineering, pp. 417–422 (2012)

Chapter 10
Extraction and Evolution of a Software Product Line from Existing Web-Based Systems

Erick Sharlls Ramos de Pontes, Uirá Kulesza, Carlos Eduardo da Silva, Eiji Adachi, and Elder Cirilo

Abstract This chapter presents a study of extraction and evolution of a software product line (SPL) from existing web-based systems. We show a set of activities: (1) to extract commonalities and variabilities from existing use case models of a cloned web-based system; and (2) to refactor and evolve a software product line that addresses the existing web-based systems. We observed several benefits in our study related to a systematic variability management and an ease customization and evolution of the SPL features. Also, we indicate that the presented activities can be part of a method for the extraction and evolution of SPLs.

10.1 Introduction

Software Product Lines (SPLs) promote large-scale reuse in the context of software development. A SPL is a family of related systems that share common features, but, according to the system (product) being considered, maintains specific features to meet the needs of a market segment [3]. A *feature* [4] is a functionality or property of a SPL that is relevant to any stakeholder. Several benefits can be observed from the opportunistic reuse of artifacts promoted by SPLs, such as: reducing time and costs with development, as well as improving the quality of final products [8].

E. S. R. de Pontes · U. Kulesza (✉) · E. Adachi
Federal University of Rio Grande do Norte, Rio Grande do Norte, Brazil
e-mail: erick@ct.ufrn.br; uira@dimap.ufrn.br; eiji@imd.ufrn.br

C. E. da Silva
Department of Computing, Sheffield Hallam University, Sheffield, UK
e-mail: C.DaSilva@shu.ac.uk

E. Cirilo
Federal University of São João del–Rei, São João del–Rei, Brazil
e-mail: elder@ufsj.edu.br

© Springer Nature Switzerland AG 2023
R. E. Lopez-Herrejon et al. (eds.), *Handbook of Re-Engineering Software Intensive Systems into Software Product Lines*, https://doi.org/10.1007/978-3-031-11686-5_10

If on one hand the SPL approach entails several desirable benefits to software development, on the other hand the proactive development of a SPL may be costly [7]. In SPL proactive development, the underlying core assets of the SPL are developed prior to the software systems (products). For this reason, there are cases in which the software systems are initially designed to meet only specific demands without anticipating their incorporation into a SPL. For these cases, there are two recommended strategies to promote the gradual adoption of SPL from existing software systems: extractive and reactive. In the extractive strategy, the development of a SPL occurs from the refactoring and combination of existing systems. The reactive strategy, on the other hand, promotes the development of a SPL by incorporating new *features* into an existing software system or SPL.

Clements [2] argues that the proactive approach is appropriate for organizations that have time and resources available to invest in a extensive and costly development process. However, when time to market is short, organizations prioritize a faster and safer transition from conventional software engineering to SPL engineering. Assunção et al. [1] conducted a systematic literature mapping that provides an overview of current research on reengineering existing systems into SPLs. The authors report that most approaches do not present explicit guidelines for conducting the whole reengineering process, nor do they explicitly address scenarios for the adoption of extractive and reactive strategies.

In this context, this chapter presents an experience report of the extraction and evolution of a SPL from existing Web software systems. These systems represent clones of each other. These clones share common features and incorporated specific features along their evolution. We found some challenges to evolve separately the different cloned web-systems, such as the difficult to integrate cloned code assets from two (or more) systems and to systematically manage their variabilities. Thus, our work also represents a migration experience of the *clone-and-own* approach of SPL development [5], as opposed to adopting an approach that promotes the systematic management of SPL variabilities. Based on the research method *Action Research* [6], this work describes in details the activities performed for refactoring and evolving a web-based SPL. The main contributions of this work are:

- An experience report of the activities conducted for the extraction and evolution of a SPL extracted from web software systems originally cloned from each other;
- Strategies for variability refactoring that can be used in web-based SPL implementations that follow the layered architectural pattern (Layer);
- Lessons learned derived from such experience.

The remainder of this chapter is organized as follows: Sect. 10.2 presents the goals of the study as well as the methodology used. Section 10.3 details the results of the study conducted for refactoring and evolving a SPL. Section 10.4 presents and discusses lessons learned while conducting the study. Section 10.5 addresses related studies. Finally, Sect. 10.6 presents the findings of the study and future work to be conducted.

10.2   Study Settings

The main aim of our study is to extract and evolve a SPL from existing software systems that were created as clones. We have used the *Action Research* method [6] to solve a real problem and to study simultaneously the experience to solve such problem. The study methodology was composed of the following activities:

1. Choose a cloned web-based software product line. This activity involves the selection set of related web-based software systems that were developed and customized to manage classrooms for different departments of the Federal University of Rio Grande do Norte (UFRN);

2. Extract the SPL from existing software systems. It consists on the extraction of the SPL core assets from existing code and documentation of the existing systems. The following activities were conducted: (i) identification of commonalities and variabilities from the set of use cases specified for the systems; and (ii) refactoring of one of the systems to address the common and variable features from two existing products in order to extract the SPL;

3. Evolve the extracted SPL After the SPL extraction and implementation, we have evolved it to address a new system (product) that maintains new features. Some code refactorings were also applied in the core assets in order to address the new features identified using use case variability analysis;

4. Analysis of results and lessons learned. After the SPL extraction and evolution activity, we analyzed the results and lessons learned of our study focusing on the benefits, contributions and challenges towards to the definition of a systematic method.

10.2.1   Target Systems

A classroom management web-based system from the Federal University of Rio Grande do Norte (UFRN) has been used in our study. Three different cloned implementations of this system was used as a base to produce the software product line. Each of them maintains specific customizations of the classroom management system that address particular needs from difference university departments. The main use cases of the systems are related to: classroom management, automatic course distribution in the classrooms, import course information, reports of the classroom management and distribution, register course calendar, etc.

Table 10.1 presents additional information of the three cloned web-based software systems that are part of our study. It shows the number of use cases, classes and lines of code (LoC).

The classroom management web-based system has been implemented using Java Web technologies. It is structured as a layered system with three different layers: (1) Graphical User Interface (GUI) layer—maintains the classes responsible to process the web requests and return the web pages. It is implemented as a set of managed

Table 10.1 Quantitative data of the studied systems (before SPL extraction and evolution)

Metric	Metric values for the 3 systems
LoC of the original systems (kbytes)	22064, 20699, 20101
Number of classes in the original systems	448, 436, 421
Number of use cases in the original systems	24, 22, 19

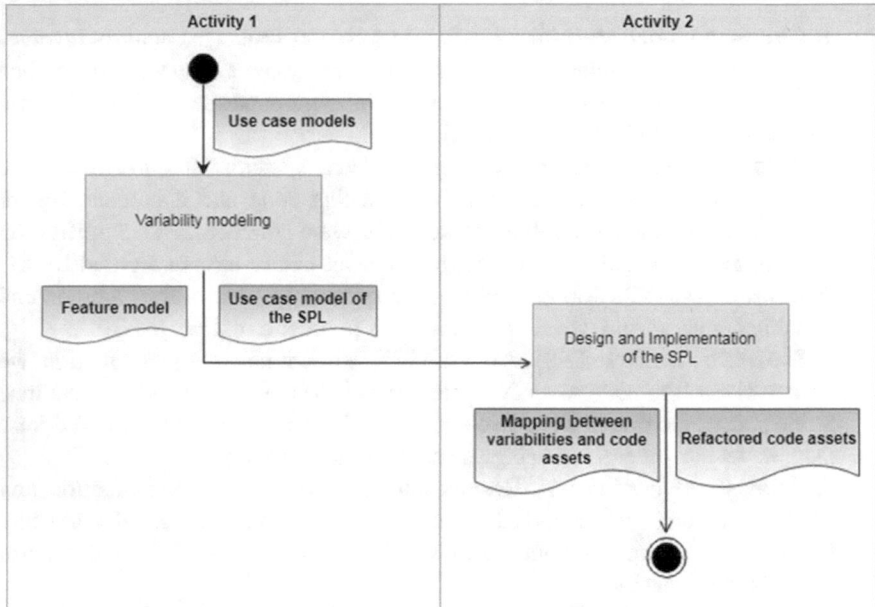

Fig. 10.1 Development activities for the extraction and evolution of the SPL

beans and dynamic web pages using the Java Server Face (JSF) technology ; (2) Business layer—responsible to specify and implement the main business services of the system. It is implemented using Java Spring technology; and, finally, (3) Data layer—maintains the classes responsible to recover and persist the information manipulated by the system using the Hibernate persistence framework.

10.2.2 Study Procedures

During the extraction and evolution of the SPL from the existing classroom management web-based systems, we have accomplished the following activities, which are also illustrated in Fig. 10.1:

1. Variability Modeling. This activity receives as input the use case models of each web system that is part of the SPL. It compares these use case models aiming to identify the common and variable use cases that the systems have. Finally, it produces as output the feature model and use case model of the software product line. During the extraction stage (Sect. 10.3.1), the use case models of two systems were compared. After that, during the SPL evolution (Sect. 10.3.2), the use case model of the SPL generated as part of the extraction stage was compared with the use case model of the third system.

2. Design and Implementation of the SPL. This activity receives as input the use case model and feature model of the SPL produced in the previous activity. It initially identifies the implementation artifacts associated to each variable features in the system used as base to implement the SPL thus producing a mapping between them. After that, it promotes the application of several refactorings to modularize the different SPL variabilities.

Next section presents and details the results of the execution of these activities. Section 10.4 presents and discuss the main lessons learned from the extraction and evolution of the SPL from existing cloned software systems.

10.3   Study Results

This section describes the main results of the SPL extraction and evolution activities from existing web-based systems. These activities varying from use case variability modelling to code refactoring of existing systems to address the SPL commonalities and variabilities.

10.3.1   SPL Extraction from Existing Systems

The SPL extraction process from existing systems involves two activities: (1) the variability modeling of the SPL; and (2) the design and implementation of the SPL by means of code refactoring of the existing systems. Next subsections detail them.

10.3.1.1   Variability Modeling

The variability modeling is driven by use cases. That is, the feature model specification is conducted based on existing use case models. In the following, we detail how the use cases were modeled and the feature model specified during the SPL extraction.

Modeling the SPL Use Cases The use case modeling begins by analyzing the existing use cases models of the software systems from which we are extracting the SPL. In the models, each use case is denoted by an ellipse with a label that represents one relevant system functionality. In the extracted SPL use case diagram

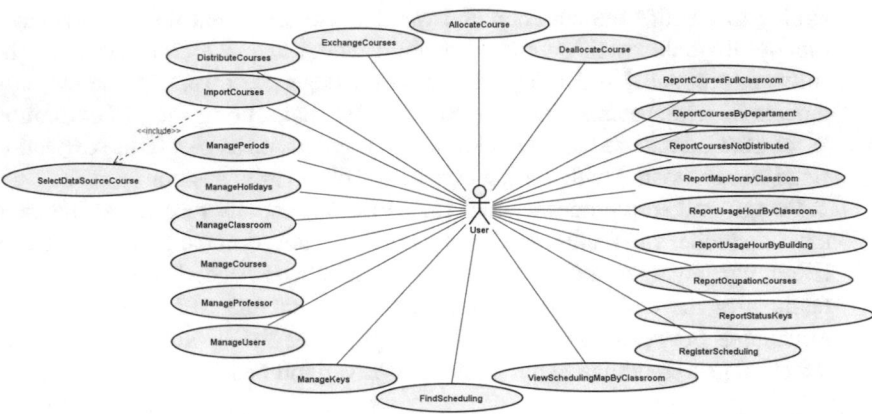

Fig. 10.2 Use case diagram of the System 01

(see Fig. 10.4) we distinguish the use cases which are commons among the software systems and the ones which are specific of each software system. We employed the package notation to visually separate the common use cases from the specific ones. Therefore, common use cases stay in the *Common* package, and the specific ones in the *Optional* package. Specific use cases can be also distinguished to be alternative or or-inclusive functionalities and placed in *Alternative* or *Or-inclusive* packages. Finally, we used the extension point notation to represent variable behavior in uses cases, as shown with use case diagram in Fig. 10.4. A variable behavior is a set of steps in the execution of a base use case that characterize system-specific user requirements.

To model the diagram in Fig. 10.4 we employed the following steps: for each use case, we observed the existence of similar use cases; and for each set of similar use cases, we created one use case in the SPL use case diagram (they are placed in the *Common* package). For example, the use cases "Allocate Course" (see Fig. 10.2) and "Distribute Course" (see Fig. 10.3) were considered as similar according to our judgment. Therefore, one use case called "Distribute Class" was created and placed in the Common package (see Fig. 10.4). Next, we conducted a fine-grained analysis of each use case aimed at identifying variable behaviors. Each identified variable behavior demanded the creation of a use case in the SPL use case diagram as an extension of the base use case. For example, we observed two variable behaviors in the use case "Distribute Course" when comparing the use cases diagram of the systems 01 and 02 which are represented by the "Distribute Course CT" and "Distribute Course CCHLA". These use cases were placed in the Alternative package as they represent mutual exclusive behaviors for the policies to distribute courses in the classrooms for each one of the university departments (CT and CCHLA). In contrast, in case they could exist simultaneously in all systems, they should be placed in the Or-inclusive package. The remaining existing use cases are all placed in the Optional package in the SPL use case diagram. For example,

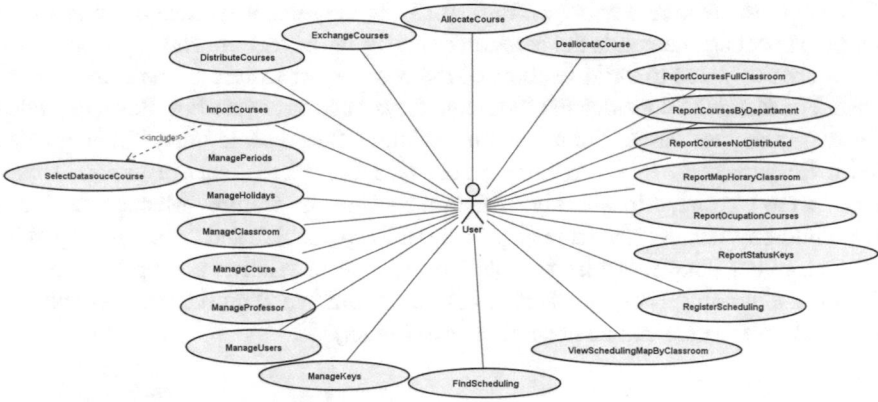

Fig. 10.3   Use case diagram of the System 02

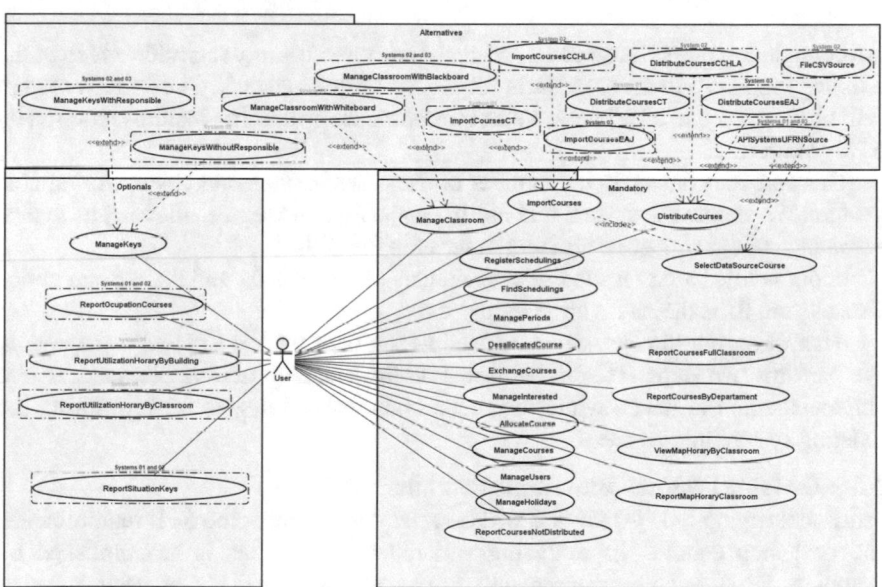

Fig. 10.4   Resulting SPL use case diagram

as there is no use case that we consider similar to the "Building Use Time Report" (System 01), we placed this use case in the Optional package.

Specifying the Feature Model The feature model is specified based on the previously created SPL use case diagram. For each use case in the diagram, we create a feature in the feature model. Specifically, for each use case in the Common package, one mandatory feature has to be created in the feature model. For example, the "Import Course" use case (Fig. 10.4) has an analog mandatory feature "Import

Course" in the feature model (see Fig. 10.13). In the same way, each use case in the Optional package demands the creation of one optional feature. Next, extension use cases are translated to child features of the counterpart feature of the extended use case. For example, consider the "Manage Keys" use case (see Fig. 10.4), extended by two other use cases: "Manage Key Without Responsible" and "Manage Key With Responsible". In the feature model (see Fig. 10.13), such a group of uses cases were translated to a group of features where the feature "Manage Key" has two children features: "Manage Key Without Responsible" and "Manage Key With Responsible". Finally, we have to define the type of relation among the children features: alternative (only one feature can be present in any product) or Or-inclusive (one or more feature can be present in any product).

10.3.1.2   Design and Implementation of SPL Through Refactoring of Existing Systems

After modeling the SPL use cases and features, it is necessary to decide which of the existing systems will serve as basis for the SPL implementation, i.e., which system will be refactored to take into account the common and specific features required by SPL products.

This choice is based on the number of use cases implemented by each available system. We choose the system that has the majority of use cases, allowing us to take advantage of existing code artifacts to develop the SPL.

In our study, based on the use case models of systems 01 and 02, we can notice that System 01 is the one with more use cases.

After choosing the system to be used as the base for the SPL implementation, we perform two steps. The first consists on the mapping of variable features into implementation artifacts, while the second concerns strategies for refactoring the existing system into an SPL.

Map Variable Features Into Implementation Artifacts

After identifying the system that will be refactored to meet the SPL requirements, the next step consists in analyzing variable features. This is accomplished by mapping SPL variable features into implementation artifacts at each layer of the system architecture. In our study, the system is divided in four layers. The presentation layer deals with user interaction through a set of classes that manage web pages state. We have a business layer that is responsible for implementing all business services and rules, while that data access layer deals with database access. Finally, the domain layer defines all entity classes of the system, representing the business domain.

Table 10.2 presents an example of mapping between variable features and their implementation artifacts, distributed among the several layers of the system. Each layer contains artifacts that can be common or variable between the systems of the SPL. Because of that, variable features do not necessarily include variation points in all layers of the system. For example, the feature *Import Courses* presents variations

Table 10.2 Mapping of the variable features to code artifacts—extractive context

Variable features	Presentation layer	Business layer	Data layer	Domain layer
Import courses	ImportCourses.xhtml ImportCourses FormBean.java	ServiceImport Courses.java (system01) ServiceImport Courses.java (system02)	TermDao.java CourseDao.java	Term.java Course.java
Distribute course	distribute.xhtml DistributeCourses FormBean.java	ServiceDistribute Courses.java (system01) ServiceDistribute Courses.java (system02)	Availability ClassroomDao.java CourseDao.java ClassroomDao.java ScheduleDao.java TermDao.java	Availability Classroom.java Course.java Classroom.java Schedule.java Term.java
Select DataSource courses	–	ImportCourses JSONSIGAA (external interface 01) ImportCourse CSVSIGAA (external interface 02)	–	–
Manage keys	RegisterKeys Formbean.java registerKeys.xhtml	ServiceRegister- Keys.java (system 01) ServiceRegister- Keys.java (system 02)	KeyDao.java History KeyDao.java Employee Dao.java	Key.java History Key.java Employee.java
Manage classrooms	new.xhtml (system 01) new.xhtml (system 02) RegisterClassroomForm- Bean.java (system 01) RegisterClassroomForm- Bean.java (system 02)	ServiceRegister- Classrooms.java (system 01) ServiceRegister- Classrooms.java (system 02)	ClassroomDao.java BuildingDao.java TypeOfClassroomDao.java	Classroom.java (system 01) Classroom.java (system 02)

only in the business layer, which indicates that this particular feature has different artifacts in this layer for the systems explored in this SPL. In a similar way, the feature *Distribute Courses* has two different implementations in the business layer, capturing the distinct business services and rules needed by the products of this SPL. The table does not present all variable features explored in this work due to its elevated number. Only those features used as example throughout this chapter are presented.

Refactoring Existing System Based on the knowledge about the variabilities of the systems, refactoring decisions must be made so that the system chosen to represent the SPL addresses all existing variations between the products. These knowledge includes where in the architecture the variability is located, the different artifacts that implement the feature (e.g. Java classes, web pages) and the type of feature (mandatory, optional, alternative, or-inclusive).

Variation points are extracted from use case models, and then used to choose one of the refactoring presented in this development activity. Changes in domain entities are addressed with the refactoring *Addition of attributes in entity*. When the variation involves the choice of one between several possibilities of communication with external systems, the refactoring *Integration with external systems* is used. Variations that involve an use case step with different business rules depending on specific products are handled by the refactoring *Interchange classes with the same interface but with distinct implementations*. However, when those variations are small, the refactoring *Interchange classes with same algorithm structure but with variation in part of it* is more appropriate. Finally, when the variation concerns the presence of a particular use case in different products, the refactoring *Control exhibition of optional features on application menu* is applied. Next we present examples of each refactoring applied to the SPL of our study (Table 10.3).

Applying the Refactoring—*Interchange Classes with the Same Interface but with Distinct Implementations* As we can see in Table 10.2, feature *ImportCourses* represents a variation at the business layer involving system 01 and system 02, in which different classes implement specific importing algorithms for extracting information about the courses of the university. In this particular case, we have applied the *Strategy* design pattern to interchange classes with the same service interface but different implementations at the business layer. Figure 10.5 presents the class diagram after the application of this design pattern in the SPL implementation. The diagram shows that a client (class *ImportCoursesFormBean* from presentation layer) uses a context (class *ContextServiceImportCourse*), which in turn contains an interface (interface *IServiceImportCourse*) that exposes different concrete algorithms for systems 01 and 02 (classes *ServiceImportCoursesCCHLA* e *ServiceImportCoursesCT*). The client informs which concrete algorithm it will use through a parameter at the constructor of the context class.

Applying the Refactoring—*Integration with External Systems* Feature *ImportCourse* interacts with feature *SelectDataSourceCourse*. The last represents two

Table 10.3 Refactorings applied over existing systems

Refactorings	Presentation layer	Business layer	Data layer	Domain layer
Addition of atributes in entity	Conditional execution and inheritanc	Strategy design pattern	–	Inheritance
Integration with external systems	–	Adapter design pattern	–	–
Interchange classes with the same interface but with distinct implementations	–	Strategy Design Pattern	–	–
Interchange classes with same algorithm structure but with variation in part of it	–	Template Method Design Pattern	–	–
Control exhibition of optional features on application menu	Usage of conditional instruction	–	–	–

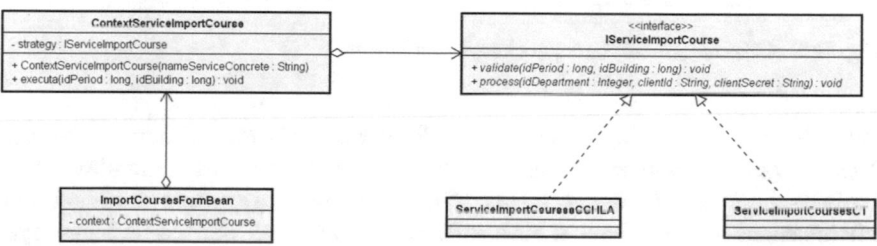

Fig. 10.5 Class diagram of the feature *ImportCourses*

possible external data sources for the SPL. The external systems are able to manipulate useful information for the SPL products, which are in a format not supported by them. In this way, in order to integrate a software product with incompatible external interface, we have employed the *Adapter* design pattern. Figure 10.6 shows the business classes related to feature *ImportCourses* of systems 01 and 02 (*ServiceImportCoursesCT* and *ServiceImportCoursesCCHLA*, respectively), and in the inferior part of the diagram, the classes that implement the adapter pattern and represent the external systems which the SPL needs to interact with. The interface *ExtractCoursesFromSIGAA*, which is used by each of the classes of feature *ImportCourses*, is responsible for providing a common view for the external systems. This interface is implemented by classes that know how to communicate with external systems and to translate the imported courses to domain objects of the SPL.

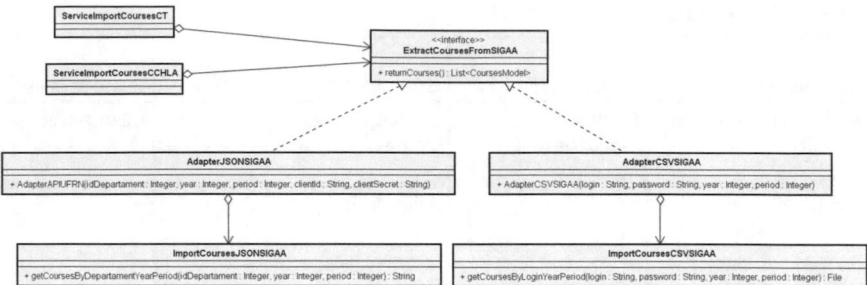

Fig. 10.6   Class diagram of the feature *SelectDataSourceCourse*

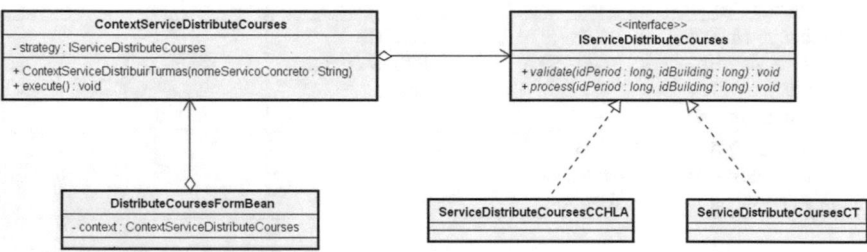

Fig. 10.7   Class diagram of the feature *DistributeCourses*

Applying the Refactoring—*Interchange Classes with the Same Interface But with Distinct Implementations* Another feature that only presents variability at the business layer is *DistributeCourses*. This is another case where the algorithms implemented for each system have different business rules at the business layer, although both systems share the same behaviour at the presentation layer. We employ the *Strategy* design pattern again, as shown in Fig. 10.7. The *Distribute-CoursesFormBean* class uses a context (*ContextServiceDistributeCourses* class) that contains a common interface (*IServiceDistributeCourses*), which expose different behaviour through the concrete classes of systems 01 and 02 (*ServiceDistribute-CoursesCCHLA* e *ServiceDistributeCoursesCT* classes). It is worth mentioning that *DistributeCoursesFormBean* class must inform which concrete algorithm it wants to use through a parameter in the constructor of the context class.

Applying the Refactoring—*Interchange Classes with Same Algorithm Structure But with Variation in Part of It* Another feature that presents variability in the business layer is *Manage Keys* (see Table 10.2). Both systems extracted from the SPL contains artifacts with different implementations in this layer. However, different from the features *DistributeCourses* and *ImportCourses* that also have variabilities in the same layer, here the variability is fine-grained. In the previous features, the code artifacts present a greater divergence of implementation (coarse-grained variability), having in common only the fact that both code artifacts present the same service interface. Thus, a different solution was used to implement each

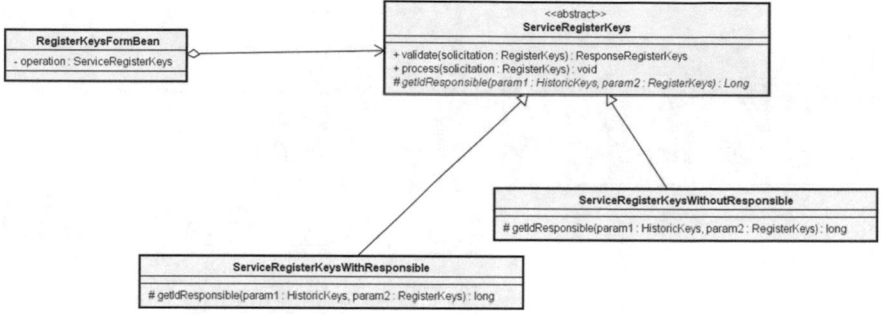

Fig. 10.8   Class diagram of the *Manage Keys* feature

variability, promoting a reuse of the common parts between the artifacts through the application of the *Template Method* design pattern. This pattern defines the skeleton of an algorithm in an operation, postponing to sub-classes the implementation of the variable steps of the algorithm without compromising its structure. Figure 10.8 shows the relationship between the classes involved in the application of this design pattern. The *RegisterKeys* class, located in the presentation layer, has an instance of one subclasses of the *ServiceRegisterKeys* abstract class, and call the *validate()* e *execute()* business methods. The method *getIdFromResponsible()* represents the variation points implemented by classes *ServiceRegisterKeys* and *ServiceRegisterKeysl*, and consists in an invocation of the abstract method *execute()*.

Applying the Refactoring —*Addition of attributes in entity* During SPL extraction, we noticed that the *ManageClassrooms* feature also presented variability between systems. In particular, there is a need for refactoring code artifacts from different layers of the SPL architecture, except the data layer. The refactorings are further complicated because it involves the domain entity *Classroom*. Four operations commonly used in traditional software development can be performed for the system entities: create, update, recover and delete. The proposed solution for refactoring the system entities is applied to each operation, although we only show it for the create operation. The presentation layer in Fig. 10.9 shows three classes related to this feature. The first class (*RegisterClassroomFormBean*) contains all code that is common for registering classrooms, while its subclasses (*RegisterClassroomWithWhiteboardFormBean* and *RegisterClassroomWithBlackboardFormBean*) deal with specific fields of the web page for each system that have classrooms with whiteboard or blackboard.

In its turn, the web page achieves variability by employing the tag *c:if* which uses the value on properties *hasWhiteboard* or *hasBlackboard* from the managed bean, as can be seen in Fig. 10.10. The *ManageClassRoomFormBean* is associated to each one of the specified variabilities (blackboard or whiteboard) in the classrooms. Figures 10.11 and 10.12 show the configuration file of JSF (faces-config.xml), which is used to define one of the two options of classrooms that the SPL provides.

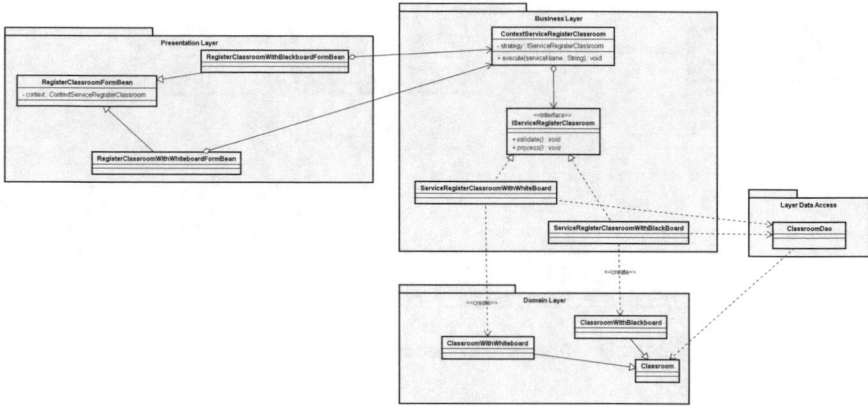

Fig. 10.9 Class diagram of the *ManageClassrooms* feature

```
1  <c:if test="${ManageClassroomFormBean.hasKindOfBoard}">
2    <li>
3      <h:outputLabel for="KindOfBoard"
4        value="#{View['cronos.form.KindOfBoard']}" />
5      <h:selectOneMenu id="KindOfBoard"
6        value="#{ManageClassroomFormBean.KindOfBoard}">
7        <f:selectItem itemLabel="--Select--" itemValue="" />
8        <f:selectItem itemLabel="White" itemValue="White" />
9        <f:selectItem itemLabel="Black" itemValue="Black" />
10       <f:selectItem itemLabel="Black/White"
11          itemValue="Black/White" />
12     </h:selectOneMenu>
13    </li>
14 </c:if>
```

Fig. 10.10 Variability in the presentation layer for the ManageClassroom feature

```
1  <managed-bean>
2    <managed-bean-name>
3      RegisterClassroomFormBean
4    </managed-bean-name>
5    <managed-bean-class>
6      br.ufrn.ct.web.RegisterClassroomWithWhiteboardFormBean
7    </managed-bean-class>
8    <managed-bean-scope>request</managed-bean-scope>
9  </managed-bean>
```

Fig. 10.11 Mapping of the *Managed Bean* in the ManageClassroom feature

The business layer employs the *Strategy* design pattern to isolate the concrete classes *ServiceRegisterClassroomWithWhiteboard* and *ServiceRegisterClassroomWithBlackboard*.

```
1   <managed-bean>
2     <managed-bean-name>
3       RegisterClassroomFormBean
4     </managed-bean-name>
5     <managed-bean-class>
6       br.ufrn.ct.web.RegisterClassroomWithBlackboardFormBean
7     </managed-bean-class>
8     <managed-bean-scope>request</managed-bean-scope>
9   </managed-bean>
```

Fig. 10.12   Mapping of the *Managed Bean* in the ManageClassroom feature

Finally, each of these concrete classes manipulates one of the domain entities *ClassroomWithWhiteboard* and *ClassroomWithBlackboard*. These classes define fields that are specific to the domain layer object, while inheriting all common attributes from *Classroom* entity.

10.3.2   SPL Evolution

To incorporate a new system into the existing SPL (reactive context), the use case model of the new system was compared with the use case model generated for the SPL. Thus, the SPL use case model generated in the extractive context was updated in order to address possible new use cases, and also possible new extension points for existing use cases, as shown in Fig. 10.4.

Next, the SPL feature model was updated to address the new use cases present in the updated SPL use case model. The same guidelines used in the extractive context were used to adequate the new use cases as features depending on the specific packages that they were accommodated. As a result of this activity, the existing SPL feature model is updated to address the new features derived from the new use cases and variabilities required by the new system incorporated into the SPL. The resulting feature model of this activity is illustrated in Fig. 10.13.

In the following activity **Map variable features in implementation artifacts**, the mapping table between variabilities and code artifacts is updated. New variabilities of the new products are included in the table and mapped to specific implementation artifacts, paying attention to the layers in which these artifacts will be created or refactored, so that they are correctly placed in the specific layers of the SPL implementation.

Finally, the activity **Apply refactoring over existing system** addresses the refactoring activities in the SPL to meet its evolving demands. The same guidelines that guide refactoring activities in the extraction context are performed again in the evolution context. The main difference between these contexts is that in the extractive context the refactoring activities are performed in one of the existing systems seeking to expose variabilities, while in the reactive context the refactoring

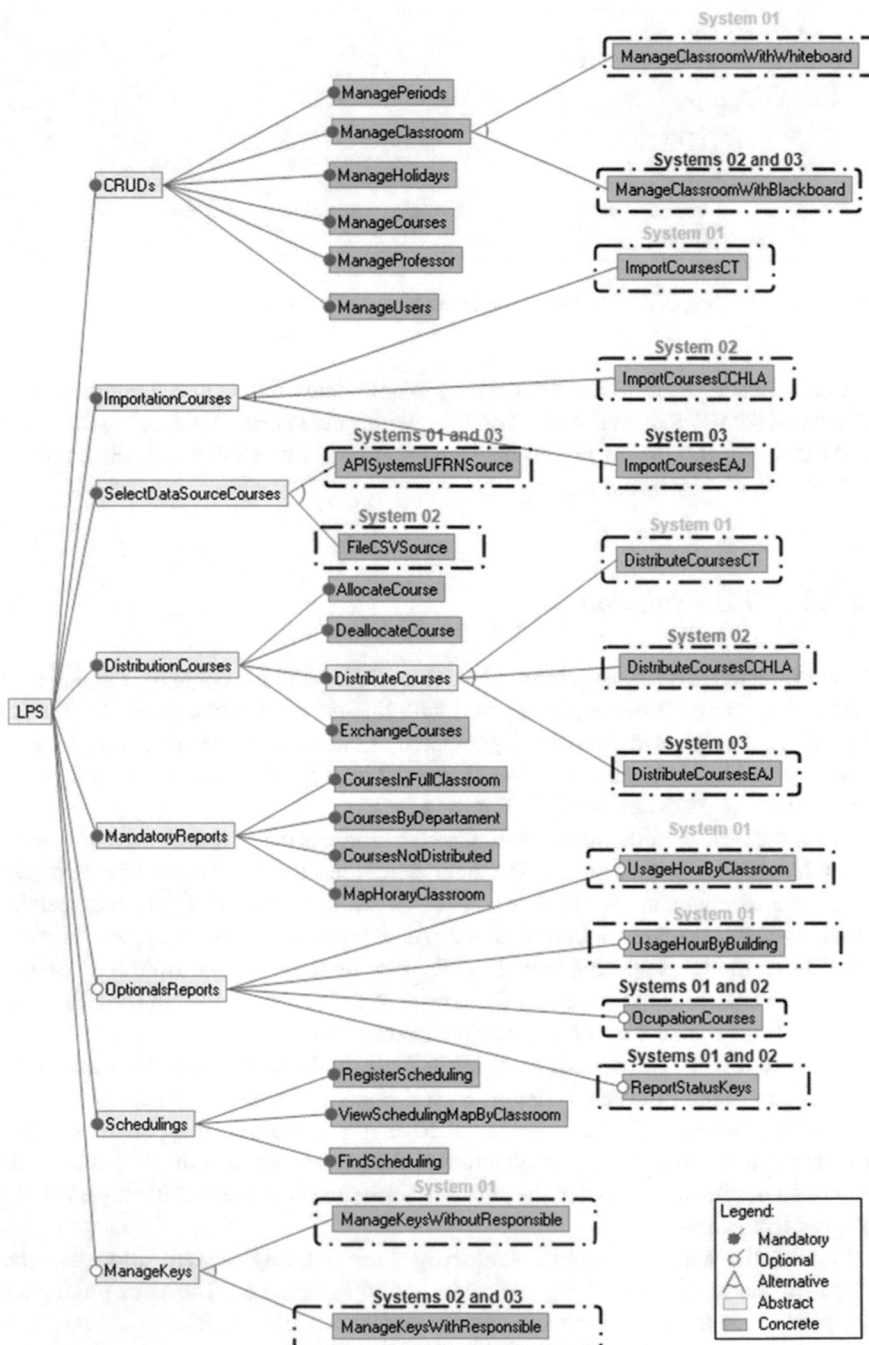

Fig. 10.13 SPL feature model

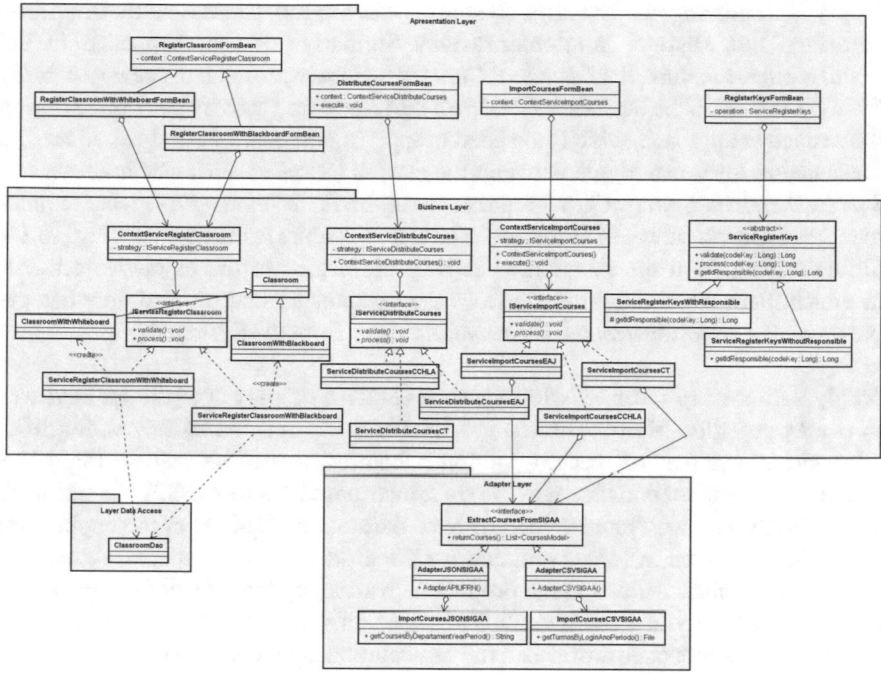

Fig. 10.14   Resulting SPL partial class diagram

activities can modify core artifacts and variabilities or even demand the creation of new code artifacts. Even in this latter scenario, the guidelines are important so that the developer knows exactly which artifacts and in which layers must be modified or created to meet the new evolution requirements demanded by the new product of the SPL.

Apply Refactoring on Existing System: Exchanging Classes with the Same Interface but Distinct Implementations   The ImportCourses feature has admitted yet another variability in the business layer—the only layer that continues to present variability in its artifacts. As the refactoring applied in this layer during the extractive approach already foresaw a mutually exclusive relationship between variable features, the class structure after refactoring did not have a strong impact, since the only change is the addition of the new subclass *ServiceImportCoursesEAJ*, as can be seen in Fig. 10.14. As already described in the extractive context, the application of the *Strategy* design pattern in this layer makes it possible to choose which of the artifacts will be selected at runtime. The *SelectDataSourceClassroom* feature, which is related to the *ImportCourses* feature, will have no impact since there was no demand for other interfaces to external systems. What happened was only the evolution of the SPL to address a new product added to the scope of the product line that needs information from external services already predicted in the extraction context.

Apply Refactoring on Existing System: Exchanging Classes with the Same Interface but Distinct Implementations Similarly to what happened to the *ImportCourses* feature, the *DistributeCourses* feature incorporated a new variability from System 03 in the business layer. With the refactoring activity performed during the extractive approach, which consisted in applying the *Strategy* design pattern, the presentation layer can toggle between the classes (*ServiceDistributeClassroomCT*, *ServiceDistributeCoursesCCHLA* and *ServiceDistributeCoursesEAJ*) which implement the business rules of this feature. The class structure is illustrated in Fig. 10.14, differentiating from the refactoring activity performed in the extractive context, in which there were only artifacts from the Systems 01 and 02, and now has the presence of *ServiceDistributeClassroomEAJ* class from the System 03.

Apply Refactoring Over Existing System: Control Display of Optional Features in the Application Menu The *UsageMapClassroom* and *SearchCurrentStatusOf-ClassroomsKeys* features become optional features, as can be seen in Fig. 10.13 because the customers of the new product incorporated into the SPL do not need them. These optional features need to have their access options in the application menu limited to the features predicted for the product being executed. According to parameter values defined in the product derivation, optional features may or may not be displayed to the system users. Thus, the solution that addresses this scenario involves refactoring code artifacts in the presentation layer on the web page in which the application menu is contained, by means of a conditional statement (tag *c:if*) to insert the necessary variation point in the application menu, as well as in the Java class, also contained in the same layer, that manages the state of the web page and provides the required parameter value for it. This implementation follows the *Conditional Execution* design pattern [11], which allows modularizing dynamic variabilities through annotative techniques.

The *ManageKeys* feature also needs to be evolved. As can be seen in Fig. 10.14, the business layer of this feature has three classes, where the class *ServiceRegisterKeys* implements the common part of this feature, leaving to its subclasses— *ServiceRegisterKeyWithResponsible* and *ServiceRegisterKeyWithoutResponsible*— implement the variable parts corresponding to the *RegisterKeysWithResponsible* and *RegisterKeyWithoutResponsible*, respectively. These subclasses share a common structure, differing only in the implementation of a part of the algorithm that is overwritten by the implementation of the *getIdFromResponsible()* method. In this way, the evolution task was facilitated when they occurred in the common part of these features, and also in the variable part. When a change was made in the common part, i.e., in the superclass, the two features were addressed at the same time. When the change was done in the variable part, that is, in some subclass, the developer focused only on the class of the specific feature in which it was performing the evolution task.

10.4   Discussions and Lessons Learned

In this section, we present discussions and lessons learned of the our study of extraction and evolution of a web-based SPL. Furthermore, several benefits achieved by the SPL approach are presented such as the improvement of the variability management and the ease of customization of new products.

Variability Management and Systematic Reuse of Artifacts With the adoption of SPL, the artifacts of existing systems have a centralized and systematic variability management, reducing the complexity of developing new products that can reuse many of the existing artifacts from the SPL. This was observed when system 03, addressed in the context of the evolution of the study, was incorporated into the SPL, adding two new features to the SPL feature model—*ImportCoursesEAJ* and *DistributeCoursesEAJ*, but whose previous refactorings have already made it possible to fit them into the SPL implementation. It is worth noting that there was an increase of about 10% in the total lines of code (LoC) for each system generated from the SPL compared to its original implementation, as well as a small increase in the number of classes. Despite the increase in the number of LoC and classes of each product, the SPL artifacts are better modularized in terms of features, which facilitates the evolution of both the SPL core classes and the variant classes of each application, as mentioned above. It is also important to note that around 70% of the core SPL source code is reused on all products (systems).

Ease of Customization of New Products Demanded by Clients As shown in Sect. 10.3, the adoption of SPL improved the product customization when it was necessary to maintain product features, allowing developers to focus on specific details of the features that they are developing, as common artifacts were already developed, thus reducing the complexity of maintenance and evolution activities. The refactoring catalog presented in the method to implement variability have helped in the organization of the implementation artifacts of *features*, which are usually spread throughout the layers of the SPL architecture. This has contributed for leaving the variability more cohesive and legible in the source code and, at the same time, less coupled together, facilitating future maintenance tasks. In general, the refactorings applied to product #3 involved two or three classes of the SPL core. It is worth mentioning that although the current SPL implementation has been created from three existing systems, its implementation now allows the easy derivation of at least 192 different products (systems). This number is calculated based on all possible combinations of four optional features (reports) and three alternative features (room management, class distribution, and input and output) present in the feature model produced and addressed by the SPL implementation.

Efficiency Gain to Update and Correct Errors The systems that were migrated to a SPL from our study were previously maintained in accordance with the clone-and-own approach [5], in which the code of an existing product (system) is cloned and adapted to meet the needs of new products and customers. However, this approach increases the complexity of developing and maintaining the artifacts of the systems, since the artifacts of each product (system) are kept separately and cannot be easily reused in a family of systems. This also causes inefficiency to perform maintenance on SPL, from updating features to correcting errors that could be propagated to all systems that are part of the SPL. In the specific case of inclusion of new features in an SPL, the application of refactorings in the SPL core allows the reuse of existing optional features, or even the introduction of new alternative features, in a non-invasive form, in new products, as we illustrated in our study.

Method for Extracting and Evolving SPL The activities presented in Sect. 10.3 represent an initial step in the definition of a method for extraction and evolution of SPLs. The *SPL variability modeling* activity could be applied to SPLs implemented for different domains and technologies since they use two widely disseminated techniques—use cases and features models. Moreover, as use cases is a very popular technique, the strategies presented for identifying similarities and variabilities in existing systems using such models can be more easily understood by development teams. On the other hand, the *Design and implementation of SPL through refactoring existing systems* activity is quite dependent on the architectural patterns and technologies used in the SPL in question. In the presented study, we have offered guidelines for refactoring certain types of variabilities that are common in SPLs implemented as a layered architecture and using Web technologies. Many of the refactorings presented can even be used in other object-oriented languages and technologies because they are based on classical design patterns. Part of these refactorings have even been applied in another study conducted earlier [12], showing their degree of generality. However, different SPL domains that use other architectural patterns or different variability implementation technologies might require other more appropriate refactoring catalogs for each scenario [10].

Definition of Test Strategies In order to allow greater reliability of the products generated from the SPL artifacts during their evolution, it is fundamental to promote the definition of test strategies during the application of refactorings. In the study presented, manual system tests were performed to evaluate the systems (products) generated from the SPL resulting from the applied refactorings. Thus, it is envisaged that in order to complement the activities of a method for extraction and evolution of SPL, it is fundamental to define test strategies that allow to evaluate the quality of both the SPL core and the products generated from it. In particular, for SPLs implemented using Java technologies like that one from our study, automated functional testing with the Selenium tool could be implemented. In addition, such tests could share a common structure and have specific parts defined according to the specificities of each product, as recommended by Linden et al. [8]. Also unit, integration and system functional tests could be defined to ensure the quality of core functionality in most critical use cases.

Limitation of the Study Despite the benefits observed with the study, it is important to note that the results found are limited to the context where it was applied—web-based systems implemented in a layered architecture and using Java technologies. Currently, the method is being applied to web-based systems developed in other languages, such as Python and PHP, in order to evaluate possible adaptations. In addition, the application of the method in our study was benefited from the domain knowledge of the main developer of the systems during the activities of domain analysis to identify similarities and variabilities of the SPL from the existing use cases of the systems.

Such knowledge is essential for the successful application of the method, which is also common in most approaches already proposed.

10.5   Related Work

The reengineering of existing software systems into software product lines has attracted attention of many software engineering research over the last years. Assunção et al. [1] conducted a systematic literature mapping to provide an overview of current research on approaches for reengineering of existing systems into SPLs. In this study, the authors observed that there is no well-established reengineering process for extracting SPLs from existing systems. In particular, they observed a lack of clear definition of the phases and activities performed in the existing research work. Despite that, the authors inferred three distinct phases based on the information and artifacts analyzed and produced in each reengineering approach identified in their mapping study: (1) detection—the phase in which existing features are identified in an existing system or set of systems; (2) analysis—the phase in which artifacts and information available are analyzed to propose a representation of the SPL; and (3) transformation—the phase in which artifacts are modified in order to obtain the SPL. Assunção et al. analyzed the mapped research work by considering the information and the artifacts analyzed and produced in each proposed reengineering approach in order to infer the above phases.

Filling the gap observed by Assunção et al. [1], our work proposes a method that explicitly defines a set of activities which serves as concrete guidelines for conducting the reengineering of existing systems into an SPL. The phases proposed by Assunção et al. are addressed by our proposed method through the following activities: Activity 1—Modeling SPL Features: deals with the identification of features in the existing systems by means of use case models comparison, resulting in a feature model representation of the SPL; Activity 2—Designing and Implementing SPL through Refactoring an Existing System: deals with the refactoring process of the existing artifacts for the SPL implementation by means of specific refactoring catalogs according to the SPL domain and adopted technologies.

Martinez et al. [9] proposed a generic and extensible framework for bottom-up adoption of SPLs. The framework relies on the tool BUT4Reuse (Bottom-Up Technologies for Reuse) that supports the following framework layers: (1) building adapters—creates, from existing artifacts, representations in the form of elements for building new reusable artifacts; (2) identification of blocks—grouping elements of existing artifacts in order to obtain greater granularity in the organization of artifacts by domain specialists; (3) identification and location of features—definition of features from blocks of elements, as well as mapping features to their implementation artifacts; (4) constraint discovery between features—identification of constraints between identified features; (5) synthesis of features model—creation and refinement of the feature model; (6) construction of reusable artifacts—enables the creation of reusable artifacts; (7) visualization—makes it possible to understand through different visions, the information produced by the other layers. Adapters are the main components of the framework. An adapter decomposes an existing artifact into elements and constructs new reusable artifacts from those elements. In the adapter, similarity metrics are defined to identify similarities and variabilities between artifacts. Since adapters are built for existing artifacts, building new reusable artifacts becomes easier. There is a great effort in the design and implementation of these adapters. In addition, there is a lack of more concrete guidelines to realize their implementations.

Similarly to our work, the approach of Martinez et al. [9] defines a set of systematic activities to develop product lines from existing software systems. However, they also mention the need to set explicit guidelines to provide more automated support for their approach. Our work differs from their approach by presenting specific guidelines that may also be applied in a bottom-up way for the development of SPLs from web systems implemented in Java, adopting both an extractive and reactive strategy. Finally, our work presents activities directly applicable to reengineering processes of legacy systems into SPLs that do not require the use of new abstractions like the adapters proposed by them.

10.6   Conclusion and Future Work

In this chapter we presented an experience report on extracting and evolving a SPL from existing web-based systems. Our experience allowed us to share a set of systematic activities which helped on the identification, refactoring and implementation of the common and variable features among existing software systems. The SPL extraction process consist of conducting a comparative analysis of use case models from the existing systems, as well as the code refactoring of several system layers to accommodate the common features and allow the easy customization of variabilities. We have observed some advantages after extracting and evolving the SPL such as, improved variability management and less burden SPL evolution when incorporating new products or features.

Currently, the presented set of activities are the base of a method to extract and evolve SPLs. The method is being applied in other domains and SPLs. It has been also evolved to include test strategies. Moreover, we are exploring the integration of our proposed method with existing SPL tools in order to improve the variability management with automated product derivation.

Acknowledgments This research was partially funded by INES 2.0, FACEPE grant APQ-0399-1.03/17, CAPES grant 88887.136410/2017-00, and CNPq grant 465614/2014-0.

References

1. Assunção, W., Lopez-Herrejon, R., Linsbauer, L., Vergilio, S., Egyed, A.: Reengineering legacy applications into software product lines: a systematic mapping. Empirical Software Engineering pp. 1–45 (2017)
2. Clements, P.: Being proactive pays off. IEEE Software **19**(4), 28, 30– (2002)
3. Clements, P., Northrop, L.: Software Product Lines: Practices and Patterns. Addison-Wesley Professional (2001)
4. Czarnecki, K., Helsen, S.: Feature-based survey of model transformation approaches. IBM Syst. J. **45**(3), 621–645 (2006)
5. Dubinsky, Y., Rubin, J., Berger, T., Duszynski, S., Becker, M., Czarnecki, K.: An exploratory study of cloning in industrial software product lines. In: 2013 17th European Conference on Software Maintenance and Reengineering, pp. 25–34 (2013)
6. Easterbrook, S., Singer, J., Storey, M., Damian, D.: Selecting empirical methods for software engineering research. In: Guide to advanced empirical software engineering, pp. 285–311. Springer (2008)
7. Krueger, C.: Easing the transition to software mass customization. In: Software Product-Family Engineering, 4th International Workshop, PFE 2001, Bilbao, Spain, October 3–5, 2001, Revised Papers, pp. 282–293 (2001) URL https://doi.org/10.1007/3-540-47833-7_25
8. Linden, F.J.v.d., Schmid, K., Rommes, E.: Software Product Lines in Action: The Best Industrial Practice in Product Line Engineering. Springer-Verlag New York, Inc., Secaucus, NJ, USA (2007)
9. Martinez, J., Ziadi, T., Bissyandé, F., Klein, J., Traon, Y.L.: Bottom-up adoption of software product lines: A generic and extensible approach. In: Proceedings of the 19th International Conference on Software Product Line, SPLC '15, pp. 101–110. ACM, New York, NY, USA (2015)
10. Neves, L., Borba, P., Alves, V., Turnes, L., Teixeira, L., Sena, D., Kulesza, U.: Safe evolution templates for software product lines. Journal of Systems and Software **106**, 42–58 (2015)
11. Santos, J., Lima, G., Kulesza, U., Sena, D., Pinto, F., Lima, J., Vianna, A., Pereira, D., Fernandes, V.: Conditional execution: a pattern for the implementation of fine-grained variabilities in software product lines. In: Proceedings of the 9th Latin-American Conference on Pattern Languages of Programming, SugarLoafPLoP 2012, Natal, Rio Grande do Norte, Brazil, September 20-22, 2012, pp. 1:1–1:17 (2012)
12. Sena, D., Pinto, F., Lima, G., Santos, J., Lima, J., Kulesza, U., Pereira, D., Fernandes, V., Vianna, A.: Modularization of variabilities from software product lines of web information systems (in portuguese). In: Proceedings of the 9th Latin-American Conference on Pattern Languages of Programming, SugarLoafPLoP 2012, Natal, Rio Grande do Norte, Brazil, September 20–22, 2012, pp. 11:1–11:15 (2012)

Chapter 11
Re-Engineering Microservice Applications into Delta-Oriented Software Product Lines

Maya R. A. Setyautami, Hafiyyan S. Fadhlillah, Daya Adianto, Ichlasul Affan, and Ade Azurat

Abstract Software with microservice architecture consists of a collection of small and independent services. Those services can be combined and modified to serve various purposes, which leads to an increase in requirement variability. The variability needs to be documented to track any changes and optimize the reusability. The issues are related to variability management, which is one of the main concerns in software product line engineering (SPLE). We propose an approach to re-engineer microservice applications into SPLE. The process comprises variability modeling, architectural design, and product line implementation. To model the variability in microservices, we use a multi-level feature diagram. The feature diagram is combined with the UML class diagram from existing systems to design a product line architecture. We utilize the UML-DOP profile that provides an extension to represent delta-oriented concepts in the UML notation. UML diagrams with UML-DOP profile are used to capture several levels of abstractions in the architectural models. These models enable traceability from requirements to endpoints implementation. The proposed approach is shown by performing a re-engineering for existing microservice-based webshop systems. The result is a microservices-based product line that can be generated into various applications.

11.1 Introduction

The microservice architecture consists of small services that collaborate with each other [16]. This architecture provides more flexibility than a monolithic architecture where changing one aspect may require the whole system's compilation. Each small service represents a specific functionality that can be modified independently to other services. Then, various services may be used and orchestrated to meet an

M. R. A. Setyautami (✉) · H. S. Fadhlillah · D. Adianto · I. Affan · A. Azurat
Faculty of Computer Science, Universitas Indonesia, Depok, Indonesia
e-mail: mayaretno@cs.ui.ac.id

© Springer Nature Switzerland AG 2023
R. E. Lopez-Herrejon et al. (eds.), *Handbook of Re-Engineering Software Intensive Systems into Software Product Lines*, https://doi.org/10.1007/978-3-031-11686-5_11

application's requirements. Therefore, it is compelling to investigate if microservice architecture can be used with huge variability and evolution of software.

Six challenges to manage the variability of microservices has been identified in [2], (1) feature identification, (2) variability modeling, (3) variable microservice architectures, (4) interchangeability, (5) deep customization, and (6) re-engineering an SPL. In software product line engineering (SPLE), variability management is a main concern [5, 17]. Several paradigms are proposed to implement SPLE, such as aspect-oriented programming (AOP) [8], feature-oriented programming (FOP) [1], and delta-oriented programming (DOP) [20]. Those paradigms show some ideas of managing part of the system concerning commonality and variability. In terms of microservices, this gives some ideas for managing common services that are used and identifying various services. Either vary because of the evolution of time or domain variation.

As each service in microservice architecture can be deployed independently and may depend on each other, single feature models might not be sufficient to capture variation. Multi-level feature models [18, 19], as used in the multi-product line (MPL) approach, can be used to model variability in microservices. An MPL consists of several product lines that share resources to create products together [10]. In multi-level feature models, several feature diagrams are defined to model variations in different perspectives. For example, a multi-level feature diagram in [18] is categorized to model different modeling spaces, i.e., problem space, solution space, and configuration space.

In previous research, we proposed a mechanism to solve the interoperability problem in MPL using a Unified Modeling Language (UML) [21]. The problem is how to enable multi variants from one product line co-exists in the same application. The UML diagram with UML-DOP profile is used to model the MPL problem. The UML-DOP profile is a UML profile that is defined based on DOP [23]. The profile enables modeling commonality and variability of product lines in the UML diagram. In this research, the UML-DOP profile is also used as a foundation to model variability in a microservice-based product line.

In line with the model, we choose the DOP paradigm to implement the microservice-based product line. In DOP, variants are implemented in delta modules (deltas). A delta can add, remove, or modify existing behavior [20] to realize different functionalities. We use one of the DOP languages, namely abstract behavioral specification (ABS). ABS is an executable modeling language that can be generated into programming languages, such as Java and Erlang [11].

In this chapter, we introduce a re-engineering mechanism from microservice applications to delta-oriented product lines. The chapter is structured as follows: Sect. 11.2 explains the variability management approach. The process starts with problem analysis in Sect. 11.2.1 to identify features. The variability model is represented with a multi-level feature diagram as described in Sect. 11.2.2. Section 11.3 proposes the architectural models that are designed with UML diagram with UML-DOP profile. Then, in Sect. 11.4, a transformation into a product line application is conducted to generate running applications based on selected features. Section 11.5 concludes the chapter and explains future work.

11.2   Variability Modeling

In this section, we explain a variability model that represents the commonality and variability of a microservice-based product line.

11.2.1   Preliminary Analysis

Before we present the variability modeling, a preliminary analysis is conducted to know the existing systems. We use microservice-based webshops as subject systems to be re-engineered into product lines. There are six webshops in [2], and we analyze four of them in this chapter.[1] Those subject systems are SockShop, HipsterShop, eShopOnContainers, and StansRobot. They sell various products and might have different features. Hence, we analyze the systems to capture the commonality and variability.

Following one of the feature modeling principles in [15]: *relying on domain knowledge and existing artifacts to construct the feature model*, we attempt to reconstruct and run the subject systems. A Linux virtual machine (VM) and a Kubernetes cluster are prepared to deploy each subject system. We perform a manual feature identification process to analyze the variability. The process comprises of three stages:

1. Simulating user interactions to identify features at the user level.
2. Reviewing the deployment configuration to identify features at the architectural level.
3. Analyzing the source code artifact to identify features at the implementation level.

First, the user interaction needs to be operated in the deployed subject systems. It is important to check all the existing and working features. For example, by simulating the flow of purchasing products, several endpoints are called consecutively. They are list and detail products, add to cart, checkout, and payment. Based on the simulation, we analyze the features in each subject system. We use an application-requirements to support the identification of commonality and variability, as shown in Table 11.1. The matrix provides a list of features for a given set of software product line application requirements [17].

The feature traceability matrix in Table 11.1 shows minor differences when compared to the result in [13], specifically for features *Order* and *Product* as denoted by the asterisk ($*$) symbol in the table. The feature *Order* is present in the Stan's Robot Shop at the user level. The feature *Product* is considered present due to its similarity to feature *Catalog* in all subject systems. Moreover, HipsterShop

---

[1] https://github.com/jacobkrueger/SPLC2020-Microservices-Challenge.

Table 11.1 Feature traceability matrix for subject systems

Features	HipsterShop	SockShop	eShopOnContainers	StansRobot
Front-end	✓	✓	✓	✓
User		✓	✓	✓
Payment	✓	✓	✓	✓
Catalog	✓	✓	✓	✓
Cart	✓	✓	✓	✓
Order	✓	✓	✓	✓*
Product	✓*	✓*	✓*	✓*
Shipping	✓	✓		✓
Email contact	✓			
Marketing	✓		✓	
Recommendation	✓			
Audit				
Currency	✓			
Location			✓	

contains a microservice named *Product Catalog* that implements features *Product* and *Catalog*.

Second, we analyze the dependencies at the architectural level by inspecting the deployment configuration of subject systems. Each system needs to run microservices in order to deliver functionalities at the user level. Thus, microservices can be considered as dependencies for one or more features. We look at the deployment-related files of each subject system to identify the microservices. For example, Docker Compose and the Kubernetes manifest file define the deployment specifications and properties. These files assist the orchestration process conducted by respective tool chains.

Based on our inspection, all running subject systems except SockShop follow the monorepo strategy on organizing the source code. The repo includes the source code of each microservice, thus making the identification process straightforward. In the case of SockShop, each microservice is identified by their Docker image in the Docker Compose file. The source code of each corresponding microservice can be found under "Microservices Demo" GitHub.[2] As a concrete illustration of how the process is conducted, suppose that we want to analyze the HipsterShop system. We reconstruct the system by following the deployment instructions. The documentation outlines the steps for deploying the example to a Kubernetes cluster using kubectl. We follow the instructions, and the microservices are successfully deployed. We access the front end to identify the features that are executed via user interactions.

By accessing the front end, we can identify related service endpoints specifying their functionality. We take notes of this endpoint to use it in the next step of identify-

---

[2] https://github.com/microservices-demo.

Table 11.2 Endpoint traceability matrix for subject systems

Features	Services	Endpoints	HipsterShop	SockShop	eShop	StansRobot
Catalog	DisplayCatalog	GetAllItems	✓	✓	✓	✓
Catalog	FilterCatalog	GetCatalog(brand)	x	x	✓	x
		GetCatalog(category)	x	x	x	✓
Catalog	CatalogItem	GetItem(id)	✓	✓	✓	✓
		GetItem(name)	x	x	✓	x

ing variability. We only focused on finding variability in the functionality of services as we implement existing services with the same framework, ABS microservices. Therefore, we do not consider variability in software quality attributes at this time.

Last, we inspect the problem in more detail by analyzing the source code artifact of each microservice in the subject systems. We explore the source code of each microservice and look for specific files that serve as endpoints. The source code files that provide endpoints usually follow common web programming idiom such as mentioning URI (e.g /orders/, /users/:id) or HTTP verbs (e.g GET, POST) in a method signature. Once we identified all endpoint methods, we reverse engineer the structural model of each subject system into a UML class diagram. Based on the class diagram, we document the endpoint methods and associate them with their corresponding microservice and feature.

To complete the source code analysis, we look for the API specification and implementation of each microservice. Since the provided subject systems do not have API specification, the endpoints are identified by analyzing the methods/-functions in the source code files. Our finding confirms that each microservice implements an endpoint that communicates using a specific data interchange format. In the case of HipsterShop, all of the microservices are using Protobuf.[3] Other examples use REST-like format that communicate using HTTP.

Based on the subject systems, we found that the endpoint methods for a feature might have different signatures across subject systems. For example, endpoint methods to display catalog (a list of all items) that are associated with feature *Catalog* have name such as getItems(), getCatalog(), listProduct(), and getAllProduct(). Since the semantic is similar, we conclude that the endpoint display catalog, which shows a list of all items, exists in all subject systems. We inspect the source code files manually to look for methods that serve the endpoints. We summarize the findings of endpoint variations in the endpoint traceability matrix. The snippet of the matrix is shown in Table 11.2. We can see that endpoints that exists in all systems are GetAllItems and GetItem(id). Another endpoint, such as, GetCatalog(category) only exists in StansRobot.

Based on the preliminary analysis, the variability model is summarized in the traceability matrix that contains detailed information about the features, services,

---

[3] https://developers.google.com/protocol-buffers/.

and endpoints from each subject system. As part of the process, we also produced a UML class diagram for every subject system [22]. The matrix serves as an input for feature modeling in Sect. 11.2.2 and the UML class diagram is used for designing the architectural model and implementation.

11.2.2 Multi-Level Feature Diagram

In this section, we explain a mechanism to model variability in a microservice-based product line. The model is represented in the feature diagram and it is defined based on the preliminary analysis described in Sect. 11.2.1. Existing subject systems are analyzed to determine the commonality and variability, yielding a traceability matrix in Tables 11.1 and 11.2. The matrix is used as an input to create the feature diagram manually.

First, we define a feature diagram based on the feature traceability matrix. The snippet of the feature diagram is shown in Fig. 11.1. Based on the source code of the subject systems, each child feature of the root feature in Fig. 11.1 is implemented as a microservice.

Each system may have different services and endpoints, as analyzed in Table 11.2. For example, feature *Catalog* has services to display the catalogs and filter catalogs. Each service also has various endpoints. In the SockShop, the available endpoints GetItemById and GetAllItems. However, the eShopOnContainers requires endpoints GetItemById, GetItemByName and FilterByBrand. If endpoint variations are included in the feature diagram in Fig. 11.1, the leaf features might have many variants.

A multi-level feature diagram can be used to manage complex systems [18, 19]. We found that we can use a multi-level feature diagram that enables modeling variations in microservice product lines. The first level captures variants of features in the problem space, and the other levels represent endpoints variations that are related to solution space. It is aligned with one of the principles of feature modeling [15]: define the specific purpose for each feature model.

In this research, we also define a different purpose for each level feature diagram. The first level feature diagram, as shown in Fig. 11.1, represents features and services variations. Fig. 11.2 is an example of another level that is used to model

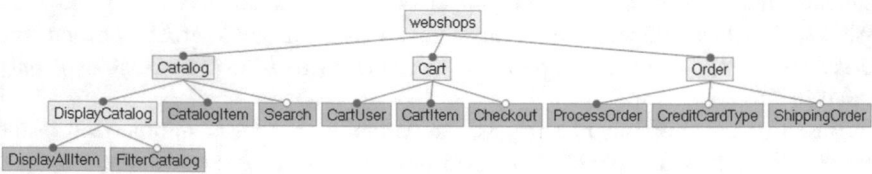

Fig. 11.1 Feature diagram: webshops domain

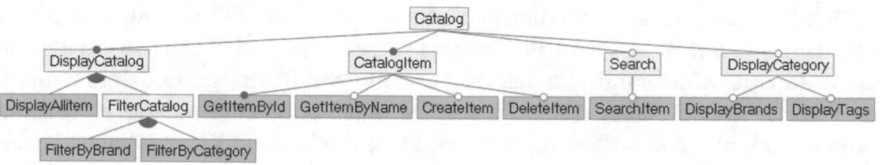

Fig. 11.2 Feature diagram: *Catalog* endpoints

endpoint variations for the feature *Catalog*. Each top child feature of a root in the first level feature diagram becomes a root feature in the other level.

In Sect. 11.2.1, endpoints for each service in the source code of subject systems are identified. Endpoints that exist in all subject systems are marked as mandatory, e.g., `DisplayAllItem`, which shows a list of all items. Endpoints that are not required by all subject systems are marked as optional. For example, service *FilterCatalog* has two endpoints: *FilterByBrand,* and *FilterByCategory*. Those two endpoints are similar, they are variations of service *FilterCatalog*, as shown in the feature diagram in Fig 11.2.

11.2.3 Multi-Stage Configurations

A feature selection process in a multi-level feature diagram can be conducted in multiple stages, called staged configuration [6]. Each stage uses a feature diagram and produces a configuration for the other feature diagram. In this chapter, the multi-stage configuration is adapted to microservices. The multi-stage configuration is performed as follows:

- Basic configuration: Choose features in the first level feature diagram (Fig. 11.1), which represents the problem domain. This configuration is mandatory.
- Advanced configuration: Choose endpoints that are related to the selected features in the previous configuration. This configuration is optional.

The basic configuration is performed in the first step by selecting services in the first level feature diagram. Based on the selected services, then the advanced configuration is conducted in several steps. For example, if four services are chosen in the basic configuration, related endpoints for each service are selected in the advanced configuration. We define the advanced configuration as an optional stage. The mandatory endpoints for the selected features are chosen if a user does not execute the advanced configuration. Based on the basic and advanced configuration, a product can be generated if all defined constraints in the feature model are satisfied.

The feature diagram is modeled using `FeatureIDE` [25]. We utilize a tool [24] to transform the feature diagram into ABS feature models. ABS use a modification of textual variability language (TVL) [4] for the feature model, called μTVL [9].

μTVL has a textual representation and a formal semantics. The example of μTVL for service *Catalog* is shown in Listing 11.1. An optional feature is denoted by keyword opt. Constraints for feature grouping can be categorized into oneof, allof, or specific cardinality. We use the obtained feature models to generate product variants. The ABS compiler is completed with a μTVL constraint checker to validate a product configuration.[4]

```
1  root Catalog {
2    group allof {
3      DisplayCatalog {
4      group allof {
5        DisplayAllItem ,
6        opt FilterCatalog {
7          group [1..*] {
8            FilterByCategory ,
9            FilterByBrand
10           ....
11 }
```

Listing 11.1 ABS feature model (μTVL)—catalog

The multi-level feature diagrams enable us to separate the perspective of the problem domain (Fig 11.1) and solution domain (Fig. 11.2). We implement a multi-stage configuration in the deployment tool, as explained in Sect. 11.4. We also add additional support to check multi-feature model constraints in the deployment tool. In future work, cross constraints for multi-feature model can be embedded in the ABS compiler. Based on selected features and services, a webshop variant from the subject systems can be generated. Therefore, the variability models are successfully constructed and potentially adopted for microservices.

11.3 Product Line Architecture

In SPLE, software architecture provides a typical high-level structure as a reference for all applications [17]. A product line architecture can be extracted from UML class diagrams and feature diagrams [3]. The result is a UML class diagram representing all variants. In this research, we also propose a variable microservice architecture design using a UML class diagram. The architecture should allow engineering and customizing different variants by systematically managing and reusing microservices [2].

We use a UML profile for delta-oriented programming (UML-DOP) [23] because the UML diagram is not designed to model product line variations. The UML-DOP profile is created by defining UML stereotypes that represent DOP notation in the UML to support SPLE modeling. Table 11.3 shows the mapping of DOP elements to UML stereotypes [23]. We extend the UML-DOP profile by defining two new

---

[4] The current version of ABS does not support multi-feature models yet. Therefore, constraints for each feature model are defined separately.

Table 11.3 Mapping of DOP elements to UML stereotypes

Element name	UML base class	Stereotype name
Core module	Package	«module»
Delta module	Package	«delta»
Module modifier	Association Class interface	«adds» «removes» «modifies» «modifiedClass» «modifiedInterface»
Modifier	Operation; property	«adds» «removes» «modifies»
Feature	Component	«feature»
Optional	Dependency	«optional»
Mandatory	Dependency	«mandatory»
Require	Dependency	«require»
Exclude	Dependency	«exclude»
Product	Component	«product»
When	Dependency	«when»
After	Dependency	«after»
Service	Component	«service»
Endpoint	Component	«endpoint»

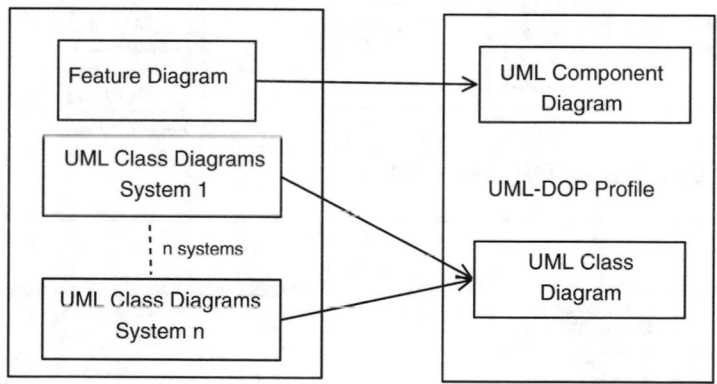

Fig. 11.3 Product line architecture design

stereotypes, «service» and «endpoint». These stereotypes are defined based on the UML component.

We define two main steps to design product line architecture, as shown in Fig 11.3. First, we design the architectural model based on the feature diagram. We use the feature diagram to derive a UML component diagram that models the high-level architecture. Second, we use the UML class diagrams from all subject systems to derive a single UML class diagram that covers all variations. UML-DOP profile enables the UML diagram to model the variations in the architectural model.

11.3.1 UML Component Diagram

As defined in Sect. 11.2.2, the multi-level feature diagram does not only represent features but also services or endpoints. The first level feature diagram representing the high-level aspects of the system is used to derive a UML component diagram, as shown in Fig 11.4. The diagram models dependencies between the different features and which services belong to a specific feature. In Fig. 11.4, a UML component with stereotype «feature» Catalog consists of several services, such as DisplayCatalog and FilterCatalog. The component Catalog is related to the component Cart by providing the interface CatalogItem.

At the lower level architectural model, we can create a UML component diagram for each microservice. For example, the UML component diagram for feature Catalog can be defined based on the feature diagram in Fig. 11.2. Figure 11.5

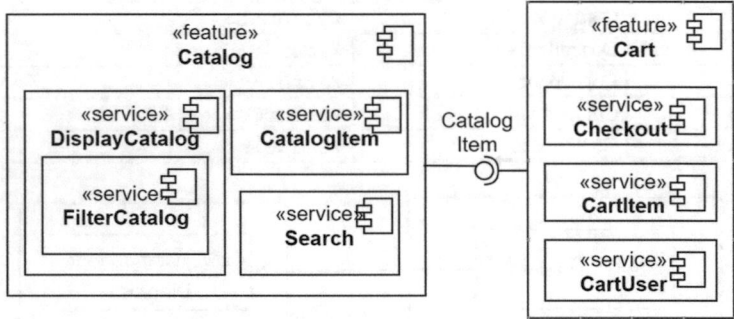

Fig. 11.4 UML component diagram—Webshop

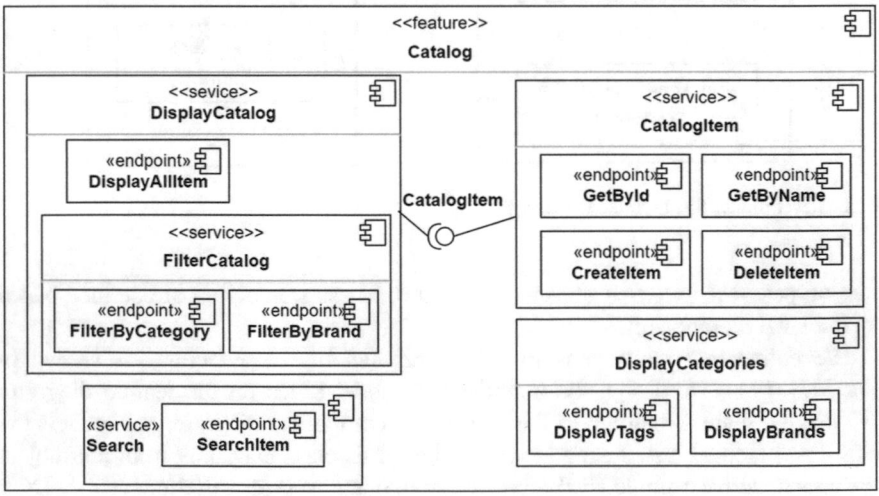

Fig. 11.5 UML component diagram—catalog

shows the UML component diagram that provides the detail services and endpoints of `Catalog`.

11.3.2   UML Class Diagram

In Sect. 11.2.1, we design a UML class diagram for each subject system during the source code analysis. Variabilities of microservices in the subject systems are captured in separated class diagrams. In this stage, we extract those UML diagrams into a UML class diagram with UML-DOP profile. Using the UML-DOP profile, the variability in the structural model can be managed systematically. In DOP approach, commonalities can be defined in the core module or delta module and variabilities are defined in the delta module. We refer to this concept to design the UML class diagram with UML-DOP profile.

Figure 11.6 shows a snippet of the UML diagram for the feature *Catalog*. All common attributes and methods are placed in the core module, see `CatalogItem` class in the «`core`» `MCatalog` package. The variants that are required by specific products are implemented in the delta module. For example, a product `SockShop` requires new fields `imageURL` and `tagString` in `CatalogItem`. Since a delta can add, remove, or modify more than one class, a delta module is modeled as a package with stereotype «`delta`».

There is a delta module `DSockCatalog` in Fig. 11.6, that consists of a new class `CatalogItem` with stereotype «modifiedClass». This class modifies the original class in the core module by adding three new attributes and a new method `getTags`. In DOP, a delta module implements a feature. The relation between a delta and a feature is defined in the delta *application condition*,

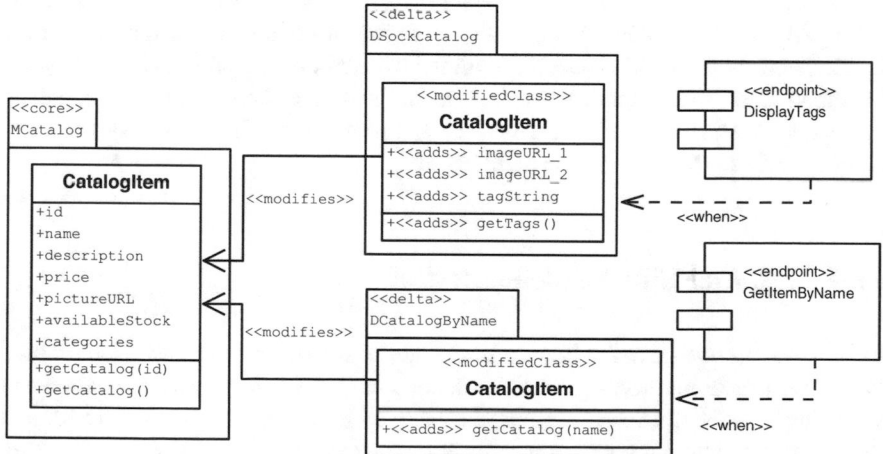

Fig. 11.6 UML class diagram: *Catalog*

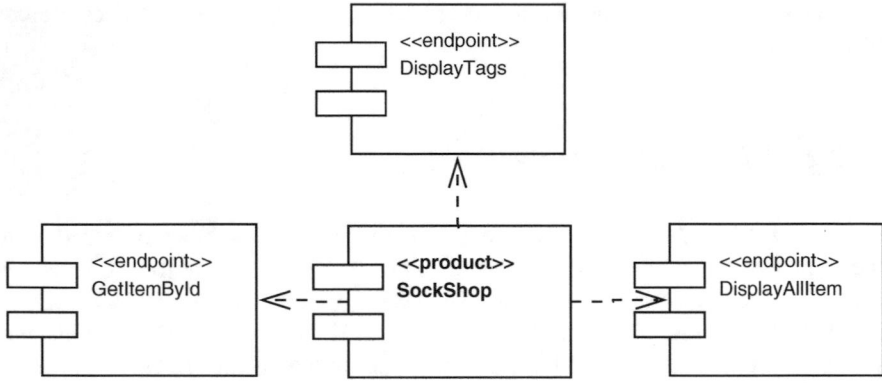

Fig. 11.7 UML diagram: product SockShop

with a keyword «when». For example, delta DSockCatalog is applied to the core module when feature *DisplayTags* is selected. Thus, in Fig. 11.6, a UML dependency with stereotype «when» connects a UML component «endpoint» DisplayTags and delta DSockCatalog.

A product consists of a list of selected features. In ABS, a product is defined in product selection language. Based on the architectural model in the UML diagram with UML-DOP profile, a product variant can be derived. We use a UML-DOP profile to visualize a feature selection for a product. For example, in Fig. 11.7, the product SockShop requires the endpoints GetItemById, DisplayAllItem and DisplayTags. Based on the feature diagram in Fig. 11.2, the endpoint GetItemById and DisplayAllItem is mandatory, and the endpoint DisplayTags is optional. In Fig. 11.6, we can see that endpoint DisplayTags is implemented by delta DSockCatalog.

We use the UML-DOP profile to represent the architectural models for microservices. As the UML-DOP profile enables the use of delta-oriented notation in the UML diagram, the architecture is straightforward to implement in DOP. A product line application can be implemented based on the defined architecture, as explained in Sect. 11.4. Based on our implementation, variants from the subject systems can be derived from the product line architecture.

11.4 Product Line Implementation

In this section, we describe how to implement a microservice-based product line. We follow the re-engineering activities defined in [12], i.e. feature identification and variability modeling (Sect. 11.2), product line architecture design (Sect. 11.3), and then transform into a product line application. Using the variability and architecture

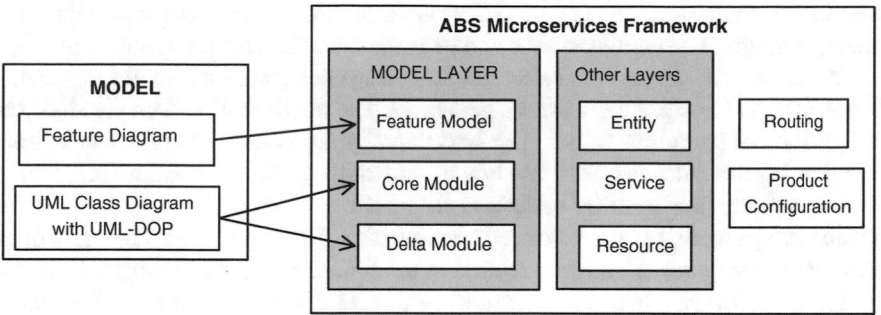

Fig. 11.8 Transformation steps

models produced in the previous sections, we implement[5] a product line application using ABS microservices [14].

We develop the webshop product line using the ABS microservices [14], a web framework based on ABS language. ABS is an executable modeling language based on DOP [9, 11]. ABS microservices framework consists of several layers, i.e., model, entity, service, resource, routing layers, to support a web-based product line development. The ABS microservices framework can produce various web applications.[6] The use of the DOP paradigm enables us to perform modification through the delta modules that can add, remove, or modify the existing implementation [20].

The implementation of core and delta modules in ABS microservices refers to the architectural model, as defined in Figs. 11.4, and 11.7. The core module consists of common implementation, and the delta modules implement optional features. In the previous research, we develop a code generator to transform feature diagrams and UML class diagrams with UML-DOP profile into ABS models [24]. The transformation steps, as shown in Fig. 11.8, are:

- The feature diagram, designed with `FeatureIDE`, is transformed into the ABS feature model.
- The skeleton of core and delta modules is generated and becomes a base implementation of the ABS microservices model layer.
- The other layers (entity, service, resource), routing, and product configuration are implemented manually.

We extend the ABS microservices framework to handle the multi-stage configurations. Each child feature of a root in the first level feature diagram (See Fig. 11.1) is realized as an ABS microservice application. Leaf features of the other level feature diagram, e.g., Fig. 11.2, are realized as functionalities and endpoints of each

---

[5] For focusing on the microservice variability, the front end interface is not yet provided. The services can be consumed using tools such as Postman.

[6] A running application using ABS microservices, called AISCO (https://aisco.splelive.id/), can automatically generate charity organization web applications.

service. To orchestrate the feature selection process, we create a deployment tool to manage multi-stage configurations and generate the microservice application [22].

We define a mechanism to select features using configuration files. By modifying these files, various products can be generated. The configuration files are stored in a specific configuration folder. The basic configuration consists of features from the first level feature diagram, as shown in Listings 11.2. Each feature selected at basic configuration must be contained inside a file `basic.json`. Based on the basic configuration, several advanced configuration files are defined. The name of an advanced configuration must be related to existing services. For example, selected endpoints in `cart.json`. as shown in Listing 11.3 configures the service `Cart`. The mandatory services will be automatically selected if users do not specify the advanced configuration.

```
1  {
2  "Cart": [
3    "CartUser",
4    "CartItem"],
5  "Catalog": [
6    "DisplayCatalog",
7    "CatalogItem"],
8  "User": "default"
9  }
```

Listing 11.2 An example of a `basic.json` file

```
1  [
2  "CartUser",
3    "CreateCart",
4    "DeleteCart",
5    "GetCart",
6  "CartItem",
7    "AddItem",
8    "UpdateItem",
9    "DeleteItem"
10 ]
```

Listing 11.3 An example of a `cart.json` file

After generating an application, users can have a running microservice application based on their current needs. Figure 11.9 illustrates the structure of a generated microservice-based application. Each application consists of several services, and each service has a JAR file and a database. The deployment tool automatically deploys each service to a specific address. Users can only access the endpoints related to the selected features. Other endpoints return an error message indicating that they do not exist. To do this, we use the delta module to adjust the routing configuration based on the selected features. ABS microservices can produce multiple variants of back-end applications with the same functionality as an API. A corresponding database to store or retrieve data needed by the API can also be generated.

Several endpoints can exist in each service, depending on the selected features in the advanced configuration. If the routing configurations are not carefully designed, conflicting endpoints between services might occur. We define a pattern `/api/<feature-name>/<endpoint-name>` to define endpoints in the

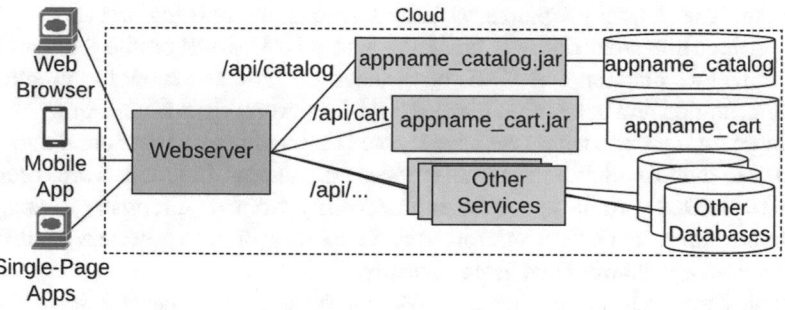

Fig. 11.9 Generated microservice-based application

microservice applications. For example, selecting endpoint DisplayAllItem in Fig. 11.2 will generate /api/catalog/display-all-item in the service *Catalog*. The /api part indicates that the endpoint is used as an API. Part <feature-name> tracks the origin of generated endpoints based on the first level feature diagram. Part <endpoint-name> indicates which leaf feature is selected in the advanced configuration step. Furthermore, using <endpoint-name> prevents generated conflicting endpoints because the name of feature in the feature diagram is unique.

The artifacts of the webshop product line implementation using ABS language are available in [22]. It is also completed with the deployment tools to generate a running application. Currently, we provide only the features *Catalog*, *Cart*, and *Order* as proof of concept to generate a running microservice application. This approach can be extended to implement other services in webshop systems. By running the solution artifacts, we evaluate that our approach provides the variants of the services as defined in the subject systems.

Our approach implements each child of the root feature in the first level feature diagram as a microservice-based product line application. Each application contains several services and endpoints. We currently do not have a reuse mechanism to share implementation for features with similar services or endpoints. This mechanism is related to the multi-product line approach that is under development in the ABS language. A new concept in ABS, called variability modules [7], can enable the reuse mechanism. Further exploration is needed to improve the mapping between services and features in our approach. Currently, we only map one feature to a service. In reality, there is a possibility that service belongs to more than one feature or vice versa.

11.5 Conclusion and Future Work

The re-engineering from the web-based microservice system into product line application is conducted based on a delta-oriented approach. The commonality and variability, which are analyzed manually, are modeled in a multi-level feature diagram. The diagram captures variations among the existing webshop systems. The product line architecture is designed with a UML-DOP profile diagram based on the feature diagram and UML class diagram. Last, we show the product line implementation and generation using the ABS microservices framework.

Based on our experience, we have learned that a multi-level feature diagram can be used to model variations in microservice applications. The models are completed with UML-DOP profile that enables traceability from requirements to endpoints implementation in DOP. Therefore, the variability of microservices in different applications can be managed systematically.

In this research, we extend the ABS microservices framework to enable the process of generating multiple services based on selected features. The deployment tool is developed to generate and deploy the application. Users only need to select features using multi-stage configurations. The deployment tool automatically generates the application and its database based on selected features. The tool also adopts the microservices approach, where each service running independently and have their own database.

We identify several possible improvements in this approach. The variations are not only in the problem domain but also in the solution domain. For example, it is possible to have variation in data interchange formats, as found in the subject systems. The communication among microservices may use different protocols and endpoint naming conventions. Thus, incorporating communication protocol variations can be considered when creating a product line for a microservice-based web application.

Currently, this approach does not focus on maintaining the security of the microservice application. The existing OAuth implementation in ABS microservices has not been tested to secure access across multiple services. To solve this problem, we consider replacing the reverse proxy by adding an API gateway and service discovery, such as Zuul[7] and Eureka.[8]

We propose using GraphQL as an alternative to access a database directly when retrieving or modifying data. GraphQL[9] is a query language, and its runtime environment provides a more descriptive and understandable query statement. Using GraphQL, we can optimize queries on each service to request only necessary attributes. When attributes are removed or added to the data, only services requesting those attributes are affected. Thus, we can minimize the number of errors or changes in the microservices due to adapting the database schema.

References

1. Apel, S., Batory, D.S., Kästner, C., Saake, G.: Feature-Oriented Software Product Lines - Concepts and Implementation. Springer (2013)

---

[7] https://github.com/Netflix/zuul/wiki.

[8] https://github.com/Netflix/eureka/wiki.

[9] https://graphql.org/.

2. Assunção, W.K.G., Krüger, J., Mendonça, W.D.F.: Variability management meets microservices: six challenges of re-engineering microservice-based webshops. In: R.E. Lopez-Herrejon (ed.) SPLC '20: 24th ACM International Systems and Software Product Line Conference, Montreal, Quebec, Canada, October 19–23, 2020, Volume A, pp. 22:1–22:6. ACM (2020)

3. Assunção, W.K.G., Vergilio, S.R., Lopez-Herrejon, R.E.: Automatic extraction of product line architecture and feature models from UML class diagram variants. Inf. Softw. Technol. **117** (2020)

4. Classen, A., Boucher, Q., Heymans, P.: A text-based approach to feature modelling: Syntax and semantics of TVL. Sci. Comput. Program. **76**(12), 1130–1143 (2011)

5. Clements, P., Northrop, L.M.: Software product lines - practices and patterns. SEI series in software engineering. Addison-Wesley (2002)

6. Czarnecki, K., Helsen, S., Eisenecker, U.W.: Staged configuration through specialization and multilevel configuration of feature models. Softw. Process. Improv. Pract. **10**(2), 143–169 (2005)

7. Damiani, F., Hähnle, R., Kamburjan, E., Lienhardt, M.: Same same but different: Interoperability of software product line variants. In: P. Müller, I. Schaefer (eds.) Principled Software Development - Essays Dedicated to Arnd Poetzsch-Heffter on the Occasion of his 60th Birthday, pp. 99–117. Springer (2018)

8. Groher, I., Völter, M.: Aspect-oriented model-driven software product line engineering. LNCS Trans. Aspect Oriented Softw. Dev. **6**, 111–152 (2009)

9. Hähnle, R.: The abstract behavioral specification language: A tutorial introduction. In: E. Giachino, R. Hähnle, F.S. de Boer, M.M. Bonsangue (eds.) Formal Methods for Components and Objects - 11th International Symposium, FMCO 2012, Bertinoro, Italy, September 24–28, 2012, Revised Lectures, *Lecture Notes in Computer Science*, vol. 7866, pp. 1–37. Springer (2012)

10. Holl, G., Grünbacher, P., Rabiser, R.: A systematic review and an expert survey on capabilities supporting multi product lines. Inf. Softw. Technol. **54**(8), 828–852 (2012)

11. Johnsen, E.B., Hähnle, R., Schäfer, J., Schlatte, R., Steffen, M.: ABS: A core language for abstract behavioral specification. In: B.K. Aichernig, F.S. de Boer, M.M. Bonsangue (eds.) Formal Methods for Components and Objects - 9th International Symposium, FMCO 2010, Graz, Austria, November 29 - December 1, 2010. Revised Papers, *Lecture Notes in Computer Science*, vol. 6957, pp. 142–164. Springer (2010)

12. Krüger, J., Berger, T.: Activities and costs of re-engineering cloned variants into an integrated platform. In: M. Cordy, M. Acher, D. Beuche, G. Saake (eds.) VaMoS '20: 14th International Working Conference on Variability Modelling of Software-Intensive Systems, Magdeburg Germany, February 5–7, 2020, pp. 21:1–21:10. ACM (2020)

13. Mendonça, W.D.F., Assunção, W.K.G., Estanislau, L.V., Vergilio, S.R., Garcia, A.: Towards a microservices-based product line with multi-objective evolutionary algorithms. In: IEEE Congress on Evolutionary Computation, CEC 2020, Glasgow, United Kingdom, July 19–24, 2020, pp. 1–8. IEEE (2020)

14. Naily, M.A., Setyautami, M.R.A., Muschevici, R., Azurat, A.: A framework for modelling variable microservices as software product lines. In: A. Cerone, M. Roveri (eds.) Software Engineering and Formal Methods - SEFM 2017 Collocated Workshops: DataMod, FAACS, MSE, CoSim-CPS, and FOCLASA, Trento, Italy, September 4–5, 2017, Revised Selected Papers, *Lecture Notes in Computer Science*, vol. 10729, pp. 246–261. Springer (2017)

15. Nesic, D., Krüger, J., Stanciulescu, S., Berger, T.: Principles of feature modeling. In: M. Dumas, D. Pfahl, S. Apel, A. Russo (eds.) Proceedings of the ACM Joint Meeting on European Software Engineering Conference and Symposium on the Foundations of Software Engineering, ESEC/SIGSOFT FSE 2019, Tallinn, Estonia, August 26–30, 2019, pp. 62–73. ACM (2019)

16. Newman, S.: Building microservices - designing fine-grained systems, 1st Edition. O'Reilly (2015). URL https://www.worldcat.org/oclc/904463848

17. Pohl, K., Böckle, G., van der Linden, F.: Software Product Line Engineering - Foundations, Principles, and Techniques. Springer (2005)

18. Rabiser, D., Prähofer, H., Grünbacher, P., Petruzelka, M., Eder, K., Angerer, F., Kromoser, M., Grimmer, A.: Multi-purpose, multi-level feature modeling of large-scale industrial software systems. Softw. Syst. Model. **17**(3), 913–938 (2018)
19. Reiser, M., Weber, M.: Managing highly complex product families with multi-level feature trees. In: 14th IEEE International Conference on Requirements Engineering (RE 2006), 11–15 September 2006, Minneapolis/St.Paul, Minnesota, USA, pp. 146–155. IEEE Computer Society (2006)
20. Schaefer, I., Bettini, L., Bono, V., Damiani, F., Tanzarella, N.: Delta-oriented programming of software product lines. In: J. Bosch, J. Lee (eds.) Software Product Lines: Going Beyond - 14th International Conference, SPLC 2010, Jeju Island, South Korea, September 13–17, 2010. Proceedings, *Lecture Notes in Computer Science*, vol. 6287, pp. 77–91. Springer (2010)
21. Setyautami, M.R.A., Adianto, D., Azurat, A.: Modeling multi software product lines using UML. In: T. Berger, P. Borba, G. Botterweck, T. Männistö, D. Benavides, S. Nadi, T. Kehrer, R. Rabiser, C. Elsner, M. Mukelabai (eds.) Proceeedings of the 22nd International Systems and Software Product Line Conference - Volume 1, SPLC 2018, Gothenburg, Sweden, September 10–14, 2018, pp. 274–278. ACM (2018)
22. Setyautami, M.R.A., Fadhlillah, H.S., Adianto, D., Affan, I., Azurat, A.: Solution artifacts on re-engineering microservices-based webshops challenge (2020)
23. Setyautami, M.R.A., Hähnle, R., Muschevici, R., Azurat, A.: A UML profile for delta-oriented programming to support software product line engineering. In: H. Mei (ed.) Proceedings of the 20th International Systems and Software Product Line Conference, SPLC 2016, Beijing, China, September 16–23, 2016, pp. 45–49. ACM (2016)
24. Setyautami, M.R.A., Rubiantoro, R.R., Azurat, A.: Model-driven engineering for delta-oriented software product lines. In: 26th Asia-Pacific Software Engineering Conference, APSEC 2019, Putrajaya, Malaysia, December 2–5, 2019, pp. 371–377. IEEE (2019)
25. Thüm, T., Kästner, C., Benduhn, F., Meinicke, J., Saake, G., Leich, T.: FeatureIDE: An extensible framework for feature-oriented software development. Sci. Comput. Program. **79**, 70–85 (2014)

Chapter 12
Understanding the Variability on the Recovery of Product Line Architectures

Crescencio Lima, Mateus Cardoso, Ivan do Carmo Machado, Eduardo Santana de Almeida, and Christina von Flach Garcia Chavez

Abstract The Product Line Architecture (PLA) of a Software Product Line (SPL) is the core architecture that represents a high-level design for all the products of an SPL, including variation points and variants. If PLA documentation is missing, it can be recovered by reverse engineering the products. The recovered PLA is a relevant asset for developers and architects, that can be used to drive specific activities of SPL development and evolution, such as, understanding its structure and its variation points, and assessing reuse. This chapter presents our PLA recovery approach and an exploratory study that investigated the effectiveness of recovered PLAs to address variability identification and support reuse assessment. We recovered the PLA of 15 open source SPL projects using the PLAR, a tool that supports PLA recovery and assessment based on information extracted from SPL products' source code. For each project, reuse assessment was supported by existing reuse metrics. The yielded results revealed that the number of products used in PLA recovery affected the variability identification, and the number of optional features affected the components reuse rate. The findings suggest that a minimum set of representative products should be identified and selected for PLA recovery, and the component reuse rate is a candidate metric for SPL reuse assessment.

12.1 Introduction

Many companies develop a portfolio of related software products, conceived to satisfy similar needs of their customers. A Software Product Line (SPL) is a set of software systems that share a mandatory and optional set of features satisfying the specific needs of a particular market segment [23]. SPL engineering supports the development and management of a product portfolio, highlighting the commonalities and variabilities, promoting reuse, and fostering customization.

C. Lima (✉) · M. Cardoso · I. do Carmo Machado · E. S. de Almeida ·
C. von Flach Garcia Chavez
Federal Institute of Bahia, Salvador, Brazil
e-mail: ivan.machado@ufba.br; esa@rise.com.br; flach@ufba.br

© Springer Nature Switzerland AG 2023
R. E. Lopez-Herrejon et al. (eds.), *Handbook of Re-Engineering Software Intensive Systems into Software Product Lines*, https://doi.org/10.1007/978-3-031-11686-5_12

The SPL adoption brings benefits, including improved product reliability, faster time to market, and reduced costs [2]. Therefore, many companies rely on less sophisticated reuse approaches during the customization of system variants. For instance, using *opportunistic reuse*, clone-and-own reuse, copy-and-paste reuse, or, ad hoc reuse [7, 15].

The development of an SPL involves the implementation of different structures, processes, interfaces, and activities, therefore a fundamental step is to define the Product Line Architecture (PLA) [18]. PLA can be defined as (1) the core architecture that represents a high-level design for all the products of an SPL, including variation points and variants documented in the variability model [23], or (2) an architecture for a family of products that describes the mandatory and optional components[1] in the SPL, and their interconnections [12].

In this context, the PLA plays an important role to allow the SPL evolution and keep complexity under control. PLA assessment can be supported by metrics to be collected during the recovery process. For instance, reuse metrics such as those proposed by Zhang et al. [33]—Structure Similarity Coefficient (SSC), Structure Variability Coefficient (SVC) and Component Reuse Rate (CRR) [33]—and the metrics proposed by [22]—Class Optional (CO), Class Mandatory (CM), and Product Line Total Variability (PLTV) could be used to provide insights about the way PLA components are reused within SPL products.

For single systems, software architecture can be recovered and documented from source code or other available information [6, 8]. Software Architecture Recovery (SAR) approaches share the goal of documenting software architecture and provide solutions to problems such as the absence of documented software architecture, and the need for detecting violations between conceptual and implemented architectures [8]. In the SPL domain the PLA provides information about the mandatory and optional components, providing useful information for software reuse. Although the architecture description is part of the SPL adoption process, not all projects have a PLA documented. The PLA recovery can help developers with the SPL evolution and maintenance tasks.

In our previous work [17], we reported the results of a literature review undertaken to investigate research work that brings together the fields of SPL and SAR. Several approaches to PLA recovery [19, 24] were identified, as well as research trends and gaps. We have found out that few SAR tools support variability identification, an essential feature for PLA recovery. Additional features such as support for PLA assessment, were not found either. Finally, these tools were mostly not available for use. These gaps motivated us to develop the PLAR Tool, a PLA recovery and assessment tool [4].

This chapter presents our PLA recovery approach and the results of an exploratory study conducted to assess the PLA recovered from a set of open-source SPL projects. The PLAR tool supported PLA recovery and assessment.

---

[1] In this chapter, we considered a PLA component as the concrete classes, abstract classes, and interfaces.

The chapter contributions are:

- We present our PLA recovery approach and tool support;
- We describe the recovery of the PLA from 15 SPL projects, and;
- We provide the assessment of those 15 PLAs through reuse metrics.

In this chapter we discovered that is not necessary to use all products to recover the PLA, the recovery process can be improved by using only the most significant configurations. The PLA recovery process described in the chapter was used on SPL projects from different domains and sizes.

The remainder of this chapter is organized as follows. Section 12.2 provides the background and definitions. Section 12.3 presents our PLA recovery approach. Section 12.4 describes the exploratory study. Section 12.5 discusses related work, and Sect. 12.6 presents concluding remarks and future work.

12.2 Background

In this section, we provide a brief background overview and definitions needed for the rest of the chapter.

12.2.1 Architecture Recovery

The recovery of different software architecture views requires the use of different extraction techniques [27]. For instance, the extraction of logical views depends on the analysis of requirements models, use cases, and activity models. In such cases, top-down processes are used because they start with high-level knowledge and aim to discover the architecture by formulating hypotheses [8]. The extraction of physical and deployment views requires the analysis of dynamic information such as logs, network traffic, configuration, and installation scripts.

The recovery of development views uses bottom-up processes because they start with low-level knowledge to recover the architecture. From source code models, they promote system understanding by raising the abstraction level [8]. In the context of this chapter, we focus on the development view provided by bottom-up processes. We recover information based on projects' source code static analysis.

12.2.2 Variability in Software Architecture

Variability is a relevant characteristic of architectures of software systems [10]. It is a key fact of "most, if not all systems" and a relevant concern for the architectures of those systems [14], that should be managed and identified early during architecting over discovering and addressed later in the life cycle [29].

Variability can be represented and assessed with the support of a documented software architecture. Variability at the architectural level can be a complex and multi-faceted concept that should be treated as a first-class citizen in a software architecture [11]. To provide software architects with an appropriate support to handle variability, it is important to figure out the likely issues they could face when carrying out variability-related tasks [9].

So far, variability has primarily been addressed in the SPL domain [5, 10]. Therefore, to address variability in SPL projects at the architectural level, the SPL community introduced the notion of PLA [1], which captures the core design of all products including variability and commonalities of several product instances.

The variability on the SPL is represented by its features [2]. However, those features can be scattered through many classes and methods implementations, this variability can be identified only by analyzing its source code structure, which is not present on the architecture. Other form variability can be inserted on the PLA by the feature is through the creation of elements (classes, inheritance, interface) and its relationships to fulfill the feature functionality. This type of variability is present on the architecture and thus, can be recovered through software architecture recovery approaches.

12.3   PLA Recovery Approach

We describe our approach for supporting the PLA recovery based on the use and adaptation of the existing single systems SAR techniques and tools. Figure 12.1 presents the approach four phases.

In ①, we gather the information about the SPL project. We download the SPL source code from the repository and organize the information according to the recovery technique and extraction tools. These techniques and tools change according to the technique used to implement the variability.

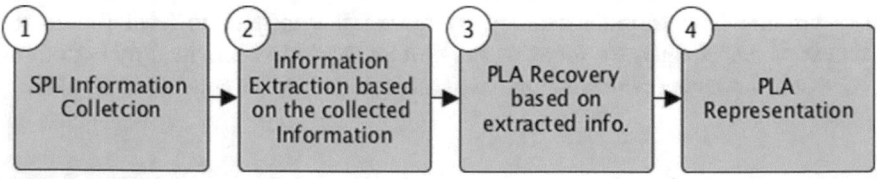

Fig. 12.1 PLA recovery main phases

We selected the extraction tool (such as Stan4J,[2] Analizo,[3] Structure101,[4] Understand,[5] and so on) according to the programming language used to implement the SPL project. Then in ②, we extracted structural information from the SPL (or/and products) source code. Based on the extracted information, we perform the PLA recovery ③ using the technique suited for the scenario (e.g., merge of the recovered information implemented by PLAR tool).

Then, we present the PLA representation ④ by providing development views that include the description of the variability at the architectural level. We used some tools to create the visualization (e.g., graphviz,[6] plantUML,[7] and so on). We also collect the reuse metrics and perform analysis of the recovered information. In our previous work [16], we provide more details about the approach phases.

12.3.1   Motivating Example

The goal of this motivating example is to illustrate our PLA recovery approach. Next we present two fictitious variants. Variant_1 was initially developed from scratch and then Variant_2 was developed by reusing the former variant using opportunistic reuse. The approach steps are presented in the following subsections.

12.3.1.1   Variant 1 Source Code Analysis and Extraction

Listing 1.1 presents the `Class_A` and `Class_B` from Variant_1. `Class_A` calls the method `foo()` implemented by `Class_B`. We grouped both classes (`Class_A` and `Class_B`) in the `package_X`.

```
1 package package_X;                        package package_X;
2
3 public class Class_A {                     public class Class_B {
4   private int test_1;                        public Class_B(){}
5
6   public Class_A(Class_B B){                 int foo(){
7     test_1 = B.foo(); }                        return 0; }
8 }                                          }
```

Listing 12.1 `Class_A` and Class_B from Variant_1

We used the Stan4J tool to extract the source code information. Figure 12.2c shows the packages of Variant_1 (higher level of abstraction). Then, in Fig. 12.2d,

---

[2] http://stan4j.com.

[3] http://www.analizo.org.

[4] https://structure101.com.

[5] https://scitools.com.

[6] https://www.graphviz.org.

[7] http://plantuml.com.

Fig. 12.2 Extracted
information from variant_1
(Stan4J). (**a**) Packages. (**b**)
Classes

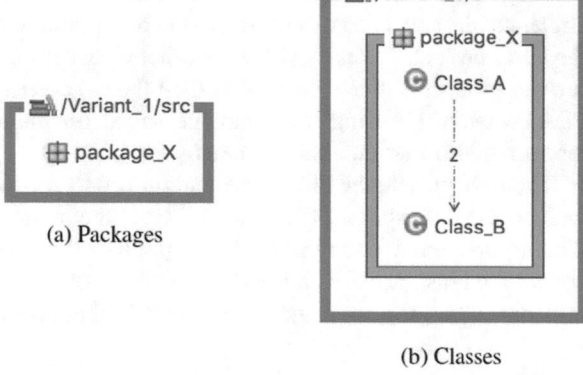

(a) Packages

(b) Classes

we extracted lower-level information. In this way, we collected information about the classes and their relationship.

12.3.1.2 Variant 2 Source Code Analysis and Extraction

Listing 1.2 presents the Class_B and Class_C from Variant_2. Class_B constructor calls the zoo() function implemented by Class_C. We organized the development project in two packages, package_X and package_Y.

```
1  package package_X;              package package_Y;
2  import package_Y.*;
3
4  public class Class_B {          public class Class_C {
5    private int test_2;             public int zoo(){
6    public Class_B(Class_C C){        return 1; }
7      test_2 = C.zoo(); }         }
8
9    int foo(){
10     return 0; }
11 }
```

Listing 12.2 Class_B and Class_C from Variant_2

Figure 12.3 presents the extracted information represented in packages (Fig. 12.3a) and classes (Fig. 12.3b). We raised the abstraction of the relationship between Class_B and Class_C to the package representation. In other words, package_X calls a method implemented by package_Y.

12.3.1.3 Application of the PLA Recovery

Figure 12.4 shows the development view (one of the outputs) of the PLA recovery approach. Moreover, we identified the variability in the architectural level.

Fig. 12.3 Extracted information from variant_2 (Stan4J). (**a**) Packages. (**b**) Classes

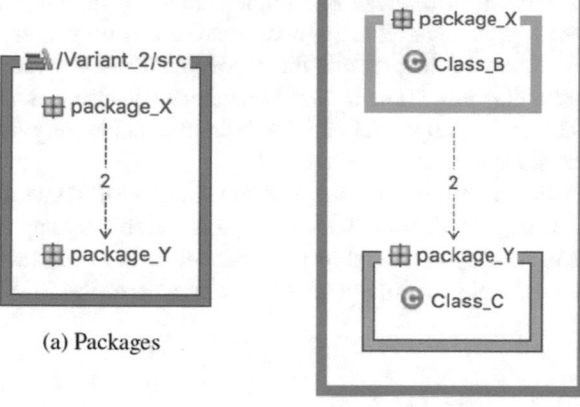

(a) Packages

(b) Classes

Fig. 12.4 Two levels of PLA recovery with variability representation. (**a**) Packages. (**b**) Classes

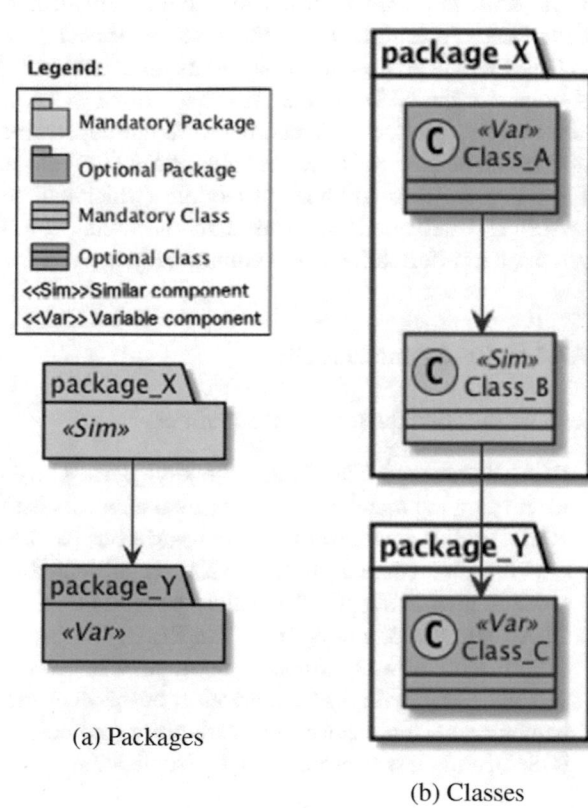

(a) Packages

(b) Classes

Figure 12.4a presents the recovered PLA represented in packages, `package_X` is mandatory because it is implemented in Variant_1 and Variant_2. On the other hand, `package_Y` is optional because it is implemented by only Variant_2.

Figure 12.4b presents the recovered PLA represented in a consolidated UML class diagram. `Class_B` is mandatory because it is implemented in both variants. `Class_A` is optional because is implemented only in Variant_1 and `Class_C` is implemented only in Variant_2.

We highlight that the implementation of `Class_B` constructor varies from Variant_1 to Variant_2. However, this variability happens in low-level. Our objective is to identify the variability in a higher level of abstraction. In this context, the low-level variability did not affect the structure of the PLA.

12.3.2 PLAR Tool

PLAR Tool[8] is a PLA recovery tool that automatizes and serves as concept proof of the PLAR technique. Its inputs are a set of MDG (Module Dependency Graph) [21] files which represent the elements and relationships from the SPL products; its output is the SPL PLA in different formats. These MDG files are extracted from the SPL products source code through dependency extraction tools such as: Analizo, DependencyFinder, STAN4J, Struct101 and many others. The recovered PLA provides information about modules(which can be represented by the system classes)[21] and relationship used in the architectural description of traditional systems, and information about commonalities and variabilities to describe PLA.

12.3.2.1 Tool Functionalities

Next, we describe the tools functionalities:

1. **PLA Recovery**—The PLA recovery process from a set of SPL products identifying the mandatory and optional elements is the main functionality.
2. **PLA Quality Evaluation support**—Metrics can be calculated using the recovered PLA information. In Sect. 12.1, we presented the metrics calculated by the tool and used to support the evaluation based on the reuse rate of PLA elements.
3. **PLA visualization support**—The PLAR Tool generates PLA representations in different formats, which is input to visualization tools. The tool provides visualizations that allow the creation of the PLA module view, highlighting the commonality (blue color) and variability (red color), of design structure matrix (DSM), and class diagrams. Each visualization was produced to follow the color

---

[8] PLAR Tool is available at: https://bit.ly/2zuzR5q.

the pattern of the module view; red represents variability while blue represents commonality.

12.3.3   PLAR Algorithm

Algorithm 3 presents the steps used by the PLAR technique to recover the PLA. The algorithm receives as input a set of products selected in the previous step. Initially, all products generated by the SPL are analyzed, individually, to identify the architecture elements. The elements could be classes, interfaces, abstract classes, relationship, and others. If the element has not been identified yet, then it will be added to the list of PLA elements; else the technique counts the number of occurrences of the element in the PLA products. The process is done incrementally, the products are analyzed in ascending order according to the files' names. However, the order does not influence the recovery results. Right after the analysis, the algorithm verifies whether each element is either present in every product instance (mandatory) or not (optional) by comparing the number of occurrences with the number of products.

12.3.4   Validation Example

To validate the PLAR Tool algorithm, we conducted a manual extraction from the DPL project using the recovery approach. The DPL is an SPL for drawing applications, more information about the project can be found on Table 12.3. To extract its architecture and verify the mandatory and optional components, we used the STAN4J tool which extracted the architecture of the products generated by DPL project.

Table 12.1 presents the classes identified in each product and the results describing if the class is optional or mandatory among the products.

Considering the information on Table 12.1, we verified that the classes Canvas and Main are mandatory because they were implemented in all the products meanwhile the classes Line and BasicRetangle are optional because they were implemented by not all the products. We proceeded the analysis verifying the

Table 12.1 DPL classes

Class	P0	P1	P2	P3	P4	P5	P6	P7	P8	P9	P10	P11	Result
Canvas	✓	✓	✓	✓	✓	✓	✓	✓	✓	✓	✓	✓	Mandatory
Line	✓	–	✓	✓	✓	✓	–	–	–	✓	✓	✓	Optional
Main	✓	✓	✓	✓	✓	✓	✓	✓	✓	✓	✓	✓	Mandatory
BasicRetangle	–	✓	✓	–	–	–	✓	✓	✓	✓	✓	✓	Optional

Algorithm 3 PLA recovery algorithm

Input: P, a collection of N variants, N > 1.

Output: PLA, a collection of mandatory and optional architectural elements

1 **begin**

2   **foreach** *variant P_i in P* **do**

3   **foreach** *element e or relationship r found on P_i* **do**

4   **if** *the element e or the relationship r has been already identified in another variants P_j, $i \neq j$* **then**

5   Add +1 on the number of occurrences of the element e or relationship r ;

6   Update the information about the variants that contains the element e or relationship r;

7   **end**

8   **if** *The element e or relationship r has not been identified* **then**

9   Insert the element e or relationship r on the PLA collection;

10   Mark the element e or relationship r as identified;

11   **end**

12   **end**

13   **end**

14   **foreach** *element e or relationship r identified on the PLA* **do**

15   **if** *the element r or relationship r is on all variants* **then**

16   Mark the element e or relationship r as "mandatory";

17   **else**

18   Mark the element e or relationship r as "optional";

19   **end**

20   **end**

21 **end**

---

relationships between those classes to check which relation are mandatory or optional among all products.

Table 12.2 presents the relationships that can happen between the classes. We also identified the relationships implemented by the products, and which is optional or mandatory. For instance, in the first line the class Canvas calls the class Line. This relationship is implemented in the products P0, P2, P3, P4, P5, P9, P10, and P111. This relationship is considered optional because it is implemented in some products. On the other hand, the relationship that the class Main calls the class Canvas is mandatory because it is implemented in all the products.

After performing the manual analysis, we recovered the architecture using the PLAR Tool and compared if the results obtained by the tool. Figure 12.5 shows the architecture recovered by PLAR Tool.

Figure 12.5 shows the architecture recovered by PLAR Tool identified the elements (classes and relation) as optional and mandatory in the same way the manual verification identified.

Table 12.2 DPL classes' relationships

Relationship	P0	P1	P2	P3	P4	P5	P6	P7	P8	P9	P10	P11	Result
Canvas > Line	✓	–	✓	✓	✓	✓	–	–	–	✓	✓	✓	Optional
Canvas > Main	–	–	–	–	–	–	–	–	–	–	–	–	N/R
Canvas > BasicRetangle	–	✓	✓	–	–	–	✓	✓	✓	✓	✓	✓	Optional
Line > Canvas	–	–	–	–	–	–	–	–	–	–	–	–	N/R
Line > Main	–	–	–	–	–	–	–	–	–	–	–	–	N/R
Line > BasicRetangle	–	–	–	–	–	–	–	–	–	–	–	–	N/R
Main > Canvas	✓	✓	✓	✓	✓	✓	✓	✓	✓	✓	✓	✓	Mandatory
Main > Line	–	–	–	–	–	–	–	–	–	–	–	–	N/R
Main > BasicRetangle	–	–	–	–	–	–	–	–	–	–	–	–	N/R
BasicRetangle > Canvas	–	–	–	–	–	–	–	–	–	–	–	–	N/R
BasicRetangle > Line	–	–	–	–	–	–	–	–	–	–	–	–	N/R
BasicRetangle > Main	–	–	–	–	–	–	–	–	–	–	–	–	N/R

Legend: [N/R] no relationship identified

Fig. 12.5 DPL SPL architecture recovered by PLAR tool

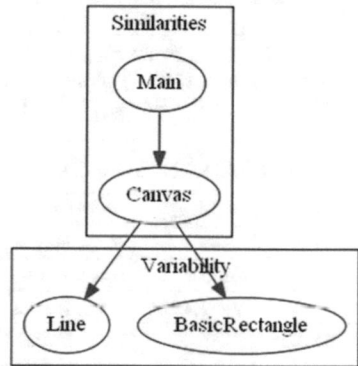

12.4 Exploratory Study

We selected fifteen open source SPL projects from different domains for this study, based on the following criteria: lack of documented PLA and source code written in Java. Table 12.3 summarizes our sample and presents the number of features (mandatory and optional), classes and products of each SPL, and the tool used for product generation.

12.4.1 Research Questions

We used the Goal/Question/Metric (GQM) approach [26] because measurement is defined in a top-down fashion, from goals to metrics. This study encompasses two related facets: *number of products impacting the precision to identify the variability*

Table 12.3 SPL projects analyzed

SPL	#Fea.	#MF	#OF	#Pr.	#Cl.	Gen.
BankAccount	6	0	6	24	2	FH
BankAccountv2	8	0	8	72	3	FH
DPL	5	1	4	12	4	NA
Desktop searcher	22	6	16	462	41	AH
Elevator	6	0	6	20	5	FH
E-mail	6	0	6	40	3	FH
ExamDB	3	0	3	8	4	FH
GOL	21	12	9	65	21	NA
GPL	38	18	20	155	15	CD
PayCard	3	0	3	6	7	FH
PokerSPL	11	2	9	28	8	FH
Prop4J	13	0	13	31	14	FH
UnionFind	10	2	8	6	4	FH
VOD	11	6	5	32	42	NA
Zip Me	7	2	5	32	31	NA

Legend: [#Fea.] Features, [#MF] Mandatory features, [#OF] Optional features,
[#Pr.] Product, [#Cl.] Classes, [Gen.] Product generator, [NA] Not available, [CD]
CIDE, [FH] FeatureHouse, [AH] AHEAD

Table 12.4 GQM model for Goal 1

Goal	Purpose	Verify
	Issue	If the number of products
	Object	Has an impact on the PLA variability identification precision
	Viewpoint	From the researcher point of view
Question	RQ1	Does the number of SPL products used in PLA recovery impact the variability identification precision?
Metrics		SSC, SVC, CRR, Optional Features, Number of products, and CO

in the PLA, and *number of optional features impacting reuse rate.* Each facet led to different research questions and hypotheses, as discussed next.

We defined two GQM models in this study, each one addressing one facet. Based on the goals, we defined the research questions and related them to the set of metrics under evaluation [22, 33].

GQM Model 1 Table 12.4 describes the GQM model for the first facet. The product generation tool provides the number of SPL products used in PLA recovery. The PLTV metric is used to estimate the total number of optional components expected in the PLA, and the SVC metric is used to calculate the overall variability of PLA components. Moreover, we verified the metrics values with different number of products in the comparison.

Table 12.5 GQM model for Goal 2

Goal	Purpose	Identify
	Issue	If there is any correlation between
	Object	The number of optional features and the component reuse rate of the PLA
	Viewpoint	From the researcher point of view
Question	RQ2	Is there any correlation between the number of optional features in the SPL and the component reuse rate of the recovered PLA?
Metrics		SSC, SVC, CRR, Optional features

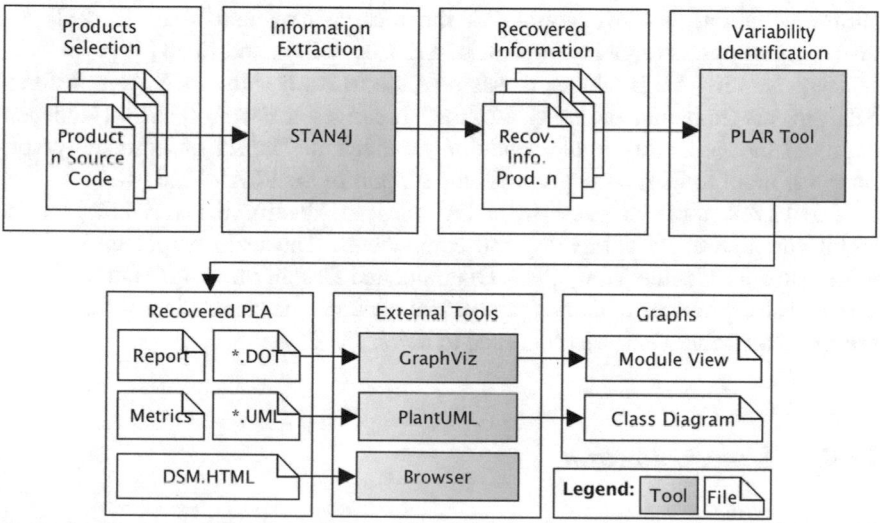

Fig. 12.6 The overall recovery process: activities, inputs and outputs

GQM Model 2 Table 12.5 describes the GQM model for the second facet. The product generation tool provides the number of optional features in the SPL. We used this information together with the SSC metric value to estimate the impact of optional features on the PLA component reuse rate.

12.4.2   Execution

Figure 12.6 shows the main activities, inputs, outputs, and tool support of the PLA recovery process executed for this study. The selected SPL projects were subject to product generation, information extraction with STAN4J, and PLA recovery with the PLAR Tool.

Only valid product configurations were used. A product configuration is valid if it obeys the SPL feature model dependencies [2]. For any SPL with a potential high number of products (e.g., Prop4J can have 5K products), we used the T-Wise method [13] (with t = 2) to generate only a subset of SPL products. T-Wise builds only the most significant products, based on the SPL feature model. Some SPL projects (DPL, VOD, Zip Me, and GOL) had existing generated products available, so that we could skip product generation.

For each selected SPL project, we extracted a module dependency graph (MDG) based on the analysis of the products' source code, with the support of Stan4J. The MDG represents the concrete classes, abstract classes, interfaces, and the relationship among them. This is done because there are different mechanisms to implement the variability (we could enlist conditional compilation, inheritance, parameterization, and overloading as the most widely used ones [3, 28]) and different composers (e.g., Featurehouse, AHEAD, CIDE, and so on [30]).

By generating the products, it was possible to recover the PLA from different SPL projects (implemented using #IFDEF directives or FeatureIDE [30]) independently of the variability implementation mechanism. The set of extracted graphs served as input to PLA recovery, with the support of the PLAR Tool [4].

The PLAR tool analyzes the MDG files to identify the variability at the architectural level by comparing the components. The main output is the PLA, represented as Module View, Class Diagram, and Design Structure Matrix (DSM). The tool also provides a metrics report, that contains the calculation of the metrics presented on Table 12.6, which is used to assess the PLA.

12.4.3 Data Collection

For each SPL project studied, the PLA was recovered. Table 12.6 presents the metrics collected using the PLAR tool. The complete data set used in this exploratory study is available at the study website.[9]

12.4.4 Descriptive Statistics

Table 12.6 presents the metric results of the recovered PLAs. The SSC metric is used to calculate the overall similarity of PLA components; the maximum value is 1. The SVC metric calculates the general variability of PLA components; the maximum value is 1. The RSC and RVC metrics are similar to SSC and SVC, respectively. However, they are used to measure the similarity and variability of relations among PLA components.

The metrics CM calculates the number of classes implementing the mandatory features and CO calculates the number of classes implementing the optional features.

---

[9] https://bit.ly/2OEZDK4.

Table 12.6 Metrics collected for the PLAs

SPL	SSC	SVC	RSC	RVC	CO	OR	CM	MR	PLTV
BankAccount	1.0	0.0	1.0	0.0	0	0	2	1	0
BankAccountv2	0.7	0.3	0.5	0.5	1	1	2	1	2
DPL	0.5	0.5	0.3	0.7	2	2	2	1	4
Desktop searcher	0.3	0.7	0.1	0.9	30	134	11	14	164
Elevator	1.0	0.0	1.0	0.0	0	0	11	29	0
E-mail	1.0	0.0	1.0	0.0	0	0	3	4	0
ExamDB	1.0	0.0	1.0	0.0	0	0	4	5	0
GOL	0.6	0.4	0.7	0.3	8	11	13	24	19
GPL	0.6	0.4	0.4	0.6	6	23	9	16	29
PayCard	0.7	0.3	0.4	0.6	2	5	5	3	7
PokerSPL	0.5	0.5	0.3	0.7	4	5	4	2	9
Prop4J	0.1	0.9	0.0	1.0	13	50	1	0	63
UnionFind	1.0	0.0	1.0	0.0	0	0	4	4	0
VOD	0.8	0.2	0.7	0.3	10	23	32	55	33
Zip Me	0.8	0.2	0.7	0.3	6	14	25	32	20

Legend: [SSC] Structure similarity coefficient [SVC] Structure variability coefficient
[RSC] Relation similarity coefficient [RVC] Relation variability coefficient [CO] Class
optional [OR] Optional relation [CM] Class mandatory [MR] Mandatory relation
[PLTV] Product line total variability

Besides, the metrics OR and MR use the same principle to calculate the number of mandatory and optional relations. It is possible to perform these calculations because PLAR analyzes the classes and relations captured in the MDG files.

PLTV is a metric that estimates the PLA variability. Table 12.6 shows the CO and OR metrics.

The CRR metric is missing from the overview presented in Table 12.6. This metric provides a measurement for each PLA component and relation, as it calculates the amount of products (ratio) that have a specific component or relation. Components with CRR of 100% indicates that the component is present in all the products. Values above 50% mean that the component was used at least in half of SPL products.

12.4.5   Answers to the Research Questions

For the first research question, we verified if *the number of products has an impact on the PLA variability identification precision.* Figure 12.7 shows SSC (darker grey) and SVC (lighter grey) metrics of four SPL projects (DPL, VOD, Zip Me, and Prop4J) collected during different stages of comparison. We selected these projects randomly from the sample. All the SPL projects presented the same patterns.

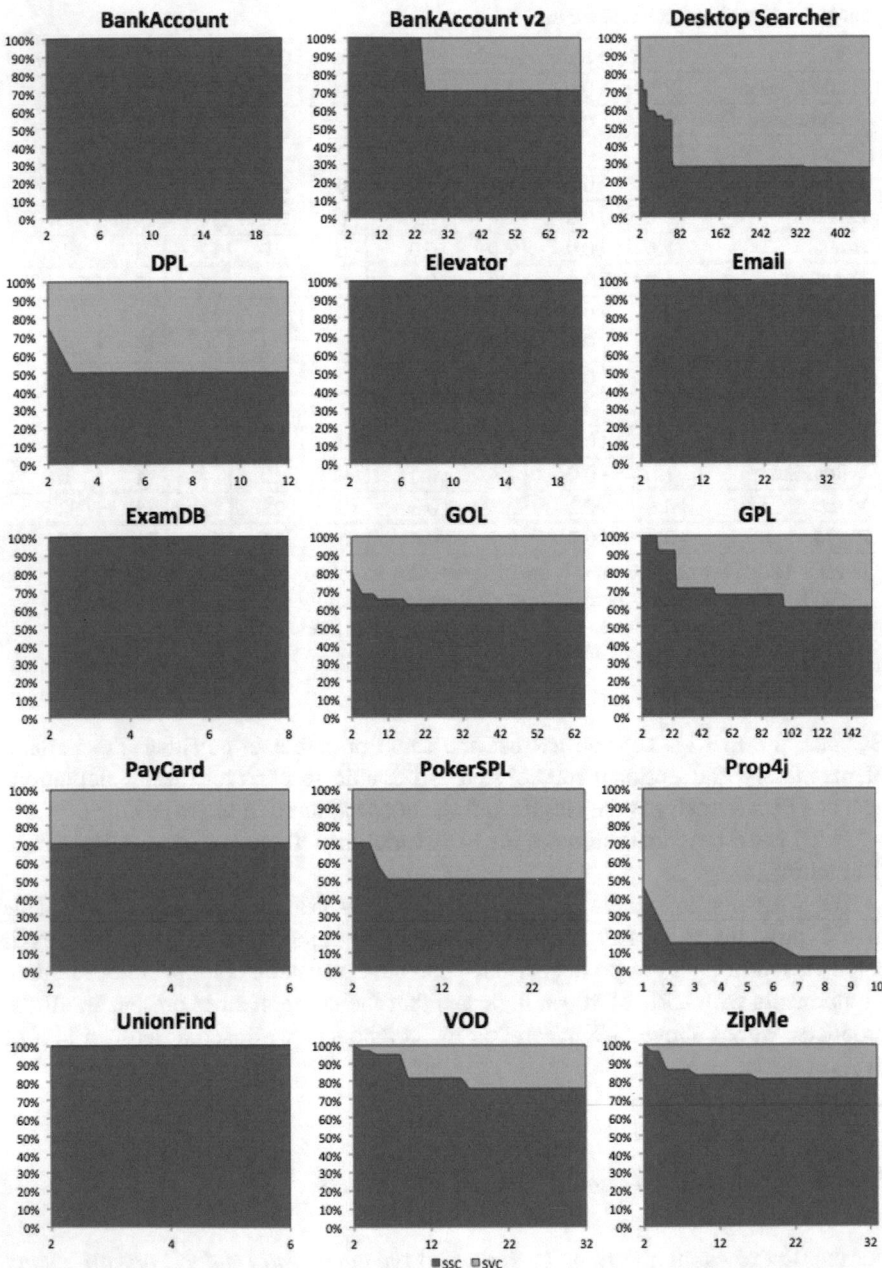

Fig. 12.7 SSC and SVC metrics according to the number of products in the comparison

We identified that the precision regarding the variability identification increased when we included more products in the comparison. This happens because, with more products, more configurations are analyzed. By analyzing all the feature combinations, it is possible to guarantee the detection of all the optional components and provide a reliable PLA.

Moreover, after a certain number of comparisons, the value of the metrics became constant. For instance, we compared 18 products aiming to recover all the variability details of the Zip Me SPL. We observed the same pattern on other SPL projects. For example, it was necessary to compare 17 products to recover all the variability details of the VOD SPL.

As the PLA recovery process examined and merged more products, the set of components and relations that comprise the PLA and metrics values tends to stabilize. The set of products (after the metrics stabilization) had a mandatory structure, with variations present in low-level details. We also identified this pattern when we analyzed the CRR values with different combination of products in the recovery.

Moreover, to answer the RQ1, in the first stage of the analysis, we performed a correlation analysis among the variables of the exploratory study (see Fig. 12.8). We identified a positive correlation (represented by the blue circles—darker colors represent stronger correlation) between the number of products and the metrics

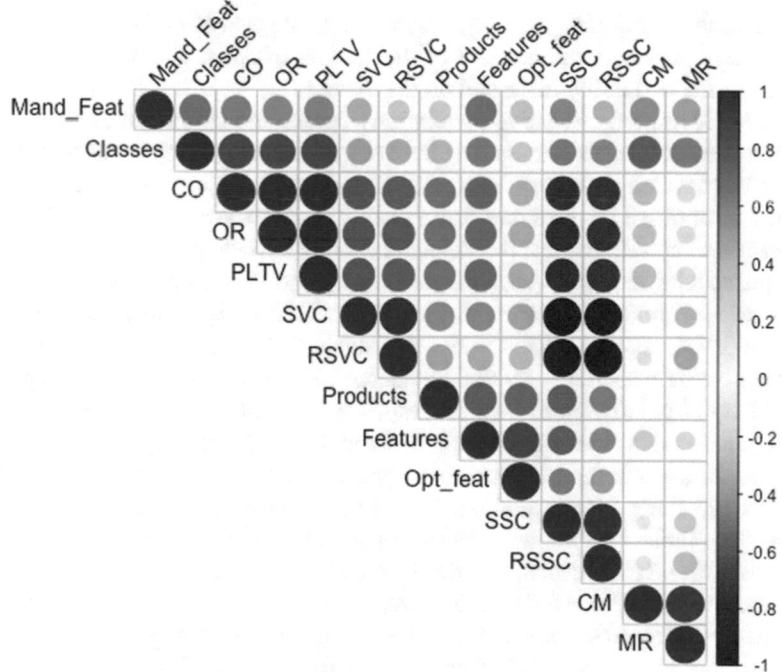

Fig. 12.8 Correlation analysis

Table 12.7 Comparisons
that rejected the null
hypothesis RQ1

Comparison	p-value
Products-CO	7.0e−03
Products-OR	7.0e−03
Products-PLTV	7.0e−03
Products-SVC	2.0e−02
Products-OF	2.0e−03

Table 12.8 Comparisons
that rejected the null
hypothesis RQ2

ID	Comparison	p-value
40	Elevator-DesktopSearcher	2.3e−03
43	GOL-DesktopSearcher	4.4e−02
49	VOD-DesktopSearcher	2.1e−03
50	ZipMe-DesktopSearcher	1.5e−03
57	Prop4J-Elevator	4.0e−05
74	Prop4J-ExamDB	1.9e−02
81	Propo4J-GOL	8.0e−04
92	Prop4J-PayCard	2.2e−02
96	Prop4J-PokerSPL	4.4e−02
100	UnionFind-Prop4J	1.9−e02
101	VOD-Prop4J	7.0e−05
102	ZipMe-Prop4J	4.0e−05

addressing the variability (CO, OR, PLTV, SVC, and number of optional features) which means that with the increase of the number of optional features we have an increase in the variability identified on the PLA.

We also identified a negative correlation (represented by the red circles—darker colors represent weaker correlation) between the number of optional features and the metrics related to commonality (SSC and RSC) which means that with the increase of optional features that commonality tends to decrease. Table 12.7 shows the *Spearman* correlation test that rejected the null hypothesis.

In the second research question, we investigated if *there is a relation between the number of optional features in the SPL and the component reuse rate of the recovered PLA*, we used the ANOVA (Analysis of Variance) to test the variables and the p-value was $1.3e-07$. Such evidence allows to reject the null hypothesis (H_{0a}) of equal population means. Therefore, it is possible to conclude that at least one PLA has CRR values significantly different from the others.

To identify the different means, we applied the Tukey test. We performed and analyzed 105 comparisons, and only 12 of them presented statistically significant differences. Table 12.8 shows p-values of the comparisons that rejected the null hypothesis (the SPLs involved in the test, and the p-value). Based on such data, we identified that Prop4J (in eight comparisons) and DesktopSearcher (in four comparisons) yielded statistical difference in CRR values among the PLAs.

According to the correlation analysis performed (see Fig. 12.8), the use of optional features impact the CRR values of the PLA by decreasing the commonality and increasing the variability. Configuring a product with optional features implies in the appearance of new classes associated with these features. Meaning that there will be new optional components in the product architecture, that are often associated with specific product configurations.

12.4.6 General Findings

Correlation Between Metrics From the overall results for the fifteen SPL projects, we noticed that when the value of SSC was high, the PLA components presented high CRR values as well. This may be a preliminary evidence for a correlation between SSC and CRR metrics.

Some Metrics Provided Support for Other Metrics The quantitative metrics CM and CO counted the number of classes implementing mandatory features and optional features. They confirmed the SSC and SVC metrics values. Moreover, ClassVP and ComponentVariable indicated if a given class or component presented a variability.CM, CO, ClassVP and ComponentVariable provided support for the SSC, SVC, and CRR metrics. The former validated and confirmed the values of the latter.

Feature Scattering and Component Reuse Rate In projects with metrics high values (Zip Me, VOD, and GOL respectively), the classes outnumbered the features, with feature scattering in a significant amount of classes. To perform this analysis, we verified how the feature selection to build each product was spread through the source code manually and compared to the metrics collected by the PLAR. The relation between feature scattering and high CRR deserves further investigation.

Select a Relevant Product of the Subset During the study execution, we identified subgroups with the same architecture. For this reason, instead of generating/selecting all the SPL products, we should select only one product of the subset. In other words, by doing this, we reduce the time of product generation and the effort of analyzing every product.

12.4.7 Threats to Validity

The following threats to validity are discussed to reveal their potential interference with our study design.

Internal Validity PLAR tool limitations [4] may have impacted the results of the exploratory study. For instance, the input for PLAR tool is a MDG file created by STAN4J and Analizo. The extracted MDG only supports "call" dependencies between modules. Inheritance relationships are not extracted.

External Validity No industrial SPL projects were used in the study; only open source SPL projects were used. To minimize such a threat, we analyzed projects widely-accepted by SPL research community, which have been used as testbeds for empirical evaluations [19].

Construct Validity The recovered PLA from the SPL projects were not verified by SPL developers. To minimize this threat, we performed a manual PLA extraction, which served as an oracle. Then, we compared the number of optional and mandatory elements obtained by PLAR tool according to the oracle. The results indicated that there was no difference in the number of elements detected.

Conclusion Validity The metrics SSC and CRR present an overview of the mandatory and optional components of a PLA by showing the presence of the components among all the products. However, low-level granularity variability in the components, such as optional with different values and different methods implementation, are not covered by these metrics. This information can give a different perspective about the CRR.

12.5   Related Work

Wu et al. [32] presented a semi-automatic PLA recovery approach. The authors defined measures to detect similarity and variability points on software products source code of the same domain to migrate to SPL. The study reports on a case study. The assumption is that legacy products of a same domain have similar designs and implementation that can be used to build a SPL. In our approach, we build the PLA from the products generated by the SPL project.

Losavio et al. [20] proposed a reactive refactoring bottom-up process to build a PLA from existing similar software product architectures of a domain. The main assets were expressed by UML logical views. The work is focused on the construction and representation of a candidate PLA followed by an optimization process to obtain the final PLA. The refactoring process was applied to a case study in the robotics industry domain. The focus of our work is the assessment of recovered PLA based on metrics analysis.

Torkamani [31] presents a novel SPL quality attribute for called Extractability. The attribute is calculated based on the weight of the reusable component over the weight of all components, a process similar to the CRR metric calculation. Extractability effectiveness on six SPLs from a iranian telecommunication company was evaluated in practice. In our study, we analyzed SPLs from different domains.

Shatnawi et al. [25] proposed an approach to PLA recovery that focused on the comparison of components (classes and interfaces) recovered from different versions of the same SPL. Our study did not use different variants derived from an already existing SPL. Instead, several variants from the same domain were used as input to our approach. For each variant, we extracted structural information from source code and collected information about variability found within classes, packages, and their relationships.

Linsbauer et al. [19] presented an approach for extracting information from sets of related product variants (structural information from SPL products source code) for recovering a feature model for the SPL. Our approach supports the extraction of structural information from the source code of sets of related variants. However, we focused on recovering the PLA for the SPL.

12.6   Conclusion

PLA recovery provides useful information for SPL developers and architects, to support maintenance and understand the implementation of SPL variability and improve the reuse. The recovered PLA components and their relationships can serve as a basis for different types of visualization that describe variability in architectural level, and for different types of analysis (e.g., identification of components that are more likely to be reused, propagation analysis during the implementation of reuse changes).

In this chapter, we presented our PLA recovery approach and the results of an exploratory study to assess the recovered PLAs from 15 open source SPL projects implemented in Java. The PLAR tool was used to support PLA recovery with the identification of commonality and variation points.

Eleven out of fifteen recovered PLAs had high CRR values indicating high reuse of components during the SPL development phase. The results provided evidence regarding a correlation between the metrics values and the components reuse rate. We aim to replicate this study by including more SPL projects to strengthen the evidence base.

As future work, we intend to automate the selection of only one relevant product of each subset. We intend to evolve the PLAR tool to address some limitations and extend the exploratory study by including more projects in the analysis.

Acknowledgments The authors would like to thank the anonymous reviewers for the thorough feedback. This work is partially supported by FAPESB grants BOL1564/2015, BOL2443/2016 and JCB0060/2016, and INES, grant CNPq/465614/2014-0.

References

1. Ahmed, F., Capretz, L.F.: The software product line architecture: An empirical investigation of key process activities. Inf. Softw. Technol. **50**(11), 1098–1113 (2008)
2. Apel, S., Batory, D., Kstner, C., Saake, G.: Feature-Oriented Software Product Lines: Concepts and Implementation. Springer (2013)

3. Bosch, J., Capilla, R.: Variability Implementation, pp. 75–86. Springer (2013)
4. Cardoso, M.P.S., Lima, C., von Flach Garcia Chavez, C., do Carmo Machado, I.: PLAR Tool - A Sofware Product Line Architecture Recovery Tool. In: 8th Brazilian Conference on Software: Theory and Practice - Tools Session, pp. 18–22 (2017)
5. Chen, L., Ali Babar, M.: A systematic review of evaluation of variability management approaches in software product lines. Inf. Softw. Technol. **53**(4), 344–362 (2011)
6. Clements, P., Garlan, D., Bass, L., Stafford, J., Nord, R., Ivers, J., Little, R.: Documenting Software Architectures: Views and Beyond. Pearson Education (2002)
7. Dubinsky, Y., Rubin, J., Berger, T., Duszynski, S., Becker, M., Czarnecki, K.: An exploratory study of cloning in industrial software product lines. In: Proceedings of the 2013 17th European Conference on Software Maintenance and Reengineering, pp. 25–34. IEEE Computer Society, Washington, DC, USA (2013)
8. Ducasse, S., Pollet, D.: Software Architecture Reconstruction: A Process-Oriented Taxonomy. IEEE Transactions on Software Engineering **35**(4), 573–591 (2009)
9. Galster, M., Avgeriou, P.: Handling variability in software architecture: Problems and implications. In: Proceedings of the 2011 Ninth Working IEEE/IFIP Conference on Software Architecture, pp. 171–180. IEEE Computer Society (2011)
10. Galster, M., Avgeriou, P.: The notion of variability in software architecture: Results from a preliminary exploratory study. In: Proceedings of the 5th Workshop on Variability Modeling of Software-Intensive Systems, pp. 59–67. ACM (2011)
11. Galster, M., Weyns, D., Avgeriou, P., Becker, M.: Variability in software architecture: views and beyond. SIGSOFT Softw. Eng. Notes **37**(6), 1–9 (2013)
12. Gomaa, H.: Designing Software Product Lines with UML: From Use Cases to Pattern-Based Software Architectures. Addison Wesley Longman Publishing Co., Inc. (2004)
13. Henard, C., Papadakis, M., Perrouin, G., Klein, J., Heymans, P., Traon, Y.L.: Bypassing the combinatorial explosion: Using similarity to generate and prioritize t-wise test configurations for software product lines. IEEE Transactions on Software Engineering **40**(7), 650–670 (2014)
14. Hilliard, R.: On representing variation. In: 1st International Workshop on Variability in Software Product Line Architectures. ACM (2010)
15. Holmes, R., Walker, R.J.: Systematizing pragmatic software reuse. ACM Transactions on Software Engineering and Methodology **21**(4), 20:1–20:44 (2013)
16. Lima, C., Assunção, W.K.G., Martinez, J., do Carmo Machado, I., von Flach G. Chavez, C., Mendonça, W.D.F.: Towards an automated product line architecture recovery: The apo-games case study. In: VII Brazilian Symposium on Software Components, Architectures, and Reuse, SBCARS '18, pp. 33–42. ACM (2018)
17. Lima-Neto, C.R., Cardoso, M.P.S., von Flach Garcia Chavez, C., de Almeida, E.S.: Initial evidence for understanding the relationship between product line architecture and software architecture recovery. In: IX Brazilian Symposium on Components, Architectures and Reuse Software, pp. 40–49 (2015)
18. Linden, F.J.v.d., Schmid, K., Rommes, E.: Software Product Lines in Action: The Best Industrial Practice in Product Line Engineering. Springer-Verlag (2007)
19. Linsbauer, L., Lopez-Herrejon, R.E., Egyed, A.: Variability extraction and modeling for product variants. Software & Systems Modeling (2016)
20. Losavio, F., Ordaz, O., Levy, N., Baiotto, A.: Graph modelling of a refactoring process for product line architecture design. In: XXXIX Latin American Computing Conference (CLEI), pp. 1–12 (2013)
21. Mancoridis, S., Mitchell, B.S., Chen, Y., Gansner, E.R.: Bunch: A clustering tool for the recovery and maintenance of software system structures. In: IEEE International Conference on Software Maintenance, pp. 50–59. IEEE (1999)
22. Oliveira-Junior, E.A., Gimenes, I., Maldonado, J.: A metric suite to support software product line architecture evaluation. In: XXXIV Conferencia Latinoamericana de Informatica, pp. 489–498 (2008)
23. Pohl, K., Böckle, G., Linden, F.J.v.d.: Software Product Line Engineering: Foundations, Principles and Techniques. Springer-Verlag (2005)

24. Shatnawi, A., Seriai, A., Sahraoui, H.: Recovering architectural variability of a family of product variants. In: Software Reuse for Dynamic Systems in the Cloud and Beyond: 14th International Conference on Software Reuse, pp. 17–33. Springer (2014)
25. Shatnawi, A., Seriai, A.D., Sahraoui, H.: Recovering software product line architecture of a family of object-oriented product variants. Journal of Systems and Software (2016)
26. van Solingen, R., Basili, V., Caldiera, G., Rombach, H.D.: Goal question metric (gqm) approach. In: Encyclopedia of Software Engineering. John Wiley & Sons, Inc. (2002)
27. Stavropoulou, I., Grigoriou, M., Kontogiannis, K.: Case study on which relations to use for clustering-based software architecture recovery. Empirical Software Engineering 22(4), 1717–1762 (2017)
28. Svahnberg, M., van Gurp, J., Bosch, J.: A taxonomy of variability realization techniques: Research articles. Softw. Pract. Exper. 35(8), 705–754 (2005)
29. Thiel, S., Hein, A.: Modeling and using product line variability in automotive systems. IEEE Softw. 19(4), 66–72 (2002)
30. Thüm, T., Kästner, C., Benduhn, F., Meinicke, J., Saake, G., Leich, T.: Featureide: An extensible framework for feature-oriented software development. Science of Computer Programming 79, 70–85 (2014)
31. Torkamani, M.A.: Extractability effectiveness on software product line. International Journal of Electrical and Computer Engineering 4(1), 127 (2014)
32. Wu, Y., Yang, Y., Peng, X., Qiu, C., Zhao, W.: Recovering object-oriented framework for software product line reengineering. In: Proceedings of the 12th International Conference on Top Productivity Through Software Reuse, pp. 119–134. Springer-Verlag (2011)
33. Zhang, T., Deng, L., Wu, J., Zhou, Q., Ma, C.: Some metrics for accessing quality of product line architecture. In: International Conference on Computer Science and Software Engineering, vol. 2, pp. 500–503. IEEE (2008)

Part III
Frameworks

Chapter 13
PAxSPL: A Framework for Aiding SPL Reengineering Planning

Luciano Marchezan, Elder Rodrigues, João Carbonell, Maicon Bernardino, Fábio Paulo Basso, and Wesley K. G. Assunção

Abstract Among the approaches to develop Software Product Lines (SPL), the extractive approach is adopted when the company has a set of similar systems that are analyzed to extract, categorize, and group their features throughout the SPL reengineering process. However, SPL reengineering scenarios differ due to different variables, such as the experience of the developers and product portfolios. Due to this diversity of options, rigorous planning of the reengineering process is critical to perform SPL reengineering. To create a planning framework to allow customization, we sought in the literature and analyzed SPL reengineering processes. We defined the Prepare, Assemble, and Execute Framework for SPL Reengineering (PAxSPL). PAxSPL aids the SPL reengineering planning by providing flexibility concerning artifacts, strategies, and techniques used for feature retrieval. This flexibility is given by allowing the choice and combination of different techniques for feature retrieval based on company related information. We conducted a case study to collect exploratory evidence about PAxSPL application into ten different products, generated from an organization's real development environment. The results indicated that our proposal helps in the assembly of a feature retrieval process according to user's needs. Furthermore, we collected evidence about the reusability of SPL assets when re-executing the reengineering process in a similar scenario.

L. Marchezan (✉)
Institute of Software Systems Engineering - Johannes Kepler University Linz, Linz, Austria
e-mail: luciano.marchezan_de_paula@jku.at

E. Rodrigues · J. Carbonell · M. Bernardino · F. P. Basso
Laboratory of Empirical Studies in Software Engineering - Federal University of Pampa, Alegrete, Brazil
e-mail: elderrodrigues@unipampa.edu.br; bernardino@acm.org; fabiobasso@unipampa.edu.br

W. K. G. Assunção (✉)
Pontifical Catholic University of Rio de Janeiro, Rio de Janeiro, Brazil

Johannes Kepler University of Linz, Linz, Austria
e-mail: wesley.assuncao@jku.at

© Springer Nature Switzerland AG 2023   319
R. E. Lopez-Herrejon et al. (eds.), *Handbook of Re-Engineering Software Intensive Systems into Software Product Lines*, https://doi.org/10.1007/978-3-031-11686-5_13

13.1 Introduction

The increasing demand for quality of software products and the concern of software development companies in lowering project costs has led to the emergence of software engineering solutions such as Software Product Line Engineering (SPLE) [51]. While several systems are now being developed from scratch (proactively) as a Software Product Line (SPL), there are still those that emerge when a company has one or more software products and wants to create an SPL out of them. Then, the extractive SPL approach [31] may be used to transform such existing software products into an SPL. This approach uses the SPL reengineering process to take several product variants and transform them into an SPL with the use of techniques, methods, and tools [6].

For companies to achieve their goals with SPL reengineering, a well-defined reengineering process is paramount. In this way, a proper process to reengineer variants into SPLs is a relevant contribution to the SPLE research field because it may reduce the effort of planning the SPL reengineering. A conventional scenario is, for example, a company that possesses an Enterprise Resource Planning (ERP) [42] system, which was developed as traditional software. As the system scope increases, the company developed and included new features to meet the needs of multiple clients. In some cases, clients may not desire all features, only a specific group. A possible solution here is to migrate the already developed system into an SPL through the application of SPL reengineering. ERP in SPL scenarios can be found in several works from the literature [16, 24, 35, 44, 47, 53]. In this SPL reengineering scenarios, the development team might not have any experience with both SPL or reengineering. In addition, the system documentation is usually outdated, and there are few artifacts available to be analyzed, mostly the source code.

A solution that is customizable according to this possible scenario may be relevant because, for instance, if the system possesses source code as an available artifact, the approach used to perform feature retrieval must give support to this artifact as a source of information. The experience of the team of practitioners that will perform the reengineering should also be considered. Also, there are additional possible scenarios to represent this problem. What if a part of the system source code could not be analyzed for some reason and the reengineering must be performed considering requirements and class diagrams only? All these concerns could be addressed by proper planning before, during, and after the SPL reengineering.

In this chapter, we present **P**repare, **A**ssemble and **Ex**ecute Framework for SPL Reengineering (PAxSPL) [37]. PAxSPL is a methodological framework with technical guidelines designed to give support to SPL reengineering planning by aiding the user on the preparation, assembly, and execution of feature retrieval. PAxSPL's goal is to assemble different feature retrieval processes for different scenarios, aiming at leveraging a high level of reuse. Our framework intent is to provide flexibility with regard to artifacts, strategies, and techniques used for feature retrieval. This flexibility is given by allowing the choice and combination of different techniques for feature retrieval based on information gathered during the framework execution. This information includes: team experiences and skills, domain engineering artifacts, requirements artifacts, product artifact types and extensions, and technologies used to develop the products. In addition, we created a set of guidelines to help PAxSPL users when performing our framework to choose the techniques that better fit their situation. More specifically, we discuss how we conceptualize the PAxSPL framework and evaluated it in a case study.

The case study was conducted to initially evaluate PAxSPL, we aimed to measure the effort required and impact of performing feature retrieval using our framework. The case study results indicated that our proposal helps the assembly of a feature retrieval process according to the user's needs. We also observed the relevance level of each artifact generated during the reengineering. Furthermore, we analyzed which activities of our framework demanded more effort from the participants. Lastly, we collected information about which artifacts generated during the case study could be reused when re-executing PAxSPL in a similar scenario with different products. This information was used for analyzing the reusability of PAxSPL artifacts.

The remainder of this chapter is structured as follows: Sect. 13.2 presents the background and related work; Sect. 13.3 presents the motivation, and details the PAxSPL framework, describing the process and guidelines for executing it; Sect. 13.4 presents a case study performed to collect exploratory evidence about PAxSPL applicability in a real scenario; lastly, Sect. 13.5 presents our conclusion remarks.

13.2 Background and Related Work

In this section, we describe SPLs and the re-engineering planning process to develop SPLs using an extractive approach. We also discuss similar works and their relation to PAxSPL.

13.2.1 Software Product Lines and Reengineering Process

There are three possible approaches to develop SPL [31]: proactive, reactive, and extractive. By using the *proactive approach*, a company plans, analyzes, designs, and develops a complete SPL including the whole scope of their products at once. With the *reactive approach*, the company incrementally develops an SPL to reach the demand for new products or emerging new requirements. An *extractive approach* can be applied when the company already has a set of system variants to be used as a starting point for the SPLE. The variants are the main source of information to identify and extract the commonalities and the variabilities. The extractive adoption of SPLs is employed by a reengineering process [6, 34]. This process is composed of three high-level phases [6]: (i) *detection*, when variabilities and commonalities among variants, represented in the form of features, are identified and extracted throughout the use of feature retrieval techniques; (ii) *analysis*, the information extracted is used to design and organize the features in a variability model, usually an FM; (iii) *transformation*, variant artifacts linked to the features, such as source code and requirements list, are refactored/modified to include variability mechanisms and create the SPL. The reengineering process may be conducted by practitioners with different expertise/experience, using different artifacts, strategies, and techniques. This lead to a variety of possible strategies for different scenarios. This variety, however, increases the complexity of the reengineering. In this sense, collecting and analyzing organizational and technical information for planning the reengineering may aid users when deciding which strategy is more adequate to their scenario. Thus, we define the SPL reengineering planning process.

13.2.2 SPL Reengineering Planning

The SPL reengineering planning includes the reengineering phases of the process defined by Assunção et al. [6], which were presented in the previous subsection. However, we expand on their process by including activities before and after the reengineering. The inclusion of these activities is needed due to the lack of flexibility for considering organizational aspects. By considering these aspects before, during, and after the reengineering (instead of only during the reengineering as in the traditional SPL reengineering process [6]), we aim to address the flexibility problem as decisions can be customized for diverse scenarios.

The basis for our SPL reengineering planning process, is the main workflow of the Prepare, Assemble and Execute (PAxSPL) framework [37, 38] (The details of the workflow are presented in Sect. 13.3). PAxSPL was proposed to support feature retrieval for SPL reengineering planning. This support is done by aiding the decisions related to the selection of strategies and techniques for feature retrieval based on technical and organizational aspects. This characterizes the SPL reengineering planning discussed earlier.

13.2.3 Motivational Scenarios

As discussed in the literature [10, 11], several challenges arise when developing SPL in organizational scenarios.[1] In this sense, when performing the reengineering of legacy systems, companies may face different challenges understanding and dealing

---

[1] In this chapter, we consider an organizational scenario to be "a certain group of engineers, having a set of system variants, knowing a specific set of techniques for analyzing features from a determined set of artifacts".

with features being extracted and modeled [25]. For illustration purposes, we can find a variety of scenarios in the ESPLA catalog [39]. One of these scenarios is presented by Eyal-Salman et al. [20], in which object-oriented (OO) source code is used for extracting features by applying three different retrieval techniques, namely FCA [50], LSI [17], and clustering [26]. Another scenario is presented by Acher et al. [1] that uses dependency analysis [30], structural similarity, and clustering as techniques for retrieving architectural FM from plugin dependencies. Although both strategies were useful for their respective scenarios, their proposals can only be used in other scenarios that share the same characteristics. These characteristics being the artifacts available (OO source code for [20] and plugin dependencies for [1]) and retrieval techniques.

In such a situation, a flexible SPL reengineering planning process may address the aforementioned characteristics of distinct scenarios. This process should allow collecting and analyzing the company information, e.g., both technical and organizational. This information can leverage understanding and conducting feature detection, analysis, and transformation. By applying such a process, a company may address the limitations of the SPL reengineering considering the organizational boundaries. We defined PAxSPL with this goal in mind. Our framework is detailed in Sect. 13.3.

13.2.4   Related Work

In this section, we present related work and discuss how PAxSPL differs from them.

Studies on Feature Retrieval studies proposing processes for feature retrieval in SPL reengineering usually focus on technical aspects and few artifacts, namely requirements, design, and source code. Requirements artifacts are used in several studies [1, 9, 40, 46], being one of the most common artifacts amongst the approaches as mapped in Assunção et al. [6]. Design models are used as input in [1, 33, 41], while source code is used in [20, 23, 28, 40]. Source code is the most used artifact for retrieving features. Domain information, however, is only used in a few studies [2, 7, 22]. This type of information may be more related to organizational than technical aspects, corroborating with our argument that such information is usually not considered when planning the reengineering. Although these approaches use different types of artifacts, their flexibility is still limited. For instance, in Bécan et al. [9] requirement artifacts are mandatory for the reengineering. This hinders the customization as scenarios where requirements are not available or outdated may not apply this approach. The approach presented in Martinez et al. [40], however, was designed to be generic regarding the artifact types, allowing the integration of new artifact types. However, this approach does not consider organizational aspects by default, as done in PAxSPL.

Customization for Different Scenarios the customization considering different scenarios and contexts allows the scalability of the approaches considering different organizational scenarios. This customization is present in approaches such as PuLSE-Eco [49]. PuLSE-Eco is part of the PuLSE framework [15], supporting SPL scoping. PuLSE-Eco allows the customization of its components. Another work, presented in Alsawalqah et al. [4], defines a set of rules for different scenarios. Their approach handles scoping costs according to the current scenario, thus, making their approach customizable. In comparison, PAxSPL offers a generic feature retrieval process as well as specific activities to collect organizational information. Furthermore, Kruger et al. [32] defined Promote-pl, a process model for adopting and evolving product lines defined based on the analysis of the literature and collaborations with industry. Promote-pl is a high level process model, that can be used for guiding users when applying SPL reengineering. In comparison to PAxSPL, however, Promote-pl does not present guidelines detailing reengineering techniques and how they may be assembled to retrieve, group and categorize features from system variants.

Furthermore, we have works that consider economical aspects of the SPL reengineering, such as cost models [13, 43] and market analysis[8]. Although PAxSPL does not focus on the economical part of SPL reengineering, we plan to evolve our framework to give support to these economical aspects in the future.

13.3 PAxSPL Framework

This section presents the motivation and details of PAxSPL framework. Our framework is composed of a process and a set of guidelines created for aiding its execution.

PAxSPL framework was defined with the goal of providing a mechanism addressing the limitations discussed in Sect. 13.2.3.

13.3.1 Process Overview

In this section, we present and detail each PAxSPL phase and activity.

13.3.1.1 Prepare

To prepare the process assembly, the information is collected in the first phase of PAxSPL.[2] The first activity is, therefore, to Collect Team Information, as

---

[2] PAxSPL is presented by using the Business Process Model and Notation (BPMN), all the figures presented in this section related with PAxSPL activities were created using BPMN 2.0 https://www.omg.org/spec/BPMN/2.0/.

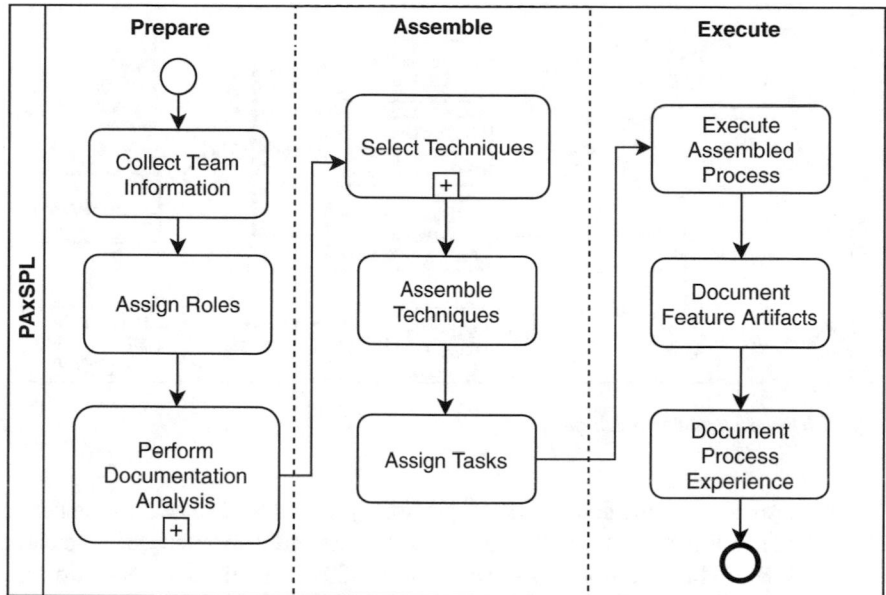

Fig. 13.1 PAxSPL main workflow

Fig. 13.1 illustrates. During this activity, information about the team is collected. This information includes the experience, skills, knowledge, and preferences of each member. The second activity is `Assign Roles` based on the information collected on the previous activity. Possible roles are: Domain Engineer, Analyst, Architect, and Developer. These roles are related with the following sub-process, which is `Perform Documentation Analysis`. Here, domain information, constraints, and glossary are collected by the `Domain Engineer`. This activity allows the user to collect and analyze information regarding SPL scoping, such as descriptions of domain models and reuse benefits and risks. Requirements information of the products is gathered by the `Analyst`. Information about architecture and artifacts is registered by the `Architect`. Also, the `Developer` may document technologies and development information. The main contribution of `Prepare` is the generation of a `Documentation Set`, composed of artifacts and information used during the `Assemble` phase. These artifacts may include product architecture, requirements, domain information, and team information. Some artifacts have a higher level of impact when choosing a technique, but they all must be used to assemble the process.

13.3.1.2   Assemble

In this phase, the information collected is analyzed and techniques are selected and assembled into the generic process. The first sub-process is to `Select`

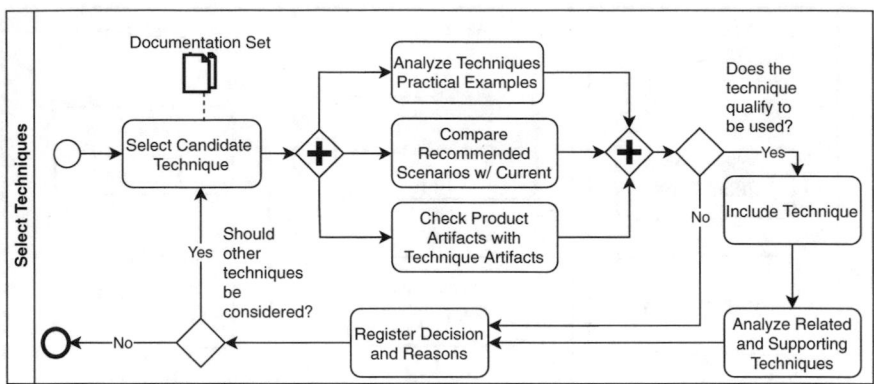

Fig. 13.2 Select techniques sub-process

`Techniques`, here, the data collected previously is analyzed to help the selection of techniques for feature retrieval (Fig. 13.2). First, a candidate technique is selected to be analyzed. This selection is made based on artifacts from the documentation set, e.g., team members experience with the technique. After the candidate technique is selected, it must be analyzed considering three points: (i) practical examples, which are examples of the technique found in the literature; (ii) a comparison among techniques recommended scenarios with current scenario, also found in the literature. The users should analyze whether their scenario contains some similarity in comparison with the scenarios on which the technique was used; (iii) users should check available product artifacts with technique artifacts, for instance, if a technique uses requirements artifacts, this type of artifact should be available. Based on the analysis performed considering those three points, the user must decide to use the techniques or not. If the technique qualifies to be used, it is included as a selected technique, then related and support techniques are analyzed to decide whether they may be candidate techniques. The decision of including or not the technique must be registered along with its reasons. If another technique is considered a candidate, then the process repeats.

The second activity is `Assemble Techniques`. In this activity, the chosen techniques are assembled inside our generic process, shown in Fig. 13.3. The generic process consists of the main activities performed during the feature retrieval process considering the literature mapped during our process creation. `Extract`, `Categorize` and `Group` are basic activities performed with the features prior to the creation of the feature model. After the end of each activity, we placed a check gateway, implying to the user that some kind of checking may be performed before moving to the next activity. The assembled process will be customized according to the scenario where PAxSPL has been applied, giving our process flexibility to be applied in different situations. To help the assembly of techniques, we created in the guidelines what we call a *priority order* attribute for each technique. This attribute shows in which step of our generic process each feature retrieval technique may best

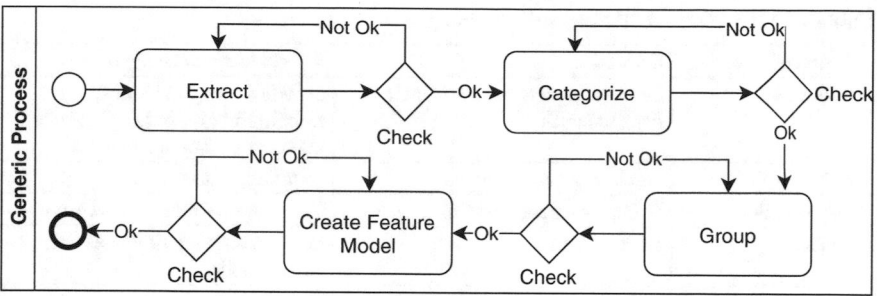

Fig. 13.3 The generic process for feature retrieval

Table 13.1 Excerpt from the guidelines checklist showing the questions related to the assemble techniques activity

Assemble techniques checklist
Is the technique priority to be assembled for extraction?
Is the technique priority to be assembled for categorization?
Is the technique priority to be assembled for group?
Are there techniques assembled for the three first activities (extract, categorize or group) of the generic process?

fit. An example of assembled process is to use FCA for extracting and categorizing features, clustering for grouping and refining them, and expert driven knowledge for validating the features, thus enabling the creation of a FM. This example briefly describes the assembled process (Fig. 13.5) generated during the case study reported on Sect. 13.4. Furthermore, the user can rely on the our supporting checklist for aiding the process execution. Table 13.1 presents part of our support checklists with the questions related to the assemble techniques activity.

The last `Assemble` activity is `Assign Tasks` where each member of the team will receive a task to perform during the retrieval process execution. These tasks are not directly related with the roles used during the `Perform Documentation Analysis` activity, they are related to the retrieval tasks (e.g., extract features). In this case, one member may perform more than one task and a task can be performed by multiple members.

13.3.1.3 Execute

During this phase, see Fig. 13.1, the feature retrieval is performed and the feature artifacts are collected. The first activity is `Execute Assembled Process`, where the assembled process is executed to detect, extract, categorize, and group the features according to the selected techniques. The second activity is `Document Feature Artifacts`, here, artifacts are documented in a structured

Table 13.2 Guideline for the clustering technique

Technique	Clustering	Formal concept analysis
Definition	Group elements based on their dependencies	Provides a way to identify meaningful groupings of objects that have common attributes
Variations	Agglomerative; divisive	Clarified; reduced
Priority order	Group >Extraction >Categorize	Extraction >Categorize >Group
Inputs	Source code	Source code; requirements list; design models
Outputs	Feature tree; feature clusters; dendrogram tree	Concept lattice
Tools	Cluster 3.0; pycluster; C clustering library	Concept explorer; galicia; FCAStone; lattice miner
Related techniques	Formal concept analysis	Clustering; latent semantic indexing
Recommended situations	Products with high level of dependencies among feature implementations	Products where elements have meaningful names
Examples	[5, 12, 14, 21, 29, 45, 52]	[3, 18, 20, 21, 54, 55]

way according to the techniques selected. Artifacts may be variability reports, feature descriptions, data dictionaries among others. Lastly, reports are created to document the experience of the process execution during the `Document Process Experience` activity. These reports may be used in future re-execution of the process (e.g., when new features emerge from clients demand, or for different software products of the same organization), reducing cost and effort.

13.3.2   Guidelines

By analyzing other SPL reengineering approaches, mapping the used strategies and artifacts, we created a set of guidelines. These guidelines contain support documentation to help to choose techniques, describe each one, give examples, supporting tools, define recommended scenarios and give a prioritization assemble order when assembling a technique into the generic process, as Table 13.2 shows. In the large amount of information found in the guidelines section of our process, we included a basic introduction to SPL and its main concepts. We also provided information about variability management and feature model notations and tools.

We only present two example of this description. More guidelines can be found in PAxSPL documentation.[3] The examples and recommended situations for each technique were collected by analyzing information mapped in [6]. With this

---

[3] https://github.com/HestiaProject/PAxSPL/wiki/Guidelines.

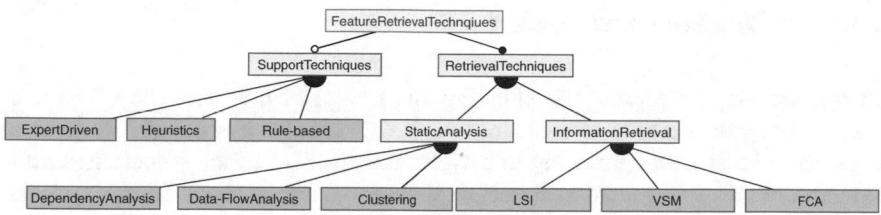

Fig. 13.4 A feature model of retrieval techniques. LSI—Latent semantic indexing; VSM—Vector space model; FCA—Formal concept analysis

documentation, we intend to give as much help as possible for the team to make the best decisions when selecting the techniques for feature retrieval. We also created a feature model of feature retrieval techniques that formalizes possible techniques and makes it possible to calculate how many different combinations can be chosen. As illustrated in Fig. 13.4,[4] we grouped the techniques based on their strategy. We have the mandatory group of Retrieval Techniques which are composed of two Or-alternatives (at least one must be selected), Static Analysis, and Information Retrieval. For Static Analysis, we have three Or-alternatives: Dependency Analysis, Data-Flow analysis, and Clustering. For Information Retrieval we also have three Or-alternatives: Latent Semantic Indexing (LSI), Vector Space Model (VSM), and Formal Concept Analysis (FCA). The second group is optional, composed of three supporting techniques: Expert Driven, Rule-Based, and Heuristics. Based on the selection of the techniques, the user would assemble them into the generic process for feature retrieval and analysis, shown in Fig. 13.3. As stated, the generic process is used to tailor the assembled process that generates the extracted features and the feature model [27].

13.4 Case Study

To evaluate PAxSPL, we conducted a case study in a real development environment to collect evidence about PAxSPL when applied in a company willing to conduct the reengineering process. We also collected evidence about the reuse capability provided by PAxSPL when performed in a different scenario. As an exploratory evaluation, this case study focused on qualitative results rather than quantitative. Thereby we formulated our objectives and data collection mechanisms.

---

[4] Dynamic analysis techniques are not being considered in this version of PAxSPL and will be included in future work.

13.4.1 Planning and Design

In this section, we present the planning and design of the case study. The main goal of the case study is to evaluate how PAxSPL helps a team with little or no experience in SPL reengineering to perform the planning of the process in a set of system variants. We wanted to collect exploratory evidence about the most relevant PAxSPL artifacts, effort to apply PAxSPL, and PAxSP'L reuse capability when re-applied in a different scenario. Based on this goal, we conducted the case study with the following objectives:

OBJ1. Analyze the impact and relevance of the artifacts generated by PAxSPL execution in terms of reengineering.

OBJ2. Measure the effort needed to perform each PAxSPL phase and activity.

OBJ3. Analyze PAxSPL reuse capability.

The impact/relevance of the artifacts generated during PAxSPL execution is measured in terms of the reengineering process (OBJ1). We measured how many times and in which activities each artifact was used. We also inquired participants about their opinion of each artifact's relevance/impact when choosing techniques for feature retrieval. The effort comparison of each phase (OBJ2) was analyzed in terms of: time spent to learn concepts needed to perform feature retrieval and analyze product documentation (`Prepare` phase); time spent to select techniques and assemble them before retrieving the features (`Assemble` phase); and time spent to perform the retrieval techniques and generate the feature artifacts (`Execute` phase); also, we considered the complexity of each activity regarding the partici-pants' opinion. To gather information for OBJ3, we considered which artifacts could be reused without any modification. We also considered the participants' opinions about artifacts reusability. To maintain the artifacts quality level for both phases, we considered artifacts quality scores from both phases when comparing the reusability results.

The ERP company owns a web-based ERP called ICode. ICode can be used for managing the registration of customers, suppliers, tax accounts, finances, schedules, products, sales, and electronic invoice generation. The system was developed using a modular architecture, composed of six different modules: registration, taxation, finances, e-invoice, schedule, and requests.

ICode was developed with Java, and its version is composed of more than two hundred Java classes (with an average of two hundred lines of code per class) and has a database with more than sixty tables. The company attends to more than fifty clients and distributes different configurations (products) of ICode according to their needs. For instance, a product may have three modules (*Registration, Finance, and Schedule*). However, this product configuration is performed in a non-systematic way. These characteristics indicate that ICode has the potential to become an SPL, being a good scenario for this case study. Therefore we decided to observe how the software engineers would perform the feature retrieval using PAxSPL.

Table 13.3 ICode modules present in each product

Modules	Used on both phases					Used only on Phase 2				
	Pd1	Pd2	Pd3	Pd4	Pd5	Pd6	Pd7	Pd8	Pd9	Pd10
Registration	✓	✓	✓	✓	✓	✓	✓	✓	✓	✓
Taxation	✓		✓	✓	✓	✓		✓	✓	✓
Finance		✓	✓		✓		✓	✓	✓	✓
E-invoice				✓	✓	✓		✓	✓	
Request							✓		✓	✓
Schedule						✓		✓	✓	

Pd—Product

13.4.1.1 Participants Profile

Concerning the participants, they were two software engineers from the company where the case study was applied. They have experience working as software developers and were grouped in a team. The team executing PAxSPL was familiar with ICode before the case study execution. Regarding their background in SPL, according to the team information report, only one member was familiar with a feature retrieval technique, FCA, while the other was considered a domain specialist because he has been working with ICode since its creation.

13.4.1.2 Case Study Protocol

The case study protocol was divided into two phases. During **Phase 1**, PAxSPL was performed in five different products of ICode. The selection of the products was based on those most used by the company clients. Although the company had this variability of products, these products were created manually by using the clone-and-own approach.

During the case study execution, these five products were analyzed and the feature retrieval process was executed. The five first products were composed of a different combination of four modules, presented in Table 13.3 (Pd1–Pd5). During **Phase 2**, we re-applied PAxSPL adding five more products, thus the participants should use ten different products of ICode as input for the feature retrieval. For **Phase 2**, we reused products one to five as well as composing six new products (Pd6–Pd10) by adding different combination of six modules, presented in Table 13.3. The modules *Schedule* and *Request* were only used on Phase 2.

During **Phase 2**, the participants could use the documentation generated during **Phase 1**, allowing to reuse the generated artifacts in a different set of system variants. We did not set any time limit for the participants, and the case study was performed during the company's working hours (8 hours a day). We still, however, registered the time spent on each PAxSPL activity.

13.4.1.3   Data Collection

To increase the precision and strengthen the validity of our case study we performed the data collection taking multiple perspectives, thus allowing triangulation [48]. Therefore, we collected data using different sources: observing and documenting information in real time, applying different surveys (Available at section "Appendix"), and analyzing PAxSPL generated artifacts. We also kept track of each artifact used during each activity, registering how often and in how many activities an artifact was used. During **Phase 2** of the case study we compared these information to achieve OBJ3.

We applied three surveys in different moments of the case study. Survey 1 was applied before **Phase 1** aiming to collect information about the participants. Survey 2 was applied before **Phase 2** to collect the information gathered during **Phase 1**, aiming to achieve OBJ1 and OBJ2. Lastly, Survey 3 was applied after **Phase 2** to collect information related to OBJ3. The artifacts were analyzed only at the end of the whole execution, aiming to measure their quality.

13.4.1.4   Quality Metrics

To measure the quality of the artifacts generated during PAxSPL execution in the case study, we adopted ten Quality Metrics (QM), presented in Table 13.4. Although there are metrics found in the literature [19], those metrics are used for specific artifacts, such as variability models or source code analyzed. For our case study, however, we intend to use metrics to analyze PAxSPL activities and its specific artifacts. Thus, we decided to define our own metrics instead of using those found in literature. At the end of the calculation, a high quality score indicates that the users applied PAxSPL as intended, while low scores would represent problems or difficulties performing PAxSPL. To calculate the total score of the QMs, we created

Table 13.4 Quality metrics

ID	Question
QM1	Are the PAxSPL mandatory artifacts well documented following their templates?
QM2	Are all the team members roles and tasks documented in the team information report?
QM3	Were all needed product artifacts documented during the documentation analysis?
QM4	Were the reasons to select or not select a technique for feature retrieval documented?
QM5	Was the assembled process documented following a process structure?
QM6	Were all the retrieval techniques output artifacts documented?
QM7	Were all feature entry points from the retrieved features documented?
QM8	Were all features from the system variants retrieved?
QM9	Was a feature diagram created to represent system variants as SPL?
QM10	Was the process execution experience documented?

three possible scores: Total (T) which scores 1, Partial (P) which scores 0.5, and
Nothing (N) which scores 0 (zero). To give more clarity about how the scores were
applied we used percentages to compare the number of artifacts generated.[5]

13.4.2   Conduction and Data Collecting

Before the case study execution, we did not provide any kind of training nor
introduction to basic SPL or reengineering concepts to the participants. At the
beginning of **Phase 1**, the participants received PAxSPL documentation and the first
five products of ICode. ICode artifacts were composed of source code, requirements
list, and some architecture diagrams. During PAxSPL execution, we observed
and documented the information that would be used to achieve the OBJs. At the
beginning of **Phase 2**, we gave to the participants artifacts from five additional ICode
products. The participants could also use the documentation that they generated
during **Phase 1**. We collected the same kind of information, allowing us to perform
some comparison between both phases. The data collected for the OBJs can be
categorized into four different categories: time spent, quality of artifacts, use and
reuse of artifacts, and the answers from the surveys. This data is detailed in the
following.

13.4.2.1   Time Spent

The case study was executed during 2 weeks. Table 13.5 details the information
about the time spent in each PAxSPL phase and activity during both phases of
the case study. In total, **Phase 1** was performed in thirteen and a half hours,
while for **Phase 2** only four and a half hours were needed. For both execution
phases, the most time consuming phase was Execute (8 hours for **Phase 1** and
three and a half hours for **Phase 2**), mainly because the Execute Assembled
Process activity, which was reduced in 3 hours. Two activities were reduced by
1 hour during **Phase 2**: Perform Documentation Analysis was performed
in one and a half hour during **Phase 1** and half an hour during **Phase 2**,
while Document Feature Artifacts reduced from 2 hours to one. Another
important information is the activities where no time was spent during **Phase 2**.
During these activities (Collect Team Information, Assign Roles and
Select Techniques), artifacts from **Phase 1** were completely reused, justifying
the time saved.

Table 13.5 Time spent in each PAxSPL activity during the case study

Activity/time spent (hours)									
	Prepare			Assemble			Execute			Total
	Collect team info.	Assign roles	Perform doc. analysis	Select tec.	Assemble tec.	Assign tasks	Exec. assembled process	Doc. feature Artifacts	Doc. process exp.	
P1	0.5	0.5	1.5	1.5	1.0	0.5	5.0	2.0	1.0	13.5
P2	0.0	0.0	0.5	0.0	0.2	0.3	2.0	1.0	0.5	4.5

P1—Phase 1; P2—Phase 2

13.4.2.2   Quality of Generated Artifacts

During the execution of PAxSPL in both phases of the case study, more than 30 artifacts [5] from PAxSPL were generated. For a in-depth investigation, at the end of the case study, we analyzed the artifacts and applied ten QMs (see Table 13.4) to look for evidence that the artifacts were generated according to the process guidelines. The score obtained from **Phase 1** of the case study was 9.5 while from Phase 2 was 10. The only difference between both phases was in QM6, where some feature artifacts were not documented during **Phase 1**.

Despite these results, the participants exposed some difficulties related to the artifacts. The first difficulty was the lack of tools for registering the information related to PAxSPL reports, e.g., Feature Retrieval Techniques Report. According to the participants, they could reduce the time spent in some activities related to these reports if such a tool was available. Secondly, the participants had difficulty understanding the feature report artifact. They expressed some problems with the current structure of the feature report template. For them, this artifact should be more graphical (e.g., a diagram) than textual.

After analyzing the results of the quality metrics, we could conclude that the comparisons of effort and reusability could be performed without any interference from artifacts with low quality because for both phases, we achieve good quality results. Among the generated artifacts, at least one was generated during each activity of PAxSPL. For the first two activities, `Collect Team Information` and `Assign Roles` we have the Team Information Report. The report was documented following its template, indicating that the process description was followed for those activities. This artifact described name of the members, their roles, experience working with SPL, and knowledge with feature retrieval techniques. The generated artifact for both phases of the case study was the same because the team members were kept the same.

Another important artifact is the assembled feature retrieval process created by the participants (using BPMN notation) during **Phase 1** and reused during **Phase 2**. In this particular case, the tasks were not assigned to a specific actor, which means they may be performed by anyone. As shown in Fig. 13.5, FCA is applied and a concept lattice is generated. This concept lattice is checked to find inconsistencies related to the documentation of the iCode versions, such as the name of features. Then, the extracted features are grouped into clusters and are checked for inconsistencies. The clusters are refined, the features are categorized and validated with the domain specialist. Lastly, the feature model is created and checked, and the process ends.

For each retrieval technique applied (with exception of expert-driven extraction) at least one artifact was generated. For instance, the concept lattices (one generated during each phase of the case study) were created using an FCA supporting tool, the Concept Explorer.[6] Figure 13.6 presents the lattice generated during **Phase 2**, which

---

[6] http://conexp.sourceforge.net/.

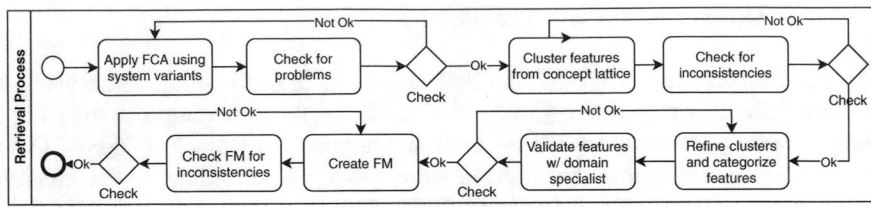

Fig. 13.5 Feature retrieval process assembled during the case study

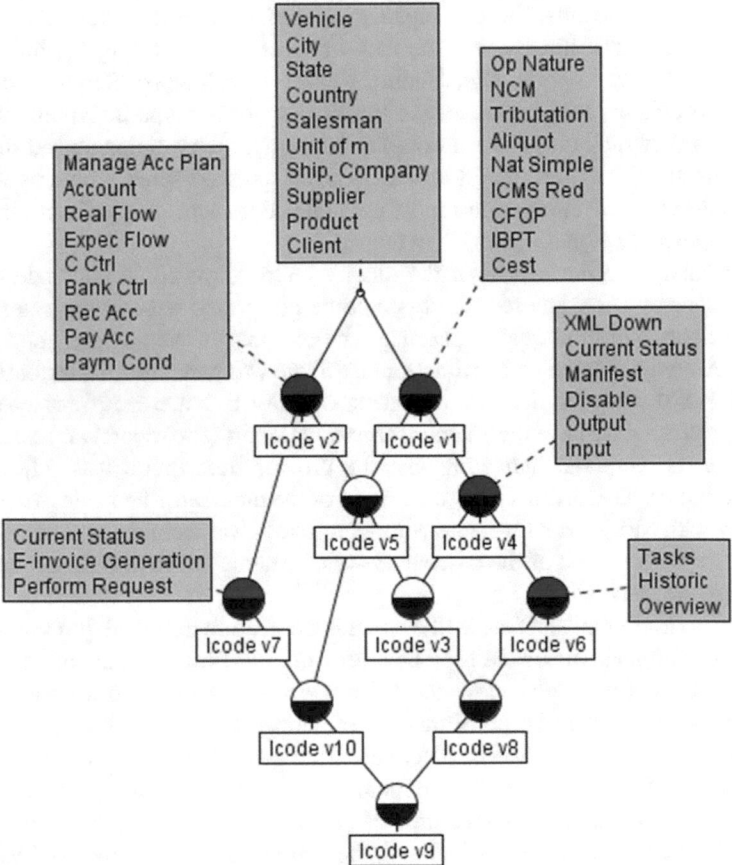

Fig. 13.6 Concept lattice of features extracted from ten different ICode products

describes an ordered hierarchy of the features extracted from ten different ICode products. In this case, the features closer to the lattice top are the ones shared by most ICode products. For instance, features *Vehicle*, *City*, *State*, *Country*, *Salesman* and the others in the top are shared among all ten products.

The final output of PAxSPL, which is the feature model of the extracted features, did not suffer many changes during both phases of the case study. The main difference between **Phase 1** (Fig. 13.7) and **Phase 2** (Fig. 13.8), was the addition of the features (*Request, Schedule* and their sub-features) extracted from the new products included in **Phase 2**. Considering the similar features, we have *Registration* and its sub-features as mandatory, because they are found in all products. *E-Invoice* and *Request* are part of an *or*-alternative group, because at least one of them must be present when the optional feature *Document* is part of the product.

Continuing, we have the abstract feature *Operations*, which is mandatory and composed of an *or*-alternative group of the sub-features *Taxation* and *Finance*. There is also the optional feature *Schedule* (only in feature model from **Phase 2**). In addition, some restrictions were documented in the feature model: if the features *Finance* or *E-Invoice* are part of a product, then the feature *Paym. Cond.* must also be a part of that product. The feature *E-Invoice* requires the features *Taxation* and *Transport*. Lastly, the feature *E-invoice Generation* requires *E-Invoice*.

13.4.2.3   Use of Generated Artifacts

We also collected the number of times that each artifact was used during each activity of PAxSPL. The most used artifacts, used in six different activities, were team information report, assembled process, process documentation, and PAxSPL guidelines. The artifact less used was the development information report. Despite these results, this information does not give enough evidence of the impact/relevance level of the artifacts, we still had to consider the survey's answers. Another type of data collected was the reusability of the generated artifacts. We documented the use condition of the artifacts during **Phase 2** of the case study. Four artifacts from **Phase 1** were reused with no need to perform modifications, namely team information report, artifacts type specification, retrieval techniques report and FM of retrieval techniques configured. In addition, six artifacts generated during **Phase 1** were updated, needing some modification during **Phase 2**. These six artifacts were the domain glossary, domain constraints list, requirements specification, assembled process, process documentation, feature report and the FM.

13.4.2.4   Participants Answers for Surveys

Survey 1 was designed to collect information about the participants and their knowledge about SPL. We asked the participants to list the most important artifacts in terms of reengineering. The cited artifacts were: team information report, requirements specification, assembled process, and PAxSPL guidelines. We also asked them to give a score (1–5) about the relevance of each artifact. These same questions were also included in Survey 3 and were used on OBJ1. We calculated the average results of each survey and then the average considering both surveys.

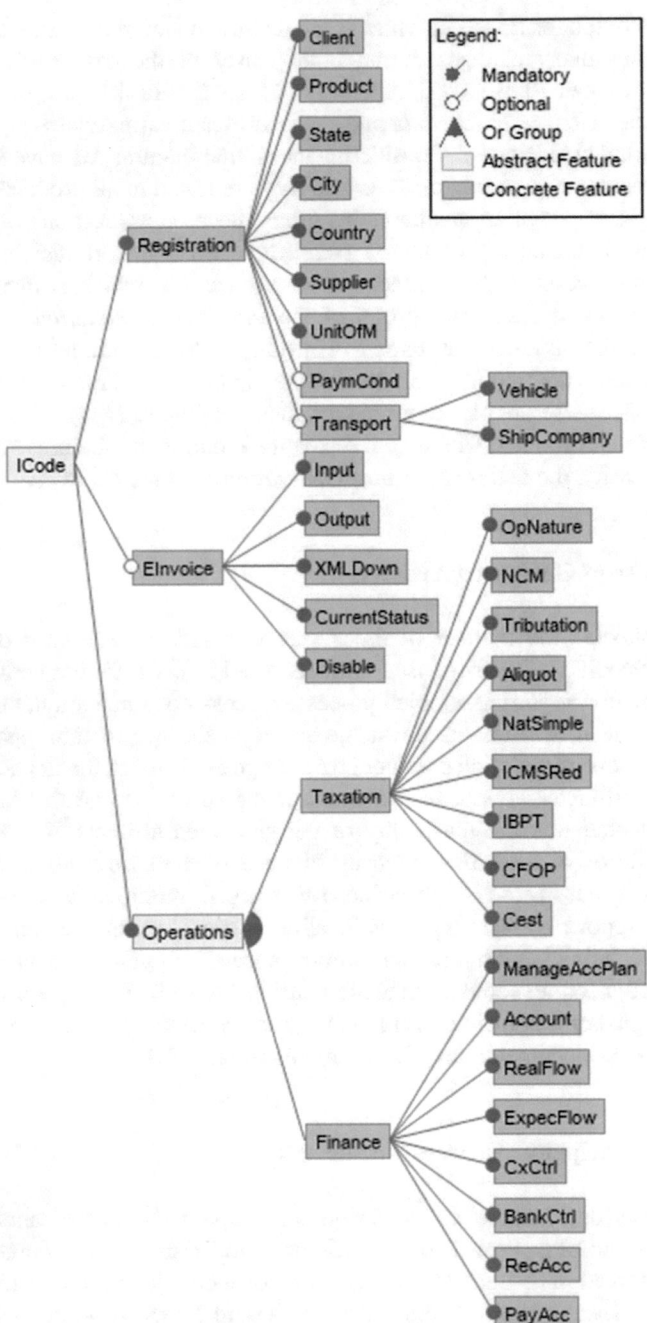

Fig. 13.7 ICode feature model from Phase 1

Fig. 13.8 ICode feature
model from Phase 2

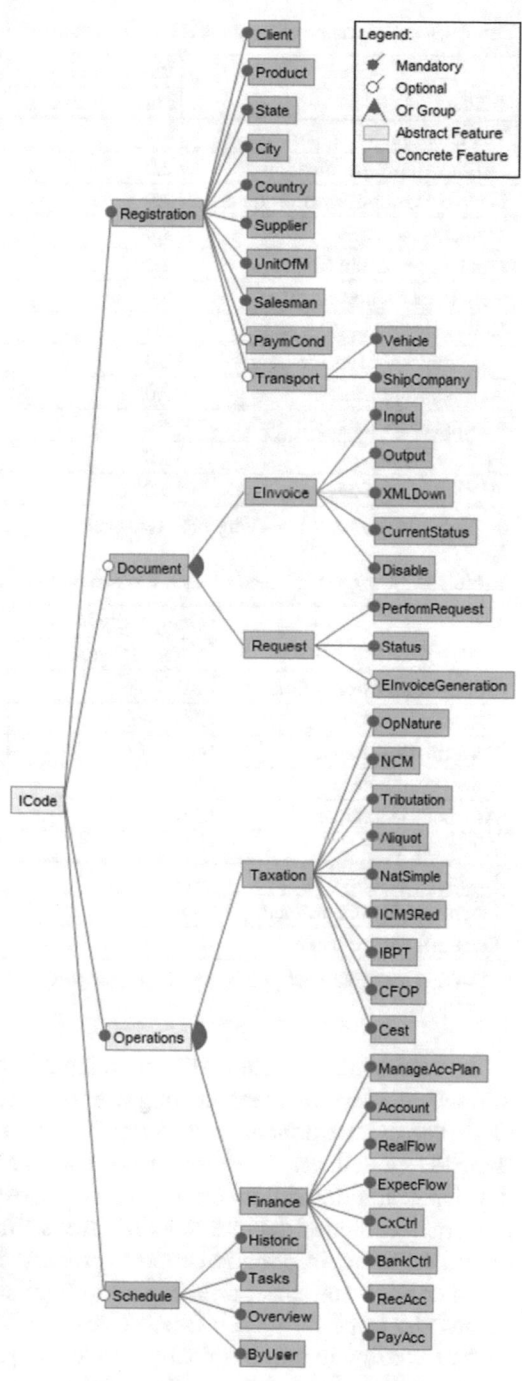

Table 13.6 Relevance of artifacts according to survey results

	Relevance level		
Artifact	Survey 2 average	Survey 3 average	Total average
Team information report	3.0	3.0	3.0
Artifacts type specification	2.0	2.0	2.0
Development information report	3.0	1.0	2.0
Domain glossary	2.0	3.0	2.5
Domain constraints list	4.0	4.0	4.0
Requirements specification	5.0	5.0	5.0
Retrieval techniques report	3.0	5.0	4.0
FM of retrieval tec. configured	2.0	2.0	2.0
Assembled process	5.0	5.0	5.0
Process documentation	4.0	3.0	3.5
Feature report	3.0	4.0	3.5
PAxSPL guidelines	5.0	3.0	4.0

1—Very low relevance; 5—Very high relevance

Table 13.7 Complexity level of each PAxSPL activity according to survey answers

	Complexity level		
Activity	Survey 2 average	Survey 3 average	Total average
Collect team information	1.0	1.0	1.0
Assign roles	2.0	1.0	1.5
Perform doc. analysis	4.0	3.0	3.5
Select techniques	5.0	5.0	5.0
Assemble techniques	5.0	4.0	4.5
Assign tasks	2.0	2.0	2.0
Execute assembled process	4.0	3.0	3.5
Document feature artifacts	3.0	2.0	2.5
Document process exp.	2.0	1.0	1.5

1—Very low complexity; 5—Very high complexity

As presented in Table 13.6, according to the survey results, the most relevant artifacts in terms of reengineering are the requirements specification, the assembled process, the domain constraints list, the retrieval techniques report, and the PAxSPL guidelines. The less relevant artifacts are: artifacts type specification, development information report, domain glossary, and the configuration of the retrieval techniques' feature model. Other artifacts can be considered as mid-level relevance: team information report, process documentation, and feature report. Another important question included in both surveys (2 and 3) was related to the complexity to perform each PAxSPL activity. The participants should give a score (1–5) according to the complexity they had to perform each activity.

Table 13.7 shows that, in the opinion of the participants, the most complex activities were: Select Techniques and Assemble Techniques. Activities

Table 13.8 Reusability level of PAxSPL generated artifacts according to survey 3 results

Artifact	Reusability level
	Average
Team information report	5.0
Artifacts type specification	5.0
Development information report	5.0
Domain glossary	3.0
Domain constraints list	2.5
Requirements specification	2.0
Retrieval techniques report	5.0
FM of retrieval tec. configured	5.0
Assembled process	4.5
Process documentation	3.5
Feature report	2.5
Feature model	4.0

1—Low reusability; 5—High reusability

such as `Collect Team Information`, `Assign Roles`, `Assign Tasks` and `Document Process Experience` have a lower level of complexity. In addition `Perform Documentation Analysis`, `Execute Assembled Process` and `Document Feature Artifacts` are categorized as mid-level of complexity to be performed. We used these information to help us with OBJ2. Survey 3 focused on questions about the reuse capability of PAxSPL, aiming to give us information to achieve OBJ3. We asked which PAxSPL artifacts from **Phase 1** of the case study provided the most level of reuse. According to the participants, these artifacts were: team information report, retrieval techniques report, and assembled process.

Table 13.8 summarizes the answers according to the level of relevance of each artifact generated during **Phase 1**. The artifacts with higher reusability are: team information report, artifacts type specification, development information, retrieval techniques report, the configuration of the retrieval techniques' feature model, assembled process and feature model. The less reusable artifacts are: domain glossary, domain constraints list, requirements specification and feature report.

13.4.3 Results and Discussion

To obtain the information required to answer the OBJs, we performed a cross-analysis among the data collected from different sources. Thus, we analyzed and merged data collected in real-time, survey answers, and generated artifacts analysis. As this case study was exploratory, our objectives are related to finding evidence about opportunities to improve PAxSPL. Cross-examination of those data is detailed in the following sections.

13.4.3.1 OBJ1: Impact and Relevance of the Artifacts Generated by PAxSPL Execution in Terms of Reengineering

To achieve this OBJ, we performed a cross-analysis in the data about the use of artifacts and Table 13.6, alongside additional information gathered during the survey answers and artifacts analysis. Considering the number of uses for each artifact in each PAxSPL activity, we could analyze how useful an artifact may be for each part of the process. This information, however, is not enough to indicate the relevance of the artifacts. Hence, by merging this information with Table 13.6, which presents the relevance of each artifact according to participant's opinion, we can identify if the use of each artifact is somehow related to its relevance. In addition, by considering the artifacts used during Select Techniques, we could indicate the impact level of those artifacts while selecting the retrieval techniques. To calculate the relevance of the artifacts, we applied a score count on them. We considered how many times an artifact was used during each PAxSPL phase (Prepare, Assemble and Execute), we also considered the total number of uses. The total number of uses from the artifacts had a range of two to six uses. Thus, the numerical range was composed of five numbers which were used when calculating the score. Therefore, if an artifact was used twice, we added 1 point to its relevance score, if it was used six times, we added 5 points.

Considering PAxSPL phases, however, the numerical range was between 0 and 4. Thus, when calculating the relevance for each phase individually, if an artifact was used four times in a specific phase it would receive a score of 5, and if it was not used would receive 1 point. We merged these points with the relevance level (1–5) given by the participants in the survey, allowing the possibility for each artifact to reach a total score of 10. Also, we considered whether the artifact was listed as the most important or not by the participants in the survey answers. Therefore, the final score of each artifact could reach a maximum of 12 points. As presented in Table 13.9, the artifacts which obtained the higher scores are team information report, requirements specification, assembled process, and PAxSPL guidelines. To categorize the artifacts, considering the reengineering, we created four levels of relevance, based on the scores:

1. − **Not relevant:** artifact was not used;
2. + **Useful:** artifact was used and scored 4 relevance points or less;
3. ++ **Helpful:** artifact was used and scored between more than 4 and a maximum of 8 relevance points;
4. + + + **Relevant:** artifact was used and scored more than 8 relevance points.

We categorized the artifacts considering PAxSPL phases individually (e.g., development information report was not used during Execute) and in general. We summarize these results in Table 13.10, showing the relevance level of each artifact for Prepare, Assemble and Execute phases, and overall relevance as well. The information in Table 13.10 indicates that artifacts such as team information reports, requirements specification, and PAxSPL guidelines are more relevant during the preparation before assembling the process. In addition, requirements specifi-

Table 13.9 Relevance score of each artifact

Artifact	Number of uses				Survey	Extra[a]	Final score			
	P	A	E	T			P	A	E	T
Team information report	4	2	0	6	3.0	✓	10	8	6	10
Artifacts type specification	2	1	0	3	2.0		5	4	2	4
Development information report	1	1	0	2	2.0		4	4	2	3
Domain glossary	2	1	0	3	2.5		5.5	4.5	3.5	4.5
Domain constraints list	2	1	0	3	4.0		7	6	4	6
Requirements specification	2	1	2	5	5.0	✓	10	9	10	11
Retrieval techniques report	2	2	0	4	4.0		7	7	4	7
FM of retrieval tec. configured	2	2	0	4	2.0		5	5	2	5
Assembled process	0	2	4	6	5.0	✓	7	10	12	12
Process doc.	0	2	4	6	3.5		3.5	6.5	8.5	8.5
Feature report	0	0	4	4	3.5		3.5	3.5	8.5	6.5
PAxSPL guidelines	2	2	2	6	4.0	✓	9	9	9	11

P—Prepare; A—Assemble; E—Execute; T—Total
[a]Listed as most relevant on survey answers

Table 13.10 Relevance level of each artifact during PAxSPL execution

Artifact	Relevance level			
	Prepare	Assemble	Execute	Overall
Team information report	+++	++	−	+++
Artifacts type specification	++	+	−	+
Development information report	+	+	−	+
Domain glossary	++	++	−	++
Domain constraints list	++	++	−	++
Requirements specification	+++	+++	+++	+++
Retrieval techniques report	++	++	−	++
FM of retrieval tec. configured	++	++	−	++
Assembled process	−	+++	+++	+++
Process documentation	−	++	+++	+++
Feature report	−	−	+++	++
PAxSPL guidelines	+++	+++	+++	+++

− Not relevant; + Useful; ++ Helpful; +++ Relevant

cation, assembled process, and PAxSPL guidelines are more important during the assembly of the retrieval process. For the execution of the feature retrieval, artifacts such as the requirements specification, assembled process, process documentation, feature report, and PAxSPL guidelines are more relevant. Considering the overall relevance, the more important artifacts are team information report, requirements specification, assembled process, process documentation, and PAxSPL guidelines.

We also analyzed the artifacts used only during the Select Techniques sub-process to categorize their impact level when selecting techniques. For this

Table 13.11 Impact level of artifacts when selecting techniques

Impact	Artifacts
High	Team information report; requirements specification;
Medium	Domain glossary; domain constraints list;
Low	Artifacts type specification; development information report;

analysis, we found important evidence in the retrieval techniques report, where the reasons for selecting a technique are documented. Considering this information, we tabulated the impact level of each artifact when deciding which technique to use for feature retrieval. As shown in Table 13.11, team information report and requirements specification have both high levels of impact. Domain glossary and domain constraints analysis have a medium level of impact when selecting techniques. Lastly, artifact type specification and development information have a low level of impact.

The cross-analysis performed to analyze OBJ1 helped us understand which artifacts are more important during the reengineering. As an exploratory case study, this gave us initial evidence about the importance of PAxSPL generated artifacts. Because this is the first time that our proposal is performed in a real development environment, this kind of feedback gives evidence to establish three preliminary conclusions:

1. **No artifact is useless**: all artifacts indicated to contribute somehow to the reengineering process, although there are artifacts that were only used in specific phases;
2. **Collect team information before starting the reengineering is relevant**: as shown in Tables 13.10 and 13.11, the team information report have high relevance when conducting the reengineering, specially when selecting retrieval techniques to be used. Despite its importance, this kind of artifact was not present in most of the studies found in the literature [6];
3. **PAxSPL guidelines are very helpful for both the reengineering, and the retrieval techniques selection:** the guidelines of our proposal were created to give additional support when performing the reengineering. The collected evidence indicates that they are fulfilling their goal.

In addition, focusing on the improvement of PAxSPL, we now have evidence that indicates which artifacts we should give more attention to. Thus, we can give focus on the activities where these artifacts are generated, improving their templates, creating supporting tools, and also indicating to future users which artifacts they could give special treatment.

13.4.3.2   OBJ2: The Effort Needed to Perform Each PAxSPL Phase and Activity

To calculate the effort, we performed a cross-analysis in the information collected in real-time (shown in Table 13.5), and the information gathered with the survey

Table 13.12 Effort score of each PAxSPL activity

Activity	Hours spent	Complexity score	Effort score
Collect team information	0.25	1.0	0.25
Assign roles	0.25	1.5	0.375
Perform doc. analysis	1.0	3.5	3.5
Select techniques	0.75	5.0	3.75
Assemble techniques	0.6	4.5	2.7
Assign tasks	0.4	2.0	0.8
Execute assembled process	3.5	3.5	12.25
Document feature artifacts	1.5	2.5	3.75
Document process exp.	0.75	1.5	1.125
Total	9.0		28.5

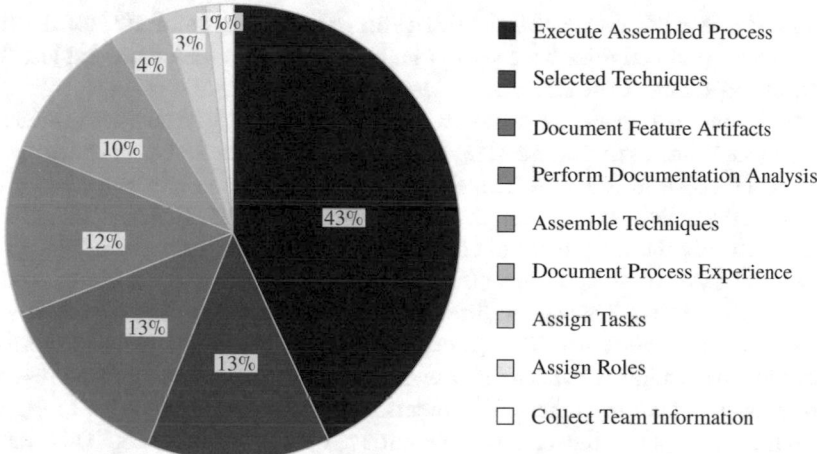

Fig. 13.9 Effort percentage of each PAxSPL activity

answers (illustrated by Table 13.7). We considered the average time spent on each activity during both phases of the case study. We also considered only the average complexity level collected in the survey answers. To merge both results, we multiplied the complexity level by the time spent and called the resulting number as an effort score. All this information is summarized in Table 13.12, showing that the `Execute Assembled Process` activity obtained the highest effort score (12.25) points. `Collect Team Information`, however, obtained the lowest score, only 0.25 effort points.

The effort percentage of each activity in relation of the total effort is shown in Fig. 13.9. `Execute Assembled Process` consists of 43% of the total effort. This first number is really expressive because this activity was also pointed as one of the most relevant in OBJ1. `Select Techniques` and `Document Feature Artifacts` represent 13% each, while `Perform Documentation`

Fig. 13.10 Effort percentage
of each PAxSPL phase

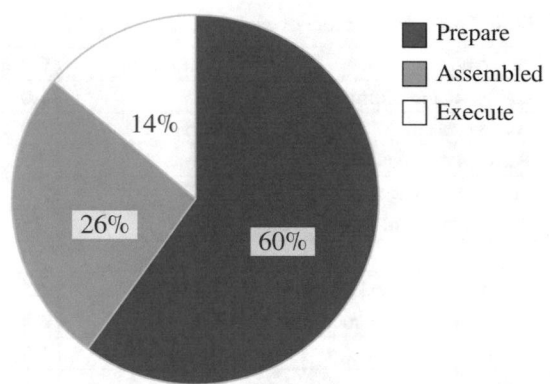

Analysis is 12%, and Assemble Techniques consists of 10% of the total
effort. These four activities have similar numbers, however, they represent less than
a half of Execute Assembled Process.

For the last activities, Document Process Experience (4%), Assign
Tasks (3%), Assign Roles (1%) and Collect Team Information (1%),
we have the opposite situation. These four activities presented less than a half effort
score than the activities we consider more balanced (between 10% and 13%).

By analyzing the total effort of each PAxSPL phase, as illustrated in Fig. 13.10,
we see that Execute represents 60%, Assemble represents 26% and Prepare
only 14% of the total. This major difference between Execute and the others were
already expected when we first created PAxSPL. Although we planned the three
phases to have similar relevance (as shown in OBJ1) the Execute phase presented
more relevance than the others. We understand that this happened due to the fact
that during this phase the features are retrieved from the products. This feature
retrieval process requires more effort and time than planning the feature retrieval, so
it is understandable why its complexity spent time is higher than the other PAxSPL
phases.

As result of the analysis for this OBJ, we formulated two conclusions:

1. **Execute Assembled Process demands more than twice the effort of other
   activities:** this conclusion give us evidence to plan to perform modification in the
   Execute phase. Although Execute Assembled Process effort difference
   should still be higher, we can look into develop supporting tools for this activity
   trying to reduce the time spent;
2. **Some activities require almost insignificant effort to be performed:** even if
   we merge the effort of Document Process Experience, Assign Tasks,
   Assign Roles and Collect Team Information the result would be
   lower than other activities. This may indicate that these activities should be
   reformulated, maybe combined with others or we could even consider to remove
   some of them from the process and reallocate its generated artifacts to other
   activities.

We aimed to identify which PAxSPL activities demand more effort. We wanted to collect evidence to compare the activities and phases of our process in terms of effort. This comparison allowed us to improve some aspects of PAxSPL. By identifying the activities that demand more effort we can give special attention to them. The results regarding the effort showed in this section are not related to the real effort needed to perform an activity. This measure, however, can be used to analyze the effort difference among the activities. In addition, we included the effort information within PAxSPL guidelines to give future users some basis about how much percentage of the total time they would spend on each activity.

13.4.3.3 OBJ3: PAxSPL Reuse Capability

To measure the reuse capability, *i.e.*, reusability, of PAxSPL, we focused on its generated artifacts. The main objective here is to understand how the re-application of PAxSPL can benefit from generated artifacts. We conducted a cross-analysis of information collected in real-time related with the reuse of artifacts and the survey answers regarding reusability (see Table 13.8). Table 13.13 shows the results of the reusability score calculation.

To calculate the reusability of the artifacts, we considered their use condition during **Phase 2** which could be: used without modification, updated, or not used. If an artifact was used without modification, it would receive 3 reusability points. If an artifact was updated, it would receive 1 reusability point. Artifacts not used would receive zero reusability points. These points were added to the reusability score (1–5) given by participants in the survey answers. We also gave 2 extra points for artifacts cited in the survey results as more important during PAxSPL re-application. As can be seen, the team information report and retrieval techniques report obtained

Table 13.13 Reusability score of PAxSPL artifacts

Artifact	Survey score	Phase 2 condition score	Extra[a]	Total score
Team information report	5.0	3.0	✓	10.0
Artifacts type specification	5.0	3.0		8.0
Development information report	5.0	0.0		5.0
Domain glossary	3.0	1.0		4.0
Domain constraints list	2.5	1.0		3.5
Requirements specification	2.0	1.0		3.0
Retrieval techniques report	5.0	3.0	✓	10.0
FM of retrieval tec. configured	5.0	3.0		8.0
Assembled process	4.5	1.0	✓	7.5
Process documentation	3.5	1.0		4.5
Feature report	2.5	1.0		3.5
Feature model	4.0	1.0		5.0

[a]2 extra points were given to artifacts listed as most important during PAxSPL re-application

Table 13.14 Reusability level of PAxSPL artifacts

Reusability level	Artifacts
High	Team information report; artifacts type specification; retrieval techniques report; FM of retrieval tec. configured;
Medium	Assembled process; process documentation; feature model;
Low	Domain glossary; domain constraints list; requirements specification; feature report;
Not Reusable	Development information report;

the maximum possible score, ten points each. Artifacts type specification and the configuration of the retrieval techniques' feature model also obtained good scores, eight points each. Requirements specification, with three points, and feature report and domain constraints list, with three and a half points each, obtained the lower results.

We created four categories to group the artifacts based on their reusability score:

1. **Not reusable:** artifacts not reused during **Phase 2** of the case study, despite its reusability score;
2. **Low level of reuse:** artifacts used during **Phase 2** and that scored 4 reusability points or less;
3. **Mid level of reuse:** artifacts used during **Phase 2** and that scored between more than 4 and less than 8 reusability points;
4. **High level of reuse:** artifacts used during **Phase 2** and that scored at least 8 reusability points.

The results related to this classification are presented in Table 13.14. We plan to include this information within PAxSPL guidelines to help future users of our process to identify which artifacts they could give focus when re-applying PAxSPL.

Based on the results of this OBJ, we formulated two conclusions:

1. **The reusability has a high impact on the selection of techniques:** among the artifacts that were categorized as having a high level of reuse, we have the retrieval techniques report and the configuration of the retrieval techniques' feature model. These two artifacts are both generated during `Select Techniques` activity. As this activity was also found to be the second needing more effort to be performed (see Fig. 13.9), the reusability of its artifacts was the main reason for the time saved (see Table 13.5) during **Phase 2** of the case study;
2. **PAxSPL reusability indicates its capability to maybe be applied using the SPL reactive approach:** if we analyze the difference between both phases of the case study, the main difference is the inclusion of new features. This scenario is similar to when the SPL reactive approach is applied in a company, e.g., new requirements arise and new functionalities are implemented. Thus, as shown in Table 13.5, the only activities that demand some time during **Phase 2** of the case study were those when new requirements or features had to be analyzed. Although our main goal was to create a process to give support to the SPL

extractive approach, the reusability results gave us initial evidence about PAxSPL benefits when applied in an SPL reactive scenario. This allows us to further investigate the real benefits when using PAxSPL in a reactive approach scenario.

13.5 Concluding Remarks

In this chapter, we presented PAxSPL, a framework that aims to aid the SPL reengineering planning. Our proposal is intended to give enough flexibility for the user's scenario by handling organizational and technical information when preparing the feature retrieval process. We defined PAxSPL by analyzing a large variety of different proposals found in the SPL reengineering literature [6], identifying their common techniques, strategies, phases, and activities. We also defined guidelines to help the PAxSPL's users when executing our framework, aiming the decision on the selection of techniques and how to assemble them into a feature retrieval process.

We conducted a case study to collect exploratory evidence about the PAxSPL applicability. In the case study, we observed PAxSPL application into ten different products from an ERP system, collecting information related with the relevance of each PAxSPL artifact, quality of PAxSPL generated artifacts, effort spent to perform each PAxSPL phase and activity, and PAxSPL reusability.

We divided the case study into two phases, during **Phase 1** the participants applied PAxSPL in five different products generated from the ERP system, while in **Phase 2** ten different products were analyzed. The analysis of the information collected during the case study gave us evidence to achieve some important conclusions:

1. In general, PAxSPL gave support to the participants when planning the reengineering. The guidelines helped the participants and guided them into customizing a retrieval process for their scenario;
2. In regard to the artifacts, they were all useful somehow. Some artifacts indicated to have a high relevance in terms of reengineering, such as the team information report, requirements specification and PAxSPL guidelines. The results also indicated that the guidelines were very helpful during the retrieval techniques selection;
3. In terms of effort to perform each PAxSPL activity, `Execute Assembled Process` received more than twice the effort of the second most effort needed activity. Also, some activities indicated to require almost insignificant effort to be performed.
4. Considering the reusability, the results indicated that PAxSPL, when re-applied in a different but similar scenario, saves time by reusing some of its artifacts.

Based on the results of the case study as well as analysis of additional research work conducted, we planned the evolution of PAxSPL. This evolution consisted of addressing the limitations identified in our work by establishing the SPL Reengineering Planning framework [36].

Acknowledgments This work was partially supported by the Carlos Chagas Filho Foundation for Supporting Research in the State of Rio de Janeiro (FAPERJ), under the PDR-10 program, grant 202073/2020. This work was partially supported by the Natural Sciences and Engineering Research Council of Canada (NSERC) grant RGPIN-2017-05421.

Appendix

Survey 1 Questions: Participants Information

1. How many times have you participated in a case study?
2. How many times have you performed a SPL re-engineering process before?
3. Regarding your technical knowledge, please check the following options: ()SPL () Re-engineering () SPL Re-engineering () Feature Model () Feature Diagrams ()Feature Retrieval Techniques
4. How is the variability of products being performed in this organization?

Survey 2 Questions: Answered After Phase 1

1. Describe any difficulty that you may had during PAxSPL execution.
2. How helpful were PAxSPL's guidelines? Not Much Helpful 1–5 Very Helpful
3. In which activities did you spend more time during PAxSPL execution?
4. Which artifacts were more used during the reengineering?
5. What artifacts were more important during PAxSPL execution?
6. What changes would you recommend for PAxSPL?

Survey 3 Questions: Answered After Phase 2

1. What were the main difficulties to re-apply PAxSPL?
2. What were the main benefits to re-apply PAxSPL?
3. In which activities did you spend more time during PAxSPL re-execution?
4. How many artifacts from the first execution the team could reuse?
5. How many artifacts from the first execution the team could reuse **without** modification?
6. How helpful were PAxSPL's guidelines? Not Much Helpful 1–5 Very Helpful
7. What artifacts were more important during PAxSPL re-execution?
8. What changes would you recommend for PAxSPL?

References

1. Acher, M., Cleve, A., Collet, P., Merle, P., Duchien, L., Lahire, P.: Extraction and evolution of architectural variability models in plugin-based systems. Software & Systems Modeling **13**(4), 1367–1394 (2013)
2. Acher, M., Cleve, A., Perrouin, G., Heymans, P., Vanbeneden, C., Collet, P., Lahire, P.: On extracting feature models from product descriptions. In: 6th International Workshop on Variability Modeling of Software-Intensive Systems, pp. 45–54. ACM (2012)
3. AL-Msie'deen, R., Seriai, A., Huchard, M., Urtado, C., Vauttier, S., Salman, H.E.: Feature location in a collection of software product variants using formal concept analysis. In: J. Favaro, M. Morisio (eds.) Safe and Secure Software Reuse, pp. 302–307. Springer Berlin Heidelberg, Berlin, Heidelberg (2013)
4. Alsawalqah, H.I., Kang, S., Lee, J.: A method to optimize the scope of a software product platform based on end-user features. Journal of Systems and Software **98**, 79–106 (2014)
5. Alves, V., Schwanninger, C., Barbosa, L., Rashid, A., Sawyer, P., Rayson, P., Pohl, C., Rummler, A.: An exploratory study of information retrieval techniques in domain analysis. In: 2008 12th International Software Product Line Conference, pp. 67–76 (2008)
6. Assunção, W., Lopez-Herrejon, R., Linsbauer, L., Vergilio, S., Egyed, A.: Reengineering legacy applications into software product lines: a systematic mapping. Empirical Software Engineering pp. 1–45 (2017)
7. Bagheri, E., Ensan, F., Gasevic, D.: Decision support for the software product line domain engineering lifecycle. Automated Software Engineering **19**(3), 335–377 (2012)
8. Bartholdt, J., Becker, D.: Scope extension of an existing product line. In: 16th International Software Product Line Conference - Volume 1, SPLC '12, pp. 275–282. ACM, New York, NY, USA (2012)
9. Bécan, G., Acher, M., Baudry, B., Nasr, S.: Breathing ontological knowledge into feature model management. Tech. rep., IRISA - Institut de Recherche en Informatique et Systèmes Aléatoires, Inria Rennes – Bretagne Atlantique (2013)
10. Bosch, J.: The challenges of broadening the scope of software product families. Communications of the ACM **49**(12), 41–44 (2006)
11. Bosch, J.: From software product lines to software ecosystems. In: Proceedings of the 13th International Software Product Line Conference, SPLC '09, p. 111–119. Carnegie Mellon University, USA (2009)
12. Chen, K., Zhang, W., Zhao, H., Mei, H.: An approach to constructing feature models based on requirements clustering. In: Requirements Engineering, 2005. Proceedings. 13th IEEE International Conference on, pp. 31–40. IEEE (2005)
13. Cruz, J., Neto, P.S., Britto, R., Rabelo, R., Ayala, W., Soares, T., Mota, M.: Toward a hybrid approach to generate software product line portfolios. In: IEEE Congress on Evolutionary Computation, pp. 2229–2236 (2013)
14. Damaševičius, R., Paškevičius, P., Karčiauskas, E., Marcinkevičius, R.: Automatic extraction of features and generation of feature models from java programs. Information Technology And Control **41**(4), 376–384 (2012)
15. deBaud, J.., Schmid, K.: A systematic approach to derive the scope of software product lines. In: Proceedings of the 1999 International Conference on Software Engineering (IEEE Cat. No.99CB37002), 99CB37002, pp. 34–43 (1999)
16. Dhungana, D., Seichter, D., Botterweck, G., Rabiser, R., Grünbacher, P., Benavides, D., Galindo, J.A.: Integrating heterogeneous variability modeling approaches with invar. In: Proceedings of the Seventh International Workshop on Variability Modelling of Software-Intensive Systems, VaMoS '13. Association for Computing Machinery, New York, NY, USA (2013)
17. Dumais, S.: Latent semantic analysis. Annual review of information science and technology **38**(1), 188–230 (2004)

18. Eisenbarth, T., Koschke, R., Simon, D.: Derivation of feature component maps by means of concept analysis. In: Software Maintenance and Reengineering, 2001. Fifth European Conference on, pp. 176–179. IEEE (2001)
19. El-Sharkawy, S., Yamagishi-Eichler, N., Schmid, K.: Metrics for analyzing variability and its implementation in software product lines: A systematic literature review. Information and Software Technology **106**, 1–30 (2019)
20. Eyal-Salman, H., Seriai, D., Dony, C.: Identifying traceability links between product variants and their features. In: 1st International workshop on Reverse Variability Engineering, pp. 17–22 (2013)
21. Eyal-Salman, H., Seriai, D., Dony, C.: Feature location in a collection of product variants: Combining information retrieval and hierarchical clustering. In: Software Engineering and Knowledge Engineering, pp. 426–430 (2014)
22. Ferrari, A., Spagnolo, G.O., Dell'Orletta, F.: Mining commonalities and variabilities from natural language documents. In: 17th International Software Product Line Conference, pp. 116–120. ACM (2013)
23. Fischer, S., Linsbauer, L., Lopez-Herrejon, R.E., Egyed, A.: Enhancing clone-and-own with systematic reuse for developing software variants. In: Software Maintenance and Evolution (ICSME), 2014 IEEE International Conference on, pp. 391–400. IEEE (2014)
24. Hamza, H.S., Martinez, J., Alonso, C.: Introducing product line architectures in the erp industry: Challenges and lessons learned. In: SPLC Workshops, pp. 263–266 (2010)
25. Hubaux, A., Heymans, P., Benavides, D.: Variability modeling challenges from the trenches of an open source product line re-engineering project. In: 12th International Software Product Line Conference, pp. 55–64. IEEE (2008)
26. Jain, A.K., Dubes, R.C.: Algorithms for clustering data. Prentice-Hall, Inc. (1988)
27. Kang, K., Cohen, S., Hess, J.A., Novak, W., Peterson, A.: Feature-oriented domain analysis (FODA) feasibility study. Tech. rep., DTIC Document (1990)
28. Kang, K., Kim, M., Lee, J., Kim, B.: Feature-oriented re-engineering of legacy systems into product line assets–a case study. In: International Conference on Software Product Lines, pp. 45–56. Springer (2005)
29. Kelly, M., Alexander, J., Adams, B., Hassan, A.: Recovering a balanced overview of topics in a software domain. In: Source Code Analysis and Manipulation (SCAM), 2011 11th IEEE International Working Conference on, pp. 135–144. IEEE (2011)
30. Klatt, B., Krogmann, K., Seidl, C.: Program dependency analysis for consolidating customized product copies. In: IEEE International Conference on Software Maintenance and Evolution, pp. 496–500. IEEE (2014)
31. Krueger, C.: Easing the transition to software mass customization. In: International Workshop on Software Product-Family Engineering, pp. 282–293. Springer (2001)
32. Krüger, J., Mahmood, W., Berger, T.: Promote-pl: A round-trip engineering process model for adopting and evolving product lines. In: Proceedings of the 24th ACM Conference on Systems and Software Product Line: Volume A - Volume A, SPLC '20. Association for Computing Machinery, New York, NY, USA (2020)
33. Kulesza, U., Alves, V., Garcia, A., Neto, A., Cirilo, E., De Lucena, C., Borba, P.: Mapping features to aspects: A model-based generative approach. In: Early Aspects Workshop, pp. 155–174. Springer (2007)
34. Laguna, M.A., Crespo, Y.: A systematic mapping study on software product line evolution: From legacy system reengineering to product line refactoring. Science of Computer Programming **78**(8), 1010–1034 (2013)
35. Leitner, A., Kreiner, C.: Managing erp configuration variants: An experience report. In: Proceedings of the 2010 Workshop on Knowledge-Oriented Product Line Engineering, KOPLE '10. Association for Computing Machinery, New York, NY, USA (2010)
36. Marchezan, L., Carbonell, J., Rodrigues, E., Bernardino, M., Basso, F.P., Assunção, W.K.G.: Enhancing the feature retrieval process with scoping and tool support: Paxspl_v2. In: Proceedings of the 24th ACM International Systems and Software Product Line Conference - Volume B, SPLC '20, p. 29–36. Association for Computing Machinery, New York, NY, USA (2020)

37. Marchezan, L., Rodrigues, E., Bernardino, M., Basso, F.P.: PAxSPL: A feature retrieval process for software product line reengineering. Software: Practice and Experience **49**(8), 1278–1306 (2019)
38. Marchezan, L., Rodrigues, E., Bernardino, M., Basso, F.P.: PAxSPL: A Feature Retrieval Process for SPL Reengineering. In: Proceedings of the 24th ACM Conference on Systems and Software Product Line: Volume A - Volume A, SPLC '20. Association for Computing Machinery, New York, NY, USA (2020)
39. Martinez, J., Assunção, W.K.G., Ziadi, T.: ESPLA: A Catalog of Extractive SPL Adoption Case Studies. In: Proceedings of the 21st International Systems and Software Product Line Conference - Volume B, SPLC '17, pp. 38–41. ACM, New York, NY, USA (2017)
40. Martinez, J., Ziadi, T., Bissyandé, T., Klein, J., Le Traon, Y.: Bottom-up adoption of software product lines: a generic and extensible approach. In: Proceedings of the 19th International Conference on Software Product Line, pp. 101–110. ACM (2015)
41. Martinez, J., Ziadi, T., Klein, J., Le Traon, Y.: Identifying and visualising commonality and variability in model variants. In: European Conference on Modelling Foundations and Applications, pp. 117–131. Springer (2014)
42. Mazo, R., Assar, S., Salinesi, C., Ben Hassen, N.: Using software product line to improve ERP engineering : literature review and analysis. Latin-American Journal of Computing (LAJC) **1**(1), . (2014). URL https://hal.archives-ouvertes.fr/hal-02397633
43. Muller, J.: Value-based portfolio optimization for software product lines. In: 15th International Software Product Line Conference, pp. 15–24 (2011)
44. Nöbauer, M., Seyff, N., Dhungana, D., Stoiber, R.: Managing variability of ERP ecosystems: Research issues and solution ideas from microsoft dynamics ax. In: Proceedings of the Sixth International Workshop on Variability Modeling of Software-Intensive Systems, VaMoS '12, p. 21–26. Association for Computing Machinery, New York, NY, USA (2012)
45. Nöbauer, M., Seyff, N., Groher, I.: Similarity analysis within product line scoping: An evaluation of a semi-automatic approach. In: International Conference on Advanced Information Systems Engineering, pp. 165–179. Springer (2014)
46. Noor, M.A., Grünbacher, P., Hoyer, C.: A collaborative method for reuse potential assessment in reengineering-based product line adoption. In: Balancing Agility and Formalism in Software Engineering, pp. 69–83. Springer Berlin Heidelberg, Berlin, Heidelberg (2008)
47. Rabiser, R., Wolfinger, R., Grünbacher, P.: Three-level customization of software products using a product line approach. In: 2009 42nd Hawaii International Conference on System Sciences, pp. 1–10 (2009)
48. Runeson, P., Host, M., Rainer, A., Regnell, B.: Case study research in software engineering: Guidelines and examples. John Wiley & Sons (2012)
49. Schmid, K.: A comprehensive product line scoping approach and its validation. In: Proceedings of the 24th International Conference on Software Engineering, ICSE '02, pp. 593–603. ACM, New York, NY, USA (2002)
50. Stumme, G.: Formal concept analysis. In: Handbook on ontologies, pp. 177–199. Springer (2009)
51. Van der Linden, F., Schmid, K., Rommes, E.: Software product lines in action: the best industrial practice in product line engineering, 2007th edn. Springer Science & Business Media (2007)
52. Weston, N., Chitchyan, R., Rashid, A.: A framework for constructing semantically composable feature models from natural language requirements. In: 13th International Software Product Line Conference, pp. 211–220. Carnegie Mellon University (2009)
53. Wolfinger, R., Reiter, S., Dhungana, D., Grünbacher, P., Prähofer, H.: Supporting runtime system adaptation through product line engineering and plug-in techniques. In: Seventh International Conference on Composition-Based Software Systems (ICCBSS 2008), pp. 21–30 (2008)
54. Xue, Y., Xing, Z., Jarzabek, S.: Feature location in a collection of product variants. In: Reverse Engineering (WCRE), 2012 19th Working Conference on, pp. 145–154. IEEE (2012)
55. Yang, Y., Peng, X., Zhao, W.: Domain feature model recovery from multiple applications using data access semantics and formal concept analysis. In: Reverse Engineering, 2009. WCRE'09. 16th Working Conference on, pp. 215–224. IEEE (2009)

Chapter 14
Bottom-Up Technologies for Reuse: A Framework to Support Extractive Software Product Line Adoption Activities

Jabier Martinez, Tewfik Ziadi, Tegawendé F. Bissyandé, Jaques Klein, and Yves le Traon

Abstract Bottom-Up Technologies for Reuse (BUT4Reuse) is a generic and extensible framework for helping in Software Product Line (SPL) adoption from existing artefacts. It supports the re-engineering of source code variants, models, requirements, or other structured formats. Currently 17 adapters are available for different artefact types. The framework covers the most relevant re-engineering activities towards extractive SPL adoption, i.e., the same framework can support feature identification and location, feature constraints discovery, feature model synthesis, and the construction of reusable assets. Well-defined extension points are provided for integrating algorithms and techniques for the mentioned activities. Similar to the case of the adapters, more than 20 state-of-the-art algorithms and techniques are currently integrated. The target users are both SPL adopters and integrators of adapters and techniques. In addition, two integrated benchmarks are proposed towards reproducible and comparable results for feature location research. This chapter presents the framework principles, supported activities, and an overview of the currently available functionalities.

J. Martinez (✉)
Tecnalia, Basque Research and Technology Alliance (BRTA), Derio, Spain
e-mail: jabier.martinez@tecnalia.com

T. Ziadi
Sorbonne University, Paris, France
e-mail: tewfik.ziadi@lip6.fr

T. F. Bissyandé · J. Klein · Y. le Traon
University of Luxembourg, Esch-sur-Alzette, Luxembourg
e-mail: tegawende.bissyande@uni.lu; jaques.klein@uni.lu; yves.letraon@uni.lu

© Springer Nature Switzerland AG 2023
R. E. Lopez-Herrejon et al. (eds.), *Handbook of Re-Engineering Software Intensive Systems into Software Product Lines*, https://doi.org/10.1007/978-3-031-11686-5_14

14.1   Introduction

Extractive Software Product Line (SPL) adoption is based on leveraging existing variants by extracting the common and varying parts into a single SPL [18]. The literature in the extractive adoption paradigm is rich in reengineering approaches for the detection of the variability and commonality among existing products, their analysis, and transformation [6]. Several case studies, ranging from source code variants to models or requirements have been reported [25]. Despite of this, the lack of tool-supported frameworks for this endeavour has as consequence that similar implementation efforts are being repeated to support different use cases. Thus, practitioners do not easily find techniques to experiment with state-of-the-art SPL adoption analyses.

It is a challenge by itself to address, within the same environment, all the SPL adoption activities. Each technique requires inputs and provides outputs at different granularity levels and with different formats complicating the integration of approaches in a unified process. In addition, the proposed approaches are often related to specific types of software artefacts. Thus, the implementation of such algorithms is usually specific to a given artefact type (e.g., source code in a given programming language), and the effort needed to re-adapt it for another type of artefact is often a barrier (e.g., another programming language or a completely different artefact such as requirement files or architecture models). There is, however, an opportunity to reuse the principles guiding these existing techniques for other artefacts. When such algorithms are underlying in a framework providing an abstraction for diverse artefact types, they could be transparently used in different scenarios.

In this context, Bottom-Up Technologies for Reuse (BUT4Reuse)[1] [29, 31] is an open-source framework for helping in extractive SPL adoption. Other frameworks like ECCO (Extraction and Composition for Clone-and-Own) [14] or the Virtual Platform [23] try to support companies to mix the benefits of clone-and-own and SPLs. As mentioned before, in the case of BUT4Reuse, the main objective is the extraction of an SPL with a minor focus on variants synchronization [36, 38], or trying to support reactive adoption approaches [18] (i.e., incrementally growing the SPL or making the SPL coexist with clone-and-own).

BUT4Reuse's main properties are threefold (1) it covers the most relevant re-engineering activities towards SPL adoption from feature identification and location, feature constraints discovery and feature model synthesis until the extraction of reusable assets. While it can be used for the analysis of single systems, the focus has been in analysing variants of systems created with clone-and-own approaches [8]. (2) Generic: It is agnostic of the artefact types of the assets or variants under analysis. This is supported by the concept of Adapters and a large set of adapters are available ranging from requirements to models and widely-used programming

---

[1] https://but4reuse.github.io/.

languages such as Java or C/C++. (3) Extensible: BUT4Reuse has well-defined interfaces (extension points) for the activities (e.g, feature location, feature constraints discovery or feature model synthesis) and its plugin-based architecture allows developers to easily integrate them in the framework. Similar to the case of the adapters, a large set of algorithms and techniques are available.

Given these properties, two main types of users are expected to use the framework [31]: (a) SPL adopters: companies with similar software products that aim to get the benefits claimed by SPL Engineering, and (b) Integrators to test concrete techniques for the different steps of extractive SPL adoption. Notably, the software engineering research community can integrate innovative techniques for comparison and benchmarking.

This chapter provides an overview of the framework and points the reader to the relevant publications for further reading. The chapter is organised as follows. Section 14.2 details the central concept of Adapter in BUT4Reuse to make the framework generic for different artefact types. Then, Sect. 14.3 presents the covered re-engineering activities and the typical workflow for SPL adopters. The extensible property is detailed in Sect. 14.4, and Sect. 14.5 discusses the current benchmarking options. Finally, Sect. 14.6 concludes and outlines future perspectives.

14.2   A Generic Framework for Different Artefact Types: Adapters

BUT4Reuse aims at supporting different types of artefacts enabling extensibility in this regard. To achieve this, it relies on *adapters* for the different artefact types. These adapters, that can be considered as a pivot language or as an intermediary abstraction, are implemented as the main components of the framework. Section 14.2.1 elaborates on the principles in adapter development, Sect. 14.2.2 presents the design of a set adapters, and Sect. 14.2.3 provides an overview of those currently available.

14.2.1   *Principles to Be Considered in Adapter Development*

The adapter is responsible for decomposing each artefact type into its constituting elements and supporting re-engineering activities including defining how a set of elements should be constructed to create a reusable asset. An adapter is intended to follow a set of principles for its implementation, illustrated in Fig. 14.1:

(1) A typical software artefact can be decomposed into distinct *elements*.
(2) Given a pair of elements in a specific artefact type, a *similarity* metric can be computed for comparison purposes.

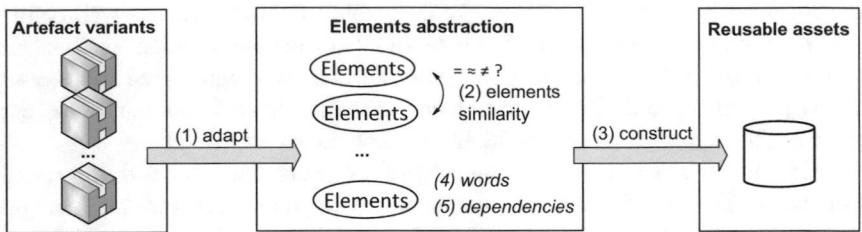

Fig. 14.1 Illustration of the principles of adapters

(3) Given a set of elements recovered from existing artefacts, a new artefact, or at least a part of it (which would be a reusable asset), can be *constructed*.

On the one hand, principles (1) and (2) make possible to reason on a set of software artefacts for identifying commonality and variability of *n* variants, which in turn will be exploited in feature identification and location activities. For instance, the elements similarity function between any pair of elements will enable to use n-way comparison techniques. On the other hand, principle (3) promises to enable the construction of the reusable assets based on the elements found in existing artefacts.

Optionally, there are another two principles that can be implemented in an adapter:

(4) An element can provide a list of *meaningful words* [37] which is particularly useful for feature identification and location activities based on information retrieval or text-based analysis. For instance, classes and methods names in source code can be related, in some cases, to feature names and descriptions.
(5) *Dependencies* can be established between elements. These dependencies define constraints, e.g., an element depends on another element. This is helpful for constraints discovery among features. For instance, an element from a feature might require an element from another feature suggesting a requires constraint. Maximum and minimum cardinalities in the relation between elements can also be defined. For example, one variant has one element "A" with two child elements, and another variant has the same element "A" with two different child elements. If the maximum number of child-parent dependencies that "A" can hold is two, it is not possible to construct a variant with four children for element "A". This is a potential indicator of alternative features. Besides its use for constraints discovery, dependencies can also be useful during construction as it also captures how an artefact can be correctly constructed.

Figure 14.2 illustrates examples of adapters dealing with different artefact types. We can see how an adapter allows the operations to adapt the artefact to elements, and to take elements as input to construct a reusable asset for this artefact type. For example, source code can be adapted to Abstract Syntax Tree (AST) elements which capture the modular structure of source code. Text files can be decomposed in different parts (e.g., lines). Models can be decomposed in Meta-Object Facility

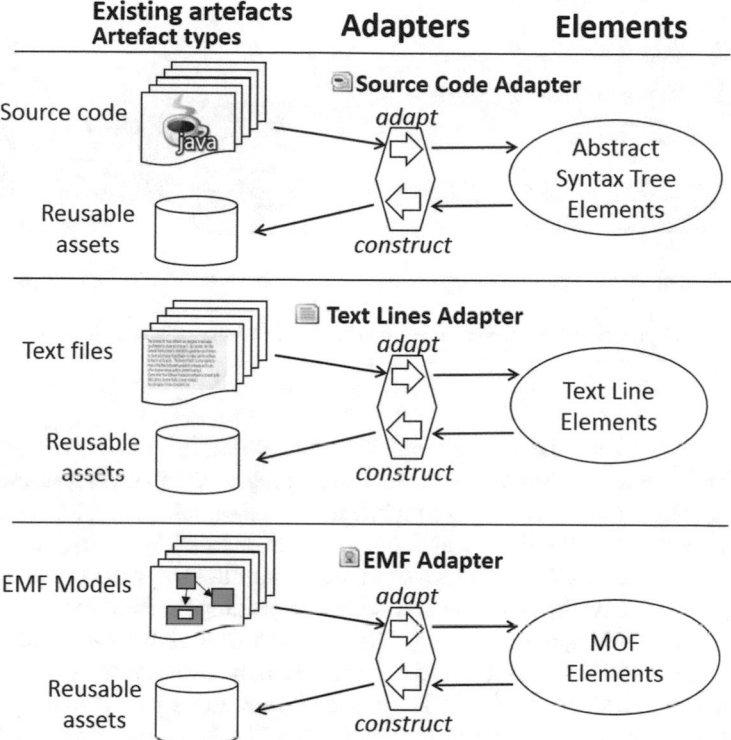

Fig. 14.2 Artefact type examples and elements representation creation through the adapters. The adapter can also construct reusable assets taking a set of elements as input [29]

(MOF) Elements [34] such as Class, Attribute and References. More details are presented next.

14.2.2 Design Examples of Adapters

Several examples of adapters are available in the source code repository of the framework, all of them using the `org.but4reuse.adapters` extension point. The currently available ones are presented in Sect. 14.2.3, however, we present here examples of adapters. More specifically, we present how we can design an adapter in terms of their elements and the implementation of the principles. We illustrate it with the adapters to analyse Text Lines, File Structures, Models, Java source code, and C/C++ source code.

Figure 14.3 presents a couple of basic adapters that are currently available. The text lines adapter, in Fig. 14.3a, only contains one element type: `LineElement`. The similarity between lines, instead of checking an exact match of the text in

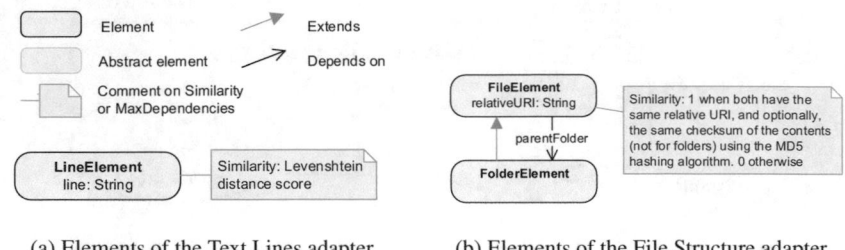

(a) Elements of the Text Lines adapter   (b) Elements of the File Structure adapter

Fig. 14.3 Examples of basic adapters. Elements of the Text Lines adapter. Elements of the File Structure adapter

the line, is based on the Levenshtein distance score [19] which will provide a normalized continuous value from 0 to 1 according to the matching characters of the string. The words retrieved from a line are based on tokenizing the string (e.g., creating segments of the line string from its white-spaces). Many user-preferences are available in BUT4Reuse to further process and filter the words obtained from the adapters. Finally, the construct is based on appending the lines to a document.

The file structure adapter, in Fig. 14.3b, also has an straightforward design. The `FolderElement` extends `FileElement` as they both share an URI (e.g., a path in the file system). Each file has a dependency to its parent folder. There is virtually no limit in the number of files within a folder, so there is no need to define cardinality constraints in this dependency. Assuming that all the variants are in the same root URI, the similarity is based on comparing the relative URIs of the files with respect to this root. This similarity is just in the name and path of the file, but not in the contents (i.e., two files in different variants are considered equal even if the contents are different). Because of this, a user-preference, defined by the adapter, is available in the framework to select if contents must be checked. In this implementation, the checksum of the contents is calculated for both files using the MD5 hashing algorithms to check if the contents are equal. Other designer could have made different design decisions to avoid to have a similarity based only in 0 or 1, e.g., using Levenshtein distance score in the file names, or, when checking the contents of the files, some kind of percentage of the lines that are equal. The words are based in tokenizing the names of the files, and the construct is based on copying the files in the given output folder.

Figure 14.4 shows the elements of the Models adapter. The details and case studies for this adapter are available [28]. The model is decomposed in its class, attribute, and reference elements which are basic entities of the MOF (Meta-Object Facility) standard [34]. MOF is a standard to support model-driven engineering in its many forms, not only UML models, so the adapter can be used for a wide set

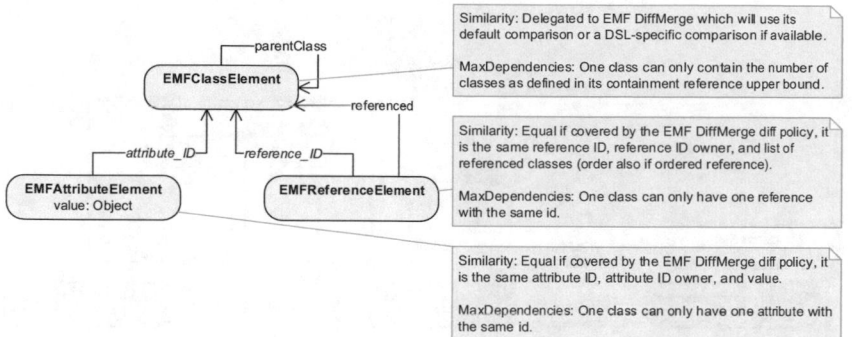

Fig. 14.4 Elements of the Models adapter

of model types. The implementation is based on the Eclipse Modelling Framework (EMF).[2]

Instead of reinventing the wheel on model elements similarity, and to get the benefit of established approaches, the similarity in the Models adapter is delegated to the publicly available EMF DiffMerge framework [13]. This extensible framework allows to define how entities of a given Domain-Specific Language (DSL) should be compared and it provides a general-purpose and configurable implementation for any DSL. For instance, the diff policy can define when certain attributes or references should be ignored (e.g., derived attributes), or which are the relevant attributes to consider a model class as equal to another class. For the constraints regarding well-formed models, the adapter implementation checks the cardinality of the containment references (i.e., the cardinality of parent child relations). Also, attributes and references can only have one value or referenced list (e.g., if a class has an attribute with ID "name", this class cannot have two "name" attributes). The words are based on the EMF label providers of the classes and the string representation of the attributes' values. The construct is based on creating a base model following the CVL (Common Variability Language) [17] annotative approach. CVL is a conceptual and tool-supported framework for variability management in models.

Figure 14.5 shows the elements defined by the currently available Java JDT adapter implementation that uses the Eclipse Java Development Tools (JDT) parser and framework.[3] Most of the elements inherit from `JDTElement`, as for example, the `CompilationUnitElement` that corresponds to the different Java files, the `TypeElement` which are the Java classes inside the compilation units, the package defined in the classes corresponds to the `PackageElement`, the `MethodElements` which are the declaration of the methods inside the classes, etc.

---

[2] https://www.eclipse.org/modeling/emf/.

[3] https://www.eclipse.org/jdt/.

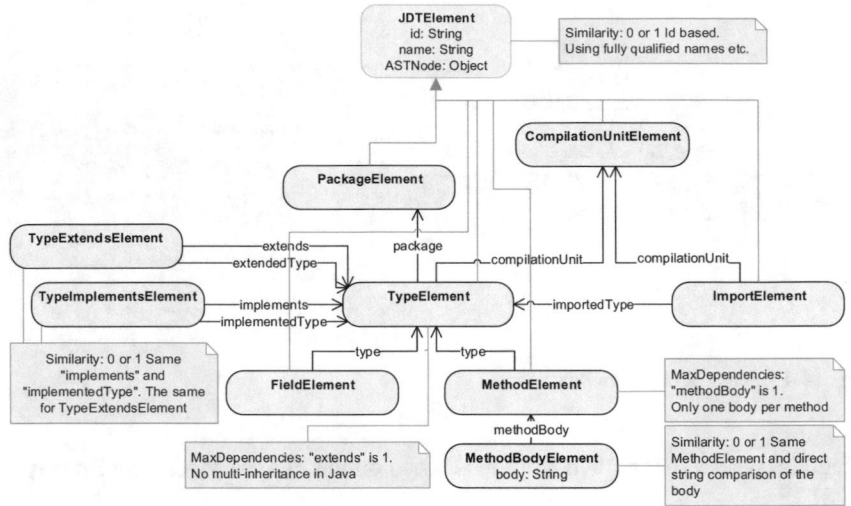

Fig. 14.5 Elements of the Java JDT adapter

The similarity function in this case is not using values from 0 to 1 but directly 0 or 1 depending if the source code qualified name (as defined in the `JDTElement` id) is exactly the same. This kind of source code adapters makes the similarity function very sensible to source code refactoring in the variants [7]. Notice also that the granularity of this adapter is not considering source code method statements separately. However, it has the `MethodBodyElement` which is a string with all the text of the method but without making distinction among statements. The similarity in this case is defined as a string comparison of this text. Depending on the desired granularity of the analysis, a refined adapter might be required. This is possible by extending or modifying the adapter. In general, the user of the framework will need to check if the selected adapter is appropriate for its task at hand and extend it or refined if needed.

The notes in Fig. 14.5 also mentions the implemented constraints. Notably, the "extends" relation to `TypeExtendsElement` only allows one entry as multi-inheritance extending from several classes is not permitted. Also, one method declaration (`MethodElement`) can only have one `MethodBodyElement`. These constraints are relevant to avoid that the adapter constructs incorrect products. To prevent this, these constraints can be used to detect other kind of constraints in the relation between implementation parts of the variants. For instance, we might have two variants with changes in the statements within the same method, then, the variation point will have two alternatives that are mutually exclusive as we cannot have both `MethodBodyElement` as part of the method. The words are based on the names of the classes, methods, etc., other designer could have chosen to also retrieve words from the source code comments or JavaDoc annotations. The construct is based on re-creating the AST based on the elements to be constructed.

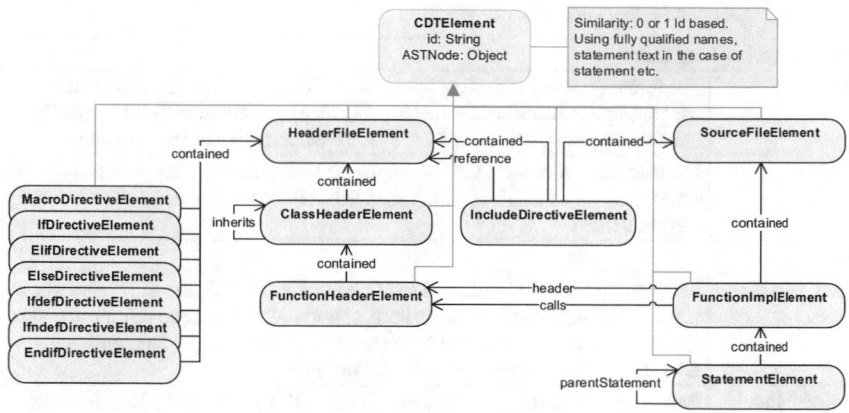

Fig. 14.6 Elements of the C/C++ CDT adapter

A similar approach is followed for the design of the C/C++ source code adapter that internally uses the Eclipse C/C++ Development Tooling (CDT) parser.[4] Figure 14.6 shows the elements of this adapter. Header files are decomposed in class headers with their function headers, as well as include and different types of source code directives. Source files are decomposed in function implementations and their statements. Contrary to the design of the JDT adapter, in this case we further decompose the methods implementation in statements and nested statements. Among the typical references in source code, the adapter captures also the "calls" within function implementations. For this, the adapter relies on the Doxygen external tool.[5]

14.2.3   Currently Available Adapters

Martinez et al. [29] detailed several specific adapters in terms of: when an artefact is adaptable by the adapter, which are the predefined elements, how the adaptation is performed, which is the similarity function between elements, which types of dependencies are defined, and how the construction is performed. Table 14.1 presents an updated list of the currently available adapters with a brief description.

The available adapters are diverse. Some of them are related to programming languages such as Java and C/C++ [16, 51] as presented before. Others are for Models such as the mentioned EMF Models adapter which is detailed in Martinez et al. [28], and a specific type of models which is the Requirements Interchange Format (ReqIF) [35]. Then, we have general structured formats for dealing with

---

[4] https://www.eclipse.org/cdt/.

[5] https://www.doxygen.nl/.

Table 14.1 List of adapters and a brief description

Programming languages	
Java	For folders or files with Java source code. There are two variants of this adapter, one is based in Ziadi et al. [51] using the FeatureHouse parser [5], but the one using JDT (See Sect. 14.2.2) supports newer Java versions
C/C++	For folders or files with C/C++ source code. Similarly to the Java adapter, an adapter based on Ziadi et al. [51] exists but the new one using CDT is more recommended
Models	
EMF Models	MOF compliant models [34]. Described in Sect. 14.2.2 and in Martinez et al. [28]. It decomposes the models in its classes, attributes, and references. The construction allows to create 150% models (n-way merge) and, optionally, CVL [17] assets for the derivation of variants
ReqIF Models	Requirements documents following the ReqIF standard [35]. ReqIF model visitor with ProR [12], and similarity using the WUP natural Language comparison technique [47]
General structures	
Text lines	Text files. Similarity based on the Levenshtein distance between strings [19]. The construct is based on appending the line strings to an empty file
Natural language text	A text file with Sentence elements. Sentence splitter using OpenNLP [4] and WUP natural language comparison technique [47] for similarity as implemented in WordNet for Java [46]
File structure	Any folder. The elements are files and folders. The similarity is based on the name and relative path to the initial folder. Optionally file contents based on MD5 hashing. Containment dependencies are considered. The construct method copies the resources in the given destination
JSON files	The elements are those of the JSON specification: Object, Key, Value, Array, etc.
CSV files	Comma-separated values file. The elements are the cells and the comparison is based on the position and string comparison. A cell depends on its row and column
Graphs	A GraphML or GML file. The elements are VertexElement and EdgeElement. Decomposition using the Blueprints Tinkerpop graph visitor [44]. Vertex dependency based on the edges. Subgraphs creation in GraphML format
Images	Image files in jpg, bmp, png, gif or ico format. Detailed in Martinez et al. [29]. It decomposes the images in its pixels with dependencies to their position in the image matrix
Specific artefact types	
Eclipse	The folder of an Eclipse installation. The elements are the plugins and files
Scratch	Scratch scripts. This adapter is an extension of the JSON adapter. It constructs a complete sb2 file with the project.json and all the needed resources (images, sounds etc.)
Music XML	Note elements adapted using a MusicXML parser. Note similarity is based on the note position in the measure, pitch and duration
JaCoCo reports	Reports created with the Java Code Coverage Library. Instead of comparing product variants, this adapter can be used analyse and compare execution traces of a program
Bytecode	Programs compiled with the Java Bytecode. For example compiled with Java, Kotlin or Scala. Details are presented in Ziadi and Hillah [52]
Android	This adapter extends the JDT adapter to also capture Android apps metadata [20]

file structures, comma-separated values files (CSV), JSON files (JavaScript Object Notation), Graphs in GraphML or GML files, etc. Then we have support for specific artefact types such as Eclipse installations, Music scores in MusicXML files, the bytecode adapter [52], an specialization of the Java adapter for Android apk files [20], and other miscellaneous adapters.

The similarity functions in the different adapters are diverse as well. For EMF models, as mentioned in Sect. 14.2.2, we rely on an existing model comparison framework, EMF DiffMerge [13], which allows the user to customize the way the similarity is calculated. For file structures, name and relative path to the initial folder are used and optionally file contents based on MD5 hashing. For elements relying in text, there are several options that we have used such as the Levenshtein distance between strings [19] or the WUP natural language comparison technique [47] as implemented in WordNet for Java [46].

In Martinez et al. [29], we discussed the effort needed to implement new adapters. We consider that the creation or modification of adapters is not complex. Specially, if we put them in perspective with the amount of possibilities for variants analysis that will be unlocked. The most challenging part of an adapter is probably the similarity function as it is a complex problem by itself. The number of implemented examples can also simplify their development.

14.3   Covered Re-engineering Activities

In this section we elaborate in the re-engineering activities for extractive SPL adoption supported by the framework. Figure 14.7 presents the concepts and complementary activities. Regarding the role of the adapter, in the *decomposition* layer (on the left side of Fig. 14.7), we illustrate how the adapter represents the strategy for the decomposition of the artefact variants into elements. As mentioned before, these elements are the abstraction used for the rest of the extractive SPL adoption process. Also, on the right side of the figure, we illustrate how the adapter construction method helps in creating the reusable assets.

The framework builds on an architecture composed of various extensible layers explained below. After the decomposition of all artefact variants in elements, the elements are grouped via block identification. Then, with the abstraction of elements and blocks, we can seamlessly chain the activities for extractive SPL adoption. In addition, we present the visualisation layer for domain experts which is a horizontal layer that covers the whole process.

We describe more in detail the different activities:

Decomposition: The first layer is the decomposition layer using the *adapters*. It is extensible by providing support for different artefact types. It enables the creation of the *elements representation* which provides a common internal representation.
Block identification: A block is a set of elements obtained by analysing the artefact variants (e.g., comparing the variants to identify common and variable

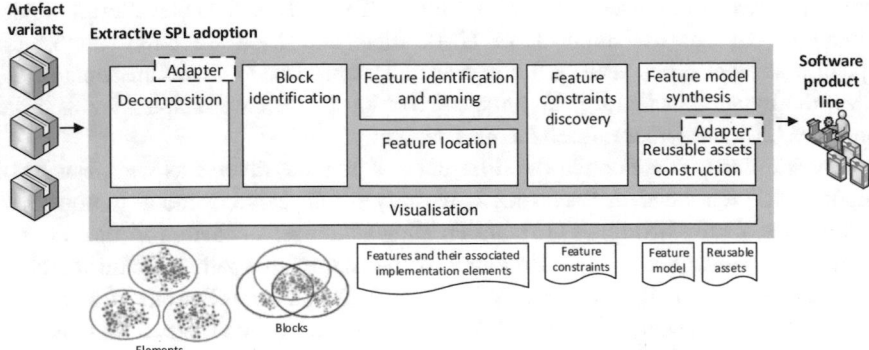

Fig. 14.7 Relevant activities during extractive SPL adoption within BUT4Reuse

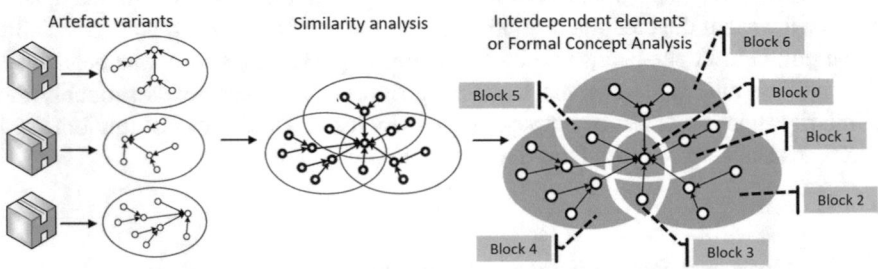

Fig. 14.8 Block identification example

parts). Blocks permit to increase the granularity of the analysis by the domain experts so that it is not needed to reason at element level. This is particularly relevant when trying to identify or locate features, and also during constraints discovery. In the context of feature identification, block identification represents an initial step before reasoning at feature level. Figure 14.8 illustrates a typical block identification approach where, after the decomposition of the variants and using the similarity functions, the blocks are identified as the different intersections of the variants.

Feature identification: The activity consists in analysing the blocks to map them to features. For instance, blocks identified as feature-specific can be converted into a feature of the envisioned feature model. In other cases, a block can be merged with another block, or we can split the elements of one block in two blocks to adjust it to identified features. To illustrate the usefulness of this, we present a recurrent issue when dealing with copy-paste-modified source code artefacts. This issue is the situation where a modification (e.g., a bug fix) is released in a set of the artefacts but not in all of them. In this case, the block identification technique could identify three different blocks: One containing the modified elements for the bug fix, one containing the "buggy" elements, and, finally, the one that contains the shared elements that were not part of the modified elements. In this case, we would like to remove the "buggy" block and merge the bug fix block with the shared block.

Also, some features are intended to *interact* with other features. A feature interaction is defined as some way in which a feature or features modify or influence another feature in defining overall system behaviour [49]. Logging feature is a common example to illustrate features that must interact with others because of its crosscutting behaviour [10] (i.e., other features might need to log if the Logging feature is present). In some cases, the implementation of the interaction needs *coordination elements* (also known as *derivatives* [21], *junctions* [50] or *glue code* among others). It is also important to consider the negations of the features, i.e., some elements can be needed when a feature is not present. In our context of extractive SPL adoption, feature interactions, and the coordination elements, must be considered.

As part of feature identification, block names should be modified by domain experts to have representative names.

Feature location: The aim is to locate the features reasoning on the list of known features and the identified blocks. Concretely, feature location techniques in our framework create mappings between features and blocks with a defined confidence. The confidence is a normalized continuous value from zero to one. For example, if the feature location technique concludes that a given feature is located in a given block with a confidence of one, it means that the technique is almost certain that the elements of this block are implementing this feature.

Constraints Discovery: The identification of constraints by mining existing assets has been identified as an important challenge for research on the SPL domain [6]. For this purpose, our framework is extensible to contribute constraints discovery approaches.

Feature model synthesis: Feature model creation demands a feature model synthesis technique to obtain comprehensible feature diagrams.

Reusable assets construction: The framework supports the step of creating the reusable assets from a set of elements using the adapter. Depending on the needs, the set of elements could correspond to a block, an identified feature, or the elements that corresponded to a located feature.

Visualisation: Visualisation and interactive techniques reduce the complexity of comprehension tasks and helps to have in-sights and make decisions on the tackled problem [9]. The visualisation layer is orthogonal to the other layers. It is intended to present to the domain expert relevant information yielded by other layers. Visualisations can be used, not only to display information, but also to interact with the results.

A typical workflow for SPL adopters is illustrated in Fig. 14.9. The preparation phase is followed by a feature identification and location phase. And then, depending on the scope, the feature model can be created, or the reusable assets can be extracted. BUT4Reuse is a framework to be used by integrators and researchers to test techniques for the different activities. The points with grey background in Fig. 14.9 can be extended by integrators. This will be further explained in next section.

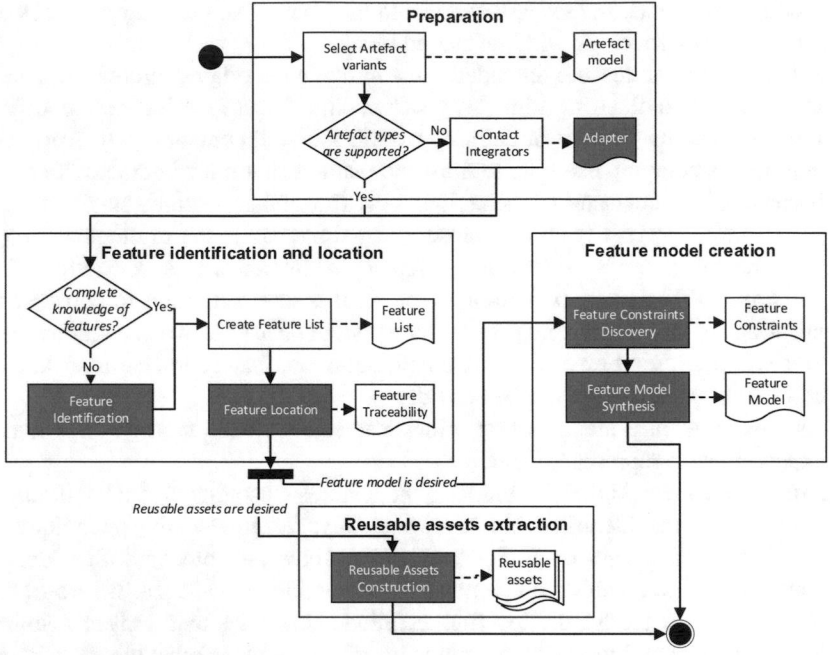

Fig. 14.9 Typical workflow for SPL adopters in BUT4Reuse. Integrators can extend BUT4Reuse at the points with grey background. Figure adapted from [31]

14.4   An Extensible Framework for Different Algorithms and Techniques

Extension points are available for the different activities presented in Sect. 14.3. In this section, we briefly present some of them with the appropriate references. The decomposition and construction activities described in Sect. 14.3 are not mentioned here as these correspond to the Adapters explained in Sect. 14.2.

Table 14.2 lists the techniques for block identification, feature identification, and feature location. For block and feature identification we can find several available techniques such as the interdependent elements technique [50] or the Formal Concept Analysis (FCA) technique [2, 41] where the objective is to separate the different intersections of the artefact variants. Other techniques are described such as using FCA and then structural splitting [24].

For feature location, current implementations try to map blocks or elements to features. Apart from the core of each feature, we are also interested in locating coordination elements belonging to feature interactions. Before applying feature location techniques, to locate these coordination elements, we implemented a method for pre-processing the feature list. This method can be optionally used to

Table 14.2 List of available techniques related to block identification, feature identification, and feature location

Block identification	
Interdependent elements	An algorithm proposed by Ziadi et al. [50] to separate the different intersections of the artefact variants
Formal Concept Analysis (FCA)	Based on FCA [15], it is another widely used approach for n-way comparison to separate the intersections of the artefact variants
FCA and structural splitting	This technique extends FCA by further splitting the obtained blocks based on the dependencies among the elements [24]. This splitting can be done through two graph analysis techniques: strongly connected components or weakly connected components
Similar elements	This technique provides the finest granularity where each element, after the similarity analysis phase, corresponds to one block. This creates a large number of blocks to be used for testing or for delegating the analysis to the following activities (e.g., feature location)

Feature identification: Mainly a manual process supported by BUT4Reuse visualisations (e.g., VariClouds [30])

Feature location	
Strict Feature-Specific location (SFS)	A feature is located in a block when (1) the block always appears in the artefacts that implements this feature and (2) the block never appears in any artefact that does not implement this feature
Feature-Specific heuristic	The same as SFS but without the second rule
Latent Semantic Indexing (LSI)	In LSI [11], the name and description of a feature are extracted to create a term query. Then, a term-document matrix is created, and the cosine similarity is calculated with the words extracted from the elements of the block. Several traditional LSI parameters can be specified by the user
SFS + LSI	Features identified as relevant for a block through SFS are then transformed into LSI documents. Then, block elements are used as query and the document (feature) with highest similarity is used as located feature for the element
SFS + Shared term	Group features and blocks with SFS and then apply a "search" of the feature words within the elements of the block to discard elements that may be completely unrelated. This one and the next two ones are detailed and evaluated in Martinez et al. [32]
SFS + TF	After using SFS, all the features assigned to a block compete for the block elements, based on term-frequency as metric
SFS + TFIDF	The same as SFS + TF but using TFIDF (term frequency–inverse document frequency)
Spectrum-based localization	A technique traditionally used for fault localization [45] but integrated in BUT4Reuse following the principles described in Michelon et al. [33]. The user can select from 33 different ranking metrics

automatically include potential derivative features related to pairwise interactions, 3-wise interactions or feature negations.

Given that we introduced the notion of the *confidence* of the located feature with a value from 0 to 1, the framework allows setting the value of a user-specified threshold. By default, the threshold is 1, i.e., only when the feature location returns 1 as confidence it will be considered as similar enough to be considered equal. A second threshold in the similarity can be introduced to define in which cases the user wants to perform a manual check to decide if they can be considered the same or not.

We integrated diverse feature location techniques [24] from which we can highlight two: The Strict Feature-Specific (SFS) technique that follows two assumptions: A feature is located in a block when (1) the block *always* appears in the artefacts that implements this feature and (2) the block *never* appears in any artefact that does not implement this feature. The second technique is Latent Semantic Indexing (LSI), a technique for analysing relationships among a set of documents [11] that has been used in feature location in the context of extractive SPL adoption [3, 40, 48]. In LSI, the name and description of a feature are extracted to create a term query. Then, a term-document matrix is created, and the cosine similarity is calculated with the words extracted from the elements of the block. Given that the amount of words can be large, LSI techniques often rely on parameters to reduce this amount. In our implementation, this can be configured for using a user-specified percentage of the words. Alternatively, the user can select a fixed number of words ignoring the least frequent ones. Combinations of static and textual-analysis feature location techniques have been also integrated and evaluated such as SFS and Shared term, SFS and Term frequency, SFS and tf-idf described in Martinez et al. [24, 32].

Table 14.3 lists the currently available techniques for constraints discovery, feature model synthesis, and reusable assets construction. For constraints discovery, the available ones are described in Martinez et al. [24] and they can be simultaneously applied during the analysis. The first one, structural binary relations, is useful for "requires" and "mutual exclusion" constraint discovery using the cardinality constraints defined in the adapters (MaxDependencies presented in Sect. 14.2 as well as the MinDependencies that can be defined). Apart from that one, there is one heuristic using FCA's concept lattices, and another using machine learning through a-priori association rules from the existing configurations.

Regarding feature model synthesis, currently, there are two available options: One that just creates a flat feature model with the feature list and another called "Alternatives before Hierarchy" that groups features based on the identified constraints [24]. Concretely, alternative groups for mutually exclusive features, and parent-child relationships based on the "requires" constraints. The created feature models can be opened in FeatureIDE [43].

Table 14.4 lists the available techniques for visualisation. The visualisation is a relevant aspect in BUT4Reuse [24]. We can find visualisations such as bars and stripes visualisations, feature location heat-maps, several graph representations (dependencies among elements in a variant, all elements from all variants using colours for each block, constraints discovered among blocks, similarity graphs among variants etc.), the pruned concept hierarchy from the FCA, or wordclouds summarising information from blocks, features, and variants [30].

Table 14.3 List of available techniques for constraints discovery, feature model synthesis, and reusable assets construction

Constraints discovery	
Structural binary relations	This is based on analysing the dependencies among the elements. The requires constraint is defined when at least one element from one side (block or feature) has a dependency with an element of the other side. The mutual exclusion constraint is identified based on incompatible maximum cardinalities of a dependency (See Sect. 14.2)
A-priori association rules	This technique uses association rule learning. It mines the relationships of the presence or absence of the blocks in the artefact variants (i.e., the configurations of the existing variants). We integrated the A-Priory algorithm as previously evaluated for this purpose in the SPLE literature [22]. Blocks information can be exported to the Weka ARFF format
FCA-based constraints discovery	When applying FCA, concepts are related through concept lattices which represent potential relations among the blocks. This technique has been presented and evaluated in research on extractive SPL adoption [1, 39, 41]. We implemented the requires dependency when there is a sub-concept that requires a super-concept according to the identified lattices
Feature model synthesis	
Flat feature model	This technique creates a feature model without any hierarchical information among features. It is based on the creation of an abstract root feature where all the features are added as subfeatures. All the constraints are added as cross-tree constraints
Alternatives before hierarchy	This heuristic is based on calculating first the Alternative groups from the mutual exclusion constraints, and then creating the hierarchy using the requires constraints. The constraints that were not included in the hierarchy are added as cross-tree constraints

Reusable assets construction: It relies on each of the adapters functionality for construction (See Sect. 14.2)

14.5   Benchmarking Support for Different Techniques

It is acknowledged the importance of benchmarking in the context of evolution of variant-rich systems [42], specially to improve the state-of-the-art through comparable and reproducible results. With such an extensible architecture to integrate different algorithms and techniques, it is natural to provide BUT4Reuse with benchmarking functionalities.

So far, the focus was on feature location techniques, notably because of its relevance during the analysis and evolution of variants. Establishing a ground-truth for feature location benchmarks based on traceability between feature and implementation elements might be also less subjective than for other activities. For example, for activities such as feature model synthesis or feature identification, the subjectivity of the domain experts might play a more important role.

We integrated two feature location benchmarks; (1) EFLBench, the Eclipse Feature Location Benchmark [32], and (2) ArgoUML-SPL Bench, the ArgoUML SPL

Table 14.4 List of available techniques for visualisation

Visualisation	
Bar diagrams	A visualiser displaying information about block elements on artefacts, blocks on artefacts, features on blocks, and blocks on features
Formal Context Analysis	A typical visualisation as result of the FCA technique [15]. It is known as the pruned concept hierarchy or the AOC-poset
Heat-map for feature location	It displays a matrix with the relation among features and blocks. Larger location confidence values are represented with darker background colours in the cells
Graphs of elements, blocks and features	Three kind of graph-based visualisations. A graph where the nodes are all the elements and the edges are the dependency relations among them. A graph where the nodes are the identified blocks and the edges are the identified constraints among them. A graph where the nodes are the features and the edges are the identified constraints between them. In all these graphs, nodes and edges are labelled with different attributes for easy graph manipulation
VariClouds	Proposed and evaluated by Martinez et al. [30], it is an approach that helps mainly for feature identification. Words from the blocks are visualised as word clouds based on TF or TFIDF metrics. The user can refine the processing of the words using and chaining several techniques (stemming, camel case splitter, synonyms etc.)
Graph of artefacts similarity	A graph where the products are the nodes and the weighted edges are based on the Jaccard similarity among them

Feature Location Benchmark [26]. They can be used independently of BUT4Reuse, but there exists helpers for their usage within the framework.[6]

Table 14.5 presents some characteristics of these benchmarks. In EFLBench the granularity of the location is coarse (component/plugin level but not the source code) so it is appropriate for information retrieval and text-based techniques. ArgoUML SPL benchmark has a quite fine granularity which is close to source code statements. This benchmark can be used for benchmarking a wider range of techniques including dynamic feature location [33]. Apart from the precision and recall metrics calculated by the benchmark, the results can be put in perspective with a recent study on the manual process for feature location to create the original ArgoUML SPL [27].

In both benchmarks, diverse scenarios are available to analyse if the technique is sensible to the number of variants, or to their level of diversity (i.e., pair-wise of the features within the set of variants). A developer of a new feature location technique just need to integrate it in the framework and use the BUT4Reuse helpers to obtain the metrics.

---

[6] EFLBench: https://github.com/but4reuse/but4reuse/wiki/Benchmarks, ArgoUML SPL benchmark: https://github.com/but4reuse/argouml-spl-benchmark_but4reuse-helper.

Table 14.5 Integrated feature location benchmarks

	EFL bench	ArgoUML-SPL bench
Scenarios	The main scenarios are the official releases of Eclipse variants. Ten scenarios are presented in Martinez et al. [32] with a number of variants ranging from 4 to 14. A generator of synthetic scenarios is also provided to evaluate the effect of the number of variants and their diversity in the feature location results	Fifteen predefined scenarios: One of them is the original ArgoUML for feature location in single systems. Another one with all possible variants (256) to assess scalability. Ten of them randomly generated with different numbers of variants. Other scenario of 9 variants with full pair-wise feature coverage. And the traditional scenario of 10 variants used in previous literature
Features	The number of features depends on the scenario but it usually ranges between 100 and 600 features. They are almost completely disjoint	Eight features with 14 feature interactions and 2 feature negations
Location granularity	Plugins. Despite that the plugins are based on source code, the benchmark focuses on a coarser granularity to represent component-based architectures. The information that is expected to be used for feature location are the plugin name, description and dependencies	Source code in terms of classes, methods, and "Refinements" of classes or methods (i.e., no need to locate the concrete statement but identifying that at least one statement corresponds to a feature in the Method, or in the Class (e.g., import statements or global variables))
Variants size	There is high diversity in the number of plugins of a variant. The scenario of the official releases had in total from 484 to 2614 plugins for all variants. Each feature is usually associated to 5 plugins with a standard deviation of around 10	A minimum of 111 KLoC and a maximum of 148 KLoC

14.6 Conclusion

Bottom-up Technologies for Reuse (BUT4Reuse) is a framework for the analysis and transformation of variants mainly focused in their transition to a Software Product Line approach. It is conceived to be generic and extensible enabling the integration of previously existing techniques in different activities, as well as enabling the integration of novel and original ones. More than 20 algorithms and techniques are currently integrated. Existing adapters for very diverse artefact types allow its quick usage. Currently, 17 adapters are available. However, a refinement of the adapters will be usually needed to adjust them to the expected level of granularity and the re-engineering needs. BUT4Reuse has been used for different case studies and two integrated benchmarks are available for the feature location activity.

The presented extensible framework open perspectives for the integration of other benchmarks for the different activities. Benchmarking results could provide evidences about the convenience of certain techniques for specific scenarios. Once available, recommendations or guidelines to select the techniques to chain in the reengineering process could be provided. In addition, capabilities for cost estimation of the reengineering process, or functionalities for SPL scoping, could be integrated to complement the technical framework with other organizational concerns.

References

1. AL-Msie'deen, R., Huchard, M., Seriai, A.D.D., Urtado, C., Vauttier, S.: Concept lattices: A representation space to structure software variability. In: 5th International Conference on Information and Communication Systems (ICICS), pp. 1–6 (2014)
2. Al-Msie'deen, R., Seriai, A., Huchard, M., Urtado, C., Vauttier, S., Salman, H.E.: Feature location in a collection of software product variants using formal concept analysis. In: 13th International Conference on Software Reuse, ICSR 2013, Pisa, Italy, June 18–20. Proceedings, *Lecture Notes in Computer Science*, vol. 7925, pp. 302–307. Springer (2013)
3. Al-Msie'deen, R., Seriai, A., Huchard, M., Urtado, C., Vauttier, S., Salman, H.E.: Mining features from the object-oriented source code of a collection of software variants using formal concept analysis and latent semantic indexing. In: The 25th International Conference on Software Engineering and Knowledge Engineering (SEKE), Boston, MA, USA, June 27–29, 2013, pp. 244–249 (2013)
4. Apache: OpenNLP. http://opennlp.apache.org (2010)
5. Apel, S., Kastner, C., Lengauer, C.: FEATUREHOUSE: Language-independent, automated software composition. In: Proceedings of the 31st International Conference on Software Engineering, ICSE '09, pp. 221–231. IEEE Computer Society, Washington, DC, USA (2009)
6. Assunção, W.K.G., Lopez-Herrejon, R.E., Linsbauer, L., Vergilio, S.R., Egyed, A.: Reengineering legacy applications into software product lines: a systematic mapping. Empir. Softw. Eng. **22**(6), 2972–3016 (2017)
7. Benmerzoug, A., Yessad, L., Ziadi, T.: Analyzing the impact of refactoring variants on feature location. In: 19th International Conference on Software and Systems Reuse, ICSR 2020, Hammamet, Tunisia, December 2–4, 2020, Proceedings, *Lecture Notes in Computer Science*, vol. 12541, pp. 279–291. Springer (2020)
8. Berger, T., Rublack, R., Nair, D., Atlee, J.M., Becker, M., Czarnecki, K., Wasowski, A.: A survey of variability modeling in industrial practice. In: The 7th International Workshop on Variability Modelling of Software-intensive Systems, VaMoS '13, Pisa, Italy, January 23–25, 2013, pp. 7:1–7:8. ACM (2013)
9. Card, S.K., Mackinlay, J.D., Shneiderman, B. (eds.): Readings in Information Visualization: Using Vision to Think. Morgan Kaufmann Publishers Inc. (1999)
10. Couto, M.V., Valente, M.T., Figueiredo, E.: Extracting software product lines: A case study using conditional compilation. In: 15th European Conference on Software Maintenance and Reengineering, CSMR 2011, 1–4 March 2011, Oldenburg, Germany, pp. 191–200. IEEE Computer Society (2011)
11. Deerwester, S.C., Dumais, S.T., Landauer, T.K., Furnas, G.W., Harshman, R.A.: Indexing by latent semantic analysis. Journal of the American Society for Information Science and Technology (JASIS) **41**(6), 391–407 (1990)
12. Eclipse: Requirements Engineering Platform. http://eclipse.org/rmf/pror/ (2014)
13. Eclipse: EMF Diff/Merge: a diff/merge component for models. http://eclipse.org/diffmerge (Accessed 2021)
14. Fischer, S., Linsbauer, L., Lopez-Herrejon, R.E., Egyed, A.: Enhancing clone-and-own with systematic reuse for developing software variants. In: 30th IEEE International Conference on Software Maintenance and Evolution, Victoria, BC, Canada, September 29–October 3, 2014, pp. 391–400. IEEE Computer Society (2014)

15. Ganter, B., Wille, R.: Formal Concept Analysis: Mathematical Foundations, 1st edn. Springer-Verlag New York, Inc., Secaucus, NJ, USA (1997)
16. Grüner, S., Burger, A., Abukwaik, H., El-Sharkawy, S., Schmid, K., Ziadi, T., Paule, A., Suda, F., Viehl, A.: Demonstration of a toolchain for feature extraction, analysis and visualization on an industrial case study. In: 17th IEEE International Conference on Industrial Informatics, INDIN 2019, Helsinki, Finland, July 22–25, 2019, pp. 459–465. IEEE (2019)
17. Haugen, Ø., Wasowski, A., Czarnecki, K.: CVL: common variability language. In: 17th International Software Product Line Conference, SPLC 2013, Tokyo, Japan - August 26–30, 2013, p. 277. ACM (2013)
18. Krueger, C.W.: Easing the transition to software mass customization. In: 4th International Workshop on Software Product-Family Engineering, PFE 2001, Bilbao, Spain, October 3–5, 2001, Revised Papers, *Lecture Notes in Computer Science*, vol. 2290, pp. 282–293. Springer (2001)
19. Levenshtein, V.: Binary Codes Capable of Correcting Deletions, Insertions and Reversals. Soviet Physics Doklady **10** (1966)
20. Li, L., Martinez, J., Ziadi, T., Bissyandé, T.F., Klein, J., Traon, Y.L.: Mining families of Android applications for extractive SPL adoption. In: Proceedings of the 20th International Conference on Software Product Lines, SPLC 2016, Beijing, China, September 19–23 (2016)
21. Liu, J., Batory, D.S., Lengauer, C.: Feature oriented refactoring of legacy applications. In: L.J. Osterweil, H.D. Rombach, M.L. Soffa (eds.) 28th International Conference on Software Engineering (ICSE 2006), Shanghai, China, May 20–28, 2006, pp. 112–121. ACM (2006)
22. Lora-Michiels, A., Salinesi, C., Mazo, R.: A method based on association rules to construct product line models. In: VaMoS, *ICB-Research Report*, vol. 37, pp. 147–150. Universität Duisburg-Essen (2010)
23. Mahmood, W., Strüber, D., Berger, T., Lämmel, R., Mukelabai, M.: Seamless variability management with the virtual platform. In: 43rd IEEE/ACM International Conference on Software Engineering, ICSE 2021, Madrid, Spain, 22–30 May 2021, pp. 1658–1670. IEEE (2021)
24. Martinez, J.: Mining software artefact variants for product line migration and analysis. Ph.D. thesis, University of Luxembourg and Sorbonne University, France (2016). URL https://tel.archives-ouvertes.fr/tel-01477423
25. Martinez, J., Assunção, W.K.G., Ziadi, T.: ESPLA: A catalog of extractive SPL adoption case studies. In: Proceedings of the 21st Int. Systems and Software Product Line Conference, SPLC 2017, Volume B, Sevilla, Spain, September 25–29, 2017, pp. 38–41. ACM (2017)
26. Martinez, J., Ordoñez, N., Tërnava, X., Ziadi, T., Aponte, J., Figueiredo, E., Valente, M.T.: Feature location benchmark with ArgoUML SPL. In: Proceeedings of the 22nd International Systems and Software Product Line Conference - Volume 1, SPLC 2018, Gothenburg, Sweden, September 10–14, 2018, pp. 257–263. ACM (2018)
27. Martinez, J., Wolfart, D., Assunção, W.K.G., Figueiredo, E.: Insights on software product line extraction processes: Argouml to argouml-spl revisited. In: SPLC '20: 24th ACM International Systems and Software Product Line Conference, Montreal, Quebec, Canada, October 19–23, 2020, Volume A, pp. 6:1–6:6. ACM (2020)
28. Martinez, J., Ziadi, T., Bissyandé, T.F., Klein, J., Traon, Y.L.: Automating the extraction of model-based software product lines from model variants (T). In: 30th IEEE/ACM International Conference on Automated Software Engineering, ASE 2015, Lincoln, NE, USA, November 9–13, 2015, pp. 396–406. IEEE Computer Society (2015)
29. Martinez, J., Ziadi, T., Bissyandé, T.F., Klein, J., Traon, Y.L.: Bottom-up adoption of software product lines: a generic and extensible approach. In: Proceedings of the 19th International Conference on Software Product Line, SPLC 2015, Nashville, TN, USA, July 20–24, 2015, pp. 101–110. ACM (2015)
30. Martinez, J., Ziadi, T., Bissyandé, T.F., Klein, J., Traon, Y.L.: Name suggestions during feature identification: The VariClouds approach. In: Proceedings of the 20th International Conference on Software Product Lines, SPLC 2016, Beijing, China, September 19–23 (2016)

31. Martinez, J., Ziadi, T., Bissyandé, T.F., Klein, J., Traon, Y.L.: Bottom-up technologies for reuse: automated extractive adoption of software product lines. In: 39th International Conference on Software Engineering, ICSE 2017, Buenos Aires, Argentina, May 20–28, 2017 - Companion Volume, Tool demo, pp. 67–70. IEEE Computer Society (2017)
32. Martinez, J., Ziadi, T., Papadakis, M., Bissyandé, T.F., Klein, J., Traon, Y.L.: Feature location benchmark for extractive software product line adoption research using realistic and synthetic eclipse variants. Information & Software Technology **104**, 46–59 (2018)
33. Michelon, G.K., Sotto-Mayor, B., Martinez, J., Arrieta, A., Abreu, R., Assunção, W.K.G.: Spectrum-based feature localization: a case study using argouml. In: SPLC '21: 25th ACM International Systems and Software Product Line Conference, Leicester, United Kingdom, September 6–11, 2021, Volume A, pp. 126–130. ACM (2021)
34. OMG: Meta Object Facility (MOF) Core Specification. http://www.omg.org/spec/MOF/2.0/ (2006)
35. OMG: Requirements Interchange Format (ReqIF). http://www.omg.org/spec/ReqIF (2013)
36. Pfofe, T., Thuem, T., Schulze, S., Fenske, W., Schaefer, I.: Synchronizing Software Variants with VariantSync. In: Proceedings of the 20th International Conference on Software Product Lines, SPLC 2016, Beijing, China, September 19–23, 2016 (2016)
37. Rubin, J., Chechik, M.: A survey of feature location techniques. In: Domain Engineering, Product Lines, Languages, and Conceptual Models, pp. 29–58. Springer (2013)
38. Rubin, J., Czarnecki, K., Chechik, M.: Managing cloned variants: a framework and experience. In: 17th International Software Product Line Conference, SPLC 2013, Tokyo, Japan - August 26–30, 2013, pp. 101–110. ACM (2013)
39. Ryssel, U., Ploennigs, J., Kabitzsch, K.: Extraction of feature models from formal contexts. In: Software Product Lines - 15th International Conference, SPLC 2011, Munich, Germany, August 22–26, 2011. Workshop Proceedings (Volume 2), p. 4. ACM (2011)
40. Salman, H.E., Seriai, A., Dony, C.: Feature-to-code traceability in a collection of software variants: Combining formal concept analysis and information retrieval. In: IEEE 14th International Conference on Information Reuse & Integration, IRI 2013, San Francisco, CA, USA, August 14–16, 2013, pp. 209–216. IEEE Computer Society (2013)
41. Shatnawi, A., Seriai, A., Sahraoui, H.A.: Recovering architectural variability of a family of product variants. In: 14th International Conference on Software Reuse, ICSR 2015, Miami, FL, USA, January 4–6, 2015. Proceedings, *Lecture Notes in Computer Science*, vol. 8919, pp. 17–33. Springer (2015)
42. Strüber, D., Mukelabai, M., Krüger, J., Fischer, S., Linsbauer, L., Martinez, J., Berger, T.: Facing the truth: benchmarking the techniques for the evolution of variant-rich systems. In: Proceedings of the 23rd International Systems and Software Product Line Conference, SPLC 2019, Volume A, Paris, France, September 9–13, 2019, pp. 26:1–26:12 (2019)
43. Thüm, T., Kästner, C., Benduhn, F., Meinicke, J., Saake, G., Leich, T.: FeatureIDE: An extensible framework for feature-oriented software development. Science of Computer Programming **79**(0) (2014)
44. Tinkerpop: TinkerPop3: A Graph Computing Framework. http://blueprints.tinkerpop.com (2015)
45. Wong, W.E., Gao, R., Li, Y., Abreu, R., Wotawa, F.: A survey on software fault localization. IEEE Transactions on Software Engineering **42**(8), 707–740 (2016)
46. WordNet Similarity for Java: WordNet Similarity for Java. https://code.google.com/p/ws4j/ (2015)
47. Wu, Z., Palmer, M.S.: Verb semantics and lexical selection. In: 32nd Annual Meeting of the Association for Computational Linguistics, 27–30 June 1994, New Mexico State University, Las Cruces, New Mexico, USA, Proceedings., pp. 133–138. Morgan Kaufmann Publishers/ACL (1994)
48. Xue, Y., Xing, Z., Jarzabek, S.: Feature location in a collection of product variants. In: 19th Working Conference on Reverse Engineering, WCRE 2012, Kingston, ON, Canada, October 15–18, 2012, pp. 145–154. IEEE Computer Society (2012)

49. Zave, P.: An experiment in feature engineering. In: Programming methodology, pp. 353–377. Springer New York (2003)
50. Ziadi, T., Frias, L., da Silva, M.A.A., Ziane, M.: Feature identification from the source code of product variants. In: 16th European Conference on Software Maintenance and Reengineering, CSMR 2012, Szeged, Hungary, March 27–30, 2012, pp. 417–422. IEEE Computer Society (2012)
51. Ziadi, T., Henard, C., Papadakis, M., Ziane, M., Traon, Y.L.: Towards a language-independent approach for reverse-engineering of software product lines. In: Symposium on Applied Computing, SAC 2014, Gyeongju, Republic of Korea - March 24–28, 2014, pp. 1064–1071. ACM (2014)
52. Ziadi, T., Hillah, L.: Software product line extraction from bytecode based applications. In: 23rd International Conference on Engineering of Complex Computer Systems, ICECCS 2018, Melbourne, Australia, December 12–14, 2018, pp. 221–225. IEEE Computer Society (2018)

Chapter 15
Systematic Software Reuse with Automated Extraction and Composition for Clone-and-Own

Lukas Linsbauer, Stefan Fischer, Gabriela Karoline Michelon, Wesley K. G. Assunção, Paul Grünbacher, Roberto E. Lopez-Herrejon, and Alexander Egyed

Abstract In order to meet highly individual and frequently changing customer requirements, engineers need to efficiently develop and maintain large sets of custom-tailored variants of systems. An approach commonly used in practice is to clone existing variants and adapt them to meet new requirements. This clone-and-own approach is flexible, intuitive and leads to quick results. However, it causes problems in the long run, as the efficient maintenance of existing variants and reuse of implementation when creating new variants become challenging for larger sets of clones. Software product line engineering addresses these problems as a structured approach for developing highly configurable systems by providing a common platform from which variants can be derived. This enables efficient reuse and maintenance, but requires large upfront investment for building the platform and training of developers. Furthermore, it is not as flexible when it comes to evolution, as changes to the platform can affect many variants at once and possible side-effects need to be considered. In this work, we propose an approach for

L. Linsbauer (✉)
Technische Universität Braunschweig, Braunschweig, Germany
e-mail: l.linsbauer@tu-bs.de

S. Fischer
Software Competence Center Hagenberg, Hagenberg, Austria
e-mail: stefan.fischer@scch.at

G. K. Michelon · P. Grünbacher · A. Egyed
Johannes Kepler University Linz, Linz, Austria
e-mail: gabriela.michelon@jku.at; paul.gruenbacher@jku.at; alexander.egyed@jku.at

W. K. G. Assunção (✉)
Pontifical Catholic University of Rio de Janeiro, Rio de Janeiro, Brazil

Johannes Kepler University of Linz, Linz, Austria
e-mail: wesley.assuncao@jku.at

R. E. Lopez-Herrejon
École de Technologie Supérieure, Universite du Québec, Montreal, QC, Canada
e-mail: roberto.lopez@etsmtl.ca

© Springer Nature Switzerland AG 2023
R. E. Lopez-Herrejon et al. (eds.), *Handbook of Re-Engineering Software Intensive Systems into Software Product Lines*, https://doi.org/10.1007/978-3-031-11686-5_15

combining the advantages of ad-hoc reuse, such as flexibility and intuitiveness, with the advantages of product line engineering, such as efficient reuse and a common platform. Specifically, we introduce data structures and operations for the automated extraction of feature-to-implementation traces from variants, and accompanying workflows for creating and evolving a portfolio of variants that resemble clone-and-own but are supported by automated reuse. We show an implementation of the discussed concepts in practice and successfully evaluate it on a research challenge.

15.1 Introduction and Motivation

Demand for custom-tailored systems increases as engineers are faced with the challenge of developing and evolving large portfolios of system variants to meet individual and frequently changing customer requirements. *Variability* is the capacity of software artifacts to vary [37]. Its effective management requires variability information, such as the set of possible variants, the features they provide, how features are related, and how they are implemented.

A common ad-hoc reuse approach for creating variants is to clone existing variants and then adapt them as needed, referred to as *Clone-and-Own* [11, 36]. The parts to be reused must first be located in the existing variants, then extracted, merged, and completed to obtain new working variants. This process is repeated for each new variant required. It is considered as flexible and intuitive, but does not scale to larger sets of variants, as bugs are propagated and reuse is hindered. In short, maintenance and evolution become infeasible for larger sets of cloned variants.

Another approach for building a variable system is *Software Product Line Engineering (SPLE)* [2, 5, 34] where reusable assets are maintained in a configurable platform from which variants are derived based on features. Advantages are efficient reuse and maintenance. However, SPLE requires large upfront investments to build the platform. Furthermore, the domain needs to be well-known and rather stable, otherwise the platform will be outdated before it starts to pay off. Changing the platform is challenging as features can interact with each other, depend on each other, and side-effects can occur because variants are not independent. Lastly, developers need special training to learn variability mechanisms.

We propose an approach that aims to combine the advantages of ad-hoc reuse (clone-and-own) and structured reuse (SPLE) while at the same time mitigating their drawbacks. We refer to this approach and its tool implementation as *Extraction and Composition for Clone-and-Own (ECCO)*. It is based on two automated operations. The *extraction operation* iteratively compares features and implementation of system variants in order to compute and iteratively refine a repository of feature-to-implementation traces. The *composition operation* uses the traces stored in the repository to compose existing as well as new system variants. A *trace* is a link between a source and a target artifact [7]. *Traceability* is the potential for traces to be established and used. The approach can be applied to support clone-and-own development with systematic reuse, as well as to support extractive or reactive product line adoption. The repository can also be used to provide traceability information to developers.

We first introduce an illustrative example that is used throughout this chapter. We then explain basic data structures and operations for the extraction of traces from variants and the composition of variants from traces. We illustrate how these operations can be applied to scenarios such as the extractive adoption or reactive extension of product lines. We then showcase a concrete tool implementation and discuss ideas for data visualization. Finally, we show an evaluation based on a data set proposed by a research challenge.

15.2 Illustrative Example and Basic Data Structures

We first introduce basic data structures using an illustrative example shown in Fig. 15.1. We use images of a person to represent the implementation of variants. An image can be considered as much an implementation artifact as source code, models, or diagrams.

Variants
A *Variant* v is a pair (C, A), where C is a configuration and A is a set of implementation artifacts. As an example, consider a set of three variants $V = \{v_1, v_2, v_3\}$ shown in Fig. 15.1. Each variant represents an image of a differently dressed person. The same variants are described formally in Table 15.1. The example shows three variants, each with its configuration $v_i.C$ and implementation artifacts $v_i.A$.

Features
We use the concept of *Features* [6] to express and manage variability. A *Feature* f is a unique identifier freely chosen by a developer to label a specific functionality. The

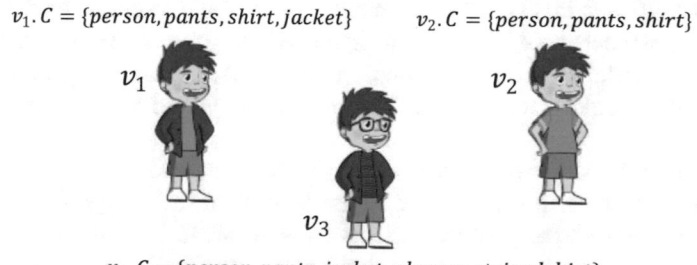

$$v_1.C = \{person, pants, shirt, jacket\} \qquad v_2.C = \{person, pants, shirt\}$$

$$v_3.C = \{person, pants, jacket, glasses, stripedshirt\}$$

Fig. 15.1 *Illustrative Example* of three *Variants* of an image showing a person, each with *Configuration* (negative features omitted) and *Implementation Artifacts* (in this case pixels)

Table 15.1 *Example:* Set of Variants $V = \{v_1, v_2, v_3\}$ as illustrated in Fig. 15.1

Variant v_i	Configuration $v_i.C$	Artifacts $v_i.A$
v_1	{person, pants, shirt, jacket, ¬glasses, ¬stripedshirt}	$\{a_1, a_2, a_3, a_4\}$
v_2	{person, pants, shirt, ¬jacket, ¬glasses, ¬stripedshirt}	$\{a_1, a_2, a_4, a_5\}$
v_3	{person, pants, ¬shirt, jacket, glasses, stripedshirt}	$\{a_1, a_2, a_3, a_6, a_7\}$

features used in the illustrative example in Fig. 15.1 are person, pants, shirt, jacket, glasses, and stripedshirt.

Configuration

A variant v is denoted by its *Configuration* $v.C$. A *Configuration* C is a set of selected (i.e., positive) or deselected (i.e., negative) features. For example, variant v_1 in Fig. 15.1 and Table 15.1 has features person, pants, shirt, and jacket and therefore configuration $v_1.C =$ {person, pants, shirt, jacket, ¬glasses, ¬stripedshirt}. A feature is therefore either present or absent. Absent features are negated. The absence of a feature can influence the implementation of a variant and thus have an effect on the features that are present.

Implementation Artifacts

A variant v is implemented by a set of *Artifacts* $v.A$. An *Artifact* a is an element in the implementation of a system. We organize artifacts in a hierarchical tree structure, which we refer to as the *artifact tree*. An artifact has exactly one parent and any number of children. Artifacts can have arbitrary dependencies to other artifacts across the tree. This artifact tree is well-suited to express most engineering artifacts, such as simple text files, ASTs (Abstract Syntax Trees) produced by programming language parsers, or EMF[1] Ecore models. A single artifact in the tree can represent a directory, a file, a line in a text file, or any other element of a variant's implementation. In the case of source code, an artifact could represent a class, a method, a field, or a single statement (i.e, it would resemble an AST). Other examples of artifacts could be elements in a UML diagram or shapes (lines, circles, etc.) in a CAD drawing. In the example in Fig. 15.1, the artifacts represent pixel coordinates and colors in an image. The artifact tree would then look as shown in Fig. 15.2.

We assume that any two artifacts a_1, a_2 can be compared for equivalence ($a_1 \equiv a_2$) as follows: two artifacts $a_1, a_2 \in A$ are equivalent ($a_1 \equiv a_2$) if a_1 and a_2 are equal ($a_1 = a_2$) and their parent artifacts are equivalent, i.e., their position in the artifact tree is the same. In the above artifact tree, the artifact with identifier 5 is equal to the artifact with identifier 7, but they have different parents and ([4] and [6] respectively) and are thus not considered equivalent.

---

[1] https://www.eclipse.org/modeling/emf/

```
[1] project [directory]
 └─ [2] person.png [file/image]
     └─ [3] [57,128] [resolution]
         ├─ [4] [0,0] [coordinate]
         │   └─ [5] [0,255,255,255] [color]
         ├─ [6] [0,1] [coordinate]
         │   └─ [7] []0,255,255,255] [color]
         └─ ...
```

Fig. 15.2 *Example:* Artifact tree of an image consisting of a project `directory` at the root, which contains an image `file` with a `resolution` of 57 × 128 pixels. Every pixel `coordinate` is stored as its own artifact node in the tree and contains its `color` as a child artifact

Table 15.2 *Example:* Set of Traces $T = \{t_1, t_2, t_3, t_4, t_5\}$ as illustrated in Fig. 15.3

Trace t_i	Presence condition $t_i.P$	Artifacts $t_i.A$
t_1	{person, pants}	$\{a_1, a_2\}$
t_2	{jacket}	$\{a_3\}$
t_3	{shirt, person ∧ ¬glasses}	$\{a_4\}$
t_4	{shirt ∧ ¬jacket, person ∧ ¬jacket, pants ∧ ¬jacket}	$\{a_5\}$
t_5	{stripedshirt, glasses}	$\{a_6, a_7\}$

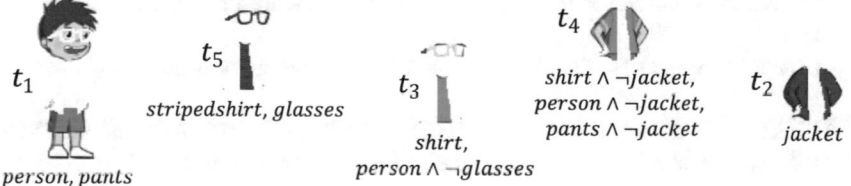

Fig. 15.3 *Illustrative Example* of the same five *Traces* shown in Table 15.2. Every trace maps implementation artifacts (in this case pixel coordinates and colors) to a set of clauses over features

Traces

A *Trace* t is a pair (P, A) that maps a set of artifacts A to a presence condition P represented as a set of clauses over features, each representing a feature or feature interaction. Table 15.2 presents an example of a set of five traces $T = \{t_1, t_2, t_3, t_4, t_5\}$ that match the set of variants V in Table 15.1. Note, that this is not a unique solution, as alternative sets of traces exist that also match the set of variants V.

15.3 Operations

Based on the above data structures we introduce operations for the extraction of traces from variants and for the composition of variants from traces.

15.3.1 Trace Extraction

The *Trace Extraction* computes a set of traces from a set of variants based on commonalities and differences in their features and implementation. As *input* it receives a *set of variants V*, each consisting of a configuration (i.e., a set of features) and an implementation (i.e., a set of artifacts). The goal is to compute a presence condition P for every artifact a. As *output* it therefore computes a *set of traces T*, each mapping a presence condition to implementation artifacts. This task is often referred to as feature location [3, 4, 9, 35].

Basic Ideas
Whether a clause c is part of a presence condition P for an artifact a depends on some fairly intuitive ideas that have been proven to work very well [31, 33]. Intuitively, for two variants A and B of a system:

- Common artifacts *likely* trace to common features.
- Artifacts in A and not B *likely* trace to features that are in A and not B, and vice versa.
- Artifacts in A and not B *cannot* trace to features that are in B and not A, and vice versa.
- Artifacts in A and not B *can at most* trace to features that are in A, and vice versa.
- Artifacts in A and B *can at most* trace to features that are in A or B.

Figure 15.4 illustrates the first rule using our running example for the two variants v_2 and v_3 shown on the left. The features these two variants have in common (person and pants) are traced to the artifacts these two variants have in common via trace t_1 shown on the right.

Figure 15.5 illustrates the second rule on the same two variants v_2 and v_3 of our running example. The features only in variant v_2 (shirt) are traced to the artifacts only in variant v_2 via trace t_3. The features only in variant v_3 (jacket, glasses, stripedshirt) are traced to the artifacts only in variant v_3, which initially corresponds to the three traces t_2, t_5 and t_6 in Fig. 15.3 and Table 15.2. This trace would be refined further and split up into the individual traces after also having considered variant v_1, as it contains jacket without features glasses and stripedshirt.

Presence Conditions
We now explain how the traces and presence conditions are computed in more detail and for any number of variants. We compute the presence condition P_a for every artifact a in the form of a disjunctive normal form (DNF) formula whose literals are

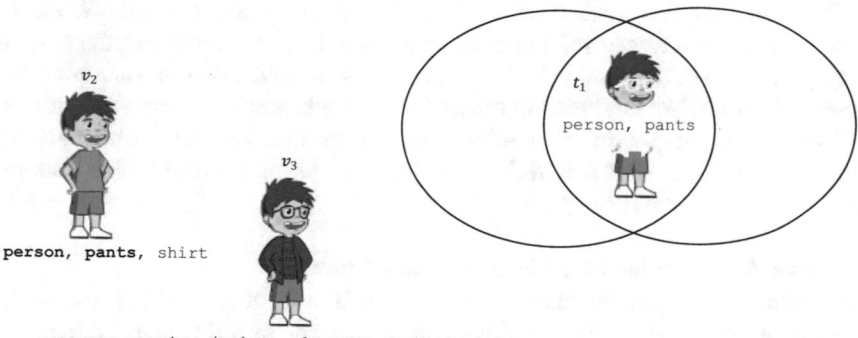

Fig. 15.4 *Extraction Illustration: Rule 1.* The parts of the implementation (pixels in this case) that are common to variants v_2 and v_3 trace to the features that are common to variants v_2 and v_3 (person and pants in this case)

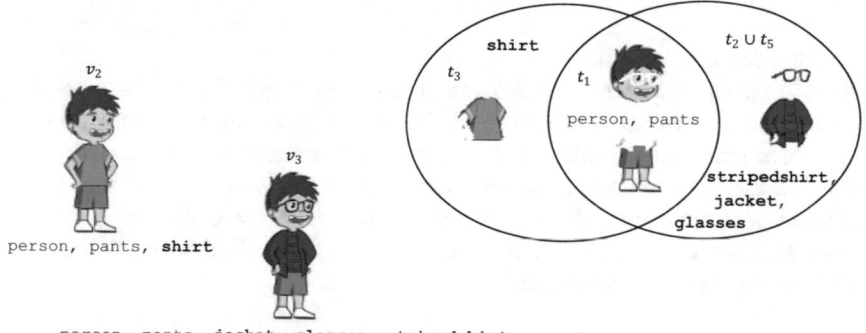

Fig. 15.5 *Extraction Illustration: Rule 2.* The parts of the implementation (pixels in this case) that are either only in variant v_2 or only in variant v_3 trace to features that are either only in variant v_2 (shirt) or only in variant v_3 (jacket, glasses, stripedshirt)

features. A DNF formula is a disjunction of clauses, where a clause is a conjunction of literals. We treat presence conditions as a set of such clauses.

Every clause can be considered as a static feature interaction [12, 14] of the features contained in the clause. This aligns with previous research in feature algebra [21], feature location [18], or the analysis of variable systems [1, 14].

We limit the maximum size of clauses in presence conditions, i.e., the number of feature literals in a conjunction, which corresponds to the number of interacting features, to a threshold that can be freely configured. This provides a major improvement to the scalability of the approach, as without a constant threshold the number of clauses would grow exponentially with the number of features. For the evaluation presented in this chapter, the threshold was set to at most three interacting features, based on previous empirical research [13, 14]. The downside to this is, that potential higher order feature interactions cannot be traced anymore.

Note, that every clause must contain at least one positive literal. While the absence of a feature can influence other features and thus have an effect on the implementation of a variant [21], it makes no sense to have a clause containing only negated features. We therefore do not include such clauses in presence conditions.

We denote the set of all conjunctive clauses that can be formed given a configuration (i.e., set of features) $v.C$ of variant v as $clauses(v.C)$. For example, $clauses(\{f_1, f_2, \neg f_3\}) = \{f_1, f_2, f_1 \wedge f_2, f_1 \wedge \neg f_3, f_2 \wedge \neg f_3, f_1 \wedge f_2 \wedge \neg f_3\}$.

Criterion for Inclusion of a Clause in a Condition

For a clause c to be contained in a presence condition P_a of an artifact a, the artifact a must be contained in every variant $v \in V$ that contains the clause c, i.e., $c \in clauses(v.C)$, and there must be at least one variant in V that contains clause c.

$$P_a = \{c \mid (\forall v \in V : c \in clauses(v.C) \Rightarrow a \in v.A) \wedge (\exists v \in V : c \in clauses(v.C))\} \tag{15.1}$$

Criterion for Likely Clause

Our technique additionally provides a smaller and more specific set of clauses $P'_a \subseteq P_a$ to which the artifacts trace more likely. This is based on our observation that, in practice, presence conditions with a logical OR between features are much less likely to occur than ones with a logical AND [31]. Therefore, a clause c' is contained in the set of likely clauses P'_a if all variants that have clause c' also have artifact a (inclusion criterion as above), and in addition, all variants that have artifact a also have clause c' (additional criterion).

$$P'_a = \{c' \mid (\forall v \in V : c' \in clauses(v.C) \Leftrightarrow a \in v.A) \wedge (\exists v \in V : c' \in clauses(v.C))\} \tag{15.2}$$

Artifact Clusters

We do not consider every artifact individually, but rather cluster artifacts, i.e., group artifacts together, that never appeared without each other in any variant and assign presence conditions to those clusters instead of every individual artifact. For example, artifacts a_1 and a_2 in the set of variants V in Table 15.1 always appear together and never without each other. We therefore group them instead of treating them individually, as shown in Tables 15.2 and 15.3.

Artifact Sequence Alignment

Our technique relies on the ability to compare any two implementation artifacts for equivalence. In cases where two sibling artifacts a_1 and a_2 (i.e., artifacts with the same parent) are not unique, the order of the artifacts is important when determining equivalence. This is the case, for instance, if the same statement appears multiple times inside a method. In such cases an alignment of the artifact sequences across variants must be performed. We adapted a Longest Common Subsequence (LCS) algorithm [10] to perform multi-sequence alignment for comparing more than two variants [13, 19], e.g., if they have the same method whose statements must be aligned.

Element Counters

We count for every clause c in how many input variants it was contained, for every artifact cluster a in how many input variants it was contained, and for every pair (c, a) of clause and artifact cluster in how many input variants both were contained together. We denote the counter value for a clause c as $\#(c)$, for an artifact a as $\#(a)$, and for a pair (c, a) of clause c and artifact a as $\#(c, a)$. These counters are sufficient to evaluate the above criterion for inclusion of clauses in a presence condition P_a of an artifact a (see Eq. 15.1).

$$P_a = \{c \in \bigcup_{v \in V} \text{clauses}(v.C) \mid \#(c') = \#(c', a)\} \tag{15.3}$$

The same principle applies to likely clauses in a presence condition P'_a of an artifact a (see Eq. 15.2).

$$P'_a = \{c' \in \bigcup_{v \in V} \text{clauses}(v.C) \mid \#(c') = \#(c', a) \wedge \#(a) = \#(c', a)\} \tag{15.4}$$

This has the advantage that it works incrementally, i.e., new input variants can be added iteratively whenever necessary simply by increasing the respective counters and already considered variants to not need to be kept. Hence, already computed traces do not have to be recomputed when a new variant is encountered. Instead, the counters are simply increased and the existing presence conditions trimmed, i.e., clauses removed for which the above conditions do not hold anymore.

Table 15.3 presents an example of the counters that match the set of variants V in Table 15.1 and the set of traces T in Table 15.2. The rows list the five artifact clusters with the total number of appearances in variants. The columns list (a subset of) the clauses $c \in \bigcup_{v \in V} \text{clauses}(v.C)$ with the total number of appearances in variants, sorted by the number of literals (i.e., interacting features). Each cell contains the number of times that the artifact cluster and the clause appeared together in a variant. For example, artifacts a_1 and a_2 appear in three variants ($\#(a_1) = \#(a_2) = 3$). The clause person also appears in three variants ($\#(\text{person}) = 3$). Finally, the artifacts and the clauses appear together also in three variants ($\#(\text{person}, a_1) = \#(\text{person}, a_2) = 3$). Therefore, the criterion for likely clauses (see Eq. 15.4) is satisfied. Similarly, artifact a_4 appeared in two variants, clause shirt appeared in two variants, and both appeared together also in two variants.

Iterative Extraction

A variant is essentially a mapping between a configuration (i.e., features) and an implementation (i.e., artifacts). A trace can therefore be considered a generalization

Table 15.3 *Example:* Subset of Counters # for Artifact Clusters (rows) and Clauses (columns)

#		person	jacket	shirt	...	jacket ∧ shirt	shirt ∧ ¬jacket	...
		3	2	2	...	1	1	...
a_1, a_2	3	3	2	2	...	1	1	...
a_3	2	2	2	1	...	1	0	...
a_4	2	2	1	2	...	1	1	...
a_5	1	1	0	1	...	0	1	...
a_6, a_7	1	1	1	0	...	0	0	...

of a variant. However, a trace is usually more specific (i.e., referring to fewer features) than a variant. It can map a single feature to its implementation artifacts, in which case we consider it a very fine trace. In cases where multiple features cannot (yet) be distinguished (e.g., because they always appeared together) a trace can contain multiple features. A variant can therefore be considered a coarse trace that maps all its features to its entire implementation. A trace t_v can be computed from a variant v as follows:

$$t_v = (\text{clauses}(v.C), v.A) \qquad (15.5)$$

The iterative trace extraction operator computes fine traces from coarse traces. It incrementally refines a set of (coarse) traces T into a set of (finer) traces T' by considering new information provided by a new trace t.

Operator 1 (Iterative Extraction) *The iterative* Extraction *operator* $extract(t, T) = T'$ *consumes a trace t (in most cases this will be a coarse trace that represents a variant) and a set of (coarse) traces T (in most cases extracted in previous iterations) to compute an updated set of (finer) traces T'.*

An existing set of traces T is iteratively refined with a new variant v to obtain the refined set of traces T' as follows:

$$T' = extract(t_v, T) \qquad (15.6)$$

Computation of Dependencies

Given a set of traces T, we can compute a set of dependencies D (i.e., *requires* relations) between these traces, and consequently between the respective features, by looking at the dependencies between the contained artifacts. In other words, based on artifact dependencies, which are given (e.g., by source code constraints), we compute dependencies between traces and therefore between the features contained in the traces. The set of dependencies D therefore contains constraints on possible feature combinations imposed by their implementation. It can be regarded as a simple variability model of a system, expressing what combinations of features can be selected to create valid configurations [19].

The set of dependencies D is computed based on dependencies between implementation artifacts in the artifact trees of traces. An artifact a_1 depends on an artifact a_2 when a_1 is contained in a_2 (e.g., a method a_1 depends on its containing class a_2) or a_1 uses a_2 in some way (e.g., a statement a_1 calling a method a_2 depends on that method). A dependency $d \in D$ is an ordered pair of traces (t_1, t_2) denoting that t_1 depends on t_2.

The set of dependencies D is then

$$D = \{(t_1, t_2) \mid \exists a_1 \in t_1.A, a_2 \in t_2.A : contained(a_1, a_2) \vee uses(a_1, a_2)\} \tag{15.7}$$

The computed dependencies can also be represented as a set of constraints in propositional logic. Every dependency represents one constraint. The propositional logic representation of a dependency $(t_1, t_2) \in D$ is

$$\bigvee_{from \in t_1.P} from \Rightarrow \bigwedge_{to \in t_2.P} to \tag{15.8}$$

The propositional logic expression for the entire set of dependencies D is then simply the conjunction of all its individual dependencies.

The set of dependencies can be visually represented as a directed graph where nodes represent traces and the directed edges represent the dependencies.

15.3.2   Variant Composition

The *Variant Composition* computes a variant v from a set of traces T given a configuration C.

Operator 2 (Composition) *The* Composition *operator* $compose(C, T) = v$ *consumes a configuration C, denoting the desired variant, and a set of traces T to compute a variant v.*

First, the set of relevant traces T' are selected from the set of all traces T:

$$T' = \{t \mid t \in T \wedge \text{clauses}(C) \cap t.P \neq \emptyset\} \tag{15.9}$$

The set of artifacts A of variant v is then:

$$A = \bigcup_{t \in T'} t.A \tag{15.10}$$

The final resulting variant v is then given as $v = (C, A)$.

Computation of Hints

In the case of intensional versioning [20], where a new variant is composed that has not existed before, we can provide a set of hints. Each hint points at a feature or feature interaction that is either missing from the composed variant's implementation (because no trace containing the needed implementation exists yet) and needs to be added, or surplus (because the needed implementation is contained in a coarse trace together with the implementation of other features) and needs to be removed.

The set of missing feature or feature interaction hints H^- for a composed variant with configuration C is:

$$H^- = \text{clauses}(C) \setminus \bigcup_{t \in T'} t.P \tag{15.11}$$

The set of surplus feature or feature interaction hints H^+ for a composed variant with configuration C is:

$$H^+ = \bigcup_{t \in T'} t.P \setminus \text{clauses}(C) \tag{15.12}$$

15.4 Workflow and Application Scenarios

The above operations can be applied to support several scenarios. Figure 15.6 gives an overview of the overall workflow by means of our illustrative example. We now illustrate the *extractive* and *reactive* product line adoption scenarios in more detail.

15.4.1 Extractive Adoption

The *extractive adoption scenario* refers to the migration ① of a set of initial (legacy, cloned) variants into the (initially empty) repository of traces. The extraction operation is invoked once per initial variant (in this case three times) to populate the repository with a set of traces. This process is often referred to as *extractive product line adoption* or *product line reverse engineering* [2].

The original variants can then be reconstructed ② using the composition operation by specifying the same configurations. The variants can be fully reconstructed based on the previously extracted traces as all necessary information is available in the repository. In the domain of Software Configuration Management (SCM) and Version Control Systems (VCS) this is referred to as *extensional versioning* [17, 20] where already known variants are retrieved.

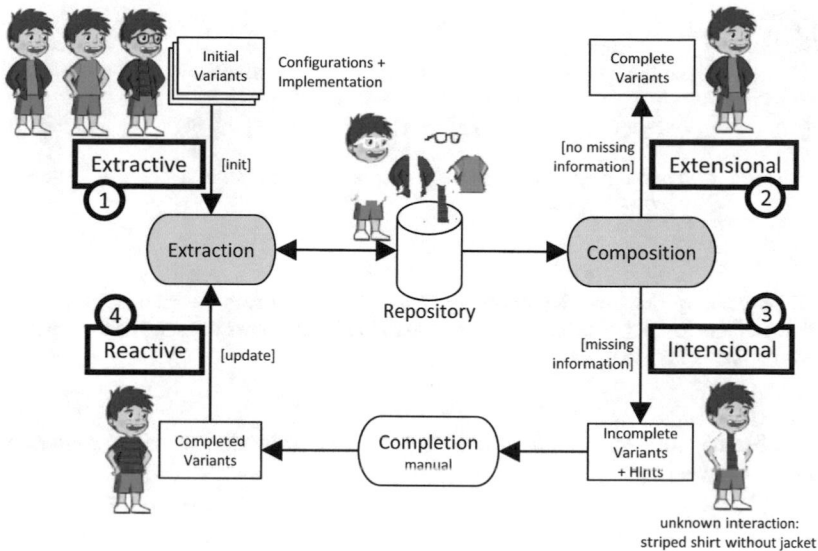

Fig. 15.6 Workflow overview

15.4.2 Reactive Extension

The repository can also be used to create new variants (with new features or new combinations of existing features) that have not existed before ③ using the composition operation. In the domain of Software Configuration Management (SCM) and Version Control Systems (VCS) this is referred to as *intensional versioning* [17, 20], where a variant with a new configuration is retrieved that has not existed before. In this case, the information in the repository might not be sufficient to construct a fully complete variant. This can lead to missing as well as surplus implementation artifacts.

In the example shown in Fig. 15.6, the composed variant is missing implementation, as it is not yet known how the stripedshirt looks underneath the jacket. Therefore, the set of missing feature interaction warnings H^- will include (among others) the hint that the interaction of features stripedshirt and ¬jacket is unknown and might require manual intervention. The developer can then manually complete the implementation of the variant (in this case by adding missing pixels) without interference from other variants. The completed variant can then be fed back into the repository ④ to update its contained traces. This process is often referred to as *reactive product line adoption* or *incremental product line construction* [2], as new variants with new features or new combinations of existing features can be added incrementally whenever needed.

Notice, that this workflow is quite similar to clone-and-own, with the difference that reuse of existing implementation is performed automatically (alleviating the

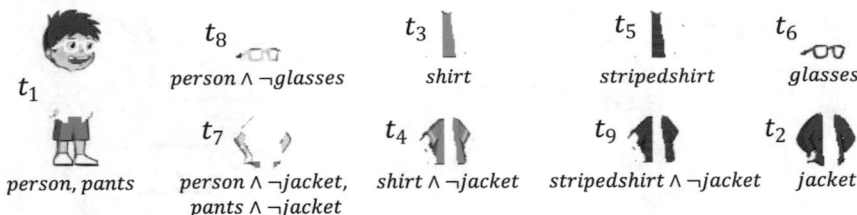

t_1 t_8 *person ∧ ¬glasses* t_3 *shirt* t_5 *stripedshirt* t_6 *glasses*

person, pants t_7 *person ∧ ¬jacket, pants ∧ ¬jacket* t_4 *shirt ∧ ¬jacket* t_9 *stripedshirt ∧ ¬jacket* t_2 *jacket*

Fig. 15.7 *Repository Content.* The repository contains a set of traces. Every trace maps implementation artifacts to a set of clauses over features. This figure shows the state of the repository after the example in Fig. 15.6

reuse problem) and no actual clones are created (alleviating the maintenance problem).

15.5   Repository Contents

Figure 15.7 shows the contents of the repository after the scenario illustrated in Fig. 15.6. It contains a set of nine traces T. Every trace $t_i \in T$ associates pixel coordinates and colors with features. Actually, the artifacts in each trace are mapped to a set of clauses over features, each representing a feature or feature interaction. For example, the middle part of the striped shirt traces to feature `stripedshirt`. The parts of the striped shirt that are potentially covered by the jacket trace to *stripedshirt ∧ ¬jacket*, as they should only be included in a variant's implementation if feature `stripedshirt` is selected and `jacket` is not selected. Another noteworthy example is the trace containing both features `person` and `pants`, which we would consider a coarser trace than the others. This is due to the fact that no variant had these two features separated, which makes them indistinguishable for now.

15.6   Tool Implementation

The approach is implemented in the ECCO (Extraction and Composition for Clone-and-Own) tool[2] available on GitHub.[3] Its core is implemented as a Java library on top of which it provides a Command Line Interface (CLI) as well as a Graphical

---

[2] https://jku-isse.github.io/ecco/

[3] https://github.com/jku-isse/ecco

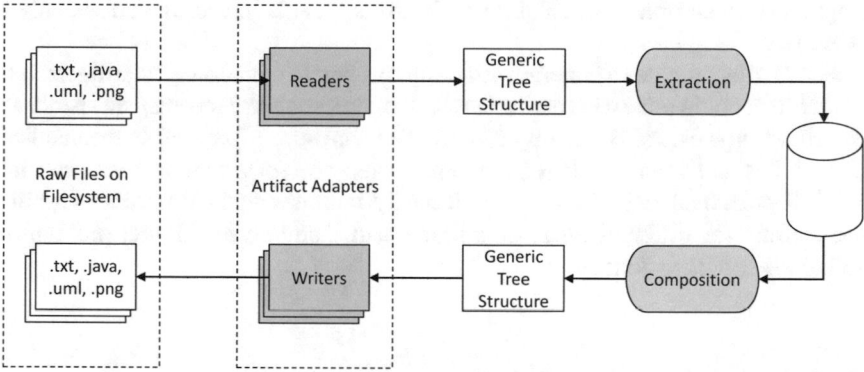

Fig. 15.8 *Artifact Adapters.* The raw files on the file system (left) are assigned to artifact adapters. Every type of file that contains variability requires a matching artifact adapter that can *read* the file contents to create the generic artifact tree structure and *write* the file contents from the artifact tree. Files for which no artifact adapter exists are treated as atomic binary files

User Interface (GUI) built with JavaFX. Additionally, a web interface[4] and a REST API are in the process of being built and also available on GitHub.[5]

15.6.1   Heterogeneous Implementation Artifacts

A repository can contain many different heterogeneous types of implementation artifacts at once (e.g., text files, source code, images, and other types of files). We keep the technique independent of the types of implementation artifacts by utilizing artifact type specific adapters that are responsible for parsing respective files and generating the generic artifact tree structure consisting of folders, files, and further file-type specific artifacts. The only requirement is that artifacts can be uniquely identified and compared for equivalence. This is achieved via *artifact adapters* as shown in Fig. 15.8. This is similar to how other approaches deal with heterogeneous implementation artifacts, most prominently BUT4Reuse[6] [29, 30]. Artifact adapters in our case consist of a *reader* and a *writer*. The readers translate specific file types into the generic artifact tree that our operators use. The writers translate the generic artifact tree back into the specific file types. There needs to be an artifact adapter for every type of file that shall be variable (i.e., whose content shall change depending on selected and not selected features). Files that are of a type for which no artifact

---

[4] https://github.com/jku-isse/ecco-web

[5] https://jku-isse.github.io/ecco-web/

[6] https://but4reuse.github.io/

adapter exists are treated as an atomic file artifact that is traced to features only in its entirety.

ECCO thus provides a generic variability mechanism. It allows for artifacts to be variable that could otherwise not be variable, as no variability mechanism specific to the artifact type exists. For example, while there are several variability mechanisms for text files and source code (e.g., a simple preprocessor), there is no appropriate variability mechanism for images. Additionally, it unifies all the different variability mechanisms for different types of artifacts and therefore avoids the problem of having to keep them consistent.

15.6.2 Graphical User Interface

Figure 15.9 shows a screenshot of the GUI. The upper part (red) shows the list of traces stored in the repository. Every trace (line in the list) has a unique identifier, an arbitrary (optional) name, a presence condition (with features as literals), and the number of contained artifacts. Selecting any number of traces (on the very right) makes it possible to preview the composed artifact tree in the lower left part (blue). Selecting a node in the artifact tree shows a preview of the actual artifact in the lower right part (yellow) if an optional viewer is provided by the respective artifact adapter to which the selected node in the artifact tree belongs. In this view, an arbitrary set

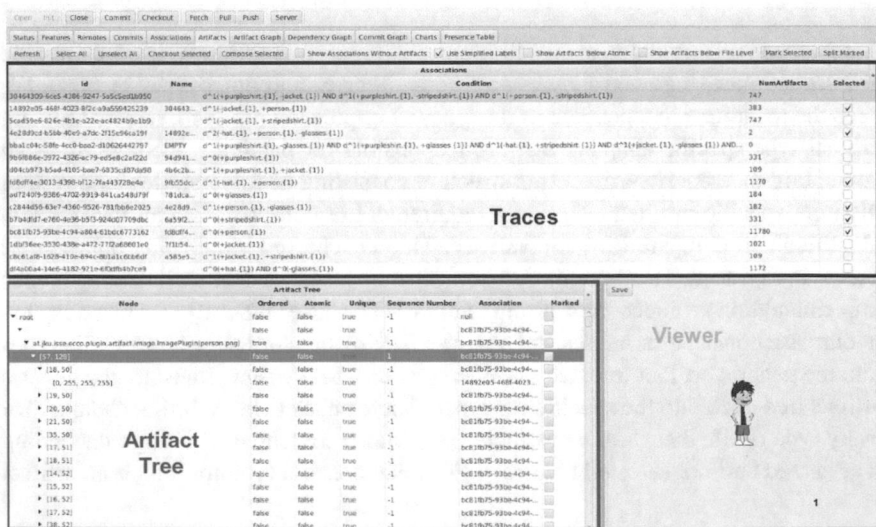

Fig. 15.9 *User Interface Screenshot* showing a list of *Traces* (with presence condition and number of contained artifacts) at the top (in red), the *Artifact Tree* (corresponding to the selected traces) at the bottom left (in blue), and a *Viewer* showing a preview of the selected node in the artifact tree at the bottom right (in yellow)

of traces can be manually selected, even ones whose conditions mutually exclude each other. During the composition of concrete variants, this selection is performed automatically based on the provided configuration and thus always consistent.

15.6.3 Data Visualization

The information in the repository is useful far beyond the composition of variants. Making this information (e.g., traceability, interactions, dependencies) available to developers provides additional benefits [24–26]. Figure 15.10 shows an alternative visualization of the artifact tree (available in both the GUI and in the web interface)

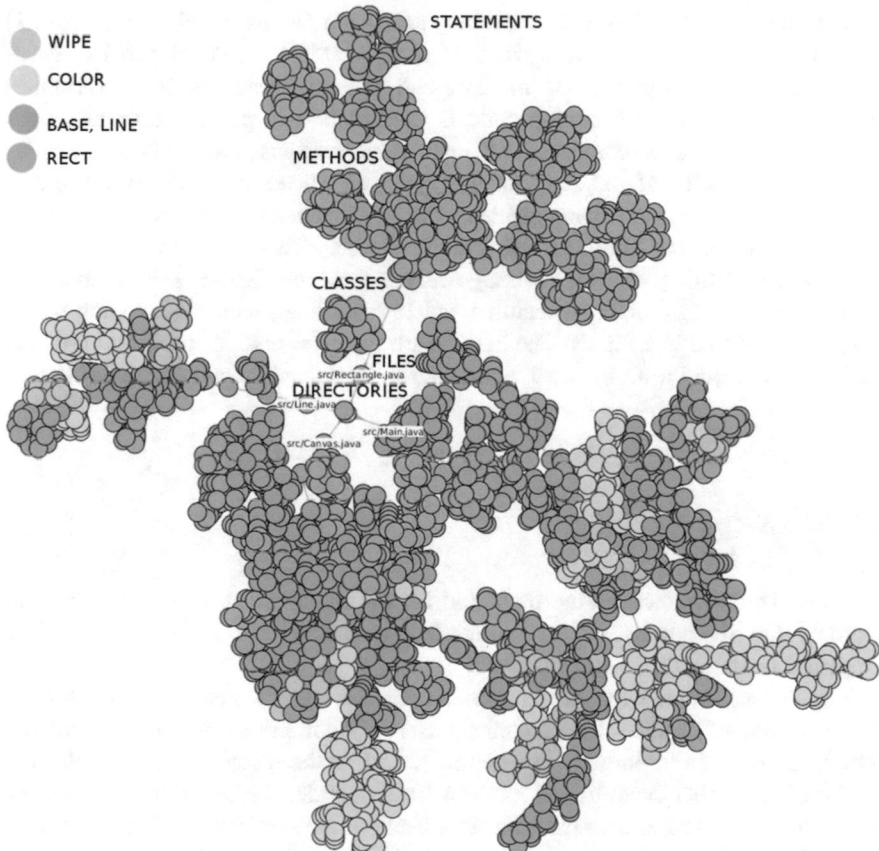

Fig. 15.10 *Artifact Tree Visualization* for a drawing application written in Java. Every circle represents a tree node (i.e., an artifact). The root of the tree is at the very center. The leaves are on the outside. Every trace is assigned a color. The artifacts closer to the root are coarser and get finer further down in the tree. From the root, artifacts represent directories, then files, classes, methods, and finally statements

of a small Java drawing application. Such a visualization is useful to get an overview of a system. It is easy to recognize in what parts of the implementation several features are tangled and which features are scattered over large parts of the implementation. If a certain region is of particular interest an option to zoom in on that region could be added. There are several visualization techniques that could be utilized given the information stored in the repository [15, 22, 23].

15.7 Evaluation

We evaluate performance and correctness of ECCO by applying it to the ArgoUML-SPL challenge case [28]. The corresponding challenge solution has already been published separately [31]. ArgoUML-SPL is one of the most used subject systems in the area of extractive SPL adoption, as shown in the ESPLA catalog [27]. ArgoUML-SPL is a software system of considerable size, developed by several developers. It is implemented in Java and uses a preprocessor as variability mechanism, i.e., its Java source code is annotated with preprocessor directives. Its implementation is composed of feature interactions and feature negations, and the granularity of the artifacts that must be traced varies from entire Java classes to individual statements inside methods. Martinez et al. propose a challenge case study based on ArgoUML-SPL at the Systems and Software Product Line Conference (SPLC) [28]. This challenge defines the ArgoUML-SPL benchmark that is comprised of eight optional features and 15 predefined scenarios ranging from a single variant to 256 variants. The benchmark provides a set of tools and artifacts, including a ground truth to allow techniques to be evaluated and compared to each other.

15.7.1 Setup

For this evaluation, we set the threshold for the maximum number of interacting features (i.e., the number of feature literals in a clause) to three, based on previous empirical research [13, 14].

Figure 15.11 shows the structure of the artifact tree created from Java files by the Java adapter used for the challenge case. It is comprised of classes at the top, which can contain imports, fields, methods, and further nested classes. Fields and methods are further decomposed into raw lines of code. It reflects the requirements of the challenge that asks to trace classes, methods and their respective refinements in the form of changes to imports, fields and lines of code. Therefore, we store classes (including nested classes), imports, fields and methods explicitly. For fields and methods we also store their children (to be able to detect refinements) in the form of raw lines of code as they can span over multiple lines. This is necessary as variability in ArgoUML-SPL is often implemented at such a fine-granular level

Fig. 15.11 Artifact tree
structure created by the Java
adapter used for the challenge
case

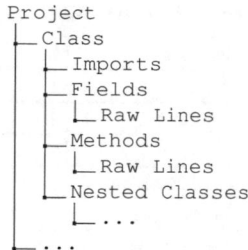

```
Project
└─ Class
    ├─ Imports
    ├─ Fields
    │   └─ Raw Lines
    ├─ Methods
    │   └─ Raw Lines
    └─ Nested Classes
        └─ ...
└─ ...
```

and annotations are not always placed in a disciplined manner [16]. Even single statements, e.g. field declarations, can span multiple lines, of which only some might be annotated with features.

15.7.2   Data Set

The ArgoUML-SPL challenge [28] provides *15 scenarios* and a *ground truth* consisting of *24 traces*. ArgoUML is an open source tool for UML modeling that is implemented in Java and was refactored into a product line [8]. It consists of *two mandatory features*: Diagrams Core and Class Diagram; and *eight optional features*: State Diagram, Activity Diagram, Use Case Diagram, Collaboration Diagram, Deployment Diagram, Sequence Diagram, Cognitive Support and Logging.

15.7.2.1   Scenarios

The challenge provides *15 scenarios* (see Table 15.4) with varying number of variants. More specifically, *Original* scenario contains only the initial ArgoUML system as a single variant from which the ArgoUML-SPL was initially created [8]. *Traditional* scenario has 10 variants, one with all the features, one with only the mandatory features, and for every optional feature one variant with only that feature disabled. *PairWise* scenario is composed of 9 variants obtained using the pair-wise feature coverage algorithm from FeatureIDE [38]. *Random* scenarios of different size (2, 3, 4, 5, 6, 7, 8, 9, 10, 50 and 100 variants) with randomly selected variants. *All* scenario has all the $2^8 = 256$ possible variants of ArgoUML-SPL obtained from FeatureIDE [38].

15.7.2.2   Ground Truth

The ground truth provided by the challenge consists of *24 traces*. It contains one trace for each of the eight individual features, two traces with a single negative feature, 13 traces with a conjunction of two features, and one trace with a conjunction of three features.

Table 15.4 ArgoUML-SPL challenge scenarios [31]

Scenario	Size	Description
Original	1	Original ArgoUML variant containing all features
Traditional	10	Variants with no, all, and combinations of 7 optional features
PairWise	9	Set of variants that covers all pairwise feature combinations
2–10 Random	2–10	Randomly selected subsets of variants
50 Random	50	Randomly selected subset of variants
100 Random	100	Randomly selected subset of variants
All	256	All possible variants of ArgoUML-SPL

15.7.3   Results

This section presents and discusses the results of ECCO being applied to each of the 15 scenarios. The results and instructions for reproducing them are publicly available.[7]

15.7.3.1   Time Performance

Figure 15.12 shows a box plot of the run time per variant (i.e., per extraction operation) per scenario, ordered by increasing number of variants. It was measured on an HP ZBook 14 laptop, with Intel® Core™ i7-4600U processor (2.1 GHz, 2 cores), 16 GB of RAM and SSD storage, running Fedora Linux as operating system. Each run time measurement includes the time it takes the *reader* of the artifact adapter to create the artifact tree from the Java source code of the variant, the *extraction operation* to refine the traces, and the storage backend to store the traces in the repository on the disk. Each scenario's average run time per variant is between 4 and 7 s. Overall, the run time per extraction operation remains quite constant. Fluctuations are most likely caused by differences in the size of variants. The total run time per scenario therefore scales roughly linearly with its number of variants.

15.7.3.2   Precision, Recall, F1 Score

To validate the computed traces, three metrics are computed *for each trace t*. They are calculated automatically by the challenge benchmark [28], which compares every ground truth trace $t_{gt} \in T_{gt}$ with the respective (i.e., same feature condition $t.P$) trace t_{ecco} computed by ECCO.

Precision is the percentage of correctly retrieved artifacts relative to the total number artifacts retrieved artifacts.

---

[7] https://github.com/jku-isse/SPLC2019-Challenge-ArgoUML-FeatureLocation

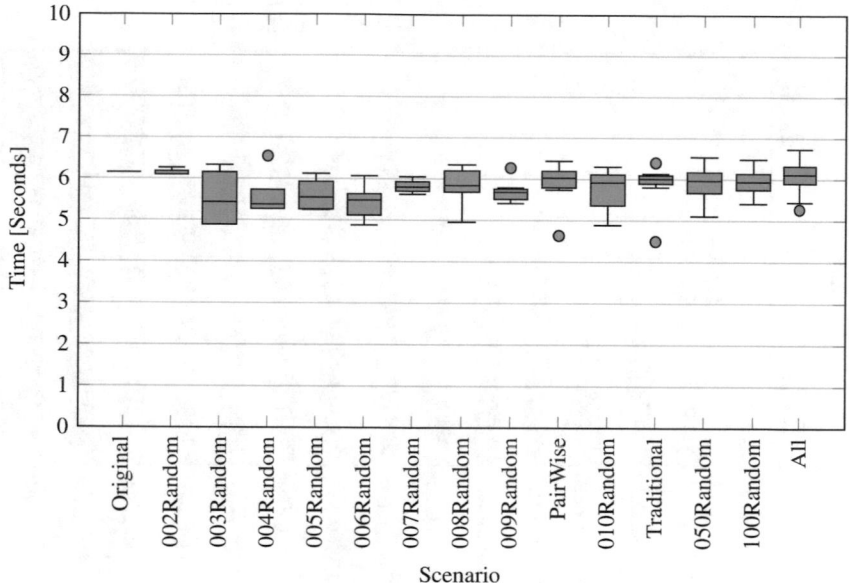

Fig. 15.12 Run Time per Variant per Scenario [31]

$$precision = \frac{TP}{TP + FP} = \frac{|t_{gt}.A \cap t_{ecco}.A|}{|t_{ecco}.A|} \qquad (15.13)$$

where TP (true positives) are the correctly retrieved artifacts and FP (false positives)
are the incorrectly retrieved artifacts.

Recall is the percentage of correctly retrieved artifacts relative to the total number
of artifacts in the ground truth trace.

$$recall = \frac{TP}{TP + FN} = \frac{|t_{gt}.A \cap t_{ecco}.A|}{|t_{gt}.A|} \qquad (15.14)$$

where FN (false negatives) are artifacts in the ground truth trace which are not
included in the retrieved artifacts.

The F1 score (F-measure) relates precision and recall and combines them into a
single measure.

$$F1 = 2 * \frac{precision * recall}{precision + recall} \qquad (15.15)$$

Figure 15.13 shows average precision, recall and F1 score over all traces per
scenario, ordered by increasing number of variants.

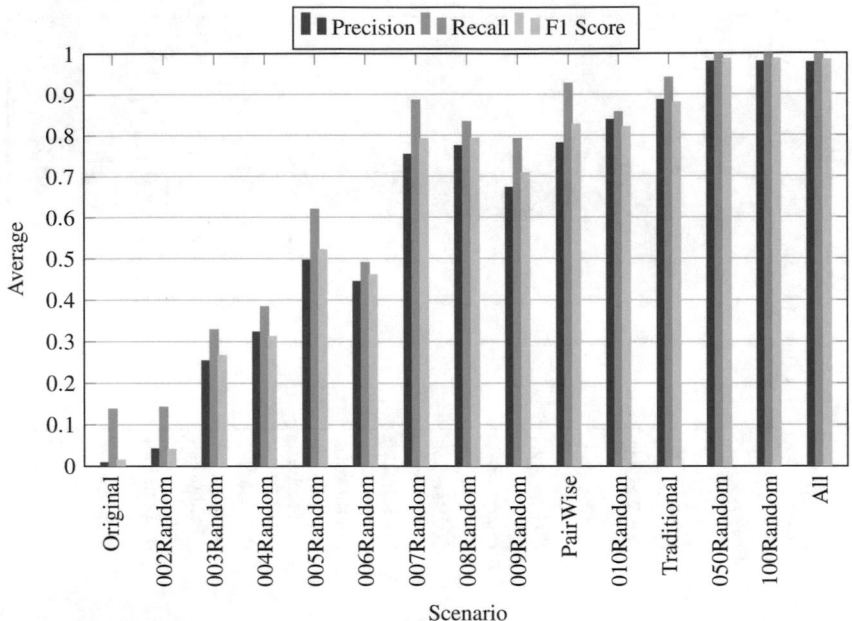

Fig. 15.13 Average Precision, Recall and F1 Score per Scenario [31]

15.7.3.3 Discussion

The best results are obtained with the largest scenarios, where 100% average recall and around 99% average precision and F1 score are achieved. Overall, the results improve the more variants are available. This is to be expected, as our technique is based on the comparison (i.e., commonalities and differences) of features and implementation of variants. As a consequence of this, scenarios consisting of only one or two variants produce quite useless results.

However, it is not generally true that more variants always produce better results. For example, the 9 random variants produce a slightly worse result than the 8 random variants. Similarly, the 10 traditional variants produce a slightly better result than the 10 random variants. This means that variants with *beneficial* configurations (i.e., combinations of features that exhibit *interesting* variability) can make up for a lower number of total variants available. There can be cases, where additional variants do not provide any new information as their variability has already been fully covered by previous variants. For example, new combinations of existing features that do not interact in any way provide no additional information. Instead, variants that combine interacting features in a new way might allow to trace the feature interaction, or variants that split up features that always appeared in combination in previous variants would allow to also split up the coarse trace (for both features) into two finer traces (one for each feature). Also, there seems to be a critical point after which the results do not improve much anymore, which is

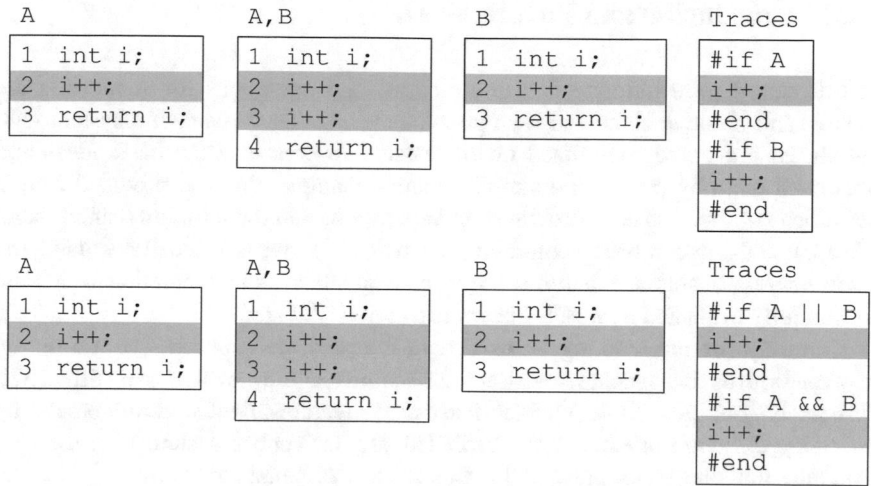

Fig. 15.14 Illustration of two valid alignments of lines (top and bottom) in three variants with two optional features A and B (left side) and the corresponding traces (right side) [31]

somewhere around 10 variants. After that, every additional variant only improves the results marginally. Beyond 50 variants the results do not even change at all anymore as nothing new can be learned from additional variants.

The few differences that remain in the results, even with all variants available for analysis, are caused by ambiguities during the alignment of sequences of lines of source code (for example, children of methods in the artifact tree) during the comparison of the implementation of variants. Alignments of sequences of lines, i.e., insertions and deletions, do not always reflect perfectly the actual changes that were performed, as anyone who has ever used a source code diffing tool, e.g. when performing merges in a VCS such as Git, is probably aware. This causes misinterpretations of changes and leads to mismatches with the ground truth in some cases. However, this does not mean that the computed traces are *wrong* as they still produce the exact same variants, it just means that there are multiple valid traces and that the one our approach computed does not match the one provided by the ground truth. This is illustrated with a minimalistic example in Fig. 15.14. It shows three variants with features {A}, {A, B} and {B} respectively and alignments of the statement i++ on the left and the corresponding traces that produce the variants in the form of annotated code on the right. The two rows illustrate two different alignments and corresponding different traces. Even though the traces (on the right) are different, the produced variants (on the left) are identical.

15.8   Conclusion and Future Work

In this chapter, we introduced data structures and operations for supporting the flexible and intuitive clone-and-own practice for creating variants of a system with automated reuse and centralized maintenance. We presented the basic ideas and illustrated them by means of a simple running example. We also provided formal definitions of the used data structures and operations and the intuition behind them. We applied the operations in common scenarios which we also illustrated using the same running example. Finally, we showed a practical implementation which we successfully evaluated on a well-known research challenge.

Currently, we are working on extending the presented concepts with a notion of evolution by introducing revisions per feature as they evolve over time [32]. Ultimately, our goal is to enable distributed, feature-oriented development by providing a feature-oriented and distributed version control system with the data structures and operations presented in this chapter as foundation.

Acknowledgments This work was partially supported by the Carlos Chagas Filho Foundation for Supporting Research in the State of Rio de Janeiro (FAPERJ), under the PDR-10 program, grant 202073/2020. This work was partially supported by the Natural Sciences and Engineering Research Council of Canada (NSERC) grant RGPIN-2017-05421.

References

1. Angerer, F., Grimmer, A., Prähofer, H., Grünbacher, P.: Change impact analysis for maintenance and evolution of variable software systems. Autom. Softw. Eng. **26**(2), 417–461 (2019)
2. Apel, S., Batory, D.S., Kästner, C., Saake, G.: Feature-Oriented Software Product Lines — Concepts and Implementation. Springer (2013)
3. Assunção, W.K.G., Lopez-Herrejon, R.E., Linsbauer, L., Vergilio, S.R., Egyed, A.: Reengineering legacy applications into software product lines: a systematic mapping. Empir. Softw. Eng. **22**(6), 2972–3016 (2017)
4. Assunção, W.K.G., Vergilio, S.R.: Feature location for software product line migration: a mapping study. In: SPLC Workshops, pp. 52–59. ACM (2014)
5. Batory, D.S., Sarvela, J.N., Rauschmayer, A.: Scaling step-wise refinement. IEEE Trans. Software Eng. **30**(6), 355–371 (2004)
6. Berger, T., Lettner, D., Rubin, J., Grünbacher, P., Silva, A., Becker, M., Chechik, M., Czarnecki, K.: What is a feature?: a qualitative study of features in industrial software product lines. In: SPLC, pp. 16–25. ACM (2015)
7. Cleland-Huang, J., Gotel, O., Zisman, A. (eds.): Software and Systems Traceability. Springer (2012)
8. Couto, M.V., Valente, M.T., Figueiredo, E.: Extracting software product lines: A case study using conditional compilation. In: 15th European Conference on Software Maintenance and Reengineering, CSMR 2011, 1–4 March 2011, Oldenburg, Germany, pp. 191–200. IEEE Computer Society (2011)
9. Cruz, D., Figueiredo, E., Martinez, J.: A literature review and comparison of three feature location techniques using argouml-spl. In: VaMoS, pp. 16:1–16:10. ACM (2019)
10. Deorowicz, S., Debudaj-Grabysz, A., Gudys, A.: Kalign-LCS - A more accurate and faster variant of Kalign2 algorithm for the multiple sequence alignment problem. In: ICMMI, *Advances in Intelligent Systems and Computing*, vol. 242, pp. 495–502. Springer (2013)

11. Dubinsky, Y., Rubin, J., Berger, T., Duszynski, S., Becker, M., Czarnecki, K.: An exploratory study of cloning in industrial software product lines. In: 17th European Conference on Software Maintenance and Reengineering, CSMR 2013, Genova, Italy, March 5–8, 2013, pp. 25–34 (2013)
12. Fischer, S., Linsbauer, L., Egyed, A., Lopez-Herrejon, R.E.: Predicting higher order structural feature interactions in variable systems. In: ICSME, pp. 252–263. IEEE Computer Society (2018)
13. Fischer, S., Linsbauer, L., Lopez-Herrejon, R.E., Egyed, A.: Enhancing clone-and-own with systematic reuse for developing software variants. In: 30th IEEE International Conference on Software Maintenance and Evolution, Victoria, BC, Canada, pp. 391–400. IEEE Computer Society (2014)
14. Fischer, S., Linsbauer, L., Lopez-Herrejon, R.E., Egyed, A.: A source level empirical study of features and their interactions in variable software. In: 16th International Working Conference on Source Code Analysis and Manipulation, SCAM 2016, pp. 197–206. IEEE (2016)
15. Illescas, S., Lopez-Herrejon, R.E., Egyed, A.: Towards visualization of feature interactions in software product lines. In: IEEE Working Conference on Software Visualization, Raleigh, NC, USA, pp. 46–50. IEEE Computer Society (2016)
16. Liebig, J., Kästner, C., Apel, S.: Analyzing the discipline of preprocessor annotations in 30 million lines of C code. In: 10th International Conference on Aspect-Oriented Software Development, AOSD 2011, Porto de Galinhas, Brazil, March 21–25, 2011, pp. 191–202. ACM (2011)
17. Linsbauer, L., Berger, T., Grünbacher, P.: A classification of variation control systems. In: Proceedings of the 16th ACM SIGPLAN International Conference on Generative Programming: Concepts and Experiences, Vancouver, BC, Canada, pp. 49–62. ACM (2017)
18. Linsbauer, L., Lopez-Herrejon, R.E., Egyed, A.: Recovering traceability between features and code in product variants. In: 17th International Software Product Line Conference, Tokyo, Japan, pp. 131–140. ACM (2013)
19. Linsbauer, L., Lopez-Herrejon, R.E., Egyed, A.: Variability extraction and modeling for product variants. Software and System Modeling 16(4), 1179–1199 (2017)
20. Linsbauer, L., Schwägerl, F., Berger, T., Grünbacher, P.: Concepts of variation control systems. J. Syst. Softw. 171, 110,796 (2021)
21. Liu, J., Batory, D., Lengauer, C.: Feature oriented refactoring of legacy applications. In: 28th International Conference on Software Engineering, ICSE 2006, p. 112–121. ACM (2006)
22. Lopez-Herrejon, R.E., Illescas, S., Egyed, A.: Visualization for software product lines: A systematic mapping study. In: 2016 IEEE Working Conference on Software Visualization, Raleigh, NC, USA, pp. 26–35. IEEE Computer Society (2016)
23. Lopez-Herrejon, R.E., Illescas, S., Egyed, A.: A systematic mapping study of information visualization for software product line engineering. Journal of Software: Evolution and Process 30(2) (2018)
24. Mäder, P., Egyed, A.: Do software engineers benefit from source code navigation with traceability? - an experiment in software change management. In: ASE, pp. 444–447. IEEE Computer Society (2011)
25. Mäder, P., Egyed, A.: Assessing the effect of requirements traceability for software maintenance. In: ICSM, pp. 171–180. IEEE Computer Society (2012)
26. Mäder, P., Egyed, A.: Do developers benefit from requirements traceability when evolving and maintaining a software system? Empirical Software Engineering 20(2), 413–441 (2015)
27. Martinez, J., Assunção, W.K.G., Ziadi, T.: Espla: A catalog of extractive spl adoption case studies. In: 21st International Systems and Software Product Line Conference - Volume B, SPLC '17, pp. 38–41. ACM (2017)
28. Martinez, J., Ordoñez, N., Tërnava, X., Ziadi, T., Aponte, J., Figueiredo, E., Valente, M.T.: Feature location benchmark with argouml spl. In: Proceedings of the 22nd International Systems and Software Product Line Conference - Volume 1, SPLC 2018, Gothenburg, Sweden, pp. 257–263. ACM (2018)
29. Martinez, J., Ziadi, T., Bissyandé, T.F., Klein, J., Traon, Y.L.: Bottom-up adoption of software product lines: a generic and extensible approach. In: SPLC, pp. 101–110. ACM (2015)

30. Martinez, J., Ziadi, T., Bissyandé, T.F., Klein, J., Traon, Y.L.: Bottom-up technologies for reuse: automated extractive adoption of software product lines. In: ICSE (Companion Volume), pp. 67–70. IEEE Computer Society (2017)
31. Michelon, G.K., Linsbauer, L., Assunção, W.K.G., Egyed, A.: Comparison-based feature location in ArgoUML variants. In: Proceedings of the 23rd International Systems and Software Product Line Conference, SPLC 2019, Volume A, Paris, France, September 9–13, 2019, pp. 17:1–17:5. ACM (2019)
32. Michelon, G.K., Obermann, D., Linsbauer, L., Assunção, W.K.G., Grünbacher, P., Egyed, A.: Locating feature revisions in software systems evolving in space and time. In: SPLC '20: 24th ACM International Systems and Software Product Line Conference, Montreal, Quebec, Canada, October 19–23, 2020, Volume A, pp. 14:1–14:11. ACM (2020)
33. Müller, R., Eisenecker, U.W.: A graph-based feature location approach using set theory. In: Proceedings of the 23rd International Systems and Software Product Line Conference, SPLC 2019, Volume A, Paris, France, September 9–13, 2019, pp. 16:1–16:5. ACM (2019)
34. Pohl, K., Böckle, G., Linden, F.J.v.d.: Software Product Line Engineering: Foundations, Principles and Techniques. Springer-Verlag New York, Inc. (2005)
35. Rubin, J., Chechik, M.: A survey of feature location techniques. In: Domain Engineering, Product Lines, Languages, and Conceptual Models, pp. 29–58. Springer (2013)
36. Rubin, J., Czarnecki, K., Chechik, M.: Managing cloned variants: a framework and experience. In: SPLC, pp. 101–110 (2013)
37. Svahnberg, M., van Gurp, J., Bosch, J.: A taxonomy of variability realization techniques. Softw., Pract. Exper. **35**(8), 705–754 (2005)
38. Thüm, T., Kästner, C., Benduhn, F., Meinicke, J., Saake, G., Leich, T.: FeatureIDE: An extensible framework for feature-oriented software development. Sci. Comput. Program. **79**, 70–85 (2014)

Chapter 16
Re-engineering Automation Software with the Variability Analysis Toolkit

Kamil Rosiak, Lukas Linsbauer, Birgit Vogel-Heuser, and Ina Schaefer

Abstract In the automated production systems (aPs) domain, software increasingly gains relevance to realize certain functionality. New system variants are created by using ad-hoc practices such as copying existing systems and customizing them to meet varying customer requirements, affecting software quality and overall maintainability in the long run. Various software systems' variability information needs to be re-engineered to decrease such problems and reestablish sustainable development. In this chapter, we present the Variability Analysis Toolkit (VAT), which is an extensible framework that allows for the analysis of control software variants with implementations adhering to the IEC 61131-3 standard. It allows the analysis of all languages included in PLCOpen, which are Structured Text (ST), Sequential Function Chart (SFC), Ladder Diagram (LD), and Function Block Diagram (FBD) and their nesting. A fully customizable metric drives the comparison process and adjusts the whole process to get results as expected. The underlying framework is extensible and supports the adaptation of the process for other artifact types. The VAT supports the detection of code clones within and the analysis of variability between variants and delivers visualization for the comprehension of the analysis results.

K. Rosiak · L. Linsbauer (✉)
Institute of Software Engineering and Automotive Informatics, Technische Universität Braunschweig, Braunschweig, Germany
e-mail: k.rosiak@tu-bs.de; l.linsbauer@tu-bs.de

B. Vogel-Heuser
Institute of Automation and Information Systems, Technische Universität München, München, Germany
e-mail: vogel-heuser@tum.de

I. Schaefer
Testing, Validation and Analysis of Software-Intensive Systems (TVA), Karlsruhe Institute of Technology (KIT), Karlsruhe
e-mail: ina.schaefer@kit.edu

© Springer Nature Switzerland AG 2023
R. E. Lopez-Herrejon et al. (eds.), *Handbook of Re-Engineering Software Intensive Systems into Software Product Lines*, https://doi.org/10.1007/978-3-031-11686-5_16

16.1   Introduction and Motivation

With an increasing interest in variants for industrial products, variability has become
a key feature of many software systems. In the domain of automated production
systems (aPs) and their control, software often remains in use for several decades
[23]. Such aPs are often controlled by programmable logic controllers (PLCs).
The majority of PLC systems today adhere to the IEC 61131-3 control systems
programming standard [3]. Long lifespans make it unlikely for engineers to predict
the entire scope of functionality [17]. When customer requirements or governing
rules in the production change, the software needs to be adapted frequently [6]. To
cope with changing requirements, engineers often use an unstructured, but straightforward reuse approach known as clone-and-own [7]. This approach saves time and
workload in the short-run, but if no documentation of variant creation is available,
problems are caused in the long-run. With an increasing number of variants, the
maintainability and evolution of the portfolio are negatively affected.

In contrast, the Software Product Line Engineering (SPLE) approach uses variant
management to enable the reuse of software artifacts in a structured and documented
fashion. Extractive SPLE is an approach for the migration of system variants from
unstructured reuse, such as clone-and-own, to structured reuse techniques [11].
Therefore, a detailed analysis of artifacts is required to identify common and different parts of the PLC software. Furthermore, the analysis of program organization
units (POUs) within a variant is also useful to detect similar artifacts that can be
extracted into library components to establish a component-based Software Product
Line (SPL). Identifying intra- and inter-system clones in the domain of aPs is a
remaining challenge and needs appropriate tool support.

In this chapter, we present the Variability Analysis Toolkit (VAT), a Rich
Client Platform (RCP) application, which allows a detailed model-based analysis
of aPs implemented in IEC 61131-3. This chapter is based on a research paper
on IEC 61131-3 clone detection [14]. In this chapter, we focus on the qualitative
point of view of our re-engineering process to show the usefulness of our results for
engineers.

16.2   The IEC 61131-3 Standard

IEC 61131-3 is an international standard for programming languages for industrial
automation [21]. It is the third part of the IEC 61131 family and a formal
specification of five programming languages, including the languages' overall
software architecture and structure.

Figure 16.1 depicts the IEC 61131-3 software model. A *configuration* represents
the highest level of a PLC controlled system and is assigned to a particular type of
control system, which includes the hardware, i.e., processing resources, memory
addresses for all input and output channels as well as the system capabilities.

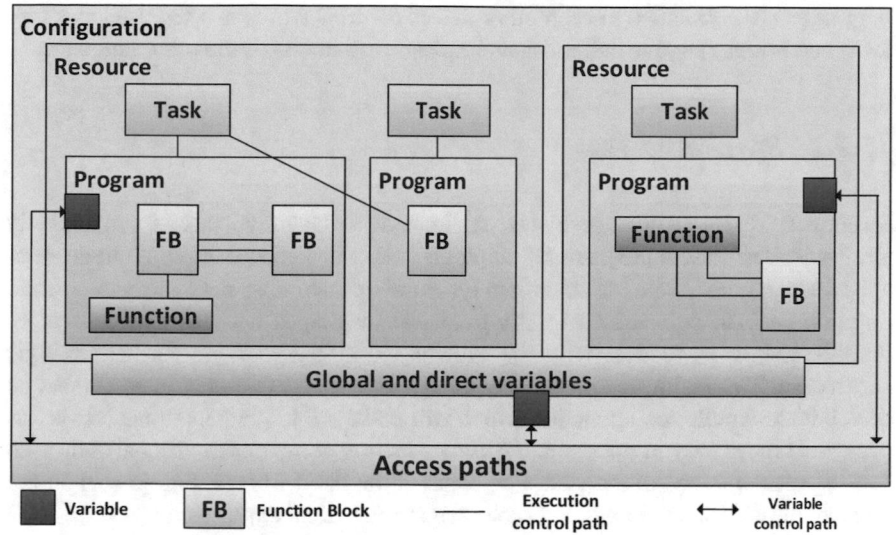

Fig. 16.1   IEC 61131-3 software model [8]

A *configuration* contains *resources*, which are a processing facility that can execute IEC programs. A *resource* can contain one or more *tasks*, which control the execution of *programs* and *function blocks*. A *program* is defined as a logical assembly of all programming language elements and constructs necessary to fulfill a control task of plant machinery. *Functions* and *function blocks* are the basic elements and contain specific implementation. *Function blocks* contain state and keep track of the execution history in contrast to *functions* that do not have state and always return the same output given the same input.

Within the IEC 61131-3, *programs, function blocks* and *functions* are called program organization units (POUs). A POU contains a declaration part where variables and data types are defined and a body part where algorithms are implemented. A POU can be implemented in one of the five defined programming languages Structured Text (ST), Sequential Function Chart (SFC), Ladder Diagram (LD), Function Block Diagram (FBD) and Instruction List (IL), which we briefly explain in the following subsections. IL is similar to assembly languages and marked as deprecated in the last version of IEC 61131-3 and no longer considered.

In contrast to other programming languages such as Java, C, or Python, the IEC 61131-3 allows implementing aPs in different languages. This approach is flexible and allows engineers to choose the programming language that they are most comfortable with. In addition, the nesting of different languages is allowed, e.g, we can call a ST in a *function block* or implement SFC *actions* in any of the IEC 61131-3 languages. Such nesting of graphical and textual languages makes the analysis challenging and requires dedicated analysis techniques. Overall the languages are alternative to each other except for SFC which is often used as a top-level control language to call artifacts implemented in one of the other languages.

16.2.1 Structured Text

Structured Text is a high-level textual imperative language that is syntactically similar to C or Pascal [13]. An ST implementation is a composition of single steps called statements. Available statement types are *for*, *while*, *if*, *case*, *assignment*, and *function call*. In comparison to the graphical languages such as LD, it is more flexible and helps to deal with the growing complexity of programmable logic controllers. The major benefit of structured text is that a complex program can be divided into smaller components, which will make ST implementations less error-prone and more easy to maintain. ST allows writing complex conditional code with less effort than in one of the other languages of the IEC 61131-3. Figure 16.1 shows an example ST implementation which assigns the logical expression $((A \wedge B) \vee C)$ to the variable D.

```
1 D := (A AND B) OR C;
```

Listing 16.1 Example of a Structured Text program.

16.2.2 Sequential Function Chart

SFC is a graphical programming language, which is based on the Graphe Fonctionnel de Commande Etape Transition (GRAFCET) standard [5] and allows to model Petri net behavior. The main components of an SFC program are *steps* with associated *actions* and *transitions* with assigned conditions. Steps represent a state of the system. They are linked to *action blocks* performing specific control actions and are connected with *transitions* to other *steps*. *Transitions* are a condition, which, when evaluate to true deactivates the *step* before the *transition* and activates the next *step*. *Actions* can be implemented in any of the IEC 61131-3 languages and are executed either when a step is activated or deactivated. Two triggers can activate a step. Either the step is an initial step specified by the developer, or all the steps above a step are active, and the connecting transition is enabled. *Steps* can be executed in parallel or in sequence. Figure 16.2 depicts an example SFC implementation. On the top, we can see the initial step marked with a double border. Initially, this step executes the non-stored (N) *Action 1*. When the first transition evaluates to true, the second step will be activated and execute the stored (S) *Action 2*. When the second transition evaluates to true, the last step is reached.

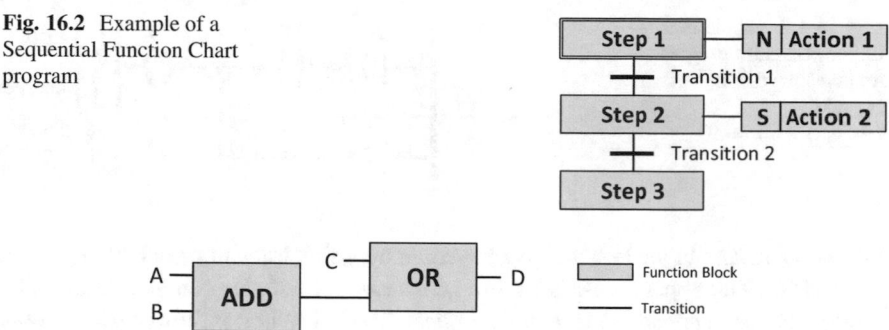

Fig. 16.2 Example of a
Sequential Function Chart
program

Fig. 16.3 Example of a Function Block Diagram program representing the logical expression $(A \wedge B) \vee C) = D$

16.2.3   Function Block Diagram

FBD is the second graphical programming language for data-flow networks and offers a way to abstract complex functions written in several code lines into boxes. Thereby can be connected to make a bigger PLC program. An FBD implementation contains a list of networks with each network representing some functionality. For the implementation of networks, we can use *Functions* such as logical AND, and *function blocks* such as timers or delays. Networks have input ports and output ports, which can be connected to *variables*, *networks* or to other *function blocks*. *Function blocks* can also execute ST code with the *EXECUTE function blocks*. Figure 16.3 depicts a FBD implementation of a network consisting of a logical AND and a logical OR *Function Block*. The resulting logical expression of this implementation is $(A \wedge B) \vee C) = D$.

16.2.4   Ladder Diagram

LD is also a graphical language for capturing program flow in a way similar to electric circuits. An LD contains a number of *networks* similar to FBD. A *network* is bounded on the left and right sides by a vertical line called the *power rail*. *networks* use *contacts*, *coils*, and connecting lines. Each *contact* represent a boolean variable, which when evaluates to TRUE, passing the condition from the left to the right *power rail*.

Otherwise, the value FALSE is propagated. On the right side of a *Network*, there can be any number of *coils*. A *coil* relays a the value from left to right and stores it in a variable. In addition to *contacts* and *coils*, the usage of *function blocks* and *programs* is allowed. Figure 16.4 shows an example of a LD *network* implementation. As we can see, this *network* is bounded on the left and right side by

Fig. 16.4 Example of a
Ladder Diagram program
representing the logical
expression
$(A \wedge B) \vee C) = D$

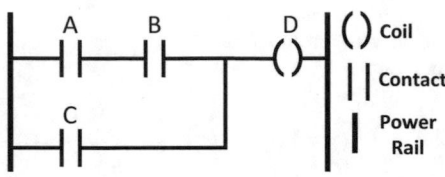

the *power rails*. On the left side, we have two outgoing transitions, which represent
a logical or. The upper *transition* starts with a *contact* with the name A followed by
contact B, those contacts expresses a logical AND. The bottom *transition* are only
connected with the *contact* C. Overall this *network* expresses the following logical
expression $(A \wedge B) \vee C) = D$.

16.3 Code Clones

Cloning artifacts is a common approach for creating new functionality within
a system and developing new system variants. This chapter uses the following
terminology for cloned artifacts, which is essential to understand our analysis
methods. A clone is a pair of similar artifacts by some definition of similarity [20].
Clones within a system occur by copying and pasting artifacts of finer granularity,
such as POUs, and are referred to as intra-system clones [9, 10]. Cloned variants
are created by copying an entire system and adapting it to fit new requirements.
This practice is called clone-and-own. Cloned systems (i.e., variants) are referred
to as inter-system clones [9, 10]. Clones can be categorized into the following four
types [1, 15, 16]:

- **Type-I Clone**: Two cloned code fragments that are an exact copy of each other
  except for changes in white space or variation in comments.
- **Type-II Clone**: Two syntactically identical fragments of code which show
  changes in the identifier names of types, literals, or functions as well as changes
  of Type-I clones.
- **Type-III Clone**: Clones can exhibit further modifications such as added or
  deleted artifacts and all modifications from Type II clones.
- **Type-IV Clone**: Semantically equivalent code fragments potentially lacking
  any textual similarity, e.g., an iterative and a recursive implementation of the
  same functionality.

We can also apply the commonly available definition of clones to IEC 61131-
3 languages. The only difference is the name of the artifacts. In the context of IEC
systems, we speak of configurations or POUs, whereas in object-oriented languages,
for example, classes and methods are common artifacts.

```
1  IF  CONDITION  THEN
2      VALUE  :=  5;
3  END_IF
```

```
1  IF  CONDITION  THEN
2      VAR1  :=  5;  //RENAME
3      VAR2  :=  7;  //ADD
4  END_IF
```

Fig. 16.5 Example structured text clone pair

Figure 16.5 shows a cloned pair of ST implementations. On the left, if the variable CONDITION evaluates to true (cf. Line 1), we assign the value 5 to the variable VALUE (cf. Line 2). On the right, the variable VALUE is renamed to VAR1 (cf. Line 2), and the if condition block is extended with an additional assignment (cf. Line 3). So these code fragments are Type III clones of each other.

As a requirement for VAT, we want to detect intra- and inter-system clones of types I to III. Our focus is on the re-engineering of aPs, which often contain many duplicated POUs (intra-system clones) or have been cloned in their entirety (inter-system clones). This work serves as the first step towards the extraction of configurable library components from intra-system clones. Furthermore, identifying common artifacts between system variants is a necessary step for the extraction of a SPL from inter-system clones.

16.4 Intra- and Inter-System Clone Detection for IEC 61131-3

To re-engineer an IEC 61131-3 system into a SPL, a detailed analysis is required to identify common and variable artifacts. In this section, we present our approach for intra- and inter-system clone detection in IEC 61131-3 systems, which allows tracking of cloned POUs within a variant and between variants. Figure 16.6 shows an overview of our intra- and inter-system clone detection approach implemented in the VAT. First, IEC 61131-3 variants are parsed into meta-model instances as explained in Sect. 16.4.1. The comparison process requires at least one model for the intra-system clone detection and two or more models for the inter-system clone detection. Models are compared based on a comparison metric ① (Sect. 16.4.2). The comparison process decomposes models down to statement-level and compares all elements pair-wise ② (Sect. 16.4.3). The difference between the intra-system and inter-system clone detection approach is the input. The intra-clone detection analysis compares each artifact within a variant with each artifact of the same variant. The inter-clone detection approach compares each artifact from one variant with each artifact of another variant. To filter relevant comparisons, the comparison results are matched ③ (Sect. 16.4.4). Finally, the matched comparison results are visualized ④ (Sect. 16.4.5).

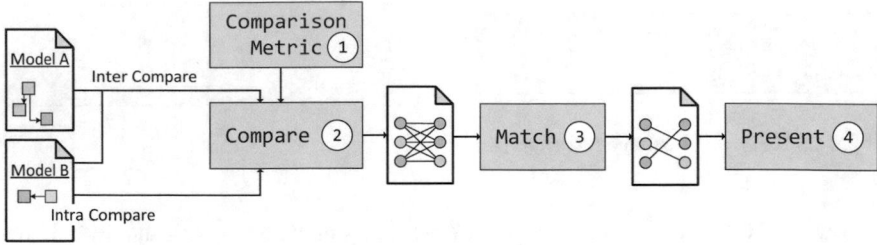

Fig. 16.6 Overview of the intra- and inter-system clone detection approach in VAT

The existing and generic model comparison tool EMF Compare[1] calculates an overall score between two artifacts based on their name, type, and attributes, but does not consider their children in order to determine similarity. In contrast, our approach also allows to define comparison metrics that also consider the calculated similarity of all child artifacts, which is propagated bottom-up, to compute the final similarity of any pair of artifacts.

16.4.1 IEC 61131-3 Meta-Model

The comparison of IEC 61131-3 programs is based on a meta-model representation of the IEC 61131-3 standard. Therefore, we created a hierarchy of meta-models shown in Fig. 16.7, expressing the entire IEC 61131-3 standard, including the software model (Fig. 16.1). The *configuration* meta-model describes the whole project on the top level, e.g., *resources*, *tasks* or the implementations. Implementations are represented in the *Language* meta-model. This allows the extension of our work with other implementation languages used in the IEC 61131-3 context, such as C or C++. Every implementation language inherits from this model and defines language specific parts. For FBD and LD, we grouped the common diagram elements in the *diagram* meta-model. Also, we modeled all logical and arithmetical expressions in a separate meta-model. All meta-models are created using the Eclipse Modelling Framework (EMF).[2] Meta-models are implemented as Ecore models and publicly available on GitHub.[3]

---

[1] https://www.eclipse.org/emf/compare/.

[2] https://www.eclipse.org/modeling/emf/.

[3] https://github.com/TUBS-ISF/variability_analysis_toolkit_iec.

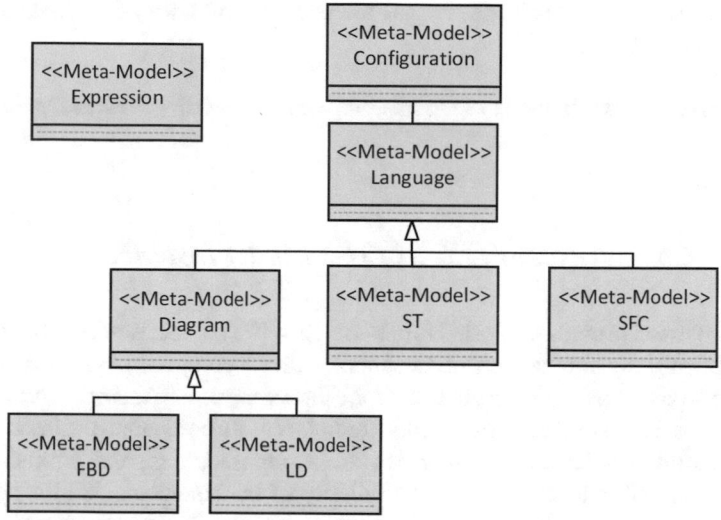

Fig. 16.7 Example metric with three attributes and one option

If-Statement		Assignment		Categorie
				Option
Condition	0.8	Assignment right side	0.5	Attribute
Nested Impl	0.2	Assignment left side	0.5	Weight

Fig. 16.8 IEC 61131-3 meta-model dependencies

16.4.2   Comparison Metric for IEC 61131-3

The comparison of IEC 61131-3 meta-model instances is driven by a fine-grained and customizable comparison metric. The comparison metric contains a set of *attributes* and *options*. Attributes are atomic comparison algorithms developed to compare the model's properties, e.g., the comparison of the names of two POUs. Attributes return a similarity value between 0.0 and 1.0, which expresses the similarity of two elements. Options are Boolean flags that enable and disable parts of the model comparison and activate or deactivate parts of the comparison process. We can also assign a weight between 0.0 and 1.0 to attributes and options to adjust their impact on the comparison metric, e.g., the implementation of a POU is more relevant than its name.

In Fig. 16.8, we present an example metric for the comparison of the code clone example shown in Fig. 16.5 that specifies how if-statements and assignments are compared. For example, it compares if-statements with an attribute for the condition and an option for the nested implementation. The attribute is weighted with 0.8 and the option with 0.2, which means that the overall similarity of an if-statement is calculated as follows:

$$similarity(if - statement) = Condition Attribute * 0.8 + Nested Option * 0.2$$

$$(16.1)$$

16.4.3 Comparison of IEC 61131-3 Model Instances

The comparison process is divided into two steps: The comparison and the matching phase. During the comparison phase, models are decomposed systematically and compared pair-wise using attributes from the comparison metric. The result of this process is a similarity tree. This tree stores all compared artifacts and the corresponding similarities. Similarities are composed, e.g., the similarity of a method declaration is the composed similarity of all statements and the similarity of the method-specific attributes such as parameters, method name, or method type. Artifact pairs, which have a composed similarity of 1.0, represent Type-I/II clones. Artifacts with a lower similarity than 1.0 and higher as an adjustable threshold are Type-III clones.

Figure 16.9 shows an example similarity tree using a metric with three attributes for the comparison of the cloned artifacts shown in Fig. 16.5. On the top level, we compare the if statements with a resulting similarity of 0.85. This similarity is the sum of the condition attribute similarity (1.0) multiplied by its weight (0.8) and the similarity of the nested implementation option (0.25) multiplied by its weight (0.2): $1.0 \times 0.8 + 0.25 \times 0.2 = 0.85$. These similarities are propagated from the bottom to the top artifacts.

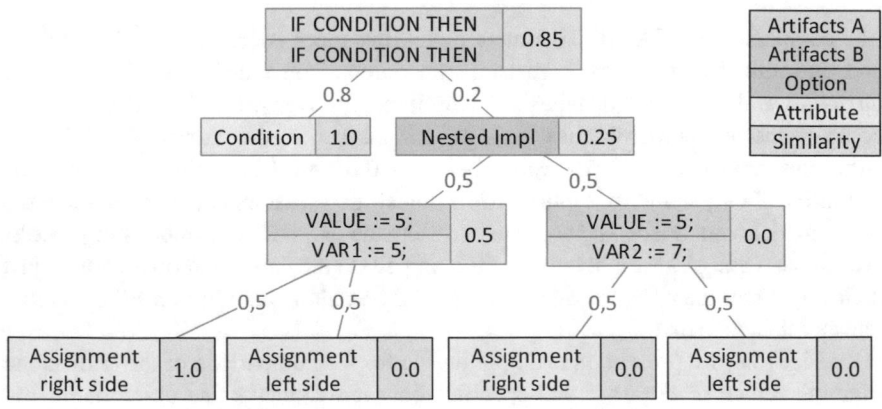

Fig. 16.9 Calculated similarity tree between the cloned ST artifacts shown in Fig. 16.5

Algorithm 1 Artifact Comparison

   Output: Result result

1 **Function** `compare` (*Artifact artA,Artifact artB*) **:**

2   **for** *Attribute attr : metric.getAttributeForElement(artA)* **do**

3   result.add(attr.compare(artA,artB)

4   **if** *artA.hasChildren()* ∧ *artB.hasChildren()* **then**

5   **for** *Artifact childA : artA.getChildren()* **do**

6   **for** *Artifact childB : artB.getChildren()* **do**

7   result.add(compare(childA,childB))

8   **return** result

Algorithm 1 shows the pseudo-code of the comparison phase. It receives two elements of type *Artifact* as input parameters. *Artifact* is a placeholder for an arbitrary meta-model element. First artifacts are compared, and comparison results are added to a result data structure (cf. Lines 2–3). If both artifacts have child artifacts, e.g., a *task* contains nested *POUs*, the child elements are compared recursively and added to the result data-structure (cf. Lines 4–7). After the comparison, the result data structure contains similarity values for each pair of elements of the first and second model on the same level of hierarchy and type. Each comparison can be considered as a triple in this result data structure described as *(ArtifactA, ArtifactB, Similarity)*.

16.4.4 Matching of Compared Model Instances

The second step in our approach is the matching phase, which filters the result data structure to get only relevant pairs of elements. We use a heuristic approach, which sorts all comparisons by similarity in descending order.

Algorithm 2 Artifact Matching

   Output: Result result

1 **Function** `match` (*Result result*) **:**

2   result = sortBySilimarityDesc(result.getComarisions())

3   **List** matchedElements = new List()

4   **for** *Comparison cmp : result.getComparisons()* **do**

5   **if** *!matchedElements.contains(cmp.getArtifactA())* ∧
            !matchedElements.contains(cmp.getArtifactB()) **then**

6   matchedElements.add(cmp.getArtifactA())

7   matchedElements.add(cmp.getArtifactB())

8   **else**

9   result.getComparisons().remove(cmp)

10   matchOptionals(result)

11   **return** result

Algorithm 2 shows the basic concept of the matching phase as pseudo-code. First, comparisons are sorted by similarity in descending order (cf. Line 2), and a list to store already matched artifacts is created (cf. Line 3). Second, we iterate over all comparisons and check if both artifacts are not already matched (cf. line 4–9). If the artifacts are not matched, we add both artifacts to *matchedElements*, else we remove the comparison from the matching. The last step is to identify the optional artifacts, which are those artifacts that are not in the *matchedElements* list (cf. Line 10). The matching approach keeps those artifacts that are relevant for the matching and removes artifacts which are already matched. This heuristic follows a greedy strategy and takes the first comparison with the highest similarity for the matching. If two comparisons have an equal similarity value, the matching only considers the first comparison during the matching phase. This first-come, first-serve strategy can lead to a matching that is not optimal, but only requires a run-time of $\mathcal{O}(n \log n)$. In contrast, the Hungarian method solves the matching problem optimally but has a time complexity of $\mathcal{O}(n^3)$.

16.4.5   Result Presentation

We present the matching result as a *family model* [2] to show the variability between two artifacts and a dependency graph to show the relationship between all compared artifacts. In Fig. 16.10, we depict a family model. The family model uses three elements to express the variability between artifacts and a hierarchical containment structure. Elements marked with a blue question mark ❓ are optional, which means that they are not contained in all variants. Elements marked with a green exclamation mark ❗ are mandatory and occur in every variant. The last element type is the alternative element, which is marked with arrows ⇆ and indicates artifacts that occur in each variant but in a modified version. On the right side, we show the details of the comparison in a details view. It shows all attributes and options used during the comparison phase, with their respective weights and the resulting similarity.

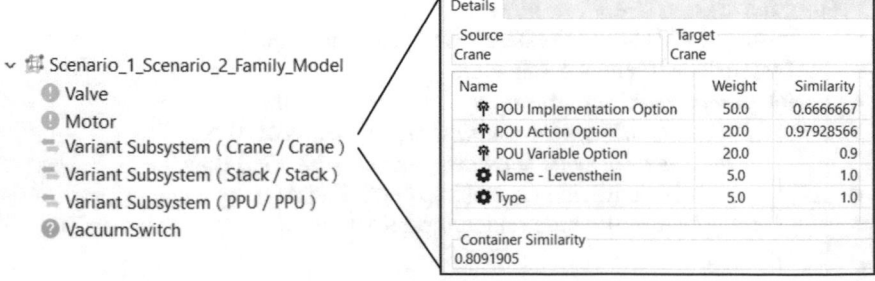

Fig. 16.10 Example of a family model on the left side with details of a selected comparison on the right side

This view supports users with detailed comparison information and makes results comprehensible.

The dependency graph presents compared artifacts and shows their dependencies. Nodes represent artifacts, e.g., variants for the inter-system clone detection approach, connected with weighted edges. Those weights show the similarity between connected nodes and can be selected to open the respective family model that shows more details. This view is available for the analysis of variants and POUs.

16.5   The Variability Analysis Toolkit for IEC 61131-3

In this section, we present the Variability Analysis Toolkit (VAT), which implements the previously described concepts. The VAT is open source and freely available on GitHub.[4] In Fig. 16.11, we illustrate the high-level architecture of the VAT. VAT is created based on the *e4CompareFramework*,[5] which is a black- and white-box framework for the creation of prototypes and developed as RCP 4 application. The framework is created modular and extensible with plug-ins which are loaded using Equinox,[6] a Java Java Open Services Gateway Initiative (OSGi)[7] implementation. Meta-models are created with EMF,[8] which contains a Java implementation of the Meta Object Facility (MOF)[9] called Ecore.[10] IEC 61131-3 implementations are exported as PLCOpenXML and parsed using an ANTLR[11] generated parser to transform the PLC software variants into meta-model instances.

In Fig. 16.12, we present the graphical user interface of the VAT, which is divided into 4 views. Models, metrics, family models, dependency graphs and feature models that are related to our process are serializable and can be managed in the project explorer, shown in the top left (1). From here, we can load stored metrics,

Fig. 16.11 High level architecture of the Variability Analysis Toolkit

Variability Analysis Toolkit			
e4CompareFramework			
Eclipse 4 RCP	Equinox (OSGi)	EMF	ANTLR
Java Virtual Machine			
Operating System			

---

[4] https://github.com/TUBS-ISF/variability_analysis_toolkit_iec.

[5] https://github.com/TUBS-ISF/e4CompareFramework.

[6] https://www.eclipse.org/equinox.

[7] https://www.osgi.org.

[8] https://www.eclipse.org/modeling/emf.

[9] https://www.omg.org/mof.

[10] https://wiki.eclipse.org/Ecore.

[11] https://www.antlr.org.

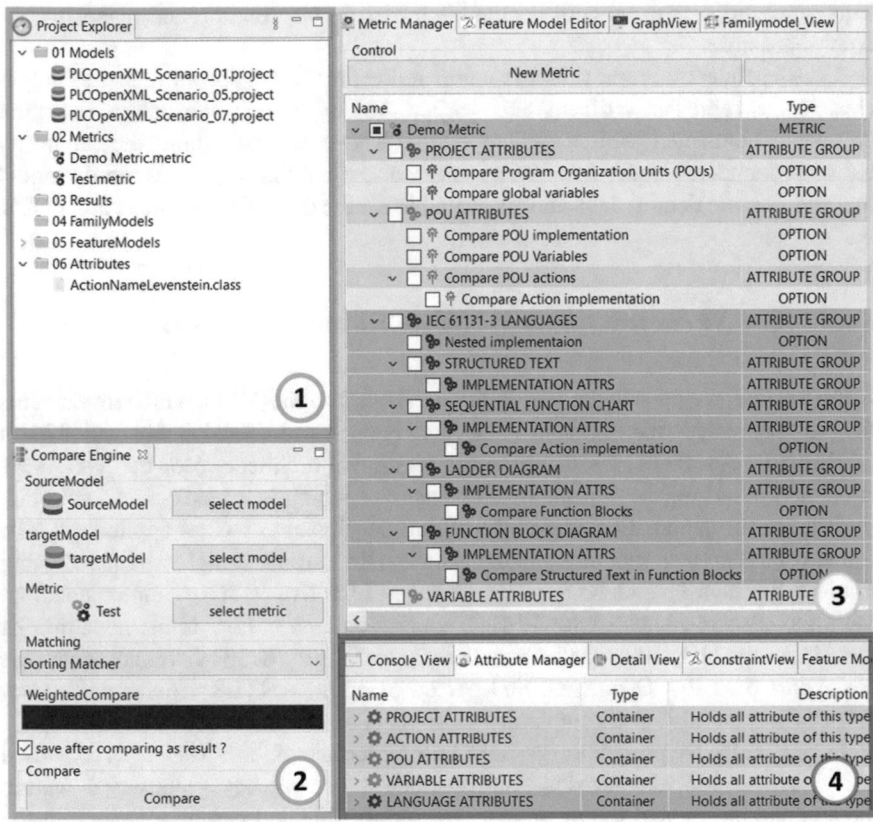

Fig. 16.12 The user interface of the VAT

inspect comparison results, and initialize the comparison process from the context menu. To adjust the comparison process, we can create a comparison metric in the *Metric Manager* ③. The comparison metric structure is close to the structure of the IEC 61131-3 software model. The metric contains *options* and *attributes*. *Options* can be activated and deactivated, and *attributes* can be added to the comparison metric by selecting them from the *Attribute Manager* ④.

In total, the *Attribute Manager* provides 66 predefined *attributes*, which are grouped into the following categories *project*, *action*, *pou*, *variable* and *language*. To adjust the relevance of attributes and options on the comparison result, we can adjust their weights supported by a *Weight Manager*. After the creation, we can store the metric, which allows us to refine the metric later or share it with other researchers.

The intra- and inter-system clone detection can be started by selecting the models from the project explorer by choosing either *project compare* or *variant compare* from the context menu. The inter-system compare process opens the *Compare*

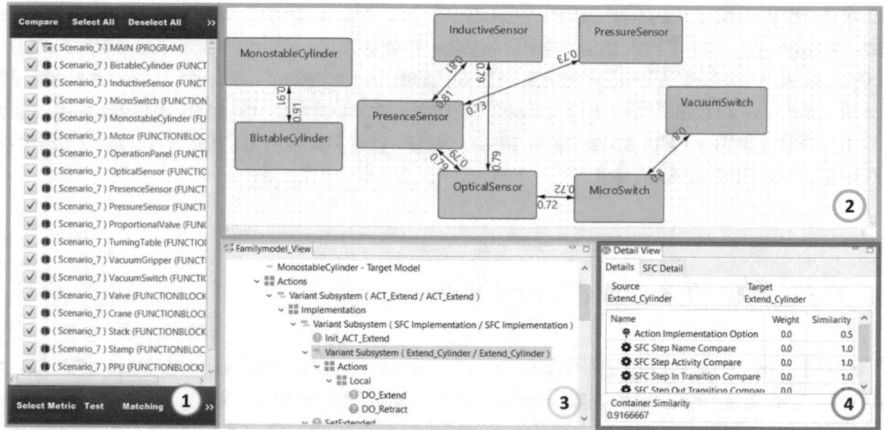

Fig. 16.13 Graphical user interface of the intra system clone detection approach

Engine View ②, which allows selecting a metric and the weights of attributes and options. The comparison process is started by pressing the compare button at the bottom of the Compare Engine View. The comparison result is presented in a family model and shows the variability between compared models.

In Fig. 16.13, we depict the intra-system compare perspective. The intra-system compare process opens the *Project Compare View* ①. In this view, all POUs from the selected models are shown, which can be selected for the comparison. We can adjust a similarity threshold, which filters all artifacts that have similarities less than the threshold to remove unrelated comparisons. To start the intra-system clone detection process, we have to select a metric and the similarity threshold. The comparison results are shown in the *Graph View* ②, which shows the similarities between compared POUs in a dependency graph. For example, the *BistableCylinder* is to 91% similar to the *MonostableCylinder* shown the left ②. For better comprehensibility of the comparison results, we can click on edge between those nodes, which opens the *Family-Model View* ③. This view shows all common ●, additional ❓, and modified ⇆ implementation artifacts. We can also select every element of the *Family-Model View* and show the comparison details in the *Detail View* ④. This view shows the similarity values of *attributes* and *options* that are used to compute this node's overall similarity.

16.6   Analyzing the Pick and Place Unit

In this section, we apply our approach to the Pick and Place Unit (PPU) and Extended Pick and Place Unit (xPPU) systems [22, 24] to illustrate the analysis with the VAT. First, we present the PPU, a universal demonstrator to show variability in the context of aPs and the extension of this system family with different sensors and safety aspects called xPPU. Second, we show our setup and methodology for analyzing the PPU and xPPU system variants, which includes the utilized comparison metric. Finally, the analysis results are presented with some detailed examples. All created family models, comparison metrics and meta-model instances of the PPU and xPPU scenarios, and a deployed version of the VAT are publicly available online on GitHub.[12]

16.6.1 The Pick and Place Unit

The Pick and Place Unit (PPU) manipulates work-pieces of different material. It is a universal demonstrator to show the evolution of aPs and is an ideal subject system for the analysis of cloned artifacts within and between PLC software systems. In total, 23 evolution steps are applied to evolve the PPU, yielding 24 different scenarios. In each scenario, a different number of POUs is added to the system. The implementation of each scenario is available online as a PLCOpenXML file on GitHub.[13] The first PLCOpenXML scenario file contains 7,790 Lines of Code (LoC) and is growing up to 39,161 LoC in scenario 24. Figure 16.14 shows the ninth

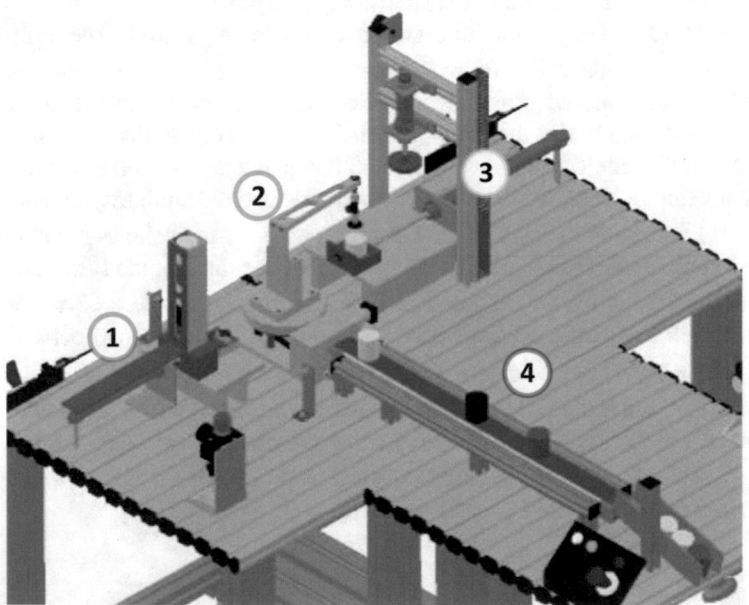

Fig. 16.14 A schematic depiction of the ninth evolution scenario of the PPUs[24]

---

[12] https://github.com/TUBS-ISF/IEC_61131_3_Clone_Detection.

[13] https://github.com/x-PPU.

PPU evolution scenario. In this scenario, the PPU has a stack ① as work-piece input, and a conveyor ④, which transports work-pieces to a ramp which serves as the output. The crane ② picks and places work-pieces between the input and a stamp ③, which stamps work-pieces. The PPU processes metal and white plastic work-pieces, which are stamped and transported to the conveyor, while black plastic work-pieces are directly transported to the conveyor. During the following evolution steps, the PPU is extended with pushers that sort work-pieces out from the conveyor, additional conveyors and safety aspects described in the xPPU scenarios.

16.6.2 Case Study Methodology

We analyze the PPU case study with the goal of detecting variation points to support SPL migration. Starting with an intra-system clone analysis, we aim to identify similar POUs, which can be refactored into library components. We then perform inter-system clone analysis on the PPU scenarios to identify commonalities between variants.

For the comparison process, we use the comparison metric shown in Fig. 16.15. Attributes and options are chosen with our intuition of importance, e.g., the

Attribut Name / Option Name	Weight	Attribut Name / Option Name	Weight
Configuration Attributes		*Variable Attributes*	
(Option) Compare POUs	0.8	Variable Name (Levensthein Distance)	0.6
(Option) Compare Global Variables	0.2	Types of Variables	0.4
POU Attributes		*Sequential Function Chart Attributes*	
(Option) POU Implementation	0.5	(Option) Compare Action Implementation	0.2
(Option) Compare POU Variables	0.2	Step Name	0.2
(Option) Compare POU Actions	0.2	Step In Transition	0.2
POU Name (Levensthein Distance)	0.05	Step Out Transition	0.2
POU Type	0.05	Step Level	0.2
Action Attributes		*Ladder Diagram Attributes*	
(Option) Action Implementation	1.0	(Option) Compare nested FBD	0.2
Structured Text Attributes		Coil Expression	0.2
Function-Call Parameter Types	0.2	Contact Expression	0.2
Function-Call Parameter Names	0.2	Power Rail Assignment	0.2
Function-Call Names	0.6	Source Elements	0.2
Assignment Left Side Name	0.25	Target Elements	0.2
Assignment Left Side Type	0.25	*Function Block Diagram Attributes*	
Assignment Right Side	0.5	(Option) Compare nested ST	0.2
If Conditions	1.0	Block Names	0.15
While Conditions	1.0	Block Types	0.15
For Conditions	1.0	Block Level	0.1
Case Conditions	1.0	Block In Ports	0.1
Exit Assignment	1.0	Block Out Ports	0.1
		Block In Ports	0.1
		Block Out Ports	0.1
Metric Category	Attribute	Option	Weight

Fig. 16.15 Comparison metric for the PPU case study

implementation of a POU has more impact on the result than the name of the POU. Based on this metric, models are decomposed down to statement level and compared. We activated the comparison of nested implementations to detect all changes. In total, we activated nine options and used 31 attributes. For example, we use three attributes for the comparison of function calls to detect detailed changes. As we can see, we compare the parameter types and the parameter names, which are weighted with 20% each, which means that the parameters have an impact of 40% on the overall result of a function call comparison. The function call name attribute contributes the last 60% of the function call comparison similarity. This comparison metric can also be used to compare other IEC 61131-3 software systems, which are implemented in compliance with the standard.

For the analysis of the PPU we use an Intel Core i7-9700k (3.6 GHz) with 16 GB of RAM, running Windows 10 64 bit.

16.6.3   Results of the Intra System Clone Analysis

To analyze the PPU and xPPU scenarios, we first parse them into meta-model instances. The parsing process is guided by a wizard, which can be started from the project explorer's context menu. The intra-system clone detection process is started as explained in the previous sections.

Figure 16.16 shows the results of the intra-system clone analysis for the PPU. The first scenario, which is the starting point of the evolution of the PPU, contains 12 POUs of which 2 are clones. The last scenario contains 46 POUs, of which 25 POUs are potential clones that are dividable into six clone clusters. In this context, a clone cluster is a set of artifacts similar to each other by the definition of code clones. In the dependency graph, a clone cluster is a sub-graph containing more than two nodes. For each scenario, we show the number of added, removed, and cloned POUs.

Figure 16.17 shows detailed results of the intra-system clone analysis of Scenario 9. On the left, we show a snippet of the dependency graph, which shows a POU clone

	PPU Intra-System Clone POU Analysis Results												
	s1	s2	s3	s4a	s4b	s5	s7	s8	s9	s10	s11	s12	s13
# Added POUs	0	1	3	1	0	0	3	0	1	0	0	0	1
# Removed Cloned POUs	0	0	0	0	0	1	0	0	0	0	0	0	0
# Added Cloned POUs	0	1	1	1	0	0	3	0	0	0	0	0	0
# POU Clone Cluster	1	1	2	2	2	2	2	2	2	2	2	2	2
Total # of Cloned POUs	2	3	4	5	5	4	7	7	7	7	7	7	7
Total # of POUs	12	12	16	17	17	16	19	19	20	20	20	20	21

	xPPU Intra-System Clone POU Analysis Results									
	s14	s15	s16	s17	s18	s19	s20	s21	s23	s24
# Added POUs	2	6	3	2	1	0	9	3	1	0
# Removed Cloned POUs	2	0	0	0	0	0	0	0	0	0
# Added Cloned POUs	1	4	1	1	1	0	8	2	0	0
# POU Clone Cluster	2	3	4	4	5	6	6	6	6	6
Total # of Cloned POUs	8	12	13	14	15	15	23	25	25	25
Total # of POUs	21	27	30	32	33	33	42	45	46	46

Fig. 16.16 Results of the intra-system POU analysis

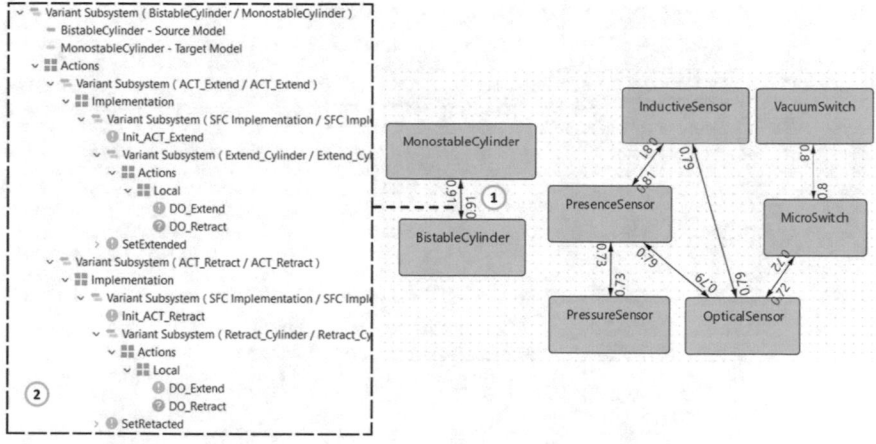

Fig. 16.17   Results of the intra-system clone analysis applied to Scenario 9

cluster and a clone. The clone cluster contains different sensors and switches. The cloned POU is a cylinder ① implementation with a similarity of 91%. Selecting the edge between those cylinders opens the family model representation, which shows detailed information about the differences of those POUs ②. As we can see, the implementation of the *MonostableCylinder* and *BistableCylinder* can be identified as a Type III clone, which is indicated by the added elements ?. In contrast, a Type II clone would only show modified elements ⇐⇒ without added elements ?. Type I clones are indicated by a similarity of 100% and only mandatory elements !. Information about common and different parts of POUs can be used to extract configurable components or to establish a component-based SPL.

16.6.4   Results of the Inter System Clone Analysis

To detect similar and different artifacts between scenarios, an inter-system clone analysis is required. In Fig. 16.18, we show all pair-wise similarities between the PPU scenarios, which are aggregated similarities from the analysis results, i.e., the similarity between two scenarios is the aggregation of the similarities of compared POUs and global variables. The similarity values decrease from left to right, which can be explained with the increased evolutionary distance between scenario pairs. High similarity differences are mostly caused by added POUs. For example, the similarity between Scenario 1 and Scenario 3 is 75.05%, the number of POUs has grown from 12 to 16 (see Fig. 16.16). Figure 16.19 shows the family model between Scenario 7 and Scenario 9. Between those scenarios, the *LargeSortingConveyor* POU is added, which is indicated by the ? element in the bottom of the family model. Also, six existing POU implementations have changed, which is indicated

					PPU Scenario Similarities							
%	**s2**	**s3**	**s4a**	**s4b**	**s5**	**s7**	**s8**	**s9**	**s10**	**s11**	**s12**	**s13**
s1	91,21	75,05	71,52	71,51	75,08	65,97	65,97	63,1	63,10	63,10	63,10	60,32
s2		81,31	77,41	77,39	81,34	71,11	71,11	67,83	67,83	67,83	67,83	64,79
s3			94,86	94,88	99,96	86,19	86,06	81,50	81,50	81,50	81,57	77,60
s4a				99,58	94,82	89,46	89,33	84,65	84,65	84,65	84,65	80,90
s4b					94,84	89,48	89,35	84,67	84,67	84,67	84,67	80,89
s5						86,16	86,03	81,48	81,47	81,47	81,47	77,58
s7							99,86	94,48	94,48	94,48	94,48	88,41
s8								94,55	94,55	94,55	94,55	88,48
s9									99,07	99,08	99,08	92,66
s10										99,86	99,78	93,33
s11											99,91	93,45
s12												93,54

			xPPU Scenario Similarities						
%	**s15**	**s16**	**s17**	**s18**	**s19**	**s20**	**s21**	**s23**	**s24**
s14	78,33	72,40	68,90	67,58	65,43	55,45	52,17	51,46	51,09
s15		91,43	86,54	84,82	81,15	67,80	63,61	62,64	62,22
s16			94,51	92,57	88,22	73,34	68,63	67,56	67,14
s17				97,18	91,73	76,07	71,18	70,05	69,63
s18					93,87	77,75	72,74	71,58	71,16
s19						82,56	77,20	75,94	75,40
s20							96,64	92,02	91,49
s21								98,20	96,46
s23									96,70

Fig. 16.18 Calculated similarities for the comparison of the PPU and xPPU

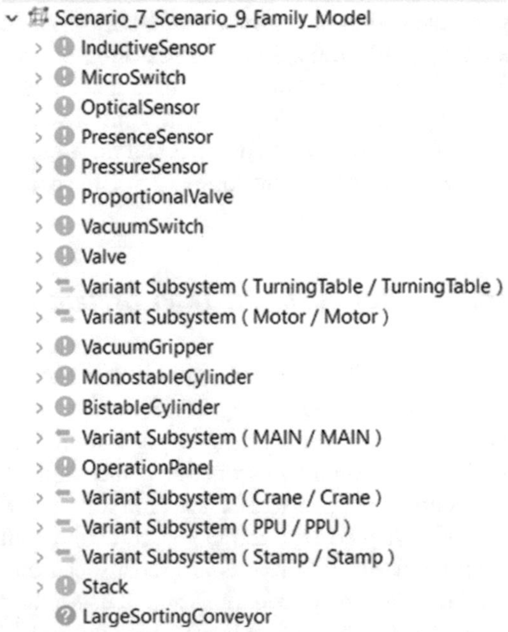

Fig. 16.19 Family model showing the comparison of Scenario 7 and Scenario 9

∨ 🏛 Scenario_7_Scenario_9_Family_Model
  > 🟡 InductiveSensor
  > 🟡 MicroSwitch
  > 🟡 OpticalSensor
  > 🟡 PresenceSensor
  > 🟡 PressureSensor
  > 🟡 ProportionalValve
  > 🟡 VacuumSwitch
  > 🟡 Valve
  > ⊟ Variant Subsystem (TurningTable / TurningTable)
  > ⊟ Variant Subsystem (Motor / Motor)
  > 🟡 VacuumGripper
  > 🟡 MonostableCylinder
  > 🟡 BistableCylinder
  > ⊟ Variant Subsystem (MAIN / MAIN)
  > 🟡 OperationPanel
  > ⊟ Variant Subsystem (Crane / Crane)
  > ⊟ Variant Subsystem (PPU / PPU)
  > ⊟ Variant Subsystem (Stamp / Stamp)
  > 🟡 Stack
     ❓ LargeSortingConveyor

by the arrows ⬅⮕. 13 POUs are mandatory 🟠, which means that they remain unchanged during this evolution step.

Overall, the pair-wise comparison's similarity values provided by the VAT seem to be reasonable considering the evolution steps between the PPU scenarios. Detailed family models support the developer in re-engineering their system variants from unstructured reuse approaches into a sustainable approach such as SPLE.

To establish the whole extractive SPLE process, an analysis of more than two scenarios is required [19]. It allows automatic processing of artifacts into a variability model such as the family model. Family models can be transformed into feature models with a high degree of detail, referred to as technical feature models (TFMs). TFM variants can be restructured into domain feature models to reduce the configuration complexity [18].

16.6.5 Quantitative Analysis

Scalability To analyse the scalability of VAT, we measured the run-time and memory consumption, which is presented in more detail in [14]. For this analysis, we used the xPPU scenarios that include more artifacts than the PPU scenarios. During the comparison of Scenario 14 with Scenario 14, 108,824 artifact pairs are created, which takes less than one second. Comparing Scenario 24 with itself, 439,030 artifact pairs are created and compared in less than a second total. Scenario 24 is the biggest scenario in the number of contained artifacts. Overall, this indicates a linear run-time. To measure the memory consumption, we used *VisualVM*,[14] a tool that provides detailed information on Java applications. We performed all pair-wise comparisons between the PPU scenarios. The initial heap size was about 850 MB, and during the comparison, the Java Virtual Machine (JVM) allocated memory to a maximum of about 1700 MB.

Correctness To evaluate correctness, we used a mutation framework to fully automatically compute recall and precision using a standard mutation-based analysis procedure. The mutation framework uses a random PPU or xPPU scenario as seed and applies random mutations to it in order to create synthetic clones. The applied mutations serve as ground truth, which allows us to compute precision and recall of our approach. As per standard for mutation analysis, the framework is configured to only use one category of mutations, i.e., either only Type II mutations such as the renaming of artifacts, or only Type III mutations such as insertions or deletions of artifacts, per model. We perform two runs with 10,000 iterations each, to determine the precision and recall for Type II and Type III mutations respectively. We also calculate the overall precision and recall over all types of mutations. Due to the parsing process which normalizes the PLCOpenXML files, we cannot detect Type I

---

[14] https://visualvm.github.io/.

Fig. 16.20 Precision and
recall measured utilizing a
mutation framework

Precision and Recall in %			
	Type 2	Type 3	Total
Precision	100	100	100
Recall	77,38	99,91	88,65

mutations, and thus not distinguish Type I and Type II clones. In Fig. 16.20 we show
the resulting precision and recall values of our comparison process. Overall, with a
precision of 100% and a recall of 88%, the detection approach can detect most of the
cloned artifacts. This indicates that our calculated similarity values are meaningful
and valuable to support engineers to refactor their variants.

16.7   Conclusion and Future Work

With an increasing demand for custom-tailored products, variability has become
an essential aspect of software systems. This also applies to automated production
systems and their control software, often implemented using the IEC 61131-3
family of programming languages. In practice, a common approach for dealing
with varying requirements and creating variants is simply cloning of source code
of entire variants and of smaller parts within variants. This chapter introduced an
approach for analyzing variants of control software comprised of arbitrarily nested
implementations of any combination of IEC 61131-3 programming languages. The
approach is implemented in the publicly available VAT framework to support the
extraction of SPLs from clones. We applied VAT to the PPU and xPPU case
studies, two automated production systems commonly used in literature as universal
demonstrators [22, 24]. First, we performed an intra-system clone analysis to
identify potential library components. The results show that our approach can
support developers in refactoring existing software systems to eliminate clones
and facilitate reuse in the small. Then, we performed inter-system clone analysis
to consider the variability between variants and provide information useful for
extractive product line adoption. Both analyses show good results and indicate that
our approach can be useful to domain experts and developers when migrating a
system into an SPL or during maintenance of software variants. The run-time and
memory consumption let us assume that our approach scales even for larger systems.
Moreover, with a precision of 100% and a recall of 88%, we think that the results
are reasonable and useful.

Other frameworks focus on the inter-system analysis, e.g., BUT4Reuse [12],
which is an adaptable bottom-up SPLE approach, or on intra-system clone detection,
e.g., NiCad [4], which is an automatic clone detection approach. In contrast, the VAT
provides a highly configurable comparison approach, which allows customization
such that results meet expectations. Moreover, we provide both an intra-system
analysis to extract reusable components and an inter-system analysis to support SPL
extraction.

As future work, we extend the approach to be applicable to sets of cloned variants instead of just pairs of variants. This is necessary to fully support extractive product line adoption for an entire variant portfolio. We also plan to further explore our approach on clones of varying granularity, ranging from entire variants over POUs down to individual instructions. This shall enable the automated refactoring of finer-grained clones into reusable library components.

References

1. Bellon, S., Koschke, R., Antoniol, G., Krinke, J., Merlo, E.: Comparison and Evaluation of Clone Detection Tools. IEEE Trans. Software Eng. **33**(9), 577–591 (2007)
2. Beuche, D.: Modeling and building product lines with pure:: variants. In: Proceedings of the 17th International Software Product Line Conference co-located workshops, pp. 147–149 (2013)
3. Commission, I.E., et al.: Programmable Logic Controllers—Part 3: Programming Languages. IEC Standard pp. 61,131–3 (2009)
4. Cordy, J.R., Roy, C.K.: The NiCad Clone Detector. In: The 19th IEEE International Conference on Program Comprehension, pp. 219–220. IEEE Computer Society (2011)
5. DIN, E.: 60848: GRAFCET, Spezifikationssprache für Funktionspläne der Ablaufsteuerung. Berlin: Beuth (2002)
6. Durdik, Z., Klatt, B., Koziolek, H., Krogmann, K., Stammel, J., Weiss, R.: Sustainability guidelines for long-living software systems. In: 28th IEEE International Conference on Software Maintenance, pp. 517–526. IEEE Computer Society (2012)
7. Faust, D., Verhoef, C.: Software product line migration and deployment. Softw. Pract. Exp. **33**(10), 933–955 (2003)
8. Iec, I.: 61131-3: Programmable controllers–part 3: Programming languages. International Standard, Second Edition, International Electrotechnical Commission, Geneva **1**, 2003 (2003)
9. Koschke, R.: Large-Scale Inter-System Clone Detection Using Suffix Trees. In: 16th European Conference on Software Maintenance and Reengineering, pp. 309–318. IEEE Computer Society (2012)
10. Koschke, R.: Large-scale inter-system clone detection using suffix trees and hashing. J. Softw. Evol. Process. **26**(8), 747–769 (2014)
11. Krueger, C.W.: Easing the Transition to Software Mass Customization. In: Software Product-Family Engineering, 4th International Workshop, *Lecture Notes in Computer Science*, vol. 2290, pp. 282–293. Springer (2001)
12. Martinez, J., Ziadi, T., Bissyandé, T.F., Klein, J., Traon, Y.L.: Bottom-up adoption of software product lines: a generic and extensible approach. In: Proceedings of the 19th International Conference on Software Product Line, pp. 101–110. ACM (2015)
13. Ramanathan, R.: The IEC 61131-3 programming languages features for industrial control systems. In: 2014 World Automation Congress (WAC), pp. 598–603. IEEE (2014)
14. Rosiak, K., Schlie, A., Linsbauer, L., Vogel-Heuser, B., Schaefer, I.: Custom-Tailored Clone Detection for IEC 61131-3 Programming Languages. Journal of Systems and Software. Volume 182 (2021)
15. Roy, C.K., Cordy, J.R.: A survey on software clone detection research. Queen's School of Computing TR **541**(115), 64–68 (2007)
16. Roy, C.K., Cordy, J.R., Koschke, R.: Comparison and evaluation of code clone detection techniques and tools: A qualitative approach. Sci. Comput. Program. **74**(7), 470–495 (2009)
17. Rubin, J., Chechik, M.: Quality of Merge-Refactorings for Product Lines. In: Fundamental Approaches to Software Engineering - 16th International Conference, *Lecture Notes in Computer Science*, vol. 7793, pp. 83–98. Springer (2013)

18. Schlie, A., Knüppel, A., Seidl, C., Schaefer, I.: Incremental feature model synthesis for clone-and-own software systems in MATLAB/Simulink. In: SPLC '20: 24th ACM International Systems and Software Product Line Conference, pp. 7:1–7:12. ACM (2020)
19. Schlie, A., Rosiak, K., Urbaniak, O., Schaefer, I., Vogel-Heuser, B.: Analyzing variability in automation software with the variability analysis toolkit.. In: Proceedings of the 23rd International Systems and Software Product Line Conference (2019)
20. Svajlenko, J., Roy, C.K.: Evaluating Modern Clone Detection Tools. In: 30th IEEE International Conference on Software Maintenance and Evolution, pp. 321–330. IEEE Computer Society (2014)
21. Tiegelkamp, M., John, K.H.: IEC 61131-3: Programming industrial automation systems, vol. 14. Springer (1995)
22. Vogel-Heuser, B., Bougouffa, S., Sollfrank, M.: Researching Evolution in Industrial Plant Automation: Scenarios and Documentation of the extended Pick and Place Unit. Tech. rep., Institute of Automation and Information Systems, Technische Universität München (2018)
23. Vogel-Heuser, B., Fay, A., Schaefer, I., Tichy, M.: Evolution of software in automated production systems: challenges and research directions. In: Software Engineering 2016, *LNI*, vol. P-252, pp. 107–108. GI (2016)
24. Vogel-Heuser, B., Legat, C., Folmer, J., Feldmann, S.: Researching Evolution in Industrial Plant Automation: Scenarios and Documentation of the Pick and Place Unit. Tech. rep., Institute of Automation and Information Systems, Technische Universität München (2014)

Chapter 17
Managing Software Product Line Evolution by Filtered Editing: The SuperMod Approach

Felix Schwägerl and Bernhard Westfechtel

Abstract This chapter introduces SuperMod, an approach and tool to support the evolution of software product lines (SPLs) by means of a filtered editing model, which is inspired by the checkout-modify-commit workflow established in version control systems. Rather than forcing the developers into editing multi variant artifacts of an SPL, SuperMod allows them to perform modifications successively in single-variant workspaces and to integrate the changes by indicating the logical scope, i.e., the affected variants, of the change performed. The SPL itself is managed automatically in a transparent repository by the system. As a consequence, developers may re-use the same engineering tools they also used for the development of the product variants prior to the re-engineering process. SuperMod furthermore orchestrates collaborative development and provides dedicated support for (without restricting developers to) model-driven approaches to SPL engineering. We illustrate SuperMod's capabilities by the well-known graph SPL example and discuss the practical benefits of the suggested solution to SPL evolution as well as its relation to SPL re-engineering.

17.1 Introduction

After having successfully re-engineered a *software product line* (SPL) from diverging variants, new challenges arise for software engineers: future changes to the SPL—regardless of which and how many variants they affect—need to be managed consistently, while we must avoid that software variants diverge from the SPL again.

Managing the *evolution* of an SPL is a difficult task: Engineers have to cope with all variants (logical versioning), they have to keep track of all changes (historical versioning), and they have to coordinate their work (collaborative versioning). Traditionally, SPL engineers use heterogeneous tools for managing different dimen-

F. Schwägerl (✉) · B. Westfechtel
University of Bayreuth, Applied Computer Science I, Bayreuth, Germany
e-mail: felix.schwaegerl@uni-bayreuth.de; bernhard.westfechtel@uni-bayreuth.de

© Springer Nature Switzerland AG 2023
R. E. Lopez-Herrejon et al. (eds.), *Handbook of Re-Engineering Software Intensive Systems into Software Product Lines*, https://doi.org/10.1007/978-3-031-11686-5_17

sions of versioning. For example, they may rely on SPL tools focusing exclusively on logical versioning, and may use revision control systems for historical and collaborative versioning.

Unfortunately, combining heterogeneous tools results in poor integration: Revision control systems are not aware of the variability of artifacts they manage. Therefore, the changes maintained by a revision control system are not related to the variant space. For example, it is not known which variants are affected by a certain change. Furthermore, coordination of collaborative work may require *merging* of changes. Merge tools not being aware of variability may produce incorrect merge results. For example, they may report merge conflicts on artifacts affected by two changes even though these changes refer to mutually exclusive variants.

This chapter introduces *SuperMod* (*Super*imposition of *Mod*els) [16], an approach and tool for managing evolving SPLs. SuperMod supports logical, historical, and collaborative versioning in a uniform way: Every change is connected to the set of variants it affects. Furthermore, collaboration support takes both logical and historical versioning into account in detecting conflicts and merging changes.

Filtered editing lies at the heart of SuperMod, which adopts the checkout-modify-commit paradigm from revision control systems. In SuperMod, an SPL engineer operates on a single version of the SPL. On checkout, (s)he first specifies the desired revision and—in a second step—the variant of that revision. When the work in the current iteration is completed, it is committed to the repository. Now, the SPL engineer has to provide a so called *ambition*, a partial selection in the variant space defining which variants are affected by the change. Thus, while working on a single variant, the SPL engineer may perform changes with a wider scope, affecting other variants, as well. SuperMod offers a convenient user interface for specifying variants and ambitions.

Finally, to support collaboration, SuperMod supports hierarchically organized repositories with optimistic concurrency control: Changes may be pushed from a local to a remote repository. If changes from another repository have been pushed to the common remote repository in the meantime, they are pulled first. In the next step, potential conflicts are resolved in the local repository, before the changes are finally pushed to the remote repository.

The rest of this chapter is organized as follows: Sect. 17.2 provides background information on relevant sub-disciplines of software engineering and summarizes the main contributions of the SuperMod approach in general terms at an abstract level. For the purpose of illustration, we give a small example of using SuperMod, based on the well-known graph SPL [9] (Sect. 17.3). The next sections are devoted to the foundations of SuperMod. Section 17.4 describes its underlying architecture, focusing on the relationships between version space and product space. Section 17.5 briefly introduces the underlying formal foundations, which are hidden intentionally from the user of SuperMod, but are essential to support model-driven, evolving SPLs. Section 17.6 sketches advanced functionality, regarding SuperMod's dynamic filtered editing model, distributed cooperation support, and well-formedness analysis. Section 17.7 puts our work into context, by discussing the connection to SPL re-engineering, the alignment with SPLE processes, and SuperMod's conceptual and technical maturity. Section 17.8 presents the conclusions.

17.2 Background and Contribution

SuperMod intersects three sub-disciplines of software engineering: *model-driven software engineering*, *revision control* (a.k.a. version control), and *SPL engineering*. This section provides a brief introduction into these sub-disciplines as well as integrative approaches, provides a discussion of commonalities and differences in terminology of SPL engineering and revision control, and concludes with the explanation of the *filtered editing* paradigm, which is at the heart of SuperMod.

17.2.1 Relevant Software Engineering Sub-disciplines

Model-driven software engineering (MDSE) [18] aims at increasing the level of abstraction, thus the productivity of software engineering. A *model* is an artifact that conforms to a well-defined *modeling language*; the abstract syntax of such languages is often provided in terms of a *metamodel*. Models should have well-defined semantics; *model transformations* describe the mapping of high- to low-level models and (eventually) to executable programs. The Eclipse Modeling Framework (EMF) [20] is a technological foundation many research applications, including SuperMod, build upon.

Contemporary *revision control systems*, such as Git [5], rely on an incremental three-stage editing model as illustrated in Fig. 17.1. First, the operation *check-out* requests the user for the selection of a unique *revision* among the set of available (i.e. previously committed) revisions. After selection, a *workspace* is populated with the artifacts belonging to the selected revision. The user may then apply arbitrary changes (stage *modify*) using the tools of his/her choice. Upon *commit*, the modified artifacts are transferred back to the repository, and a new revision is created transparently; this revision is *immutable* in that it can be safely retrieved later from the repository even if new revisions are created later.

Fig. 17.1 Editing model of revision control systems

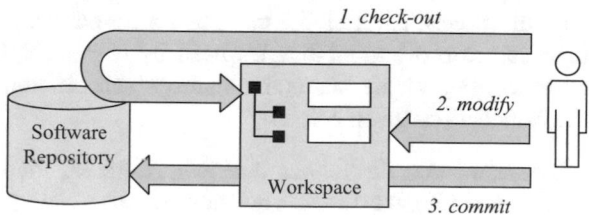

Software product line engineering (SPLE) [12] denotes an organized reuse process for the systematic development and maintenance of *variants* being members of a product family. Traditionally, two SPLE phases are distinguished: In *domain engineering*, a *variability model* is defined which captures common and discriminating properties of product variants; frequently, *feature models* [7] are used for this purpose. Based on the variability model, a *platform* of reusable artifacts is developed. In *application engineering*, the platform is used to build a specific product variant, which is defined by a *feature configuration* (a selection of features from the feature model).

17.2.2   Integration of Sub-disciplines

Partial integration of MDSE, SPLE, and revision control has been attempted earlier. *Model-driven SPL engineering* (MDSPLE) approaches [6] represent both the variant space and the product space as models. Commonly, so called *150% models*—models annotated with variability annotations—come into play, but there exist other approaches relying, e.g., on model transformations [2] or delta modeling [14]. Usually, revision control is not addressed by MDSPLE approaches.

Model version control [1] subsumes the lifting of versioned elements from line-oriented to structured model-based artifacts, such that differences between versions are described by higher-level operations. This also increases the quality of merging [21]. Model version control focuses on revision control of models, but does not take variants into account.

Finally, *integrated version control* provides a version model which allows to express historical versioning (revisions), logical versioning (variants), and collaborative versioning in a uniform framework. The feasibility of this approach was demonstrated e.g. by ICE [23], which is based on feature logic, and UVM [22], which employs propositional logic for the same purpose. However, both systems were applied to file-based artifacts rather than to models.

17.2.3   Comparison: SPLE and Revision Control

Although both disciplines deal with *versions*, the combination of SPLE and revision control is less covered by the literature and deserves a deeper analysis. We here compare the terminologies used by both disciplines in order to provide an understanding of the key commonalities and differences. Table 17.1 summarizes the explanations given below:

- The compared disciplines deal with different kinds of versions and therefore address different *intents*. In revision control, a change evolves a given revision into

Table 17.1 Comparison of revision control and SPLE concepts. Modified from [16]

Aspect	Description	RevCS	SPLE
Intent	Type and purpose of versions	Revisions (superseding)	Variants (co-existing)
Version space	Defines the available versions	Revision graph	Feature model
Version rules	Constrain the version space	(Implicit)	Feature constraints
Option	Unit of version selection	Revision	Feature
Choice	Unique and consistent version	Revision selection	Feature configuration
Change scope	Implications of a change	(Commit message)	Feature ambition
Visibility	Version membership of an artifact	(Automated)	Presence conditions

a successor, which is supposed to supersede the original one. This is in contrast to SPLE, where different variants of a product co-exist intentionally.

- SPLE and revision control adopt different approaches to organize the *version space*. In revision control, *revision graphs* consist of revisions which are connected by relationships expressing their historical evolution. In SPLE, feature models are used to define both features and their hierarchical and cross-tree relationships.
- Version selection is constrained by *version rules*, which are implicit in revision control (e.g., the selection of a revision implies the changes associated with predecessor revisions), whereas feature models allow to freely define parent/child or cross-tree constraints.
- The disciplines significantly differ with respect to how versions are constructed from their units of selection (*options* for revisions or features, respectively). In revision control systems, one may select exactly one out of an enumeration of available revisions, whereas feature models allow an individual decision for every feature, as long as the feature model constraints are satisfied.
- The term *choice* denotes a unique and consistent version selected from the set of versions available in the version space. In revision control, a specific revision is selected. In SPLE, a feature configuration is defined which assigns a unique selection state (selected or deselected) to each feature from the feature model.
- The *scope of a change* delineates the set of versions to which the change may be applied. In revision control systems, the scope is defined only implicitly and informally by a commit message. If the revision control system was aware of the variant space, the scope could be defined explicitly by an ambition, which delineates the set of product variants to which the change may be applied.
- Independently of the representation of the product space, the versioned artifacts must be associated to the version space in order to decide for their *version membership*. Revision control systems manage version membership automatically, whereas many SPLE approaches utilize presence conditions, which denote user-editable logical expressions over the elements of the feature model.

The SuperMod approach presented in this paper aims at an *integrated* solution treating revision control and SPLE equally. This is in contrast to related approaches, where revision control is provided on top of SPLE support or vice versa. For instance, the *VariantSync* [11] approach assumes clone-and-own SPLE development and provides synchronization operations on top, which basically adopt the revision control role. Conversely, [10] presents a tool that exploits GitHub's branching model in order to realize collaborative SPLE on top of revision control.

17.2.4   Filtered Editing and Variation Control

Conventional approaches frequently represent SPLs as 150% artifacts, i.e., super-impositions of all product variants. Unfortunately, management of these artifacts causes considerable complexity: SPL engineers are forced to consider all product variants simultaneously. This complexity becomes evident e.g. in C programs with conditional compilation, which is employed extensively in a variety of applications such as the Linux operating system.

In response to this problem, Sarnak et al. [13] introduced the concept of *filtered editing*. Rather than applying a change to a multi-version source artifact directly, a similar change is applied to a *view* of it. From this actual modification, a source-level modification is derived and transparently applied to the *source*. Figure 17.2 illustrates the concept and hints why filtered editing may be more convenient than direct multi-version editing; in the modification sketched, the user may focus on the relevant parts of the product (e.g., the box, which is modified into a hexagon), whereas the irrelevant parts (rounded rectangle and oval) are filtered out.

Figure 17.2 furthermore distinguishes between a *read filter*, which determines the view displayed in the editor, and a *write filter*, which delineates the scope of a change. Different proposals have been made concerning the relationships between read and write filters. If both filters are equal, the view contains exactly those product variants to which the change applies. In contrast, the original approach by Sarnak et al. uses the read filter to define a unique variant, while the write filter defines the set of product variants to which the change is applied. This approach simplifies the view, but assumes that the user may accurately determine the scope of the change.

Filtered editing recently experienced a revival in the shape of *variation control systems* [19], which transfer editing model and other concepts from revision control

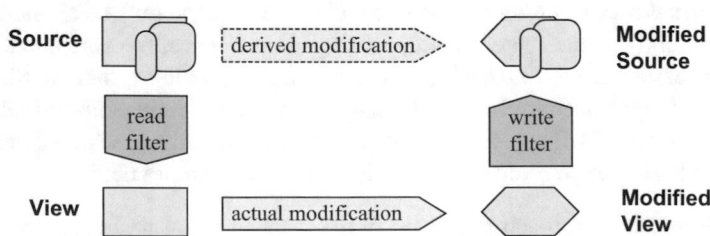

Fig. 17.2 Concept of filtered editing

to variability management, typically by adding higher-level variability management mechanisms to the plain filtered editing model.

17.2.5 Contribution

SuperMod (*Super*imposition of *Mod*els) [16] provides a conceptual framework and tool support for managing evolving model-driven SPLs. In contrast to previous work, our approach achieves full integration of MDSE, SPLE, and revision control.

Externally, SuperMod provides different abstractions for historical and logical versioning (revisions and variants, respectively). Intentionally, these abstractions are familiar to users of revision control systems and SPL engineers. For historical versioning, SuperMod offers revision graphs; logical versioning is supported through feature models. Internally, both historical and logical versioning are mapped to a *uniform version model* being founded on propositional logic. In addition, SuperMod supports collaborative versioning (through a collaboration model inspired by Git), which is mapped to the uniform version model, as well.

SuperMod extends the check-out/modify/commit paradigm of revision control systems which was illustrated in Fig. 17.1. The whole SPL, including all of its product variants, is kept under revision control. However, the user is never exposed to the complexity of 150% models, with their superimposition of all product variants. While the repository maintains an internal representation of the superimposition of all product versions (revisions and variants), only a single product version is checked out into the workspace.

SuperMod's filtered editing approach provides for a read filter which is defined in two steps: First, a revision of the SPL is specified. Second, a product variant is selected by configuring the feature model for that revision. The editing iteration is terminated with a commit operation, whose write filter determines the scope of the change. The scope is defined by a feature ambition, which specifies the set of variants to which the change performed in this iteration applies. Thus, although the user edits a specific product variant, the scope of the change may be much wider (e.g., all variants including a feature which was implemented in the current iteration). In this way, multiple maintenance may be avoided: There is no need to repeat the same change in different variants.

In the workspace, the user may edit (EMF-based) models, as well as text-based artifacts, with EMF models being the primary focus. During the editing iteration, the user may work with his/her favorite tools, which are agnostic to revision and variation tools. Thus, existing tools may be reused—an important property shared with traditional revision control systems. In particular, SuperMod supports MDSE in the workspace, allowing to reuse any EMF-based tool.

From the SPLE perspective, SuperMod proposes a radical shift away from classical SPLE processes, which distinguish sharply between domain and application engineering. The paradigm underlying SuperMod is denoted as *product-based product line engineering*: The SPL evolves through iterations on specific product variants. There is no explicit distinction between domain and application engineering, and there is no need to switch between these levels. An iteration with a wide scope may be considered to belong to domain engineering, while an iteration with a narrow scope (in the extreme, a single product variant) may be allocated to application engineering. However, the scopes are arranged in a continuum: The user may specify an adequate scope at any intermediate level between all product variants and a single product variant.

17.3   SuperMod by Example

We now demonstrate the usage of the tool SuperMod by a running example, an adaptation of the standard *Graph* SPL [9]. In this section, we intentionally focus on the user's perspective and leave some concepts of SuperMod unexplained. The subsequent three sections will clarify and more formally describe how SuperMod works internally.

The editing model in action is exemplified by an iteration that addresses the realization of the optional feature **Weighted**, distinguishing weighted from unweighted graphs. The versioned artifact is a simple class diagram that describes the static structure of graphs. Six preceding revisions have already been performed in the version history of this example.

In the top left corner of Fig. 17.3, the latest revision 6 of the *feature model* before executing the iteration is shown. By definition, the feature model is hierarchical, starting with the root feature **Graph**. This feature contains two mandatory subfeatures **Vertices** and **Edges** (filled circles), which in turn contain optional features **Colored** and **Directed** (empty circles).

During check-out, a *feature configuration* is requested from the user. In the example, all features are selected, except for **Directed**, which is deselected. As a consequence, a class diagram representing colored, undirected graphs is exported into the workspace.

Now, the workspace—which consists of the feature model and the class diagram—may be modified arbitrarily. In our example, the fictional user adds an attribute **weight** of type **Double** to the class **Edge**. Furthermore, the same class is renamed into **WeightedEdge**. The change shall be connected to a new feature **Weighted**, which is added to the feature model below **Edges** also during the *modify* step.

The connection between the change to the model and the newly introduced feature is established during *commit*, where a *feature ambition* is requested from the user. In contrast to check-out time configurations, feature ambitions are *partial*, i.e., they may leave features unbound (gray). In our case, exclusively **Weighted** is selected positively since the change is immaterial to all other features (i.e., it could have been equivalently applied to an uncolored, directed graph). The changes are, furthermore, associated with the new revision 7, which is transparently introduced to the revision graph.

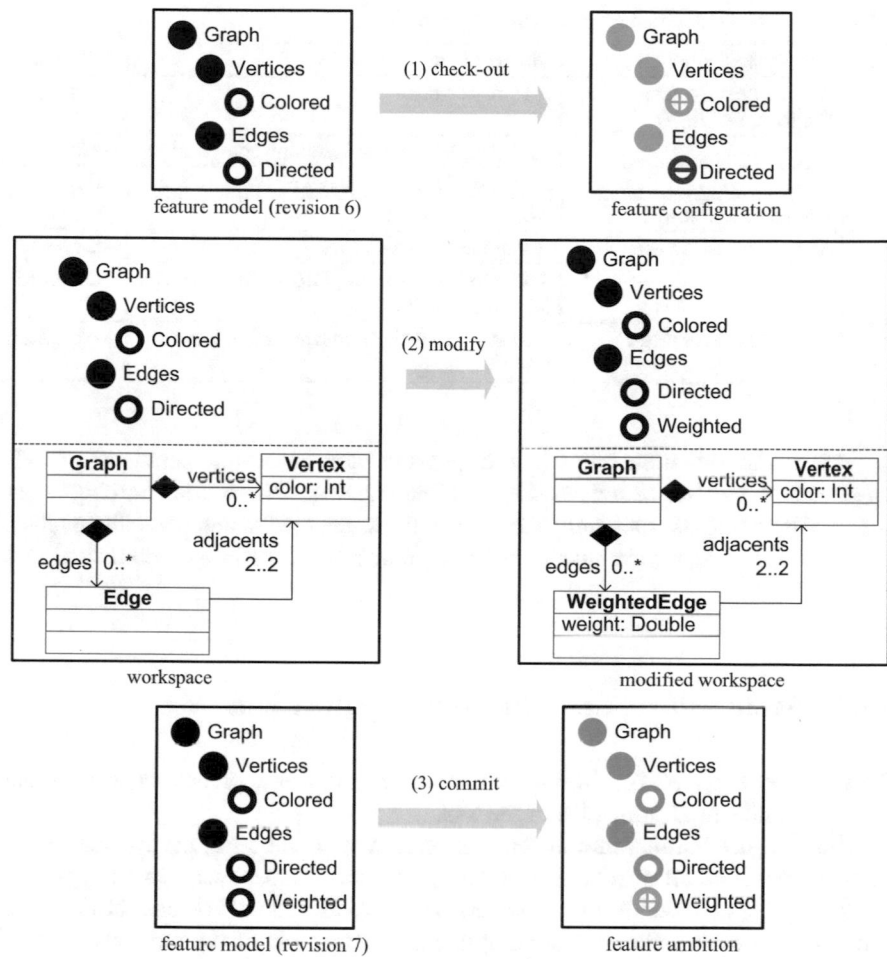

Fig. 17.3 An example iteration of filtered editing using SuperMod

As a consequence of the performed iteration, attribute **weight** and the alternative class name **WeightedEdge** will become available in the workspace if a revision greater or equal than 7 is selected and the specified feature configuration includes a positive selection for the feature **Weighted**.

As explained above, this iteration is actually part of a larger version history, where other features have been realized using the equivalent workflow. Table 17.2 summarizes the version history of previous examples. In the column *feature ambition*, we use the following notation: positively selected features (green in the graphical representation) are prefixed with the symbol +, negative (red) features with −, and unbound features are not mentioned. Please note that undirected edges are implemented by a negative binding of feature **Directed**.

Table 17.2 Full revision history of the running example

Rev.	Changes to feature model	Changes to domain model	Ambition
1	Add features Graph, Vertices, Edges	Add class Graph	+Graph
2	–	Add class Vertex and incoming composition	+Vertices
3	–	Add class Edge and incoming composition	+Edges
4	Add feature Colored	Add attribute color	+Colored
5	Add feature Directed	Add reference adjacents	–Directed
6	–	Add references source, target, rename Edge into DirectedEdge	+Directed
7	Add feature Weighted	Add attribute weight, rename Edge into WeightedEdge	+Weighted

This example demonstrates how SuperMod pioneers a new paradigm in SPL engineering: *product-based product line engineering*. Rather than forcing users into manipulating internal multi-variant notations, SuperMod automatically evolves the SPL by managing changes to specific product versions in an incremental and iterative way.

17.4 Architectural and Functional Foundations

This section explains the editing model underlying the approach as well as the internal architectural principles of the tool.

Tying on the notions introduced alongside with Table 17.1, the *version space* defines the set of all available revisions or variants, respectively. In analogy, the *product space* here denotes *what* is versioned, i.e., the actual contents of the SPL. Although we used a simple class diagram in the example of the previous section, SuperMod is by no means restricted to particular modeling languages or tools. It rather supports arbitrary Eclipse projects that may consist of model, source code, configuration files, etc. Nevertheless, we call these contents the *domain model*.

In SuperMod, the feature model plays a dual role by being part of both the version space and the product space, which are therefore not disjoint. Obviously, the feature model evolves over time, and therefore, multiple revisions of it exist. The feature model is therefore part of both the version space and the product space; it is versioned by the revision graph and provides versioning of the domain model. Figure 17.4 depicts a simplified conceptual model of SuperMod's repository contents.

The layered structure of the repository directly influences the *editing model* provided by our approach (Fig. 17.5). SuperMod inherits the incremental check-out/modify/commit model from revision control and enhances it with variability management functionalities; version selection is performed in the revision graph first, and then in the feature model. Phrased in terms of filtered editing, the feature

Fig. 17.4 Coarse architecture of a SuperMod repository

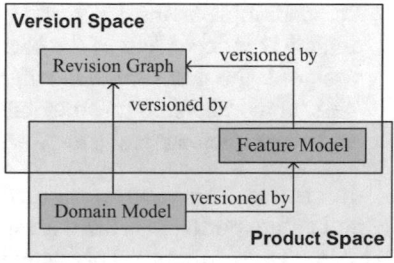

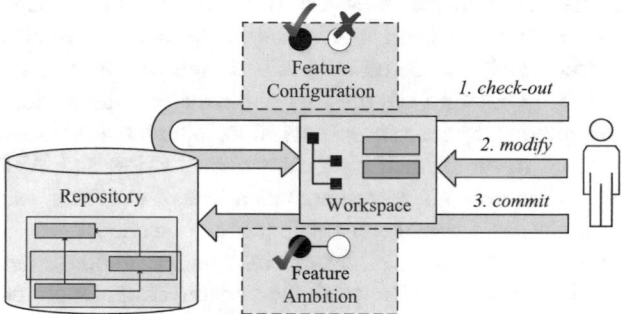

Fig. 17.5 SuperMod's filtered editing model

configuration constitutes a (single-variant) read filter, while the feature ambition—which may cover a set of variants—defines a write filter.

The operations constituting an editing iteration are explained below:

Check-out. The user performs a selection in the version space. In the revision graph, the selection comprises a single *revision*. In the selected revision of the feature model, a *feature configuration* has to be specified. As mentioned above, a feature configuration defines a selection state—either *selected* or *deselected*—for every feature of the feature model.

Once the user has provided this information, a single-version working copy of the repository contents, filtered by the selected revision and variant, is exported into the workspace.

Modify. In the workspace, the user may apply a set of changes to the single-version domain model and/or to the feature model. In many cases, these changes are conceptually related, e.g., a feature is introduced and its implementation is provided in the domain model.

Commit. Upon request, the iteration is finished and the changes are written back to the repository. For this purpose, the user must provide information in both dimensions of the version space. First, for the revision graph, the user may enter a commit message that documents the change in prose. Second, in the feature model, the user is prompted for a so called *feature ambition*, a partial selection in the feature model to delineate the logical scope of the changes applied to the domain model.

In ambitions, a third selection state, *unbound*, is allowed, denoting that a feature is independent of the change performed. The more features get *unbound* assigned, the more variants will be affected by the change. During the commit, version membership information inside the repository is updated automatically, and a newly created revision is submitted to the repository.

In the definitions above, we used phrases like "a filtered copy of the repository contents is exported into the workspace", or "the updated workspace is transferred back to the repository". This would suggest that the artifacts of the repository be represented in the same way as they are in the workspace. Though, SuperMod distinguishes between an *external* representation, which is presented to the user as the workspace, which can be directly edited, and the *internal* representation, which is intentionally hidden from the user and managed automatically inside the repository. The internal representation can store alternative values for different versions of a detail of an artifact, e.g., class names Edge and WeightedEdge. Internally, the product space is represented as a tree of elements, each carrying a *visibility* that defines its version membership (see next section).

Distinguishing between internal and external representation brings two major advantages: On the one hand, arbitrary (single-version) editing tools may be utilized in the workspace, without having to make them "SuperMod-compatible" in any way. On the other hand, the repository internally offers *unconstrained variability*, i.e., multi-version artifacts need not necessarily conform to single-version rules dictated, e.g., by the metamodel of the utilized modeling language. The mapping between internal and external representation is fully transparent.

Once again, we would like to remind the reader that SuperMod also supports regular text files, which are persisted as such in the workspace. Within the repository, a multi-version storage model for texts is provided. Text is managed in a line oriented way and stored as a directed acyclic graph. By default, this representation is assumed for all non-model (e.g., source code and configuration) files.

17.5   Formal Foundations

In Sect. 17.2, we introduced generalizations for different terms used in revision control and SPLE, respectively. For instance, both revisions and features can be interpreted as *options*, i.e., units of version selection. In this section, we show how these commonalities are systematically exploited by SuperMod in order to map high-level concepts such as revision graphs, feature configurations, presence conditions, or commit messages onto a formally sound theoretical base layer. This base layer in turn is an extension to the *Uniform Version Model* (UVM) originally described in [22]. Rather than giving a full formal introduction—which can be retrieved in [16]—we here provide instances for the instrumentation of this base layer, referring to the running Graph example introduced above.

Options Both revisions and features are mapped to *options*, which can be either selected or deselected in a given version. The *option set* of the running example can be written as:

$$O = \{r_1, r_2, r_3, r_4, r_5, r_6, r_7, f_{Graph}, f_{Vertices}, f_{Edges}, f_{Colored}, f_{Directed}, f_{Weighted}\}$$

Version Rules The feature model may impose constraints (e.g., parent/child, mandatory root, requirement or mutual exclusion) on the selection of features. These constraints can be straightforwardly translated into propositional logic. Similarly, the revision graph defines version dependencies via its edges: a revision is only applicable if its predecessor revision is selected, too. All these rules must be satisfied by *choices* (see below) in order to be consistent. For our running example in its state after revision 7, we can derive the following version rules:

$$R = \{r_2 \Rightarrow r_1, r_3 \Rightarrow r_2, r_4 \Rightarrow r_3, r_5 \Rightarrow r_4, r_6 \Rightarrow r_5, r_7 \Rightarrow r_6, f_{Graph}, f_{Vertices} \Leftrightarrow f_{Graph},$$

$$f_{Edges} \Leftrightarrow f_{Graph}, f_{Colored} \Rightarrow f_{Vertices}, f_{Directed} \Rightarrow f_{Edges}, f_{Weighted} \Rightarrow f_{Edges}\}$$

Choices The term *choice* abstracts from a version selection in the revision graph and thereafter in the feature model. A choice is internally represented as a conjunction of positive or negative occurrences of options. For the choice used at the beginning of our example iteration 7, we can derive the following expression:

$$c = r_1 \wedge r_2 \wedge r_3 \wedge r_4 \wedge r_5 \wedge r_6 \wedge f_{Graph} \wedge f_{Vertices} \wedge f_{Edges} \wedge f_{Colored} \wedge \neg f_{Directed}$$

Notice that SuperMod selects revisions 1 until 5 transitively when the user selects revision 6; this is due to the version rules $r_2 \Rightarrow r_1$ etc. introduced above. Furthermore, the choice, referring to revision 6, does not include a binding for feature **Weighted**, which is introduced only during the *modify* phase of iteration 7. Finally, the bindings for feature options must satisfy the version rules derived from the feature model, i.e., the specified feature configuration must be consistent (and complete; unbound features are not allowed).

Ambitions In our theoretical base layer and its precursor UVM, an *ambition* describes a *set* of versions to which a specific change applies. This is reflected in the fact that the option binding of an ambition, in contrast to choices, is in general *partial*. It must comply to the version rules inasmuch as the ambition must not contradict the version rules (constraints); e.g., an ambition must not include a binding $\cdots \wedge \neg f_{Graph} \wedge \ldots$ because there exists no valid choice in which the mandatory feature **Graph** is deselected.

Coming back to our running example, when committing revision 7, the user selected feature **Weighted** positively, while leaving all other features *unbound* (cf. grey boxes in Fig. 17.3). The following expression for the ambition a is derived from this selection:

$$a = r_7 \wedge f_{Weighted}$$

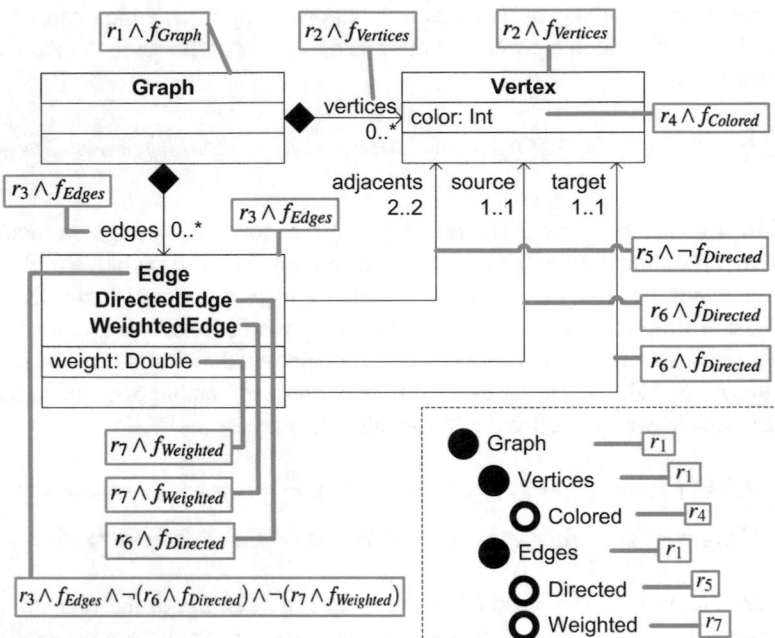

Fig. 17.6 The internal repository representation of the example, including the feature model in the bottom right corner

Visibilities As mentioned in Sect. 17.2, the term *visibility* abstracts from both revision membership information, which is managed transparently in revision control systems, and manually edited presence conditions as usually provided in SPLE. In our theoretical framework, visibilities are expressions in propositional logic over the options of the version space. Visibilities are intentionally hidden from the user and managed entirely automatically by SuperMod based on the ambitions derived from user defined change scopes (i.e., feature ambitions). This happens according to three generic *update rules*, which can be summarized in a simplified way as follows:

- For inserted elements, assign as initial visibility v the ambition a: $v := a$
- For deleted elements, "subtract" the ambition from its previous visibility v_{old}: $v := v_{old} \wedge \neg a$
- Updates are broken down into insertions and deletions.

Figure 17.6 depicts the repository-internal product space after revision 7 has been committed. Keep in mind that the product space consists of both the feature model and the domain model, and that this is an internal multi-version representation that is entirely hidden from the user. For this reason, it is possible, e.g., that one class carries three different names (e.g., Edge, DirectedEdge, and WeightedEdge).

Section 17.6.3 explains how SuperMod ensures that one of these names is uniquely selected when checking-out a version.

Attached to product space elements, visibilities are depicted in the figure. These visibilities have been created automatically by the aforementioned ambition mechanism based on user-defined feature ambitions.

The visibilities depicted in the bottom right corner illustrate that the feature model does not depend on itself: The ambitions occurring as sub-expressions in its visibilities are purged from options referring to features; for instance, in revision 7, rather than the full a defined above, SuperMod applies $a' := r_7$.

Referring back to the domain model, visibilities tell the evolution history of specific model elements. For instance:

- Features **Graph**, **Vertices** and **Edges** were all introduced in revision 1 and not modified thereafter.
- Class **Graph** was introduced in revision 1, where feature **Graph** was selected positively in the ambition.
- Reference **adjacents** was introduced in revision 5 for those feature configurations that do *not* include **Directed**.
- Class **Edge** was renamed twice: first, into **DirectedEdge** under the scope "all revisions since 6 where **Directed** is selected", and second, into **WeightedEdge** under the scope "all revisions since 7 where **Weighted** is selected" The rename operations are broken down into the insertion of a new name (e.g., **Weighted-Edge**, ambition $r_7 \wedge f_{Weighted}$) and the deletion of the old name **Edge**, which was originally inserted under the ambition $r_3 \wedge f_{Edges}$.

Taken together, SuperMod provides uniform management of historical evolution and logical variability based on a solid theoretical formalism. The complexity of this formalism is, however, not forwarded to the end users, who may perform their version definitions (choices, ambitions) based on well-known abstractions such as revision graph and feature model.

17.6 Advanced Functionality

So far, in the preceding sections, we made some idealistic assumptions, e.g., that the tool is used by a single user in a disciplined way and that modifications made in several iterations do not contradict with each other. In this section, we briefly explain on a lower level of detail three advanced concepts that make SuperMod applicable to realistic scenarios. First, dynamic filtered editing is aware of evolutionary paradoxes that can be introduced by the fact that the feature model, based on which the workspace choice is created, may change by itself. Second, we introduce multi-user operation. Third, both filtered editing and collaboration may cause product conflicts, whose detection and resolution is guided by SuperMod.

17.6.1   Dynamic Filtered Editing and the Operation Migrate

The filtered editing model presented here extends the state of the art [13, 19] by allowing the co-evolution of the version space—more precisely, the feature model—and the product space. As the choice, which defines the workspace contents, is derived from the version space, this might cause several types of consistency problems. For instance, what happens if the user deletes a feature that is currently selected in the choice? How is the precise relationship between feature configuration and feature ambition, given the fact that they may refer to different revisions of the feature model (after check-out and before commit, respectively)?

The *dynamic filtered editing model* [16] supports the aforementioned evolution scenario by providing eight dedicated consistency constraints as well as four consistency-preserving operations that guarantee that these constraints are satisfied. SuperMod provides instant feedback and disallows the definition of, e.g., a feature configuration or feature ambition that would violate a constraint. The four operations include *check-out*, *commit*, a modified *edit feature model* action which ensures satisfiability, and an additional operation *migrate* that deserves deeper explanation.

Although we claimed that revision control systems follow an iterative three-stage workflow, consisting of *check-out*, *modify*, and *commit*, this does not strictly coincide with reality. Rather, the check-out is often omitted because the user just proceeds with the current workspace that has been committed before. Transferring this to SuperMod, this would imply that the user wants to keep the current feature configuration by default after commit. Albeit, the configuration may have become inconsistent or incomplete, e.g., due to the introduction of new features. In such cases, the operation *migrate* steps in. This operation can be invoked after commit and proceeds automatically in many cases by transferring missing selection states from the feature ambition. In the rare case of ambiguities, migration involves user selections of undecided features in order to complete the current feature configuration. Unless aborted intentionally, migration obviates the *check-out* for the subsequent iteration.

17.6.2   Multi-User Operation by Distributed Versioning

SuperMod is a fully-fledged distributed revision and variation control system; in addition to the aforementioned *inner loop*, consisting of check-out, modify, and commit, which are executed on a repository that is locally stored in the project metadata of the corresponding user, it provides an *outer loop* to synchronize different copies of a repository. Figure 17.7 sketches that the outer loop is realized by two additional operations, *pull* and *push*, inspired by the popular revision control system Git [5]. In its current state, SuperMod assumes a central remote repository that is synchronized with an arbitrary number of local repositories belonging to different users.

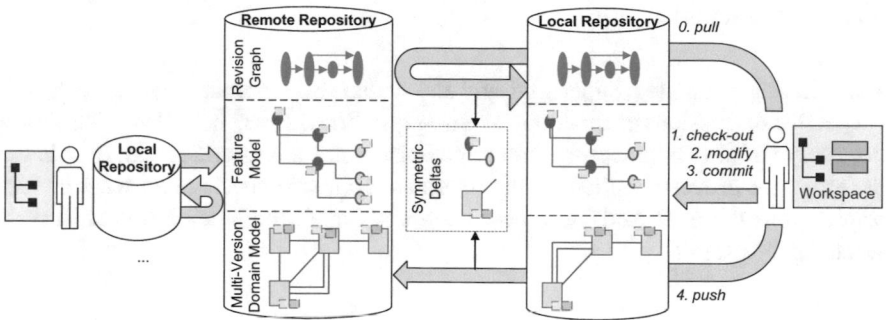

Fig. 17.7   SuperMod's distributed versioning approach

Collaborative versioning traditionally raises a follow-up problem: concurrent modifications. SuperMod handles them in an *optimistic* way, i.e., rather than disallowing them by locks, three-way merging comes into play as soon as the version history branches out. Due to their multi-version internal representation, repositories can always be merged without conflicts. However, after a merge, the subsequent check-out operation, which converts the merged contents into the external representation, is not guaranteed to be successful, and *product conflicts* may occur (see below).

17.6.3   *Product Conflict Detection and Resolution*

Besides collaboration, SuperMod is aware of a second source of product conflicts, namely the combination of optional features. In our running example, such a conflict would occur upon the selection of a variant that includes both features **Directed** and **Weighted**: two candidate class names, **DirectedEdge** and **WeightedEdge**, contradict with each other. Conflicts from either source are handled in a uniform way which we summarize as *product-based product line analysis*.

The strategy provided by SuperMod is twofold: First, if a product conflict is detected during check-out, it is immediately resolved non-interactively by a predefined strategy (e.g., "the most recent change wins"). In the subsequent *modify* step, the automatically applied resolutions are explained to the user by means of *workspace markers*. The user may either accept the automatic decision or provide an alternative resolution in the editor of his/her choice. After all product conflicts have been resolved, the repaired state is written back to the repository by commit. This also means that product conflict resolution is always scoped with the feature ambition specified at commit, while variants outside this scope may still be affected by the same or similar product conflicts.

17.7 Discussion

After having presented SuperMod and the underlying approach, we provide ret-rospective discussions responding to three questions: First, how does SuperMod connect to SPL re-engineering, and which pieces are missing? Second, how is the development process implied by the presented approach special, and what are the implications thereof? And third, how mature is SuperMod when it comes to real-world applications?

17.7.1 Connection to SPL Re-engineering

Let us draw a connection between the SPL re-engineering approaches described in other chapters of this book and this chapter, whose focus is SPL evolution.

As sketched in Fig. 17.8, we consider SPL re-engineering as an activity embed-ded into a chain of four activities. Firstly, during *single product development* (1), a software product is developed without the need for and the awareness of variability. Eventually, variability comes into play (often without the stakeholders being aware of it), inevitably leading to *divergence* of different *product variants*, e.g. by branching the development repository. Once the developers realize the overhead of having to manage multiple related variants, they decide to *re-engineer* the variants into an SPL. SPL re-engineering *converges* the variants into an *SPL* (3). The focus of this chapter has been put on the fourth activity, *SPL evolution* (4). Once available, the derived SPL is inevitably subject to changes, which address, e.g., the whole SPL, specific features thereof, or the introduction of new features.

Although resulting in the undesired divergence of product variants, activities (1) and (2) have two decisive advantages over (4). The *cognitive complexity* of

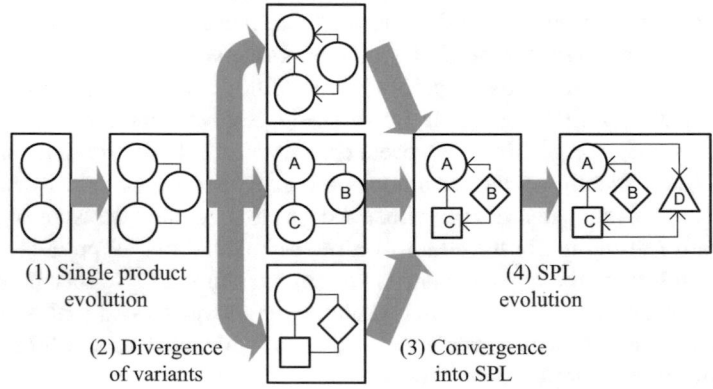

Fig. 17.8 SPL re-engineering and SPL evolution in context

development is lower because developers can focus on single variants rather than having to edit multi-variant SPL artifacts. Moreover, for editing, developers may use arbitrary tools optimized for the utilized programming or modeling language. In contrast, many state-of-the-art SPL tools require the developers to express variability by means of difficult, external concepts such as *deltas* [14] or *150% models* [4]. As a consequence, the economical advantages gained by integrating the variants into an SPL must be partly paid back by a less comfortable editing workflow.

The SuperMod approach promises to lower this cognitive barrier almost to the level of difficulty exposed by the activities (1) and (2). SPL evolution is decomposed into a series of changes, which are performed in *single-variant workspaces*, where the tools employed for single product development can be reused without any restrictions. These changes are propagated to the SPL automatically, such that it is guaranteed that the SPL is kept in a convergent state. Taken together, SuperMod combines the advantages of single-variant development (i.e., tool independence and product-based development) with the power of SPL management (i.e., multi-variant editing and convergence of the product family).

17.7.2 Alignment with SPLE Processes

In the literature, we can find several examples for SPL-specific software development processes, most of which extend traditional single-variant development processes, which in turn range between plan-driven and agile. A rather plan-driven approach has been proposed by Pohl et al. [12]; it assumes the aforementioned distinction between domain and application engineering and organizes both phases into the classical development activities (analysis, design, implementation, testing). Each domain engineering activity produces artifacts, which are reused by corresponding application engineering activities. Both phases can be iterated in order to respond to customer feedback; however, these iterations are rather long-running and, in general, refer to multiple features. Especially the first iteration of the SPL is developed in a *big-bang* fashion.

In contrast, the SuperMod approach suggests a radically different workflow with two decisive properties. First, the SPL evolves in a *product-based* way, where domain engineering is derived from a series of small increments. Second, as the running example suggests, the SPL is developed *feature by feature*, or, more generally, change by change, where each change is described by a feature ambition. Interestingly, this matches the principles of *agile software development* quite well. Among others, the *agile manifesto* [3] postulates "early and continuous delivery" and encourages developers to "welcome changing requirements". Like SuperMod, agile software development is a highly incremental and iterative activity. *Agile SPLE* [17] is more and more acknowledged by the literature.

Regardless of the underlying development process, Krueger [8] suggests three *adoption paths* to SPLE based on different premises. First, *proactive* SPLE matches the big-bang approach mentioned above. The SPL and most features thereof are planned carefully in advance. The decision that the software is going to be developed as an SPL is made early and consciously, using adequate variability-aware tools from the beginning. This is in contrast to *extractive* SPLE, where the product line is derived from many diverging variants after a certain period of time. SPL re-engineering techniques are well-suited for this task. Third and last, the *reactive* adoption path assumes that the SPL already exists and focuses on responding to feedback to individual products. The aforementioned iterative and incremental nature of SuperMod suits the properties of the reactive adoption path well. In particular, the product-based approach eases the transition from *proactive* to *reactive* SPLE.

17.7.3   Conceptual and Technical Maturity

We have seen how SuperMod pioneers a new paradigm in SPLE, *product-based product line engineering*. This brings several advantages that are of practical relevance:

Tool Independence.   Conceptually, SuperMod works in a purely state-based way; to compute the difference between check-out and commit, specific model or text differencing strategies are applied. Technically, SuperMod is an Eclipse plug-in that is compatible with arbitrary text or modeling editors. It does neither prescribe a certain interface that editing tools must comply to, nor require the employed tools to be aware of multi-version editing. This important property has been transferred from version control systems.

Reduction of Cognitive Complexity.   As SuperMod users are faced with single product variants only, they may focus on the elements being relevant for a specific change, while other elements are filtered out. This property, which has been confirmed in several case studies [16], scales with the complexity of the variant space involved.

Uniform Revision and Variation Control.   The same tool is provided for the management of revisions and variants, respectively. Every change is documented with both a historical (the revision) and a logical (the feature ambition) scope.

Incremental SPLE.   The development process associated with SuperMod is highly incremental. As a consequence, developers may start with a minimal set of features and add and refine them step by step. As mentioned above, for the same reason, the approach presented here aligns well with agile development principles.

Although having been successfully employed in several academic case studies [16], SuperMod must still be considered as a research prototype rather than a production-ready tool. First of all, many operations that belong to the standard repertoire of version control systems are missing. These include user authentication, pessimistic locking, difference reports, forking, etc. As far as SPL analysis is concerned, SuperMod is restricted to ensuring the syntactical correctness of checked-out product variants, but semantical consistency is not checked by any means.

With regard to the integration with SPL re-engineering, SuperMod is currently not able to import extracted SPLs from any format. This problem is amplified by the fact that there exists no standard, or even de facto standard, for representing (model-driven or text-based) SPLs across tools. As a consequence, there is a gap between *extractive* and *reactive* SPLE—and therefore between SPL re-engineering and SPL evolution—which cannot be completely closed by SuperMod.

17.8 Conclusion

The SuperMod approach contributes a new paradigm of SPLE: *product based product line engineering*, which blurs the distinction between domain and application engineering and aligns with agile SPLE processes. *Dynamic filtered editing*, which adopts the check-out/modify/commit cycle from version control and allows SPLE engineers to perform a change affecting multiple variants in a single variant populating the workspace, constitutes a key mechanism for realizing product-based product line engineering. In this way, SPL engineers are shielded from the complexity implied by the superimposition of multiple variants, which are exposed at the user interface as, e.g., 150% models in other SPLE approaches. Another key contribution consists in the integrated management of revisions and variants, resulting in fully-fledged support of *evolving model-driven SPLs*.

As it stands, SuperMod is a research prototype which was applied in rather small case studies, including the graph SPL which served as a running example in this chapter. Thus, application of SuperMod to *industrially relevant case studies* is an important next step towards an evaluation of its functionality, user interface, and implementation. Furthermore, from the re-engineering perspective concepts and tools should be developed which support the transition from products that have potentially evolved into different variants, into a systematically managed SPL. Here, we should note on the side that SuperMod itself is a product line (to a limited extent), which also supports single product evolution (revision control) and thus could be used in the first phase of SPL re-engineering, prior to the transition into an SPL.

Resources

The Ph.D. thesis of the first author provides an in-depth description of the SuperMod approach [15]. The interested reader is also referred to a journal article covering concepts, theory, tool support, and case studies [16].

The source code of SuperMod is publicly available on GitHub.[1]

A stable SuperMod build is available as a modular package of Eclipse plug-ins on an update site.[2]

When running in multi-user mode, SuperMod requires a server-side application, which may be installed as Tomcat servlet using a pre-built web archive.[3]

An archive of three Eclipse projects that contain the raw primary data of the evaluation case studies is available.[4]

References

1. Altmanninger, K., Seidl, M., Wimmer, M.: A survey on model versioning approaches. IJWIS **5**(3), 271–304 (2009)
2. Apel, S., Kästner, C., Lengauer, C.: Language-independent and automated software composition: The FeatureHouse experience. IEEE Trans. Software Eng. **39**(1), 63–79 (2013)
3. Beck, K., Beedle, M., van Bennekum, A., Cockburn, A., Cunningham, W., Fowler, M., Grenning, J., Highsmith, J., Hunt, A., Jeffries, R., Kern, J., Marick, B., Martin, R.C., Mellor, S., Schwaber, K., Sutherland, J., Thomas, D.: Manifesto for agile software development (2001). URL http://www.agilemanifesto.org/
4. Buchmann, T., Schwägerl, F.: Ensuring well-formedness of configured domain models in model-driven product lines based on negative variability. In: I. Schaefer, T. Thüm (eds.) 4th International Workshop on Feature-Oriented Software Development, FOSD '12, Dresden, Germany - September 24 - 25, 2012, pp. 37–44. ACM (2012)
5. Chacon, S., Straub, B.: Pro Git, 2nd edn. Apress, Berkely, CA, USA (2014)
6. Czarnecki, K., Antkiewicz, M., Kim, C.H.P., Lau, S., Pietroszek, K.: Model-driven software product lines. In: R.E. Johnson, R.P. Gabriel (eds.) Companion to the 20th Annual ACM SIGPLAN Conference on Object-Oriented Programming, Systems, Languages, and Applications, OOPSLA 2005, October 16-20, 2005, San Diego, CA, USA, pp. 126–127. ACM (2005)
7. Kang, K.C., Cohen, S.G., Hess, J.A., Novak, W.E., Peterson, A.S.: Feature-oriented domain analysis (FODA) feasibility study. Tech. Rep. CMU/SEI-90-TR-21, Software Engineering Institute, Carnegie Mellon University (1990)
8. Krueger, C.W.: Easing the transition to software mass customization. In: F. van der Linden (ed.) Software Product-Family Engineering, 4th International Workshop, PFE 2001, Bilbao, Spain, October 3–5, 2001, Revised Papers, *Lecture Notes in Computer Science*, vol. 2290, pp. 282–293. Springer (2001)
9. Lopez-Herrejon, R.E., Batory, D.S.: A standard problem for evaluating product-line methodologies. In: J. Bosch (ed.) Generative and Component-Based Software Engineering, Third International Conference, GCSE 2001, Erfurt, Germany, September 9–13, 2001, Proceedings, *Lecture Notes in Computer Science*, vol. 2186, pp. 10–24. Springer (2001)
10. Montalvillo, L., Díaz, O.: Tuning github for SPL development: branching models & repository operations for product engineers. In: D.C. Schmidt (ed.) Proceedings of the 19th International Conference on Software Product Line, SPLC 2015, Nashville, TN, USA, July 20–24, 2015, pp. 111–120. ACM (2015)

---

[1] https://github.com/se-ubt/supermod.

[2] https://github.com/se-ubt/supermod/raw/master/update.

[3] https://github.com/se-ubt/supermod/raw/master/artifacts/supermod-server.war.

[4] https://github.com/se-ubt/supermod/raw/master/artifacts/studies.zip.

11. Pfofe, T., Thüm, T., Schulze, S., Fenske, W., Schaefer, I.: Synchronizing software variants with variantsync. In: H. Mei (ed.) Proceedings of the 20th International Systems and Software Product Line Conference, SPLC 2016, Beijing, China, September 16–23, 2016, pp. 329–332. ACM (2016)
12. Pohl, K., Böckle, G., van der Linden, F.: Software Product Line Engineering - Foundations, Principles, and Techniques. Springer (2005)
13. Sarnak, N., Bernstein, R.L., Kruskal, V.: Creation and maintenance of multiple versions. In: J.F.H. Winkler (ed.) Proceedings of the International Workshop on Software Version and Configuration Control, January 27–29, 1988, Grassau, Germany, *Berichte des German Chapter of the ACM*, vol. 30, pp. 264–275. Teubner (1988)
14. Schaefer, I., Bettini, L., Bono, V., Damiani, F., Tanzarella, N.: Delta-oriented programming of software product lines. In: J. Bosch, J. Lee (eds.) Software Product Lines: Going Beyond - 14th International Conference, SPLC 2010, Jeju Island, South Korea, September 13–17, 2010. Proceedings, *Lecture Notes in Computer Science*, vol. 6287, pp. 77–91. Springer (2010)
15. Schwägerl, F.: Version control and product lines in model-driven software engineering. Ph.D. thesis, University of Bayreuth, Germany (2018). URL urn:nbn:de:bvb:703-epub-3554-3
16. Schwägerl, F., Westfechtel, B.: Integrated revision and variation control for evolving model-driven software product lines. Software & Systems Modeling **18**(6), 3373–3420 (2019)
17. da Silva, I.F., da Mota Silveira Neto, P.A., O'Leary, P., de Almeida, E.S., de Lemos Meira, S.R.: Agile software product lines: a systematic mapping study. Softw., Pract. Exper. **41**(8), 899–920 (2011)
18. Stahl, T., Völter, M., Bettin, J., Haase, A., Helsen, S.: Model-driven software development - technology, engineering, management. Pitman (2006)
19. Stanciulescu, S., Berger, T., Walkingshaw, E., Wasowski, A.: Concepts, operations, and feasibility of a projection-based variation control system. In: 2016 IEEE International Conference on Software Maintenance and Evolution, ICSME 2016, Raleigh, NC, USA, October 2–7, 2016, pp. 323–333. IEEE Computer Society (2016)
20. Steinberg, D., Budinsky, F., Paternostro, M., Merks, E.: EMF: Eclipse Modeling Framework 2.0, 2nd edn. Addison-Wesley Professional (2009)
21. Westfechtel, B.: Merging of EMF models - formal foundations. Software and Systems Modeling **13**(2), 757–788 (2014)
22. Westfechtel, B., Munch, B.P., Conradi, R.: A layered architecture for uniform version management. IEEE Trans. Software Eng. **27**(12), 1111–1133 (2001)
23. Zeller, A., Snelting, G.: Unified versioning through feature logic. ACM Trans. Softw. Eng. Methodol. **6**(4), 398–441 (1997)

Part IV
Perspectives

Chapter 18
Challenges and Potential Benefits of Adopting Product Line Engineering in Start-Ups: A Preliminary Study

Mercy Njima and Serge Demeyer

Abstract Software start-ups have gained attention from the software engineering research community in the recent past. However, the systematic adoption of existing engineering practices for use in start-ups has not attracted that much attention. The smooth transitioning towards software product lines in particular can be a major stumbling block for start-ups that must broaden their product portfolio to deal with divergent demands imposed by the market and the costs of maintaining their products. We conducted a preliminary study within two software start-ups, which revealed the motivating factors and benefits that would lead to the migration from a single product into a product line. Despite the benefits, tackling the challenges foreseen and the identification of features and their relations in the current product is the crucial first step towards implementing an appropriate highly-configurable product portfolio.

18.1 Introduction

In the start-up world, competition is becoming both more intense and more wide spread [39]. Most companies depend on mission-critical systems to manage customer interactions, speed up delivery of goods to their destinations and manage finances in complex business environments [24]. Often these companies compete on small differences in quickly introduced, innovative services. Accomplishing key business goals such as satisfying the customer, achieving time to market with products and services or controlling costs have direct implications on the way these companies choose to develop and use software systems for competitive advantage. Success therefore means that the products and services that rest upon a software

M. Njima
University of Antwerp, Antwerpen, Belgium
e-mail: mercy.njima@uantwerpen.be

S. Demeyer (✉)
University of Antwerp – Flanders Make vzw, Antwerpen, Belgium
e-mail: serge.demeyer@uantwerpen.be

© Springer Nature Switzerland AG 2023
R. E. Lopez-Herrejon et al. (eds.), *Handbook of Re-Engineering Software Intensive Systems into Software Product Lines*, https://doi.org/10.1007/978-3-031-11686-5_18

base must get their software "faster, better and cheaper". Faster as the software has to meet a market window. Better as the software has to serve the requirements of the process it is to support and later, do so with few failures. Cheaper as the software has to make economic sense to produce and maintain. To meet these conditions, the software must be produced more efficiently or large portions must be reused [24].

Traditional development approaches are preferred with ad-hoc reuse mechanisms used to introduce variability [33]. It is common practice in industry to apply Clone and Own approaches, replicating an existing system and adapting it according to the new requirements [13, 42]. However, while this ad-hoc practice comes with low effort, is easy to use and enables a quick time-to-market, information about commonalities and differences amongst the cloned systems is lost impeding the maintenance and evolution of the typically large number of variants [31]. Despite having low adoption costs and allowing independence from other developers, cloning easily leads to inconsistencies, redundancies, and lack of control [1]. In addition, the complexity and size of software products are rapidly increasing due to the market's evolution. The higher the products' diversity is, the bigger the complexity and challenges for an organization are. The following list summarizes typical problems which can arise as complexity of products increases as reported in [48]:

- The same functionality is developed at different places.
- The same changes are repeated at different places.
- Identical features behave differently depending on the particular product.
- Updating products and managing changes are challenging tasks.
- Maintaining products requires too much effort and resources.

Thus, long term reliance on cloning is discouraged in favor of systematic and strategic reuse offered by a software product line engineering approach with a central platform integrating all reusable assets [1].

Start-ups, in general, do not care about the long term but most of them aspire to become non-start-ups someday. A potential difference between start-ups and established organizations is that in an established organization the project sponsor and the project team are from the same organization, thus share the same goals to serve customers, improve internal efficiency, and fulfill the organization's mission. However, start-ups are often funded by outsiders. Thus, their goals may not always be aligned [26, 46].

In this context, this study aims to present results of an empirical study to investigate the potential to adopt software product line engineering in start-ups. The results can contribute to a better understanding of product line adoption in start-ups by documenting barriers, best practices, and experiences with insights to guide future investigations.

The remainder of this chapter is organized as follows. Section 18.2 summarizes the background information and related work are provided. Section 18.3 presents the research approach applied. Section 18.4 presents a discussion of the results. Section 18.5 discusses the validity of this study. Section 18.6 reports on the study conclusions, implications and future work.

18.2   Background

Software product line engineering has been adopted as a large-scale development approach that enables the efficient development of related software systems from a common set of core assets in a prescribed way [8]. Software product lines can therefore be beneficial to companies developing software products with common or similar features between the products. As a result a wide variety of companies have substantially decreased the cost of software development and maintenance, time to market and increased the quality of their software products [6]. A software product line comprises a set of software-intensive systems that can be distinguished by their commonalities and differences in terms of features. A feature in this context is a user-visible increment in functionality [33]. Based on (de-)selecting features, a particular variant can be tailored and generated based on the developed core assets. Usually, software development does not start with a software product line engineering approach, because it induces high upfront costs and it is mostly unclear whether a vast amount of variants are needed.

18.2.1   Start-Up Ecosystems

The definition of a start-up is ambiguous, as there are no commonly accepted terms. For most people the image that gets conjured up when they hear the word start-up is: "scrappy outsiders, possessed by a unique genius, took outrageous risks and worked incomprehensible hours to beat the odds" [40]. Coleman et al. describe software startups as unique companies that develop software through various processes and without a prescriptive methodology [9]. Ries defines a start-up as a human institution designed to deliver a new product or service under conditions of extreme uncertainty [40]. Klotins et al. define software start-ups as small companies created to develop and market an innovative and software-intensive product with the aim to benefit from economies of scale [27]. For Paternoster et al., start-ups are freshly created companies with no operating history and mainly oriented towards developing high-tech and innovative products, aiming to grow their business in highly scalable markets [38].

Even though there is no consensus on the definition of the software start-up term, many share an understanding that software start-ups deal with uncertain conditions, grow quickly, develop innovative products, and aim for scalability. Different definitions emphasize distinct aspects, and consequently may have varying implications for how studies that adopt them should be designed, e.g., who qualifies as study subjects, or which factors are worth exploring [50].

Start-ups typically develop early software versions to test and validate emerging ideas to avoid wasteful implementation of complicated software which may be unsuccessful in the markets [51]. They aim to spend as little time as possible on activities that have an uncertain contribution to customer value [26]. Under these conditions, often the extra effort required to design and implement software with optimal design is considered unaffordable and a potential waste of time and effort [47]. Start-ups often make sub-optimal design decisions to allow them to get to market quickly and this strategy allows the start-up to put their product in users hands faster, get feedback, and improve [36]. If and when the developed product or service is successful, then a start-up focuses on maintaining and modifying the software to meet the user needs by adding new features. As the number of features increases so does the complexity of their development and maintenance, hence a systematic reuse approach is necessary. One of the best ways to tackle this problem is the early adoption of a software product line approach.

18.2.2 Software Product Line Engineering in Start-Ups

Start-up software companies usually start with a single idea in search of market fit and thus with a single product or service. Over time, if the company is successful, the product matures and the management sees that it can use the same idea (or slight variations of it) to develop a new set of products or services [29]. However, during this process most start-ups still have scarce financial resources, so they cannot invest heavily in development. Thus, they must make reuse a reality.

A few stages of start-up development can be identified as inception phase, stabilization phase and growth phase [10, 14]. In the inception phase, the start-up is searching for ways to make business. In the stabilization phase, the organization starts gradually to find its way of working and the amount of uncertainty decreases. In the growth phase, the start-up goes through a series of changes and needs to restructure itself to support growth in all areas: business, personnel, the scope of the product, etc. At the stabilization phase most start-ups are considered scale-ups. When the products evolve, features need to be added, removed, turned into modules or separate products [11]. This requires attention to the architecture and implementation.

Software product lines offer companies a systematic way to reuse existing assets and capabilities rather than repeatedly developing new assets for new customers. They use architectures, designs and implementation techniques that make features modular and independent so that they are easy to reuse, remove, turn into modules or separate products. Although the advantages of using product lines are compelling, implementing a product line requires a lot of effort and resources and very little work has been done to bring software product lines effectively to start-ups.

Start-ups share some characteristics with other contexts such as small companies but present a combination of different factors that make the development environment different [38]. In order to distinguish between start-ups and other established organizations, Klotins examines the commonly used terms used to characterise start-ups [26]. Understanding to what extent software start-ups are different from established organizations is central to transferring the best engineering practices from other contexts to start-ups. If start-ups are different, the differences need to be explored to develop start-up specific engineering practices. If start-ups are not different, further research needs to emphasize the transfer of the best engineering practices from other contexts to start-ups.

Conventional wisdom says that software product lines may be fine for large organizations, but not for small ones such as start-ups. Start-ups cannot afford the upfront costs. Further, the burdensome processes, the strict organizational roles, and the tedious planning all run completely counter to a start-up's lean culture [16]. Many of the well-known and most publicized software product lines come from large companies [52]. These organizations boast hundreds of developers, with ample budgets to cover an experiment or two with a new and untried paradigm. If it fails, it is not as though the company will be in danger as there is always a bit of risk involved with a research and development project. For start-ups, research and development is considered a luxury [12]. Experiments are not for start-ups where every product has to strike "market gold" for the company to survive.

No wonder the conventional wisdom views software product lines as a game only for the heavyweights but this assumption is wrong. There is evidence that the majority of small, especially very small software organizations, are not adopting existing standards as they perceive them as being orientated towards large organizations and studies have shown that small firms' negative perceptions of process model standards are primarily driven by negative views of cost, documentation and bureaucracy [32, 44]. In fact, software product lines offer many start-ups their last best hope for success. Time to market and economy of production are two of a product lines' best assets, and both are many times more critical and the primary goals for a start-up [19]. Of course, even the largest software house would like to cut costs and get products to market sooner, but the large companies enjoy reputations that help them entice customers to wait for an announced product. After release, large volumes help pay for large development staff. Start-ups for the most part have neither a global reputation nor the expectation of global-sized volume to provide a cushion. Their road to success lies through the tricky territories of turning out products that are "impossibly customized, in an impossibly short time, using an impossibly small staff"[16].

18.2.3   Related Work

In 2014, Paternoster et al. performed a systematic mapping study highlighting the lack of relevant research addressing software engineering in start-ups [38]. Unterkalmsteiner et al. published a research agenda identifying further research directions in the area [50]. In the period following these works, an increasing number of empirical studies on software start-ups have been conducted and analyzed focusing mainly on exploring engineering contexts and used practices [18, 19, 21, 27, 28, 49]. At the same time, systematic adoption of existing engineering practices such as software product line engineering for use in start-ups has attracted little attention.

Heymans et al. present the project PLENTY whose aim was to adapt software product lines engineering for small and medium sized companies which can not support huge investment and risks [48]. They list some specific problems associated with the adoption of software product lines in small and medium companies and propose suggestions to prevent these problems.

Gacek et al. present the experience of a small company in Germany as they adopted and used software product lines to help their business grow successfully into a new market area. The case study reports on the history of the company, how it came to adopt product lines as its prominent development strategy, the role of the key individuals involved, and how they met and overcame various technical challenges [16].

Hanssen et al. presented a case study of a software product company that had successfully integrated practices from software product line engineering and agile software development [22]. They show how practices from the two fields support the company's strategic and tactical ambitions. The findings from this study are relevant to software product companies seeking ways to balance agility and product management. In addition, the findings inform on the practicalities and effects of agile software product line engineering as an interesting approach to industrialized software engineering.

Hetrick et al. presented their experience of incremental transitioning to software product line engineering to bypass the typical up-front adoption barrier of high costs [23]. The company made a small initial investment and were able to start a chain reaction in which the tactical and strategic incremental returns quickly outpaced the incremental investments, making the transition pay for itself.

Bastos et al. reported on a multi-method study, where results from a mapping study, industrial case study and also expert opinion survey were considered to investigate software product line engineering adoption in the context of small and medium sized enterprises. The study documented evidence observed during the transition from single-system development to a software product line engineering approach [3].

In the "Software Variant building" project, Knauber et al. transfered product line concepts to six small- and medium-sized enterprises by applying the Product Line Software Engineering method, PuLSE [29]. They report on the experience and lessons learned from 24 months of work including first results within the companies.

Nazar et al. used an ethnographic approach at a small company in China to investigate how well the software product line approach would work for a small organization [35]. They addressed the challenges faced by the company and suggested potential improvements to ensure that the company reaped the benefits of software product line engineering.

Ghanam et al. provided a comprehensive taxonomy of the challenges faced when a medium-scale organization decided to adopt software platforms in order to achieve high levels of reuse and improve quality [17]. They report on the need to investigate the issues and challenges organizations face when transitioning to a software platform strategy. The work reveals how new trends in software engineering (i.e.

agile methods, distributed development and flat management structures) inter played
with the chosen platform strategy.

There exists a significant body of knowledge on the transitioning to software
product lines for large companies. The overview of the related work illustrates
that some initial investigations have been conducted on small and medium sized
companies and almost none for start-ups. Software start-ups are quite distinct from
traditional mature software companies, but also from micro-, small-, and medium-
sized enterprises, introducing new challenges relevant for software engineering
research [20, 50].

18.3   Research Design

In recent years, there has been a growing interest in empirical research in software
engineering [43]. One of the main reasons is that the analytical research paradigm
is not sufficient for investigating complex real life issues, involving humans and
their interactions with technology [3]. While such a large gap between research and
practice presents many opportunities, it also brings many potential pitfalls. Without
a mature body of theoretical knowledge to use as a guiding light, systematic research
becomes somewhat more difficult. It is recommended that in instances where the
study is broad, exploratory and where limited research currently exists, it is vital
that the researcher parses the research project into a set of clearly defined steps [3]

In order to evaluate the start-ups potential for software product line adoption,
we conducted in-depth semi-structured interviews to identify the strategies applied
in relation to reuse and in general the perception towards software product line
engineering practices. We followed the guidelines presented in [43, 45]

We targeted software start-ups that develop a software intensive product or
service and are adopting the latest technology trends to create a competitive
advantage in the market. In the first stage of the study, we established contact
with individuals in the two start-ups to request their participation in this study.
Specifically, we sent personalized emails to the individuals describing the scope
and objectives of the study. We asked for interviewees with experience in software
development and product management processes. All of the participants in this
study were volunteers, and no compensation of any form was offered or paid. We
informed the participants that the assessment being conducted was part of a doctoral
research project and that neither the identity of an individual nor of the start-up
would be disclosed in the resulting thesis or in any research publications. In order
to protect the privacy of the two start-ups, they will be referred to as "A" and "B".
To form a broad view of a start-up and its processes, we interviewed individuals
from different teams and at different ranks / roles from two start-ups based in two
different countries, see Table 18.1.

We created an interview guide based on the software product line engineering
concepts and areas of interest that we deemed necessary to explore during the
interviews. All the interviews were face-to-face interviews and followed an open-

Table 18.1 Interview participants

Role	Co.	Country	Segment	Development practices
Senior product manager	A	Belgium	Data/Telecom	Agile
Developer	A	Belgium	Data/Telecom	
CEO / Developer	B	Netherlands	Automation/Services	No formal process, some agile
Business/Tech analyst	B	Netherlands	Automation/Services	

ended interview style. At the beginning of each interview, we started with a short introduction to familiarize the interviewees with the scope of the research. The introduction carried more depth than the introductory e-mails, and the interviewees had a possibility to ask for more details. The interviews themselves were 2 hours long. All the interviews were recorded with a digital voice recorder, so that any of the information collected would be captured and only correct information would be used when analyzing the results. After the interviews, the recordings were transcribed.

This study was conducted in light of the following research questions:

1. *To what extent is the migration to software product line engineering useful in practice for start-ups?*
2. *What are the major challenges that would be faced while adopting software product lines in a start-up?*
3. *How do we evaluate a start-ups readiness for the adoption of software product line engineering approaches?*

18.4 Results and Discussion

In this section, we report the findings from the interviews. Firstly, the events in the context of the study are captured by the perception of the researchers based on observations, interviews and experience. We started by reading notes and transcribing the recordings of the interviews. We developed and analyzed the ideas arising from the concepts in the collected data. Further, we used our knowledge and experience in the software product line domain to further strengthen our analysis. We thoroughly checked the start-ups' websites in order to extract useful information and to verify whether we had missed anything. In the end, we compared our findings to the existing literature in order to identify similarities and differences.

We found out that start-ups heavily employ Clone and Own approaches and reuse software artifacts only when necessary. We also noticed that one of the start-ups we interviewed has similar products but are not developed from a common platform. However, the start-ups were hesitant to commit to software product line engineering when they could not see the obvious, short-term return on investment.

We now present results concerning the research questions.

Research Question 1 To what extent is the migration to software product line engineering useful in practice for start-ups?

Multiple preconditions must be satisfied if a software product line engineering approach is to be profitable, but the most fundamental of these is that the market for the products be predicted accurately [22]. In addition, product management is more complicated due to complex dependencies between product variants and the scope of the platform especially in cases where agile practices are employed.

We found that the start-ups applied some agile software development practices mainly iterative development, scrum meetings, sprint demo meetings and release planning. Agile software development lies at the other end of the plan-based spectrum. Agile software development focuses little on planning and expects limited predictability. Further, it does not address issues of reuse. Hence, it contrasts sharply with the plan centered software product line engineering approach. While software product line engineering supports the strategic objectives of the organization, agile software development primarily benefits tactical ambitions, for example, addressing the immediate demands of customers or targeting smaller-scale development efforts [22]. However, Table 18.2 summarizes how the software product line engineering approach corresponds to some principles of the Agile Manifesto and how the two approaches can complement each other [4, 22, 53].

There are three widely recognized ways to adopt a software product line engineering approach. None of them is the best approach in all cases, it depends on the context in which a start-up operates [5, 34].

In the proactive approach the reusable assets are developed prior to any product development. This approach is efficient in a very stable domain where the organization has lots of experience. The biggest risk is that over time, before some products in the product line can be built, changes in the business climate or in the domain and product definitions will render useless some of the assets already created as usually happens in start-ups.

In the reactive approach the reusable assets are harvested from products after they are built and deployed. Initially the product is built like any single-product development effort. As other products are built they use assets harvested from the products that have been built so far. The set of reusable assets evolves into a more useful collection over time. This approach reduces the risk that assets will become obsolete. Every asset is used at least once.

The incremental approach is a compromise between the the proactive and reactive approaches. The set of assets is built in scheduled increments. The increments are usually defined to provide assets needed for a set of products scheduled to be produced in the near future. The risks of the other two approaches are present here in reduced form but still present.

Time to market and economy of production are two of software product line engineering best assets, and both are many times more critical for a start-up [19]. Start-ups report on attempts to leverage on cutting-edge technologies with the aim to gain a competitive advantage such as faster time-to-market or additional features. Given the information in Table 18.2, we can see that software product lines offer

Table 18.2 Comparing agile software development and software product line engineering

Agile software development	Software product line engineering
Priority on early and continuous delivery of valuable software	Dependent upon SPLE approach adopted. A reactive model supports early delivery of valuable software
Simplicity—the art of maximizing the amount of work done	Same—but by using reuse as vehicle for eliminating work. In a reactive SPLE approach, the risk of doing unnecessary work is reduced
Sustainable development. Maintain a constant pace indefinitely	SPLE promotes sustainable development at a larger scale
Continuous attention to technical excellence and good design enhances agility	SPLE platforms encode technical excellence and design to support rapid product derivation

start-ups a great opportunity to meet both their business and software development goals.

Research Question 2 *What are the major challenges that would be faced while adopting software product lines in a start-up?*

We captured a set of challenges that the interviewees thought they would encounter during the adoption of software product line engineering approach and we present some thoughts on how they can be handled with ideas from existing literature [3].

- **High initial cost of adoption:** to overcome this barrier, the incremental and minimally invasive transition strategy should be employed to maintain low initial costs and meet pre-defined milestones [30, 37].
- **Autonomy of developers:** start-up developers usually work autonomously and own different features of the products (micro products). In order to transition to software product lines, developers would need to collaborate and find similarities among the features they develop.
- **Unpredictability:** Mainly due to the rapid change in technology. Keeping up with the technological changes and advancements is the only way that start-ups can stay ahead.
- **Lack of organizational maturity:** start-ups work under heavy constraints. They need to be very flexible and fast in their reaction to customer requests, thus limiting their openness to long-term planning. A culture of continuous learning would help.
- **Unclear product vision:** before adopting a software product line engineering approach, a start-up should have a clear plan for future products in the portfolio and identification of new opportunities.
- **Ad-hoc development process:** the start-ups did not have a systematic procedure to follow during software development. Some basic principles and practices of software engineering should be introduced to overcome this barrier through training and guidance.

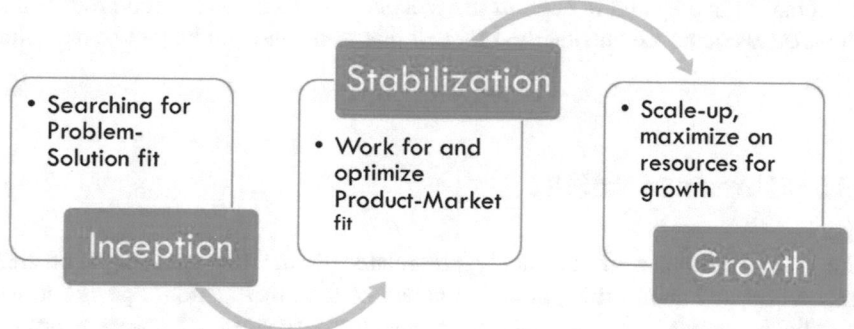

Fig. 18.1 Start-up life-cycle phases as indicators of readiness for the adoption of software product line engineering (SPLE). Life-cycle phases based on [10]

Catal et al. present other challenges that a company might face that would be worth investigating [2, 7, 25].

Research Question 3 *How do we evaluate a start-ups' readiness for the adoption of software product line engineering approaches?*

One of the early indicators that a start-up might be ready to transition to software product line engineering is the life-cycle phase in which the start-up is in. As seen in Fig. 18.1, in the stabilization phase a start-up is working to optimize the product-market fit. In the growth phase, a start-up is maximizing on resources that might help it grow. These goals match with the software product line promises of decreased time to market, increased product quality, decreased product risk, increased market agility, increased customer satisfaction and ability to effect mass customization.

In order to evaluate whether a start-up is ready to transition to software product line engineering, the development team should be able to identify features and their variation points. During the course of the interviews, the interviewees pointed out some features in their products and their commonalities. They were also open to performing a systematic and ongoing software product line scoping exercise in order to foresee future requirements. Even with the expected difficulties, these start-ups appear to be well positioned to adopt a software product line engineering approach due to the relative ease of feature and variability information extraction from single software systems.

Other than a willingness to transition, the interviewees' responses are not a good criteria to evaluate readiness for adopting a software product line. A good approach to assess readiness would be the use of the Product Line Potential Analysis framework [15]. A Product Line Potential Analysis decides in a half-day workshop whether the software product line approach is suitable for a given set of products and their market using a structured interview based on a questionnaire. Another option would be the APPLIES framework [41]. This framework detect signals that could motivate a company to adopt a product line approach and assess the extent to which the company is prepared to support the practices necessary to adopt a product line. These assessments are outside the scope of this study and will be part of our future work.

18.5   Threats to Validity

The main limitations of this study are related to the limited sample of start-ups investigated and to the qualitative nature of the investigation. Specific threats to validity include construct validity related to the concept of software product line engineering, external validity with respect to the limited contexts analyzed, and reliability of the results affected by the high level of interpretation that both interviewees and researchers might have injected in the study [43].

To mitigate construct validity, we held an introductory session with the participants in the start-ups to clearly define and align on what software product line engineering is. We gave concrete examples, used the up to date definition of software product line engineering reported in [8], and asked the participants to share examples in order to test whether their understanding matched the community's definition. Additionally, we asked and probed the claims made by inquiring for additional concrete examples.

To mitigate the external validity threat, we collected information from two different countries. In addition, we approached start-ups from different industrial sectors and interviewed people holding a spectrum of organizational roles as seen in Table 18.1. Furthermore, we acknowledge this threat by carefully avoiding to generalize our results. These limitations can be considered acceptable in light of the exploratory purpose of this study. We preferred to gain a deep and rich understanding of the context of a few cases to build a holistic first theory rather than surveying the topic on a high level only. We plan to expand our sample in the future, to reach a higher degree of external validity.

18.6   Conclusion and Outlook

This study contributes to the growing interest in software engineering activities of software start-ups. Start-ups have several advantages over large firms. They are much more flexible, innovative and can adopt the changes in business environment very quickly. On the other hand, they produce their products under severe time constraints and with a lack of resources which creates a set of unique challenges. This exploratory study set out to provide a first understanding of how software start-ups reason about variability and migrating to software product line engineering techniques. Through interviews with four software professionals in two start-up companies, we identified the opportunities and challenges that these start-ups would face in transitioning to software product line engineering approach.

The results reveal that software product line engineering has the potential to supply start-ups with sufficient resources to support various business and software development needs. In this paper, we have described (1) the motivating factors that would drive a start-up to adopt software product line engineering, (2) the various ways in which the challenges can be tackled (3) the favourable consequences of migrating to software product line engineering.

The transfer of scientific and technological knowledge from universities to start-ups is very much needed to make start-ups competitive and also to fill the gap in the software engineering practices of which software product line engineering is a large part.

Acknowledgments The authors of this paper would like to thank all practitioners who found time and motivation to share their experiences. This work is supported by Flanders Make vzw, the strategic research centre for the manufacturing industry.

References

1. Antkiewicz, M., Ji, W., Berger, T., Czarnecki, K., Schmorleiz, T., Lämmel, R., Stănciulescu, t., Wasowski, A., Schaefer, I.: Flexible product line engineering with a virtual platform. In: Companion Proceedings of the 36th International Conference on Software Engineering, ICSE Companion 2014, pp. 532–535. ACM, New York, NY, USA (2014)
2. Bagheri, E., Gasevic, D.: Assessing the maintainability of software product line feature models using structural metrics. Software Quality Journal **19**(3), 579–612 (2011)
3. Bastos, J.F., da Mota Silveira Neto, P.A., OLeary, P., de Almeida, E.S., de Lemos Meira, S.R.: Software product lines adoption in small organizations. J. Syst. Softw. **131**(C), 112–128 (2017)
4. Beck, K., Beedle, M., van Bennekum, A., Cockburn, A., Cunningham, W., Fowler, M., Grenning, J., Highsmith, J., Hunt, A., Jeffries, R., Kern, J., Marick, B., Martin, R.C., Mellor, S., Schwaber, K., Sutherland, J., Thomas, D.: Manifesto for agile software development (2001). URL http://www.agilemanifesto.org/
5. Böckle, G., Muñoz, J.B., Knauber, P., Krueger, C.W., do Prado Leite, J.C.S., van der Linden, F., Northrop, L., Stark, M., Weiss, D.M.: Adopting and institutionalizing a product line culture. In: G.J. Chastek (ed.) Software Product Lines, pp. 49–59. Springer Berlin Heidelberg, Berlin, Heidelberg (2002)
6. Bosch, J.: Maturity and evolution in software product lines: Approaches, artefacts and organization. In: Software Product Lines, Second International Conference, SPLC 2, San Diego, CA, USA, August 19–22, 2002, Proceedings, pp. 257–271 (2002)
7. Catal, C.: Barriers to the adoption of software product line engineering. SIGSOFT Softw. Eng. Notes **34**(6), 1–4 (2009)
8. Clements, P.C., Northrop, L.: Software Product Lines: Practices and Patterns. SEI Series in Software Engineering. Addison-Wesley (2001)
9. Coleman, G., O'Connor, R.V.: An investigation into software development process formation in software start-ups. Journal of Enterprise Information Management **21**(6), 633–648 (2008)
10. Crowne, M.: Why software product startups fail and what to do about it. evolution of software product development in startup companies. In: Engineering Management Conference, 2002. IEMC '02. 2002 IEEE International, pp. 338–343 vol.1 (2002)
11. Dande, A., Eloranta, V.P., Kovalainen, A.J., Lehtonen, T., Leppänen, M., Salmimaa, T., Sayeed, M., Vuori, M., Rubattel, C., Weck, W., et al.: Software startup patterns-an empirical study. Tampereen teknillinen yliopisto. Tietotekniikan laitos. Raportti-Tampere University of Technology. Department of Pervasive Computing. Report; 4 (2014)

12. Deeds, D.L.: The role of R&D intensity, technical development and absorptive capacity in creating entrepreneurial wealth in high technology start-ups. Journal of Engineering and Technology Management **18**(1), 29 – 47 (2001)
13. Dubinsky, Y., Rubin, J., Berger, T., Duszynski, S., Becker, M., Czarnecki, K.: An exploratory study of cloning in industrial software product lines. In: 2013 17th European Conference on Software Maintenance and Reengineering, pp. 25–34 (2013)
14. Eloranta, V.P.: Towards a pattern language for software start-ups. In: Proceedings of the 19th European Conference on Pattern Languages of Programs, EuroPLoP '14, pp. 24:1–24:11. ACM, New York, NY, USA (2014)
15. Fritsch, C., Hahn, R.: Product line potential analysis. In: R.L. Nord (ed.) Software Product Lines, pp. 228–237. Springer Berlin Heidelberg, Berlin, Heidelberg (2004)
16. Gacek, C., Knauber, P., Schmid, K., Clements, P.: Successful software product line develop ment in a small organization (2001)
17. Ghanam, Y., Maurer, F., Abrahamsson, P.: Making the leap to a software platform strategy: Issues and challenges. Information and Software Technology **54**(9), 968 – 984 (2012)
18. Giardino, C., Bajwa, S.S., Wang, X., Abrahamsson, P.: Key challenges in early-stage software startups. In: C. Lassenius, T. Dingsøyr, M. Paasivaara (eds.) Agile Processes in Software Engineering and Extreme Programming, pp. 52–63. Springer International Publishing, Cham (2015)
19. Giardino, C., Paternoster, N., Unterkalmsteiner, M., Gorschek, T., Abrahamsson, P.: Software development in startup companies: The greenfield startup model. IEEE Transactions on Software Engineering **42**(6), 585–604 (2016)
20. Giardino, C., Unterkalmsteiner, M., Paternoster, N., Gorschek, T., Abrahamsson, P.: What do we know about software development in startups? IEEE Software **31**(5), 28–32 (2014)
21. Giardino, C., Wang, X., Abrahamsson, P.: Why early-stage software startups fail: A behavioral framework. In: C. Lassenius, K. Smolander (eds.) Software Business. Towards Continuous Value Delivery, pp. 27–41. Springer International Publishing, Cham (2014)
22. Hanssen, G.K., Fígri, T.E.: Process fusion: An industrial case study on agile software product line engineering. J. Syst. Softw. **81**(6), 843–854 (2008)
23. Hetrick, W.A., Krueger, C.W., Moore, J.G.: Incremental return on incremental investment: Engenio's transition to software product line practice. In: Companion to the 21st ACM SIGPLAN Symposium on Object-oriented Programming Systems, Languages, and Applications, OOPSLA '06, pp. 798–804. ACM, New York, NY, USA (2006)
24. Jacobson, I., Griss, M., Jonsson, P.: Software Reuse: Architecture, Process and Organization for Business Success. ACM Press/Addison-Wesley Publishing Co., New York, NY, USA (1997)
25. Kircher, M., Schwanninger, C., Groher, I.: Transitioning to a software product family approach - challenges and best practices. In: Software Product Line Conference, 2006 10th International, pp. 9 pp.–171 (2006)
26. Klotins, E.: Software start-ups through an empirical lens: are start-ups snowflakes? In: Proceedings of the International Workshop on Software-intensive Business: Start-ups, Ecosystems and Platforms (SiBW 2018), Espoo, Finland, December 3, 2018., pp. 1–14 (2018). URL http://ceur-ws.org/Vol-2305/paper01.pdf
27. Klotins, E., Unterkalmsteiner, M., Chatzipetrou, P., Gorschek, T., Prikladniki, R., Tripathi, N., Pompermaier, L.: A progression model of software engineering goals, challenges, and practices in start-ups. IEEE Transactions on Software Engineering **PP**, 1–1 (2019)
28. Klotins, E., Unterkalmsteiner, M., Gorschek, T.: Software engineering in start-up companies: An analysis of 88 experience reports. Empirical Software Engineering **24**(1), 68–102 (2019)
29. Knauber, P., Muthig, D., Schmid, K., Widen, T.: Applying product line concepts in small and medium-sized companies. IEEE Software **17**(5), 88–95 (2000)
30. Krueger, C.W.: New methods in software product line development. In: 10th International Software Product Line Conference (SPLC'06), pp. 95–99 (2006)
31. Krüger, J., Al-Hajjaji, M., Schulze, S., Saake, G., Leich, T.: Towards automated test refactoring for software product lines. In: Proceedings of the 22Nd International Systems and Software Product Line Conference - Volume 1, SPLC '18, pp. 143–148. ACM, New York, NY, USA (2018)

32. Laporte, C.Y., Alexandre, S., O'Connor, R.V.: A software engineering lifecycle standard for very small enterprises. In: R.V. O'Connor, N. Baddoo, K. Smolander, R. Messnarz (eds.) Software Process Improvement, pp. 129–141. Springer Berlin Heidelberg, Berlin, Heidelberg (2008)

33. Li, Y., Schulze, S., Saake, G.: Reverse engineering variability from natural language documents: A systematic literature review. In: Proceedings of the 21st International Systems and Software Product Line Conference - Volume A, SPLC '17, pp. 133–142. ACM, New York, NY, USA (2017)

34. McGregor, J.: Agile software product lines, deconstructed. Journal of Object Technology **7**, 7–19 (2008)

35. Nazar, N., M. J. Rakotomahefa, T.: Analysis of a small company for software product line adoption — an industrial case study. International Journal of Computer Theory and Engineering **8**, 313–322 (2016)

36. Nguyen-Duc, A., Wang, X., Abrahamsson, P.: What influences the speed of prototyping? an empirical investigation of twenty software startups. In: H. Baumeister, H. Lichter, M. Riebisch (eds.) Agile Processes in Software Engineering and Extreme Programming, pp. 20–36. Springer International Publishing, Cham (2017)

37. Nóbrega, J.P., De Almeida, E.S., Lemos, S.R.: A cost framework specification for software product lines scenarios. 6th Workshop on Component–Based Development (2006)

38. Paternoster, N., Giardino, C., Unterkalmsteiner, M., Gorschek, T., Abrahamsson, P.: Software development in startup companies: A systematic mapping study **56**(10), 1200–1218 (2014)

39. Pe'er, A., Keil, T.: Are all startups affected similarly by clusters? agglomeration, competition, firm heterogeneity, and survival. Journal of Business Venturing **28** (2012)

40. Ries, E.: The lean startup : how today's entrepreneurs use continuous innovation to create radically successful businesses. Crown Business, New York (2011)

41. Rincón, L., Mazo, R., Salinesi, C.: Applies: A framework for evaluating organization's motivation and preparation for adopting product lines. In: 2018 12th International Conference on Research Challenges in Information Science (RCIS), pp. 1–12 (2018)

42. Riva, C., Rosso, C.D.: Experiences with software product family evolution. In: Sixth International Workshop on Principles of Software Evolution, 2003. Proceedings., pp. 161–169 (2003)

43. Runeson, P., Höst, M.: Guidelines for conducting and reporting case study research in software engineering. Empirical Softw. Engg. **14**(2), 131–164 (2009)

44. Sánchez-Gordón, M., Colomo-Palacios, R., de Amescua, A., O'Connor, R.: The Route to Software Process Improvement in Small- and Medium-Sized Enterprises, pp. 109–136 (2016)

45. Shull, F., Singer, J., Sjøberg, D.I.: Guide to Advanced Empirical Software Engineering. Springer-Verlag, Berlin, Heidelberg (2007)

46. Suominen, A., Hyrynsalmi, S., Seppänen, M., Still, K., Aarikka-Stenroos, L.: Software start-up failure: An exploratory study on the impact of investment. In: IWSECO (2017)

47. Terho, H., Suonsyrjä, S., Systä, K.: The developers dilemma: Perfect product development or fast business validation? In: P. Abrahamsson, A. Jedlitschka, A. Nguyen Duc, M. Felderer, S. Amasaki, T. Mikkonen (eds.) Product-Focused Software Process Improvement, pp. 571–579. Springer International Publishing, Cham (2016)

48. Trigaux, J.C., Heymans, P.: Software product lines: State of the art (2003)

49. Tripathi, N., Klotins, E., Prikladnicki, R., Oivo, M., Pompermaier, L.B., Kudakacheril, A.S., Unterkalmsteiner, M., Liukkunen, K., Gorschek, T.: An anatomy of requirements engineering in software startups using multi-vocal literature and case survey. Journal of Systems and Software **146**, 130 – 151 (2018)

50. Unterkalmsteiner, M., Abrahamsson, P., Wang, X., Nguyen-Duc, A., Shah, S.M.A., Bajwa, S.S., Baltes, G.H., Conboy, K., Cullina, E., Dennehy, D., Edison, H., Fernández-Sánchez, C., Garbajosa, J., Gorschek, T., Klotins, E., Hokkanen, L., Kon, F., Lunesu, I., Marchesi, M., Morgan, L., Oivo, M., Selig, C., Seppänen, P., Sweetman, R., Tyrväinen, P., Ungerer, C., Yagüe, A.: Software startups - A research agenda. e-Informatica **10**(1), 89–124 (2016)

51. Waseem, M., Ikram, N.: Architecting activities evolution and emergence in agile software development: An empirical investigation - initial research proposal. In: Agile Processes, in Software Engineering, and Extreme Programming - 17th International Conference, XP 2016, Edinburgh, UK, May 24–27, 2016, Proceedings, pp. 326–332 (2016)
52. Weiss, D.M., Clements, P.C., Kang, K.B., Krueger, C.W.: Software product line hall of fame. 10th International Software Product Line Conference (SPLC'06) pp. 237–237 (2006)
53. Yau, A., Murphy, C.: Is a rigorous agile methodology the best development strategy for small scale tech startups? Tech. Rep. MS-CIS-13-01, Penn Engineering (2013). URL http://repository.upenn.edu/cis_reports/980

Chapter 19
Re-engineering Legacy Systems as Microservices: An Industrial Survey of Criteria to Deal with Modularity and Variability of Features

Luiz Carvalho, Alessandro Garcia, Wesley K. G. Assunção, Thelma Elita Colanzi, Rodrigo Bonifácio, Leonardo P. Tizzei, Rafael de Mello, Renato Cerqueira, Márcio Ribeiro, and Carlos Lucena

Abstract Microservices is an emerging industrial technique to promote better modularization and management of small and autonomous services. Microservice architecture is widely used to overcome the limitations of monolithic legacy systems, such as limited maintainability and reusability. The re-engineering of monolithic legacy systems into microservice-based architectures has been receiving great attention from industry and academia lately. However, there is little knowledge on how professionals perform microservice extraction to conduct the re-engineering process. In particular, there is not much information of how legacy features should be modularized and customized as microservices, while managing variability, to fulfill customer needs. In order to address this gap, we performed a study composed of two phases. Firstly, we conduct an online survey with 26 specialists that contributed to the migration of legacy systems to a microservice architecture. Secondly, we conduct individual interviews with seven participants of the survey. The results reveal that criteria related to modularity such as coupling, cohesion, and reuse are considered useful during the microservice extraction. Half of the

L. Carvalho (✉)
Pontifical Catholic University of Rio de Janeiro, Rio de Janeiro, Brazil

Present Address: University of Luxembourg, Luxembourg, Luxembourg
e-mail: lmcarvalho@inf.puc-rio.br

A. Garcia · C. Lucena
Pontifical Catholic University of Rio de Janeiro, Rio de Janeiro, Brazil
e-mail: afgarcia@inf.puc-rio.br; lucena@inf.puc-rio.br

W. K. G. Assunção (✉)
Pontifical Catholic University of Rio de Janeiro, Rio de Janeiro, Brazil

Johannes Kepler University of Linz, Linz, Austria
e-mail: wesley.assuncao@jku.at

© Springer Nature Switzerland AG 2023
R. E. Lopez-Herrejon et al. (eds.), *Handbook of Re-Engineering Software Intensive Systems into Software Product Lines*, https://doi.org/10.1007/978-3-031-11686-5_19

participants dealt with systems with variability during the extraction. Moreover, they stated that variability is a key criterion for structuring the microservices.

19.1 Introduction

Most of the software systems used in industry nowadays are long-lived applications. These legacy systems usually rely on obsolete technology and have undergone extensive maintenance along the years, leading to decaying and degradation of their architecture [48]. In addition, these systems usually have a monolithic architecture, with strongly connected and interdependent components tangled into a single unit [36, 53]. Due to their monolithic architecture and existing technical debt, legacy systems are difficult to extend and include innovation, hampering digital transformation, and requiring great maintenance resources [7, 23, 40, 45]. On the other hand, a legacy system represents a long term massive investment that cannot be discarded. To remain competitive and preserve the existing investment, many companies have been modernizing these monolithic legacy systems [32]. In this context, a trend observed in the industry is the re-engineering of monolithic architectures to microservice-based architectures [8, 20, 24, 36, 54, 57].

Microservices are granular and autonomous services that work together by communicating via lightweight protocols [41]. As a principle, microservices are independent of each other, allowing developer teams to freely choose and combine different technologies and establish their own development cycle [15]. To integrate such technologies and services developed by different teams, microservices are highly interoperable [26]. Microservices make easier the implementation of complex business rules, as for example, the coordination among a Java, a PHP, and a COBOL application, developed by different teams [47, 59]. Yet, microservice architecture promises other benefits, such as reducing maintenance effort, increasing

T. E. Colanzi
State University of Maringá, Maringá, Brazil
e-mail: thelma@din.uem.br

R. Bonifácio
University of Brasília, Brasília, Brazil
e-mail: rbonifacio@unb.br

L. P. Tizzei · R. Cerqueira
IBM Research, São Paulo, Brazil
e-mail: ltizzei@br.ibm.com; rcerq@br.ibm.com

R. de Mello
Federal Center for Technological Education of Rio de Janeiro, Rio de Janeiro, Brazil
e-mail: rafael.mello@cefet-rj.br

M. Ribeiro
Federal University of Alagoas, Maceió, Brazil
e-mail: marcio@ic.ufal.br

availability, simplifying the integration of innovative features, enabling continuous delivery and DevOps, optimizing scalability management, as well as reducing the time to market [20, 36, 41, 53, 57].

The literature usually supposes that service-based architectures, and consequently microservices, should meet some attributes to satisfactorily fulfill their purpose [14]: (1) scalability, enabling optimization in the use of hardware resources to meet high demand services; (2) multi-tenant efficiency, offering transparency in the use of shared services, since the service should optimize the sharing of resources and also isolate the behavior of different tenants; and (3) variability, where a code base provides common and variable functionalities to all tenants, reducing maintenance and system evolution effort as customized features can be easily delivered.

In this sense, technical literature suggests that different microservices work satisfactorily with the first two attributes [20, 36]. However, the literature is scarce in relation to the use of variability to allow the customization of different services. A possible explanation for the lack of discussion regarding microservices' variability may be the fact that this technology was initially conceived in the industry and only in the last years have had the attention of academia.[1] Besides, recent pieces of work highlight the need of new studies addressing the management of microservices' variability [3, 11].

Configurable systems are widely developed in the industry to manage variability, as for example, Software Product Lines [35, 43]. By the use of configurations, customizable products can be generated to meet demands related to different types of hardware, different types of platforms (e.g., mobile, web, or desktop), serving different customers or market segments, and the like [46]. An example of a software product line is the Weather InSights Environment (WISE) from IBM, migrated from a monolithic system and currently composed of 13 configuration options to meet the needs of different customers [50, 54]. In order to manage different configurations, WISE combines a software product line architecture and microservice architecture.

To provide a better understanding of the context of reuse and variability management in microservices, we conducted a first investigation through a survey with practitioners involved in the re-engineering of legacy systems into microservice-based architecture [11]. This chapter extends this preliminary study by further describing how practitioners consider variability, reuse, and customization to identify microservices. For this purpose, we analyzed the answers given by 26 practitioners, in which 13 practitioners reported dealing with variability during the extraction of microservices. Regarding the variability criterion, the survey participants stated that variability was a key criterion for structuring the microservices. The results also reveal that criteria related to modularity, such as coupling, cohesion, and reuse, are considered useful for supporting the microservice extraction. Moreover, we performed seven interviews with practitioners aiming at

---

[1] https://martinfowler.com/articles/microservices.html.

obtaining an in-depth understanding of the criteria employed for migrating legacy systems to microservice architecture. The evidence collected suggests an increase of requests for customization after microservice extraction in systems that were not initially configurable. We also identified patterns used in microservice architecture to implement the customization.

The remainder of this chapter is organized as follows. Section 19.2 addresses the main concepts involved in this work. Section 19.3 details the survey and interview studies. Results and discussion are presented in Sect. 19.4. Section 19.5 addresses related work. Finally, Sect. 19.6 presents some final remarks.

19.2   Background

This section presents the main concepts involved in this work. They are about microservice-based architecture, software customization and variability.

19.2.1   Microservices

Microservices are small and autonomous services that work together [41]. A microservice is expected to have a fine granularity [15]. Microservice is also expected to be autonomous: (1) it should consist of service highly independent from others, and (2) it should enable an independent choice of technologies, such as the programming language, database, communication protocol, life cycles, and the like. Tools like docker[2] and kubernetes[3] have favored the process of deploying, horizontal scaling, and managing these microservices in cloud infrastructures.

However, the fine granularity of microservice architecture leads to more elements communicating over the network. The network protocols expected are lightweight protocols [41]. The lightweight protocols provide reliable communication without business rules, in contrast to heavy communication protocols. For example, a common lightweight protocol for synchronous communication is HTTP and AMQP for asynchronous communication. As noted by previous studies, there are several options for protocols [41, 53]. Inappropriate choices may lead to greater network overhead in communication or even impact on a development effort. In this way, choosing a communication protocol becomes a challenge [53]. Moreover, the microservice architecture ideally has a database per microservice in a decentralized data model [33, 41].

---

[2] https://www.docker.com/.

[3] https://kubernetes.io/.

Previous work report experiences in which microservices were not developed from scratch but from legacy systems [20, 24, 36]. The migration from a legacy system to microservices is perceived as challenging by developers who have experienced it [36, 53]. In this way, the monolithic legacy system represents a valuable source of information in the decision-making process. A previous study indicates that developers and architects usually adopt the source code of the legacy system in migration to microservice architecture [21]. In order to extract microservices from a legacy system, approaches were proposed using criteria observed in source code [27, 29, 37], generally using coupling and cohesion criteria. Other approaches also recommend observing the database schema [41].

However, there is a lack of common understanding of which criteria were useful to specialists in the migration process to microservice architecture in an industrial context. This lack includes the comprehension of variability usefulness in the migration process when the legacy system is a configurable system or software product line.

19.2.2   Customization and Variability

Functionalities and quality properties that individual customers require from a software system can differ. In this context, microservices should allow tenant-specific configuration and customization. However, the tenant-specific adaptations may affect all layers of the application, such as the business rules and database schema. Furthermore, tenants do not only have different requirements regarding functional properties, but they can also require different non-functional requirements of service properties such as privacy or performance [39]. In this context, one particular problem is related to managing the variability, for instance, different microservices can be freely combined or provide the same functionality in different variations, but may be deprecated or offline at any point in time [3].

To achieve such customization, the industry must deal with software variability, which is the ability of a system, an asset, or a development environment to be changed, customized, or configured for use in a particular context, supporting the production of a set of artifacts that differ from each other in a pre-planned fashion [4]. A high degree of variability in software applications allows it to be used in a broader range of contexts. Thus, the software is more reusable.

Variability can be viewed as consisting of two dimensions: space and time [10]. The space dimension is concerned with the use of software in multiple contexts. For example, different system variants to meet customers' needs, some products in different hardware devices, etc. This dimension is related to multiple products in a software product family. The time dimension is concerned with the ability of software to support evolution and changing requirements in its various contexts. For example, enabling new features of a new system version to a group of users.

19.3   Study Design

The goal of our study is to characterize the usefulness of different criteria previously discussed in empirical studies for extracting microservices (e.g. cohesion, software reuse, software variability) in the decision-making process, from the perspective of specialists. These specialists are experienced in migrating existing systems to microservice-based architecture. In what follows, Sect. 19.3.1 presents the study phases (survey and interview), population, and sampling. In addition, Sect. 19.3.2 shows the instruments used in the study phases, and Sect. 19.3.3 presents the rolling out the survey and interview.

19.3.1   Study Phases, Population and Sample

Our exploratory study is composed of two phases: (1) an exploratory survey [34] with specialists, and (2) individual interviews with specialists who answered the survey.

We developed a search plan [38], aiming at identifying a representative sample of the target audience. The target audience of our survey are practitioners and industrial researchers with a background in migrating monolithic legacy systems to a microservice architecture. In the first execution of our study [12], we used the results of two mapping studies [1, 42] as the source of sampling to identify practitioners with experience in migration to microservice architecture to respond to the survey. Next, we performed a forward snowballing search [58] in studies that cited the referred mapping studies. For performing this search, we used Google Scholar.[4] In our recruitment strategy [38], we invited the authors to participate in the survey and we requested that they submit the survey to the specialists, i.e., the original subjects of the empirical studies.

Variability was not a criterion analyzed in our previous study [12]. This was due to the low number of participants who have worked with some legacy systems that contained variability (e.g. configurable systems) that were migrated to microservice architecture.

Thus, we decided to expand the source of sampling for increasing the sampling size in a systematic way [38]. Since a third mapping study about microservices [22] has been published during our investigation, we expanded our literature review and also considered the results of this more recent work. Moreover, we also opted by re-sending the initial invitation for increasing the number of responses.

Results only related to variability criterion were presented in our previous work [11]. Among them, half of the survey's participants indicated they had previous experience to identify microservice candidates in the presence of variability and

---

[4] https://scholar.google.com/.

three patterns to implement variability in microservice architecture were identified during the interviews. In the current study, we present the results and analysis of all the eight criteria, named coupling, cohesion, communication overhead, reuse potential, requirements impact, visual models, database schema, and variability. After execution, our search plan resulted in the recruitment of 90 subjects.

19.3.2   Instrumentation

Survey We organized the questionnaire items into three groups [34]. The first group is composed of questions for characterizing the survey participants. This group of questions is presented in Table 19.1. Among others, we asked the subjects' academic background, development experience, and position in the current job. More specifically, we asked about their background in migrating legacy systems to microservices.

The second group of questions has the objective of perceiving the usefulness of different criteria, such as coupling, cohesion, and variability, in the extraction of microservices from legacy systems. These questions are shown in Tables 19.2 and 19.3. The list of criteria (e.g., coupling, reuse) used to ask participants were extracted from automatic approaches and empirical studies referenced by the three mapping studies [1, 22, 42] or studies found in snowballing. Commonly, these

Table 19.1 Survey questions about characterization of respondents

Question	Type of answer
Name	Open question
Email	Open question
What is your academic background?	Choice: HS, Grad, Master, PhD, Other
How long have you been developing software? (years)	Positive number
What is your position in your current job?	Open question
How many migration processes to a microservice architecture did you participate in the past (e.g., in architecture decisions, programming tasks, and others)?	Positive number
How many migration processes to a microservice architecture are you currently participating (e.g., in architecture decisions, programming tasks, and others)?	Positive number
How many migration processes to a microservice architecture did you only observe in the past (e.g., examination, analysis, review, consulting, and others)?	Positive number
How many migration processes to a microservice architecture are you currently observing (e.g., examination, analysis, review, consulting, and others)?	Positive number
What is (are) the domain(s) of the systems that underwent migration(s) to a microservice architecture with your involvement?	Open question

Table 19.2 Specific questions to all the criteria of second group

Criterion	Definition	Question	Answer's options
Coupling	The manner and degree of interdependence between software modules [25]	How did you measure coupling?	*Checkbox:* 1. The structure of the source code 2. Program execution 3. Others
Cohesion	The manner and degree to which the tasks performed by a single software module are related to one another [25]	How did you measure cohesion?	*Checkbox:* 1. The structure of the source code 2. Program execution 3. Others
Communication overhead	Overhead is related to the amount of time a computer system spends performing tasks that do not contribute directly to the progress of any user task [25]	How did you measure overhead in future network communication between extracted microservices?	*Checkbox:* 1. The structure of the source code 2. Program execution 3. Others
Reuse potential	Reuse is the use of an asset in the solution of different problems [25]	How did you measure reuse?	*Checkbox:* 1. The syntax of the code 2. Code duplication 3. Others
Requirements impact	Software Requirements is a software capability needed by a user to solve a problem or achieve an objective [25]	What is (are) the software requirements considered (if any)?	*Open and Likert Scale:* 1. Textual
Visual models	A visual representation for visualizing, specifying, constructing, and documenting system's artifacts [25]	What was (were) used visual representations?	*Open:* 1. Textual
Variability	The ability to derive different products from a common set of artifacts [2]	Which implementation approach for variability was (were) used?	*Checkbox:* 1. Parameters 2. Design patterns 3. Frameworks 4. Components 5. Version control 6. Build systems 7. Pre-processors 8. Feature-oriented programming 9. Aspect-oriented programming 10. I did not use variability

Table 19.3 Common questions to all the criteria of second group

Question	Type
Feel free to justify the usefulness (or not) of the criteria in the decision-making process	Open question
What tool(s) was (were) used for measuring or analyzing the criteria?	Open question

empirical studies cited some criteria that were used to identify and for extracting microservices from legacy systems. However, these criteria were scattered across several empirical studies and there is a lack of validation and generalization of their usefulness in different re-engineering cases. In other words, case studies or reports usually present a few criteria related to one or two systems with a lack of (1) generalization of your usefulness and (2) the union of a greater number of criteria. Besides that, a last open question was requested in the second group of questions requiring participants to provide other criteria and their usefulness, whether they exist.

We used a five-point Likert scale associated with the following levels of usefulness, from the least to the most: (1) Not useful—it was not useful at all, (2) Slightly useful—it was only useful to a small degree, (3) Moderately useful—it was not considerably usefulness, (4) Useful—it was considerably usefulness, (5) Very useful—it was indispensable.

To avoid misinterpretations, we provided in the questionnaire a formal definition of each criterion as presented in Table 19.2. The database schema criterion is not shown in Table 19.2 because it had no specific question, that is, only common questions were applied as shown in Table 19.3. The definition given for this criterion was that a database schema is the description of a database [17].

We also asked the participants to justify their answers. Besides, we want to understand how each criterion was analyzed or measured. In this order, we asked whether developers consider existing tools sufficient to support the migration process, as shown in Table 19.3.

For each criterion investigated, we applied particular questions, based on its characteristics. Coupling, cohesion, and communication overhead are usually measured through static and dynamic analysis [31, 52]. In this way, we asked whether the participants use one of these approaches or both. For reuse, we asked whether this criterion is measured through the syntax of the source code and by the incidence of duplicated code. Regarding software requirements, we questioned whether non-functional and functional requirements are used. Regarding visual models, we asked about the type of artifacts commonly used to represent the system in higher levels of abstraction. Regarding variability criterion, we questioned about the mechanisms or approaches used to implement variability (e.g., design patterns or conditional compilation).

The third group of questions asked about the sufficiency of the existing tools to support the microservice extraction, and cases where the extraction may have failed. The questions of the third group are presented in Table 19.4 and they are all open questions.

Table 19.4 Questions in the third group

Question
Do you believe that existing tools are sufficient to support the migration process?
Was there any case that the extraction of the microservice was not successful (led to a high overhead communication between microservices, data inconsistency, or some other problems)?

Interview In the second phase of the study, all participants in the survey were invited to an individual interview. That is, each interview was conducted with a single interviewee per time. The goal of this phase was to understand the pre and post characteristics of the migration process to a microservice architecture.

For the execution of the interview, we chose a semi-structured approach. That is, combine questions in which expected answers are quantified (structured) and questions that only suggest the theme (unstructured) [49]. Regarding the questions, the participants were firstly questioned with open and general questions about more high-level themes, in an unstructured way. For example, explaining about the legacy system that was migrated or that is being migrated to microservice architecture. After that, we posed them quantitative questions. For example, the number of microservices extracted. This approach was chosen by observing those survey participants who had an experience mean of 15.77 years in software development. Moreover, the seven participants have been involved in the migration process to the microservice architecture. Among the questions, we investigated the following themes: (1) legacy systems, (2) migration process, (3) variability, and (4) tools. As aforementioned, we asked about variability as the survey responses pointed out that variability was present in 50% of the migration processes. We were interested in discovering how they implement and manage the arouse variabilities.

The interviewees were informed that they were free to ask questions about the study. They were also stimulated to talk about their personal experiences in migration to a microservice architecture, independently of whether it is related to questions asked. Each interview was conducted by an interviewer and a researcher performing the role of a scribe that took notes, while a single interviewee spoke.

19.3.3 Rolling Out the Survey and Interview

The survey was executed from January to March 2019. From the subjects recruited, we collected answers from 26 participants, resulting in a participation rate of 29%, which is considered a good participation rate when sampling voluntary participants out of the convenience [55]. Among these participants, 13 (out of 26) also answered our questions related to software variability.

We invited all survey participants to an interview. We have conducted seven interviews until July 2019, which allows us to better catch pre and post information about the migration process to microservice architecture. Also, during the analysis of the responses of the survey, we identified that a significant part of the migration processes involved variability or microservice customization, which lead us to ask about these two topics. The interviews were conducted using video conference tools with a duration of around 1 h.

19.4 Results and Analysis

We present the results and their analysis next. Section 19.4.1 addresses the characterization of participants who answered the survey. Sections 19.4.2 and 19.4.3 present an overview of the survey results and detailed discussion about the criteria adopted during the microservice extraction, respectively. Sections 19.4.3.1 and 19.4.3.2 address our findings about variability and microservice customization.

19.4.1 Participants Characterization

The vast majority of the respondents had already concluded their participation in at least two migration processes (a mean of 2.5 and median of 2.0) and most of them are actively participating in at least one project (a mean of 1.3 and median of 1.0) where the microservice extraction is currently underway. Besides that, participants observed at least one process (a mean of 1.5 and a median of 1.0) and they are observing at least one migration (a mean of 1.5 and a median of 1.0). Survey respondents' experience may be evidenced by previous and ongoing activities with the migration process to microservice-based architectures. Also, the respondents have extensive experience in software development. The time in years the participants have been developing software is considerably high: (1) the mean is 15.77 years and median is 15 years, and (2) with a maximum of 35 years and a minimum of 3 years. Our sample of respondents is diversified in terms of the roles that they play in their company: developers (42%), architects or engineers (23%), team leaders (19%), and industrial researchers (19%). The participants were involved in the migration process of systems from different domains, such as: bank services, e-commerce, education, military, government, insurance, weather forecast, and Enterprise Resource Planning (ERP).

Interview participants are experienced professionals since they are invited from the survey's respondents. All of them have previous experience with microservices migration. The mean experience with the software development process is of 14 years, with a minimum of 5 years and a maximum of 30 years. The median is of 10 years. The subset of respondents had already concluded their participation (a mean of 3.0 and median of 2.0) and are actively participating with a mean of 0.9 and a median of 1.0 where the microservice extraction is currently underway. Besides that, participants observed extractions with mean of 0.9 and they are observing at least one migration with a mean of 0.7.

19.4.2   Perception of Criteria Usefulness

We found that at least four criteria (including variability when applicable) were perceived as useful or very useful in 81% of participants' responses. Besides, no participant reported less than three useful criteria. These findings contrast with previous approaches for extracting microservices based on the adoption of one or two criteria [18, 27, 29, 37, 41]. For instance, Newman [41] indicates the use of the database schema to identify the boundary of microservices. Whilst the others use coupling and cohesion in automated approaches.

Figure 19.1 summarizes our results about the criteria usefulness through a stacked bar plot, where the colors represented range from gray dark to gray light. According to the Likert scale presented in Sect. 19.3.2, 1 means that the criterion is not useful whereas 5 means that it is very useful. For instance, about half of the answers were fixed as useful.

The criteria that are classified as most useful (median 4) by the survey participants to extract microservices from legacy systems are cohesion, coupling, and reuse. The participants also consider functional and non-functional requirements (such as performance) useful (median 4) during a migration process. In addition, communication overhead, database schema, and visual models are considered moderately useful (median 3). As previously observed in our preliminary study [12], these results prevail in the larger sample considered in this work.

In this study and in Carvalho et al. [11], we analyzed variability in the first phase (survey). These analyzes indicated variability as a useful criterion. The second phase of the study (interview) also provided relevant results about the process of migrating to a microservice architecture. These studies made clear the importance of modularity and the request for customization of the extracted microservices.

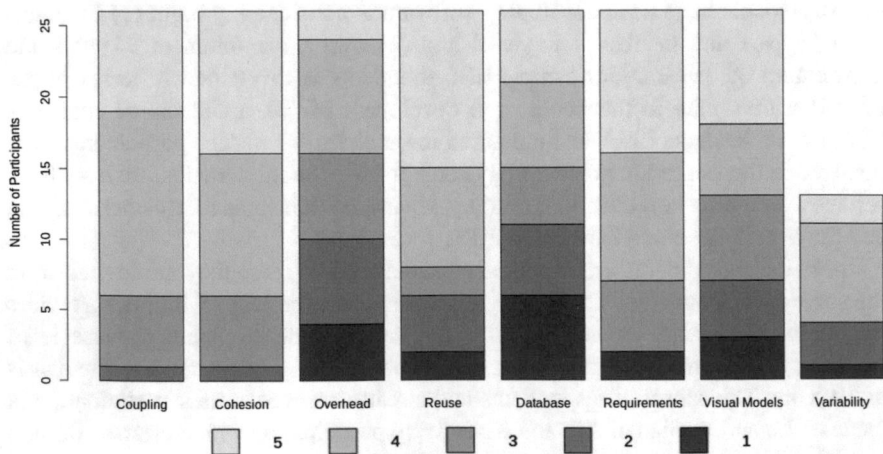

Fig. 19.1 Answers of the criteria usefulness. The colors, from gray dark to gray light, represented the Likert scale, in which 1 means that the criterion is not useful and 5 means that it is very useful

Regarding the third group of questions, 65% of the survey participants stated that tools are not sufficient to support migration to microservice architecture. They described during related open questions of each criterion the lack of tools to analyze properly each criterion and the adaptation of existing tools that had been originally designed to other goals. In addition, 50% of participants reported previous experience of unsuccessful extraction of microservices. That is, extractions that they directly participated in (e.g., developer) or observed (e.g., team manager).

19.4.3 Detailed Results and Analysis

In this section, we provide a detailed analysis of each investigated criterion. The modularity criteria (**coupling, cohesion, and reuse**) are considered relevant during the efforts to migrate a legacy system. Only 4% of the respondents do not consider cohesion and coupling relevant, while 23% consider that reuse is not a relevant criterion during a migration effort.

One of the respondents stated that it is hard to decompose a legacy system into microservice architecture, when the structures present a high degree of coupling: "When code structures are tightly coupled, decomposing them into autonomous units (microservices) is harder, so this affects the decision to migrate the architecture or not." Reducing coupling might be also one of the principles used during the migration process, as another participant made clear: "We moved from a monolithic system with all classic problems of tightly coupled interfaces to a modular architecture, which solved many of these problems."

Cohesion was also considered a relevant criterion to identify candidates for microservices. However, identifying the "right" level of cohesion is also considered a challenge. That is, it seems difficult to break legacy system components into one or more microservices, with well-defined boundaries. One of the respondents stated: "I think that delimiting the ideal functional size of each microservice is one of the most challenging parts of the whole process. And cohesion is one very important tool to help. I usually reason about the cohesion of a module to decide whether it should be an autonomous service or whether it should be together with some other module in the deployment unit."

The participants reported the use of different tools and techniques for identifying coupling and cohesion, ranging from manual assessment to existing static analysis tools and dynamic techniques. As far as coupling analysis is concerned, 42% of survey participants used tools, 81% used the structure of the source code, 20% used the program execution, and 15% used the structure of the source code and the program execution. As for cohesion analysis, 46% of participants used tools, 81% used the structure of source code, 31% used the program execution, and 27% used both.

Several participants also pointed to reuse as "one of the driving forces for conducting a specific migration scenario", which aims to "reduce code and logic duplication." Interestingly, this opinion contrasts with the perspective of another respondent, which state that "Though arguably a good reason to create new microservices, I haven't witnessed any project in which its main motivation is reuse. The most common solution to this problem was software libraries instead." Therefore, for some migration contexts, the use of microservices was envisioned as a possible alternative for reducing code duplication among different systems.

Modular identification of microservices can interact somehow with other criteria, such as **communication overhead and database schema**. However, participants reason about communication overhead and database schema less often they do with modularity along the microservice extraction. For instance, the participants considered that communication overhead is not as relevant as the set of modularity criteria during the decomposition of a legacy system into a microservice architecture. Only 38% of the respondents consider communication overhead as useful. The other 38% of the respondents state that this criterion is either not useful or not considered useful to a small degree, while 24% are neutral.

This view is clear when the respondents stated that "The communication was not a concern and the benefits of extracting the microservices overcome the communication overhead between the components." and "We didn't try to design a solution thinking about a possible communication overhead. A better approach should be, after identifying an overhead, redesign the current decomposition." In fact, several participants reported that reasoning about communication overhead became a concern only after the microservices were fully defined and the migration was completed.

The respondents also present some insights on dealing with possible issues involving communication overhead. For instance, a respondent stated the use of caching mechanisms: "The ErlangMS service bus works with a cache to minimize the overhead of communication between repeated calls to microservices." Another participant also emphasized that in a case of performance reduction due to the complexity, the microservices' extraction and deployment strategy could be modified. "Sometimes a more complex and time consuming service is separated in a new one, and it can be executed in a different server which is more robust and works on demand." In the interview, all participants that fully completed microservice extraction reported the cache usage, but this need was not observed before microservice extraction. In this way, 86% of interview participants that finished the microservice extraction used cache to reduce overhead in the network and 24% to reduce overhead in the database in a migrated microservice architecture.

Finally, one participant also suggests that, in the cases where it is possible to use a private network to support all microservices communication, the overhead criterion is not so relevant. "The communication between the services will occur in a private internal network with good network speed, so I think the side effect of decomposition is not relevant in this sense."

All the interviewees reported avoiding the use of data interchange between microservices by the database. This strategy was only violated when the network communication overhead between microservices was high to the point of violating certain expectations associated with non-functional requirements. For instance, communication between microservices using databases might generate data inconsistency. It was noticeable that this form of communication using a database has worse coupling than done by well-defined interfaces. Thus, database communication between extracted microservices was always the last option of the participants interviewed. This confirms the result obtained in a survey, that better modularity is a desired characteristic in a microservice architecture.

Regarding the communication protocol, interviews confirmed the use of lightweight protocols as HTTP, AMQP, and Kafka. These protocols are associated with specification languages to define the microservices interfaces such as OpenAPI,[5] Avro,[6] or another domain-specific language created in-house.

The **requirements** criterion was classified as useful criteria (median 4) by the practitioners. Regarding the most cited and useful criteria are functional requirements. The second and third more cited and useful non-functional requirements are performance and security. These results confirm the preference of experienced practitioners to modularity criteria insofar as the functional requirements have central importance in the microservice architecture. For instance, each microservice is expected to modularize a core functionality [33]. The non-functional requirements are less cited by experienced practitioners, despite their relevance. This can be motivated by the lack of tools to measure them previously to microservice extraction as also observed in the overhead and database impact criteria.

Visual models were reported by the participants as a moderately useful criterion (median 3.5). Regarding the assets adopted in the process of migrating to a microservice architecture, the most cited were UML diagrams, such as class, use case, and component diagrams. Besides, practitioners also indicated the usefulness of less formal visual resources as drawings on whiteboards.

Regarding the systems under the process of migrating to a microservice architecture, the interviewees indicated the characteristics of the systems. All the interviewees reported the migrated systems as legacy systems. Among the characteristics, maintenance problems, out-of-date technologies, and high business importance were the most indicated.

Finally, our results point that experienced practitioners have great attention to criteria related to modularity during the microservice extraction. However, once the migration is completed, practitioners become increasingly concerned with communication overhead and database schema. These facts may be caused by the need for tools to previously measure the impact on network overhead and database schema, and the lack of appropriate tools in the process of migrating to a microservice architecture. Moreover, the results also suggest that automated approaches [13, 18, 19, 28–30, 37, 60] are oversimplified insofar as experienced practitioners usually consider at least four criteria, while the automated approaches usually adopt one or two criteria to indicate microservice candidates. In what follows, we present results and discussions about variability criterion as it has an important role for re-engineering features as microservices.

---

[5] https://swagger.io/docs/specification/about/.

[6] https://avro.apache.org.

19.4.3.1 Variability

From the 26 participants, 50% have never considered variability. For these respondents, the domain they work does not require the ability to derive different products from a common set of artifacts [2]. Their intention was to specifically migrate a single software system to a microservice architecture. However, the other half of the participants have answered that their legacy systems, which were the target of microservice extraction, had variability. Thus, these respondents were able to answer about the usefulness of variability along the migration to a microservice-based architecture.

Among the participants with previous experience to answer on the usefulness of this criterion (13 out 26, see Fig. 19.1): (1) four ($\approx$31%) considered it as not relevant by assigning values of 1 or 2 in the scale, and (2) nine ($\approx$69%) of the participants considered it as useful or very useful. There is no response with moderate usefulness. Among those that considered variability important, one participant said: "It was useful to identify the variabilities and features of each product". Other participant said that "There are three systems that will be affected by the migration and we need to ensure the differences among them and how these differences can be handled by the migration process". In this way, most participants considered variability useful or very useful in the migration process to the microservice-based architecture.

Regarding the variability implementation approaches, the most common ones are those shown in Table 19.5. In the last column of the table, we present the total and approximate percentage in which they were cited. Version control was the most common variability implementation approach used in legacy systems, i.e., before migrating to microservice architecture. One may consider version control the most simplistic approach for implementing variability once it leads directly to the management of copy and paste of the source code or additional artifacts to generate different products.

Variability management approaches that are more robust are less common, like the use of aspect-oriented programming and feature-oriented programming. That is, approaches that are software product line specific or extending the adopted

Table 19.5 Variability implementation approaches

Approach	Total ($\approx$Percentage)
Version control	10 (77%)
Design patterns	8 (62%)
Framework	8 (62%)
Components	7 (54%)
Parameters	6 (46%)
Build systems	5 (38%)
Aspect-oriented programming	4 (31%)
Feature-oriented programming	2 (15%)
Pre-processor	1 (8%)

programming language. Moreover, all the respondents reported using two or more approaches for implementing variability, with a mean of 4.5. For example, combining parameters in an interface that instantiate a variability point with a design pattern in the source code that implements the interface and theirs respective variability point.

Finally, we found that no participant mentioned the adoption of systematic approaches for supporting variability management. This finding corroborates the statements from technical literature addressing the lack of approaches available for supporting variability management and microservice customization in configurable systems [3, 11], as discussed in detail in the following section.

19.4.3.2 Microservice Customization

In this section, we discuss the approaches used by developers to implement the customization that emerged after the migration process to the microservice architecture. During the interviews, we asked the participants whether the extraction allowed that some microservices could be used in different contexts.

To our surprise, four out of seven interviewees said that some customization was required after the migration process to the microservice architecture. Different groups inside the same enterprise or customers of software system requested the customization. In the four mentioned cases, the participants previously answered in the survey that the systems had no variability before the migration to microservices. This finding suggests that the process of migration to microservice architecture increases the systems' capacity of customization. This capacity is probably achieved by increasing modularity and interfaces available to its customers.

Regarding the other three participants of the interview, two of them reported in the two study phases that: (1) the system had variability before the migration to a microservice architecture, (2) and the system preserved its variability after the migration. In one case, the variability in the migrated system relied on design patterns and parameters in the interface to identify a tenant [39]. In the third case, the migration process was still underway. However, it was expected that some microservices would not exist or have their behavior drastically modified in different usage contexts. In the third case which there was no variability before or after the migration, the software system was completely developed. After that, it was migrated for a single customer and it will not be used by different groups of the enterprise.

During the interviews, four participants reported that the migration to microservices was not made to turn the system more easily customizable or lead to higher customization requests. However, after the migration, customization requests were made by different clients or groups within the same enterprise. Among the four participants that reported an increase in post-migration customization, three of them described which approaches were adopted to implement variability in a microservice architecture. The other participant reported that the need for customization only emerged after the microservice extraction, however, he did not observe or participate in the process of implementing or managing the customizations.

We describe below the three implementation approaches employed to deal with the customization required after the microservice extraction: *Copy and Paste*, *Big Interface*, and *Filter to the Different Platforms*.

Copy and Paste was adopted after the migration process to microservice architecture by one of the participants. That happened when customizations in the interface of extracted microservices began to be requested by different groups within the same enterprise. In this reported case, the developers decided to copy the microservice implementation and perform the customization. Thus, the copied microservice coexists with the original (inclusive at runtime). Changes are performed in both microservices by the original developers when maintenance over mandatory features is required. It was also reported that the code of test cases is submitted to the same copy and paste process and it is managed in the same way. The copy and paste approach is often used in the industry as it promptly promotes the reuse of verified functionalities as reported by Dubinsky et al. [16].

Big Interface was also an adopted solution. In this case, certain consumers of the microservice APIs needed additional information or the same information in different formats. To fulfill this demand, the developers just included all required information in already existing APIs. However, it should be noted that this solution raises well-known issues related to the big interface problem [9].

Filtering to the Different Platforms is an approach that uses an intermediary microservice between other microservices and consumers, similar to a gateway microservice. This intermediary microservice has the sole purpose of filtering the outputs for specific platforms. The case described by the participant had three different platforms, named mobile, web, and desktop, that need customized information from the same microservice. For example, when a consumer uses a mobile platform, the user interface returns more targeted and lean responses to these devices. That is, it was a filter of the original outputs from the target microservice interface with its customization for the different platforms. This pattern seems to be a form of resolution to mitigate problems from the previously presented approach.

We also asked the interviewed participants about the integration between the extracted microservices and the legacy system. From the five experiences reported in which the migration process was concluded before the interviews, the interviewees described that, in four cases, the microservices were extracted by following an incremental process. That is, some microservices were extracted and integrated with the legacy system and their behavior was observed. A similar result was described by Francesco et al. [21].

In these integrations were common to use feature toggles or similar mechanisms to switch between the legacy system and the integration between extracted microservices. In summary, a feature toggle is a variable used in a conditional statement to guard code blocks, with the aim of either enabling or disabling the feature code in those blocks for testing or release [5, 44]. This was used in production environments for the problems reported or observed by the team monitoring the transition to the new architecture. By this approach, it is possible to make a fast return to the stable version (legacy system). In general, microservices requiring database access (usually a key-value database) are used as filters to choose the switch between adopting only the legacy system or the extracted microservices integrated with the legacy system. Among the survey participants, 43% reported steps addressing the integration between the legacy system and the extracted microservices. In most cases, the effort reported for performing these steps were medium or high. During the interviews, one participant reported using this switching strategy between both versions for a small portion of their users.

19.5   Related Work

In this section, we present other surveys and interviews conducted with practitioners aiming at understanding the migration process of legacy systems to a microservice-based architecture.

Francesco et al. [21] interviewed and applied a questionnaire to developers. Their main goals were to understand the performed activities as well as the challenges faced during the migration to microservice architecture. In this way, the study participants reported what are the existing system artifacts (e.g., source code and documents) used to support the migration. The main reported migration challenges were: (1) the high level of coupling, (2) the difficulty of identifying the service boundaries, and (3) the microservice decomposition. However, they did not specifically analyze the usefulness of the extraction criteria addressed in our survey. Moreover, our work also reinforces some findings. For instance, the fact that migration is performed incrementally more frequently and the intensive use of the source code.

Taibi et al. [53] also conducted a survey with developers to characterize the motivations behind the migration to microservices and addressing expectations. The main motivations reported was the improvement of maintainability, scalability, and enhancing delegation of team responsibilities. The survey participants also reported difficulties in the migration process, such as decoupling from the monolithic system, followed by migration, and splitting of data in legacy databases. Nevertheless, the previous study did not investigate the criteria directly observed during the microservice extraction.

Wang et al. [56] conducted a mixed-method study that includes interviews and a follow-up online survey to gather experiences, challenges, and lessons learned by organizations in the post-migration phase of a legacy system to a microservice architecture. They found that practitioners choose to refrain from using multiple programming languages for implementing their microservices once this practice hinders reusability. Another interesting finding is that, in several cases, practitioners focus on resource consumption and intended deployment infrastructure when identifying microservice candidates. However, their study did not systematically investigate which criteria the practitioners apply during the microservice extraction.

In addition to the previous empirical studies, Assunção et al. [3] proposed six challenges of variability management for microservices to call the attention of both research communities of software product lines and microservices. Aiming at overcoming these challenges, Benni et al. [6] analyzed service dependencies as feature dependencies, at the feature, structural, technological, and versioning level, to assess the interchangeability of services. These authors concluded that the six community-selected use-cases are non-interchangeable systematically by default and new approaches are need. Also aiming to overcome the challenges, Setyautami et al. [51], reported the experience of performing feature identification in the subject systems by introducing a mechanism to model variability and designs a software product line architecture based on existing features. In addition, they transformed some subject systems into a product line application by using delta-oriented programming to generate running applications based on selected features.

Despite the existence of a few studies addressing the migration to microservices, the different sources of evidence available point out that this practice is beneficial although challenging. In this way, one can see that our study bridges some important gaps, investigating in depth the decisions made by specialists during the process. These findings may be used, for instance, in the design of technologies for supporting an effective extraction of microservices from legacy systems.

19.6 Final Remarks

This chapter reported an exploratory study conducted with experienced practitioners on the migration process of legacy systems to microservice-based architecture. In a survey questionnaire, we asked participants about the perceived usefulness of a set of extraction criteria. These criteria were previously identified from empirical studies, guidelines, and automatic approaches. The results revealed that specialists usually pay great attention to criteria addressing the system modularity. However, we also found that practitioners become more concerned about criteria addressing communication overhead and database access after the migration. Besides, we also found the study participants experienced in dealing with variability during the migration process tend to consider variability as useful or very useful to extract microservices.

After the survey, we invited the participants to a follow-up interview. In this second phase, we could identify more detailed characteristics of the decision-making process involved in extracting microservices. We could ask about communications chosen, desired modularity, customization requests after the microservice extraction, and the mechanisms used by the participants to deal with post-migration customization. Our results brought evidence that the relationship between variability and microservice extraction is non-negligible. Besides, we observed that re-engineering a legacy system to a microservice-based architecture often enables new customization opportunities. In this matter, the main finding of our study addressing customization is that the extraction of microservices leverages the customization of legacy systems, including those whose legacy version lacked variability.

For future works, our study presents key results to build more realistic approaches to support developers in the task of microservice identification relied on legacy systems. For instance, we proposed and evaluated an automated approach [13] considering five criteria that were observed in this survey and interviews. In this sense, this study should continue to influence and guide the building of new and better approaches, whether automatic, semi, or manual. Moreover, previous approaches to microservice extraction do not make use of the variability criterion. We believe that our study can call attention of practitioner to use the criterion of variability during the re-engineering of legacy systems and motivate the proposal of new approaches that consider this criteria to support the extraction of microservices.

Acknowledgments This study was partially funded by CNPq grants 151723/2020-6, 434969/2018-4, 312149/2016-6, 408356/2018-9 and 428994/2018-0, 421306/2018-1, 309844/2018-5, CAPES grant 175956, the Carlos Chagas Filho Foundation for Supporting Research in the State of Rio de Janeiro (FAPERJ) grants 22520-7/2016, 010002285/2019, and PDR-10 program 202073/2020, FAPPR grants 51152 and 51435, and FAPEAL grants 60030.0000000462/2020.

References

1. Alshuqayran, N., Ali, N., Evans, R.: A systematic mapping study in microservice architecture. In: International Conference on Service-Oriented Computing and Applications (SOCA), pp. 44–51 (2016)
2. Apel, S., Batory, D., Kstner, C., Saake, G.: Feature-Oriented Software Product Lines: Concepts and Implementation. Springer Publishing Company, Incorporated (2013)
3. Assunção, W.K.G., Krüger, J., Mendonça, W.D.F.: Variability management meets microservices: Six challenges of re-engineering microservice-based webshops. In: 24th ACM Conference on Systems and Software Product Line: Volume A - Volume A, SPLC '20. Association for Computing Machinery, New York, NY, USA (2020)
4. Bachmann, F., Clements, P.C.: Variability in software product lines. Tech. Rep. CMU/SEI-2005-TR-012, Carnegie Mellon University - Software Engineering Institute (2005)
5. Bass, L., Weber, I., Zhu, L.: DevOps: A software architect's perspective. Addison-Wesley Professional (2015)
6. Benni, B., Mosser, S., Caissy, J.P., Guéhéneuc, Y.G.: Can microservice-based online-retailers be used as an spl? a study of six reference architectures. In: 24th ACM Conference on Systems and Software Product Line: Volume A - Volume A, SPLC '20. Association for Computing Machinery, New York, NY, USA (2020)
7. Bisbal, J., Lawless, D., Wu, B., Grimson, J.: Legacy information systems: Issues and directions. IEEE Software 16(5), 103–111 (1999)
8. Bucchiarone, A., Dragoni, N., Dustdar, S., Larsen, S.T., Mazzara, M.: From monolithic to microservices: An experience report from the banking domain. IEEE Software 35(3), 50–55 (2018)
9. C. Martin, R.: Agile Software Development, Principles, Patterns, and Practices, 1st edn. Pearson (2002)
10. Capilla, R., Bosch, J., Kang, K.C.: Systems and Software Variability Management: Concepts, Tools and Experiences. Springer Publishing Company, Incorporated (2013)

11. Carvalho, L., Garcia, A., Assunção, W.K.G., Bonifácio, R., Tizzei, L.P., Colanzi, T.E.: Extraction of configurable and reusable microservices from legacy systems: An exploratory study. In: 23rd International Systems and Software Product Line Conference - Volume A, SPLC '19, pp. 26–31. ACM, New York, NY, USA (2019)
12. Carvalho, L., Garcia, A., Assunção, W.K.G., de Mello, R., de Lima, M.J.: Analysis of the criteria adopted in industry to extract microservices. In: International Workshop on Conducting Empirical Studies in Industry and International Workshop on Software Engineering Research and Industrial Practice (CESSER-IP), pp. 22–29. IEEE Press, Piscataway, NJ, USA (2019)
13. Carvalho, L., Garcia, A., Colanzi, T.E., Assunção, W.K.G., Pereira, J.A., Fonseca, B., Ribeiro, M., Lima, M.J., Lucena, C.: On the performance and adoption of search-based microservice identification with tomicroservices. In: The 36th IEEE International Conference on Software Maintenance and Evolution (ICSME) (2020)
14. Chong, F., Carraro, G.: Architecture strategies for catching the long tail. MSDN Library, Microsoft Corporation pp. 9–10 (2006)
15. Dragoni, N., Giallorenzo, S., Lafuente, A.L., Mazzara, M., Montesi, F., Mustafin, R., Safina, L.: Microservices: Yesterday, Today, and Tomorrow, pp. 195–216. Springer International Publishing, Cham (2017)
16. Dubinsky, Y., Rubin, J., Berger, T., Duszynski, S., Becker, M., Czarnecki, K.: An exploratory study of cloning in industrial software product lines. In: European Conference on Software Maintenance and Reengineering (CSMR), pp. 25–34. IEEE (2013)
17. Elmasri, R., Navathe, S.: Fundamentals of Database Systems, 6th edn. Addison-Wesley Publishing Company, USA (2010)
18. Escobar, D., Cárdenas, D., Amarillo, R., Castro, E., Garcés, K., Parra, C., Casallas, R.: Towards the understanding and evolution of monolithic applications as microservices. In: XLII Latin American Computing Conference (CLEI), pp. 1–11 (2016)
19. Eski, S., Buzluca, F.: An automatic extraction approach: Transition to microservices architecture from monolithic application. In: 19th International Conference on Agile Software Development: Companion, XP '18, pp. 25:1–25:6. ACM, New York, NY, USA (2018)
20. Fowler, S.: Production-Ready Microservices, 1st edn. O'Reilly Media (2016)
21. Francesco, P.D., Lago, P., Malavolta, I.: Migrating towards microservice architectures: An industrial survey. In: International Conference on Software Architecture (ICSA), pp. 29–2909 (2018)
22. Francesco, P.D., Lago, P., Malavolta, I.: Architecting with microservices: A systematic mapping study. Journal of Systems and Software **150**, 77–97 (2019)
23. Ganesan, A.S., Chithralekha, T.: A survey on survey of migration of legacy systems. In: International Conference on Informatics and Analytics. ACM, New York, NY, USA (2016)
24. Gouigoux, J., Tamzalit, D.: From monolith to microservices: Lessons learned on an industrial migration to a web oriented architecture. In: International Conference on Software Architecture Workshops (ICSAW), pp. 62–65 (2017)
25. ISO: ISO/IEC/IEEE 24765: 2017(E): ISO/IEC/IEEE International Standard - Systems and software engineering–Vocabulary. IEEE (2017)
26. Jarwar, M.A., Ali, S., Kibria, M.G., Kumar, S., Chong, I.: Exploiting interoperable microservices in web objects enabled internet of things. In: International Conference on Ubiquitous and Future Networks, ICUFN, pp. 49–54. IEEE (2017)
27. Jin, W., Liu, T., Cai, Y., Kazman, R., Mo, R., Zheng, Q.: Service candidate identification from monolithic systems based on execution traces. IEEE Transactions on Software Engineering pp. 1–1 (2019)
28. Jin, W., Liu, T., Cai, Y., Kazman, R., Mo, R., Zheng, Q.: Service candidate identification from monolithic systems based on execution traces. IEEE Transactions on Software Engineering, pp. 1–1 (2019)
29. Jin, W., Liu, T., Zheng, Q., Cui, D., Cai, Y.: Functionality-oriented microservice extraction based on execution trace clustering. In: International Conference on Web Services (ICWS), pp. 211–218 (2018)

30. Kalia, A.K., Xiao, J., Lin, C., Sinha, S., Rofrano, J., Vukovic, M., Banerjee, D.: Mono2Micro: An AI-based toolchain for evolving monolithic enterprise applications to a microservice architecture. In: Proceedings of the 28th ACM Joint Meeting on European Software Engineering Conference and Symposium on the Foundations of Software Engineering, ESEC/FSE 2020, p. 1606–1610 (2020)

31. Knoche, H.: Sustaining runtime performance while incrementally modernizing transactional monolithic software towards microservices. In: International Conference on Performance Engineering (ICPE), pp. 121–124. ACM, New York, NY, USA (2016)

32. Knoche, H., Hasselbring, W.: Using microservices for legacy software modernization. IEEE Software 35(3), 44–49 (2018)

33. Lewis, J., Fowler, M.: Microservices: a definition of this new architectural term (2014). URL https://martinfowler.com/articles/microservices.html. Accessed 2019-11-29

34. Linaker, J., Sulaman, S.M., Maiani de Mello, R., Höst, M., Runeson, P.: Guidelines for conducting surveys in software engineering (2015)

35. Van der Linden, F., Schmid, K., Rommes, E.: Software product lines in action: the best industrial practice in product line engineering. Springer Science & Business Media (2007)

36. Luz, W., Agilar, E., de Oliveira, M.C., de Melo, C.E.R., Pinto, G., Bonifácio, R.: An experience report on the adoption of microservices in three brazilian government institutions. In: XXXII Brazilian Symposium on Software Engineering (SBES), pp. 32–41. ACM, New York, NY, USA (2018)

37. Mazlami, G., Cito, J., Leitner, P.: Extraction of microservices from monolithic software architectures. In: International Conference on Web Services (ICWS), pp. 524–531 (2017)

38. de Mello, R.M., Travassos, G.H.: Surveys in software engineering: Identifying representative samples. In: International Symposium on Empirical Software Engineering and Measurement (ESEM), pp. 55:1–55:6. ACM (2016)

39. Mietzner, R., Metzger, A., Leymann, F., Pohl, K.: Variability modeling to support customization and deployment of multi-tenant-aware software as a service applications. In: Workshop on Principles of Engineering Service Oriented Systems (PESOS), pp. 18–25. IEEE Computer Society, Washington, DC, USA (2009)

40. Miller, J.: Spending on legacy IT continues to grow, but there is light at the end of the tunnel (2018). URL https://federalnewsnetwork.com/ask-the-cio/2018/08/spending-on-legacy-it-continues-to-grow-but-there-is-light-at-the-end-of-the-tunnel/

41. Newman, S.: Building Microservices, 1st edn. O'Reilly Media (2015)

42. Pahl, C., Jamshidi, P.: Microservices: A systematic mapping study. In: International Conference on Cloud Computing and Services Science (CLOSER), pp. 137–146 (2016)

43. Pohl, K., Böckle, G., van Der Linden, F.: Software product line engineering: foundations, principles and techniques. Springer Science & Business Media (2005)

44. Rahman, M.T., Querel, L.P., Rigby, P.C., Adams, B.: Feature toggles: Practitioner practices and a case study. In: 13th International Conference on Mining Software Repositories (MSR), pp. 201–211. ACM, New York, NY, USA (2016)

45. Ransom, J., Somerville, I., Warren, I.: A method for assessing legacy systems for evolution. In: Proceedings of the Second Euromicro Conference on Software Maintenance and Reengineering, pp. 128–134 (1998)

46. von Rhein, A., Grebhahn, A., Apel, S., Siegmund, N., Beyer, D., Berger, T.: Presence-condition simplification in highly configurable systems. In: 37th International Conference on Software Engineering (ICSE), pp. 178–188. IEEE Press, Piscataway, NJ, USA (2015)

47. Richards, M.: Microservices vs. Service-Oriented Architecture. O'Reilly (2015)

48. Seacord, R.C., Plakosh, D., Lewis, G.A.: Modernizing Legacy Systems: Software Technologies, Engineering Process and Business Practices. Addison-Wesley Longman Publishing Co., Inc., USA (2003)

49. Seaman, C.B.: Qualitative methods in empirical studies of software engineering. IEEE Transactions on Software Engineering 25(4), 557–572 (1999)

50. Segura, V.C.V.B., Tizzei, L.P., d. F. Ramirez, J.P., d. Santos, M.N., Azevedo, L.G., d. G. Cerqueira, R.F.: Wise-spl: Bringing multi-tenancy to the weather insights environment system. In: 5th International Workshop on Product Line Approaches in Software Engineering (PLEASE), pp. 7–10 (2015)
51. Setyautami, M.R.A., Fadhlillah, H.S., Adianto, D., Affan, I., Azurat, A.: Variability management: Re-engineering microservices with delta-oriented software product lines. In: 24th ACM Conference on Systems and Software Product Line: Volume A - Volume A, SPLC '20. Association for Computing Machinery, New York, NY, USA (2020)
52. Tahir, A., MacDonell, S.G.: A systematic mapping study on dynamic metrics and software quality. In: ICSM, pp. 326–335 (2012)
53. Taibi, D., Lenarduzzi, V., Pahl, C.: Processes, motivations, and issues for migrating to microservices architectures: An empirical investigation. IEEE Cloud Computing 4(5), 22–32 (2017)
54. Tizzei, L.P., Nery, M., Segura, V.C.V.B., Cerqueira, R.F.G.: Using microservices and software product line engineering to support reuse of evolving multi-tenant saas. In: 21st International Systems and Software Product Line Conference (SPLC), pp. 205–214. ACM, New York, NY, USA (2017)
55. Torchiano, M., Fernández, D.M., Travassos, G.H., de Mello, R.M.: Lessons learnt in conducting survey research. In: CESI, pp. 33–39. IEEE Press (2017)
56. Wang, Y., Kadyala, H., Rubin, J.: Promises and challenges of microservices: an exploratory study. Empirical Software Engineering (2021)
57. Watson, C., Emmons, S., Gregg, B.: A microscope on microservices (2015). URL http://techblog.netflix.com/2015/02/a-microscope-on-microservices.html. Accessed 2019-11-29
58. Wohlin, C.: Guidelines for snowballing in systematic literature studies and a replication in software engineering. In: International Conference on Evaluation and Assessment in Software Engineering (EASE), pp. 38:1–38:10. ACM, New York, NY, USA (2014)
59. Yuan, E.: Architecture interoperability and repeatability with microservices: An industry perspective. In: International Workshop on Establishing a Community-Wide Infrastructure for Architecture-Based Software Engineering, ECASE, pp. 26–33. IEEE (2019)
60. Zhang, Y., Liu, B., Dai, L., Chen, K., Cao, X.: Automated microservice identification in legacy systems with functional and non-functional metrics. In: 2020 IEEE International Conference on Software Architecture (ICSA), pp. 135–145 (2020)

Chapter 20
Evolution in Software Product Lines: An Overview

Leticia Montalvillo and Oscar Díaz

Abstract As any other software system, Software Product Lines (SPLs) evolve to attend to changing requirements (e.g. unforeseen issues, new market trends, etc). SPL specifics make evolution even more demanding than for traditional applications. The larger number of all, assets, dependencies, years of validity (lifecycle) and people involved, bring scalability and coordination concerns. This often requires intermediary stages where changes are first considered for some artifacts, and next, propagated to the rest of the SPL. This scenario might rise tensions between domain engineering, in pursuit of quality and reuse effectiveness, and application engineering whose agenda is pushed by time-to-market and customer pressures. During SPL evolution, this might lead to eventual asynchronicities between core assets and SPL products. both core assets and products might evolve separately until they are later synchronized. In this chapter we provide an overview on the main processes and activities involved in SPL evolution while reporting on existing research efforts. We start by setting the general framework, to next delve into the two main processes for synchronizing core asset and products, namely, backward propagation and forward propagation.

20.1 Introduction

Once Software Product Lines (SPLs) are conceived (e.g. through re-engineering existing software variants), evolution comes into play [5, 15]. The term "evolution" is overloaded with diverse concerns in the SPL literature: migrating legacy systems into SPLs [28], refactoring to account for SPL erosion [28], or bug fixing [48, 55]. For the purpose of this chapter, "evolution" refers to the adaptation of the SPL as *a result of changing SPL requirements* [6]. The present chapter builds up from our

L. Montalvillo (✉) · O. Díaz
Faculty of Informatics of San Sebastian, University Of the Basque Country, San Sebastián, Spain
e-mail: lmontalvillo@ikerlan.es; oscar.diaz@ehu.eus

© Springer Nature Switzerland AG 2023
R. E. Lopez-Herrejon et al. (eds.), *Handbook of Re-Engineering Software Intensive Systems into Software Product Lines*, https://doi.org/10.1007/978-3-031-11686-5_20

systematic mapping study on the topic [36], with the aim to provide a more synthetic and pedagogical view on SPL evolution concerns.

A first question is what makes SPL evolution different from *traditional* software evolution. Though techniques can be similar, SPLs bring scalability concerns, i.e.

- large number of assets. SPLs aim to build a family of products, not just a single product. This implies a larger number of stakeholders with potentially competing (evolving) requirements;
- high number of dependencies between assets. Assets are defined at different levels of variability and levels of abstraction. This complicates traceability. Specifically, the following difficulties for achieving traceability in SPL have been identified [62]: (i) the large number and heterogeneity of documents when compared to traditional software development; (ii) the need to have a basic understanding of variability consequences under all development phases; and (iii) the need to establish relationships between product members (of the family) and the product line architecture, or relationships between the product members themselves;
- additional level of collaboration. Transitioning from a product-centric approach to a SPL involves creating dependencies between assets (e.g. products and core assets), and hence, between teams responsible for those assets. This introduces new collaboration demands that did not exist earlier, e.g. when using *clone&own*, there is no need to match agendas and priorities of the distinct teams involved;
- large life-span. SPLs are long-term investments. This lengthy life-span should encourage a more effective control over SPL evolution to avoid SPL decay [63];

These specificities increase the complexity of SPL evolution w.r.t. traditional applications. SPL evolution is what goes from SPL adoption to SPL maturity. In their infancy, SPLs strive to fix defects. At adulthood, SPLs might have less defects, but their wider customer base more likely increases the chances for new functionality requests. The bottom line is that reaching a mature SPL is hardly a one-shot effort but rather the result of a many year-long journey [26]. Hence, SPL evolution might require intermediary stages, as they are first initiated with a partial core-asset baseline that is first refactored from (a subset of) existing product variants, and next, gradually enlarged with newer functionalities. The objective of this chapter is to provide an overview on the main processes and activities involved in SPL evolution while reporting on existing research efforts. We start by setting the general framework (Sect. 20.2) to next delve into the two main process, namely, *backward propagation* (Sect. 20.3) and *forward propagation* (Sect. 20.4).

20.2 SPL Evolution: A Brief on Main Concepts

SPL engineering aim to support the development of a whole family of software products through *systematic reuse* of shared assets [10]. The keyword here is "systematic reuse". To this end, SPL development is commonly split into two interrelated processes: Domain Engineering and Application Engineering (see

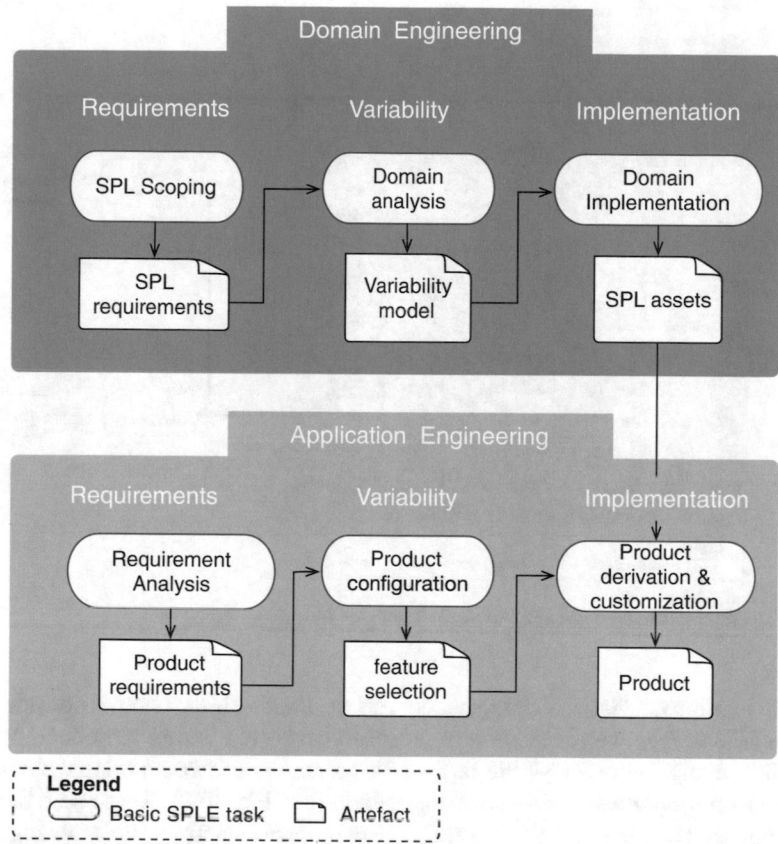

Fig. 20.1 Basic software product line engineering (SPLE) process

Fig. 20.1). Domain Engineering (DE) does not result in a specific software product, but prepares artifacts (a.k.a core-assets) to be used in multiple, if not all, products of a product line. That is why DE is said to target *development for reuse*. On the other hand, Application Engineering (AE) targets *development with reuse*. That is, AE has the goal of developing products by reusing the core-assets from DE where possible. In the simplest case, customer's requirements are mapped to feature selection based on the features identified during DE. This selection constitutes a *product configuration*, which resolves variability by selecting or eliminating named features. Based on the product configuration, the *product derivation* process yields the products along the feature-to-code mappings. However, sometimes, core-assets can not be reused "as is" but they need to be adapted to the product's specifics (a.k.a. "*product customization*". Rationales for product customization might be timely reaction to market events or urgent customer requests [12, 23, 52].

But "systematic reuse" is not a one-shot endeavor. It is a constant throughout the SPL lifecycle. SPL changes should be accounted for along the same "systematic

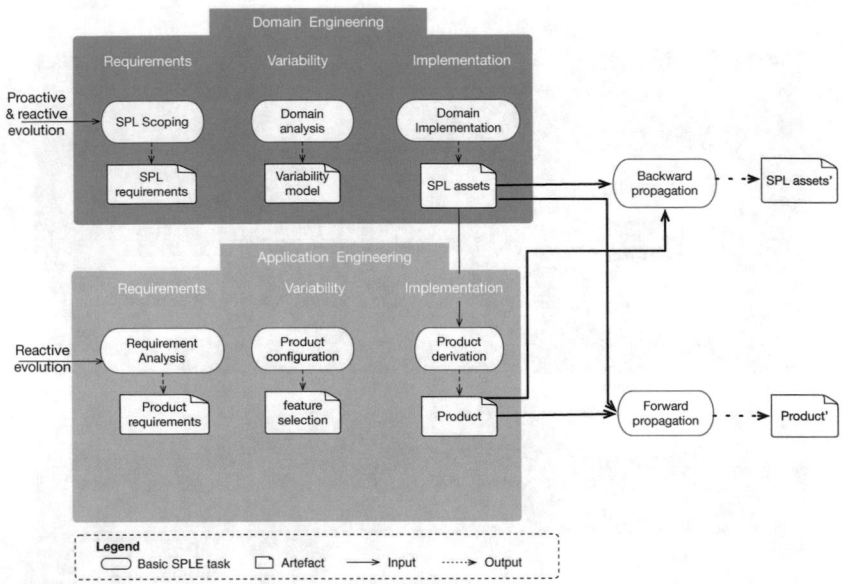

Fig. 20.2 Basic SPLE process complemented with evolution processes

reuse" leitmotiv. That is, changes, no matter their origin, should consider the whole SPL scope, even if they were originally triggered within a product. To this end, SPL evolution overlays the basic SPL process with two additional activities: *backward propagation* & *forward propagation* (see Fig. 20.2). These activities are superimposed on top of traditional software maintenance activities like testing. That is, SPL assets must certainly go through testing (e.g. checking feature dependencies) before being consumed during Application Engineering. Likewise, products might also need to be tested if bespoken code is permitted. Yet, what is new about SPL is the need to propagate the decision. Products are not longer isolated artifact. Nor are core assets. Indeed, some product upgrades might make perfect sense, product wise, yet being turned down because they do not match the SPL growing strategy. Next, we focus on this SPL specific.

Backward Propagation During *Application Engineering* new requirements can emerge due to unexpected *customer* petitions (a.k.a *reactive evolution*). These requirements can be handled in two different places: within the AE realm or within the DE realm. If changes are urgent, AE might be forced to create product-specific artifacts (i.e. "*product customization*". Here, application engineers might tune existing core-assets or even create new artifacts to meet product specifics. This might solve the urgency, but "systematic reuse" pushes those product specifics to be eventually ported to DE to consider their usefulness and co-existence with the rest of the core assets. How do SPL evolution cope with such a scenario? Let us imagine a core asset C is of importance for a set of ten products, and may be reused "as is", without any change. However, for the next three products, the same core asset

C must be changed to a certain extent. How could A be considered, whether there are C, C', C" and C"'? For these incomplete developments, "feature toggles" can be used [47]. Rather than polluting C code with conditional statements, "nascent features" are integrated but annotated with a toggle. In this way, toggles behave as feature annotations in SPL code: preventing code from being considered unless the feature toggle is on. During development, a developer can enable the feature for testing and disable it for other users. Feature toggles are a time-honored way to keep latent capabilities of an application in a Continuous Integration setting where applications are deployed continuously. This promotion of product specifics to DE is referred to as *backward propagation* (see Fig. 20.2).

Forward Propagation During *Domain Engineering* new requirements can be anticipated for future needs (a.k.a *proactive evolution*). Core-asset upgrades may be propagated to existing SPL products. In the heart-beat sync strategy, products can be updated with core-asset latest versions after the whole set of core assets have been tested out. The downside is latency: even if a core-asset upgrade is ready for production, it cannot be reused by products until the next "heart-beat baseline" [7]. If products are allowed to customize their local copies of the core assets then, a manual merge is required [27], which might cause mismatches between the two versions leading to the so called integration hell [38]. Such propagation problems can easily knock a product project off-schedule [24]. In practice, the upgrade delay differs significantly for the different products, as reported by Jepsen et al. [24]: "While some tend to upgrade rather quickly, some do not upgrade for a long time, even when not close to a release. However, access to new features and bug fixes is only available by upgrading".

Next sections provide additional details about these two processes.

20.3 Backward Propagation: Evolving SPL Assets out of Product Customization

Backward propagation is the process whereby product-specific assets developed during AE are ported up to the DE realm. This section accommodates *backward propagation* as a change process along Yau's mini-cycle[65] for single system evolution, which consists of four main tasks, namely: *identify change, analyze and plan change, implement change*, and *verify change*. We adapt Yau's change mini-cycle to account for *backward propagation* specifics within DE (see Fig. 20.3). Specifically:

- **Identify change.** This step deals with identifying product customizations. This requires to *monitor products* and keep track of the customization effort (i.e. the effort spent by application engineers on adapting core assets or creating new product-specific assets). In this way, engineers can know how exactly derived

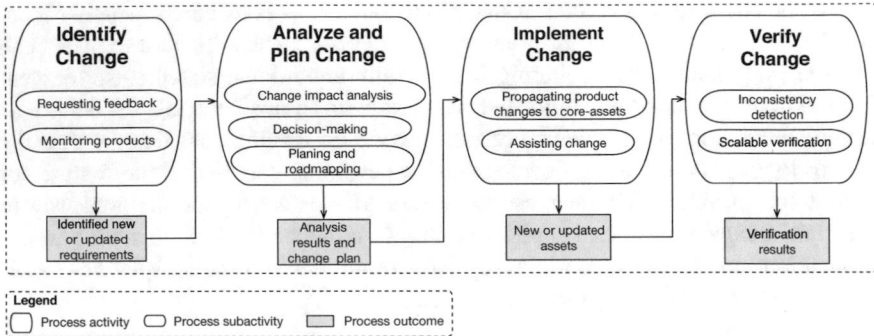

Fig. 20.3 Backward propagation evolution process

products are changing the reusable core-assets; which are the most changed core-assets; or which are the products most customized.

- **Analyze and plan change.** This step deals with analyzing which of the previously identified *product customizations* deserve to be promoted to the core-assets base, and when it should be achieved. This requires to balance between the costs of refactoring and merging product customizations into the core-asset base, and the benefits of having them as reusable assets. Herein, cost models, impact analysis and risk assessments should be in place to support the decision.
- **Implement change.** This step deals with revisiting *product customization* code but now from a reusable perspective. Refactoring and adaptation might be needed to make customizations ready for reuse in other SPL products.
- **Verify change.** This step deals with verifying and validating that propagated product customizations do not affect the SPL in unexpected ways.

Next subsections provide details on each step, together with references to related literature.

20.3.1 Identify Change

This step identifies changes coming from the product side. Two approaches are described in the literature:

- Requesting feedback. Here, application engineers provide feedback to domain engineers on changed assets. To foster product engineer feed-backing, Carbon et al. [8] adapt an agile practice, "planning game", to SPLs [44]. By means of so-called *reuse stories*, product engineers are instructed to provide concrete suggestions about how to improve SPL assets.
- Monitoring products. Rather than requesting direct feedback from engineers, another option is to monitor code repositories. This approach is illustrated in [37]. Here, Git repositories, product branches specifically, are mined in the search

for product customizations. Product customizations are next characterized in terms of the number of LOCs added/deleted and broken down by feature. This data is visualized through alluvial diagrams to spot which products customize which features, and vice versa, how features are being customized by the SPL products. Montalvillo et al. [37] help to inform about customizations but they do not offer heuristics about which specific customization to promote as core assets. One heuristic would be to look for "similar customizations": the larger the number of products with a similar customization, the higher the chances for this customization to be refactored and promoted into the core-asset realm. This approach is illustrated in [32] where the Levenshtein function is used to assess similarity among customizations from different products.

20.3.2 Analyze and Plan Change

This step deals with analyzing which of the identified changes deserve promotion. This decision requires careful analysis and planing, since it will affect the whole SPL. Three main steps are included: (1) *change impact analysis* where the scope and implications of promoting each change are considered; (2) *decision-making* on whether to perform that change; and (3) *planning* and *road-mapping* for the selected changes.

Change Impact Analysis (CIA)

SPLs encompass artifacts at different levels of abstraction: Variability Models (VMs), SPL architecture or code artifacts. CIA might be conducted vertically (i.e. from more abstract to more concrete) but also horizontally (e.g. among code artifacts due to feature dependencies). No matter the direction, propagation requires traceability mechanisms to be in place. Next, we focus on changes on the VM, e.g. adding a new feature to account for a new functionality found in a product customization. Being one of the most abstract artifacts, its changes ripple down the whole SPL ecosystem. Specifically, changes in the VM model might impact:

- the variability model itself. Changes in the variability model might impact existing features due to existing feature dependencies (e.g. *excludes*, *includes*, and *feature associations*). Paskevicius et al [42] resort to Prolog rules to assess the impact of feature model changes.
- the SPL architecture. Ideally, features in the VM should have a counterpart in the SPL architecture (e.g. a component). If these traces are made explicit (by means to a feature-to-SPL-architecture mapping), CIA can assess which architecture elements risk to be affected by the VM changes at hand. Heider et al. [20] present an industrial case study where they identify engineers' desired trace links when performing CIA in a component-based SPL. They further discuss implications for a tool support CIA based on the Eclipse IDE.

- code assets. Determining the actual code assets being impacted by VM changes is not always easy. Industrial experiences have stressed the difficulty to determine how implementation is affected when VM constraints are modified [31].
- product configurations. VM upgrades impact existing product configurations. Some examples follows: introducing new features enlarges the configuration space, hence additional testing might be needed; modifying constraints between features can turn some configurations invalid, hence questioning the VM change itself. Thüm et al. [60], Dintzner et al. [16] and Murashkin et al. [39] introduce tools for CIA of VM upgrades on product configurations.

Decision-Making

Say domain engineers have identified tens of product customizations worth being considered for the next SPL release. These requests might most likely "belong" to distinct product teams (and hence customers), each expecting "their changes" to be promoted as SPL core-assets. This rises the question of how to achieve consensus among stakeholders and on which grounds:

- Achieving consensus among stakeholders. To this end, *WinWin* models are proposed for traditional software development [4]. SPL wise, *WinWin* models are introduced in [19]. First, key stakeholder roles are identified (e.g., salesperson, product engineers, customers, managers). Next, negotiation clusters are set (e.g., development, market, management). For each negotiation cluster, stakeholders describe their individual objectives and expectations as *win* conditions. If all stakeholders concur on a *win* condition, then the condition is turned into an *agreement*. Otherwise, stakeholders identify conflicts, risks, or uncertainties as *issues*. Stakeholders seek *options* to overcome the collected issues and explore tradeoffs as a team. *Options* can then be turned into *agreements* that capture mutually satisfactory solutions. A more sophisticated approach blending both *WinWin* and *Question Options Criteria* models[1] are introduced in [61].
- Predicting the cost of a change. In predictive analytics, predictive modeling creates statistical models of future behavior. These models can later be used to estimate costs for the different SPL evolution scenarios (e.g., fix a feature, add a new feature, etc). As an example, Peng et al. [43] assess the profit that a change would bring based on the following estimates: (1) the probability that the change will emerge (estimated by analyzing the market and the technological trends), (2) the volume of the change (the number of products affected by the change), and (3), the added customer value for each product (estimated by multiplying the price and the relative value of all the impacted problems identified in change impact analysis)

---

[1] *QOC* models arrange decision making along four steps. First, define the issues (*questions*). Second, identify available solutions (*options*). Third, define the criteria (e.g., estimates about development efforts, benefits and risks) to rate the available options. Finally, a decision (*option*) is selected on this basis.

- Assessing the risk of a change. Risk is an expectation of loss, a potential problem that may or may not occur in the future. Engineers should anticipate possible issues risen all along the change chain as resulted from CIA. For component-based SPLs, Annosi et al. [2] present an industrial experience on risk management when updating components COTSs.[2] The upgrade may surface incompatibilities with other components resulting into unforeseen side effects. Authors build a decision model that considers expert knowledge and dependencies between SPL architecture elements (i.e. existing components) and the COTS candidates.

Planning and Road-Mapping

At this point, "the change backlog" has several change candidates whose costs and risks have been assessed. These changes are now competing for attention and resources. Roadmaps and release plans can help DE on this endeavor. **Roadmaps** provide a high vision on products and features that the SPL would offer from some years to come. The aim is to manage stakeholder expectations, and generate a shared understanding across the teams involved. On the other hand, a **release plan** is a detailed plan of the next SPL release, which clearly states which change requests are going to be delivered, when is this going to be finished, and who is responsible for implementing it. It differs from road-mapping in that it signifies that there are a subset of selected requirements to be implemented, and there are committed resources to implement such requirements. Road-mapping and release planing is not specific to SPLs, but the literature offers some example for SPLs:

- Road-mapping. For SPL evolution, a roadmap provides a global vision of the SPL with features and products to be offered some years from now. Savolainen et al. [51] suggest key factors for effectively road-mapping, including decomposing features into sub-features (to better understand feature inter-dependencies), mapping features to component versions (to understand how features are mapped to code), and prioritizing features based on the value that each product gives to each feature. Alternatively, Pleuss et al. [45] and Schubanz et al. [54] advocate for the use of Feature Models to frame change requests where "the what" and "the why" of the change is documented.
- Release planning. SPLs are characterized by handling a large number of assets. This leads [58] to specify release plans as matrixes with different layers. Each layer accounts for different SPL release facets: prioritized product features, allocated requirements for each component, estimated development effort, scheduled dates, test plans cases, and delivered product configuration. Layers might help to arrange release concerns, yet not clear how to prioritize each concern. Prioritization can be based on distinct criteria: costs and benefits [41], constraints on available resources to conduct the requirements (e.g., person months until

---

[2] Commercial Off-The-Shelf (COTS) are pre-packaged solutions usually acquired to a third-party for a fee.

next release) or dependencies between requirements (e.g., one requirement includes/excludes another) [21].

20.3.3 Implement Change

This step deals with integrating changes (i.e. product customizations) into the core-asset base. Note that domain engineers do not consider product changes at the time the change happened (i.e. when application developers made the change), but at a later stage (i.e. when they trigger a *backward propagation* process). This means that, from all of the candidate changes that products have made, domain engineers need to *cherry-pick* the interesting ones first, and next, *merge* them into the core-asset base. SPL wise:

- cherry picking. The use of *diff* algorithms is being explored in [9] and [57]. For model-based SPLs, these works introduce *diff* algorithms that output the list of changes that a product has performed since derived from the SPL. The *diff* spots changes as additions of interfaces, deletions of connectors and any other changes in the model. Domain engineers can next cherry pick those changes of interest, and with a *model merge* algorithm, integrate those changes into the SPL architecture model. At code level, the reasoning about what changes to *cherry-pick & merge* needs to be conducted in terms of features (variation points) and not in terms of classes or methods. In annotation-based SPLs, variation points are hidden within the code, and unfortunately, available VCSs' *cherry-pick* operation does not act upon variation points (features) but code snippets. Mapping those code snippets to their corresponding variation points can be error prone and time consuming. Tools to help in this endeavor are being proposed for Git [35, 38], Subversion [1], and a home-made VCSs [59].
- merging. Reconciling different changes frequently implies adapting and refactoring. How is this operationalized very much depends on the kind of artifact at hand. For VM, two main approaches are being studied: preventive and curative. The former avoids engineers from performing "forbidden" edits to the VM [50]. The curative option allows the edits but support restore actions when the VM turns incorrect after the change[18, 46]. If the artifact to be changed is code, the difficulty stems from the lack of tools that consider SPL specifics. For example, domain engineers might not be aware of the errors that a given change might rise until they derive the products and found it. In this sense, authors provide tools for domain engineers so that they are aware of compilation errors in composition-based SPLs [13], and the ripple effects that a change brings in annotation-based SPLs [49].

20.3.4   Verify Change

Once changes have been conducted, the SPL needs to be revalidated to ensure its integrity. First, *inconsistency detection* techniques serve to determine whether the core-asset base is in a consistent state (i.e. no mismatches exist among SPL assets). Engineers need support for detecting and resolving inconsistencies within and between the numerous SPL artifacts [64]. Second, the provided SPL functionality needs to be reverified to check whether the previously existing functionality is still working as expected (e.g. through regression testing). The challenge here rests on scalability. Hence, *scalable verification* seeks ways to lower the set of tests that need to be run in order to ensure that all products are still working as expected. Back to the SPL literature:

- Inconsistency detection between different kind of assets. Jahn et al. [22] develop a consistency checker that raises warnings about any inconsistency between the variability model and the SPL architecture. Say, that an element from the SPL architecture model does not have any counterpart element in the VM. The tool suggests the engineer how to resolve such inconsistencies by proposing edits to the variability model (e.g., a new feature should be added). In the absence of SPL architecture that represents the SPL implementation, consistency between the VM and the code assets can directly be checked. Vierhauser et al. [64] build a consistency checking framework where developers are given feedback about VM constraints being violated by their code counterparts. If we move to the configuration space, tools are been devised to check whether existing products configurations are preserved upon feature changes [29]. Finally, if the focus is on SPL architectures, several authors rely to architecture evaluation techniques to detect inconsistencies between the SPL architecture, and the source code [40], [22], [25], [17]. This, compares the SPL architecture model with the actual implementation at code level. Possible outputs include: the architectural element converges (if it exists in both the architecture and the source code), the architectural element diverges (if it is only present in the source code) or the architectural element is absent (if the element is only present in the architecture). Next, SPL architects can interpret the results based on the total numbers of convergences, divergences and absences.
- Scalable verification has to do with reducing the number of both core assets and products that need to be re-verified. Regression testing is a type of software testing used to determine whether new problems are the result of software changes. To lower the number of products to run regression tests to, the commonalities and similarities between products' configurations can be analyzed. The idea is to determine the minimal set of products such that the successful verification of such a reduced set implies the correctness of the entire SPL [30, 53]. Alternatively, model checking approaches automatically verify if a *system* satisfies a given *property*. In SPLs, a *system* is a product. A *property* can be anything concerned with safety, liveness of the program (e.g the absence of deadlocks), or behavior. As an example, consider a coffee-machine SPL. A property would be that the total

cost of a drink is always less than 2$. When a new feature is added to the SPL (e.g. the possibility to pay with credit card), all the products need to be model checked to verify this property is still met. This can be very time consuming for large number of product configurations. Cordy et al. [11] argue that if the newly introduced feature has the peculiarity to add functionality to a product without altering its previous functionality (a.k.a a *conservative* feature), this may drastically reduce the number of products to verify. Authors propose theorems to determine which products can be left out for verification when such *peculiar* features are introduced.

20.4 Forward Propagation: Evolving Derived Products Out of Core-Asset Changes

Forward Propagation is the process whereby *enhancements to SPL core-assets* are ported to Application Engineering, i.e to already derived products. *Forward propagation* serves both for *configuration repair* (synchronize products' configuration when the variability model changes) [3] and for *product upgrade* (propagation of the latest versions of reusable assets to products) [27]. The time to conduct the upgrade very much depends on the nature of the upgrade as well as the product-team agenda. While some tend to upgrade rather quickly, others might delay the decision specially when close to the product's release [24] (Fig. 20.4).

Forward Propagation is not that much different from the evolution of traditional traditional products. This explains why there exists fewer number of studies. Similar to the previous section, we resort to Yau's change mini-cycle [65] to frame backward-propagation specifics within AE (see Fig. 20.3).

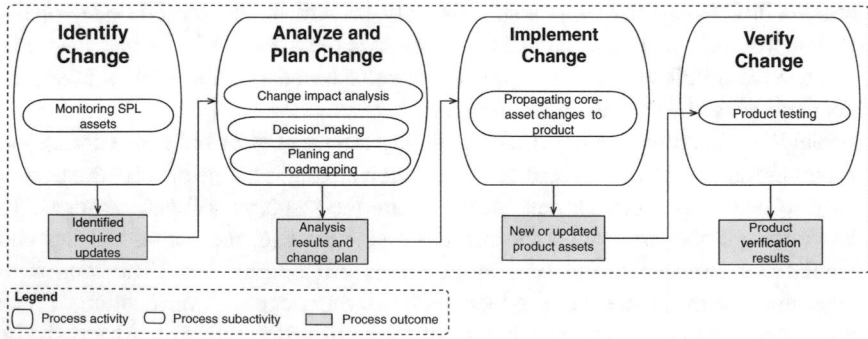

Fig. 20.4 Forward propagation evolution process

Identify Change

This step deals with identifying *core-asset updates* of interest for the product at hand. This requires to *monitor core-assets* to identify changes that might impact existing products. Michalik et al. detect which product configurations are turn invalid after changes in the VM. The tool informs product owners about the number of core-asset changes that might be required to *re-valid* products' configuration [33]. For co-evolution scenarios, Montalvillo et al. [35] introduce a tool on top of GitHub that help to assess which core-asset upgrades from the last release might be of interest for the product at hand. Using a *diff*-like visualization, product engineers can inspect, at a glance, which are the new changes conducted.

Analyze and Plan Change

This step analyzes which of the previously identified *core-asset updates* deserve to be readily propagated to products. For instance, bug fixes might be readily integrated. By contrast, if the enhancement is not so critical for the customer, functional enhancement might be delayed till it better fits the developers' agenda.

Implement Change

This step integrates *core-asset updates* into the product at hand. For fully-configurable SPLs where products are solely derived from the configuration model, this step is void. However, for co-evolution scenarios where both core assets and products might evolve separately till the next sync point, this step might imply costly refactoring and merging of the upgraded core-assets with the product code. In this sense, means have been proposed for propagating core-asset changes to already derived products. Different scenarios have been considered by the literature, namely:

- VM changes propagate to product configuration. On VM changes, product configurations might no longer be valid. Hence, application engineers would need to restore their product's configuration so that it is compliant with the new version of the VM. This might be hard for large VMs. Barreiros et al. [3] introduce algorithms to work this out, based on the distance between the original configuration and a potential repaired configuration. The algorithm suggests those with the minimum distance.
- SPL architecture propagate to products. Architectural traces (i.e., those that trace elements from the SPL architecture to products) become vital to determine how a product architecture should be updated. Michalik et al. [34] seek to abstract the level at which this process is conducted. Ideally, SPLs include an architecture model. However, this is not always the case for products where the architecture might be hidden within the code assets. This leads Michalik et al. to follow a modernization-like approach where the product's architecture model is first obtained from the product's code; next, this model is enhanced with the updates available in the SPL architecture model; and finally, the so-obtained enhanced

model is mapped back to code. The enhancement stage is conducted by comparing the current product's model and the SPL architecture model. These differences will lead product engineers to manually update products. For products that do have the architecture model available in the first place, Chen et al. [9] and Shen et al. [57] provide *model diff & merge* algorithms.

• Code asset changes propagate to products. Here, Version Control System (VCS) operations (i.e. branch, merge, cherry-pick) serve to automatically propagate core-asset updates to already derived products. Note that products reuse a subset of the core-assets. Hence, engineers are interested in only those changes that impact the product at hand. Different authors tackle this problem at the VCS level [56], [35].

Verify Change

This step verifies that changes do not break the product. Engineers can resort to traditional techniques (e.g. regression testing). A specific risk is that of bloatware where products end up keeping unnecessary assets. This superfluous code may be harmful in safety critical domains, hindering runtime performance. This is investigated in [14].

20.5 Conclusion

SPLs' long life-cycles inevitably lead customer needs to differ from those of their inception. But SPLs' complexity risks SPL products to be unable to react at the appropriate speed, jeopardizing one of the SPL rationales: time to market. This chapter provides an overview of the issues risen during SPL evolution. Domain engineering and product engineering also frame SPL evolution where traversal activities might be needed to keep both realms in sync. This means that changes might have their origin in either of the two realms, but next, the impact should be evaluated/propagated to the other realm. This complicates matters. Unfortunately, there exists a lack of tools to support these activities. To the best of our knowledge, none of the most widely used SPL frameworks (i.e. *Gears* and *pure::variants*) fully sustain SPL evolution in terms of analyzing, planning, implementing and verifying change. Time has come to shift the focus from adoption to evolution to accompany SPLs in their long life-cycles.

References

1. Anastasopoulos, M.: Increasing efficiency and effectiveness of software product line evolution: an infrastructure on top of configuration management. In: Proceedings of the joint international and annual ERCIM workshops on Principles of software evolution (IWPSE) and software evolution (Evol) workshops, Amsterdam, Netherlands, August 24–28, 2009, pp. 47–56 (2009)

2. Annosi, M.C., Penta, M.D., Tortora, G.: Managing and assessing the risk of component upgrades. In: Proceedings of the Third International Workshop on Product LinE Approaches in Software Engineering, PLEASE 2012, Zurich, Switzerland, June 4, 2012, pp. 9–12 (2012)

3. Barreiros, J., Moreira, A.: A cover-based approach for configuration repair. In: 18th International Software Product Line Conference, SPLC '14, Florence, Italy, September 15–19, 2014, pp. 157–166 (2014)

4. Boehm, B.W., Bose, P.K., Horowitz, E., Lee, M.J.: Software requirements as negotiated win conditions. In: Proceedings of the First IEEE International Conference on Requirements Engineering, ICRE '94, Colorado Springs, Colorado, USA, April 18–21, 1994, pp. 74–83 (1994)

5. Bosch, J.: Maturity and evolution in software product lines: Approaches, artefacts and organization. In: Software Product Lines, Second International Conference, SPLC 2, San Diego, CA, USA, August 19–22, 2002, Proceedings, pp. 257–271 (2002)

6. Botterweck, G., Pleuss, A.: Evolution of software product lines. In: Evolving Software Systems, pp. 265–295 (2014)

7. Breuche, D.: Product line engineering. https://productlines.wordpress.com/2011/12/20/strategies-for-releases-development-and-maintenance-in-product-line-part-2-release-and-maintenance/ Last accessed: 1 March, 2018

8. Carbon, R., Knodel, J., Muthig, D., Meier, G.: Providing feedback from application to family engineering - the product line planning game at the testo AG. In: Software Product Lines, 12th International Conference, SPLC 2008, Limerick, Ireland, September 8–12, 2008, Proceedings, pp. 180–189 (2008)

9. Chen, P., Critchlow, M., Garg, A., van der Westhuizen, C., van der Hoek, A.: Differencing and merging within an evolving product line architecture. In: Software Product-Family Engineering, 5th International Workshop, PFE 2003, Siena, Italy, November 4–6, 2003, Revised Papers, pp. 269–281 (2003)

10. Clements, P., Northrop, L.: Software Product Lines: Practices and Patterns. Addison-Wesley Professional (2001)

11. Cordy, M., Classen, A., Schobbens, P., Heymans, P., Legay, A.: Managing evolution in software product lines: a model-checking perspective. In: Sixth International Workshop on Variability Modelling of Software-Intensive Systems, Leipzig, Germany, January 25–27, 2012. Proceedings, pp. 183–191 (2012)

12. Deelstra, S., Sinnema, M., Bosch, J.: Product derivation in software product families: a case study. Journal of Systems and Software **74**(2), 173–194 (2005)

13. Delaware, B., Cook, W.R., Batory, D.S.: Fitting the pieces together: a machine-checked model of safe composition. In: Proceedings of the 7th joint meeting of the European Software Engineering Conference and the ACM SIGSOFT International Symposium on Foundations of Software Engineering, 2009, Amsterdam, The Netherlands, August 24–28, 2009, pp. 243–252 (2009)

14. Demuth, A., Lopez-Herrejon, R.E., Egyed, A.: Automatic and incremental product optimization for software product lines. In: Seventh IEEE International Conference on Software Testing, Verification and Validation, ICST 2014, March 31 2014-April 4, 2014, Cleveland, Ohio, USA, pp. 31–40 (2014)

15. Dhungana, D., Neumayer, T., Grünbacher, P., Rabiser, R.: Supporting evolution in model-based product line engineering. In: Software Product Lines, 12th International Conference, SPLC 2008, Limerick, Ireland, September 8–12, 2008, Proceedings, pp. 319–328 (2008)

16. Dintzner, N., Kulesza, U., van Deursen, A., Pinzger, M.: Evaluating feature change impact on multi-product line configurations using partial information. In: Software Reuse for Dynamic Systems in the Cloud and Beyond - 14th International Conference on Software Reuse, ICSR 2015, Miami, FL, USA, January 4–6, 2015. Proceedings, pp. 1–16 (2015)

17. Duszynski, S., Knodel, J., Lindvall, M.: SAVE: software architecture visualization and evaluation. In: 13th European Conference on Software Maintenance and Reengineering, CSMR 2009, Architecture-Centric Maintenance of Large-SCale Software Systems, Kaiserslautern, Germany, 24–27 March 2009, pp. 323–324 (2009)

18. Guo, J., Wang, Y., Trinidad, P., Benavides, D.: Consistency maintenance for evolving feature models. Expert Syst. Appl. **39**(5), 4987–4998 (2012)
19. Heider, W., Grünbacher, P., Rabiser, R.: Negotiation constellations in reactive product line evolution. In: Fourth International Workshop on Software Product Management, IWSPM 2010, Sydney, NSW, Australia, September 27, 2010, pp. 63–66 (2010)
20. Heider, W., Vierhauser, M., Lettner, D., Grünbacher, P.: A case study on the evolution of a component-based product line. In: 2012 Joint Working IEEE/IFIP Conference on Software Architecture and European Conference on Software Architecture, WICSA/ECSA 2012, Helsinki, Finland, August 20–24, 2012, pp. 1–10 (2012)
21. Inoki, M., Kitagawa, T., Honiden, S.: Application of requirements prioritization decision rules in software product line evolution. In: 5th IEEE International Workshop on Requirements Prioritization and Communication, RePriCo 2014, Karlskrona, Sweden, August 26, 2014, pp. 1–10 (2014)
22. Jahn, M., Rabiser, R., Grünbacher, P., Löberbauer, M., Wolfinger, R., Mössenböck, H.: Supporting model maintenance in component-based product lines. In: 2012 Joint Working IEEE/IFIP Conference on Software Architecture and European Conference on Software Architecture, WICSA/ECSA 2012, Helsinki, Finland, August 20–24, 2012, pp. 21–30 (2012)
23. Jensen, P.: Experiences with product line development of multi-discipline analysis software at overwatch textron systems. In: 11th International Software Product Line Conference, SPLC 2007, pp. 35–43. Overwatch Textron Systems (2007)
24. Jepsen, H.P., Beuche, D.: Running a software product line: standing still is going backwards. In: Software Product Lines, 13th International Conference, {SPLC} 2009, San Francisco, California, USA, August 24–28, 2009, Proceedings, pp. 101–110 (2009)
25. Knodel, J., Muthig, D., Naab, M., Lindvall, M.: Static evaluation of software architectures. In: 10th European Conference on Software Maintenance and Reengineering (CSMR 2006), 22–24 March 2006, Bari, Italy, pp. 279–294 (2006)
26. Kolb, R., John, I., Knodel, J., Muthig, D., Haury, U., Meier, G.: Experiences with product line development of embedded systems at testo AG. Proceedings - 10th International Software Product Line Conference, SPLC 2006 (01), 172–181 (2006)
27. Krueger, C.W.: Towards a taxonomy for software product lines. In: Software Product-Family Engineering, 5th International Workshop, PFE 2003, Siena, Italy, November 4–6, 2003, Revised Papers, pp. 323–331 (2003)
28. Laguna, M.A., Crespo, Y.: A systematic mapping study on software product line evolution: From legacy system reengineering to product line refactoring. Sci. Comput. Program. **78**(8), 1010–1034 (2013)
29. Leopoldo Teixeira Vander Alves, P.B., Gheyi, R.: A product line of theories for reasoning about safe evolution of product lines. In: Proceedings of the 19th International Conference on Software Product Line, SPLC 2015, Nashville, TN, USA, July 20–24, 2015, pp. 161–170 (2015)
30. Lity, S., Lochau, M., Schaefer, I., Goltz, U.: Delta-oriented model-based SPL regression testing. In: Proceedings of the Third International Workshop on Product LinE Approaches in Software Engineering, PLEASE 2012, Zurich, Switzerland, June 4, 2012, pp. 53–56 (2012)
31. Livengood, S.: Issues in software product line evolution: complex changes in variability models. In: Proceedings of the 2nd International Workshop on Product Line Approaches in Software Engineering, PLEASE 2011, Waikiki, Honolulu, HI, USA, May 22–23, 2011, pp. 6–9 (2011)
32. Mende, T., Beckwermert, F., Koschke, R., Meier, G.: Supporting the grow-and-prune model in software product lines evolution using clone detection. In: 12th European Conference on Software Maintenance and Reengineering, CSMR 2008, April 1–4, 2008, Athens, Greece, pp. 163–172 (2008)
33. Michalik, B., Weyns, D.: Towards a solution for change impact analysis of software product line products. In: 9th Working IEEE/IFIP Conference on Software Architecture, WICSA 2011, Boulder, Colorado, USA, June 20–24, 2011, pp. 290–293 (2011)

34. Michalik, B., Weyns, D., Betsbrugge, W.V.: On the problems with evolving egemin's software product line. In: Proceedings of the 2nd International Workshop on Product Line Approaches in Software Engineering, PLEASE 2011, Waikiki, Honolulu, HI, USA, May 22–23, 2011, pp. 15–19 (2011)
35. Montalvillo, L., Díaz, O.: Tuning github for SPL development: branching models & repository operations for product engineers. In: Proceedings of the 19th International Conference on Software Product Line, SPLC 2015, Nashville, TN, USA, July 20–24, 2015, pp. 111–120 (2015)
36. Montalvillo, L., Díaz, O.: Requirement-driven Evolution in Software Product Lines: A Systematic Mapping Study. The Journal of Systems and Software (2016)
37. Montalvillo, L., Díaz, O., Azanza, M.: Visualizing product customization efforts for spotting SPL reuse opportunities. In: Proceedings of the 21st International Systems and Software Product Line Conference, SPLC 2017, Volume B, Sevilla, Spain, September 25–29, 2017, pp. 73–80 (2017)
38. Montalvillo, L., Díaz, O., Fogdal, T.: Reducing coordination overhead in spls: peering in on peers. In: Proceeedings of the 22nd International Conference on Systems and Software Product Line - Volume 1, SPLC 2018, Gothenburg, Sweden, September 10–14, 2018, pp. 110–120 (2018)
39. Murashkin, A., Antkiewicz, M., Rayside, D., Czarnecki, K.: Visualization and exploration of optimal variants in product line engineering. In: 17th International Software Product Line Conference, SPLC 2013, Tokyo, Japan - August 26–30, 2013, pp. 111–115 (2013)
40. Murta, L.G.P., van der Hoek, A., Werner, C.M.L.: Archtrace: Policy-based support for managing evolving architecture-to-implementation traceability links. In: 21st IEEE/ACM International Conference on Automated Software Engineering (ASE 2006), 18–22 September 2006, Tokyo, Japan, pp. 135–144 (2006)
41. Noor, M.A., Rabiser, R., Grünbacher, P.: Agile product line planning: A collaborative approach and a case study. Journal of Systems and Software **81**(6), 868–882 (2008)
42. Paskevicius, P., Damasevicius, R., Stuikys, V.: Change impact analysis of feature models. In: Information and Software Technologies - 18th International Conference, ICIST 2012, Kaunas, Lithuania, September 13–14, 2012. Proceedings, pp. 108–122 (2012)
43. Peng, X., Yu, Y., Zhao, W.: Analyzing evolution of variability in a software product line: From contexts and requirements to features. Information & Software Technology **53**(7), 707–721 (2011)
44. Planning Game agile practice Http://c2.com/cgi/wiki?PlanningGame. Last visited: 2015-12-11
45. Pleuss, A., Botterweck, G., Dhungana, D., Polzer, A., Kowalewski, S.: Model-driven support for product line evolution on feature level. Journal of Systems and Software **85**(10), 2261–2274 (2012)
46. Quinton, C., Pleuss, A., Berre, D.L., Duchien, L., Botterweck, G.: Consistency checking for the evolution of cardinality-based feature models. In: 18th International Software Product Line Conference, SPLC '14, Florence, Italy, September 15–19, 2014, pp. 122–131 (2014)
47. Rahman, M.T., Querel, L., Rigby, P.C., Adams, B.: Feature toggles: practitioner practices and a case study. In: Proceedings of the 13th International Conference on Mining Software Repositories, MSR 2016, Austin, TX, USA, May 14–22, 2016, pp. 201–211 (2016)
48. Ribeiro, M., Borba, P.: Recommending refactorings when restructuring variabilities in software product lines. In: Second ACM Workshop on Refactoring Tools, WRT 2008, in conjunction with OOPSLA 2008, Nashville, TN, USA, October 19, 2008, p. 8 (2008)
49. Ribeiro, M., Borba, P., Kästner, C.: Feature maintenance with emergent interfaces. In: 36th International Conference on Software Engineering, ICSE '14, Hyderabad, India - May 31 - June 07, 2014, pp. 989–1000 (2014)
50. Romero, D., Urli, S., Quinton, C., Blay-Fornarino, M., Collet, P., Duchien, L., Mosser, S.: SPLEMMA: a generic framework for controlled-evolution of software product lines. In: 17th International Software Product Line Conference co-located workshops, SPLC 2013 workshops, Tokyo, Japan - August 26–30, 2013, pp. 59–66 (2013)

51. Savolainen, J., Kuusela, J.: Scheduling product line features for effective roadmapping. In: 15th Asia-Pacific Software Engineering Conference (APSEC 2008), 3–5 December 2008, Beijing, China, pp. 195–202 (2008)

52. Schackmann, H., Lichter, H.: A cost-based approach to software product line management. In: International Workshop on Software Product Management, IWSPM '06, Minneapolis/St.Paul, Minnesota, USA, September 12, 2006, pp. 13–18 (2006)

53. Scheidemann, K.D.: Optimizing the selection of representative configurations in verification of evolving product lines of distributed embedded systems. In: Software Product Lines, 10th International Conference, SPLC 2006, Baltimore, Maryland, USA, August 21–24, 2006, Proceedings, pp. 75–84 (2006)

54. Schubanz, M., Pleuss, A., Pradhan, L., Botterweck, G., Thurimella, A.K.: Model-driven planning and monitoring of long-term software product line evolution pp. 18:1–18:5 (2013)

55. Schulze, S., Lochau, M., Brunswig, S.: Implementing refactorings for FOP: lessons learned and challenges ahead. In: 5th International Workshop on Feature-Oriented Software Development, FOSD '13, Indianapolis, IN, USA, October 26, 2013, pp. 33–40 (2013)

56. Schulze, S., Schulze, M., Ryssel, U., Seidl, C.: Aligning Coevolving Artifacts Between Software Product Lines and Products. Proceedings of the Tenth International Workshop on Variability Modelling of Software-intensive Systems - VaMoS '16 pp. 9–16 (2016)

57. Shen, L., Peng, X., Zhu, J., Zhao, W.: Synchronized architecture evolution in software product line using bidirectional transformation. In: Proceedings of the 34th Annual IEEE International Computer Software and Applications Conference, COMPSAC 2010, Seoul, Korea, 19–23 July 2010, pp. 389–394 (2010)

58. Taborda, L.J.M.: Generalized release planning for product line architectures. In: Software Product Lines, Third International Conference, SPLC 2004, Boston, MA, USA, August 30-September 2, 2004, Proceedings, pp. 238–254 (2004)

59. Thao, C., Munson, E.V., Nguyen, T.N.: Software configuration management for product derivation in software product families. In: 15th Annual IEEE International Conference and Workshop on Engineering of Computer Based Systems (ECBS 2008), 31 March - 4 April 2008, Belfast, Northern Ireland, pp. 265–274 (2008)

60. Thüm, T., Batory, D.S., Kästner, C.: Reasoning about edits to feature models. In: 31st International Conference on Software Engineering, ICSE 2009, May 16–24, 2009, Vancouver, Canada, Proceedings, pp. 254–264 (2009)

61. Thurimella, A.K., Bruegge, B.: Evolution in product line requirements engineering: A rationale management approach. In: 15th IEEE International Requirements Engineering Conference, RE 2007, October 15–19th, 2007, New Delhi, India, pp. 254–257 (2007)

62. Vale, T., de Almeida, E.S., Alves, V., Kulesza, U., Niu, N., de Lima, R.: Software product lines traceability: A systematic mapping study. Information & Software Technology **84**, 1–18 (2017)

63. van Gurp, J., Bosch, J.: Design erosion: problems and causes. Journal of Systems and Software **61**(2), 105–119 (2002)

64. Vierhauser, M., Grünbacher, P., Heider, W., Holl, G., Lettner, D.: Applying a consistency checking framework for heterogeneous models and artifacts in industrial product lines. In: Model Driven Engineering Languages and Systems - 15th International Conference, MODELS 2012, Innsbruck, Austria, September 30-October 5, 2012. Proceedings, pp. 531–545 (2012)

65. Yau, S.S., Collofello, J.S., MacGregor, T.M.: Ripple effect analysis of software maintenance. In: International Computer Software and Applications Conference, pp. 71–82 (1978)

Glossary

Clone-and-own refers to an opportunistic reuse practice where a system is copied and modified to create a new variant. The development life cycle of these variants are independent of the rest and their synchronization during maintenance and evolution is challenging.

Configuration refers to a selection of features in a way that the variation points of a configurable system can be resolved.

Constraints discovery or extraction is the activity of enriching the knowledge about the variability of a system by adding new constraints. This activity helps to prevent invalid configurations of features.

Feature is a functional or non-functional characteristic of a system that is relevant in a domain. In a variability management context, some features can be optional, representing the differences among variants. Features are then increments of a system with their own requirements, design, implementation, and maintenance and evolution needs.

Feature identification is the activity of discovering the relevant features of a system or family of systems when complete information is not available.

Feature localization is the activity of establishing traceability links between features and the software artifacts (e.g., source code fragments) that implement them.

Feature model is a widely used formalism in variability management to define the configuration space of a family of systems. It is usually depicted as a tree-like structure, called a feature diagram, where the nodes are the features and the hierarchy are the parent-child relationships among them. These relationships are extended with a notation to express optional or mandatory features, alternative or 'or' group of features, complemented with cross-tree constraints (e.g., 'requires' or 'mutual exclusion') and constraints defined with formulas using Boolean logic.

Feature model synthesis is the activity of defining the feature model structure that fits best with the stakeholders' understanding of the system variability.

© Springer Nature Switzerland AG 2023
R. E. Lopez-Herrejon et al. (eds.), *Handbook of Re-Engineering Software Intensive Systems into Software Product Lines*, https://doi.org/10.1007/978-3-031-11686-5

Re-engineering   is any activity that transforms existing systems or processes with the goal of improving their quality. In the context of this handbook, we refer to re-engineer software intensive systems to achieve higher levels of systematic reuse. This usually requires reverse engineering activities from the initial systems as a prior task to the actual restructuring or refactoring.

Reuse   is using existing software engineering assets for creating or evolving software systems.

Reverse engineering   refers to the analysis of systems to create higher level representations of them such as their components' structures and relationships. These abstractions support systems comprehension and re-engineering tasks.

Software Product Line   is a platform to derive system variants from a common and managed set of core assets. Thus, the platform is based on a Software Product Line architecture with reusable or configurable components. The set of the system variants, derived from a platform, is also referred to as the Software Product Line.

Software Product Line Engineering   is a paradigm to achieve systematic reuse in the derivation of variants following organizational and technical measures. At organizational level, the domain engineering teams are responsible to define the desired variability and preparing the core assets, while the application engineering teams are responsible for the configurations and the derivation process. At technical level, it is based on implementing a Software Product Line platform enabling mass customization.

Variability   refers to the capability of a software system or artifact to be configured or adapted. This non-functional property aims to satisfy different customers, market segments, or operational contexts.

Variability management   is the activity of defining and handling variability and commonality within a family of software systems during its life cycle.

Index

Printed in the United States
by Baker & Taylor Publisher Services